Peiresc's
MEDITERRANEAN WORLD

Peiresc's
MEDITERRANEAN WORLD

Peter N. Miller

Harvard University Press

Cambridge, Massachusetts
London, England
2015

Copyright © 2015 by Peter N. Miller
All rights reserved
Printed in the United States of America

First printing

Library of Congress Cataloging-in-Publication Data is available from
the Library of Congress.

ISBN: 978-0-674-74406-6

For my wondrous Livy and Sam

ꝫ

Although my profession seems far removed from knowledge of the stars we can not be completely forbidden consideration of them, because of our nature: "man was given a lofty countenance and was commanded to behold the skies."

—Peiresc's dedication to Queen Marie de' Médicis, quoting from Ovid, of his never-completed study of the moons of Jupiter, ca. 1612

Contents

Note on the Text

Peiresc's original language and that of his correspondents has been preserved as much as possible. Where his idiosyncratic seventeenth-century orthography and that of his many secretaries may puzzle readers I have tried to reassure them with [*sic*]. Where it is likely to lead readers astray I have silently corrected the spelling.

The spelling of names in particular is vexing, especially given the tendency for the same name to be reused within successive generations of the same family, and the prevalence of family businesses in Marseille's maritime world. I have generally tried to standardize orthography, and generally tried to follow current conventions. But not always. In one particular case, that of the Magy brothers, I have always referred to the Marseille-based brother as "Jean-Baptiste," while the Cairo-based Jean is usually referred to as "Magy" and only sometimes as "Jean Magy."

Peiresc's own convention was to underline passages of importance. These have here been rendered in italics, which is our convention for emphasis. Italics have also been used to render foreign terms of art. I trust the reader to distinguish between the two uses.

But what of the Mediterranean of the historian?

—FERNAND BRAUDEL, *The Mediterranean and the Mediterranean World in the Age of Phillip II*

For everything that matters is to be found in the card box of the researcher who wrote it, and the scholar studying it assimilates it into his own card collection.

—WALTER BENJAMIN, *One-Way Street*

Introduction

*T*he artists who depicted Nicolas Fabri de Peiresc (1580–1637) from life—Louis Finson, Claude Mellan, and perhaps Anthony Van Dyck—all seem to have been attracted to his eyes. In the portrait done by Finson, around 1613, and still in Aix-en-Provence, the slight tensing of the eyebrows combined with the sag of the lower eyelids creates an atmosphere at once expectant and melancholy, and the blue of his irises jumps out all the more (Figure 1a–b). Tradition has it that Van Dyck, the young student of Peiresc's friend Rubens, passed through Marseille in 1625, probably during a brief visit from Palermo to Genoa.[1] The grisaille portrait and the engravings that derive from this visit show the forty-five-year-old Peiresc standing, with his hands together, fussing at the books piled in front of him. But in the immobility of his face, the still more deep-set darkness of the eyes pulls in the viewer, like some gravitational force. It is almost as if the artist is telling us that of all this scholar's tools, the eyes are the most powerful. And if one looks very, very closely, one sees that even in the engraving there is a twinkle in those eyes (Figure 2). Twelve years later, however, in the charcoal drawing done by Mellan on his way back from Rome, and now in the Hermitage, the sparkle seems to have gone. Peiresc has become old (Figure 3). Mellan pares away the lower torso. His hands are no longer visible, and all energy, all movement, all meaning are communicated by the eyes, which, even without their joy, have lost none of their expressiveness. They had seen more in the intervening twelve years, and they seem to have grown larger.[2] The lids are heavier and the whole effect somehow more reflective.

> It is certain that this person possesses in all fields as much knowledge as any one person in his own, nor can I possibly imagine to myself how one head could suffice for so many different things.[3]

Peiresc is the most thrilling intellectual personality in that lost French generation between Montaigne and Descartes. Brought up in an aristocratic family with a long administrative tradition and trained as a

Figure 1a–b.
Louis Finson, portrait of
Peiresc. (Académie des sciences,
agriculture, arts et belles-
lettres d'Aix-en-Provence)

lawyer, Peiresc inherited his uncle's seat in the Parlement of Provence,
where he functioned as a judge. But his passion was for learning—of all
sorts—and his drive and range brought him to the attention of the greatest
scholars in Europe: Galileo, Gassendi, Grotius, Scaliger, Casaubon, de
Thou, Saumaise, Schikard, Kircher, Doni, Naudé, Selden, Camden,

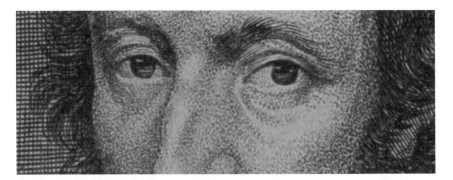

Figure 2. Lucas Vorsterman after Anthony Van Dyck. (Private collection)

Cotton, Campanella, Mersenne, Rubens. They became his friends, correspondents, and intellectual partners. He was equally at home with politicians, cardinals, and merchants: more of his letters went to Secretary of State Loménie de Brienne than to any other single correspondent, and his most famous letters were sent to Cardinal Francesco Barberini, pleading for him to beseech his uncle, Pope Urban VIII, for leniency toward Galileo—both old correspondents of Peiresc's. Peiresc struck the pose of the prophet, warning that prosecuting Galileo for his intellectual commitments would look to future generations like the Athenians' condemnation of Socrates. More than a century after Peiresc's birth, Pierre Bayle, the leader of Europe's Republic of Letters, described Peiresc as his direct predecessor, the "Procurator-General" of letters. Several centuries later still, he seems to us like its prince. But we would be wise to include charm as one of his attributes: one cannot make so many friends, and make out of them such a mighty intellectual apparatus, without a compelling personality.[4]

Yet, unlike Montaigne's, for example, Peiresc's charm is not so obvious. He does not speak to "us" the way his great predecessor does from out of hours of reading and reflection. He is, rather, always in conversation with contemporaries, sometimes named and often unnamed. Amid the sounds still audible at this distance, one must listen carefully for his charm, or, let us say, his voice. What is interesting in Peiresc is the way he thinks, and unlike Montaigne, to stay with this example, he does not talk about his thoughts. Yet they are there, on paper, and as a musican might do for a composer, it is in the notes themselves that the creator is brought back to life.

Figure 3.
Claude Mellan,
drawing of Peiresc.
(Photograph © The
State Hermitage
Museum/photo by
Vladimir Terebenin)

Peiresc's vast erudition and insatiable curiosity were celebrated by contemporaries—the memorial volume produced just after his death by his Roman friends contained elegiac poems in all the world's known languages, including Quechua, Coptic, and Japanese—and made him a byword for posterity.[5] His curiosity, I confess, is what grabbed me so long ago. And my astonishment was exactly that of Rubens before me: how could any one person speak so knowledgeably about so many things? From astronomy and botany through glyptics, numismatics, and sigillography and all the way on to zoology, there are few subjects in which Peiresc was not in some way present.

If I were an antiquarian, I would have eyes only for old things, but I am a historian. Therefore, I love life.[6]

When Henri Pirenne made the point to Marc Bloch in Stockholm in 1928 about the antiquarian as someone alienated from the present and dead from the waist down, he was trafficking in a venerable commonplace. From Shackerly Mermion's play *The Antiquary* (1641), if not before, and from George Eliot's Casaubon in *Middlemarch* (1871), and on after, antiquaries were associated with the worst kind of dry-as-dust scholarship, if not seen ultimately as traitors to life itself.[7] But when Arnaldo Momigliano two decades later launched the revival of the study of antiquarians and antiquarianism, he struck off in a different direction. Far from engaging with the representation of the antiquary's dire symbolic status, Momigliano focused attention on his scholarly practices. In this vision, antiquarians emerged as key contributors to how modern historians worked from, say, Gibbon onward. In his Sather Lectures, delivered at Berkeley in 1963, Momigliano placed Peiresc at the heart of this phenomenon, describing him as "that archetype of all antiquarians."[8]

To talk about "antiquarianism" today is to address this complex phenomenon. We can begin with the linguistic context: in antiquity, the *antiquarius* had to do with the writing of texts, especially the preservation of old texts. From this we retain our notion of the antiquarian as the seller of old or secondhand books. In the Renaissance, the *antiquarius* was the lover of old things—hence the "antiquariat" or "antiques" dealer of today. In the sixteenth and seventeenth centuries, the love of antiquities gave way to the study of *antiquitates,* the ancient systems that those physical remains once comprised.

And so, when Jacob Spon, a medical doctor from Lyon who was a leading antiquarian of the second half of the seventeenth century, wanted to make sense of what had already in his time become a substantial body of scholarship, he sought linguistic clarity in neologism. Abandoning the already vexed "antiquarian," he opted for "archaeologia" or "archaeografia," which he defined as "the science of what the Ancients wanted to teach posterity about their religion, their sciences, their history and their politics, by the original monuments which they have left us." This science had eight parts: numismatics, epigraphy, ancient architecture, iconography (including sculpture), glyptography, toreumatography (the study of reliefs), bibliography, and angeiography. This last he called "a vast and prickly" field that included weights, measures, vases, domestic and agricultural utensils, games, clothing, "and a thousand other things whose study does not easily fit in the previous sciences." It is in this messy realm that Spon presented Peiresc as his model.[9]

In the past two decades there has been a veritable explosion of work on the early modern European study of antiquities—an online bibliography put together by Joseph Connors records over seven hundred entries—and much new work showing that people have been trying to access the past through its physical remains since prehistory and around the globe.[10] And though most clear as an early modern phenomenon, it was Momigliano himself who suggested that there was also a *longue durée* and a connection not just to the nineteenth century, and antiquarianism's decay into the modern disciplines of art history, archaeology, anthropology, sociology, and history of religion, but even to the twentieth.[11] Does antiquarianism not still work today through what we call "material culture"?[12]

The importance of evidence and, in particular, the evidentiary value of material culture is a legacy of early modern antiquarianism. In moving beyond the text to the artifact, antiquaries also inaugurated a different principle which we have inherited. For the notion that it was interesting and valuable to increase the number of sources and diversify their points of view is central to our working notion of "research." In the sixteenth and seventeenth centuries, historians of the ancient world tended to rewrite ancient historians, while the antiquaries juxtaposed texts and objects in order to answer questions inaccessible from only one of these standpoints. Histories of Late Antiquity and the Middle Ages, as they came to be written in the seventeenth and eighteenth centuries, borrowed from the antiquarian model. With Gibbon and Winckelmann, so Momigliano himself taught us, the writing of history conclusively incorporated these notions of material evidence and research. Once we grasp this, then understanding antiquarianism becomes crucial because it takes us to the heart of understanding the practice of historical scholarship from the Renaissance right up to the present.

> To do exact research . . . in order to see what I am missing and to choose what it would be worth the effort to have researched . . . who did the research, for the love of me . . . I will do the research on the Admiralty . . . and will do everywhere the most precise research that I could. . . . I have by the same research happily encountered a copy that I once had had transcribed of the particular statutes of Marseille . . . where I had done a little research.[13]

In this book we will not engage directly with antiquarianism as the study of antiquities. Instead, we will follow Momigliano himself, who in the very same lecture that presented Peiresc as the archetypal antiquary also linked Peiresc with Galileo on the common ground of close observation.[14] This is the track we will take. We will be thinking about the family resemblances between antiquarianism and analogous research practices. Momigliano's hint has since fired careful exploration of the parallel empirical approaches of antiquaries and medical doctors.[15] The new scholarly literature on objectivity and precision has deepened our awareness of the contiguity of antiquarian and natural philosophical investigations in the seventeenth century but also of antiquarian and ethnological inquiry.[16] People like Peiresc, who studied both antiquities and astronomy, might not have referred to their astronomical work as "antiquarian," or even thought about it as such. But we might well want to know what, epistemically, could connect these approaches when pursued by the same person.

To answer this we need to know much more about how cultures of observation and curiosity intersect with cultures of historical research. When we catch Peiresc attentively recording artisanal practices in the Parisian "Jewel House," does he do this as an antiquary who had studied the making of ancient tripods or weights and measures?[17] Or are his antiquarianism and his "material attentiveness" both species of something else? His English admirers in the Hartlib Circle might have used the word "virtuoso" to refer to this conjunction. Robert Hooke, so similar to Peiresc in so many ways, used the term "natural antiquary" to refer to the empirical study of nature.[18] When we find Peiresc bringing the same precision and experience to his interactions with Marseille's merchants and mariners, what are we to call it?[19]

Here we return to Pirenne and Bloch in Stockholm. They were certain that "antiquarian" implied alienation from the present. And so by definition there could be no connection between the Peiresc in his study in Aix and the Peiresc on the quays of Marseille. But can we be so sure? Peiresc collecting coins and Peiresc collecting shipping times, Peiresc describing sculptures and Peiresc describing how to circumvent quarantine rules, Peiresc comparing gems and Peiresc comparing profit margins were, after all, the same person. And beyond biographical facts, and beyond the continuity of scholarly practices, there is something else. Michael Shanks proposes rereading Momigliano's dichotomy between history and antiquarianism so that history becomes what happened in the past, whereas antiquarianism is about the past-in-things that remains alive in the present. If antiquarianism is, then, the vision of the past that is experienced in our present—completely inverting Pirenne's "thesis"—then Peiresc in Marseille may be much closer to Peiresc in Aix than we might otherwise assume.[20]

Beyond the question, then, of whether Peiresc was archetypal and how, is a much broader one about the varieties of "research" practices in the seventeenth century. This actually seems to have been Peiresc's own preferred term to describe his activity. We find him frequently using both the verb form—*rechercher*—and the abstract and specific nouns—*recherche* and *recherches*.[21] But for the proper noun he does not use *chercheur*, or "researcher," preferring the untranslatable term *curieux*, perhaps best rendered as "person curious of things." This term far outpaced his use of others related to erudition or antiquarianism.[22]

> We saw here the Sr de la Rivière, come on the same ship [the *navire Dauphin*], who was 8 months with him [Ambassador Marcheville] in Constantinople, during all these disorders, of which he gave us yesterday such a full relation that it would require a great book, and not a simple letter, to convey it to you.[23]

All of Peiresc's projects are "situated": he could not have studied antiquities without his Roman friends; could not have become an astronomer without his time spent in Padua; could not have studied botany without his contacts in Montpellier and Leiden. And he could not have made the contribution he did to the beginning of oriental studies without his connections in Marseille, in Toulon, and along the Provençal coast. This was probably Peiresc's biggest intellectual legacy. Through his own research, and through his determined support of his friends' intellectual ambitions, Peiresc was a key figure in advancing the study of the languages and literature of the ancient and contemporary Near East. Books, objects, and manuscripts flowed through him to scholar-colleague friends in Rome, Paris, Leiden, and Oxford, always leaving a trace—and sometimes much more—in the fertile soil of his own archive.[24]

Between Peiresc in Provence and his friends in the Levant stretched the vastness of the sea. But for a person of great charm, and one who took seriously the meaning and obligations of "friendship," a very important concept and category in the seventeenth century, this physical space was also a human space. If we were to ask how it was possible for a person sitting in metropolitan Provence to have acquired so many things and written so many letters to such faraway places, the answer would be "people."[25]

So, no Levant without the Mediterranean. And as I began to think about the Mediterranean I realized that Peiresc's was not an accidental Mediterraneanism, but a conscious vocation. His work on the physical sea, its tides and currents and mountains and winds, was intertwined with attention to its human inhabitants in just the same way that he would describe a tulip that was sent him which was yellow with a red border and streaks of red as "like the coat of arms of Pope Urban V," who ruled in Avignon during the Babylonian Captivity of the fourteenth century.[26] But it was Mediterranean Provence that captivated Peiresc from early on: the relationship between the House of Barcelona and counts of Provence, the Provençal empire of the Angevins in Italy and Greece, and the Provençaux who went on Crusade and settled in the Kingdom of Jerusalem.[27] Indeed, a description of this project stands at the key juncture in Gassendi's *Life of Peiresc* when he moves from an account of the man to one of the researcher.[28]

But there was still more. As I peered ever more deeply into Peiresc's surviving archive and as my eyes began to acclimate to its darker corners, I found traces, and then whole tranches, of letters to the local people who literally made his intellectual life possible. And I realized that there was a human level at which the "what" and "how" questions, which I for so long had kept apart, could not be separated. If I really wanted to understand what Peiresc was doing, then his work as a scholar and his work as a man of action had to be brought together. Biography is the typical format in which we bring together the many parts of a single life, however distinct and sometimes even disjunctive they might be. If the spheres of the intellectual and the material can be brought together in the life of one man, might it not also be possible to join intellectual and material history on a larger scale? And could these two registers, of the biographical and the conceptual, be integrated? This book is just such an attempt.

> The fruit man came by. My Father gave him an order on the account of the tenant at Belgentier, who paid up quickly, and brought yesterday to Father the 27 écus remaining of the Easter rent, with the fruits of the Priory which aren't worth sending to Paris and the graftings which we will send, along with those of Marseille and with the figs.[29]

The house Peiresc was born into, during an outbreak of plague in 1580, sits today amid a park in the village of Belgentier, in the narrow valley of the Gapeau, off the D554 about ten miles north of Toulon. The current owners say that something of the kitchen survives in the lower floor of the modest chateau now on the site, but it is hard to say. The gardens in which he walked, worked, and planted are now divided, with some belonging to the chateau and the rest, over the fence and across the gurgling stream, to the municipality. In the corner of the garden is a ruined tower. The local tradition holds that this was the place from which Peiresc made his astronomical observations, sitting up late into the night with his friends, among them Pierre Gassendi, his future biographer and future professor of astronomy at the Sorbonne; Salomon Azubi, the rabbi of Carpentras; and Simon Corberan, his book-binder and factotum. There is a Rue Peiresc, a Place Peiresc, a Parc Peiresc, and a Chateau Peiresc. The blank façade of the church bears a modern fresco painting of Louis XIV's visit to the town in 1660 with Peiresc's chateau and gardens as backdrop. Off to the side is a passably identifiable portrait of Peiresc standing and watching the proceedings alongside a telescope.[30]

Aix, where Peiresc was the brightest star in a bright local firmament, has commemorated him with a portrait bust on a plinth across from the cathedral, with a street across from where the palace once stood and the *parlement*, to which Peiresc belonged, used to meet, and with a plaque on the site of his house. (The bar currently occupying the ground floor is an unlikely form of remembrance for such an ascetically inclined man.) His portrait hangs above the dais in the meeting room of the Academy of Aix, in the Musée Paul Arbaud. The remains of his body lie in a crypt in the Dominican church, on the other side of the remodeled palace square. In 1794 the French Revolution claimed the tomb inscription and monument to Peiresc that had been erected only sixteen years earlier. From the beginning of the nineteenth century we can date the "Renaissance of Peiresc": first with publication of some of his letters and then with the eventual National Edition of 1888–1898.[31]

> The rumor of the abolition [of taxes] which the Monsignor the Cardinal of Lyon obtained for that city gave hope for a total grace, not only for Lyon but for all the neighboring people who could benefit from it, and principally for those of our coast, who have their most important connections there. Things having to do with the sea are so close to our heart.[32]

There is no site in Marseille that we can definitively assign to Peiresc (nor is there a statue, street, or square, save for a short, nondescript *allée*

Figure 4. Civitates Orbis Terrarum, vol. 2, 1575. (Bibliothèque Nationale de France)

in a characterless and distant suburb). We do know that he was inside the monastery of St. Victor because we have the copies he made of its inscriptions. But for the rest, if we perch above the city like the imaginary travelers in Franz Hogenberg and Georg Braun's depiction of Marseille from the south in *Civitates Orbis Terrarum* (Figure 4), published only six years before Peiresc's birth, we have to imagine Peiresc circulating along the quays, and climbing up and down the steep lanes of Le Panier to visit his merchant friends, one "near the Fountain" in the neighborhood of St. Jean, a sailors' haunt where the new Museum of the Mediterranean rears up; another at the Place Vivaux, at the foot of the hill; and a third at the "Place of St. James of Spain" near the Church of St. Martin, hard upon the course of the now-destroyed old city walls.[33] But it is the building in the center of the view, in the middle of the Quai du Port, the building Walter

Benjamin saw shining like "a signet ring on a fishwife's hard finger," that was Peiresc's chief destination in Marseille: the Hôtel de Ville.[34] For it was there that the archives of the city were kept, and thus it is there that the imagination finds its firmest footing.

> I have been held in such diversions or laziness during these last months, aside from certain required necessities, that I have not been allowed at all to take back up the books on maritime matters. But I have not failed, however, to seek out better examples of them than mine. I was thinking of going to dig in the archives of Marseille, but I have not been able to find the time, to my great regret. I have not yet lost, however, the hope, and await still the response from other places. For out of love of me the officers of Marseille have written even to Barcelona itself on this subject.[35]

In this book I use Peiresc's archive to tell a story about the maritime, commercial Mediterranean of the first decades of the seventeenth century, and in particular the Mediterranean world as it looked from Marseille. Astonishingly, for a city of its importance—France's leading port, one of Mediterranean Europe's for centuries, and possessed of rich public archives—Marseille of the early seventeenth century has simply not been studied. In part, this is because of the gaps in those archives for Peiresc's period relative to earlier and later ones. With so many other riches to mine, and with the tendency of economic and political historians to focus on long runs of documents, Peiresc's Marseille has all but disappeared. There is also the tendency to think that in previous times, as in our own, France was synonymous with Paris. But Peiresc's provincial life and his archive—a private archive—afford us this missing, rich vision of Marseille as a living city. The intensity of his engagement in Marseille's maritime activity means that we can read his papers for precious details of its commerce.

We can learn, for instance, the names of merchants and ship's captains and artisans that are often lacking in the public record. And we find these commercial men doing the kinds of things that no public record of their activities would ever contain: helping a great local scholar carry out his intellectual investigations and intellectual projects hundreds, and even thousands, of miles away.

And yet, however promising our reversal of perspective—looking at wider Mediterranean events through a single telescopic lens—there is the ever-present threat of distortion. For, however rich, Peiresc's data are only one man's vision, with all the obvious limitations. Even the very premise of mobilizing his archive for wider investigation threatens us with a historiographical *mise-en-abîme:* there will always be some detail that will escape scrutiny, some piece of knowledge that will be missed. In that sense, this book, even if too long, is still only a beginning. Our consolation must be that this problem was his problem, too.

> He was so unwearied in writing, that he presently noted down, whatever he met with. To say nothing of his Letters, which were very many in number, most full of Learning and commonly very large. . . . Moreover, whatsoever he noted down, he did it upon a new or fresh leaf of paper that if anything were afterwards to be added, it might be done without confusion. And he always wrote on the top of the leaf, or the upper part of the margin, the Subject or Title of what he was to note down, in a large character (with which commonly he inserted proper names, and other words, which in the ordinary letter could not so well be read, or so soon found out) and he added the year and the day, and if he received it from some other, he premised the Author's name.[36]

Peiresc's archive lives today, mostly, in the Bibliothèque Inguimbertine in Carpentras, whose 1950s-era front rooms serve now as the municipal library, catering to students, old-age pensioners, and those with time on their hands. It holds 119 volumes of manuscripts of Peiresc's letters, reading notes, memoranda, and excerpts, by far the largest share of a surviving archive of about 77,000 pieces of paper. The volumes vary little in size, ranging from 370 mm × 270 mm (14.5" × 10.6") down to 310 mm × 230 mm (12.2" × 9"), and are in a uniformly good state of preservation; some of the more disordered volumes have been conserved only in the last two decades. Gassendi tells us, and the archive confirms, that Peiresc kept his pages loose, tied together in bundles, so that they could be untied and new materials inserted in the appropriate place as needed. Traces of this filing system are still visible (Figure 5). But while the researcher at Carpentras—or Paris or The Hague or anywhere else an original Peiresc manuscript volume can be found—will meet up with a *bound* book, this was not Peiresc's reality. The material today, in fact, bears the relationship to Peiresc's working archive that a dead body does to the living.[37]

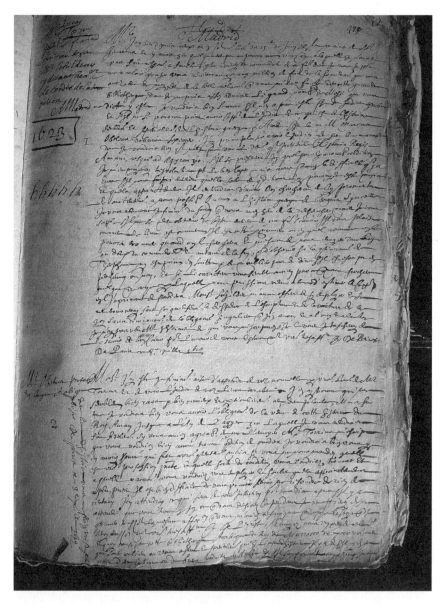

Figure 5. Sample *mise-en-page* with later filing key. Peiresc to Torrius. CBI, MS. 1876, f. 420r. (Bibliothèque Inguimbertine, Musées et Bibliothèques de Carpentras)

Still, it is miraculous that this body has largely survived the accidents of time. While Peiresc's 5,000-odd books and 18,000 coins and were snapped up by collectors after his death, along with his objects and rare manuscripts (such as those of Provençal troubadours), his working papers were ignored.[38] They remained in Aix, and almost entirely in the hands of family and friends. Gassendi published a catalog of these papers in his *Life of Peiresc*, and with only some deviations, the list can be traced through to present-day holdings.[39] There are essentially two kinds of materials, volumes devoted to correspondence—approximately seventeen in number—and those that represent work-in-progress—approximately 107.[40] These latter include what are essentially "notebooks," such as Peiresc's log of astronomical observation, or the Antelmi brothers' meteorological records from Fréjus, or reading notes from medieval documents in the *Trésor des Chartes*, memoranda on an encyclopedic range of issues, and draft essays, whether on the history of the parlement in France or ancient tripods. The proportion is important; with so much attention devoted to studying early modern correspondence, it is worth remembering that for most scholars the letter, like the printed piece, rests atop a foundation of erudite paper.

I call this an "archive" quite self-consciously because Peiresc collected all this material and then organized it for use. This paper was the arsenal he drew upon, a kind of tool for thinking: his "paperware" for our "software."[41] In keeping his archive, Peiresc was only doing unto himself what he did unto others: he demonstrated a deep familiarity with the organization of different French archives and attended to the physical location of documents—where in the various chambers they were found—and their preservation—in what type of compartment, of which color, and so on.[42] If the work of Peter Stallybrass has led a generation to think about the "material text," here is a whole archive, and an archival practice, treated already as "material" by its seventeenth-century author.[43]

Peiresc, in short, presents to us an early image of the "archives man."[44] He thought himself so well known for frequenting archives that he once used this as cover when on His Majesty's Secret Service.[45] The preservation of his own archive, more or less in situ, and more or less as he left it, after all these hundreds of years, enables us not only to reconstruct an early modern learned life but almost to feel as if peering over his shoulder with his pen paused in midthought. I say "thought" because while Peiresc wrote down his thoughts, and while he shared them with friends—a form of scribal publication—he did not publish them in *printed* form.

I received your three [letters] at the same time this morning around 9 o'clock.[46]

Even with all this paper, the archive cannot be mistaken for reality itself. For instance, from this sentence we learn that Pierre Fort, Peiresc's Marseille-based banker, received three letters from him on 31 January 1630. A day later, Fort wrote again, mentioning receiving four letters from Peiresc, two each on 28 and 30 January.[47] None of these letters survives, nor are they even listed in any of Peiresc's various archival formats. If the volume of communication mentioned here is even slightly representative of these two men's frequency of interaction—the closeness of their working relationship and the sensitivity of the transactions they discussed suggest it is—then they must have exchanged hundreds of letters. Yet all we possess are two letters from Peiresc to Fort and two from Fort to Peiresc. The same would be true for Peiresc's other key Marseille merchant banker, the mysterious Hugh Masse (or Mace) de Gastines, someone Peiresc mentions frequently but whose more direct traces are almost all missing: only three of Peiresc's letters to him survive, and six from him to Peiresc.

This imbalance, then, between what there was and what there is suggests that even at its current scale, the Peiresc archive reflects not only the inevitable losses to accident but also deliberate omissions. Were some materials too sensitive to be kept? Did his heirs seek to protect themselves—or burnish their hero's reputation for intellectualism—by omitting all of these tiresomely practical letters? We cannot be sure. But our uncertainty means that as much as we can rely on what the archive does tell us, we must remember that it does not tell us everything. If Peiresc's work, and our study of him, seems like a model of Benjamin's practice of transferring note cards, then we must also acknowledge that the notecards do not tell us everything we want to know.

On desireroit scavoir . . .

"One would want to know . . ." This phrase recurs over and over again in the Peiresc archive. It is usually followed by a list of questions, all of which take the form of a research agenda devoted to a particular problem. Sometimes Peiresc sent the list to a correspondent, but just as often he wrote it as a "memo to self" and retained the original in the archive, whereas with his letters, it was the original that he sent and the copy that he retained for the archive. The phrase can be taken as Peiresc's motto, reflecting his omnivorous curiosity, his programmatic focus, and his constant use of questions to mark out fields of knowledge. He was also not afraid of receiving negative answers or of playing with ideas, though the fact that he often begged his interlocutor's forgiveness for his "conjectures" suggests that even among those who knew him well he expected some resistance to his approach.

The story of "Peiresc and the Mediterranean" is the thread that runs through the entire archive, uniting not only the bodies of knowledge that Peiresc so doggedly plumbed but the different kinds of knowledge that he possessed. There is, of course, Peiresc the scholar, helping us to understand the role of empirical engagement in early modern natural philosophy and the role of collection, description, and comparison in the pre-disciplinary human sciences.[48] But there is also the Peiresc who knows his way among the rough-and-tumble of a hard-edged port city, who knows how to finagle his goods out of quarantine—the Peiresc who knows his way around a maritime cosmos stretching from the Hôtel de Ville to Alexandria, Aleppo, and beyond. In this conjunction we see why the Mediterranean Sea was the great historical laboratory for the twentieth century: from Aby Warburg and Henri Pirenne in its first decades, to Fernand Braudel, whose masterwork was published at exactly its midpoint, to Michael McCormick, Peregrine Horden, and Nicholas Purcell at its very end (Chris Wickham's book appeared in 2005 to conclude the Mediterranean's century). Like its name, the kind of scholarship that this sea has elicited focuses on everything that is "between": between people, places, things, and times but also between intellectual disciplines, subfields, and historiographies.

> And whereas he was accustomed in a peculiar manner, to bind up into bundles, such Letters as he received according to the variety of Persons, Places or Times: he first writ upon each, who wrote the same, from whence, what year, month and day; and subjoyned a brief Index of the chief matters, which in reading he had marked with a line drawn under them; for by this meanes he was holpen, both to answer the same more distinctly and speedily; as also to finde the same, if at any time he went to seek any thing in his Letters.[49]

The archive itself seems to mark what was especially significant about Peiresc. For once we step outside print publication as the mark of a writer, we see that if Peiresc was anything, he was a writer. Every day he wrote for hours; those letters, notes, and memoranda were written by him, though many of the excerpts and all of the copies of letters were the work of his secretaries, only one of whose name is known: François Parrot. His ideas came to life in his hands—and this makes his decision to organize his thoughts in letters all the more understandable, since even as a conversation with absent friends, letter-writing remained a species of conversation. The archive he left was his literary creation. This realization led me to want to put as much of his raw materials as possible into the text of this book, in as unmediated a form as possible, though at the same time knowing that some mediation is inevitable. Peiresc published only once, and even then anonymously, but his life surely makes clear that print publication is not the only way to know a writer or to identify him as one.[50]

The specific group of letters and related materials that I focus on in this book are those to his Mediterranean correspondents. The period of their creation, the decades from 1620 to 1640, is especially interesting: Venice had lost its dominance in the Levant; Marseille had moved in but would, in turn, be challenged and displaced by the Dutch and the English. But just then, at that brief moment, the Ottoman Mediterranean was presided over from Marseille, whose ships proliferated in the ports of the southern and eastern Mediterranean shores.

The bulk of Peiresc's letters that traveled the roads of the sea are found in two distinct dossiers covering the period 1627–1637 and organized around the names "Jean Magy," Peiresc's longtime agent in Cairo, and "François-Auguste de Thou," son of the great historian Jacques-Auguste, who traveled in the Levant between 1627 and 1629 before returning to France and eventually, a decade later, after being passed over as ambassador extraordinary to Constantinople, being executed by Richelieu as a conspirator. Magy managed the two missions to the Levant undertaken in the years from 1629 to 1633 by Peiresc's friend and confessor Théophile Minuti. Between 1633 and 1636 Peiresc was in close communication with a group of Capuchins in Egypt. From 1635 to 1637 he leaned heavily on a Flemish Discalced Carmelite based in Aleppo.

While Peiresc's letters to his eastern contacts reveal much about his intellectual interests, they are surrounded by clusters of letters to merchants, officials, diplomats, and mariners based in Marseille, the content of many of which seems prosaic: quotidian details about ships and shipping, packaging, winds, disruptive threats, finances. In other letters Peiresc drew his correspondents deeper into his intellectual world, sharing ideas and setting them tasks to execute elsewhere. To the historian, all these letters are a treasure trove, documenting an extremely close relationship between a scholar and a maritime merchant community. There surely were other close encounters of this sort in early modern Europe, but they have not left their trace, or else have not been sufficiently studied.

Just as Aby Warburg saw in the portraits that the merchants of the Florentine Quattrocento commissioned not just individual identity but the commitments—authority, strength, innovation, piety—of the class that made Renaissance Florence, we might see in the Peiresc archive the moral portrait of Marseille's merchants of the early seventeenth century, who left us little else. We see their engagement in the cause of "curiosity," their desire to collaborate in the pursuit of the new, and their range of geographic visions. The letters, excerpts, and dossiers in the Peiresc archive may well be their monument, just as the Sassetti Chapel or the façade of Santa Maria Novella are those of Florence's merchant rulers:[51]

> And then I had gone a long time without receiving any, when the servant whom M. d'Agut sent expressly to Lyon broke open the ice, as it were, and brought me one of 19 November all virgin, without having been passed through vinegar [a precaution in time of plague], soon followed by five others, of 9, 16, 23, 30 October and 6 November, which came almost at the same time, although by different routes, some via Marseille and others via Salon, and the two oldest, and nevertheless the most tardy, via Aix, where they had gone by mistake, and were soon followed by two others of 4 and 18 December come in a similar way, one from Marseille and the other from Salon, with which we had such beautiful books and such curious papers, and such a good part of news of the world, that it seemed to us, after a long absence, that we were all of sudden brought back to the middle of the Louvre, and of the Academy [of the Dupuy]—although in reality we were so distanced from them, and almost confined to the middle of a desert.[52]

In the 1950s Fernand Braudel organized a book series for the Centres de Recherches Historiques, a unit of the VIème section of the École Pratique des Hautes Études, entitled *Affaires et gens d'affaires.* The books published the correspondence of merchants with a learned commentary. In his preface to a volume on a late sixteenth-century Marseille merchant family, Braudel explained that the letters' value lay in "being thus compared to similar documents and plunged back into an economic history of the sixteenth century as seen day by day, explained by its actors."[53] In his study of a Portuguese merchant family in that same series, José Gentil da Silva proclaimed that while letters are the "flesh and bones" of history, their very quotidian detail could be fully grasped only by a historian capable of perceiving in the everyday a kind of "poetry."[54]

What is this poetry, and what is its place in the historian's craft? As Braudel put it in that same preface, "[The letters' interest,] if I am not mistaken, is to insert us into the heart of the practices and realities of merchants' everyday lives: these realities, on their own or because of their repetition, often go beyond the merely anecdotal detail."[55] The poetry is in the detail, of daily life and of daily thought, brought from a past person to our present across a vast expanse of time. Reading Iris Origo's exactly contemporary *Merchant of Prato* we sense the poetry; it is the way in which the details of Francesco Maria Datini's life in letters resonate with our own and so enables us to feel that the enormous distance between us can be bridged, even a little bit.[56] Writing to a young student of his in 1856, Jacob Burckhardt explained that "if you want to remain a poet" while still studying history it was necessary "to love in a completely personal way" both human beings and the "singular phenomena" of existence. He intended this for himself, too; elsewhere he wrote that history was, "in great measure, poetry."[57]

Yet this is an elusive poetry. It has no motto, like Ovid's haunting "Tempus Edax Rerum, tuque invidiosa vetustas, omnia destruitis" (You, Time, devourer of things, and you, invidious age, destroy all), which looms over the antiquaries clambering in a landscape of ruins in Herman Posthumus's moving painting of 1536 (Figure 6).[58] It has no philosopher, like Nietzsche, who explained that "in Antiquity philology was in no way a science, but only a general passion for every kind of knowledge." The revival of antiquity, he continued, was marked by "the sentimentality of ruins, especially Rome's, and in excavations this longing [*Sehnsucht*] was satisfied."[59] And it does not yet have its historian: even the man who did the most to re-create the merchant world of the Mediterranean, S. D. Goitein, paid little attention to it.

> My name is well-enough known all along the coast of this province so that if the navires and *barques* on which you have loaded my things dock at ports other than Marseille, I could still recover what is mine.[60]

If we are to find the poetry in Peiresc's maritime world, then in the spirit of Burckhardt we will have to follow the names. In the scores of

Figure 6. Herman Posthumus, "Tempus Edax Rerum."
(Liechtenstein. The Princely Collections, Vaduz-Vienna)

unfamiliar names of merchants, factors, and captains, we will find the
Tempus Edax Rerum of commercial life. In Peiresc's archive are long-
forgotten structures—families, networks, broken partnerships, and shat-
tered projects. Mostly, though, it is Nietzsche's "longing" that lingers: the
close encounter with lives at the limit of remembrance, clinging to our
world often only by their names, and these sometimes only by virtue of
Peiresc's having recorded them. We read their names—there are so many
of them—and think about how very real they were and how utterly forgotten they are, just one step short of complete oblivion.

Historians use names all the time. We use them to invoke persons,
to say something about their geographical origin, or profession, or religion. More broadly, we use names to identify, to localize, and to catego-
rize. "Toponymics" is the auxiliary science of place names, while "onomastics" serves for personal names. But both of these seek the answers
found in names; "namescape" seeks the questions, and thus their prompt
to the historical imagination.

Peiresc's names point us in two different directions, and in this book
we shall follow them both. The first takes us to a philological reconstruction of the day-to-day practice of a Mediterranean vocation in the 1620s

and 1630s through the lens of Peiresc papers. Section 6 follows Peiresc's letter-writing to the Levant day by day for the last ten years of his life; such a reconstruction makes it clear that his was not an "accidental Mediterraneanism," a story that could have happened anywhere. For it is the sea that focuses us on the intricate and extensive web of relations binding Peiresc to the practical men of Marseille, its merchants, mariners, officials, and ship's captains. Nicholas Purcell has shown how the term "thalassography" can describe the kind of history in which the sea serves as a "stage" for the human. But he also suggested, perhaps tongue in cheek, that "thalassographies" did not have to be about seas but about the systole and diastole of human mobility and connectivity that characterizes life in and on the sea. What the jest elides are the serious historiographical stakes in the practice of thalassography: that looking at the sea can tell us a lot about human life on land.[61]

This points us to the second broad argument I make in this book, perhaps a little less obviously. The tenuous preservation of names in a scholar's private, unpublished archive is an invitation to think about the differences between historical research and history-writing. The presence of all those names is not so unusual: anyone who has worked through large quantities of original source materials knows full well just how disorienting the experience can be of wandering the paths of even a well-tended archive. A name, for a researcher, is both monad and metaphor: it stands for the whole class of past things that once existed but about which we start out knowing almost nothing.

> The solution of these problems will generally lead to the reformulation of the whole mode of questioning along the following lines: how is the question "What was it really like?" [*Wie es denn eigentlich gewesen sei?*] susceptible not just of being scientifically answered, but of actually being put[?] . . . A science in conflict with the language of its own investigations is an absurdity.[62]

While most history books relay the past to us as a story, researchers know that the past comes to us not as story, but as proper nouns: as discrete facts that are not themselves inscribed within any story. Four hundred years ago, Francis Bacon perceived this very clearly. In his *Advancement of Learning* (1605) he talked about scholarship that drew from "names" and also from "passages of books that concern not story." Bacon's contemporary and Peiresc's correspondent, Jean Besly, lamented that nothing in the genealogical research he did contained "a narrative worthy of the public" ("narration digne du public"). Neither Bacon nor Besly gave any indication as to how one actually might write history from this type of source.[63]

The historiographical intervention that this book intends to make lies, then, not only in what it says, but *how* it says it. I have ordered its thirty-six sections so as to move, on one axis, from the historiographical present to the historical past and then back again, and, on the other, out from Marseille and eastward across the Mediterranean. Some of these sections are diachronic, some synchronic, and some microhistorical. Some are very short, some are very long, and one, the day-by-day narrative of Peiresc's letters to the Levant over a ten-year period, could almost stand as a book on its own. While it is relatively uncommon for writers—and even less common for historians—to attempt to match the structure and style of a work to its subject matter, Peter Matthiessen's novel of Caribbean sailing, Arlette Farge's history of the eighteenth-century Parisian street, Karl Schlögel's *Moscow 1937,* and Rayner Banham's book about driving in Los Angeles show that it can be done beautifully and for a purpose: writing as a cognitive tool.[64] Behind them all stands László Moholy-Nagy's *Marseille Vieux-Port* (1929), a portuary kaleidoscope in ten minutes and thousands of faces.

The mimesis I am attempting here also extends from macro to micro structure. The act of "reconstruction"—what antiquaries did and what I will sometimes do here—requires some names and dates and actions to be registered in the account even if they do not register as "plot." In a way, this marks a difference between seventeenth- and twenty-first-century expectations of historical writers: we now expect an interventionism that leaves us with an ordered account. What does not fit is left out. But when Goethe called his book on color theory (*Farbenlehre,* 1812) a "kind of archive," he was alerting his readers to the difference between his book and what they were used to reading. Those of you interested in experiencing something of the confusion of prospecting in a seventeenth-century archive and of struggling with a different kind of reading can follow Peiresc from day to day and from section to section. Those seeking a tighter, more focused, more argued—and more familiar, modern—historiographic experience can instead turn directly to the thematic sections, especially those dealing with his Mediterranean network. These include "Marseille's Merchants," "Financing, Disbursing, Reimbursing," "Ships' Captains and *Patrons,*" "People in Motion," and "Endpoints." Even in the thematic sections you, the reader, should expect to find a greater-than-usual proportion of detail to argument.

I hope that for you, the reader, the benefit of this effort to bring the interpretive performance into some relationship with the materials upon which it draws—in Benjamin's terms, the respective card boxes of different generations of researchers—will be a closer encounter with the past as it comes down to us and a better understanding of how the historian works. But there are benefits for the writer, too. For me, writing this way has opened up the possibility of a "counter-history," a rebalancing of the familiar relationship between research and narrative that better exposes the craft practices—and struggles—of the historian. Benjamin, who surely knew whereof he spoke, saw in the patient work of historical reconstruction a "weak messianic power," which is to say, capable in some small way of bringing the dead back to life—or, in secular terms, reversing the Second Law of Thermodynamics.[65] But as Momigliano wrote long ago and Mark Phillips more recently, by the eighteenth century those conducting historical research had to learn to write connected narratives about the past or risk being cast aside as having no value for the present.[66] Antiquaries as a group never made the leap, and so discussions of their approach and the issues it raises have tended to happen only in their absence.[67] How, then, to write a book about the past—a book we would recognize as "history"—from "passages of books that concern not story" while preserving the look and feel of the encounter with those passages? This is the real challenge to which this study of Peiresc and the Mediterranean has brought me in the end: the redemption of a research culture by the literary imagination.

> And therefore, as when he himself enquired into any thing, or questioned another about it, he would not omit to enquire into every thing which concern'd the same; even so, when he desired any thing to be sought into and observed, by others, either near at hand or far off, he alwaies gave order, that it should be veiwed all manner of waies, so that no circumstances, if possible, might lie hid, which he therefore was commonly accustomed exactly to set down in writing.[68]

The "past," as Pierre Nora reminds us, which overflows the categories of "history" and "memory," is an increasingly large part of contemporary reading, writing, and viewing.[69] "Research," the process of recovering that wide past, is our chief tool for engaging with this complex twining of past and present. But research takes us into a world of detail, inevitable incompleteness and nonlinearity. Byron, reflecting on the antiquarian endeavor in *Childe Harold,* put words to our condition: "we but feel our way to err."[70] If storytelling reflects our need to organize our knowledge into modes of explanation (or refutation) that make sense of this world, then it will always need to elide or flatten some of the detail. Research, however, remains closely bound up with what we do not know, as well as what we do. That is why it is so important to me to make research both the content *and* the form of this study. It is a way of explaining without simplifying; of getting closer without pretending that we are ever going to arrive back at a past that is whole.

Nor can we pretend that the kind of narrative history-writing invented by Gibbon and Winckelmann did not triumph over other varieties. We cannot tell a story without narratives of some sort. (With this, I accept that the historian's role is to interpret sources, not just to publish them.) But perhaps we can use narrative in such a way as to evoke Peiresc the researcher. The different lines of inquiry he carried out through copying, annotating, memo-making, essay-writing, and corresponding do not converge on a single point, and probably could not. Peiresc's research for his history of Provence is as brilliantly variegated as that of the best-trained twentieth-century historian, but when Peiresc actually wrote his *History of Provence* it came out looking like any other chronicle. Orhan Pamuk planned to write *The Museum of Innocence* as a catalog of objects, but ended up writing a traditional narrative. Somewhere between these positions, between notes and the novel, we historians may find a way to tell our readers a story, and at the same time, perhaps by thinking with Peiresc, show them how stories about the past are made.

When Jacob Burckhardt first began thinking of himself as a cultural historian, he defined the practice as a focus on the background, rather than the more obvious foreground.[71] But in Peiresc's life and work these elements are so intermingled, the details of communication so central to the correspondence, and the intellectual projects so dependent on the realities of maritime practice that exploring Peiresc's Mediterranean can also offer a way of experimenting in a different kind of cultural history.

> You are not content to furnish them with rare manuscripts and other relics of a venerable Antiquity which could be found in Europe in

order to aid them in perfecting their works, but you have taken pains
to research all that is most curious in the Levant.[72]

I have long loved the historian's craft. My years exploring Peiresc's
archive have filled me with admiration for his intelligence, but even more
for his keen ability to use a question to tease out the kind of information
that did not seem evident on the surface of things. Archaeologists are
among the best at wringing every last bit of information out of artifacts,
largely because they often have so few and have to work so hard to find
them. I have learned much from them, and treat what I have found in my
tell with the same kind of attentiveness.

I first met R. G. Collingwood as a philosopher of history long before I learned he was an archaeologist, and before I saw that he derived
his vision of the seventeenth-century revolution in historical method from
the same turn to material culture that made the antiquaries, for Momigliano, unsung heroes of the modern study of the past. Unlike Momigliano,
however, Collingwood focused not on the sources, but on the ways the
historian reads them. Imagination, inference, conjecture, and, above all,
questioning were for Collingwood essential tools for grasping the past.
Because grasping the past in this way was the task of the historian, it requires us to find a way into the minds of those we study. "There is only
one way in which it can be done," Collingwood tells us, and that is "by
re-thinking them in his own mind." I have tried to do this here.[73]

Because of the riches of Peiresc's archive I have been able to reconstruct his Mediterranean life day by day. This was, after all, how he lived
it. I also realized that much was nevertheless missing, and much that was
there left me bewildered. My bewilderment, too, reflected something of
Peiresc's experience and our own, living in time as we must. But when I
organized the material by theme, making sense of what was otherwise
lost in the simultaneous but fragmentary unfolding of many plots, it became harder to see how it could all have been coordinated by one person,
integrating conversations with several hundred correspondents over more
than a decade. It was clear that both perspectives, the diachronic and the
synchronic, were needed. I knew that the choice of structure would shape
the possible story that could be told. Seeing its implications made me want
to have it both ways.

But then the problem of internal organization presented itself. Could
all the significant themes of Peiresc's Mediterranean be divided into chapters? Or was the entire endeavor really one chapter with many sections?

Here the experience of the archive itself—Bacon's "passages of books that concern not story," or the researcher writing rather than the storyteller writing—provided the solution. I decided that I wanted to bring to the reader as much of the researcher's experience as possible of working in the archive. That is why, in addition to the way the text is constructed and the way I have tried to tell this story, I have also assembled a detailed table and a series of charts that offer the reader an opportunity to go even deeper into the atomic structure of the argument (see Appendixes B and C).

To push my material to the limit I was willing to allow for a degree of centrifugal force usually not tolerated in academic history writing, both within each section and cumulatively. Working in any archive confronts the researcher with many possible narratives, but the conventions of practice require her to impose only one of them on those unruly facts, So, too, in this book there are many narrative lines that do not all perfectly connect. I wanted to reproduce the sense of gaps—as in the fragmentary character of part of the diachronic narrative—as well as the historian's sense of disorientation, of never quite catching every word of the conversation. The goal was to frame a large-scale accounting through many discrete, connected narratives, but neither to reduce them to one story nor to remove the reader too far from the words in the archive. This meant creating a structure in some tension. The historian knows that not everything adds up and that even in the best cases of documentation there is much that cannot be known. *Tristram Shandy* marks out the extreme example by leaving blank space where nothing can be said.

> All over his writings there are traces of wreckage: projects not carried out, promises of articles never written, and ideas which were never developed. (Gertrud Bing of Aby Warburg)[74]

In the Mellan drawing of 1636, Peiresc's eyes dominate. By then, his body had been ravaged by illness. But those eyes had seen much. They had peered into distant space through telescopes, and into the smallest things of the earth with microscopes. They had examined books, manuscripts, coins, plants, chameleons, and many other objects, some for the first time, some for the first time since antiquity. There is a touch of melancholy to Mellan's vision. Of course, for any thoughtful person the accumulation of years adds on a layer of sadness, if not an outright burden of suffering. There is also the possibility that the kind of work in which Peiresc immersed himself, the reconstruction of the past from its incomplete and broken fragments, brought with it a sense of the inevitable imperfection of things. This was Walter Benjamin's interpretation of Flaubert's lament, to a friend, that "few people could imagine how sad one had to be to undertake to bring Carthage back to life."[75]

For our man, there was also an inescapable set of biographical facts. Though he had learned much, and had advanced the learning of others, he must also have come to recognize by the end that some of his grandest projects would never come to fruition, even though he had spent his lifeblood on them. There were his observations of the moons of Jupiter, every night from late 1610 to mid-1612, and his investigation of ancient weights and measures, which filled a volume of notes and hundreds of pages of letters, and his study of the Roman Calendar of 354, whose oldest surviving copy he had obtained and which is now lost, and the "Gem Book" that he and Rubens began but never completed, and the complete publication of all the Samaritan versions of the Pentateuch in Hebrew, Aramaic, and Arabic, and his *History of Provence*, which saw some of his most brilliant research but which he could not find a way to bring into his written narrative.

And, of course, there was that "great book" about Marseille and the Mediterranean. This one he lived so intensely from day to day that there was never a question of writing it as a book. Instead, there are notes to self, memoranda, plans, lists, excerpts of reading, and letters, all of which he preserved as records from a life in progress. Peiresc, who was so aware that scholarship was an intergenerational project and that it was not one's obligation to finish a work but only not to despair of it, ended up having to leave his own materials to be made sense of by scholars of the future.

I have spent many years on the tell that is this archive. I have surveyed it. I have dug exploratory trenches. I have excavated for season after season, exposing long-buried remains. And always I have returned to the work table to turn the finds over and over, sometimes trying to piece the fragments together, other times satisfied simply with contemplating the pieces. Only now, after all these years, can I see them as if through Peiresc's eyes.

I ᘓ
Prologue: Algiers, June 1932

Once upon a time—about eighty years ago now—a group of Corsican-born Frenchmen living in Algiers decided to create a society that would promote the Corsican contribution to the French North African empire. The name chosen for the society and for its journal, *Bastion de France,* was the name of a French *comptoir,* or "concession," first established in the mid-sixteenth century and destroyed and rebuilt several times over the course of the next one. For a time, from 1628 to 1633, its governor was a Corsican-born Marseillais named Sanson Napollon. The journal had a relatively short life span—eight numbers over three years— and typically contained news of the community, some historical vignette or preservationist article, the occasional advertisement, and a section devoted to "Documents." In the first number, for example (1929), the documents section contained Napollon's 1631 report to Cardinal Richelieu on the importance of Bastion de France to the defense of maritime France.[1]

In 1932, on the eve of the three hundredth anniversary of Napollon's attack on the Genoese garrison of Tabarka, in which he was to lose his life, the society undertook to refurbish the site of Bastion de France and to put up a statue to Napollon's memory. They also got the idea—we do not know how—to devote the documents section of the journal to letters to Napollon from Peiresc.

In the April 1932 issue of the journal (*Bastion de France* no. 7) there is a brief notice announcing to readers the discovery, "after much research, of a veritable documentary treasure at the Bibliothèque Inguimbertine of Carpentras."[2] These included forty-two letters from Peiresc to Jean Gazille, who lived in Napollon's house in Marseille during the latter's absences in Algiers and Paris; to Lazarin de Servian, Napollon's deputy at Bastion de France; and to Napollon himself.

In the next—and as it turns out last—issue of the journal, published in June 1932, a selection of seven small notices was published. They are disparate in content, and include only one letter from Peiresc to Napollon, the ostensible core of the project.[3] The unsigned introduction to these pieces begins dejectedly: "We hoped to find in the minutes and copies of the correspondence of Peiresc some important documents; our expectation was a little disappointed." The anonymous voice acknowledged also having had some difficulty with the handwritings.[4]

Now, there is a great deal of material on Napollon in Carpentras (see Section 14, "Sanson Napollon"; Section 28, "Corsairs"; and Section 29, "Ransoming"). That so few items were deemed interesting enough to publish suggests that the person making the selection did not really understand how Peiresc worked. The avoidance of the letters is particularly telling: to see their value, one would have to read them for more than a narrative. Had the person who undertook this project taken the trouble to acquaint himself a little more deeply with Peiresc's practices, he would have found additional letters intended for Napollon but sent to others. Beyond Napollon, one could have learned much about Peiresc's deep interest in North Africa and the role of people like Napollon in his system. But these leads were never grasped. Whoever was looking for Napollon never understood how Peiresc managed his Mediterranean correspondence network.

The Peiresc-Napollon materials were published without a byline. But we do know that the person who had published those documents on Napollon in the 1929 issue of the journal was a young member of the Société Bastion de France, then teaching in Algiers, and an expert in this period. It is likely that he was the one chosen to direct this project. His name was Fernand Braudel.

This raises a question: What might the history of scholarship in the twentieth century have looked like if Braudel had understood the practicalities of Peiresc's Mediterranean-wide operation?[5] Could we imagine how someone with Braudel's sense for the material dimension of history might have tackled the practice of a seventeenth-century scholar? What might a historian with Braudel's inclinations have done with someone like Peiresc who himself paid so much attention to materiality, from the world with which he associated and the objects he studied, right down to the care with which he chose the paper on which he wrote?[6] What might one great student of the Mediterranean have done with the life and work of another? Later Braudel would show acute sensitivity to correspondence as a window into the breadth of past life.[7] But in the 1930s, he seemed to have had little interest in the Peiresc archive and little sense for how it could function as a window onto the same Mediterranean of commerce, navigation, and practice on which he would later focus through the public records of Simancas, Venice, and Dubrovnik.

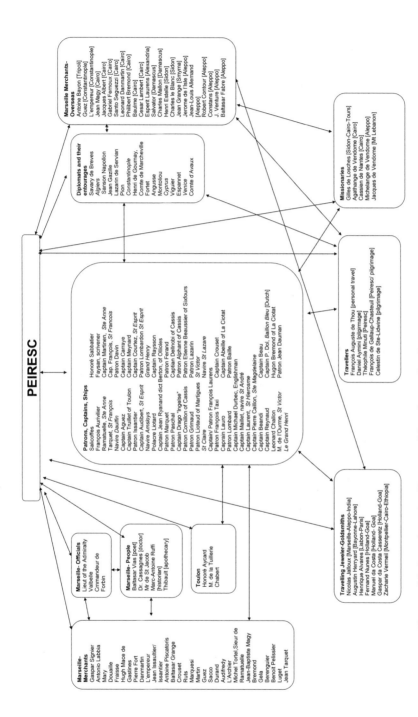

Figure 7. Chart of Peiresc's web. (Prepared by the author)

Braudel's failed encounter with the Peiresc archive calls to mind his failed encounter in the 1950s with S. D. Goitein, the great scholar of another Mediterranean trove: the Cairo Geniza.[8] Both of Braudel's near-misses mark a fault line in the history of historical scholarship in the twentieth century. I first came to study Braudel's interest in the Geniza and Goitein's work on it because I was looking for ways of thinking about Peiresc's Mediterranean network and archive. Studying Goitein's accomplishment showed me how scraps of conversations about everyday business dealings from hundreds of years ago could be turned into evidence by a historian asking the right questions.[9] For a brief period, Goitein was still "under the spell of the living *Annales* tradition" and felt the pull of structural explanation.[10] Looking in the other direction, Braudel in the Peiresc archive could have found the material culture of cultural history. A Braudel who had learned to decipher the Mediterranean world of Peiresc's archive in the 1930s might also have learned to pay closer attention to the individual's voice and experience when writing his history of the Mediterranean world. Goitein learned this in his Geniza's fragments, but his *Mediterranean Society* stopped short of story. And so, nearly a century later—a century full of historical exploration and innovation—we come back to this missed encounter, and to a question: What kind of history could Braudel have written had he fully understood Peiresc? (Figure 7).

2 ❧

Marseille-Aix

*A*ix and Marseille have always been the two cities of Provence: the one royal, learned, official, the other commercial, maritime, inevitably a little heteroclite. The courts and the university marked the one, the docks and the *chambre de commerce* the other. Scholarship has paid more attention to the scholarly than to the practical world, at least for the early modern period—perhaps a result of lingering, even if unselfconscious, corporate solidarity. Marseille was one of the most important cities in early modern Europe but, astonishingly, its students today have no general history of the period 1600–1650, and the closest thing to it, the relevant volume of the *History of Commerce in Marseille,* is over sixty years old.[1] In Braudel's *Mediterranean,* there are only a few pages about Marseille amid the hundreds devoted to Venice, Ragusa, Genoa, and Spain.[2] Anyone specifically interested in French commerce in the Levant in the seventeenth century must still reach for a book that was written in the 1890s.[3] Braudel wrote in the preface to an edition of Marseille merchant letters in 1953 that "one should not be shocked at the head of such a publication by the absence of a bibliography of books and sources consulted," because there were none to consult.[4] This remains more or less true today.[5]

Maritime Marseille has been studied for the Middle Ages and the eighteenth century.[6] Marseille during the civil wars of the sixteenth century has received its canonical treatment.[7] But Marseille of the early seventeenth century remains abandoned.[8] There is a problem here to be explored.

Studies of Peiresc have likewise ignored Marseille. Peiresc lived and worked in Aix, and Gassendi identified him for posterity as the "Senator of Aix-en-Provence." Today, there are many remembrances of Peiresc in Aix and Toulon, the two cities in which (or near which) he lived. But there is almost nothing in Marseille. Aix as the intellectual capital of Provence seems to make an appropriate home for the great intellectual. Marseille as a scrappy, commercial, maritime city seems somehow incompatible with a sickly, rather delicate, archive man.

But if the two cities are now joined by a motorway into a kind of "metropole," and their universities now welded into a single institution (one of whose parts, until 2010, used to be called the "Université de la Méditerranée"), in the seventeenth century they were close enough together for travelers to make the journey in a few hours.[9] And even if the scholarly literature on Peiresc has barely noticed, a huge part of his intellectual life was channeled in and through Marseille.[10] Once one looks, one finds in his work a very strong commitment to the history and life of this city, more, perhaps, even than to Aix. From an early age there were trips to Marseille, trips that have left their mark in his papers, with drawings of sculptures and copies of inscriptions.[11] And the visits continued when Peiresc was an adult.[12] Peiresc had, of course, many correspondents in Marseille, many more in fact than are found in the log of his outgoing mail, and some of them much more frequent recipients of mail than has been preserved. It was in Marseille that Peiresc acquired practical goods, such as salt, medicaments, and melons.[13] It was in Marseille that he sought leather from the Levant, probably for covering his books—though in May 1626, at least, his search was disappointed.[14] Marseille also supplied his artistic needs. He obtained from Marseille a frame for Rubens's drawing of the Great Cameo of France, which he had from a Flemish ébéniste working in St. Victor; "a sculptor, my friend," came from there to repair a crack in his cast of the cameo on the del Monte–Barberini, now Portland, vase.[15] And, of course, Peiresc worked—"dug," to use his term—in the archives of Marseille.[16] The archivists in turn were part of his knowledge community.[17] Finally, Marseille mattered to Peiresc because that is where he did his banking (see Section 13, "Financing, Disbursing, Reimbursing").

Peiresc's ramifying connections to Marseille brought him into a political relationship. His brother, Vallavez, was often enough in Marseille to be installed as the city's "Viguier," a ceremonial chief officer, for the year 1633–1634, suggesting also a recognition of the brothers' relationship to the city.[18] A few years after Peiresc's death, in 1642, Pierre Fort, the Marseille merchant who handled his affairs, was named Viguier and was ceremonially presented by none other than Vallavez.[19] We also find Peiresc at home gossiping about Marseille's politics, whether with Vallavez in 1625 or with the bishop in 1626.[20]

Peiresc also cast himself as a defender of the traditional liberties of the city. In a long letter to Vallavez written early in 1626, which he warned Vallavez to use with prudence or "all will burn in an instant," he outlined the terms of the assault on the city's privileges by Duke of Guise, then governor of Provence and the last admiral of the Levant. In Marseille, Peiresc wrote, "no one can any longer live with the accustomed liberty because M. de Guise wants them to do what he pleases and nothing else, and if anyone speaks against, he is threatened, and up to the consuls themselves."[21]

But beyond friendship, people, and even money, what bound Peiresc to Marseille and the Mediterranean was sentiment. Writing in 1636 to his closest friends, the Dupuy brothers, he recounted the visit of their nephew, Christophe, en route to Rome. Christophe had stopped in Aix and was out and about, visiting at the cabinet of Peiresc's friend Boniface Borilly, but aside from that, "there was hardly anything else worth seeing" in Aix. "But," he continued, "if he goes on to Marseille, the first view of the sea would be capable of taking from him any regret about the want of a legitimate subject for the rest of his trip."[22]

Such were the bonds of sentiment, to the point where he used the phrase "our Mediterranean Sea."[23] Nor was this a meaningless formula. Writing to de Thou in Paris, he offered that "things having to do with the sea are so close to our heart": *Les choses de la Marine nous sont si à coeur.*[24]

3 ↝

Marseille and the French Mediterranean

*T*o place Peiresc into this Mediterranean, we begin and end in Marseille. For he even described the seas between Italy and Spain as the "Mare Phoccium," in honor of Marseille, the city of the Phocceans.[1] If Braudel recognized Marseille only as the falling counterweight to the rise of Holland and England, and dated this swing to 1620, it might be an optical illusion, related to the relative paucity of the kind of sources he used for the decades immediately following.[2] But it might also be the result of his having failed to look at—or perhaps not knowing how to look at—the one source that sheds the most light on the commercial life of Marseille in the 1620s and 1630s, the Peiresc archive, rich as it is with information about human agents and their economic practices. If this is not serial history, it is a history of people engaged in "communications and commerce," Michael McCormick's redefinition of the subject of economic history.[3]

Marseille was France's gateway to the Mediterranean. It was from Marseille that merchant ships sailed and diplomatic embassies came and went. If we can reimagine the first part of the seventeenth century in terms of a "French Mediterranean," Marseille would be its undisputed capital.[4] Its commercial activity increased sixfold during this period.[5] To the extent that Peiresc's Mediterranean is co-extensive with this French Mediterranean, it shares the same capital city.

The story of Peiresc and Marseille begins with François Savary de Brèves. De Brèves was the leading figure in the French oriental politico-commercial-cultural establishment—the first French "orientaliste," we might say—circa 1600.[6] De Brèves entered the spotlight in 1598 when he was accredited French ambassador to the Sublime Porte, a position which he held until 1604. He was responsible for a renewal of the capitulations, the treaty terms between France and the Ottomans first granted by Sultan Suleiman to François I. Peiresc's archive preserves a copy of the capitulation the Sultan granted to France and de Brèves in 1604, which amounted to an augmentation of the agreement of 1598 by 34 articles, now binding Ahmed, son of the late Emperor Mehmet who had conceded the previous agreement, to guaranteeing many new commercial privileges for Marseille.[7] In 1605, de Brèves left Constantinople to return to Europe—via Syria, Lebanon, Palestine, Egypt, and North Africa.[8] This trip resulted in a book published posthumously in 1630.[9] In 1609 he received from the king the absentee consulship of Cairo, which he subsequently leased out for income.[10]

De Brèves's second ambassadorial posting was no less significant than the first: the Holy See. The Rome of the late Counter-Reformation was itself marked by an awakening to the existence and importance of Eastern Christianity.[11] De Brèves's experience of that world and his new encounter with this one led him to the idea of employing some of the young Maronites come to Rome to study at the Maronite College (founded 1583) to translate Roman Catholic texts into the languages of Eastern Christianity (Arabic, Turkish, and Syriac). With this was founded the "Typographia Savariana." When de Brèves returned to France in 1614, he took with him the idea of sponsoring translations from oriental languages, only now, in a secular setting, substituting the language of contemporary empire, Persian, for the language of early Christianity, Syriac. The printing operation, in turn, was to be located at the center of an entire institute for advanced oriental studies. His cousin by marriage, the great historian and political figurehead Jacques-Auguste de Thou, was recruited to help convince others of the wisdom of so proceeding in terms of a French "interest" in the Near East, and not out of a religious motivation.[12]

De Brèves stood at the crossroads of many policy axes—trade, negotiation, crusade, and protection of Christian holy places. He thus articulated most concisely the turning point that the Peiresc archive documents again and again. Writing to Pierre Brulart, vicomte de Puysieux and secretary of state for foreign affairs in 1619, de Brèves explained that he was advocating on behalf of "the subjects of the King trading on the seas of the Levant or, to say it better, on the Mediterranean Sea."[13] "Levant," like "Outremer," was a word from a past in which East was separated from West by a long, mythical space of conflict. De Brèves saw the "Mediterranean" that connects as the more appropriate term now that the Turkish military threat had receded. And that Mediterranean was made physically manifest by the spread of Marseille merchants throughout the Ottoman Empire.

It is no surprise that the first person to see the Mediterranean as a world to be studied and reflected on, not merely lived in, was someone whose intellectual goals were closely intertwined with Marseille and its commerce.[14] "Our Mediterranean Sea" was how Peiresc put it.

We know that de Brèves met Peiresc very early—in Marseille, in fact, upon his return to France from North Africa. Peiresc writes to Malherbe in November 1606 that M. de Brèves had arrived in Aix and was hosted by Guillaume du Vair (1556–1561), who had recently become Peiresc's *patron*. Du Vair was a politician—First President of the Parlement of Provence after Henri IV's reassertion of control over Provence and later keeper of the seals under the queen mother and regent, Marie de' Médicis, but also the vector through which Justus Lipsius's "neostoicism" came to France. De Brèves "recounted the marvels of those oriental lands," and bore gifts for the king and queen.[15] In 1614, returning from his next posting, in Rome, de Brèves again met Peiresc in Marseille. A memo in the archive records the date as 1 June 1614, under the title "Passage de Mr De Brèves." De Brèves remained in Marseille until Monday the 23rd, when he went to Aix and visited with President du Vair and Peiresc all that day and the next.[16] Responding to news of favorable negotiations between Marseille and Tunis in 1617, de Brèves offered his assistance should it be desired.[17]

De Brèves also appears frequently in Peiresc's archive.[18] One of these traces is an undated policy paper entitled "On the Alliance with the Turk" ("Sur l'alliance avec le Turc").[19] Peiresc's position at court, in the entourage of du Vair, meant that he was part of—and would have been seen by others to be part of—the "Mediterraneanist" faction at court."[20]

De Brèves advocated close relations with the Turks because of the "notable Traffic" that French subjects had in Ottoman territory. The Marseille-based trade had cut deeply into that of the Venetians and the English, leading them to work together against the French. Venice was in a constant state of war with the Ottomans and did not want another Christian state on good terms with its enemy. Similarly, the Spanish, being compelled to defend an extended empire—in Sicily and southern Italy as well as interests in North Africa—were forced into the role of antagonists. Not so France. De Brèves's chief point was that a pro-Ottoman policy was important for much more than the condition of merchants in the Levant; it counterbalanced the much greater menace of Spain in the western Mediterranean, and without it there would be immediate and negative consequences for French coastal traffic and political freedom of maneuver.[21] We could sum up de Brèves's view of the Ottoman challenge in the western Mediterranean with words from a letter he wrote to the consuls of Marseille: "I hope that this will not prevent the project already begun—of living well with those people of Algiers and Tunis—from being happily concluded."[22]

France's "Turkish" policy went back to Francis I's decision to develop one as part of his chess match with the emperor Charles V. It came to include permitting the Ottoman fleet to winter at Toulon in 1543–1544. What de Brèves's position represents is the coming predominance of commerce, rather than military conflict, as the main form of the interaction between West and East. The Peiresc archive gives out onto a commercial maritime world that is neither some sideshow nor a "history from below" to balance the grandeur of a "Lepanto." Because of the transformation of the Mediterranean in the first part of the seventeenth century from a zone of military conflict to one of commercial contact, it is the main story.

A similar document, again undated but focused on Rome, emphasizes the western Mediterranean. It begins from the value to France of maritime Provence—"the advantage which God gave us over all the princes of Europe . . . the position that your County of Provence gives you, rich as it is in good and great ports, and an infinite number of excellent mariners."[23] To block Spain, and thus to change the balance of power in Europe, de Brèves urged the king "to think in good conscience about the affairs of the sea." Because Iberia was so far from Italy, and "inasmuch as there is neither access to nor communication with Italy except by this route," Provence held the key to Spanish power.[24]

This vision of the strategic importance of maritime Provence is one that Peiresc would share, and spread, among his circle of friends and correspondents. In the second and third decades of the seventeenth century, de Brèves stood as the éminence grise behind a number of scholars and a variety of initiatives. He remained, as well, a potent force in the family of de Thou, advising the late president's son, François-Auguste, when he planned his own trip to the Levant in 1627.[25] Another protégé was Sanson Napollon, a Corsican-born citizen of Marseille (see Section 14, "Sanson Napollon") who served as consul in the Levant, negotiator with the dey of Algiers, and finally governor of the *comptoir* of Bastion de France. He represented the activist, Mediterraneanist position at court.[26] In fact, when Napollon was engaged in a complex negotiation with Cardinal Richelieu about the French position in negotiations with Algiers, de Brèves advised him. When they were both in Paris, Napollon visited de Brèves, and when Napollon returned to Marseille, de Brèves wrote to him.[27] Presenting Napollon to the consuls of Marseille, de Brèves affirmed that his care for the commerce of Marseille was "praiseworthy."[28] The pace of their letters and de Brèves's repetitiveness in them suggests resistance on the part of

Marseille to the main provision of the negotiations: release of Turks en-slaved in the galleys.[29]

While Napollon was in Paris, Peiresc relayed his letters to his agent and house-sitter in Marseille, Jehan Gazille, sometimes along with those of de Brèves to a business partner in Marseille.[30] And when he was not in Paris, but in Marseille, Peiresc forwarded letters from de Brèves to him, via a cousin of Peiresc's.[31] Finally, when de Thou was planning his trip, he turned, presumably on de Brèves's advice, to Napollon (via Peiresc) for letters of recommendation to the French consuls in the Levant and to Ottoman officials of his acquaintance.[32]

Peiresc served the de Brèves "faction" even after de Brèves's death. Writing to Gabriel Fernoux (Peiresc's habitual spelling was "Farnoux"), vice-consul in Cairo and a de Brèves appointee, Peiresc reported that de Brèves's death had complicated a scheme in which he was engaged with the widow de Brèves ("Madame La Comtesse de Brèves") to secure the position of her son, the abbot of Montmajour, near Arles.[33]

Peiresc's involvement in the affairs of the "House of de Brèves" seems entangled with those of Napollon and the Mediterraneanist faction. Thus, the same letter to Gazille of May 1629 that commiserated about the ru-mors being spread in Provence about Napollon's attempt to drive up the price of wheat from his "Bastion de France" by selling it to the enemy Genoese immediately segued into a report that Madame de Brèves was displeased that her agent in Marseille was planning to dump unsold pieces of scarlet cloth in Algiers. Peiresc asked Gazille to see if he could not find some use for it—that is, buy it—and suggested he speak with Peiresc's own merchant-banker in Marseille, who was already involved in the whole af-fair and could give him some advice.[34]

And as late as 1635, when trying to win de Thou's support for a plan that emerged from discussions between Peiresc and the Marseille-based jeweler Benoit Pelissier about setting up an entrepôt at Mocha on the Red Sea (see Section 35, "Where Mediterranean Meets Orient"), it was de Brèves's name that Peiresc invoked. It would be difficult, Peiresc wrote, to find someone better equipped for a project of this sort than Pelissier. Whatever start-up costs were involved could be covered by the king or the younger M. de Brèves.[35] The legacy of de Brèves was France's Medi-terranean vocation.

Peiresc, within this general approach, came to see Provence's distinc-tive relationship to the Mediterranean. He famously described his life in Provence as a kind of desert, telling the Dupuy brothers that he was cut off from books "no less than if we were amidst the sands of Libya."[36] Similarly, in a letter recommending his friend Dr. Cassagnes of Marseille to a Parisian doctor in 1634, he described as an "original sin our common birth in this contemptible place, and a sterile land, and so neighboring to the Barbary Coast." Thus far, the imagery of proximity to North Africa is all negative. It is the parenthesis that follows that makes all the difference to the interpretation: "which is separated only by a canal of the sea." In other words, Provence and Africa were neighbors, and the Mediterranean hardly an obstacle at all, since a canal connects as well as divides.[37] And Peiresc actually saw this proximity as his advantage, weighing his distance from Paris against his "commerce"—the word and its connotations are his— with Rome and the Levant, "which was not of the most common."[38]

This feeling was translated into a scholarly interest in "les livres de la marine."[39] We know of Peiresc's intense study of Mediterranean maritime law, beginning in 1627. Peiresc was, as I have argued elsewhere, the first student of the *Llibre del Consolat de Mar.*[40] He even claimed to have had the officers of Marseille write to Barcelona on the subject.[41] The archives of Marseille were where he went to see "if there was not anything curious there on the subject."[42] He had made transcriptions of many of the statutes of Marseille devoted to the marine, and these included a discussion of the admiralty and the "consuls de mer."[43]

As ever with Peiresc, the past was tied in to the present, and research to practice. Peiresc paid attention to the political-economic dimension of maritime commerce not only for France but also in a wider European perspective. In his archive we find an "Edict on Commerce," or the "Royal Edict for establishing a commerce in France by sea and land to the Levant, Ponant and Long-Distance Voyages in general," dated to July 1626.[44] This proposes setting up a trading company and presents piracy as a major threat.[45] The document was signed by Louis XIII and countersigned below "par le Roy de Lomenie"—showcasing Peiresc's close connection with the secretary of state.[46] Then there is a document of 1627 coming from the Senate of Danzig, in the Hansa, proposing establishment of a "compagnie generale de commerce" that would create a structure for selling Spanish imperial goods through a northern German network, as Peiresc describes it on the flyleaf. It was framed by *"intelligent people practiced in commercial matters" ("persone intelligenti, e prattiche negl'affari del commercio").*[47] Peiresc also obtained a document from the Spanish side, "The Advantages and Conveniences that the King of Spain will receive from the Admiralty of Seville." This is actually referred to in the Danzig *mémoire,* with its articulation of an alternative to the Dutch carrying trade.[48]

It would seem that Peiresc was collecting data on other attempts to set up state-backed trading companies in the light of Loménie's and Louis XIII's declared interest in doing the same. Equally of the moment, Peiresc's archive preserves a memo he drew up on the fisheries. Peiresc was responding to the desire of those already fishing in the Mediterranean to pass into the Atlantic. He sought on their behalf letters patent from the king to protect them against any obstacles or prohibitions ("inhibitions et deffances"). For instance, he sought a declaration from the king permitting one Jerome Baudin, native of Martigues, resident in Marseille, to assemble as large a fleet as he desired and pass through the Straits of Gibraltar to fish off the Spanish coast.[49] He also intervened with Gabriel d'Aubespine, the bishop of Marseille, to thank him on behalf of "this province" for intervening with the king and with Richelieu on behalf of "the reestablishment of trade in our seas." In this, Peiresc appears as a crucial spokesman for a Mediterraneanist, commerce-oriented policy, very much in the tradition of de Brèves.[50]

Peiresc used his familiarity with Alphonse-Louis du Plessis de Richelieu, bishop of Aix and later cardinal of Lyon, and brother of the more famous cardinal-minister, to champion the danger to the exposed Provençal coast.[51] Peiresc stressed how much the wealth of Lyon was connected to that of Marseille, thus simultaneously invoking the connectivity of commerce and casting himself as the defender of Marseille.[52] Once open warfare had broken out with Spain, these letters to Alphonse-Louis were filled with details of naval maneuvers, troop movements, rumors from Spain and Genoa—likely enough intended for the eyes of the bishop's brother in Paris.[53]

Peiresc collected information on the Spanish navy. From 1627 came not just the report of a visit by a flotilla of Spanish (including Portuguese and Neapolitan) naval vessels but also detailed information about the size and armament of the flagships. Peiresc made a point of preserving all these data.[54] Spanish ambitions in the western Mediterranean were of course of particular interest to Peiresc. Two documents report on the arming of a flotilla at Sardinia for a descent somewhere along the French coast in autumn 1634.[55] The outbreak of open war between France and Spain in 1635 drew Peiresc deeper into purely naval matters. In a letter to Aycard of June 1635 he conveyed news he had from Holland of a plan to outfit a squadron of thirty ships for an attack on Spain, perhaps even passing through the straits to target Valencia or Barcelona.[56] The letters to Loménie from just before the outbreak of war through the Spanish seizure of the Isles de Lerins are full with detail about Spanish naval maneuvers.[57]

But Peiresc could also think strategically about Mediterranean affairs. He explained to Sabran, the French consul in Genoa, how control of these coastal islands was part of a broader set of developments. For if this land grab was not repulsed soon, it could be extended to other parts of the coast, most notably the port of Maguelone on the outskirts of Montpellier. Second, introducing still another Mediterranean, Peiresc reported that at Barcelona flat-bottomed boats were being specially constructed for this purpose. Third, he explained that this Spanish strategy was modeled on that used at Hormuz at the other end of the Mediterranean world, where they had "for so long held out in the face of the King of Persia and all of his forces, and other similar places that they occupied" along the coasts of Barbary and the Indies. Fourth, to eject them from the isles, he mused, perhaps tongue in cheek, would require the forces of the sultan himself ("Il fallut que le grand Turc sortist de Constantinople qu'il faudroit de la facon pour les arracher de noz isles"). Finally, concluding the letter, Peiresc commiserated with Sabran on the role of the Genoese in facilitating Spanish western Mediterranean policy.[58]

And yet, Peiresc was also keenly aware that a wider war in Europe would draw attention away from the Mediterranean theater. "If France did not have elsewhere other greater affairs on its hands, one could embark with the confidence that recognizing the importance of those of the Levant, one would make preparations as one ought," he wrote to de Thou in February 1635. But the eyes, ears, and attention of French policymakers were, indeed, elsewhere.[59]

The merchants of Marseille were part of his world.[60] In this, Peiresc very much represented the continuation of de Brèves's viewpoint; he also maintained contacts with several of de Brèves's people. Welcoming the Venetian Santo Seghezzi to the consulate in Cairo, Peiresc sang the advantages of having a worldly Venetian at that posting; he made as if to hang all of France's eastern trade on the Cairo staffing. (Peiresc first mentioned Seghezzi as the Venetian consul in Cairo in a letter to de Thou of 25 April 1629.)[61] Seghezzi's credit would help advance "commerce not only in Egypt, but much further beyond, as it was at other times, as much in Africa and Ethiopia, as in Arabia and even to India, having much practice in Moucal [Mocha] and other places in the Red Sea."[62] Peiresc described Seghezzi in another letter of December 1634 as a native Venetian coming "not of the Republic's noblility, but of those who are subjects." Seghezzi had worked to elevate the Venetian position in Egypt and was now keen to do the same for France. Peiresc adopted the declinist language of the Marseille merchants: Seghezzi could "reestablish commerce, which was going to complete ruin in that land."[63]

The quarrel for the consulate in Cairo in 1634–1635 deeply engaged Peiresc (see Section 33, "Peiresc's Mixing in Cairo's Consular Politics"). Writing to Giovanni Alvise (sometimes Alviggi) Gela, Peiresc recalled de Brèves, whom he described as "more interested than anyone else" ("piu interezzato d'ogni altro")—in the seventeenth-century sense of "engaged"—and sure to have been a supporter of Seghezzi.[64] Peiresc's invocation of de Brèves in this context connects the latter to a web of French policy-making through Gabriel Fernoux, to whom de Brèves had leased the vice-consulate of Cairo, to Seghezzi in Cairo, to Gela back in Marseille, to Napollon in Algiers, and, of course, to Peiresc in Aix. With Seghezzi now embroiled in controversy over the consulate with Albert and Bermond, it cast those to whom Peiresc appealed on his behalf, notably de Thou, as implicit heirs to the same Mediterraneanist position. Two years earlier, Peiresc would turn to de Thou as a friend of Provence at court and the cause of the "restablissement du commerce." But describing de Thou's interest—or projecting it onto him—with the very same words he used to describe his own, Peiresc wrote, "Maritime matters are so close to your heart that I do not doubt at all that you will willingly make yourself useful on this occasion as I humbly ask you."[65] Treating de Thou as part of the "team," Peiresc went into detail about Seghezzi, whom, it turns out, de Brèves had handpicked in Constantinople as a future consul.[66] Moreover, when de Brèves took control of the vice-consulate of Cairo, he had supplanted a Venetian who had possessed it for more than ten years, "which is to say that there would be nothing new should another Venetian have it."[67]

De Thou was presented as ambassador extraordinary to Constantinople in January 1635, but after months of delay never left Paris.[68] Indeed, Peiresc, and all his friends, urged him not to go out of fear for his safety.[69] Nevertheless, were de Thou to have studied the language and manners of the Turks, Peiresc held, he would have become an even greater expert than de Brèves.[70] Peiresc also offered advice on how to remove the incumbent ambassador Philippe de Harlay, comte de Césy, and liquidate his debts, showing his command of the details of recent business history.[71] Word that de Thou would be able to meet with Sr. de la Picadière, an old

Ottoman hand, cheered him immensely, "since many believe that he had as many grand intentions to make himself useful there as had the late M. de Brèves."[72] Again, for Peiresc, de Brèves was always the standard. If we needed one last proof of de Brèves's pivotal role in this entire narrative of French Mediterraneanism—not so much as a person as a position—it would be that the letters from Gela to his brother-in-law Seghezzi that were intended for de Thou in Paris were actually addressed to de Brèves's secretary—and this in 1635, a full seven years after his death.[73]

The most substantial example of Peiresc's involvement in French maritime strategy—and French Mediterranean strategy in particular—is his role in the preparation of the Seguiran Report.[74] In a letter of December 1632 to Secretary of State Loménie in Paris, Peiresc mentions a public audience that Cardinal de Richelieu had held that very morning "pour la surintendance de la marine."[75] In March 1631, Richelieu had promulgated the Règlement du roi sur le fait de la Marine, which effectively abolished the ancient office of the Admiral du Levant. Then, in September 1632 he had the king appoint Peiresc's brother-in-law Henri de Seguiran (in 1615 Seguiran had married Peiresc's sister from his father's second marriage) as his *lieutenant géneral en l'intendance de la Marine*.[76] With a pension of 1,500 livres per year, this was no small reward to the Seguiran-Fabri clan. Peiresc, we know, was close to Seguiran and worked on behalf of the latter's son, his nephew, whenever possible.[77]

Seguiran needed a cartographer, and we know that Peiresc tried to get Gassendi appointed. When he turned down the offer, Jacques Maretz, professor of mathematics at Aix, was next approached, and he accepted. His appointment, too, was likely at Peiresc's suggestion.[78] Maretz, Seguiran, and an entourage then began an inspection of the Provençal coast, undertaken between 11 January and 17 March 1633. Seguiran delivered his "Report" to Richelieu that spring; it was published only in the nineteenth century.[79]

But only in Peiresc's archive do we find a second memorandum, also by Seguiran, filed by Peiresc under the title "1633. Avril. COSTE MARITIME DE PROVENCE."[80] Was this annex actually produced by Peiresc? Or to Peiresc's taste and in response to his questions? We do not know. It supplements the description of the portuary facilities and shipping found in the Seguiran Report with a specific account of the history and current state of French Mediterranean trade. The report presents the rise and incipient decline of Marseille from about 1570, and linked in *contrapasso* to the state of Venetian trade. The tense, cold peace between Venice and the

Ottomans after Lepanto was said to provide Marseille with its opportunity, "and it was from then that there began the richness and opulence" of the city.[81] Once in the door, the Marseillais were able to hold off Venetian attempts to reclaim their position, aided by the role Marseille had already assumed as way-station for Flemish and English Mediterranean shipping.

The Seguiran Report very clearly maps out where Marseille merchants were involved and how deeply. Thus, to Alexandria there sailed fifteen *vaisseaux* or barques and goods worth 900,000 livres tournois (l.t.), to Sidon eight vaisseux or barques and goods valued at 480,000 l.t., and to Alexandretta twenty *polacres*, vaisseaux, and barques with 2,400,000 l.t. worth of merchandise. To Smyrna there sailed twenty vaisseaux, polacres, and barques with 360,000 l.t. of goods, to Constantinople ten vaisseaux with 300,000 l.t., and to Antalya ("Satalie") four or five barques bearing 135,000 l.t. Cyprus was the destination for four or five barques and 81,000 l.t., while Crete and Patras were negligible trading partners. All in all, eighty to eighty-five vessels sailed annually to the Échelles bearing goods worth 4.68 million l.t. and returning with around 4.5 million l.t. in goods.[82]

The Seguiran Report makes it clear that Marseille's main Levantine connections were in Aleppo and Alexandria. But at a certain point—in the last decades of the sixteenth century—the northerners had entered the Levantine market directly. This historical account is not found in the body of the Seguiran Report.[83] But in the annex to the report, found only in Peiresc's copy, the author demonstrates a sense not only for history but for sociology and economics. The reign of Henri IV, the annex tells us, marked something of a reprieve for Marseille because of the new markets for silk—the luxuries sought after by a peacetime society and an elaborate court culture.[84]

Even more, the author of the Seguiran Report—whoever the actual author was—understood that the success of Marseille directly resulted from the kind of maritime traffic the port received. That Marseille displaced Venice in the first decades of the seventeenth century was directly related to the speed of Marseille's lighter, smaller, faster ships and the greater number of them plying the seaways. These allowed the Marseillais to make three trips in the time it took for the Venetians to make one. When de Thou was leaving Constantinople for Smyrna, he confidently announced that he would send news from there, "because there are always boats for Marseille."[85] Louis Deshayes de Courmenin, one of the diplomatic fixers

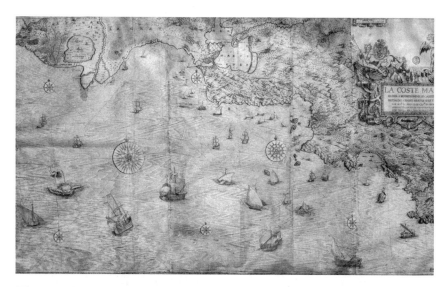

Figure 8. Jacques Maretz's map of the "Côtes Maritimes de Provence," detail. (Bibliothèque Nationale de France)

sent by the French to solve the problem of the Échelles in the 1620s, explicitly contrasted the bulky Venetian ships—whose seaworthiness was so suspect that they spent huge amounts of time in port—with the "much smaller and very much lighter" Marseille ships; "aside from that," he added, "the sailors of Marseille are so skillful and are so well practiced for the Mediterranean that they are esteemed as highly there as the Dutch are on the Ocean."[86]

For those whose histories of the Mediterranean are built around volume of cargo, this contemporary emphasis on speed suggests an alternative hierarchy of value. The writer of this report provides us with a seventeenth-century vision of the Mediterranean, one that Horden and Purcell invented, in their own terms, almost four centuries later.[87] But there is one further twist. The author explains that since the majority of the goods picked up in the East were textiles ("drap"), paper, and other sundry goods, the carrying capacity of the vessels was less meaningful than their frequency and speed. For someone like Peiresc, whose trade goods were paper, coins, and the occasional trinket, agility would have mattered more than capacity. For a material history of Peiresc's intellectual life, then, it is clear that Marseille offered an excellent base: greater frequency and speed of shipping meant that his letters, manuscripts, and memoranda could go farther and faster than had he been based elsewhere. Proof of this is found within the archive itself: when one of Peiresc's correspondents in Sidon sent not paper but a "demi-ton" of "vines and other trees of the most curious of all the land," he had to send them on a Flemish vaisseau because the small lateen barques of Marseille, once loaded with their regular cargo, had no spare capacity.[88]

One cannot separate this distinction between ship types and trading patterns from Maretz's depiction of the "coast of Provence" in the accompanying map (Figure 8).[89] Its most striking feature is the amount of space given over to the depiction not of the zone where water meets land—the coast proper—but of the water itself. On the water—as if turning water into land, and sea into roads—Maretz has arrayed 114 ships, each with enough detail to enable us to identify them. There are the vaisseaux or navires, with four masts, four square sails, one lateen, a square poop, and a capacity of 150 to 300 tons; the polacres, with three masts and mixed lateen and square sails; the barques—by far the most common type—with three masts and lateen sails and a capacity of 50 to 100 tons; and the tartanes, with one great mast, two or three sails according to whether they were used for fishing or trade, and a capacity of approximately 50 tons. And then there were the local, small craft—leyts, palanguiers, yssauges, and sardiniaux.[90]

If the Seguiran Report sees the interest in maritime trade with the Levant from the Provençal side, we know that Peiresc also wished to see it from the Egyptian side. From a letter to de Thou of May 1635, we know not only that Fernoux, the vice-consul in Cairo, stopped by chez Peiresc but that Peiresc commissioned from him a mémoire on the "present state of the commercial affairs of the Levant." Fernoux produced a succinct document that Peiresc read and sent back with a request for some small additions, including one of a series of statistical surveys that Peiresc collected (see Section 32, "Before Statistik").[91]

4 ❧
Contingency

*I*t is only a small piece of paper, printed with some official-sounding boilerplate and intended for a specific use. On close reading we see that it is a prefabricated declaration, dated to 1625, from the consuls of the city of Marseille affirming the health of the bearer of the document, with space left for names to be added in by hand. Official-looking seals and coats of arms would be added when the certificate was signed and executed. It was intended to be used once and then discarded, perhaps its rag content recycled into new paper (Figure 9).

This copy is blank, seemingly never employed for its intended purpose. But it was used all the same. For on the back, in Peiresc's hand, we find in large letters the words "LETTRES SAMARITAINES". Peiresc briefly tells us what this means: "the original Samaritan letters written to the late Scaliger (whom he calls Sullarin the Frank) from Aza [Gaza] by Eleazar the High Priest of the Samaritans in the year 998, Friday, 20 Seba, which is January, of the Reign of the Ishmaelites Agerus, who are the Turks. This corresponds to 1590 A.D. according to Scaliger's calculation."[1]

Scaliger had written to the Samaritans seeking information about their calendar in the context of his research project on world chronology, *De Emendatione Temporum* (1583). In response to a letter of 1584 in which the leaders of the Samaritan community had included their calendar, Scaliger asked a series of questions about Samaritan rituals. Their reply, written in 1590 but never to reach Scaliger, is what Peiresc summarizes here.

We know that the loss of the letters, and that of an accompanying Samaritan Pentateuch (actually a hexaglot Psalter), continued to bother Scaliger because in February 1606 Peiresc wrote to him, taking upon himself the task of recovering the books that had gone down with the foundering of the *St. Victor*, out of Marseille. If "M. Ostagier" of Marseille proved unable to provide any information as to its whereabouts, Peiresc wrote, "I will employ all my friends in Marseille who trade with the Levant to seek to recover it."[2] In his biography of Peiresc, Gassendi provided the context:

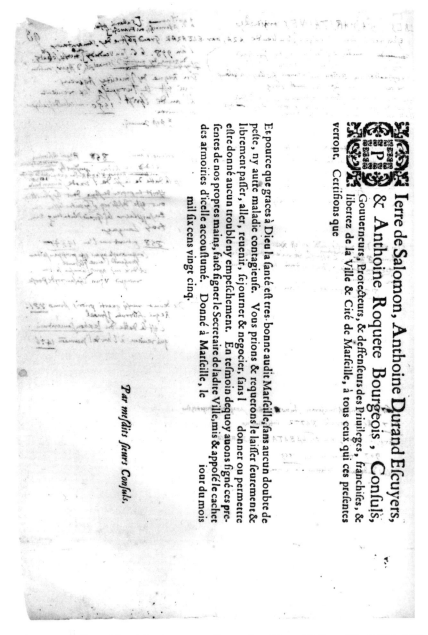

Ierre de Salomon, Anthoine Durand Escuyers, & Anthoine Roquete Bourgeois, Consuls, Gouverneurs, Protecteurs, & deffenseurs des Priuileges, franchises, & libertez de la Ville & Cité de Marseille, à tous ceux qui ces presentes verront. Certifions que

Et pource que graces à Dieu la santé est tres-bonne audit Marseille, sans aucun doubte de peste, ny aucune maladie contagieuse. Vous prions & requerons le laisser seurement & librement passer, aller, reuenir, sejourner & negocier, sans l donner ou permettre estre donné aucun trouble ny empeschement. En tesmoin dequoy auons signé ces presentes de nos propres mains, faict signer le Secretaire de ladite Ville, mis & apposé le cachet des armoiries d'icelle accoustumé. Donné à Marseille, le   iour du mois mil six cens vingt cinq.

Par mesdits sieurs Consuls.

Figure 9. Printed health clearance from the City of Marseille PBN, MS. Lat. 9340, f. 93v. (Bibliothèque Nationale de France)

Scaliger had sometime intreated him, that he would renew his commerce which he had established in the East, by the Agencie of *Pater Ostagerius,* who was in times past his Host at Marseille, for the buying up of Samaritan, Aegyptian and Arabick books; grieving that of the space of fifteen years which he had spent in Holland, he had not heard a word of the Samaritan Pentateuch, which *Ostagerius* had promised to endeavour to procure for him. *Peireskius* therefore, having indeed formerly endeavoured somewhat in that businesse, did now bestir himself more earnestly, giving order that the foresaid book, among many others, should be bought in Egypt and conveyed to him. But the ship in which it was coming was pillaged by Pirates, and the book could not be recovered, but was utterly lost.[3]

Years went by. Scaliger died. Peiresc pursued the interest in oriental studies that had bloomed during his visit to Venice in 1600, when he had first made contact with Scaliger. We find him discussing Arabo-Norman coins with Casaubon in 1606 and Gabriel Sionite in 1617, and the Samaritan Pentateuch with Joseph Leschassier in 1617. In that year, the young *parlementaire* moved to Paris and the court as secretary to the keeper of the seals, and began to develop the legendary correspondence network that fed his intellectual omnivorousness. But it was really only after Peiresc's return to Provence in October 1623, with his renewed proximity to Marseille, that the Mediterranean route to the Orient opened out before him. From not long after this, we can document the beginnings of his encounter with the Islamic coins and Indian gems in the collections of Marseille merchants.[4]

And that is when our story picks up again. For after all those many years, the Samaritan letters to Scaliger came into Peiresc's possession. That scrap of paper with boilerplate from the parlement about the sanitary regime tells this story. On the back, repurposed as scrap, Peiresc had written that the letters "had fallen into the hands of the late Sr. Genebrard and then of the late Paul Hurault Archbishop of Aix and finally of Sr Billon, who sent them to M. Galaup from whom I have had them. In August *1629*" (Figure 10).[5] Peiresc tells us no more about this transmission, but from their respective death dates—Génébrard, the *ligueur* archbishop of Aix, was banned by the Parlement of Aix in 1596 after Henri IV retook the city, and died in 1597; his successor Paul Hurault died in 1624—we can surmise that the letters reached Aix before 1596 but then sat in Hurault's possession for two decades.[6] Peiresc then sent the originals of the letters

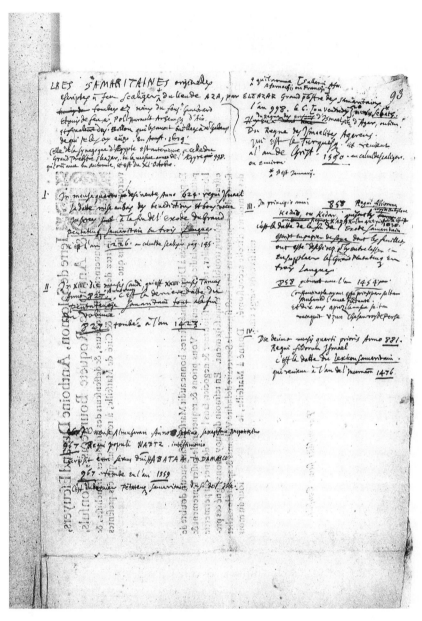

Figure 10. How the Samaritans' letters to Scaliger fell into Peiresc's hands. PBN, MS. Lat. 9340, f. 93r. (Bibliothèque Nationale de France)

to Paris to assist Father Jean Morin with his publication of the Samaritan Pentateuch and Targum.[7] Before sending them away, Peiresc had them copied and then translated into Hebrew and Latin.[8]

After this introduction, a rupture in time repaired, Peiresc proceeds as if nothing had happened with an enumeration of his four Samaritan pieces and their dates as given in the volumes' colophons. The Triglot, bought by Daniel Aymini and Théophile Minuti in Damascus in 1629 and left as a bequest to Cardinal Francesco Barberini—and now in the Vatican Library as MS. Barberini-Orientalia 1 with the gift embossed on the most elaborate of Peiresc's bindings—was written in 1226. The other Samaritan Pentateuchs were written in 1243 and 1454. The fourth title referred to a lexicon.[9]

But something had indeed happened, and elsewhere in the echo chamber of the archive, we catch a hint of how Peiresc processed this extraordinary recovery. An exactly contemporary letter was sent to the Captain Roubaud who had brought to Marseille François-Auguste de Thou's Egyptian purchases, but only after they had spent eight days in the sea when his ship foundered. The goods had been menaced by thieves but now had made it to port. Peiresc "wondered at the luck of these poor things to have passed, through the mercy of the sea [and then] through that of thieves." Peiresc knew from his seafaring friends that the sea had personality and volition.[10]

As Savary de Brèves, the French ambassador to the Sublime Porte, understood, "Mediterranean" and "Levant" were connected, geographically, semantically, and mechanically. We might imagine Peiresc's archive as a window opening onto the sea, just as we might imagine the Archive of the Chambre de Commerce of Marseille, bulging with letters from French consuls around the Mediterranean, as another such a window. But unlike the consul, who might see only what passed before his own very narrow window in Smyrna or Alexandria, Peiresc's field of view was larger. Nor was his perspective entirely passive; his archive reveals the efforts he made to expand that vision, to acquire new perspectives, to shape the very possibilities of his inquiry. It is in the practical details of commerce, correspondence, and communication that we see our man in action. Those lines tracing the return of a lost document from across the sea and through a port's merchant community to a neighboring city's ecclesiastical and aristocratic hierarchy mark for us the rhumb lines of Peiresc's Mediterranean.

5 ✑
Peiresc's Letters

*T*he past decades' interest in the "Republic of Letters" has brought renewed attention to learned correspondence in early modern Europe.[1] In this revival, Peiresc has come to seem paradigmatic for the whole enterprise, as in his position at the head of the 2007 volume *Correspondence and Cultural Exchange in Europe*.[2] Diplomatic missives, *avvisi*, and newsletters have themselves now become the subject of careful attention.[3] At the same time, merchant letters, after decades of neglect, have become a focus for scholars of medieval and early modern commerce.[4] What of the comparison, then, between merchant and learned letters?

It is no exaggeration to claim that the notion of a "Republic of Letters" has been built upon the letter. The letter-writing of Erasmus or of Lipsius has formed the subject of repeated inquiries.[5] Peiresc's fame, such as it is, is a result of his activity as letter-writer. While it is difficult to generalize from the thousands of Peiresc's letters that survive, we can make some observations about his letter-writing practice.

First, Peiresc's letters are almost entirely in vernacular languages: French and Italian. Even when writing to an Englishman, William Camden, who insisted on his preference for Latin, Peiresc wrote in French. Second, while Peiresc was capable of extreme politeness, especially with new correspondents, and was well versed in the language of friendship, obligation, and gift-exchange, he was always ready to slip into a casual register that drew on Provençal words, popular maxims, and idiosyncratic French. Most of all, he aligned his literary style to his correspondents: more formal to the formal, more familiar to the familiar.

This brings us to an important point. If one leafs through any of the volumes of merchant letters that Braudel published in the 1950s—for example, the *Lettres de negociants marseillais: Les Frères Hermite (1570–1612)*—and compares them to Peiresc's, one is struck by their very close resemblance.[6] All are focused on tasks, or problem-solving. They pay close attention to the modalities of communication itself. They scatter personal or local news on the periphery of the main theme. They use politeness as a way of engendering obligation. These similarities are all the more striking when one considers that the scholar's tasks are, generally, learned and the merchant's economic, even if in Peiresc's Mediterranean letters this distinction is frequently eroded. Peiresc is as attentive to the cash flow he needed to keep his learned project afloat, or to the details of shipping news, as he is to the specific questions or books or objects he pursues over such great distances. Peiresc was no merchant, but these are what we call "merchant letters."[7]

We can follow this convergence of subject matter, medium, and style still further, into Peiresc's Mediterranean correspondence. The surviving log of Peiresc's outgoing correspondence (Paris, Bibliothèque Nationale MS. Nouvelles acquisitions français 5169) begins in 1623, just before his return to Aix from Paris, and peters out in 1632, just before his second return to Aix, this time from a retreat to his country house at Belgentier, near Toulon, in the face of an outbreak of plague. From the log, we see that of approximately 1,066 bundles of mail, almost exactly the same number went to Provence (384) as to Paris (382).[8] The importance of Provence to Peiresc is a reminder that scholars have tended to overemphasize glamorous long-distance correspondence at the expense of the local. In the last decade of his life, after moving back to the South, Peiresc's correspondence became much more heavily oriented around Provence—and a fortiori his face-to-face intellectual life.

Peiresc's Mediterranean lives in these letters, especially those found in volumes 1874 and 1876 of the Bibliothèque Inguimbertine in Carpentras (Figure 11). If any place could be described as the "Cairo Geniza" of the early modern Republic of Letters, this would be it.[9] These papers, about two hundred folio pages in all, form but a small part of the "gigantic machine" of letters and letter-writing that has long been seen as exemplary for the early modern European Republic of Letters writ large.[10] While all of Peiresc's correspondence is arranged—and he arranged it—alphabetically, he also grouped letters to "the entourage," as Agnès Bresson termed it, around the person he viewed as the primary addressee. In these volumes, which contain the core of his Mediterranean correspondence, the letters cluster about two figures: Jean Magy and François-Auguste de Thou. Around them we find letters to those who took materials from Aix, those in Marseille who handled quayside details, the *patrons* who owned the ships, the captains who sailed them, and then, at the other end, the consuls, merchants, and journeymen who created the connections and the contexts in which the travelers operated. Once Peiresc had put into place

Figure 11. CBI, MS. 1874, contains most of Peiresc's letters to the Levant from 1634–1637. It is a fairly representative-sized volume and has recently been conserved. (Bibliothèque Inguimbertine, Musées et Bibliothèques de Carpentras)

this epistolary filing structure, he folded into it letters to a third traveler, Father Celestin de St. Lidwine, and to the Marseille merchants in Aleppo who supported him (1635–1637).

These dossiers contain 597 letters, to 148 recipients. We can establish a full reckoning of Peiresc's correspondence to the Levant if we add in letters to some of these same people scattered elsewhere through his archive, as well as additional letters to correspondents in the Ottoman Mediterranean, such as the French ambassador in Constantinople, the comte de Marcheville (21 letters), or the French captive-turned-renegade in Tunis, Thomas d'Arcos (28 letters)—but not the latters' handler in Toulon (225 letters). The breakdown of the fuller numbers, 753 letters to 184 recipients, is given in parentheses in the following text and in Charts B.1–B.11, which appear in Appendix B.

Peiresc wrote 260 (324) letters to recipients in Marseille, 73 to Cairo, 32 (46) to Constantinople, and 29 (37) to Aleppo (Chart B.1). Of his correspondents, Jean-Baptiste Magy, a merchant based in Marseille, received the most, 57 (59), and his brother Jean in Cairo 25. Father Théophile Minuti, whom Peiresc sent on trips to the Levant in 1629 and again in 1631, received 51 (Chart B.2). This same number was sent to Giovanni Gela in Marseille, the brother-in-law of the Venetian who was another of Peiresc's correspondents in Cairo, Santo Seghezzi, who received 11. The Guez brothers were the recipients of 19 (24) letters, of which 9 (12) went to the brother in Marseille and 10 to the one in Constantinople. Peiresc addressed 18 (20) letters to Baptiste Tarquet, vice-consul for Syria (but largely resident in Marseille) and 15 to Père Agathange de Vendôme, one of the Capuchin missionaries who were key figures in his Levantine enterprise. (The most important of these was Père Gilles de Loches, whom Peiresc first met upon his return from Cairo in 1633, on his way to Tours, and to whom he then addressed 43 letters.)

Of course recipients received different quantities of mail over time (Chart B.3). Letters to Minuti, for example, peaked during his two visits to the Levant, in 1629 and 1632. Similarly, those to F. A. de Thou track his travels in the Levant, while those to Peiresc's Aleppo correspondents rise with the importance of Aleppo to his work in the mid-1630s.

By profession, the role of merchants is dominant (Chart B.4). There are 282 (330) letters to merchants and another 43 (85) to diplomats, all of whom, aside from the Ambassador Marcheville (21 letters), were merchants exercising consular offices in the Levant. There are a further 15 to merchants owning ships *(patrons)* and 11 (14) to captains. There are 108 (109) to missionaries and 46 (50) to travelers, most of these to Théophile Minuti. In terms of recipients, the role of merchants is equally predominant: more than three times as many recipients are merchants than the next category, the missionaries. Diplomats, who are often also merchants, constitute the third-largest group of recipients (Chart B.5). The largest number of letters were sent in 1635 (135/163), 1636 (109/112), and 1634 (91/111). These years represent a strong rebound from the disruptions still affecting the trade of Marseille following the outbreak of plague the previous year— only 31 (39) letters sent in 1631 after 64 (71) in 1630 (Chart B.6). Mapped on to location, we see again that it is in the period 1633–1636 that we find a visible spike in the letters sent to the Levant in particular. The increasing flow of correspondence in 1628, 1629, and 1630 is evident, as is its dramatic ebb during the years of plague and disruption in Provence (1631–1632) and then subsequent rebound. We can also track the change in destinations over time, with the rise of Aleppo being perhaps the most notable (Chart B.7 and Table B.1).

Looking at the two main dossiers of letters, we find the largest number
of letters sent in July (69) and August (58), but these may not indicate anything other than variation from somewhat less propitious months for
travel such as December (56), February (54), or October and November
(53) (Chart B.8). The inclusion of transport information from elsewhere
in the Peiresc archive does not significantly change the picture. The months
with the largest number of letters are now February (85) and May (80),
but the second tier remains consistent (July 74, December 66, October 76,
and November 59) (Chart B.9). Looking even more specifically at letters
to the Levant, we see no difference between letters sent in the summer
months— 22 (23) and 23 (28) in July and August—and the winter—22 (27)
and 21 (41) in December and February (Chart B.10). Letters to the Levant were sent in batches. Jean Boutier, in his study of Étienne Baluze,
used the term "constellation" to describe the shape of these letter-groups.[11]
For they exist ad hoc, called together for a particular purpose, namely,
the departure of a given vessel, to a specific location, at a predetermined
time, with a set array of players. In these constellations we find letters to
key figures like "the traveler," surrounded by those to all the many players
who made the communication possible—lackeys, merchants, fixers, *patrons*, captains, diplomats, consuls, and others. There were 116 (140 in
the wider archive) of these batches sent over the ten years from 1627 to
1637. The visualization of Peiresc's letter-groups demonstrates the same
shape as his general correspondence. The years that see the fewest shipments moving across the Mediterranean from Marseille are 1631 and
1632 (3 batches), after which there is an upswing that mirrors that of the
Mediterranean correspondence as a whole: 25 in 1635, 25 in 1636, and
20 in 1634 (Chart B.11).[12]

Surveying this activity, one wonders how Peiresc managed to keep
track of it all. Each of these letters, written to different people in different
places, required attention to a specific context. Gassendi's description of
Peiresc's filing practices contains the solution: writing was Peiresc's form
of mnemotechnic, and the various finding aids he employed—titles, in-
dexes by title, underlining, annotations on the flyleaves of letters—were
all ways of making it easier for someone, even someone possessed of prodigious memory, to keep track of data and people on the move. But in
the end, the letters themselves were the tools used to keep track of the
letters. And so letters sent to Constantinople with a merchant but never
answered meant that Peiresc would direct the follow-up investigation to
that same merchant. Or, as with Théophile Minuti, Peiresc used the be-

ginning of each letter to review the recent history of letters sent or received.[13] Peiresc employed these techniques to keep track of the living history of his correspondence network.

But it was the movement of people, first and foremost, that led Peiresc
to the Levant. In *Peiresc's Orient* I examined this through the lens of his
pursuit of books, ideas, and learned interlocutors, many of whom lived
elsewhere in Europe. Here my concern is with exactly how Peiresc got
hold of those objects. What I have found is that his "intellectual" project
was inseparable from the realities of economic activity in Provence in the
1620s and 1630s. The story of Peiresc's oriental studies is, then, as much
part of a Mediterranean history as of the history of scholarship. Peiresc
belonged to the Republic of Letters, but also to an entire "portuary complex" consisting of merchants, bankers, *patrons,* captains, travelers,
and, yes, scholars.[14]

Many of these people are unknown today, the "almost anonymous"
whose names survive only because they are found in this log. Who were
André Rive, Sandin, Astruc, Emeric d'Ieres, la Fayé, Estienne, and le
Gascon? We know nothing of them except that from time to time they
played some role—perhaps the least important thing in their daily lives
but the one that has earned them a kind of immortality all the same—in
conveying Peiresc's letters from his doorstep in Provence toward his recipients in Syria and Egypt.

6 ॐ
Writing to the Levant, 1626–1637

*T*he seventeenth century marked the emergence of oriental studies as a mature intellectual discipline in Europe. Books of serious technical sophistication were published; university chairs founded; courses of study stabilized. But most of this happened in the second half of the century. The first half, especially its early decades, was still "predisciplinary," marked by the independent and idiosyncratic efforts of individual scholars in particular lines of inquiry.

Peiresc is central to this predisciplinary chapter. His close ties to the titans of the previous generation, Scaliger and Casaubon, and to contemporary giants such as Grotius, Saumaise, and Kircher, put him at the heart of this development. But it was actually his engagement with scholars at the rockface in less frequented quarries that enabled him to leave his mark. Peiresc's work in support of research on the Samaritans, for example, played a decisive role in the *editio princeps* of their Targum but also in the aquisition of multiple manuscripts of the Samaritan Pentateuch for European collections. Indeed, the first six pieces of Samaritana to enter the French Royal—later National—Library were all from Peiresc's collection. And behind these acquisitions lay hours of letter-writing and thinking, the organization of two expeditions, and international diplomacy at a high level. Peiresc's efforts on behalf of Arabic, Hebrew, Ethiopic, and Coptic were less comprehensive, but just as enthusiastic.

None of this would have been possible without the active collaboration of the merchant community of Marseille. For Peiresc, after his youthful travels, was a landlocked orientalist. It was only through his friends down the road in Marseille that he was able to command and organize the vast enterprise that fed information and artifacts back to Europe, and through him, to those scholars who could best make use of the material. With this step from Scaliger to people like the "Barthélemy" who owned "The Vine of the Souk" *(La Vigne de la Souque)* in Marseille, we move into a "vernacular" space where theory and practice, text and experience run together. This is Marseille as "Porte d'Orient": the Mediterranean gateway to the East.

How Peiresc played this intellectual role in Europe could be told as a story by taking his letters to the Levant, concentrating on those in the two dossiers clustered around the travels of de Thou and Jean Magy, ranging them in chronological order, and recounting their content. We can do this on an almost unparalleled scale, day by day for ten years (1627–1637). And yet even in this relentless diachronic structure we cannot escape the reality of asynchrony. The days, weeks, or months that separated the writing of a letter from its reception and reading means that the historian reconstructing this story needs to make certain decisions and assumptions about what constitutes a chronological narrative—and whose chronology is being recounted. In the end, the inescapable lacunae, false starts, and endings without beginnings teach us something essential about the impassable parts of the frontier between researching what happened and writing a story that makes sense to others.

1626

The narrative begins with François-Auguste de Thou (1607–1642), son of the great historian Jacques-Auguste de Thou and a protégé of the brothers Jacques and Pierre Dupuy, close friends of the de Thou family for two generations.[1] At nineteen, the same age at which Peiresc left for Italy, the young de Thou did likewise. His first steps are documented in a letter from Peiresc to Pierre Dupuy on 8 November 1626, which places him at Lyon on the way to Venice. Peiresc mentioned writing letters of introduction for him to his friends Lorenzo Pignoria in Venice and Cardinal Francesco Barberini in Rome.[2]

1627

Just a little later, in early January 1627, Peiresc wrote to his "fixer" in Rome, Louis de Bonnaire, telling him of a priest, recommended "by one of my best friends," who wanted to go to Jerusalem. His name was Daniel Aymini, a Recollet (a member of the French reform order of the Franciscans) who was also related to Peiresc's friend, neighbor, and fellow orientalist François de Galaup, the sieur de Chasteuil.[3] Peiresc was sending the "memoranda" and hoped that Bonnaire would duly arrange matters with the appropriate clerical authorities. Aymini possessed "a knowledge of oriental languages such that he could make fine observations in that land."[4]

In February 1627, meanwhile, de Thou was in Rome, proceeding on to Naples. By April, from Fontenay Jacquet, master of the Royal Post in

Lyon, Peiresc had heard that de Thou was already en route to Venice.[5] De Thou was, in fact, still in Rome, from whence he replied to Peiresc's letter as if to a master: he would serve with devotion "when your commandments will give birth to mine."[6]

The lightning bolt struck in midsummer. In his letter of 23 July 1627, de Thou shared with Peiresc his idea of traveling to "outre mer." Peiresc was very troubled by this, in a sweetly paternalistic way. He responded by way of a story, telling of a Minim priest then with him who had just returned from a trip to the Levant. In Jerusalem he was dogged with plague, which killed his traveling companions before his eyes. He then fled to Cairo, where he allowed himself a day to see the pyramids, but then hurriedly left, taking the first ship sailing to Marseille. On the last stretch of his voyage, between La Ciotat and Marseille, his ship was attacked by a Spanish galley, and all his goods, including antiquities purchased in Egypt, were lost. Trying to frighten de Thou, Peiresc acknowledged that however curious he himself was about those lands, "when I thought about the plague, and the barbarism that is incompatible with every sort of good curiosity, I had to change my advice."[7]

The plot lines of de Thou and Aymini intertwined in a late August letter to Bonnaire, which began with Peiresc's hope that de Thou had received his cautionary letter, and then turned to Aymini. Peiresc thanked Bonnaire for the letter he had obtained from the "patriarch of Jerusalem" on Aymini's behalf. Nevertheless, because of the plague, Aymini had decided to defer his voyage for the year. This allowed him more time to obtain a permission from the general of his order.[8] By the end of October, Peiresc was reconciling himself to de Thou's trip, recommending to him the assistance that Cardinal Barberini could provide, as well as the specialized numismatic skills of people like Claude Menestrier, one of Peiresc's Roman agents.[9]

De Thou departed from Livorno for Venice a little after 23 November 1627.[10] Peiresc was still thanking Bonnaire for his work on behalf of Aymini at the end of December and beginning of 1628—suggesting that the paperwork had not yet been completed.[11] At the same time, Peiresc was writing to the younger Camerarius at The Hague, where his father was ambassador of the king of Sweden to the United Provinces. Peiresc asked the son for information about the state of Arabic studies there after the death of Erpenius. A friend of his had gotten hold of "a very curious" book of Islamic law, both religious and secular, and Peiresc was looking to have it translated.[12]

1628

De Thou reached Venice by the beginning of the new year 1628.[13] In the meantime, Peiresc was mobilizing a group of Provençal government officials and Marseille merchants to function as de Thou's network in the East. We can follow this through Peiresc's log of outgoing correspondence. On 13 February 1628, we find letters from the premier president of the Parlement of Provence, Anne de Forbin-Meynier, baron d'Oppède, addressed to the consuls of Alexandria, Aleppo, Sidon, and Chios; from Guez in Marseille to his brother Guillaume, a merchant in Constantinople, with 1,000 livres; from M. Valbelle, the lieutenant of the admiralty, to that same Guez in Galata; and from Pierre Viguier, consul of Syria (resident in Marseille), to Vice-Consul Olivier in Aleppo, Vice-Consul Jacques Estelle in Sidon, and Blanchot in Alexandretta.[14] All this was already in place when Peiresc wrote to de Thou in mid-February 1628. Peiresc explained that along with his letter, de Thou would be receiving one from Valbelle and others for the consuls of Alexandria, Aleppo, and Sidon and for the merchant Guez in Galata. He noted that letters were written in parallel by the consul of Syria and president of the Parlement of Provence to their formal contacts.[15]

The only person in this web Peiresc had not yet been able to contact was Sanson Napollon, who possessed good knowledge not only of Turks in general but of the high ministers of the sultan in particular, with whom he had negotiated. Napollon's familiarity with the "Intendant des Jardines & plusieurs Bassaux" made him a valuable ally. Peiresc would also have Napollon write to a Turkish "Capiggy" in Marseille and have him, in turn, write on de Thou's behalf to his superiors. Napollon happened to have been in Toulon arranging the ransom of Christians from the Regency of Algiers but was due back in Marseille that very day.[16] Interestingly, Peiresc "activated" Napollon by linking de Thou's trip with the work of the former French ambassador to Constantinople, Savary de Brèves—suggesting that he believed this carried special weight with Napollon.[17] Indeed, Napollon responded immediately, writing in the next week to both Constantinople and Chios.[18]

It is in this first letter outlining a Levantine itinerary that Peiresc mentioned to de Thou the importance he attached to the collecting of manuscripts in Samaritan characters, as well as medals and coins with Samaritan inscriptions. Peiresc invoked the memory of the late Scaliger—de Thou's father's best friend—as justification for this inquiry.[19] This represents the earliest documentation of Peiresc's mature interest in the

Samaritans, and links this story to the plan to publish the Samaritan Pentateuch as part of the polyglot bible project just underway in Paris.[20]

By the time these words were written, not to mention read, de Thou had left Venice. He departed on 4 February on a Venetian ship sailing to Smyrna via Zante and Crete, attended by the brother of M. Servien, a *maître des requêtes* at court.[21] It was an eventful voyage. Eight days out from Venice, the weather changed, the wind turned, and the ship had to make for Kefalonia, where it was stuck for thirty days. It finally made it to Zante, where it had to wait another twenty-two days while a convoy of Venetian ships gathered and loaded freight, before sailing four days to Crete. There, no doubt desperate, de Thou abandoned the Venetian flotilla and switched to a Dutch ship going to Gallipoli. This took sixteen more days. In Gallipoli he switched again, this time to a postal caïque, and reached Constantinople in two more days.[22]

In Constantinople, while waiting for final preparation of his quarters at the ambassador's residence, de Thou stayed in Galata in the home of the merchant Guillaume Guez.[23] Peiresc received letters from Guez and de Thou written on 28 May, delivered via Lyon. A still more recent letter from the ambassador in Venice informed Peiresc of de Thou's plan to leave Constantinople by the end of August. This led Peiresc to suggest a side trip to Delos to study the ruins of the temple of Apollo.[24]

A letter of Peiresc to de Thou from late summer 1628 turned directly to the Polyglot Bible project in Paris. Peiresc seems to have realized that de Thou's presence on the spot, like that of Pietro della Valle a little over a decade earlier, could be translated into purchases. Peiresc briefed his correspondent on della Valle's acquisitions—in the process confusing della Valle's Samaritan Targum and his Coptic purchases ("quelques fragments du Pentateuque en langue Aegyptienne antique avec la version Arabique a Regione")—but always thinking of what new material could be found: "And if in any part of Egypt or Ethiopia there remained any vestige or relic of the ancient Egyptian language, even if corrupted, as Italian is of Latin, vulgar Greek of the ancient, and those of the Basques, Bretons and Welsh of the ancient Gallic or Breton, because people are now curious about this, in Rome as in Paris."[25]

Peiresc served as the relay station for the Dupuy brothers' attempt to stay in contact with de Thou, forwarding their letters to Guez in Marseille, who sent them on to his brother in Constantinople.[26] Peiresc received de Thou's letter of 2 July—sent, probably at the end of the month, along with a letter of 24 July by Guez—in early September.[27] Peiresc thanked Guez not only for sending his letters on to Alexandria, "since this is the regular route from Constantinople" ("puis que c'est la routte ordinaire de Constantinople"), but also for providing him with the names of those involved: Captain Roubaud, who was carrying the letters, and a Sr. Aubert in Alexandria who was to receive them.[28]

In mid-December 1628, Peiresc wrote to de Thou, saying that he had just received his packet dated 30 October, sent from Sidon and received by Baptiste Tarquet in Marseille by way of Estelle in Sidon. From this he learned of de Thou's plan to leave for Jerusalem the next day (1 November). Peiresc was very pleased to hear of his happy meeting in Sidon with an unnamed Capuchin father and their decision to work together to seek out manuscript books. Those indicated in the letter seemed to Peiresc "worthy indeed" of his taste, and "principally that history of the Saracens which, if it was other than the one given us by Erpenius some years ago," would be worth a great deal. The book about travel to Mecca would, he thought, make worthwhile reading for Holstenius with his interest in geography and Arabic, while that on Turkish laws was less engaging but would certainly "have enough to exercise those who are curious about this material" ("avoit de quoy exercer les curieux en cette matiere").[29]

Erpenius was a big fish; Peiresc had had some correspondence with him in 1617 and returned to this material again in 1628 when working in Marseille on Islamic coinage.[30] But it is the stray reference to a Capuchin in Sidon that is actually the most interesting feature of this letter. Peiresc himself followed it up in the parallel letter written to Estelle, consul in Sidon. He asked that this Capuchin be funded on his account, with reimbursement coming via Tarquet in Marseille.[31]

A letter to this as-yet-unidentified Capuchin followed. It is most likely Gilles de Loches, the learned priest who arrived at Sidon in 1626 and moved to Egypt in 1631 before returning to France in 1633. He met Peiresc in Aix on his way back, in July of that year, and became one of his relied-upon specialists on oriental language and culture. This letter marks the beginning of their relationship. Peiresc tells of learning about him and his virtue from de Thou. He explained the arrangement he was making with Estelle so that he would have all that might be neceessary to buy "those good books" that he might come across. Above all, Peiresc was interested in Samaritan things, "and principally their chronicles, if any of them might fall into your hands, and some vocabulary and grammar, if they could be found, as well also as the Egyptian books of the Jacobites and Copts, which have their Pentateuch in their language with the

Arabic translations." Peiresc also asks for a particularly careful transfer of whatever inscriptions he might come upon, "in whatever language it could be, whether Greek or Latin or Phoenician." He understood that one league from Beirut there was a rockface near the sea inscribed with many Greek and Latin letters whose transcription he wanted. Perhaps, he ventured, the authority of Emir Fakhr-al-Din II could be useful in obtaining it.[32] Finally, as if to complete the tour of his intellectual horizon, Peiresc asked after any information about the families of the Kingdom of Jerusalem that could amplify the manuscript he had just acquired (the fourteenth-century *Lignages d'Outremer*).[33] Guez, who had his own contacts, was able to inform Peiresc of the news of de Thou's visit to Jerusalem, which was only described as a possibility in Peiresc's last letter from de Thou, dated 30 October.[34]

1629

Peiresc was still in possession of only sketchy facts in early January 1629 when he wrote to the French ambassador to Venice repeating the date of a 1 November departure for Jerusalem.[35] By then, it seems that Peiresc was hatching a new idea: to send his own man, with his own program, to the Levant. The man was his close friend and confessor, a Minim from Provence, Théophile Minuti. Minuti seems to have been a native of Brignoles, died in 1662, and probably lived in Aix at the convent of the Minims. We first get wind of this plan in a letter of 14 February from Peiresc to Father Jean François, provincial of the Minims in Provence, based in Marseille. Peiresc thanked him for his approval in releasing Minuti to travel to the Holy Land.[36] On this same day, Peiresc wrote to his acquaintance Baptiste Tarquet in Marseille, notifying him of Minuti's impending voyage and asking him for a raft of relevant recommendations (as he had done for de Thou the previous year). Peiresc also asked Tarquet to intervene with "votre grand amy," the provincial of the Minims, to whom he had written, asking that Minuti be released to go on pilgrimage, since he had already obtained the pope's permission.[37] Also on that same day Peiresc wrote to Jean l'Empereur, consul of Jerusalem (though resident in Constantinople), informing him that Minuti was ready to go. He had not forgotten all the good things l'Empereur had done for him, or his promise to serve whenever needed. Minuti, Peiresc allowed, would be carrying a letter from his brother of Marseille. Peiresc asks for Minuti to be protected but also to be granted permission to see l'Empereur's collection of curiosities, and in particular his ancient Greek and Syriac medals and whatever else he possessed with Samaritan inscriptions. All this, Peiresc added, would help him with something he was now working on ("un petit ouvrage que j'ay par les mains"). He would be glad to have copies cast by a goldsmith or other worker who would be able to make them.[38] For whatever l'Empereur lacked—and could not purchase because there was "some Jew or other Curious person" who would not sell—Peiresc would be satisfied with "a parallel description and examination." Alternatively, if a goldsmith or some other craftsman could make a cast of the unobtainable object, he would also be happy with that. Some of the items he wanted were so broken that three or four would have to be assembled in order to get a sense of what a complete one would have looked like.[39] (L'Empereur's collection of precious and semiprecious gems, from "Georgia, India and Moldavia," made news of his imminent return "en Chrestienté," conveyed to Peiresc by his nephew, M. l'Empereur of Marseille, all the more desirable.)[40]

The provincial of the Minims gave his affirmative answer quickly, and by 26 February Peiresc was writing back with thanks.[41] Minuti was then at Marseille and Peiresc wrote to him there, pleased at his warm reception by Tarquet and l'Empereur. Peiresc mentioned that he had prepared several memoranda for him but hoped to see him first "because it is much more difficult to render in writing all that I could tell you."[42] This letter was accompanied by others to Marseille contacts, especially thanking both Tarquet and l'Empereur. To the latter, Peiresc noted that he had also asked Vallavez to express his gratitude in person.[43]

In March 1629, preparing for Minuti's departure—which would, in the event, be delayed until June—Peiresc drafted a series of letters to Egyptian-based Marseillais. To Fernoux, the vice-consul, Peiresc began by lamenting the recent death of de Brèves but then moved directly to Minuti's pilgrimage and the need he would have for assistance. Fernoux was asked to help with his researches "and particularly in the research that he desired to do concerning some books that could be encountered in the Samaritan and Egyptian languages among the families who are in Cairo and, it is said, of the Samaritans and Copts, together with some other kinds of antiquities that one could find there."[44] At this same time, Peiresc wrote also to Cesar Lambert, Gastines's partner in Egypt, while alerting Gastines, Jean-Baptiste Magy, and Fraisse in Marseille to Minuti's impending departure. Peiresc asked Lambert to help Minuti, who was going "on pilgrimage to Jerusalem" "and hoped to be able to go to Egypt," where he would be doing some research on old books and antiquities. Peiresc was counting on Lambert to furnish the monies necessary for this. He also asked Lambert to keep him apprised of what was being spent and sent via Lambert's own network. It is worth noting, in passing, that Peiresc presents Minuti's trip not as an expedition but as a pilgrimage, and he uses this language not only with Minuti's clerical superiors but also with his own merchant friends.[45] Peiresc asked Messers. Mary, Douaille, and Fraisse, who were among his financiers, to write to their correspondents in Egypt in favor of Minuti.[46] In this same batch of letters, Peiresc also wrote to the Marseille merchant Salicoffres, alerting him to Minuti's passage and asking for his assistance in case Minuti wished to return to Provence with a mummy.[47]

But it was in the accompanying letter to de Gastines that Peiresc talked livres and écus, including a request that a line of credit up to fifty écus be extended to Minuti for purchases reflecting the priorities outlined in the memoranda he now possessed. De Gastines was asked to include something about reimbursement in any letter of recommendation that he would himself draft for Minuti. That de Gastines was handling the finances suggests his new centrality for Peiresc in Marseille and the role of Minuti's mission in its crystallization.[48] The blanket recommendation letter drawn up by Tarquet on behalf of Minuti, dated 10 March 1629 at Aix and therefore suggesting Peiresc's hand, was copied into Peiresc's register. It urged assistance to the person of Minuti, who was expected to be passing through Sidon, and assistance with funds necessary for the acquistion of the "antique curiosities [*curiositez anciennes*] that M. Councillor Peiresc wants to recover."[49]

In early March, Peiresc was commiserating with de Thou about his scary adventures. Peiresc informed de Thou of affairs at court.[50] Peiresc remained very much unsure of de Thou's whereabouts and well-being, having heard that he had been involved in two shipwrecks but having received no letter from him since October 1628. Writing to d'Avaulx, the French ambassador at Venice, Peiresc hoped to learn more.[51] Finally, in early April, he could write to Guez that he had finally received a letter from de Thou of 25 February 1629 written from Alexandria upon his return from Cairo and Mount Sinai.[52] It was to fund Minuti through his brother Guez of Constantinople that Peiresc authorized a letter of credit for Guez of Marseille that was filled by a Meynard of Bordeaux.

It was, therefore, this first expedition that left in the archive a concrete indication of Peiresc's source of funding and how it was operationalized.⁵³ We can track this whole procedure very clearly through Peiresc's correspondence log. On 4 April 1629 he sent three letters to Marseille:

1 To Meynard "with the order to withdraw 1000 l.t. [livres tournois] from Sr. Guez and to present the *lettre de change* of 1500 l.t. to Sr Fraisse"

2 To Guez "with the order to pay to Sr Maynard [*sic*] the 1000 l.t. from the *lettre de change* of Sr. Tallevant"

3 To Fraisse "with the order to pay 158 l.t. to Sr. de Gastines, 75 l.t. to Sr Bargues, & to reimburse himself and keep the remainder until receiving a new order"⁵⁴

At the beginning of April, Peiresc wrote to Tarquet in Marseille that he had just learned from Paris of de Thou's shipwreck on the way from Constantinople to Sidon but that de Thou was by now on his way back home.⁵⁵ In the postscript he asked about the possibility of sending Minuti to Sidon and thence to the Holy Land.⁵⁶ By mid-April Peiresc could write back to the Ambassador d'Avaulx in Venice to inform him that the information he had given last time about de Thou's arrival in Ragusa after the shipwreck was false. In the interim Peiresc had received a letter from de Thou written from Alexandria on 25 January where he was waiting to take ship for Malta, and another after his return from Mount Lebanon, Damascus, Jerusalem, Mount Sinai, and Cairo.⁵⁷

On 21 April, Mathieu Passarius, head of the Province of St. Louis which, comprising Provence, lower Languedoc, and Roussillon, was directly responsible for the Minims of Provence, wrote to Peiresc acknowledging and confirming Minuti's plan to go on a learned pilgrimage.⁵⁸ A week later, Minuti was expected to be gone, with Livorno as his destination.⁵⁹ On 25 April 1629, Peiresc wrote to de Thou in Rome, reporting what he had heard about de Thou's adventures from Aubery in Rome, and from President d'Oppède in Aix, who had it from Fernoux in Cairo— about the two shipwrecks, and the route back via Malta and Messina.⁶⁰ The story of de Thou's shipwreck off the southern coast of Anatolia had come via Ambassador de Césy in Constantinople to Paris; from there the Dupuy brothers had sent the original to him in Aix. He also thanked the Lord for delivering de Thou from the "great perils" that de Thou had faced when after leaving Nazareth his party was attacked by bedouins in the hills of Samaria.⁶¹

From Rome we are able to follow de Thou's progress across the western Mediterranean. Aubery reports that from Commander de Souvray he learned that de Thou arrived at Siracusa on 19 March, and from his host had learned that de Thou, who had also lodged with him, had just left on the "Malta felucca," which departed weekly with passengers for Malta.[62] By 1 June, Peiresc had learned more details of de Thou's itinerary: his plan to go from Malta to Trapani in Sicily and thence, via Sardinia and Mallorca, to Barcelona and back to Marseille; of his sending his goods directly back from Malta to Marseille; and of their shipwreck near Messina.[63]

At this very moment, as Peiresc was preparing for de Thou's return from the Levant, he was in the final stages of organizing for Minuti's departure. On 14 May he wrote to Estelle, the vice-consul in Sidon (via Tarquet), asking him to cover Minuti's necessaries as he had for de Thou and promising to reimburse and indemnify him at Marseille for "all charges, expenses and other rights, and profits or emoluments and maritime revenues" ("tous charges remises & autres droicts & proffitz ou esmoluments & avantages maritimes"). This was Peiresc's customary language and includes the range of fixed and hidden costs in contemporary long-distance maritime trade. Peiresc also informed Guez in Constantinople of Minuti's departure; even though he was not planning to travel there, Peiresc wanted Guez alerted, in case he could be helpful.[64] And Peiresc similarly wrote to Jean Espannet, vice-consul in Cyprus, informing him of Minuti's passage even though he was taking a different route, just "in case he landed there" and some assistance would prove helpful.[65]

Minuti must have been with Peiresc when these letters were written—he may even have carried them to Marseille—because we have another letter, to Tarquet, written the very next day (15 May), which began with the apology that Minuti left late the previous evening and Peiresc stayed up late "making for him the mémoires for his voyage" ("a luy faire des mémoires pour son voyage"). This left no time to write to him. Peiresc feared that the barque Tarquet ordered for Minuti would sail immediately. Turning from future back to past, Peiresc added that he had gotten a report from Rome dated 5 May saying that de Thou was in Siracusa in Sicily on 12 March and from there was going to Malta. De Thou was now in Rome.[66]

A letter to Minuti himself that must have been written just after his departure from Aix accompanied "many" letters of recommendation and memoranda and instructions for the recovery of these singularities.[67] Peiresc cautioned him not to talk to anyone about these instructions, or about the box of medals, casts, and engravings that was attached. These were intended as tools to assist Minuti when shopping for Peiresc in the Levant. Peiresc here demonstrates his commitment to comparison as the only form of establishing authenticity. Perhaps thinking about how this secrecy might have sounded to the priest, Peiresc added, "This little zealousness does no one any harm." Time would teach Minuti how to recognize those who could be trusted from those who could not.[68]

By the end of May, Peiresc had received a letter from de Thou, dated Malta, 3 May. De Thou was fine, but he passed along word of the sinking of the ship belonging to Captain Roubaud on which was charged his "little Turkish box full of curiosities" ("petit coffre à la Turquesque tout plain de curiosités"). Peiresc passed this news on to Valbelle, in his capacity as lieutenant of the admiralty, in the hope that Valbelle would be able to discover what, if anything, was known of its possible whereabouts.[69]

All this time, Minuti was still in Marseille, waiting for the barque *Mont Carmel* of Captain Bartolle to set sail.[70] While there, Peiresc connected him with de Gastines and explained that there was no harm in showing him the secret instructions and memoranda that Minuti was carrying, since it might enable de Gastines to assist him better. De Gastines could connect him to Lambert and Fernoux in Egypt, and he himself was going there soon. All this was a measure of Peiresc's confidence in de Gastines.[71] Peiresc wrote to him again at Marseille on 4 June.[72] Minuti must have set sail not long after, for he arrived in Sidon on 28 June, having traveled nonstop.[73]

At just that same time, mid-June 1629, de Thou finally reached Marseille.[74] But, in a huge disappointment for Peiresc, de Thou did not stop to visit with him at Aix. De Thou left immediately for Montpellier to salute the king at the close of the parlementary session and then passed back through Marseille but again without coming to visit, this time leaving a letter for the Dupuy brothers with de Gastines. He then took ship for Rome.[75] The reasons for this behavior remain unclear. To Dupuy, de Thou indicated that he had explained all to Peiresc; the latter's letters to Dupuy show Peiresc grasping for an explanation.[76] (De Thou again avoided meeting Peiresc upon his return from Rome in December 1629.[77] There remains no obvious explanation for this behavior.[78])

After de Thou's departure for Italy, Peiresc urged him to return before the onset of Rome's malarial summer.[79] But on 7 July de Thou was in Genoa, heading down the Tyrrhenian coast to Rome; as for Minuti, there had been no news since he had set sail.[80] De Thou's Turkish coffer, however, did make it back to Marseille. Captain Roubaud had managed to fish it out of the water. Peiresc's letter to him of 26 July was full of directions about salvaging it as best as possible. He wanted the box turned over to de Gastines, who would get it to Valbelle, the lieutenant of the admiralty. De Gastines would pay all the relevant fees. If there were any bundles of letters, even if they were damaged, Peiresc wanted them, since if de Thou came to visit him they would serve as the basis for discussion.[81] Although the box had to be dried out as soon as possible, Peiresc explained to Valbelle in a parallel letter that because the coffer had been in the sea for eight days, drying it out too rapidly could result in its ruination upon exposure to air.[82]

Peiresc's concerted thinking about conservation practices appears in full in a letter to Captain Roubaud of 1 August, after de Gastines brought him the coffer and the crocodile skin. He thought that the curiosities would be lost, but some held up surprisingly well, including an old vellum book, while other materials, especially paper, could not be salvaged, the pages being all stuck together. The medals were in good shape, though they emerged so shiny that someone not well versed would have thought them modern objects, though he was sure they were not. As possible future practices, Peiresc suggested plunging the retrieved objects into sweet water immediately after taking them out of the salty, and then drying them completely. Or, he thought, "one could rub them with a bit of olive oil for correcting the salinization of the sea water." The damascened daggers rusted, and the crocodile skin was ruined by the salt water but could be replaced.[83]

A more detailed damage report appeared in a letter to de Thou from later that summer. The Arabic book, which Peiresc thought a Koran because of its being so carefully copied and ornamented, was only slightly discolored, though others, especially a Coptic text, were heavily damaged. The pages of this latter were stuck together. Peiresc was going to have them washed in the hopes of separating them but understood that this was a hazard. He then reviewed the condition of the daggers and coins.[84] To Aubery, Peiresc made the positive identification of the volume as a Koran, and acknowledged its importance: "I am not surprised that you have so desired and so long pursued this Koran." Because it had been wrapped in so many different envelopes it had hardly gotten wet.[85]

Minuti's first letter to Peiresc from the Levant was written from Jerusalem—"from the Holy Sepulchre, and Mt. Calvary"—on 20 July. He had stayed in Sidon from 28 June to 8 July and then departed for Jerusalem. But already in Sidon he began looking for Peiresc's desired

Samaritan materials. His principal interlocutors were Jews; those in Sidon had no Samaritan materials, but told him that he would have success in Damascus. A Jewish doctor he met in Jerusalem said he would write to the "Jews of Nablus" on his behalf—there was a large Samaritan community there. On his voyage south, Minuti had passed through Nablus, "which is the land of the Samaritans," on a Saturday and thus was unable to meet them.[86] The presence and role of the Jews was one reality; the enduring imagery of the Crusades was another. The presence of the two Provençal sailors at the Holy Sepulchre led Minuti to muse about the "laziness" of the French: "If our good King (to whom God gave a long and happy life) came to this land with only 20,000 men he would be master of all Palestine." Emir Fakhr al-Din, based in Sidon, he mused, would gladly look the other way for 12,000 horses.[87]

Our second documented evidence for Minuti's safe arrival in the Levant comes from Antoine Piscatoris, a Marseille merchant who passed along a letter from Minuti dated 30 August. In it, Minuti explained how he had packed up the medals purchased for Peiresc in Damascus in paper envelopes and put them in a small gilded coffer that also contained a box full of little curiosities for Peiresc's half-sister, the wife of the president of the parlement Henri de Seguiran. Because it was not completely full, he had filled it with fine cotton from Damascus as a gift for her.[88] Peiresc greedily asked Piscatoris for news and asked him to send it to Fort, to de Gastines, or to Baltasar Grange, all at Marseille, who would then convey it to him via Judge Chabert or Commander de Forbin, both at Toulon.[89]

Piscatoris also seems to have had some legal troubles, for in this same letter Peiresc offered to speak with Valbelle on his behalf. One suspects this service functioned as something of a quid pro quo.[90] Peiresc immediately wrote to M. Granier, a royal councillor and lawyer in the Admiralty of the Levant, that is, one of Valbelle's underlings, explaining that Piscatoris had just returned from the Levant and was worthy of compassion given how he assisted his friends in those parts. Peiresc asked him to take great care with his case, for "the love of me" and because of the "very particular obligations and inclination" which he had to Piscatoris. Peiresc reserved the postscript to tell the father that he had just responded to a letter of the son—Peiresc had helped him get into the Benedictine seminary of St. Louis at Toulouse earlier that year.[91] Peiresc also weighed in with a letter to Valbelle's mother, and to his deputy—Valbelle being away just then—lending his name to Piscatoris's case.[92] Peiresc sent a note to Piscatoris himself, telling him that he had done what Piscatoris had asked him to do and that he had no doubt that his contacts would work on his behalf. Peiresc ended by asking for news of Captain Bartolle.[93]

That same day, however, Peiresc must have learned of Bartolle's arrival at Toulon en route to Marseille. He wrote thanking Bartolle for all that he had done to help Minuti on his passage to the Holy Land. Peiresc invited the captain, at a less busy time for him, to come and visit in the country at Belgentier for a proper debriefing. Peiresc concluded by discussing the means of his getting the goods and of the captain's getting reimbursed. Peiresc also asked if Bartolle knew the whereabouts of Patron Cornillon of Cassis, to whom Minuti had entrusted letters for him.[94]

With the onset of plague, the merchants of Marseille scattered. De Gastines went to Cassis, Tarquet to Toulon. It is to there that Peiresc writes a long and interesting letter, summarizing and filling in much that is unsaid in the other six letters he wrote on 6 November.[95] Tarquet's of 30 October from Toulon had come to Peiresc with Minuti's of 29 August from Sidon. Several days earlier Piscatoris had brought him a still more recent letter with news of Minuti's embarcation for Damiette in Egypt, and his visit to the site near Beirut where he had copied out the inscriptions Tarquet had mentioned in a previous letter. Peiresc also thanked Tarquet for making good the 45 piastres that Estelle had advanced to Father Théophile and which Peiresc offered to reimburse immediately once Tarquet converted the sum to French money, and added the "droictz maritimes," which he would pay at the rate of all the other goods on the barque. The money, or some portion of it, had been used for the purchase of a book that he now awaited impatiently, Bartolle having told him that there was something for him on the *Grand Henry*. Minuti had, in addition, mentioned that Patron Cornillon of Cassis was charged with bearing him some letters from Jerusalem and other items which he wanted as soon as the boat docked.[96]

On 13 November, Peiresc had in hand a letter from Minuti (he also distributed letters Minuti had written to his relatives in Aix and Bras, a small town in the Var), saying that he was in good health, had gone to Egypt, and was now returning via Constantinople to Rome.[97]

All this time, Peiresc had been focused on Minuti's trip. Daniel Aymini had left earlier. In early September 1629 he wrote to Peiresc, reporting on the trip he took with Minuti from Sidon to Damascus. They went looking for Samaritan and Syriac books and ancient coins. In Damascus they found a Bible in Samaritan, Arabic, and Hebrew, all written in Samaritan characters. It was imperfect, and the missing pages were being filled in by the

Maronite father from whom they purchased it. The volume would return to Marseille on the *Grand Henry,* which was expected at Sidon any day. Galaup-Chasteuil, for whom on the side they were shopping for Syriac Bibles, had wanted a smaller format but "there remained but few examples in Mt. Lebanon." Aymini thanked Peiresc for providing him with the means to see the Holy Land and for allowing him to see the memoirs written for Minuti, which would better enable him to serve Peiresc. The rest of the letter complains about the way the Recollets—a French reform of the Franciscans and Aymini's order—were treated there by the French Capuchins. Speaking the language of those memoirs, Aymini argued that Minuti could provide a "tesmoin oculaire"—an "eyewitness"—for what he was saying.[98] The *Grand Henry* also carried a letter from a Charles Blanc which accompanied a gift of grafts of fig trees and cut vines.[99]

It is only in November 1629 that Peiresc was reminded of Aymini. On the 16th of that month, Peiresc wrote to him at length. He began by acknowledging a letter received the previous June, containing a box of artifacts acquired at the Church of the Holy Sepulchre and other sacred places. Peiresc explained that he would have replied had he expected Aymini to remain there longer. He had only just now received via Captain Bartolle a second letter of Aymini's from Sidon, dated 2 September. It arrived along with others that he conveyed to addresses in Tarascon, Arles, and Aix (Sieur Galaup de Chasteuil). Bartolle also delivered the case sent by Minuti that was full of books, medals, and other curiosities. This led Peiresc to invite Galaup to come and examine the materials, which included the two New Testaments in Syraic, one written on "Damascus paper" in small format and the other on parchment in large format, which Peiresc thought authentic and about five hundred years old.[100] Peiresc also kept a copy of the letter Aymini wrote to his relative Galaup-Chasteuil. In it, Aymini reported on the acquisition of a Syriac New Testament. The Jews, from whom they sought old books, seemed "assez ignorant." There was, though, a Jew named "Abraham Emias, who governs the affairs and the spirit of the Emir Aly," whom he thought could be helpful in the future.[101]

Aymini's relative, François Sieur de Galaup-Chasteuil, must have been interested in oriental studies already, or else Peiresc would not have thought it worth sharing these materials with him. Soon enough—with the embassy of de Marcheville in 1631—Galaup would depart for the East, gravitating to Lebanon, where he remained until his death thirteen years later, acquiring for himself the name of the "Solitaire du Mont Liban."[102] The growth of his oriental interest is intertwined with that of Peiresc. It began in 1629 with Peiresc inquiring of Tarquet whether there was a ship being fitted out for Sidon, since that was where Galaup-Chasteuil wished to go.[103] Peiresc repeated the question a couple of weeks later, while also engaging the consuls of Marseille to smooth the way.[104] In August, Peiresc had told Galaup that he was waiting "impatiently" for the translation of the Samaritans' letter to Joseph Scaliger that had just fallen into his hands.[105] These are the famous letters sent by the Samaritans in response to the questions sent by Joseph Scaliger in 1590 (see Section 4, "Contingency"). The letters had finally fallen into the hands of one of the very few people in Europe who knew what they were and how they came to be.

In October 1629, Peiresc told Galaup that he had in Aix the Samaritain Pentateuch of Pietro della Valle which he was sending on to Jean Morin, editor of the Samaritan material in the Paris Polyglot Bible. He was also planning to send Morin a copy of the Samaritans' letter to Scaliger and was waiting for the translation Galaup had promised.[106]

In his letter of November 1629, Peiresc effusively thanked Aymini for the pains he had taken to make the trip to Damascus with Minuti. But his principal gratitude was for the acquisition of the Bible in three languages, all in Samaritan characters. This is the first mention of Peiresc's famous Samaritan Triglot, bequeathed upon his death to Cardinal Barberini, and now Vatican Library, Barberini-Orientalia MS. 1.[107]

Missing pages in the books that he hoped would be a grammar and lexicon led Peiresc to spell out, in detail that is a goldmine for the historian, exactly what he wanted to know about the Samaritans. This letter, in effect, drafts Aymini into the project that Peiresc had outlined for Minuti almost a year earlier. Peiresc asks Aymini to make "the most exact research" that he could among the poor Samaritan priests of Nablus ("Naplouze"). Estelle or Charles Blanc, both based at Sidon, would be activated to provide him with the money he needed. "It is necessary that you get to know some of those Samaritan priests, and flatter them as much as you could in order to extract it and all the other books that you could have in this language, principally all that could be found concerning sacred or profane history, and the rules under which this sect lives, above all that which concerns their calendars and rituals, and if they have anything of astronomy in their language, do not let any of it escape you." Peiresc counted on Aymini already having some familiarity with its characters, or being able to acquire it easily.[108]

Turning from texts to objects, Peiresc advised Aymini to buy whatever medals he could find because it would be impossible for him to distinguish between good and bad. Peiresc wanted anything in Samaritan characters, whatever the size and whatever the metal. He thought that "if one dug up the ground around Jerusalem and Samaria" one would find things.[109] Peiresc had tried to advise Minuti of this as well. Yet one of the coins he had bought, despite all Peiresc's preparation, was actually a coin made by Jews using modern Hebrew characters. Though they were worthless, "I know however that the Jews make a big deal of these amongst themselves. I have decided to send it to you in order to help you if the occasion should present itself to acquire the friendship of one of those Jews there who have lots of other medals and by means of this gift could more easily be persuaded to part with theirs for money, especially those which are written in Samaritan characters, of which they are customarily more possessive than of the others."[110] Peiresc seems to have understood that these "Samaritan" coins were actually Judaean coins of the Second Temple and Bar-Kochba revolt period, when the paleo-Hebrew script was used epigraphically.

Peiresc went on to add that if Aymini wished to work on his behalf, there was much to be done in researching the "calendars" of the Eastern Christians. By this it seems that Peiresc meant not only calendar as list of days, but calendar as shorthand for "chronology," or chronological reckoning.[111] Peiresc noted that he wanted something as detailed as possible: "It is necessary that you take the trouble to have them translated and write down the translation yourself as you can in the *franc vulgaire* [the lingua franca of the ports] or another as best as can be done."[112] In advising Aymini's work on Samaritan and Coptic, Peiresc alerted him to the differences between majuscules and miniscules, the names of individual characters, and their numerological values. If possible, Peiresc wanted a line or two of writing in each of these languages. In case it turned out that the Samaritans had no old books with different characters—as he thought they should—then Aymini was to gather up as complete an alphabet as possible.

Peiresc was always a comparatist, and so from the Samaritans—perhaps ripe for this treatment because of their use of ancient Hebrew script and its relationship to Phoenician, all of which Peiresc learned from his mentor Scaliger—Peiresc turned toward other Near Eastern languages.[113] "If you could have in parallel the calendars of the Turks and Persians and other sects of our Christians, and extract from it the interpretation, it should not be neglected. And if you could choose very beautiful Damascus paper of the same size on which you will have these calendars transcribed each

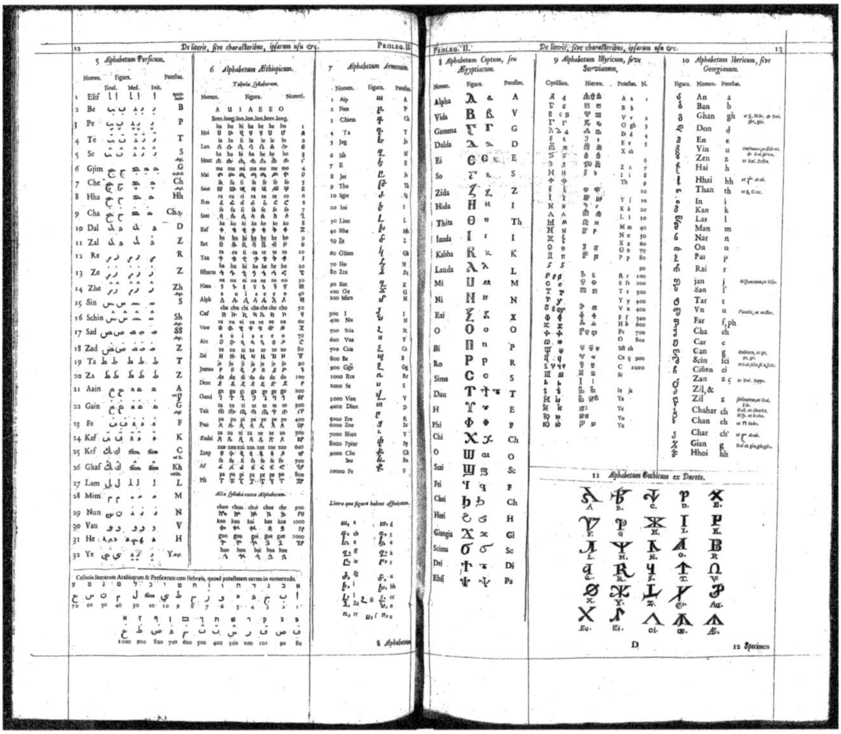

Figure 12. Chart of languages from Walton's *Prolegomena* to the London Polyglot Bible, vol. 1, pp. 12–13. (Divinity School, Yale University)

in its own notebook in order to then organize them according to my wishes, along with the alphabets of each kind." This fantasy was achieved—if not on the fine paper dreamed about by Peiresc—by Bishop Walton in the part of his *Prolegomena* to the London Polyglot Bible treating the history of scripts (Figure 12).[114]

The same ship that was carrying this letter to Aymini also carried others to two Provençal merchants based, respectively, in Sidon and Damascus, Charles Blanc and Jacques Meynier.[115] Peiresc thanked Blanc for all the assistance he had provided Minuti and Aymini, as well as for the gifts of local grapes and bananas ("raisins de damas, figues d'Adam"). Most of all, though, he stressed the importance of the book that had been purchased at Damascus before being consigned by Minuti to Blanc for shipping to Gastines at Marseille, "who is in charge of my affairs" ("qui a soign de mes affaires"). For a complete version of the book Aymini had bought, Peiresc was prepared to spend an additional fifteen or twenty écus.[116] Meynier, at Damascus, was apparently the one involved in the purchase of the Samaritan Triglot. Peiresc thanked him for his intercession with the Maronite Father Michael, who sold it.[117] Estelle, who was Peiresc's manager in Sidon, was thanked profusely and promised immediate reimbursement via Tarquet in Marseille. Although Aymini remained in the Levant for only a little while longer, and though he had only some familiarity with what Peiresc wanted, if he found other things or indeed antique medals of the sort that Minuti had sent, Estelle was authorized to advance him up to a further twenty écus. Peiresc concluded by saying that he had not yet received any reply from the Capuchins in Sidon to whom he had written.[118]

But for a fuller account of how Meynier, Minuti, and Aymini acquired the Samaritan Triglot, we need to turn to a letter written by Peiresc to Galaup-Chasteuil, dated 10 November 1629. In it, Peiresc explained that the previous day he received a packet from Aymini that described how in Damascus he had entered the library "of a very learned Turkish monk where he purchased for me a Samaritan Pentateuch in three languages, Arabic, Samaritan and Hebrew, all written in Samaritan characters." The book was being sent on a later boat, which filled him with anxiety, since this other ship had not yet come in.[119] The Syriac New Testaments acquired by Aymini were for Chasteuil, his relative.

In the meantime, however much Galaup was fired by the Syriac materials, Peiresc bemoaned his lack of interest in the Samaritans, which was his main focus. "But you are so versed in these oriental languages that you would understand everything there from half a word—when you will look." Peiresc wanted Galaup's help in order to compare the different copies of Samaritan materials.[120]

A week later, Peiresc wrote again to Galaup. He was able to report that he received the case sent back by Minuti containing two Syriac New Testaments, including the little one "written on old Damascus paper, covered in wood and very well preserved." This was the one Aymini had written to him about.[121] But Minuti also wrote that he had found a second in large format—in folio, much older and more authentic, "being written on parchment." His regret was that it lacked a table of contents or an index, the concluding part of the volume being lost. Nevertheless, it was a precious book, having "the illustrations of the early Christians of the Annunciation, Resurrection, etc., which show it being of six or seven hundred years old, in my judgment, and according to the knowledge that I have drawn from Greek and Latin manuscripts of the same century." From the fact that the volume was incomplete from the back, Peiresc deduced that it had been badly bound and the last quires had over time been worn away. Peiresc concluded by inviting him to his home; he even offered to send a horse for him or to have Vallavez bring him the following week.[122]

On 18 November 1629, Peiresc wrote to Tarquet, summarizing the information contained in the many letters he had just written to all those who had helped Minuti. Peiresc singled out the contribution of Aymini, who is "very intelligent about books" and whom he had commissioned "to research some supplements to what I have received" thus far.[123] It was for this that he had authorized Estelle to support him, and was reimbursing him for the 45 piastres already spent—but he also wondered how much all this might come to. He concluded by thanking Tarquet for passing along the note of Jacques de Vendôme, another Recollet, and the guardian of the Convent at Nazareth, who reported from Rome, where he was visiting, that de Thou was planning to return soon to France via Provence.[124]

It was at this point, full of excitement at the acquisition of these Samaritan materials, that Peiresc wrote to Hugo Grotius in Paris, noting that he had seen a little mémoire drawn up by Grotius outlining the books Jacob Golius recovered in the Levant. To Grotius, Peiresc signaled his interest in the preservation of Greek philosophical works—Avicenna and the supplement to Aristotle's *De Animalibus*—rather than the Koran or even the historical chronologies, which he usually was so intent upon.[125]

Writing again to Galaup at the beginning of December, Peiresc thanked him for the impressions and translations of the Hebrew medals sent by Minuti and approved his plan to send a digest of the Samaritan letters before making a word-for-word translation. Peiresc added that he sent to Lyon for the Bibles Aymini wanted. Peiresc added his hope that Galaup would wish to contribute his expertise in Syriac to the making of a new polyglot bible that was just under way in Paris. He added that he was still waiting for the Samaritan Triglot but expected it the next month.[126]

In mid-December, Peiresc wrote again to Tarquet. The letter seems triggered not by receipt of Tarquet's of 10 December but rather Minuti's of 30 September and another, undated, of Estelle's. Peiresc was sorry that Tarquet had not applied for the reimbursement of the money he lost through Estelle's generosity to Minuti (i.e., the interest lost). He noted that Minuti's letter of 30 September did not say that the book he was waiting for had actually left Sidon on the *Grand Henry*. If Tarquet had newer news of the ship's passage, Peiresc was desperate to have it. Finally, Peiresc admitted to being "greatly vexed" ("fasché") by not being told of de Thou's arrival in Marseille with time enough to go there and greet him.[127] As we have seen, de Thou's travels seemed to have been a constant source of disappointment for Peiresc.

Writing to Estelle, Peiresc was full of gratitude for his solicitousness on behalf of Minuti—which included feeding him at his own table in Sidon. He had not written to Minuti when replying to Estelle's letter of 3 September, thinking that he was on the way to Damiette, which had been his initial plan. Peiresc was sorry that his letters had gone astray. Believing that his letters were reaching Estelle, Peiresc said he would employ the same means to communicate with Jacques Meynier in Damascus and Charles Blanc in Sidon. In a postscript, Peiresc turned back to the book bought in Damascus and said to be on the *Grand Henry*. If it were not, Peiresc wanted Estelle to write to Meynier in Damascus and ask him to have the copyists make haste or else to send what was ready and to fill in the rest at their leisure. Finally, Peiresc wanted his good wishes conveyed to Aymini and to those Capuchins mentioned by de Thou to whom he had written but from whom he had not yet gotten a response.[128]

It was, in fact, to de Thou that Peiresc's last letter of 1629 was written. Peiresc was bitterly hurt that for a second time de Thou passed through Aix-Marseille without seeing him. Peiresc blamed de Gastines for not alerting him—this was more polite than blaming de Thou himself. But Peiresc was unable to suppress completely his feeling of hurt: "I have also taken pains to patiently take such a great mortification that you have given me by this blow, and I beseech you to grant pardon to a sensitive man when he is touched so deeply, if he is to escape from the resentment that I would not know how to suppress."[129]

As for de Thou's things, the "Corbelle Turquesque" was maltreated by the thieves who fished it out of the water near Messina. Peiresc put the contents into a box he had made so that it would hold up better on the overland route (some books had already been sent to Dupuy, and others remained at Aix while he tried to decipher them). Peiresc also put into the box some other books that the Dupuy brothers wanted, including Peiresc's important volume of the *Eclogues* of Constantine Porphyrogenitus. Only the crocodile skin remained in Aix while Peiresc waited for a better one to be obtained from Alexandria or Cairo. Peiresc explained that he had sent Dupuy a list of all the things he had gathered up from Toulon and Marseille, as well as from Aubery in Rome, as well as eighteen or so little copper coins, some engravings, and bronze figurines.[130]

(A crocodile skin worthy of de Thou was finally found by Jean Magy in Cairo in 1636. It weighed 255 pounds.[131] Peiresc discussed it in a letter to him of July 1636. He described it as of a "truly extraordinary size" compared to all the others he had seen. Nevertheless, Peiresc felt obliged to point out that the person who had "salted" the animal did not know how to handle the leg, which was corrupted. "It is true," he wrote, "that your brother found a man who handled it quite well with lavender flowers. But when one wishes to handle these animals for conserving them, it is necessary instead of common salt to use nitric salt ["sel nitre"], or the saltpeter from which one makes gunpowder, and to dissolve it in water for filling the head and all the concavities with this water. For this strongly defends against corruption and stench."[132])

Had de Thou made the detour of nine leagues from Marseille to Belgentier—others, Peiresc wrote, would have gladly come fifty—he would have seen all the things that had already been recovered from the Levant and been able to talk with his friends. Peiresc then summarized some of his recent recoveries. The Samaritan materials included a dictionary and fragments of a grammar potentially useful to Father Jean Morin, who was just then undertaking the venture of an edition of the Samaritan Pentateuch for the Paris Polyglot Bible project.[133] Peiresc was waiting for another book purchased for him in the Levant and expected to arrive in January. It cost him "only 45 piastres"—a sizable sum that Peiresc thought a bargain all the same. He told him of the Minuti mission—a "poor friar to whom I had given some little thing for his voyage to the Holy Land"—who met up in the Levant with Aymini and went with him to many places searching for books—the metaphor is "digging" ("fouiller")—before they finally "trapped" this one. After telling de Thou all this, Peiresc could not hold back, concluding that he told him all this "for a little revenge, for you not thinking it worth it to come and see me in our little rural hermitage."[134] And even this barb did not fully drain his bitterness. For in a postscript Peiresc began, "After having signed my letter, a small relic of the spirit of revenge (honest, however) made me take up the pen so as not to omit at all, as I had wanted, a bit of boastfulness capable of giving some little displeasure to someone unable to resist the curiosities of nature and antiquity." What follows is a quick survey of some high points of his own collection of natural (plants, fossils, shells, pearls) and human antiquities (including the tripod just dug up in Fréjus).[135]

1630

The Samaritan Triglot, which surely would have been one of these highlights, arrived in Marseille on 27 January 1630. It came with a letter from Estelle in Sidon. He explained that from his previous letter, of 31 October, Peiresc would have learned that Estelle loaned Minuti 50 piastres. This could be made good to Baptiste Tarquet. Minuti had also charged Estelle with shipping a Syriac book he had purchased at Damascus. At his departure from Sidon Minuti gave the money, which was about 30 piastres, to Aymini, who had acquired the book from a Venetian who charged him 31 piastres. The book was consigned to Estelle's nephew François Aurivelier for delivery to Peiresc.[136]

Aurivelier, a merchant, was charged to explore the files of the chancellery at Sidon.[137] (One wonders: what did Peiresc think he might have found there?) Peiresc's letter to him, after the obvious and immediate expression of thanks, focused entirely on the cost of the book and how much Peiresc owed (Fort, he wrote, would take care of all the details.) He explained how Aymini paid out 31 piastres to a Venetian who seized the book and that Minuti gave Aymini 30 piastres for this out of the 50 that had been furnished by Estelle to Minuti and which Pierre Fort paid out to Baptiste Tarquet on Estelle's wishes. If the additional parchment pages to fill out the Triglot cost a further 5 or 6 piastres in addition to the 30, then Peiresc would reimburse Aurivelier as well, through Fort.[138] Peiresc had received the document from Fort for the discharge of the goods and sent it on the very next day.[139] Fort himself wrote to Peiresc on 31 January and 1 February. He reported the arrival of the Samaritan Pentateuch and, via Tarquet, the completion of payment for it. The book itself arrived some time between 28 January and 2 February, when Peiresc acknowledged receipt. He had some concern about missing medals.[140]

Other coins arrived not long after, sent by Mallon, "Master Surgeon in Damascus," to his respondent, the apothecary Thibault, in Marseille.[141] Apparently, it was de Thou who had met Mallon on his trip to the Levant and conveyed Peiresc's interest in coins and medals. Mallon followed up and sent this box, as he would eventually others, via Peiresc's merchant channels, back to Marseille.[142] Peiresc summarized this shipment in a letter to Mallon of 20 February 1630. He had received Mallon's of 1 December 1629 from Damascus along with the box of coins, and that of Thibault of Marseille of 11 February along with the box itself. Many of the coins were written in Samaritan characters, others in Greek. Peiresc wanted Mallon to remain on the lookout for Samaritana.[143]

Writing on the same day to Aymini, Peiresc summarized the recent arrivals: via Aurivelier of Aymini's letter of 10 December with the Samaritan Pentateuch and a box of coins, and another via Thibault of his letter of 7 December with Mallon's box. He had also received from Aurivelier the books and coins that Minuti sent via Estelle, and from Marseille another of his, with a box full of devotions and relics. That he had not yet acknowledged reception was a result of his having to go attend the king in Languedoc—a reminder that Peiresc had a "day job" as a judge—and then was unable to return to Aix because of the plague—a reminder that in the seventeenth century even judges and scholars lived only a hair's breadth away from upheaval.[144]

Peiresc's major concern was with the Samaritan Triglot. He knew that there were many gaps in the text and part of the delay in his receiving it had to do with having new sections copied in Damascus. While he thought Minuti right to try to have them copied from other texts and then inserted, those who were given this task did not do a good job, using, for example, paper rather than parchment. Peiresc also feared the hand of that unnamed Venetian who had sold it in the first place and might have wished to invade his turf ("courut sur mon marché"). He was only sorry that Mallon let some other Samaritan books get away: "For in that language I work with everything that can be had at a moderate price, principally books of chronology and history," but also calendars and religion. Peiresc treated Samaritan as a culture and language and not just a script, perhaps overvaluing its importance.[145] And vexed as he was by the gaps in his Pentateuch, he announced that he was willing to pay for another, older, more complete one. He had already told Estelle to renew his credit; Minuti's 45 piastres were replenished and Tarquet gone off to the Levant with instructions to pay out as was needed.[146]

Peiresc gladly thanked Estelle in another letter written on 20 February, but was mostly concerned with ensuring that he was reimbursed with advantage, something that was being stonewalled by Aurivelier, who would take no money. Peiresc also wished to ensure that their communication was not blocked by the plague-related closures and commercial disruptions that had hit Provence. Finally, he had received no confirmation that either Estelle or the unnamed Capuchin father to whom he had written had ever received his letter.[147]

On 22 February 1630 Minuti wrote to Peiresc from Livorno. Peiresc answered on 3 March, and reviewed their correspondence since Minuti's departure. With Minuti's of the 22nd came those of Fernoux, Lambert, and Jean Magy from Egypt, and d'Espiot from Rome. The letter Peiresc sent on the 19th via Lieutenant Valbelle had not reached Minuti because Valbelle was now in Paris. From Patron Bartolle he had received the box, letters, and kittens consigned to him. Some time later he received Minuti's letters from Jerusalem by Patron Cornillon of Cassis. With the *Grand Henry* came the Samaritan Pentateuch and two boxes of antiquities from Aymini and Mallon. The latter's request for drugs had been met, but Peiresc had not gotten the graftings, large raisins, and bananas that Charles Blanc of Sidon was supposedly sending. Peiresc had asked Blanc's uncle in Marseille, M. Marquesi, to check but had not yet gotten a response in writing and was led to understand that he might not. He might even have made off with them, Peiresc wrote to Minuti, and "preferred to give them to someone else than to me."[148]

From these details, Peiresc turned to the project of Samaritan research. Aymini and Estelle had informed him that "a Venetian Cretan had invaded my market and during the absence of Sr. Meynier who went off to a village, and had bought from a Maronite my poor Samaritan Pentateuch for the 31 piastres, in the same state you had it." This was the volume with errors and lacunae and missing pages and different hands. Peiresc had not thought these major drawbacks. Nor did the Venetian, who paid the Maronite exactly the same amount that the Maronite had asked from Aymini to repair these lacunae! Now neither Aymini nor Minuti could get it from him.[149] Mallon had told him that there were more Samaritan books on the market and he did not want to lose any more. Mallon had not bought them because he did not know what Peiresc wanted. This had now been spelled out to him.

Peiresc had heard that there was another Pentateuch floating around Rome. It was mentioned as being in the possession of an Observant Franciscan. If it was complete and reasonably priced, Minuti was to buy it. Peiresc would secure funding via Bonnaire in Rome. Meanwhile, Peiresc was very grateful for the paper quires sent by Minuti which enabled him to put together a nearly complete Samaritan lexicon. He urged Minuti to come visit as soon as possible because it would take too long to obtain a detailed account of the trip in writing.[150]

This letter was sent to Minuti at Rome, along with a second, to Bonnaire, and included a recommendation to all their mutual friends in Rome, including Francesco Barberini.[151] In a second, short letter to Minuti which accompanied that to Bonnaire, Peiresc explained that he had omitted mention of all the Samaritan materials out of fear that it would put Barberini in ill humor, "for fear of undertaking to sending them to him, because in these matters what goes to Rome once does not easily leave." Peiresc also alerted Minuti to Pietro della Valle's Samaritan and Coptic materials.[152]

In early March 1630, Aymini wrote again to Peiresc from Sidon. In January, Aymini had sent back a packet of coins with a friend, a surgeon from La Ciotat named François Estoupan, who promised to bring it directly to Belgentier. Aymini feared that since Estoupan was traveling through Livorno he might not have reached Peiresc yet. In the meantime, meeting the baron d'Alegre, who had been deputized by the Grand Duchess of Tuscany to negotiate with Fakhr-al-Din, and who was proceeding forthwith to Damascus, Aymini commissioned him to purchase an old Samaritan Pentateuch. Meanwhile, Aymini was planning to visit Jerusalem before returning to France, and on his way would stop in Nablus and negotiate with the Samaritans. Aymini praised the merchant Charles Blanc, who had provided him with the funds to purchase medals, and who had sent back plants and fruits—more of those bananas—with the baron d'Alegre, who had since returned to Europe on a Flemish ship.[153] Blanc's own letter added that if he encountered "here some curiosities to your taste" he would not hesitate to acquire them and send them on, acting "with the diligence of Father Daniel." Blanc regretted that the almond trees from the garden of Fakhr-al-Din could not even be transported to Damascus, let alone to Marseille.[154]

Minuti stayed in Rome, but the ships that brought him over reached Marseille in mid-April. Peiresc sent letters to the captains who carried letters from Aymini and Blanc.[155] A third letter from that day was sent to Barthélemy Issaultier, scrivener of the polacre *Notre Dame de la Consolation,* who brought back the mummies Minuti had purchased for Peiresc.[156] Peiresc had heard from Aycard of Minuti's passage through Toulon and wrote immediately, urging him to avoid Marseille on account of the quarantine regime.[157] But on a fisherman's word that all was well, Captain Sarde conducted his ship straight back to Marseille where it and all its contents were promptly quarantined. Peiresc had sent a horse to Cassis for Minuti on the 17th. A friend of Peiresc's from Martigues had told him that Minuti had passed through the Isles de Marseille; if Minuti had disembarked there, his goods could have avoided being caught up in Marseille's quarantine regime.[158] Instead, Peiresc now had to urge Minuti to come immediately to Belgentier, where Galaup-Chasteuil already was, eager to see the Samaritan Triglot and the other one purchased by Aymini.[159] The goods, however, had to remain behind.

Peiresc summed up some of these movements in a letter to de Thou of 29 April 1630, a letter that was to accompany a package for him brought from the Levant by Aymini. Peiresc also passed along the word that de Thou's crocodile was slowly drying out.[160]

From Aymini's letters, and those of Charles Blanc, Peiresc learned of the efforts of the Tuscan baron d'Alegre on his behalf.[161] To recover the little plants the baron had brought from the Levant on the same Flemish boat, Peiresc wrote to a French merchant based in Livorno asking him to send the trees, in their tubs, either on French galleys or on the same Flemish boat, addressed to de Gastines at Cassis, but if necessary to Toulon or St. Tropez as well. The letter itself went via Toulon.[162] We can trace the arrival of these little trees through letters written by Peiresc to Honoré Tourtel, sieur de Ramatuelle of Sixfours, and the merchant Truillet of Toulon, both on 16 June 1630. Apparently, the tubs came from the Levant via Livorno on the polacre of Patron Alphant, arriving around 8 June. Peiresc's challenge was to figure out where it had unloaded, whether at Sanary, near Sixfours, or somewhere else on the coast. Peiresc was pleased to send a "cart or the mules" once he knew where it was.[163]

The Recollet, Jacques de Vendôme, whom Peiresc described as "Guardian of Nazareth," was in Cassis in June 1630, about to return to Sidon. As of then, Peiresc had still been unable to retrieve the cases Minuti had brought back with him in April, and also the Coptic books.[164] Peiresc wanted to know on whose barque he was traveling, having heard that it belonged to Viguier and was going to Sidon.[165] Peiresc had letters for him from de Thou, and sent them along to Toulon. Peiresc added ones for Aymini to travel on that Sidon-bound ship.[166]

Peiresc's letters to de Thou from June 1630, while the plague raged in Cassis, were dominated by logistics—how to get mail to Jacques de Vendôme, whether there was time to catch him at Toulon or whether it was necessary to write directly to Sidon, and whether de Gastines had failed to forward some mail. Peiresc also gave an update on the conservation of de Thou's box and its contents. Finally, he turned to the Arabic and Coptic books that were the subjects of his keenest concern: "I hold that these Arabic and Coptic books could be very useful to the public, and if we had had people versed in these languages we could have willingly had them work on it . . . and in fact, I think that this Arabic Bible could be just right for the edition which M. Le Jay" is making—the Paris Polyglot Bible project. For the Coptic books, there were some conservation issues, but Peiresc was hopeful about their eventual recovery.[167]

Amid the worries of plague and his constant effort to maintain a functioning communications system, Peiresc was negotiating with Rome. From Marchand, his "expeditionnaire," he was waiting to receive the new concordat with the novitiate of the Jesuits of Bordeaux. Peiresc advised that it be sent to Paris, either to Aubery de Mesnil or Denis Guillemin, prieur de Roumoulles, "who manages the affairs of my Abbey of Guîtres." But the most interesting thing about this letter is that it reveals that Peiresc was preparing for a second Minuti expedition. For we find him asking Marchand to expedite "an indulgence for the visiting of the Holy Sepulchre and other overseas places." He had gone and made "really excellent observations" ("des observations tres excellentes"). Peiresc wanted to send him back again. Peiresc gave explicit instructions to Marchand about what he wanted in the document. He wanted to phrase things so as to discourage his order from assigning him a traveling partner, but if it were necessary, the choice should be Minuti's. Peiresc suggested that the permission be sent to Father Guillaume Barmie, who gave Minuti his permission the first time. If there were problems with the bureaucracy, Bonnaire was to seek the intervention of either Cardinal Bentivoglio or Cardinal Barberini, though Peiresc thought it more diplomatic not to force Barberini to plead with his uncle the pope or with the general of the Minims. Marchand could tell them that this voyage "is not at all like those commonly made by the religious, and that he succeeded in it with benefit for the good of belief in God and the veneration of those holy places and for other things concerning antiquities and the church."[168] Peiresc himself wrote to Cardinal Barberini, asking for a safe conduct for Minuti to visit the Holy Sepulchre and "other holy places."[169]

And even as Peiresc laid the groundwork for Minuti's next trip, he was entertaining the new French ambassador to Constantinople, Henri de Gournay, comte de Marcheville. The latter had come from Toulon to Belgentier with Peiresc, and though called away promised to return in the next fortnight. Peiresc reported to de Thou on Marcheville's commitment to learning and desire to travel with scholars in his retinue. Peiresc hoped to entice Holstenius and Gassendi to this task; Marcheville hoped to leave the following November.[170]

Over the summer of 1630, Peiresc wrote to Minuti twice, about goings on in the country and about borrowing some Hebrew books that Galaup-Chasteuil desired.[171] The most notable event was the visit of two Portuguese "jewelers" ("lapidaires") en route to India, one of whom was the brother-in-law "of your celebrated Alvarez of Paris," or so Peiresc wrote to de Thou, with the result that "this miserable place is now become the great postal road, or the routes of the ambassadors to Rome, to Constantinople (and, if I would dare say) the Indies."[172]

Peiresc's Marcheville plan seemed to firm up in the early autumn of 1630, so that Peiresc could report to Galaup that Gassendi was preparing astronomical instruments in order to make observations in Constantinople and Alexandria.[173] At the same time, Aymini had written to Peiresc on 7 August from Sidon by way of Captain Maillet to explain that he would soon be sending some coins and antiquities with Jean Berard on the *St. Jerome* of Captain Laurent; by early October Peiresc had received the letter and sent Minuti to retrieve them from Marseille.[174] Peiresc passed along to Minuti the news that Mallon was leaving Damascus for Aleppo and that Aymini was planning to go to Jerusalem for Christmas and stay through Easter.[175] All this while, however, the cases that Minuti had brought back from Egypt remained locked away in the quarantine in Marseille. Now that the threat of plague was over, he wrote to Barthélemy Issaultier in Marseille asking him to get the cases back.[176] Peiresc had them by the end of the month.[177]

In Aymini's next letter to Peiresc, written at the beginning of September, he summarized his activities of the previous months; by way of Captain Grimaud he had sent back a Samaritan book (a Pentateuch, in fact) and a number of medals. Charles Blanc had provided sufficient funds to cover the medals, but not the book. Blanc left Sidon without paying the balance owed to his friend, Michael of Damascus, some 20 piastres. Five years later, Father Michael would write to Minuti at Marseille, complaining bitterly about this "shame."[178] Blanc, meanwhile, had now come across a second and even better Samaritan Pentateuch. It belonged to one of "our" Flemish fathers in Jerusalem, Aymini wrote. He—Father Adrianus Bachers—was keen that it pass through a hereditary channel; Aymini wrote that he, Aymini, was just as determined to be able to keep it. Bachers had many coins, too, though he claimed that they were pledged to a cardinal. Aymini concluded that he hoped to be at the Holy Sepulchre for Christmas and the New Year, and there "to put into execution your first *relation* for the convenience of all nations that are there within." With this glancing reference, omitted from the edition of the letter published by René Lebègue—himself always ready to accuse Tamizey de Larroque of cutting, pasting, stitching, and otherwise violating the integrity of the letters he published—we are confronted with one of Peiresc's most audacious plans: an investigation of the music of the Eastern Christians, undertaken within the Church of the Holy Sepulchre, where each of the Eastern denominations had its chapel. The project unfolds over the course of several letters and many years.[179]

How much of this project derived from Peiresc himself, and how much from his conversations with Mersenne, who was then at work upon his *Harmonie Universelle,* is hard to determine. But we do know that the combination of travel to the Levant and discussions with Mersenne was responsible for Peiresc turning to Giovanni Battista Doni with questions about Arab music. He had met Doni in 1625, when Doni came to France in the entourage of Cardinal Francesco Barberini, and they had stayed in contact. In December 1631, responding to a letter of Peiresc's, Doni undertook to send him an Arabic manuscript on music. Doni did not think much of what was written in Arabic about music, aside from the theory that was derived from the Greeks and from exceptional authors such as Avicenna.[180]

Peiresc seems to have received Aymini's letters by the beginning of November.[181] On the twentieth of that month he wrote to Tarquet that he had heard from Sidon that reimbursement had still not been made for the monies laid out by Estelle for purchase of the first Samaritan Pentateuch, or to Meynier for the second one.[182] In December 1630 Peiresc was *still* trying to get from Minuti the name and "qualité" of the people who furnished the 31 piastres for the first Pentateuch, and the 20 for the second.[183] The box of coins sent by Mallon was also still causing similar problems. On that same day Peiresc wrote to a M. Sauvine, scrivener on the navire of Patron Lombardon, thanking him for taking the box from Mallon in Aleppo. Peiresc had learned of his indebtedness to him only belatedly: from a letter of Mallon's that accompanied the box. That letter, however, was sent by mistake to Perrier at Aix and was only just brought to him. The box, Peiresc writes, and any other letters he carried, was to be delivered to Fort at Marseille, who would reimburse any related costs.[184] That same day, still looking east, Peiresc wrote to Christofle de Bermond just back from the Levant, thanking him for the assistance he provided to Fernand Nunes ("Sr Fernandez") and Manuel da Costa.[185]

1631

Peiresc's response to Mallon occupied him in January and February 1631. On 23 January he wrote to Fort saying that the package of books for Mallon was now ready and asked him to find out about shipping to Alexandretta (the port nearest Aleppo). Peiresc wanted to know the name of the ship, the captain, the person to be charged with the package, and when the ship was planning to sail so that he could gather the other letters to be sent on it.[186] He wrote to Mallon in February—presumably after receiving this information—with a summary of their communications thus far. Peiresc reported receiving the box with sixty-six copper coins—Peiresc's coin inventory identifies Mallon's purchases as "Greek" coins—along with the letter of 20 September 1630, after a slight delay. He had, however, been able to locate in Aix, Marseille, and Toulon nearly every book of surgery on Mallon's list, and the book he could not find he would search for in Lyon and send later.[187]

Peiresc then followed with a much longer letter in which he spelled out in detail exactly what he wanted by way of coins and books, and how Mallon should choose the correct ones.[188] Mallon had acknowledged receiving from M. l'Archier in Alexandretta the letter of Peiresc's saying that he had a packet of books from M. Fort; Mallon asked that the packet be handed to "M. Franege or his companion to take with the caravan."[189] (By August 1632 Peiresc had found the last book, that of "Duc" or "Sr de" Laurens, which he was now readying for shipment.[190] Notice of receipt of the book was sent by Mallon on 1 November 1632 and reached Peiresc at the beginning of April 1633.[191])

In March 1631, the comte de Marcheville was making plans for the departure of his embassy. Peiresc informed Galaup-Chasteuil that Holstenius did not receive permission to go but that Gassendi was getting ready.[192] Peiresc told Minuti on 3 March to be ready for Marcheville's imminent departure—the first real indication we have that Peiresc planned for Minuti to travel back to the Levant in the ambassadorial retinue.[193]

Amid preparations for departure, Peiresc also welcomed back Daniel Aymini. Peiresc hoped to get him to Belgentier as soon as possible, but Aymini was waiting in Marseille for the *Dauphin* to fully unload. Peiresc told him that de Gastines would arrange his transportation to Belgentier. It was only nine leagues, but the road was rough, so it was advisable to leave in the morning. Aymini was asked to bring his instructions and travel mémoires, whether they were finished or not.[194] Aymini arrived on the 1st with another father of his order from Constantinople, bringing along a Samaritan Pentateuch and some coins. He wanted to see Minuti, who was away for the festival of St. François de Paule (founder of the Minims).[195]

Peiresc seems to have been trying to gather his local oriental studies circle but was frustrated that while he was hosting Aymini neither Minuti nor Galaup-Chasteuil, who claimed that he had to take care of his mother, could join him.[196] Another two priests returning from the Levant, this time from Jerusalem, were hosted by Minuti in mid-April, while Peiresc announced the imminent departure of Marcheville. Gassendi, just then, announced that he would be unable to depart until September and that he wished to take the route to Constantinople through Germany and Hungary. (Did this mean that he was already seeking to excuse himself?)[197] Aymini and his traveling partner—a Recollet named Joachin da Goa— must have gone to Marseille, where they met Benoit Pelissier.[198] On the same day, writing to them in Marseille, Peiresc apologized for Galaup-Chasteuil's failure to show up.[199] In late May, Peiresc was writing to Thomas d'Arcos in Tunis, accompanying his three letters with two tuns of wine— suggesting the desperately thirsty state of his correspondent in that dry land.[200]

In early June, Peiresc heard from both Minuti and his brother Vallavez of the arrival of Marcheville in advance of sailing, but since he would have to spend forty days before departing to fulfill quarantine rules, it left time enough for encounters.[201] Peiresc took advantage of this time to advise Pelissier on opportunities for meeting the ambassador.[202] On 1 July Peiresc wrote to Pelissier announcing that he was planning to travel to Marseille.[203]

With Marcheville's—and therefore Minuti's—impending departure, the rhythm and direction of Peiresc's correspondence changed. As at Minuti's first departure, we find a series of letters being written to Marseille merchants in the East. If his first trip focused on the Sidon-Aleppo-Damascus connection, Peiresc now turned to Constantinople. L'Empereur was reminded that two years ago Peiresc had written to him on Minuti's behalf but that the latter had not made it to Constantinople. Peiresc asked if Minuti could now be shown some of his "singularités" and, in particular, his medals. In the postscript we learn that Galaup-Chasteil had finally decided to travel east with Marcheville as well.[204] Guez, to whom Peiresc also wrote, was the money person, being told to furnish up to 100 écus, with a "*lettre de change* on my account or that of M. de Gastines of Marseille."[205] Peiresc apologetically wrote to Minuti that he was too unwell to travel to Marseille and so was sending his brother with the "memoirs, instructions and prints that you had from the other time with some little additions," and also letters for Guez and l'Empereur.[206]

From Vallavez's visit to Marseille to bid farewell to Minuti, Peiresc learned that Baptiste Tarquet was also about to depart for Sidon. This sparked another flurry of letter-writing. Peiresc reminded Tarquet of his policy of reimbursing all charges and "profits maritimes." But he also reminded him that he had never received a reply from the Capuchin mentioned by de Thou.[207] Peiresc renewed his contact with Jacques Estelle, as well, recalling gratefully the kindnesses he had performed for Minuti once before.[208] Peiresc also added a new contact, Jérôme de l'Isle, who had helped Aymini acquire a Samaritan book. De l'Isle was apparently a friend of de Gastines (Peiresc thanks him for his affection for "M. de Gastines and me") and had a brother in Marseille through whom reimbursement was effected. Peiresc was writing to notify him of Minuti's passage and to secure his assistance. (Peiresc also reminded him to insure his goods, unlike Marquesi, a loss that still pained him.)[209]

At the end of the year, Peiresc reviewed the current position of the players in this drama for the benefit of de Thou, himself just back from a diplomatic trip to England and the Low Countries. He began by complimenting de Thou on his worthy elevation to "Counselor to the King in his State Council and Master of Requests." He conveyed the news that that there were letters waiting for him (Peiresc) in Toulon that had come from Constantinople dated 29 October containing news of Marcheville's arrival, though not, apparently, of the formal audience that should have occurred already. As for Minuti, Peiresc reported having received a letter from him from Chios of 24 August, telling of a visit he made with the ambassador to Delos, while the ship was anchored at Chios. He recounted marvels of not only its colossus but also the measures of amphitheaters "and other great structures, all of marble." There were so many monuments and inscriptions that it seemed that the island must once have been covered by them. But the ambassador moved too quickly for Minuti to make even one copy. He had also wanted to do a tour of the island by felucca. At Chios, Minuti saw terebinths and took "la Therebentine Mastiche," which the Turks guarded with uncommon care—indeed, mastic is found only on Chios. There was a monastery and there were religious, but no books.[210] Delayed in Chios by the *tramontana*, their ship eventually reached Tenedos, from which the anxious-to-arrive ambassador switched to a faster caïque for the last stage of his journey to Constantinople.[211]

1632

Peiresc continued trying to serve Dr. Mallon in the first months of 1632. Fort retrieved a packet from Mallon dated 7 September and sent via the apothecary Thibault. It came with a box containing nine little copper coins.[212] Peiresc gave Fort a standing order to pass along to l'Archier permission to advance him up to 40 écus. (It turned out, however, that l'Archier never made the short trip from Alexandretta to Aleppo—but we learn of this only later.)[213]

The letters from Minuti began to arrive in early 1632. Peiresc received Minuti's of 14 and 17 December, and Guez's of 12 December, acknowledging them all in a letter to Guez of late March 1632.[214] The next batch of letters from Minuti came via Aycard of Toulon. On 6 August 1632 Peiresc wrote to Aycard, thanking him for sending Minuti's letter, which detailed his plan to go to Sidon, accompanied by Aycard's nephew Jean Salvator. (This, Peiresc surmised, must have pleased Aycard, who had been worried that Salvator would try to return to Europe from Constantinople, with all its seditions and riots.)

Summarizing for Aycard's benefit, Peiresc reported that Minuti had written to him on 14 April by way of Hugon Bermond of La Ciotat. Minuti said that he had sent six pigeons, none of which had arrived—or survived, as Peiresc speculated they might have been eaten en route. Also, Minuti said that he had sent a beautiful and exceptional Turkish writing desk ("escritoire Turquesque fort gentille, et fort extraordinaire").[215] Peiresc's complaint about the too-rigorous enforcement of the quarantine against Captain Raysson was successful, and his cases were released on 14 August.[216]

By 22 August, Peiresc could report to Minuti that he had received everything.[217] The writing desk was of tortoise shell, so beautiful that he was sending it to Paris to one of his friends who could use it better—and, one need hardly add, appreciate the gift. The other items Minuti sent were quickly but lovingly enumerated—another book, a vase, flowers, and "damasquined wood." Peiresc commented on the generosity of l'Empereur for making one of his vases available to Minuti for examination.[218] As for the more ephemeral commerce—news of Constantinople—Peiresc was unprepared for *"the relation of such great disorder."* Though Chasteuil had said this of the Holy Land, Peiresc was surprised that it was also true of the capital of a great empire.[219]

Peiresc made sure to write to Guez in Constantinople, thanking him for advancing money to Minuti.[220] Peiresc had rushed to write to Minuti and Guez because Ramatuelle had told him that his boat, the *Ste. Anne*, was to set sail at 10:00 a.m. on 23 August. A day's delay enabled Peiresc to write more fully to Minuti. First, he acknowledged receiving Minuti's letter of 29 May. It came with two boxes, and Peiresc enumerated the contents in some detail. He also noted receiving relations from Minuti in his letters of 14 and 17 December 1631, 25 February 1632, and 13–14 March 1632. Ramatuelle's ship was carrying letters for Chasteuil—Peiresc was sorry that Minuti felt Chasteuil was of "barbarous humor"—Marcheville, l'Empereur, and Guez. Honoré Sabatier, Minuti's host in Constantinople, had originally been forgotten, but the omission was now being made good, thanks to the delay.[221]

The letter of 23 August to Minuti was almost completely focused on the realm of the practical, on terms from everyday life as used by artisans and makers. Peiresc told Minuti about the visit just made to him by Cesar Lambert, who came with forty or fifty glass objects, some medals, and some vases made of precious stones. Peiresc offered to buy half a dozen if Minuti could find an exact match, which he could do by first measuring and then comparing the content of the vases. To this end, Peiresc sent him a cast of one of Lambert's vases. The type came from India, Peiresc wrote, "and the Turks use it to drink *eau de vie*." He had seen a half-dozen like it, and they nested one inside the other.[222] For a match, Peiresc was ready to pay up to around 20 écus. Peiresc gave Minuti permission to act quickly "because I like much more those which come ready-made from India, whose peoples are so greatly exact and scrupulous about observing a certain measure and proportion." For that reason he specifically asked Minuti not to buy something made in Constantinople, but rather to ask around the jewelers' shops to see if he could find one made in the form of a bowl or drinking cup and then try to borrow it in order to measure its liquid contents, using the copy of Lambert's as a measure. And after Minuti had done all this, Peiresc hoped he would be able to write up a little mémoire, with the quality of the material of each, the price one could have it at, and the name of the merchant who had them.[223] This would enable others, such as Guez or Sabatier, to buy them for him.

Most of all, Peiresc wanted to know the names used for these vases. To get them, he suggested that Minuti go to the commercial world of Constantinople. As someone who had himself frequented the artisans' shops of Paris to learn from them how things were made, and as someone who as a collector had purchased objects from merchants, Peiresc advised Minuti to explore the shops of Constantinople with diligence.[224] Looking for vases, he told Minuti to seek out those who sold *eau de vie*—which Peiresc distinguished from the apothecaries and druggists who sold more precious liquors—and those who marked all measures by public authority. These, he thought, would be the ones who would know the names of the different-sized vases and their contents.[225] And if Minuti had "the patience and the pleasure," Peiresc wanted the names of all the liquid measures in use "if not for wine, at least for *eau de vie* and any other liquid that was legal for them to drink." If, in addition to the Arabic and Turkish names for the measures, there were any Greek names in circulation, he wanted to know them, too.[226] A visit to the jewelers could turn up material for his study of symbols; Peiresc mentioned a porcupine in particular.[227] But Peiresc also advised Minuti to go "to the *boutiques* or *maisons*" where weights and measures were fabricated to seek out old and discarded examples, and to the workshops of those who cast bronze and copper to look for old fragments of metalware.[228] He also advised visiting foundries. If on one of these visits he saw some fragment of copper or bronze that was to be used in making some new bronze piece, and if it was "a pretty thing, very elaborate and well worthy of being preserved," and he could have it for little above its metallic value, Minuti was to buy it. In conclusion, Peiresc lamented that during the recent outbreak of plague a ship loaded with old bronze fragments from an Aegean island, which was long awaited, in the end bypassed Marseille and discharged its cargo in Spain, where he could not see it. And all this advice, it seems, was fueled by a memory that had become a mantra: in Rome, as a young man, he'd had "no difficulty in going into one of those shops and carrying out two big baskets of old bronze fragments."[229] These many years later he was suggesting that Minuti do the same. And, of course, working in the realm of the practical would enable Minuti to find out the "vernacular names of those same measures, and the translation that your dragoman could make for the one and the other in lingua franca would complete" his inquiry.[230]

In early September, Minuti wrote about his arrival in Constantinople. He had expected to depart quickly for Sidon but Galaup-Chasteuil, his traveling partner from Provence, seemed to have different ideas. Galaup was afraid of the cost of traveling and so lingered four months longer than expected in Constantinople (making a total of nine months altogether). Minuti ate at his table, "but this was at my expense, and to put it better, at yours." And since Galaup ate only one meal a day, between 11:00 a.m. and 1:00 p.m., it fell to Minuti to feed not only him, but also Galaup's servant. Hence his need to borrow 50 piastres from Guez. He had gotten so disgusted with this state of affairs that he decided to leave Galaup there and simply return to Provence. Galaup then told him he had decided to retire to Mount Lebanon and abandon the world. During this time he associated only with a priest—whom Minuti did not name—and a doctor, Salvator, who happened to be the nephew of Honoré Aycard, Peiresc's man in Toulon. Minuti also noted that Galaup had given himself over almost entirely to astrology. From Constantinople, Minuti wrote many letters to Peiresc—none seem to have arrived—and sent a box with Issaultier containing onions, bulbs, and the Hebrew Polyglot Bible printed the previous century in Constantinople. With that, he departed for Damascus. Minuti's plan was to go to Cyprus in November and spend the winter there looking for manuscripts, returning to Cairo in the spring before heading back to Provence.[231]

In mid-September, the ambassador Marcheville wrote to Peiresc, offering his diligence and assistance with commerce throughout the Eschelles, "where my charge gives me some communication."[232] A month later, in early October, Peiresc wrote to Aycard in Toulon that he had read in a letter of Galaup-Chasteuil's written in Constantinople on 14 July that Aycard's nephew Salvator had gone with Minuti to Sidon. The letter was rich in details of schedule and itinerary; they had left on a Turkish *caramoussaire* with a Greek crew that sailed on 23 June, and then changed to a warship sailing to Rhodes from whence, on 22 July, they headed to Sidon on one of the barques called *sambaquiers* which were powered by both sail and oars. By the time they made this crossing, Peiresc wrote, the Ottoman navy had "cleaned up" that coast from pirates.[233] Peiresc added that he thought writing to Sidon was the best policy for the future, but Aycard replied that Guez, who had written from Constantinople on 8 August, believed that Minuti and Salvator were going to be in Sidon for only a short time before leaving for Jerusalem.[234]

By 17 October, Peiresc had received from Lieutenant de Valbelle a letter of Minuti's from Sidon dated 7–8 September, which came along with one from Salvator. Minuti reported that Galaup-Chasteuil was planning to go up to Mount Lebanon in four days while he would be taking the road to Damascus with the idea of returning by the end of October in order to sail on the *St. François* of Sr. Tarquet, which would be carrying the cases of purchases Minuti had made for Peiresc. Minuti explained that he had already given Issaultier a box of curiosities for Peiresc and a note from Salvator for Aycard.[235] On 18 October 1632, Peiresc wrote to Issaultier, newly returned from Sidon on the barque of Captain Maillet, asking for the box. Peiresc wanted it discharged to M. Fort or to the lieutenant of the admiralty, Valbelle. This very letter was to authorize the discharge. Peiresc also wanted to know when he departed from Sidon in order to estimate Minuti's location—since Minuti had written that he was leaving the next day for Damascus and Galaup-Chasteuil in four days for Mount Lebanon.[236] To Guez of Marseille, Peiresc wrote on that same October day. Apparently, Guez had said that letters from Constantinople were going to Toulon, but Aycard in Toulon reported receiving a letter from Guez via Marseille.[237] This kind of variability seems typical.

Minuti's case had been held up in quarantine, but when Peiresc finally got hold of it, he found everything in good shape and unopened.[238] The note from Salvator to Minuti, which he had mistakenly included in the envelope of Minuti, said that all was well in Damascus, where he had not found any other doctor except a Jewish surgeon, even though the city was great, rich, and populous. He urged Minuti to come and visit. Peiresc told Aycard that he would ask Minuti to try to persuade Salvator to come home.[239]

Mail from Minuti dribbled in. On 5 November, writing from Sidon, he summed up his stay in Damascus: what he bought, who would manage his purchases, and who would be bringing Peiresc his installment of grapes and bananas.[240] On 6 November Peiresc received from Issaultier, who had it from the navire *St. Barthélemy,* which had got in only the day before, a very old letter from Minuti written in Constantinople on 23 June, two hours before his departure for Sidon with Salvator.[241] Minuti's letter of 5 November 1632 would not, in fact, reach Peiresc until February 1633. In it Minuti wrote that Salvator remained in Damascus waiting for the caravan from India to see if he could find for Peiresc "some very curious things." As for Minuti, he planned to visit Jerusalem for Easter after returning from Cyprus.[242]

1633

All the while, Peiresc was keeping track of responses to letters he had sent. And where there were no, or only limited, responses, as with those letters sent to Constantinople with Sabatier in August 1632, he asked that Sabatier look into their delivery status.[243] In a contemporary letter to Guez in Marseille, Peiresc asked that the letters for Minuti, at least, be redirected to Sidon, as he had already left Constantinople. He noted that a *lettre de change* from Minuti for 50 piastres sent on by Guez's brother, Guillaume, in Constantinople had not yet arrived; when it did he would immediately honor its account.[244]

At some point early in 1633, Minuti must have gone, probably by ship, from Sidon to Antalya ("Satalie"), for in his letter of March 1633 Minuti reports taking ship in Antalya for northern Cyprus. Meanwhile, two stray pieces of paper in Minuti's hand suggest that he did not immediately begin that voyage, for they record Greek inscriptions found in the village of Cladie and in Konya, which Minuti describes as the "capital city of Caramanie (Karaman)"—the southeastern region of Anatolia just north of Antalya. Minuti, in short, must have done some sightseeing.[245]

But then, returning to Antalya, he found a boat and set out. Somewhere between the southern Anatolian coast and northern Cyprus, his ship, full of Maronites and Greeks, was attacked. The *patron* of the attacking barque was from Martigues and the crew was almost entirely Provençal (twenty-five of the twenty-seven; the other two were Venetian and Maltese). All their goods were taken, including the "50 dozen red caps" entrusted to him by the Marseille merchant Jean-Louis Allemand for conveyance to a Venetian at the salt flats in Cyprus. The passengers were dumped on the Cypriot coast and left to fend for themselves. They scavenged in the forest for three weeks on mushrooms and roots until rescued by a passing Turkish ship. Minuti remained on Cyprus and carried out the survey work he had planned, traveling around the island looking for Greek manuscripts—following up on Peiresc's idea from 1627. He concluded that some authorization from the patriarch in Constantinople himself would be necessary to get access to the monastic library at Paphos as well as that of the archbishop of Nicosia, both of which had fine materials but were closed to him.[246] He then got himself to Sidon, where he checked on previous shipments and prepared to return to Damascus to look for a Syriac Bible and some gift for Vallavez to present to his daughter-in-law. If he were to stay longer in the East he would need a cloak, since he had been left buck naked ("tout beau nu") by the corsairs. He complained of a kind of rheumatism-like cold from sleeping rough, but said that he looked forward to being purged by Dr. Salvator in Damascus. He would wait there for the arrival of the caravans from India, China, and Persia in the hope of finding something good. He would not go with the maître d'hôtel of Marcheville, who was working his way toward Egypt while shaking down French merchants for an extra 2 percent to help defray the ambassador's debts.[247]

Writing from Damascus one month later, Minuti informed Peiresc of a near-disaster that occurred in the harbor of Sidon. The *Ste. Barbe,* which had been loaded by Minuti with books for Peiresc before he departed for Cyprus, was accidentally fired upon by the poop gun of a polacre riding at anchor, and the captain's cabin burned. As he expected the captain to have taken responsibility for Peiresc's goods, this was potentially a disaster. But it turned out, Minuti continued, that "during our voyage from Cyprus to Sidon I had given the captain ["gardien"] of the polacre to drink from that good Cypriot wine in order that he would take special care of our cases, so at the same time that he had loaded his things on the vessel he placed the said cases in the hold" of his boat and they were, therefore, saved.[248] In Damascus, Salvator was keen to go to Persia, and Minuti wrote that he, Minuti, "would be pleased to accompany him," so long as his Uncle Aycard approved, "for to go there all alone, I would not dare to undertake such a voyage."[249]

From Damascus, Minuti repeated the list of items sent from Sidon and noted in his last letter from there, adding that the two Turkish vests were cherry colored, and the 96 *picqs* of Damascus cloths (taffetas) were different from those of France.[250] At this point, Minuti awaited Peiresc's instructions, "otherwise I will take the road to Cairo, which I know by heart, and from there to Provence."[251]

Writing again only a week later, Minuti reported on the arrival in Damascus of an Indian prince and his two white cats, the strangling of the basha of Aleppo, and the arrival of two young men he knew from Constantinople who were heading to Cairo but had Persia as their ultimate destination. He "would be very pleased to accompany them" if Peiresc agreed—but he had to do so quickly or he would lose them. The caravans from Baghdad and India had still not arrived—suggesting that they had been held up by Arab bandits. The Mecca caravan, in turn, was to depart in eight days, and was composed of fifty thousand people. That to Cairo was even larger.[252]

Still having had no word that the letters he sent with Ramatuelle had reached their destinations—Marcheville's of February had come via Lyon and made no mention of the others—by the end of April Peiresc asked the ambassador to find out whether they had been received (Ramatuelle of course said that they had been delivered). Peiresc informed Marcheville that M. de Chasteuil in Lebanon was working away on Syriac and Arabic and that Minuti still planned to visit the Holy Sepulchre. Peiresc was exceedingly pleased to learn from Marcheville of the plan to establish a consul in Athens who would be able, on the side, to participate in the search for antiquities. Peiresc thought there would be great riches of inscriptions, though perhaps not much else (one wonders: did he not know of the Parthenon?). As for coins, he wanted only those that had been recently disinterred, for he was aware that there was a practice of shipping old coins to the Levant and then burying them in order for them to be "rediscovered" as antiquities and sold for a much higher price.[253] As for manuscript books, Peiresc did not have to tell him about the riches that could be found at Mount Athos, or other monasteries or hermitages.[254]

At the beginning of May, Mersenne wrote to Peiresc asking him to inquire from the consul of Aleppo, "or someone else of your cognizance," about the kind of notes used in Eastern Christian music. And if the informant could write down some of their chants with the notes, it would be all the better. Mersenne was interested in Arab, Turkish, and Persian music, as well as the names of their notes and of their instruments. He had failed to secure any of this thus far from Rome, Venice, and Constantinople.[255] Mersenne also sent Peiresc engravings of specific instruments, and Peiresc promised to send them off to the Levant along with Mersenne's questions.[256]

On 12 May 1633 Peiresc wrote to Jacques de Vendôme that the packet from Lebanon containing letters given to him on 3 February, another of Galaup-Chasteuil's written on 10 January, and one from Vendôme himself written on 8 March had arrived in Marseille the previous Saturday (7 May). Deputies of the city had been sent to Constantinople eight to ten days earlier, and Peiresc charged them to recommend to Marcheville the interests of the Recollets—Vendôme's order. Peiresc also pledged to write explicitly to the consuls of Marseille to urge the city's help, insofar as it was possible, for his order.[257]

The letters Minuti wrote on 15 March from Sidon and on 10 and 18 April 1633 from Damascus arrived in Marseille in early June with the polacre of Captain Carrayre, who also brought Peiresc two cases of books, a box of anemones, and a very attractive male cat—"the female having fallen into the sea."[258] Peiresc began by cautioning Minuti against going farther east, and then turned to the question of Samaritan materials. He was very grateful to "this good old man" for the Samaritan Arabic texts that Minuti had acquired and would gladly trade for them printed Arabic versions of the Pentateuch and New Testament. Peiresc was also adding, for potential use in trade, a copy of Cunaeus's "republique des Juifs"—*De Republica Ebraeorum* (1617)—a description of Constantinople, and possibly an Arabic grammar. De Gastines would be sending to him at Sidon "two sacks of Boysgency paper"—showing us that Peiresc made his own

paper—on the *St. François* of Captain Maynard.[259] Peiresc affirmed that
he had received everything that Minuti had sent from Constantinople,
both with Issaultier and before. He was especially pleased by the Hebrew
Pentateuch in four languages printed in Constantinople by Soncino in
1557.[260] Peiresc asked Minuti, if he were going to Egypt, to seek out a
mummy, whole and complete, for Cardinal Barberini. On the question
of books, Peiresc referred to the role of the Greek patriarch, the notorious
Cyril Lucar, who was actively playing off the various interested European
parties.[261] Lucar had just sent to the king of England a book obtained
from Egypt, a Greek Old and New Testament written by a woman
around the time of the Council of Nicaea, and including at the end the
Letter of St. Clement to the Corinthians, which had been lost for the
past one thousand years. "If it is necessary to the use the credit of this
Patriarch, it would be better to do so with the monks of Mt. Sinai or
those Hermites of St. Macaire and other Greeks of Egypt, where the
books are not subject to corruption and where it does not rain but rarely."
Peiresc wanted polyglot bibles—tritaples, octaples, and others.[262] Finally,
Peiresc wanted "all that you can gather up in Samaritan, and in Coptic"
("tout ce que vous pourrez recueillir en Samaritan, et en Cophte"). If
Minuti could find an Arabic version of the Letters of St. Paul and Acts of
the Apostles, he would not object to paying more than the usual ("n'y
plaignez pas un peu plus d'argent que le commun").[263]

But, Peiresc explained to Minuti, he would only pay for books, medals,
and antiquities, not expensive silks.

> Now, I regret the money on this sort of merchandise more than the
> contrary: I hold it well employed on books, antiques and other cu-
> riosities from which one can learn something and above all, on
> what could be for your study and your particular uses. For which I
> would always hold all which I could contribute very well employed.
> I say this on account of the great bale of Persian damask from Da-
> mascus and the piece of pale red-orange silk you have sent to us at
> your arrival in Sidon, from which we have not been as much per-
> suaded as by the single little box of medals and, even more, by the
> two books.[264]

Finally, in one of Minuti's letters, Peiresc learned of the proposal of
Aycard's nephew Salvator to go off to Persia with Minuti, and two other
"very curious young men" whom they had met in Constantinople. Minuti
wanted to go, but only with Peiresc's approval. Peiresc, in turn, put the

decision squarely in Uncle Aycard's lap.[265] Presumably Aycard said no, because Minuti returned to Provence.[266]

Jean-Louis Allemand, in Syria, was thanked for supporting Minuti (Allemand's letter of 29 April was received, along with those of Minuti and the cat, by way of Captain Carrayre).[267] Peiresc sent a similar note of appreciation to Tarquet.[268] To Philibert de Bermond, French consul in Cairo, Peiresc now wrote for the first time. Since Minuti was going to diverse places in the Levant where he would be needing protection and assistance, both for his person and for his interests—and for Peiresc's "petites curiositées"—Peiresc was hoping that Bermond would be prepared to exert himself on Minuti's behalf. Peiresc presented himself as the "particular servant of your family" ("serviteur particuliere de votre maison"), mentioning his father and two brothers.[269] A longer version of this same letter was sent the following week—apparently Peiresc had been under the impression that Bermond was planning a visit to Aleppo, and so he wrote at the first opportunity. But as he, Peiresc, was not sure if this were true, he was also writing to Egypt.[270] In the end, Christofle Bermond of Marseille did write to his brother Philibert, the French consul, on Minuti's—and Peiresc's—behalf.[271]

The summer of 1633 was a busy one for Peiresc. At the beginning of July, Jean Magy, returning from Cairo, visited for a few days with Peiresc at Aix.[272] Sometime in July, Salomon Azubi, the rabbi of Carpentras, visited with Peiresc, and the two spent nights doing astronomical observations and the days studying rabbinics.[273] At the end of the month—Peiresc wrote down the dates, 25 and 26 July on a mémoire—the Capuchin Father Gilles de Loches stopped to visit with Peiresc on his way from Cairo back to Tours.[274]

Jean Magy brought Peiresc gifts and documents. These are summarized in a mémoire drafted up by Magy showing that they discussed Ethiopia, gifts from India, and the situation in Egypt. Magy had also named for Peiresc a suite of individuals—Europeans of various countries—who now lived in Cairo and could be contacted.[275]

This meeting with Magy was catalytic; in addition to writing to and for Minuti, Peiresc would address letters to those whom Magy had told him about. Peiresc asked him about ways of writing to Zacharie Vermeil in Ethiopia, and whether Magy could find out more about the Basha of Suakin, the Egyptian port on the Red Sea.[276] He also wrote directly to some of those others based in Cairo and named by Magy in the mémoire. One was a "Sr. dottore medico d'Andalusia," who turned out to be the same Mustafa Aquin whom he had met in du Vair's company in

Aix, so long ago.[277] Peiresc plied Aquin with questions that touched on the literature, antiquities, and nature of Egypt but focused on weights and measures.[278] No answer came back. Three years later Peiresc was asking Magy if Mustafa Aquin (or "Hakeem") had ever returned to Cairo from Damascus.[279]

Peiresc also wrote to another medical doctor, "M. le Gris."[280] To this le Gris he stressed his fascination with vases and weights and measures, especially those of the ancients. Peiresc attributed to the Muslims great precision on account of possible medicinal uses. He had therefore asked Magy to send him the most complete and thoroughly examined account possible. He now wished le Gris to "verify the investigation" and "to add the names for the weights as for the measures according to the different denominations of the diverse peoples who live in your quarters or who frequent them and, when there is access, the merchants of India or Ethiopia or Nubia and other places still further from our trade." He wanted le Gris "to interrogate them carefully by way of translators if they have weights and measures similar to those in Cairo whether finer or cruder."[281]

Another person mentioned by Magy was a goldsmith named Bertier. Peiresc wrote to him on the same day. He wanted to know more about the colored stone vases that Magy had mentioned. Magy specified that Bertier would be able to acquire some for him for the least amount of money.[282] Others mentioned in the memorandom were Simone Dimo, vice-consul of the Venetians at Rosseto, and Giacomo Alvyse of Messina in Cairo. Peiresc wrote to them on the same day.[283] He asked Alvyse about the acquisition of a mummy and about petrifications from the Red Sea, of which he was said to possess a large collection.[284]

Preparing already for the next stage of his campaign, in the middle of July Peiresc asked Ramatuelle to retain an amount of credit on his account—Peiresc mentioned around 100 piastres—to be used for buying things in Egypt. Peiresc cautioned, however, against giving out too much money too soon.[285]

With Magy heading back to Cairo, Peiresc returned to the issue of Minuti's spending. Controlling costs was important because, he wrote, "my purse is so small and my curiosity so vast" ("Ma bourse est si petite & ma curiosité sy vaste"). For this reason it was essential that he "follow my little commissions as punctually as possible and not to order goods beyond my instructions, especially when they are of considerable value." Minuti had sent fur vests and silk pieces which had gotten ruined. The money would have been "much better employed on books or antiquities or other things referred to in those mémoires."[286]

By the end of August 1633, Minuti's plans had changed drastically. He had returned to Sidon from Damascus in order to leave for Provence because of "the *wars* that day after day are fomented throughout Palestine." But the planned trip to Aleppo of Roger, Marcheville's maître d'hôtel, had given him the courage to go along. Minuti expected that they would be joined by some other French merchants on account of the "great danger because of the wars and other maladies that reigned and still reign in the city." Minuti anticipated Salvator arriving from Damascus in a fortnight bearing some rosebushes from one of the chief gardens of Damascus. These would be sent to Peiresc along with a white and yellow jasmine. Tarquet, apparently, did not think they could be repotted at this season of the year and so would be shipped immediately. Allemand, meanwhile, had some other grapes for Peiresc, unsure as he was if those he had sent the previous year had been received. Finally, Minuti wished to thank de Gastines for the winter-weight cloth he sent. Unfortunately, Minuti added, "in this land I have not found anyone who knows how to make our clothes."[287]

By September, letters of mid-May (the 18th) had just arrived from Guez and l'Empereur in Constantinople. There had been no "commodité de passage" between Provence and Constantinople all summer, and with a ship now ready to set sail, Peiresc could not summarize in such a short time all that had happened in the interval.[288] L'Empereur had written to Peiresc about gemstones come from Georgia, India, and Moldavia. His nephew, M. l'Empereur of Marseille, explained that he would be returning soon to Europe, or as Peiresc put it, "en Chrestienté."[289]

To Sabatier, who had been serving as his staging agent in Constantinople, Peiresc summarized the state of communications as of mid-September 1633. From Sabatier's of 16 April, Peiresc had learned that Minuti did receive at Sidon the letters that were originally addressed to him at Constantinople by the ship *Ste. Anne*. But Peiresc himself received nothing from Sabatier, or from any of the others to whom the ship carried mail, except for the ambassador. He complained at the time to Ramatuelle, who said the letters would come, as indeed they did.[290]

By 2 October, Peiresc had received Minuti's letters from Sidon dated 24 August and 1 September in which, among other things, Minuti praised Salvator for helping him during his two months' illness in Damascus. Minuti had decided, Peiresc wrote to Aycard, to return home before meeting the "Maître d'hostel" of Marcheville, who happened to be in

Sidon, and the two of them then traveled to Aleppo together.[291] Peiresc wrote again to Minuti in early October, acknowledging receipt of his letters of 26 August and 1 September and thanking him again for all his assistance.[292] At the same time, in the same shipment of letters, Peiresc offered his thanks to Tarquet, Salvator, and Allemand for their help to Minuti, and for the fruit, flowers, and textiles they sent him.[293]

By the fall, Peiresc could inform Minuti that the captain who had robbed him was from Ollioules, near Toulon, and had been identified by Aycard as Jean Raynaud, called "Betton." He had, Peiresc noted, lost more in the punishment than he had gained in the theft, his goods being seized at Malta: "Thomas de Mayo, the merchant of Messina who gave the barque to the said Betton, with 250 pieces of eight to load wine, knowing of his piratical ways went to wait for him at Malta and seized his barque."[294]

Being the victim of corsairs only heightened Peiresc's concern for Minuti's physical security, given what Peiresc understood of the civil strife in the Lebanon and the safety of the roads between Sidon and Damascus. Nevertheless, he hoped that word of a peace arrangement would improve conditions. Peiresc passed along Aycard's report that his nephew, Salvator, was "resolved" on a "voyage to the Indies." Peiresc hoped that Minuti could dissuade him; the way was difficult and full of dangers. To hammer home the point, Peiresc passed along the news that "poor Nicolas Gilloux [Jaloux] died on the road, to my great regret." This trip had "too much danger and too little money" ("trop de danger & trop peu d'argents").[295]

If Minuti were to go to Cairo, however, he would find there prepared for him a series of memoranda and instructions that had been sent on with Magy. Most of these concerned books that Gilles de Loches had identified as capable of being found in Cairo. For Minuti's eyes only was a memo indicating how much Peiresc was willing to spend and what his purchasing priorities were.[296]

In August 1633, Peiresc had written to Gassendi with the news that he was expecting within a fortnight a response by "a great Turkish musician" to questions posed originally by Mersenne about music.[297] Now, two months later, he came back to Mersenne's general question, but pointed in a different direction, one hinted at in an earlier letter to Aymini. Writing to Minuti, he asked him "to make an effort to get some . . . memoranda of the music of the Dervishes or Turks and Arabs and the 'Basilien' Greeks."[298] Peiresc added in a postscript that he had learned that these Basilien Greeks "have ritual books of St. John of Damascus and that one of them, a great musician, put them into musical notes. It is necessary to have a really complete piece even if it were only a hymn or a psalm with their musical notes and an interpretation of their value by someone who knows a little of our music." He was hopeful that this person could be found in Aleppo, Jerusalem, or elsewhere.[299] Peiresc expected that this information would be useful for Mersenne and for Giovanni Battista Doni, who were working on the same things. "You will have," he continued, "portraits of their instruments in order to show those with which they chant in Lent or rather a piece of that sort."[300] This is a very important statement for this visionary project of what today we might call ethno-musicological research.

In this same shipment of letters, Peiresc sent a thank you note to Salvator for helping Minuti through his illness at Damascus, as well as for the plants and medals that had just reached him via Aycard.[301] Peiresc also sent a more general thank you to Tarquet, whom he treated as someone with authority in the French East.[302]

Peiresc's long letter to Magy in Egypt, written after learning from Magy's Marseille-based brother, Jean-Baptiste, of his safe arrival there on 20 August, was of a different sort. Its depth and seriousness shows clearly that Peiresc related to his correspondents in different ways. Peiresc told of meeting with the Capuchins at Aix. They had informed him that of all the foreigners in Cairo, the Venetian Santo Seghezzi was "the most curious." There was also an existing relationship, since Magy's brother in Marseille was already linked to Sr. Gela, who happened also to be—in the small world of Mediterranean merchants—Seghezzi's brother-in-law. Seghezzi was not so philo-French, Peiresc, wrote, as to want to be naturalized—unlike Jean Magy. But Peiresc did want to recruit him to his research team. This seems to be a first mention of Seghezzi, who had clearly charmed the Capuchins. Peiresc authorized Magy to make the contact if he thought it worthwhile. Peiresc had heard that "he had acquired a lot of credit in that country among those who have books, as well as with the others. And that he was curious, to the point that he had in his home cassia trees, mirabolans, and a cabbage apple that gives fruit twice when they are pruned." In other words, at this point Peiresc viewed Seghezzi as a familiar kind of European merchant-collector.[303]

Peiresc then added to Magy that he had omitted specific instructions about his music research project. He was attaching them to this letter (they are now missing). In exchange, he wanted "a mémoire concerning the music from over there." Magy was to find someone who could provide him with what Peiresc wanted to know about the chants of the Greeks,

Copts, Turks, and Arabs.[304] In the postscript, Peiresc casually mentioned that the naturalization process for Magy's wife and son was underway—this must have been discussed during his just-concluded visit home.[305]

A first letter to Seghezzi followed immediately, beginning with the recommendation made by the Capuchins.[306] This letter having missed the boat, Peiresc wrote a second one, mentioning the research trip of Minuti ("aux recherches qu'il faict pour moy") and asking if Seghezzi could use his contacts with the Turks to assist these purchases, with, of course, the usual insistence on reimbursement.[307] For the same boat, Peiresc passed along to the merchant Allemand the bad news that the entire value of the missing caps was consumed in legal fees at Malta, where ownership of the ship was claimed by Thomas de Mayo of Messina, who had put it at the disposal of Raynaud of Ollioules.[308]

Another letter written that day was to Jacques de Vendôme. Peiresc had just a couple of days earlier received his of 15 June, brought back by Napollon the Younger of Marseille. Peiresc was very pleased to learn of the progress made by Galaup in both Syriac and Arabic, and was reassured, too, of his physical well-being amid the civil disturbances in Lebanon.[309] Peiresc reviewed some of the Arabic sacred texts he was interested in—the New Testament, apart from the Acts of the Apostles; the Letters of St. Paul; and some chapters of the Apocalypse, all of which he already possessed.[310]

It is in the postscript that Peiresc turned to the matter of now-pressing importance: the Eastern Christian chants. There were "two great men," he wrote, one in Rome and one in Paris—Doni and Mersenne—who needed to know about music used in the Levant. And because—this was Peiresc's idea, we recall—at the Church of the Holy Sepulchre all the Eastern sects had chapels, he reasoned that one could go there and capture an entire spectrum of musical tradition. Peiresc asked Jacques de Vendôme to go, or to send someone to go "and mark on a paper"—to record in musical notation—the chants of the Greeks, Copts, Maronites, Nestorians, Abyssinians, "and all others who could be practicing in that place." In one day, Peiresc thought, especially if it was a holy day, one could hear them all. If Father Jacques could manage to acquire a hymnal or psalter with notes and their characters, that would be ideal. Peiresc was quite specific: this should be in their language with a "repetition in our characters and notes for . . . approximating the pronunciation and tone of their words in their language." Father Théophile would have carefully made depictions of various instruments—Mersenne's engravings, no doubt—but for

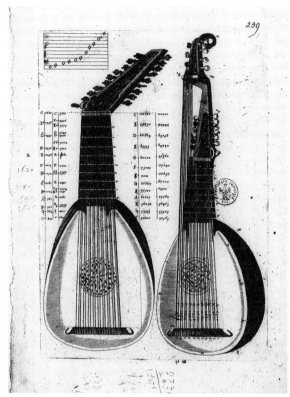

Figure 13.
One of the suite of engravings of musical instruments sent by Mersenne to Peiresc for expedition to the Levant. PBN, MS. 9531, ff. 238–288 at n499. (Bibliothèque Nationale de France)

those not depicted, Peiresc wanted their portraits, and "if possible with their dimensions." He called this "a little mémoire on the music of those parts" ("un petit mémoire de la musique de cez pais là").[311]

The navire still not sailing, Peiresc had more time to elaborate on the musicological project in another letter to Minuti. Peiresc's previous letter was sent to Aleppo "with the mémoires of the music of those lands, to help good Father Mersenne, and with the sample engravings of those instruments to show to those curious about music and to induce them to communicate the depictions and dimensions of theirs and, if it is possible, some relation or instruction on the proportions of their tones, notes and characters of the music and the way of singing and playing their instruments."[312] Peiresc kept copies of some of these engravings (Figure 13).[313] He thought that either at Sidon or at the court of Emir Fakhr-al-Din, Minuti would be able to locate someone "who combines singing and playing the instruments who could give you some instructions about this."

Peiresc could not at the moment lay his hands on the mémoire that Mersenne had sent him, as it had gotten mixed up among his papers. But he said that he had learned at Paris of a lawyer from Marseille, a Conseiller Imbert, who had more than 20,000 francs tied up in the Aleppo trade and was on very good terms with the monks of St. Basile there. Among them was one named Scaffa who had a number of excellent Greek manuscripts, "specifically on the subject of music." But, Peiresc added, he was "very jealous" and had shown his treasures to few others. Peiresc thought that if one could use some friend of his, without giving away the idea ("sans tesmoigner d'avoir ce dessein"), it might be possible to see them and, perhaps, even copy them.[314] The body of the letter concluded with news of Galaup and his supposed progress in Syriac and Arabic.

As in the letter to Jacques de Vendôme, Peiresc utilized the postscript of this letter to Minuti to call attention to the project he was piggybacking on Mersenne's, that is, studying the liturgical music at the Church of the Holy Sepulchre: "If there was a way of communicating this mémoire on music to someone going to Jerusalem, in the Holy Sepulchre where there are so many different sorts of Christians this could be the perfect place to mark the differences in the chants of the Greeks from the Copts, Armenians, Maronites, Abyssinians and others. If one could meet there someone a little cognizant of our music so that he could put in our musical notes the melody of these different songs of all these peoples and to transcribe separately the notes of each according to their writing in order to compare them with ours."[315] Peiresc added that Jacques de Vendôme had been alerted to this project and could assist him.

In a second postscript, as if inspired by the concluding reference to Jacques de Vendôme, Peiresc reported having asked him to utilize his "habitudes" in Mount Lebanon to look for the letters of St. Paul in Arabic and those of other Apostles, along with the Acts of the Apostles and the Apocalypse. Peiresc added, "I am also writing to him for the mémoire on music, so that if possible he may find it in Jerusalem at the Holy Sepulchre."[316]

The very next day, Peiresc told Mersenne that he had made inquiries in Aleppo, Sidon, Egypt, and Jerusalem, where he specifically sought the comparison of "our music" with that of "the Greeks, Copts, Abyssinians, Armenians, Maronites and others chanting in the same space of the Church, although in different chapels and possibly at different times, and with different notes or characters." He had also asked to see if anyone in the suite of Fakhr-al-Din knew anything about Western music because of the opportunities afforded by the emir's stay in Livorno.[317]

Thinking about other people's music led Peiresc to call up memories of his own encounter with "world music." From Mersenne's question about notation and his inflection of it toward comparison, Peiresc turned to "the whole art that these peoples could bring to music" ("tout l'art que ces peuples peuvent apporter à la musique"). He began with what he had heard about: that one day a week the dervishes dance "I do not know how many hours in turning to the sound of some harmony." He had himself seen the Persian ambassador playing the guitar "rather jauntily" for the pope in Rome in 1601. In Provence, he continued, and likely enough it was in Marseille, "I have heard the Moors sing very melodiously, because they generally have a great disposition to it, and have the curiosity to retain an air which I found very unusual and rather agreeable." He also reported meeting a man named "la Feuille" who claimed having been in the Indies and who was, in fact, the only one able to make music from an ivory horn that came to Peiresc from the Far East.[318]

Peiresc saw that in his project of doing comparative music history at the Church of the Holy Sepulchre in Jerusalem lay the fulfillment of Mersenne's. For the musicians themselves, hearing the music of the different traditions of chant, were the ones best placed—and most trained to execute—Mersenne's scheme of recording information about musical notation in the Eastern traditions.[319]

In a letter immediately following, to a Gilles de Loches already back in Tours, and surviving only in fragments, Peiresc conveyed the news of Vermeil's military exploits at the Ethiopian court and asked for "a brief relation" of the most curious things that de Loches had seen in the Coptic libraries.[320] This adumbrates the two main projects of the next year, the approach to Ethiopia via Vermeil and the focus on Coptic materials in the monasteries of Wadi Natrun.

In his very next letter to Minuti Peiresc reviewed the recent history of their correspondence. We understand that Peiresc did this in each letter in order to indicate to the recipient which letters had been written but not yet received. Thus, Minuti's letter of 1 September said that he was at Aleppo, with "M. Rogier, Maître d'hostel" of the ambassador. Peiresc wrote to him at Aleppo and sent a duplicate to Sidon. But it turned out that he had sent the engravings of musical instruments that were intended to serve as the starting point for the investigation of the Eastern Christian chants only to Aleppo and not to Sidon. Peiresc now presented Minuti with a precise set of questions. First of all, he wanted Minuti to record the names that the local people gave to the European-like instruments, assuming there was any resemblance at all: "That would be, for our lutes, our theorbo, our viole, our violin, our espinette, our trumpet, our flutes, our cornets, our drums and others." He wanted the names in Arabic, Turkish, Syriac, Armenian, Coptic, "and other oriental languages, and also if they (the informer or informers) knew to give the etymologies of the names in their language in order to know out of what these names were formed." If Minuti could learn this, Peiresc concluded, "there would be nothing more to find out." To create some incentive, Peiresc said that this research would serve not only Father Mersenne but also Cardinal Barberini.[321]

To Jacques de Vendôme, presumably in Syria, Peiresc wrote on 28 October with news from Rome that Cardinal Barberini had delegated his major domo, Mgr. Scamarola, the bishop of Candia, to handle the pension for Giorgio Amira, the patriarch of Lebanon. After outlining to Vendôme his many connections in Rome, Peiresc abruptly turned back to the question of music. "I asked of you last time," he wrote, "to give us some information about the different kinds of chant and music of the different sorts of Christians and other religions who practice in those lands. You will do us a great favor to send it to us as soon as you can." He then repeated the additional request he had made of Minuti for a matching of names to instruments, and in as many languages as possible.[322]

We learn more of Minuti's doings in the last months of 1633 from his letter to Peiresc of 21 October, which formed the substance of one that Peiresc wrote to Aycard on 17 December 1633. Minuti planned to spend the winter in Constantinople. He wanted to go there for two reasons. The first was to acquire letters of authorization from the patriarch that would open for him the doors of the libraries of the archbishop of Cyprus and the abbey of Nicosia, with their rich collections of manuscripts. The second was to see the collection of Jean l'Empereur before his departure and perhaps acquire something from it. From Constantinople Minuti would proceed to Cyprus in early spring and then go to Egypt so that he could be back in Provence in August.[323]

Although traveling with a member of the ambassador's household, Minuti had to depend upon the goodwill of Jérôme de l'Isle for the funds needed to provison for the caravan trip. He explained to Peiresc that de l'Isle, who was the son-in-law of Sanson Napollon, was involved in a suit against another merchant, Jehan Jaine, who had exchanged 2,000 good piastres for counterfeit ones, which de l'Isle was then caught using in Sidon and for which he was penalized at 100 percent and more. Minuti left it all to Peiresc's "prudent and sage discretion."[324]

The caravan left for Constantinople on 24 October.[325]

In the postscript of a letter written to de Loches in mid-December, Peiresc mentions the Coptic books in the hands of Della Valle in Rome, and his desire that de Loches produce for him a grammar and vocabulary in order to crack this code.[326]

A long letter to Jean Magy of 21 December presents the full picture of Peiresc's commitments at the end of the year 1633. Peiresc began by saying that he had received Magy's letter of 24 September only two days earlier, and was pleased to learn of his safe arrival in Egypt. He expressed pleasure at what Magy had told him of the marriage of Vermeil with the emperor of Ethiopia's daughter. He treated this news as a means of testing the possibility of extending his Mediterranean communications network into Ethiopia. The questions he posed to Magy treat people, and their accounts, as evidence; they represent, therefore, an attempt to develop criteria for a source criticism of ethnographically derived information. First off, he wanted to know the date of the wedding celebration and its consummation. If this proved impossible, then he wished at least to know when the news reached Cairo. Was it brought by qualified people? These sometimes traveled by caravan, in which case it would be good to jot down their names because the reliability of the claim was linked to the credibility of the claimant. It would also be necessary to identify the kind of caravan it was, and the place from which it set forth, whether from the Abyssinians themselves, or the Magrabins or "Dakydxri," or from the coast of Yemen, or Moucal (Mocha or al-Mokka), or even the Indies.[327]

Peiresc reported to Magy about meeting de Loches in July of 1633. He was now back in Tours, and his traveling partner, Césaire de Rosgo, in Belle Isle, where he was preaching in Breton, and described his auditors as "poor people a little more barbarous and less polished or civilized than the French."[328] Peiresc reminded Magy about "Sequeti the Venetien" and described him as being well inclined to France. He encouraged Magy to use him.[329]

Peiresc then turned to weights and measures. He wanted Magy to examine and mark them with care, focusing on the basic type which possessed three feet and was used for heating water, "which is below" ("qui est par dessoulz")—referring to the mémoire drawn up at their last meeting—and which served for other uses "and mysteries." He thought these could easily be found among those in charge of heating, the "Chauderonniers." "I desire to see how they created it. And with time," he continued, "little by little you could work on other things or articles from your mémoire." Money for this purpose could easily be found on either Magy's credit or his own.[330] In other words, Peiresc was viewing the summary mémoire as a potential agenda for research projects. In the postscript, Peiresc added that Minuti passed from Aleppo to Constantinople by caravan in October. The plan was for him to go from there to Cyprus, and in the spring proceed from there to Cairo before returning to Provence in August.[331]

Peiresc made sure to thank Jean-Baptiste Magy in Marseille for making his brother's letter available to him, and to convey a letter for Santo Seghezzi and another to Seghezzi's relative, Gela of Marseille.[332] The letter making contact with Seghezzi, and referring to the kind words about him said by de Loches, was written on this same day. Peiresc mentioned the search for old books and the names of Minuti and Magy.[333] To Gela, Peiresc began by noting that having learned that Seghezzi could help him with books, and that he had no aversion to assisting the French, he wished to establish a relationship. Peiresc was offering—through his relative—a pledge for his willingness to do what he could on Seghezzi's behalf.[334]

A long letter to Minuti of 23 December 1633 closed the year. Peiresc was happy to learn of his voyage to Constantinople in his letter of 21 October and that of M. de l'Isle in the letter of 7 November. He had been afraid when Minuti was in the Holy Land and wished for his speedy arrival in Constantinople; but now that he had learned of the civil disruptions there and in Syria, he wished Minuti to be gone from the Levant as soon as possible. Peiresc then reviewed the contents of the box he had lately received from Minuti, devoting special attention to the medals.[335]

In exchange for M. de l'Isle's help, Peiresc promised to to put himself out on his behalf, and to send letters to Grenoble "where is his affair" and where he had "some powerful friends." He would of course also write to him at Aleppo to thank him for his kindnesses to Minuti during his stay there. M. Issaultier had still not come to collect from Peiresc the reimbursement for the monies he had advanced to Minuti. Even after running into Peiresc "in the palace" the other day—no doubt at Aix—Issaultier could not be prevailed upon to take Peiresc's money.[336]

Peiresc admired how Minuti had managed the logistics of his forty-day-long trip from Aleppo to Constantinople—"a Lent much more austere than the others," Peiresc thought ("un caresima bien plus austere que les autres"). Peiresc assumed he had seen many pretty cities along the way, or at least "great ruins and broken down houses of pretty cities that had once been in this Asia Minor."[337] As sorry as he was that Minuti could not tarry to investigate these more fully, he was delighted that Minuti had made it safe and sound to Constantinople. And even after the fire there, he expected that in so rich a city Minuti would be able to find "some old ancient bronze vase according to my earlier mémoires and instructions sent on ahead." With Sr. Montolieu, in the ambassador's retinue, he had sent some "little instructions" on this subject to Marcheville. For vases, he wanted especially those of precious materials, and he especially wanted to see models. In any event, he counted on Minuti to know his humor; he had "an extreme passion" for all that was "the most curious in the matter of books, antiquities and curiosities of nature." This was the rule he was to follow when viewing collections in Constantinople such as that of M. l'Empereur.[338]

But if there were no way to find out if and when l'Empereur would come home, Peiresc suggested to Minuti that he could push for the communication of copies, or impressions, for what could not be transcribed, painted, or molded, whether "by relation or written description" ("par relation ou description par escript"). This is a good catalog of the different technologies of reproduction that Peiresc employed.[339]

It was in the midst of this very long letter, one of Peiresc's longest, that—ironically!—he offered a clear statement of the priority of conversation over writing. He mused that it would be so much easier to learn about l'Empereur's collection once either l'Empereur or Minuti was back in Provence: "In conversation one can much better argue and make oneself understood. And it would be difficult to put in writing all that could be well said, above all about books and all sorts of ancient writing." If Minuti could come faster that would be best, "because I would leave soon for Marseille, and would go even further, to see something and learn there a thousand rare things that I would otherwise never know." The message for Minuti was unequivocal.[340]

Peiresc was pleased that Minuti was going to Egypt, and reminded him that he went armed with many letters of recommendation. But he reminded him also that as long as he appeared to be a Frenchman he would get nowhere. He had to disguise himself as an Englishman if he were to get "the cordial and confidential recommendation—which," he adds, "you will as little know how to do as to play the minister rather than the priest or monk."[341] This is an astonishing declaration of the power—or perceived power—of the English already in the early 1630s.

Instead, in Egypt and on the way to Egypt, Minuti would have to be willing to make offers to people about services. Peiresc mentioned "Monte Santo" and Cairo, and St. Machaire and Mount Sinai, and in terms of people "above all among the Copts, as well as among the Greeks" ("mais sur tout parmy les Cophtes, aussy bien que parmy les Greeks").[342]

In Constantinople, Peiresc asked that Minuti seek out a copy of Abraham Farissol's *Iggeret Orchot Olam*, the Jewish geographical treatise published first at Ferrara in 1524 and then at Venice in 1586, which could not be had among the Jews of Italy for fear of the Inquisition. It was reprinted in Constantinople by the same house—Soncino—that had brought out the Pentateuch in four languages, "which you sent me last year." Peiresc did not think the Jews would object to selling it. It would do a big favor to "a great personality among my friends who wrote on this material and proof (both in Italian and in Hebrew), if you could find them and in most complete form that you could."[343] This probably refers to Salomon Azubi, the rabbi of Carpentras.[344]

Returning to the sad story of Minuti's encounter with corsairs, Peiresc had learned from Venice that their galleys had seized Provençal pirates. He had written to the French ambassador at Venice who was working on their liberation to see if these were the ones who captured Minuti and if there were some way to "give satisfaction" to Allemand for his losses.[345]

Peiresc advised Minuti to ingratiate himself with the English and Dutch ambassadors because of their close relationship to the Greek patriarch, Cyril Lucar. Minuti would have to proceed discreetly "for fear that they would play some bad turn on you, surreptitiously, in order to take over your conquests . . . a mark of jealousy towards me, or rather towards M. [Marcheville?] and the whole country. That is why it is necessary to proceed in this very discreetly and with great mental reserve, communicating your research as little as possible."[346]

Turning to another of Peiresc's key themes, weights and measures, Peiresc reminded Minuti of his desire for an investigation of the measures used in Constantinople for liquids and solids. He wanted a relation of the various names employed for objects in both Arabic and Turkish. This parallels the inquiry he made of Jean Magy concerning the weights and measures of Cairo and Yemen. The inclusion of Jewish and any lingering Latin terms from the medieval Latin empire in Constantinople gives the broadest vision of Peiresc's project.[347] The breadth of Peiresc's vision seemed to him to distinguish his approach from those of predecessors or contemporaries: "My research is far removed from all that Arias Montanus and all the other moderns have written."[348]

Peiresc was keen to have the balance or "the great Trebouchet" used for weighing and measuring pearls and other gems. He also wanted their names in Turkish and Greek and whatever else Minuti could learn of the use of these machines or instruments. Peiresc wanted to know if there were any public standards where weights and measures were kept in a safe place to calibrate all the others.[349] Turning from weights and measures to vases, he wanted to know if Minuti had seen in any of the principal mosques ancient vases of marble, alabaster, or other precious stones or metals that possessed inscriptions in Greek or Latin, with vegetal or other forms of ornamentation. He wanted Minuti to measure their content with water in it. But Minuti was to be "very particular and ardent" ("aussy friand & jaloux") to acquire the measurements of all sorts of other containers.[350]

Peiresc concluded by saying that he was sending the letter to Lyon to connect with the *ordinaire* to Venice. But he was also sending a duplicate via Marseille which would contain copies of the engravings of the musical instruments Mersenne wanted identified. Peiresc was also sending copies of the accompanying letters to the Constantinopolitan merchants Guez, l'Empereur, and Sabatier.[351]

That letter to l'Empereur followed exactly the line laid out in the letter to Minuti: Peiresc thanked and praised him and then asked for a visit on his way back, and if there were no plans for an immediate return, Peiresc asked for access to copies of some of the pieces in his collection. "Our insatiable curiosity" could be a little slaked if he were to offer a view of it to Father Théophile so that if he judged that there was something for his studies, a copy or mold or engraving could be communicated to him.[352] Peiresc was sorry that the letter l'Empereur had consigned to M. du Mesnil Jourdain never reached him; all he had received was a letter of 18 May 1633, to which he had responded immediately by way of Sr. de la Rivière, who embarked upon the *Dauphin*.[353]

The letter to Guez was a normal piece of courtesy, noting that Minuti was returning to Constantinople and so Peiresc was renewing his compliments and gratitude, as well, of course, as his expectations of assistance.[354] This exact same content was likewise the theme of a parallel letter to Sabatier.[355]

A letter to Marcheville in Constantinople went with all these. The ambassador's servant, M. Fortet, had brought Peiresc a very interesting document on the difference between Muslim sects. It was the Italian version of "this little sketch of the different Muslim sects by Memet Enim Ben Sadredin." Peiresc declared himself willing to spare no funds to obtain a transcription of the original Turkish text. He also thought it was à propos to inquire into the "quality and status of the author, in which time he lived, who he is, [and] to whom he addressed his work, in order to guarantee the truth of the work and that it was not forged at pleasure as part of a design to derogate from the Muslim religion." This is another example of Peiresc's applying source criticism to "news," as well as an utterly astonishing bit of sympathy for the reputation of Islam in the early seventeenth century—or at least an awareness of the many motives that existed for misrepresenting it. M. Fortet had told him that either Marcheville or the translator, one "Jacob Romany"—likely a Jew—possessed the original, and thus could make a copy for him.[356] After a survey of the situation on the European front for the benefit of the distant diplomat, Peiresc turned to his main theme: how the return of Minuti to Constantinople again put Peiresc in the ambassador's debt.[357]

Finally, all of these letters were accompanied by one to the French consul at Smyrna, whom Peiresc did not know but who, Peiresc understood full well, occupied a communications hub with equally good access to Constantinople and the Levantine coast away to the south. Peiresc was sending these letters to him for him to find the most secure way to the ambassador or to Sabatier.[358] This is a good illustration of the way in which the surviving archive maps out not just space but also time—the different stages of a path of transmission.

1634

On the first day of 1634, Peiresc wrote to Jean Magy with a set of instructions about finding and identifying papyrus along the Nile's banks.[359] A contemporary letter to Gela thanked him for putting in a good word with Seghezzi.[360] Another long letter to Minuti followed on 9 January. Peiresc began by saying that he had written fifteen days earlier by way of Venice only to realize that one of his servants had failed to include "the mémoire on music." It was now being sent with this letter. A ship had just arrived from Constantinople, having left there on 21 November—too soon, Peiresc thought, for Minuti to have reached the city with the Aleppo caravan.[361]

At the end of January 1634, Peiresc informed de Loches that he had received a letter from Jacques Albert in Cairo, "whom you know," promising him "a very exact relation of what he had of the land of the Abyssin-ians, from a Jesuit Father as from Sr. Vermeil, about whom he did not tell me of such a great fortune as rumor has it." Albert did say that he was beloved by the emperor.[362]

Peiresc received Minuti's letter of 10 December from Constantinople via the ordinaire of Lyon, describing his caravan trip from Aleppo and his favorable reception by the Provençal community at Constantinople: l'Empereur, Guez, Sabatier, and the ambassador himself. He was plan-ning to write to Minuti at Cyprus and at Egypt, both stops on his way back to Europe.[363]

In February 1634, turning to Egypt, Peiresc acknowledged Albert's long letter with one of his own. In particular he thanked Albert for the information he had offered about Vermeil. He noted that he would now have difficulty believing what everyone else said because "you speak so soberly" and actually had some relation with him. Peiresc wanted to know more.[364] He observed that while Albert had asked on Vermeil's behalf for illustrated books suitable for cross-cultural communication to a king, he had himself added content he thought was appropriate, such as military and civilian architecture in France and Germany. Peiresc believed that Jo-seph Baulme of Marseille had already shipped most of these books to him. In another ten or twelve days there would be another ship available to carry the final cargo. Peiresc added that if the price of "liberté de com-merce" with Vermeil was allowing the "Bassas" of Egypt to skim off the books they liked, he was willing to pay it, as he would then just get re-placement copies for Vermeil.[365] Peiresc left it up to Albert to decide whether the lead medals were just too heavy and too base to send on the long over-land trip.

The question of European books for Vermeil in Ethiopia immediately raised to Peiresc's mind the matter of comprehension. He thought that the Marolois book of fortifications, with its geometric figures, would be immediately accessible, even without knowledge of the words, "because the engraving is very well done, and capable of really entertaining the eye, and it has a great ability to make understandable the rules of the art only through the view when one cannot speak the language of the country." Moving to the next item, Peiresc thought it unlikely that there were no books of mathematics in Ethiopia, given what he had heard of the great quantity of books in the library at Mount Amara and among the Ethi-opians in Cairo and the desert monasteries of Wadi Natrun. His train of thought then wandered from Vermeil to his own collecting. If these

libraries "were well visited and examined one would find very curious
pieces from which we would not fail to extract some fruit." He would
write to Vermeil in order to get him to "employ his credit" in this
manner. The key word in Peiresc's letter is "exchange"—"what we could
give him in exchange."[366] Peiresc ended the letter by adding his urging
that Albert be of service to Minuti on his way back through Egypt, especially in the matter of books, for which Jean Magy had been equipped
with a series of mémoires.[367]

Writing to Magy himself a week later, Peiresc summarized the whole
history of contacts between Albert and Vermeil.[368] He thought that if
Minuti happened to arrive in time, he could review the instructions about
the books Peiresc wanted and "edit" them before they were forwarded
on to Vermeil.[369] But while Peiresc thought the mémoires would usefully
instruct Minuti and Albert, he was quite clear that "all these mémoires
and instructions are not to be communicated to others if it is possible, for
fear that they will use me to make the merchandise I want more expensive for me, and to give information to those men who take their side, as
has happened many times already and which leaves me frustrated." Therefore, he continued, "the less that M. Albert could be able to see, the
better" ("le moins que M. Albert les pourra faire voir sera la meilleur"),
and only he and Minuti were to see the whole. Peiresc realized that this
was awkward but that it was better to be free from future regret, "since it
is this way today with your friends and theirs, who tomorrow for other
interests could find it to their advantage to break with you and join those
who could make them your enemies, and will side with them, especially
in that country where the government depends on such barbarous people."
Peiresc again warned Magy about the perils of the market. He was not
even to pretend that he was buying on Peiresc's account, since that would
also have the effect of heating up the whole market for antiquities and
"could even impact on your other affairs, of which I would be very sorry."[370]
Thinking aloud, Peiresc concluded "that one can never be too reserved
in every sort of negotiations where even a little jealousy and competition
could arise in the search for goods, and especially for those that are curious, such as books."[371]

Peiresc went on to say that he had heard that there were two Arabic
books on plants known to the curious in Cairo. One was called "Maleyia"
and the other "Ebenbitar." For this latter, Peiresc cautioned that it not
be the abridgement, which already existed in the West.[372] To ensure that

the right volume was acquired, Peiresc counseled working with a native informant. But he also advised trying to get the autograph copy of the manuscript. Peiresc offered up to 20 écus for the right edition. As for the Ethiopian books, Magy was to use the mémoire as a "check list" and make a mark in the margin every time he found a title.[373] What Magy could not locate in the libraries of Cairo he was not to expect to retrieve from Ethiopia because of the limited communications that existed, with perhaps just one visit a year from pilgrims on the way to Jerusalem. But even if little came from there, Peiresc held out the possibility that books could still move: "I think that it may well be as if passed through a sieve by means of very strange and distant lands." Magy was not to give up, especially "if it were to be found true that Sr. Vermeil had acquired there such credit as you have said." Peiresc's enthusiasm for Vermeil did not blind him to the likely reality of making contact: "I doubt it a little." And yet, it was indeed possible that if not the emperor's favorite—Vermeil, or a Vermeil-like figure—Peiresc could well have been thinking about other adventurers of his acquaintance, such as Herryard in Lahore (see Section 35, "Where Mediterranean Meets Orient")—could have acquired "some free access to the person of the King or that of his principal ministers" yielding "instructions, mémoires, inventories" and even some of the specific pieces he had asked for, and this would more than repay all their efforts.[374]

Peiresc also wrote a long letter to Joseph Baulme in Marseille on that same day concerning the shipment of books and portrait medals of the current and previous king to his uncle Jacques Albert for Vermeil. Peiresc thought that medals would be more appreciated in Ethiopia than engravings. The letter includes a fascinating discussion of the behavior of customs officials in Egypt. Peiresc noted that he was sending a square-ish box that looked like a packet of letters, but was actually filled with a certain flower water that was believed "over there" to have medicinal purposes. Peiresc asked Baulme to acquire a certificate that would ward off the customs officials. Nevertheless, he thought it even better if the captain or someone else could hide it so that it not be seen, reducing the risk of its being tampered with and damaged by the clumsy and "unreasonable" customs officials. Of course, if Baulme judged that it was safe to put the case on the manifest for the officials to identify, the decision was his to make.[375]

These long and important letters to Magy and Baulme, with their wide implications, went along in a shipment with a letter to Seghezzi drawing him into Peiresc's world of book shopping.[376]

Having discovered that he had omitted the principal mémoire concerning books desired from Ethiopia, Peiresc had de Gastines's deputy quickly take it to Patron François Laure, who was then departing for Egypt.[377] Peiresc also wrote directly to Alexandria, to Esperit Laurens, the vice-consul and father-in-law of Baulme of Marseille, asking him to oversee careful handling of the books and boxes by the customs officials there, in so far as it was possible, just as he had asked the son-in-law. Peiresc explicitly mentioned the breakable container of flower water.[378] As was his custom, Peiresc also wrote a courtesy note to the captain of the polacre, Laure.[379] And, equally careful, he wrote a second note to Baulme, this telling him what he had written to Laure and Laurens. In it he blamed the omission of the mémoire on books on the haste inspired by Laure, who "gave the other date to my man; the muleteer wanting to leave, he forgot the mémoire."[380] Finally, Peiresc, in his haste, nevertheless wrote a brief note to Minuti informing him that there were instructions awaiting him in Cairo with Magy and that duplicates had been sent both via Venice to Marcheville and directly to Cairo.[381]

Another letter to Minuti was written to go via Lyon to Constantinople in case Minuti stayed longer there than he had initially planned. This illustrates how Peiresc tried to plan for chance and change in his long-distance correspondence. Peiresc informed Minuti that if he were planning to return via Chios there was a Sieur Mille of Marseille who possessed many ancient medals that had been dug up by one of his friends, and was worth visiting for purchase or trade. Otherwise, Peiresc told Minuti about his friend, Father Saqui, who, against Peiresc's exhortations, was convinced that he had to visit the Indies. He went via Rome, but his *tartane* was caught in a tempest and blown from Civitavecchia to Sardinia, whence he was forced to backtrack to Genoa. "By which," Peiresc concluded sagely, "you can see that he courted fortune right here, as much as in a distant land." Peiresc ended the letter expressing his excitement to see Minuti's mémoire of his caravan trip across Anatolia.[382]

Peiresc wrote to Magy on 12 March with the information that the box of books for Vermeil had traveled east with Captain Laure, along with letters for him and Albert. But he had also just heard from de Loches that in Cairo he had met a Copt who told him that he was the one who had sold Pietro della Valle a vocabulary and grammar and that there were more of these to be had there. Peiresc wanted Magy to investigate.[383]

Another traveler intrudes himself into our story at this point. Peiresc tells us of a Father "Gaugerics de Marquaiz" (Marquez?) who was a Jaco-

bite Christian sent by the general of his order to Constantinople and the
Holy Land to report on the conditions of his brothers there. Peiresc wrote
to Guez and to Sabatier asking them to help him with necessities, as they
had done for Minuti.[384]

In March, Peiresc was writing to Minuti in Constantinople. By mid-
April he had received the letter Minuti wrote from Civitavecchia on
20 March. Peiresc was very worried about the fate of Marcheville and relieved that Minuti was no longer in Ottoman lands, for in a letter of
25 March from Livorno he had received news from an English ship that
had departed Constantinople on 5 February that Marcheville had been
condemned to death, a sentence that was commuted in lieu of a ransom
of 100,000 piastres paid by the European ambassadorial community but
to be reimbursed over time by the French trading community. This hit
like a storm in Marseille, "where all the people in maritime trade will be
lost if the commerce is cut this suddenly and without the capacity to recover their resources engaged in the Levant."[385]

In early May, Peiresc told Gilles de Loches about a Venetian translator, Giorgio the Armenian, "who would have undertaken research into
Coptic and Abyssinian books for the love of me. And that he had begun
an inventory of all that could be found over there in the places to which
he had access." The problem was that his boss, the Venetian consul, had
just transferred him to Damiette indefinitely, delaying, for a time at least,
the search for the Book of Enoch, which Peiresc desperately sought. This
Georgio had even offered to return to Europe ("en Chrestienté") to deliver the Enoch, if necessary.[386]

A long letter to Magy in Cairo thanked him for the many items that
came on the *St. Esprit*. Among them was a "music book" that gave him
great pleasure, with only the slight regret that the illustrations on the two
or three final leaves were separated from the texts needed for their expli-
cation. Nevertheless, it led Peiresc to conclude that the Muslims must have
very good books on music. "And if the person from whom you got this
[book], whom you named in your letter as Jann Lazaravam, if I read it
aright, or that music master of Cairo named on the back cover of the book
Sici [*sic*] Ottoman, are curious to have books of our music of Christendom,
I will send them some of the most melodious, both of Paris and of Rome."[387]
"The book of Music by Chemsedin of Sidon" was by then in Paris in the
hands of Mersenne.[388] Its trajectory then led to Claude Hardy, to Gabriel
Sionite, back to Mersenne, and then to Gilbert Gaulmin, to Jacques Dupuy,
back to Peiresc, and then on to Doni in Rome. A copy was made in Rome

and sent to Golius in Leiden. When the original returned from Rome, its secrets still kept, it was then sent off to Saumaise, again for Golius.[389]

In a parallel letter to de Loches, Peiresc expanded, noting that the book was about ancient Greek music and began with a discussion of geometrical figures representing proportions and tones, with different colors to help distinguish them more easily. Peiresc wrote that he "had never seen this in all the printed books and manuscripts which passed through my hands. This made us recognize that, among these barbarous peoples, there had to be truly liberated spirits."[390] He himself had heard the Moors singing "excellently well" in Rome, many years before.[391]

Peiresc explained that he informed Seghezzi that Minuti had been given "the principal research," while Giorgio the Armenian, then in Damiette, had been tasked with making an inventory of books so that he could more efficiently choose what he liked.[392] Peiresc put himself at Magy's service in some affair—presumably legal but otherwise unexplained—unfolding around him in Provence and promised to spare nothing on his behalf. Peiresc also explicitly thanked him for "so many curious opinions," as well as for his "good offices" in organizing the shipment to Vermeil.[393] On 18 June Peiresc responded to Mersenne's of 14 May, which asked Peiresc what musical material he should send via Magy in Cairo to local music masters. Peiresc suggested some of his own works, and some contemporary music. He also proposed that Mersenne not worry about whether these were in French or Latin, as there were "among them very learned *Grenadins* who had taken all their degrees at Salamanca, including theology, of which I knew one among others whom I saw here before the expulsion of the Moriscos"—referring to the "Andalusian Doctor," Mustafa Aquin.[394] Peiresc again asked after the doctor in a letter to Magy in Cairo. He also signaled his debt to the *capigy* Abu-Bekher ("Coagy Aboubequer") for his "bonnes recommandations" as well as his desire to pay it off.[395]

By the end of July 1634, Minuti was home, and Peiresc was writing to him at Aycard's in Toulon.[396]

In September, Peiresc was writing to Magy thanking him for working on behalf of Agathange de Vendôme in getting the chasuble for the monks of St. Macaire. This was part of a swap of religious goods for manuscripts that would culminate the next year in the exchange of a European-made chalice for a polyglot Psalter. Peiresc urged Magy not to wait on Giorgio the Armenian, both because he was away and because his time would have to be bought in rare books for the Venetian consul, which Peiresc was loath to do. If Magy could find things without him, or by means of the Capuchins, that would be the best.[397] Minuti, Peiresc wrote, was "in no condition to return so quickly to your parts as he had thought, so that it will be necessary to try to do without him."[398] With this we are offered a glimpse of what must have been Peiresc's plan: a permanent back-and-forth of Minuti to manage affairs on the ground in the Levant as his lieutenant.

In December 1634, Jean-Louis Allemand, the merchant whose caps Minuti was bringing to Cyprus on that ill-starred voyage, wrote from Sidon to Minuti at the convent of the Minims in Marseille. He had a last packet of books and letters to deliver to Minuti, and had held off out of uncertainty as to whether Minuti would be going back to the Levant—though Aycard had already made clear his "little good will to see the Levant again." He was now sending them to Marseille.[399]

Nevertheless, the projects Minuti had set in motion continued to register in Peiresc's correspondence. In October 1634, Peiresc was receiving mail *from* Constantinople for Minuti; in this case it was a letter from M. l'Empereur conveyed by his servant Honoré Huguen.[400] Fernoux's opinion, sent all the way from Cairo, was that "the Turks have no art of music, and do not sing except naturally but they do make beautiful concerts pleasant to the ear."[401] Writing back, on 3 November, Peiresc declared that whatever the common view, their musicians were "very learned, grounded in their field, and capable of shaming the greatest musicians of Europe."[402]

1635

At this point we encounter the third of Peiresc's key figures in the Levant, and the only one not emerging from his own circle of friends. Pierre Golius, brother of the great Leiden orientalist Jacob Golius, and known after his conversion to Catholicism and taking of orders as Father Celestin de St. Lidwine of the Discalced Carmelites, enters Peiresc's world in 1635. He was a very interesting figure, and in many ways representative of an age in which thoughtful people moved around the Mediterranean as if on the lake it was becoming.[403]

Peiresc alerts him to his interests, as was customary in first letters: Greek and Latin inscriptions, but also those in oriental languages, as well as plants and animals. The specificity comes in the postscript, and the topic is the music history project launched during the second Minuti mission: "If you would encounter, by chance, whether among the Greek monks or the dervishes, some book on music, a little old, not only in Greek, but in Arabic or other oriental language, principally of those where might be preserved some notes of ancient music, I would willingly employ my money." Jacob Golius had offered what he possessed, an Avicenna and something else in Arabic, and Peiresc possessed a third book, the one with the colored-in notes that had come from Cairo. But Peiresc had heard that there was a Greek priest in Aleppo who had a great collection of manuscripts but was jealous of them. Peiresc wanted above all a very careful transcription of an ancient mansucript containing three hymns of Dionysus, "which are behind Aristides," along with the notes, because they were corrupt in all the extant editions. If Celestin could do this, it would be a service not only to him but to the entire learned world, to whom he would have given "a means for restoring this beautiful secret of antiquity."[404] This letter occasioned others to Peiresc's Aleppo respondents: to Robert Contour and Jean-Louis Allemand, on the 5th and 6th of January 1635.[405]

Another, more fleeting line of inquiry, Cyprus, seems to have fallen apart as a site for Peiresc's research. It had attracted his attention in 1627 as a possible source of Byzantine and Crusader materials. By 1635, with the death of Jean Espannet, Peiresc seems to have lacked assets on the ground. But because Espannet had told Peiresc about the possibility of finding books in the mountains, and because Minuti had explained to him that Charles Blanc, in Sidon, had a close relationship with Espannet, Peiresc tried to turn Blanc into a source for Cyprus.[406] Trying to win Blanc's cooperation, Peiresc explained that he would pay the "costs of recovery and the maritime profits" ("droictz de remise & les proffictz maritimes") at the same rate as the merchandise come on the ship that would be carrying the items, "like I always do."[407]

In April 1635, Father Celestin received Peiresc's of early January. He responded by sending Peiresc "some Arabic book on the science of music."[408] Later in April, Peiresc wrote again to Father Celestin, and to his brother in Leiden. To the latter, he expressed his pleasure at being asked by Saumaise to send his colleague's letters to Syria.[409] To Father Celestin, he began by thanking him for his letter of 17 February. He apologized for distracting him from his worship, "howevermuch there was there a way to bring all things to the greater glory of God" ("combien qu'il y ayt moyen de rapporter toutes choses à la plus grande gloire de dieu"). This, he thought, was especially true of "the observations of nature and its most marvelous effects, where Divine Providence always appears most admirable."[410] Peiresc turned from a general presentation of the sympathy between religion and nature to a more precise discussion of why he studied nature:

> Because the appearance of those lands could furnish great arguments and means of penetrating a little further in natural philosophy than those who study it commonly think possible today, totally differently than the ancients did, but possibly not better than them, seeing that the book of nature is the book of books and that there is nothing more conclusive than the observations of the things themselves whose course is so constant, whatever vicissitudes or revelations or changes there could be, nor any place where the grandeur of God would more appear.

This is Peiresc the citizen of the 1630s, speaking the language of his friends Galileo and Mersenne—or are they speaking his? But Peiresc went even further. It was observation, he concluded, that "is capable of enabling us to raise up the human spirit, when everything is well measured and examined as it ought to be."[411] This is research as the ultimate therapy: done carefully, science served the soul.

With this, Peiresc turned to Pliny's discussion of the topography of Antioch and Seleucia Pieriae, and of the temple of Jupiter on Mount Casius. After a description of the ancient site and its ruins, Peiresc suggested an expedition there "with some janissary or other persons lined up for the safety of your group." He was happy to subsidize the bodyguard.[412] Mount Casius had long been associated, he wrote, with the veneration of Jupiter. There were likely to be inscriptions and architectural ornaments to study. But a high place like that was also an ideal location for astronomical observation, and Peiresc devoted most of the letter to explaining in some detail how to do observation by instruments, all in preparation for the upcoming eclipse of August 1635. He also explained how these observations could facilitate the calculation of longitude.[413] From astronomy, Peiresc turned to Mediterranean topography and a long disquisition on the shape of mountains in the region of Alexandretta.[414] Then Peiresc discussed the temple itself, with its supposed chasm and vapors. Only at the last did he raise issues having to do with the history of architecture and ornament.[415]

Peiresc was also keen for a report on Father Celestin's neighbor, the sieur de Galaup-Chasteuil. But in 1635 some of this news—of his trip to Jerusalem, for instance—came with news of another bishop, Isaac in Mount Lebanon. In a letter to a M. Hazard, otherwise not part of Peiresc's network but a colleague of Gaulmin the Persianist in Paris, Periesc wanted to know more about him, and as usual with Peiresc, the questions define the content. He wanted to have "all the instructions you could provide concerning the age, *country*, good manners and teaching of that Bishop Isaac, in what place you came to know him, and especially, of the knowledge that he might have of Arabic, Latin and other languages. And if he has interests more curious than common, and where he obtained his title of bishop, in what task you have seen him, and what is the subject of his visit to Rouen."[416]

In July 1635, Peiresc was thinking of music. From Sergio Gamerio, the Maronite and nephew of the patriarch Amira, who had been living with him in Aix, Peiresc obtained a plan of the chant used by the Maronites.[417] He learned that the liturgical music of the Maronites shared a common origin with that of Arab music.[418] He also received another volume containing three musical treatises from Father Celestin in Aleppo.[419] Peiresc wrote to de Loches that this volume could supplement the little book he had from Magy, "from which I think that one can draw much more fruit than one would believe, if there were a means of interpreting it well, because of the notes and colored figures which could supply a plethora of secrets about the ancient music of the Greeks, whose memory and knowledge are buried and completely lost."[420]

Peiresc was indeed very pleased with that little Arabic book of music sent by Magy. It contained excerpts of Avicenna and that "Saphadin, a very famous musician of that people and the inventor of their musical notation."[421] At the end of his letter to Celestin, Peiresc noted that there was in it some Persian that was hard to decipher.[422] Peiresc would be even happier if Celestin could find for him the big folio volume collecting all the most celebrated Arabic authors and treatises on music. But Peiresc really wanted Celestin to see if the person who had the volume and sold it could reconstruct for him a table of contents. If he were a dervish, then Peiresc expected that he had a knowledge of music, like "the majority of those dervishes." Above all, what Peiresc wanted to know was whether there were any Greek authors who were translated into that volume and whether they could be translated out of it, especially out of the Persian, whose terms of art "are not intelligible to men very learned in these oriental languages."[423] In itself, this last is an interesting commentary on the state of things in Europe.

In his letter of early August 1635, Celestin responded to Peiresc's proposal to use Mount Casius as a site for both archaeological and astronomical observation. There were "three or four very high mountains" between Antioch and Alexandretta, and he was not certain which was which.[424]

Peiresc wrote again to Celestin in mid-October, briefly and in haste, only to have something to send with Captain Reynaud. This same ship also carried a letter to Pierre and Jean Constans, de Gastines's "correspondants" in Aleppo, who were to close the circuit between Peiresc and Celestin, as well as a letter from Golius in Leiden to his nephew.[425] In the background, we find a letter to Venture in Marseille, to whom Peiresc sent a case of books via the muleteer of Sisteron, Melchior Magnan, for Constans to consign to Celestin, as well as a letter to Golius in Leiden.[426] In this parallel letter to Golius, Peiresc spelled out the details of his project for a simultaneous eclipse observation around the Mediterranean basin.[427]

Writing to Father Celestin in November, Peiresc focused on eclipse observation. He had just orgnized a Mediterranean-wide eclipse observation, which Celestin missed. But Peiresc remained optimistic about getting Celestin *and* his Aleppan colleagues to contribute observational data in the future. Even one reliable result could be compared with other observations to establish longitudes and yield the real distances of places and "an infinity of other great things praiseworthy in our century and to posterity." Celestin had told him that there were old dervishes and other learned men "very curious about good books in all sorts of sciences, and especially mathematics." Peiresc wanted him to find out if they also had books on astronomy, which included listings of eclipses and other observational phenomena of the past. Peiresc wanted to be able to compare their information with European data, such as the Alphonsine Tables, a Hebrew version of which he had Rabbi Azubi translate for him, beginning in the summer of 1633. If any of these books were available for purchase he would not try "to spare a single piece of silver." He also wanted Celestin to copy down the basic details of the observation, namely, "the moments of each phase that were observed, coordinated with the height of some star appropriate to the situation of the place where the observation was made in order to know the latitude and the height of the pole, and more or less the longitude, as well as the quality of the instruments that were used to take these dimensions." Peiresc reminded him that he would like basic measurements such as the height of the sun at the solstice and the height of the pole star on a certain day, which could be used for the observation of future eclipses in that same place. Peiresc offered to make European observational data available to the local astronomers, "to give them pleasure in the comparison with ours," as well as to send them good books on this subject that he thought likely to be intelligible, even in a foreign language. Peiresc is fully permeated by the idea of a shared community of inquirers, irrespective of religious or cultural differences.[428]

Peiresc then turned to another problem, the lack of Persian readers in contemporary France. Peiresc urged Father Celestin not to limit himself to Arabic tuition, but to study Persian as well. Why? Because it was in Persian, Peiresc believed, and not in Arabic, that one would find the most books in the Levant in the important subjects of mathematics and history.[429] How Peiresc acquired this information—or opinion—is difficult to determine.[430] At this point in the seventeenth century, the Europeans interested in the world of Islam seem to be avoiding the question of Islam.

Finally, in the postscript to this important letter, Peiresc focuses in on a particular individual with whom he wanted some contact. He understood that in Aleppo "there was a Sherif named Mehmet Eltacaoni who was a great *curieux* of mathematics" and had an important library. Peiresc asked for a catalog of the mathematical books and above all "ancient astronomy"—which he sharply contrasted with "judicial astrology." Peiresc volunteered that he would gladly send him anything "to acquire his familiarity and correspondence." If Celestin could get the chance to catalog his books, especially the books on history, or those of other curious people in Aleppo, he would be especially grateful.[431] How did Peiresc learn of this bibliophile? In a letter of July 1635 from Cairo, Father Agathange de Vendôme informed him of a Mohammed Eltacaoni, "a *curieux* of mathematics, who has a beautiful library of books in different oriental languages."[432]

Only a few days later, learning that Patron Lombardon was about to sail for Syria, Peiresc wrote to Celestin again, picking up where the last letter left off, with "Cherif Eltacaoni." Peiresc had some specific questions. Did his library contain any ancient Arabic versions of Greek military treatises, and especially the *Tactics* of Urbicius? Was there anything by Epicurus, "who was not as bad as many wanted to believe, on the false rumor or equivocations about the word *voluptas* under which they conceived nothing less than sensuality." This defense of Epicurus obviously reflected the hours Peiresc spent talking with Gassendi, whose epochal biography of Epicurus was already in the works.[433] And then Peiresc turned back to the beginning of the previous letter, exhorting Celestin to do astronomical observation in places like Antioch, Aleppo, Jerusalem, and Constantinople.[434] This is exactly the cartographic reform plan that inspired people like Greaves a decade later.[435]

Music remained at the heart of Peiresc's interest in Syria. Less than a week later (22 November) Peiresc wrote again to Father Celestin. Peiresc had just received Celestin's letters of 29 September and 2 October. That of 29 September described an eclipse observation (difficult), the nature of intellectual life in Aleppo (limited), and negotiations for the purchase of the large volume of Arabic music manuscripts (failed).[436] The problem in the latter, according to Peiresc, was tactical—by acknowledging its value, Celestin made it easier for the price to be bid up.[437]

The main content of this long letter, however, has to do with the eclipse observation performed during the summer. Celestin was without the instruments that Peiresc had prepared for him—de Gastines was away during the summer and his *commis* never passed along the material—but other observations were performed in Aleppo, by the Capuchin Michelange de Nantes, and by Balthasar Claret, chancellor of the French consulat. Peiresc stressed how important these were, "totally different from that of plants and other natural things," and added "that when one makes it a little routine, there is nothing so simple."[438]

Father Celestin had, apparently, taken Peiresc somewhat seriously and tried to go to Mount Casius. Peiresc, in fact, was not happy about this, first because of the danger posed by the rude inhabitants of the place, and second because of the cost.[439] Peiresc again offered a careful description of "how to" do these observations, based in part on recommendations from Schikard of Tübingen.[440]

Peiresc's further explanation sheds light on many aspects of the cost structure of scientific exploration in the Levant at this time: "For me, the expense of a trip of one day's journey from Aleppo was more than 80 écus (because to reimburse the indemnity here it is necessary to return an écu for a piastre). For that reason, to wait for the day of the eclipse at the site and return with all the company it was necessary to spend a thousand écus, which would be to pay too dearly for the copy of an ancient inscription that could be transcribed there." Though Celestin did not belong to those "weak and superstitious folk" who searched for supposed treasures, his actions did feed into popular suspicion of him, his party, and indeed all the French. "That is why I have renounced all the schemes that I could have had, and beseech you not to think about it any more."[441]

Finally, Peiresc focused in on a single person who helped Celestin, "the venerable old dervish" he had mentioned but whose name he had not. Peiresc insisted that the man's name needed to be known because even were it his sole virtue, his assistance to the two Goliuses, the one in Leiden and the one in Syria, "well merits that his name, his country and his praiseworthy qualities not now be ignored." He could also help inform Peiresc if there were other men of science in the vicinity. "And it would be necessary to know," Peiresc continued, whether any "people of their nation" had made observations of celestial phenomena such as eclipses that could be compared with those made by the ancients. Again Peiresc turned back to names: "And if one could not learn their names, and where they lived, and become friendly with them."[442] This is one of the most profound and self-conscious comments by Peiresc on the importance of names and naming, and we will return to it, and to Father Celestin's answer, below.

But on that same November day in 1635, Peiresc wrote to three other members of the French merchant community in Aleppo. Robert Contour seems to have been the merchant to whom Peiresc looked to manage Father Celestin's affairs. Peiresc's letters to him offer a clear example of how he relied on merchants, and on the particular skills he associated with them. Peiresc began by thanking him for "knocking some sense into those good fathers" ("jetter sens a cez bons peres") who had wanted to undertake such a journey, innocently, for "love of him" and "for the public good." It is clear from Peiresc's expression of lasting gratitude and willingness to serve that the two had not been in contact beforehand. Peiresc was especially grateful for Contour's willingness to assist the Capuchins. He asked Contour to help make sense of Father Michelange's eclipse observations. He explained that he wanted to see all the work, and not just the cleaned-up numbers, "since in these matters, even the faults and equivocations very often also serve." Peiresc hoped that Contour would not mind working with and checking up on the Capuchin father who had "too much charity and naiveté" ("a trop de charité & déingenuité").[443] To encourage the merchant's participation, as well as to justify his seeming obsession with detail, Peiresc acknowledged that it might take some work to convince the priest "to let him see the whole 'tissue' of his observation" ("à me laisser voir la tisseue entiere de son observation"). With all these data Gassendi and Schikard, whom he described as "the two greatest mathematicians of the century" ("les deux plus grandz mathematiciens du siècle"), could fix things afterward.[444] As Peiresc wrote, "quite often one has so profited from noting the faults, that one had to choose the supposition and assertion that seemed false and leave the correction to follow."[445] This is, indeed, Peiresc's vision of the enterprise of scholarship: better to put something out into the Republic of Letters and get it corrected. Most important was to communicate.

Peiresc then went on to spell out for Contour the fullest scope of his Mediterranean-wide project, which included observations done by Father Michelange in Syria, Chasteuil in Lebanon, Agathange de Vendôme in Egypt, Thomas d'Arcos in Tunis, and then a whole host of well-known scholarly colleagues in Italy, France, Germany, and the Netherlands. Its purpose was practical: to redraw the map of the Mediterranean.[446]

In the postscript, Peiresc returned to the issue at the beginning, the attempt to observe the eclipse from some remarkable location. He thought Aleppo was fine, even without looking for some mountain, which might arouse unwanted curiosity. Doing it at Jerusalem or some other celebrated place was best.[447] A second postscript tells Contour of the competitive market for texts in Aleppo. Father Celestin had lined up a collection of Arabic authors on music, but then the brother of the owner took it. The brother claimed he was going to Persia, but Peiresc thought that no one would brave the civil disobedience there just to deliver a book.[448]

In a letter to still another Aleppo merchant, Pierre Constans, written on the same day, 22 November 1635, Peiresc returned to the aborted trip to Mount Casius. Peiresc thanked him for heading off the planned expedition for two main reasons: how the natives would have reacted to seeing such an expedition, and how much it would have cost.

> I would not have preserved the dream of such a plan if I could have predicted the unfounded anger, but being at the word and whim of such barbarous and defiant people, and of such bad faith, nothing can be held as safe, and one must abstain from even the most innocent actions when they are a little outside the mainstream. That is why I request and conjure you, insistently, to not suffer that the good Father Celestin, nor Sr. Claret, and even less your other sirs, nor others of your friends or of mine, should ever commit to the unfortunate trip to that mountain where nothing could come of it

but ill and displeasure, among such great superstition and the per-
fidy of the world. . . . What's important is that the thing is not worth
risking for whatever it is, nor taking so much trouble just to see a
grotto or some figures or inscriptions.[449]

Thus much for the first explanation.

The second focused on cost and the limits of Peiresc as *patron:* "Beyond that I am too small a partner for such casual expenses, and then that
company not having gone but the first day's journey from Aleppo had nevertheless spent 86 piastres, so that at this proportion the voyage would
have cost me a thousand or twelve hundred piastres to which I would have
been found too short." Celestin's vision was "extravagant—a bit too grand
for me—which would serve to advise me for the future no longer to do
this project."[450] Peiresc explicitly asked Constans to "break up the party"
any time he saw there was the danger of an action that would expose the
participants to extortion and persecution.[451]

Peiresc thanked him for his help and for "the use you have made
of Sr. B. Claret whom I think a person of singular merit in his profession." Balthasar Fabre was chancellor of the consulate in Aleppo and
Balthasar Claret was an apothecary in Aleppo. Their names are sometimes found on the same document. Peiresc seems to have confounded
the two.[452] Peiresc desired to make his acquaintance. He then turned directly to the 105 piastres he owed, which would be reimbursed to Venture
in Marseille.[453]

To Claret himself, Peiresc repeated his concern about the expedition
on account of the lurking dangers. With people so "superstitious and of
such bad faith," almost anything could serve as a pretext to do ill. Peiresc
went on to note the difference between their eclipse observations. Finally,
he added that he had looked at Claret's drawings and plans and wished
him only to trouble himself ("il ne fault pas profaner votre main a moins
que . . .") with the most ancient structures and best architecture.[454]

Finally, writing on that same day to Jean Venture in Marseille, who
held the connection to Aleppo, Peiresc acknowledged the various letters
he had just received from Aleppo, as well as all those he had just written
back. He was still waiting for a letter of Father Michelange, and he asked
Venture to check with the superior of the Capuchin convent in Marseille
to see if the letter wound up there. He added that he was sorry that Venture received any bill at all as port costs should have been charged to de

Gastines—suggesting that Venture had a well-known role in the Aleppo trade.[455]

1636

A much longer letter to Balthasar Fabre followed six months later, in May 1636.[456] It was a reply to one now missing, and is one of the more characteristic and important Peiresc ever wrote to the Levant. Peiresc began by clarifying his financial status and intellectual interests.

> I am not the person they wanted you to believe, not for the means (because I do not have 8,000 piastres to spend on useless matters), nor for the curiosity, which consists not at all in learning news of the world. Because I am not of the quality or of the condition to spend time on it, or to make it capital, and even less to be charged costs which could have been avoided.[457]

Peiresc knew that there were those who misunderstood his commitment to research. He wished now to spell out on what he would spend, and in what range.

> Also, I would be happy if you could disabuse those who would call this [limitation of mine] into doubt, and believe the false word that is spread out there by people who do not know me at all, and take me for someone else. It is true that I am a little curious, but it is principally only for books appropriate for aiding the public, and consequently for antiquities, when they can be had at such a moderate price that my little purse can aspire to it without inconvenience, or indeed when there is some way to have faithful portraits or drawings of those which are not on the market, and especially when there is some ancient Greek or Latin inscription of the sort that is often found on the front of temples, or on ancient marbles, or weights, I will not hold back, when it only takes a little, the cost of a painter to draw them, if the cost is not too considerable.[458]

Peiresc then turned to the expedition to Mount Casius that he had proposed in his letter to Father Celestin of autumn 1635. Father Celestin had planned an herborising trip there to gather rare seeds. Peiresc had asked him to take his route near that cavern in order to transcribe whatever he could of those inscriptions, and to defer the trip until the time of the eclipse (in August 1635) in order to make obsevations there, the height of the mountain lifting the observers above any possibly interfering ground fog. Also, the place was known in antiquity for the sun rising a quarter of an hour earlier there than elsewhere, making it especially appropriate for an eclipse observation.[459] "But the jealousy and bad faith of those who govern in that land is not compatible with any worthy plan, however innocent. And the good father wanted to add and put into the party a few too many men who made too much of a noise among such untrustworthy people who are so fond of occasions and pretexts to extort *avanies* and ransoms from good people."[460] Peiresc was therefore extremely grateful to his comrade there, M. Contour, for preventing this trip and forestalling any potential conflict. Peiresc also thanked Contour for his role in trying to acquire the music book that someone else swooped in and purchased. Nevertheless, the plan was not completely without positive issue, showing that "all these things, which seem trifles, are not always, however."[461] We see here the role of merchants serving as "chaperones": as practical fixers making sure that the unworldly missionaries do not get harmed, or worse.

Another aspect of their role is in the eclipse observation itself. Fabre's observations were reliable enough to be plotted alongside those done by Peiresc and Gassendi in Aix, both places with fixed longitude and latitude, and thus enabled a reduction of the distance between Marseille and Alexandretta by one third, or "8 or 900 miles" (he later amends this to 100 miles).[462] Peiresc ended this letter asking Claret to inquire if additional observations could be made by other people in Aleppo—Peiresc refers to one "Hasan."[463]

By the time he wrote these words, Peiresc was in receipt of Father Celestin's most recent letter from Aleppo, dated 25 February. He was very disappointed that Patron Lombardon had lost the four-volume Arabic dictionary (Giggaeus's *Thesaurus Linguae Arabicae, Arabice et Latine* [Milan, 1632])—the same as had been lost by Patron Baille on the Nile between Alexandria and Cairo the previous year—and with it Peiresc's instructions for observing the eclipse of 20 February 1636, and "the marvelous fruit which could be hoped for from similar observations for reforming geographical and marine charts." Peiresc's reply rehearsed the results of the previous year's eclipse observations: reducing the distance from Marseille to Aleppo "by a good third" ("d'un grand tiers") as well as dimensions of the globe itself.[464]

In Aleppo, Father Celestin was in one of the most Western-penetrated of the Levantine cities.[465] In a letter to his brother from early in 1636, Celestin talked about the book world in Aleppo. In September 1635 he had compared it unfavorably with Damascus and, especially, Cairo.[466] Interestingly, in July 1635, Father Agathange de Vendôme had compared Cairo unfavorably with Aleppo![467] Now, where his resources ran short, there was a whole circle; Celestin explained to his brother that the dervish had written to friends of his in Damascus for a more accurate edition found there in the library of Fakhr al-Din ("Bibliotheca Ficardini").[468] And we have already overheard Peiresc asking after Sherif Mehmet Eltacaoni—whose ungarbled name was al-Sayyid al-Taqwā or al-Taqwanī, a rival bookseller and dealer. In the final letter Celestin wrote to Peiresc, on 22 August 1637, two months after Peiresc had died but obviously before the news had reached Aleppo, Celestin explained that he had written to "Mohamed Eltacwii" asking for a catalog of his library, as Peiresc had requested, and that "Eltacwii" had promised to deliver it but thus far had not. He was a "truly a werewolf, and a fraud," not only to "my Master the Dervish Ahmed, who was familiar with these practices for many years, but I even know it from experience."[469] Al-Taqwā is similarly described as a fierce, even deceitful, competitor in the Aleppo book market in a letter from Darwish Ahmad to Edward Pococke of 1636 or 1637.[470]

As for that dervish, already in his letter to Peiresc from September 1635, Celestin referred to "an old derivish, my master" as especially versed in geography.[471] Writing to Peiresc in late February 1636—the letter traveled under the same cover as a letter to his brother, explaining why a copy of the brother's letter is today among Peiresc's papers—Father Celestin announced that he had taken for his Arabic teacher "an old and very learned Dervish"("hominem senem Dervisium doctissimum"). For six years this man had taught Arabic daily to "some student" who had ended up spending 5,000 pieces of gold building up a library of Arabic texts—and shipped it all back to England, whence he had returned the previous month. This man, named here as "Magister Pocock," was "most expert" in Hebrew, Syriac, Greek, Arabic, Persian, and other Oriental languages. Now that Pococke was gone, Celestin hoped to have more access to this teacher.[472]

It is from Pococke, perhaps the most important Arabist of the seventeenth century, whose work has received careful treatment in the recent work of Gerald Toomer, that we find the key to this dervish's identity. He was al-Darwish Ahmad ibn al-Hajj Husam al-'Akalshani. As Celestin's letters make clear, his close relationship with Edward Pococke when he was chaplain of the Aleppo Company was known to the community of interested Europeans in Aleppo.[473]

Peiresc's reflections on the book market in Aleppo, where his purchasing power ran up against English, Venetian, Persian, and local merchants with deep pockets, also suggests, indirectly, the richness of the Aleppo scene.[474] The Peiresc archive, like that of Pococke, allows us to catch a glimpse of intellectual life in these Ottoman provincial cities in the first half of the seventeenth century. Would that these slanting rays from the West were matched by those from the East! But my efforts to find comparable Ottoman sources reflecting on the encounter with European figures such as Father Celestin, or the merchants in Aleppo and Damascus on whom Peiresc relied, have thus far failed.[475]

In this environment, Peiresc suggested that a little subterfuge might be necessary to win out, explaining that a small deception was no big crime in matters as urgent as getting the right book: "I am sorry that you have lost the help that you could have received in your little consultations on oriental languages from your Mister Pokak. But since he is so jealous in the matter of books and so unsociable, I am not sorry that he has quit the field and the show, and I think rather that you will now have very good fortune, and perhaps even better than with those fraternal negotiations." Moreover, he was comfortable with Celestin's having used 60 piastres on his account, "because it could serve as an excuse and quittance to him who would like to claim it back, when you could say that you had sent it to me in France even though you were still using it. These little officious lies are not big crimes that one has to abstain from in an emergency for the health of a good book, which is sometimes comparable to that of a person because it is the sanctification and work of an author's whole life."[476] Peiresc's sense of a calling, and of a responsibility of the present to the past embodied in a book, is clear and it inspired those who worked with him.

The book in question, for which Peiresc was prepared to pay the princely sum of 60 piastres—the Samaritan Triglot only cost him 31—was a Hebrew Bible. It was said by Celestin to be six hundred years old, which put it, according to Peiresc, "at the time, more or less exactly, of the Massoretes who worked on the Hebrew Bible." Still, Peiresc feared that it was something "more recent than 300 years and composed in Spain rather than the Levant, if I am not mistaken." Celestin could clarify this if he were able to find other examples.[477] Peiresc's association with Jean Morin and the Paris Polyglot Bible, as well as his conversations with Rabbi Azubi, seems to have given him a detailed history of manuscript versions of the Hebrew Bible.

The competition between Pococke and Celestin for books clearly excited Peiresc the book hunter. He retained a copy for himself of a list of Arabic manuscript books that Pococke obtained in Aleppo from "Mehmet"—probably "Eltaconi," or Sayid al-Taqwā.[478] The list of titles that Father Celestin sent back to his brother in Leiden on the Dutch *Galleon Bleu* followed separately.[479]

Peiresc was extremely grateful for Celestin's transcription and translation of the treatise on music—"I thank you infinitely for all the good will that you have had for me in this, and also the care that you are willing to take in transcribing the musical treatise." He was especially glad because it contained technical terms ("cet art a des termes particulieres") that were more Persian than Arabic and which could not be translated in Europe, as opposed to where he was, in the presence of "Sr. Mehmet, votre Drevis," and other local people learned in mathematics. Again, the pursuit of musical texts reveals the limited state of Persian knowledge in Europe at the time. Peiresc was certain that the treatise would make a fine present for M. Golius his brother.[480]

But as good as it felt to get this musical text, Peiresc concluded, it was not the thing that most excited him. This, rather, was the history not only of the "Sarracin dynasties"—what Erpenius had written about—but of what came before, as well. It was especially in having it from the Arab side that was interesting to him: "according to the traditions of countries very different from what the Greeks had written."[481] We find this interest in looking at a familiar issue from the "other," Arab, side equally significant when Peiresc turned to the history of the Crusades.[482]

After history, Peiresc said that he was most interested in astronomy, by which he meant ancient authors such as Hipparchus and Ptolemy. He explicitly contrasted this "true astronomy" ("vraye Astronomie") with "all those suppositions and superstitions of the astrologers and makers of horoscopes which are nothing but vanities" ("toutes cez suppositions et superstitions des Astrologues et faiseurs d'horoscopes qui ne sont que vanitez"). And within astronomy he took the greatest pleasure in observation, because comparison of ancient and contemporary observations could "serve to regulate the movements of the heavens, which are the most worthy object of our eyes."[483]

Peiresc was also interested in philosophical texts that were available in Arabic, in particular those of Democritus and Epicurus. He explained why: "I understand that in the East there are sects that are mixed with Islam, and which have retained I do not know how many maxims and entire books." With this, he continues, "you will find there, I am sure, something totally different from what the poor Epicurus is accused of, when one stops at the noise without wanting to know more." Peiresc is here suggesting, no doubt on the advice and account of Gassendi, that there might be missing parts of Epicurus's teaching that survived in Arabic only and which could change the perception of his philosophy. Peiresc rose up in his defense: "Since it is believed that in putting his Supreme Good on *voluptas* he was nothing but debauched, and yet there was nothing so chaste as his *voluptas* of the spirit and not of the senses, nor so temperate, as he lived for the most part but of bread and water, like the old Anchorites." If Celestin could find any fragments Peiresc would not "spare at all his little purse" ("espargnez point ma petite bource"). *"Voilà,"* he concluded, "what you asked to learn about my taste." We can therefore take this as a self-conscious attempt by Peiresc to portray his interests for another person, just a year before his death.[484] As for his friends, he was seeking music books for Golius, books on animals for Saumaise, and Samaritan Bibles for Father Morin and Gabriel Sionite.[485]

Peiresc was full of confidence in Celestin. We know that in May 1636 Peiresc was happily serving as the link between Father Celestin and his brother Jacob, the professor, in Leiden. A *lettre de change* had arrived and Peiresc saw to its being delivered to Celestin.[486] In June, Peiresc could write to Golius that he was sending to him a copy of the little book of music that had come from Magy in Cairo and was notable for using colored notes. Peiresc likened it to ancient chromaticism. It was a poor copy, forcing Peiresc to explain about the role of colors. The Arabs did not simply transmit; they also added—something that Peiresc would have preferred they had not. On the other hand, this meant allowing a creative role for Arab music theorists, not viewing them as mere nonreactive vessels in the transmission of knowledge. Where there were difficult terms of art, Peiresc hoped that Golius would be able to unravel them by making the comparison to other texts he knew.[487] Peiresc wished to send a second musical book which was a compilation of different texts, "but the piece was envied of us by others who took advantage of the simplicity and goodness of Father Celestin, perhaps to carry it to England."[488] Again, all hands pointed to Pococke.[489]

Peiresc's involvement in Arab music must be located not only in the context of his oriental studies but also, as we have seen, in that of his friends Mersenne and Doni in ancient Roman music. He noted that some of the "Maitres de Musique" found Arab music unappealing. But he thought it was a question of acclimation, just as the taste for beer, wine, cider, cheese, "and other foods of high taste" were all acquired "and often incompatible to those who were not accustomed to it." Surveying the different musical traditions of the Italians and the French, he saw just this selective accommodation through "accoustumance."[490] This suggests again, just as in his studies of imagery, the importance of cultural history for Peiresc as an arena in which one could see how change happens over time.

Traffic to Aleppo seems to have been disrupted that summer. Peiresc complained to Celestin in August 1636 that his communications had been frustrated. First, there was the loss of Patron Lombardon's barque and then Peiresc's discovery that some of his letters had never left Marseille. And now he had learned that no ship would be traveling to Alexandretta for two to three months.[491] On 29 November, Peiresc wrote to Golius that he had just received Father Celestin's letter of 30 September. The letters that had been in that same packet for Golius and his uncle Hemelarius had been lost when the messenger carrying the letters was robbed by the Arabs between Aleppo and Alexandretta.[492]

1637

At the turn of the new year, Constans wrote to Peiresc on the burning of the papers of Michelange de Vendôme while he was away in Lebanon. This destroyed most of Vendôme's eclipse observations. Constans was only able to salvage those of 19 August 1636. He also asked Father Michelange for his "book of music" and was promised an even older one, but "since he is a man of high taste who has a large number of books without order," Father Michelange did not know how to find it before his imminent departure for Baghdad.[493]

Only in March 1637 do we have Peiresc again reporting on the arrival of a packet of new letters. In his, Celestin records that Constans had given him 4 piastres and two telescopes ("lunettes de porte veue") that Constans had purchased for him from a Venetian.[494] This suggests that Peiresc was still employing the strategy of using merchants and missionaries to carry out his research agenda when he died on 24 June 1637. What we do not find is Peiresc in direct correspondence with Ottoman or Arab scholars. Unlike Pococke, for example, we possess no record of Peiresc's ongoing relationship with a local non-European *érudit*. Nor, in fact, do we find him seeking one out. Peiresc met Turks, North Africans, and Arabs who were passing through Provence, but he did not direct his pen to seek them out in their lands. Why? Peiresc was a marvel of curiosity. We know that. But with this question, have we here discovered one of his limits?

7

Peiresc's Names, or, On Reading the Namescape

"Nicolas-Claude Fabry de Callas": this is how he signed his first three letters between 1602 and 1604 to the great Dutch botanist Carolus Clusius (Charles de l'Escluse). Then, in the postscript to the fourth, of 25 February 1604, he asked Clusius to address his letters to "Sr. de Peirests, chez monsr. le conseiller de Callas." But only two days later, he signed the very next letter "N. C. Fabry," and the next two letters, of 15 February and 25 August 1605, "N. C. de Peirets." Only in the last preserved letter, dated 15 February 1606, do we find the now-familiar "Peiresc" scrawled at the bottom of the page. He explained to Clusius that his new name was the Provençal form of the old Latin: "Our little village of 'Peiresc' is called 'Castrum de Petrisco' in the old cadasters."[1]

Peiresc paid close attention to other people's names as well, sometimes even to names from very long ago. In his dossier on Marseille we come across an excerpt documenting a Pierre de Cerveris buying half a windmill from Jean, Jehannet, and Samsette Pascal in 1390; a Bertrand d'Agout of Marseille conveying the Chateau of Cabriès to Olivier d'Agout his brother, and to his nephew Bertrand a house in the part of Marseille "long called" Jerusalem; and the commune of Sixfours purchasing the right to make olive oil on the property of the abbey of St. Victor.[2] Peiresc's sensitivity to the names of ordinary people, far from being a novelty, reflects a commonplace form of attentiveness to ancient inscriptions, with their praise of famous men.[3]

When Peiresc's great contemporary asked, "What's in a name?," he, and not only his star-crossed Juliet, was pushing back at the enormous accumulated weight of names in old Europe.[4] And yet, that very weight poses a problem for us as historians. On the one hand, names provide an unmediated link to the past, an anchorage amid a sea of strangeness. Who has not experienced this power of proximity when reading or wandering through the past? On the other hand, sometimes, as when walking in a cemetery, the profusion of names without reference only intensifies our experience of distance.

Benedetto Croce put exactly this problem at the heart of his attempt to define the difference between history and what he called "chronicle." His main point was that all history was intimately connected to the present through the mediation of the historian, who, no matter his professionalized self-denial, is inevitably someone living "now" and not "then." It is in this context that Croce asks what would be involved in writing about a period for which one lacked documentary sources. One might possess, as in the example he gives of Hellenistic painting, a series of names, artists, or artworks. But without the survival of the art objects themselves these "are empty names, and empty anecdotes, empty descriptions of their subjects, empty judgments of approbation or reproof, and empty chronological ordering." The names are empty because they do not connect to any determinate reality.[5] Without a way to assess who the person was or what the artwork was, the emptiness of the name marks an "irrevocable past." Real history lives through the present, according to Croce; "chronicle," which we might think of as an account of names only, is a form of pastness that is not history, though it partakes of some outward attributes of it.

The distinction is parallel to the one usually offered between antiquarianism and history. But unlike the modern historical discipline as currently constituted, Croce also allows for his distinction to be undone by the very practice of research. For when we attach documents to names, we connect names to realities, and thence to our questions about the past and our concerns in studying it. This amounts to a form of resurrection, and indeed Croce writes that "bringing forth history from the chronicle would be as much as bringing forth the living from a cadaver."[6] His contemporary, Aby Warburg, also linked names with resurrection, writing of the power of archival scholarship: "As we cast about for indirect ways of bringing the record to life, historical nominalism at long last comes into its own. Even so superficial a fact as the knowledge of Catarina's maiden name restores her to us as a living personality, part of the massive edifice of Florentine family life."[7]

This same problem of naming and what cannot be said lies close to the heart of Ludwig Wittgenstein's almost exactly contemporary *Tractatus Logico-Philosophicus*. Here, the challenge came from Frege and Russell and was connected to problems of meaning and language, not history. But when Wittgenstein writes, "In a proposition a name is the representative of an object," we might read, "In a book about Marseille, de Gastines is the name of a character who is a merchant." And when he continues by declaring, "Objects can only be *named* . . . I can only speak *about* them: I cannot *put them into words.* Propositions can only say *how* things are, not *what* they are," we might hear, "Naming the characters of Marseille and putting them into propositions is all we can do with them. We cannot get to them, or to Marseille itself."[8] And yet, even if we cannot speak about some things—this is the point of the *Tractatus* as a whole— Wittgenstein does give the historian of names some hope when he writes, "One name stands for one thing, another for another thing, and they are combined with one another. In this way the whole group—like a tableau vivant—presents a state of affairs."[9]

What can we do with that "tableau vivant"? Does it silently, coldly, stare back at us, like the figures on Keats's Grecian urn, defying comprehension?[10] Or can, as Croce suggests, the practice of research breathe some life back into these dry names? Insofar as research reconstitutes something of that former "state of affairs," it may be, as Wittgenstein says, that "his name does not lose its meaning when the bearer is destroyed."[11]

To the extent that so many of the names in these ten years of letters are unidentified, and so many others not much beyond a name, they mark the frontier of the silence that the historian cannot penetrate. But, to the extent that we can say something about some of them, and to the extent that future research offers the prospect of saying more, they live again. This sense of mission must have been what Walter Benjamin intended when he mused that "historical construction is dedicated to the memory of the nameless."[12]

Carlo Ginzburg is the historian who seems to have best taken up this challenge. Already thirty-odd years ago he put the importance of names at the heart of his manifesto on behalf of microhistory, seeing the primary utility of naming in its treatment of the subaltern with the dignity of the elite. It was the politics, rather than the epistemology, of naming that concerned him then.

But more recently, in an essay on antiquarianism, Ginzburg comes to the epistemological side of Croce's challenge, and puts names at the very center of the historian's vocation. Ginzburg's key text comes from the *Ars Historica* collection, Francesco Robortello's *De Historica Facultate,* originally published in 1548. Setting out to distinguish between poetry and history—like any good student of Aristotle—Robortello says that epic poetry tells one story whereas history tells many. But then he does something entirely his own: he extrapolates from the many stories that history tells to the importance of names as markers of past actions—"what

Alcibiades said or did." History is a story full of names ("history preserves the true names"), while poetry does not need to give names, and
bad history fails to give them ("often great shadows are cast on things on
account of the distortion of a name"). Robertello even took his own advice seriously and devoted an entire tract to the study of Roman names, *De
Nominibus Romanorum,* also published in 1548.[13]

From the name as the distinguishing feature of history-writing, Robortello deduced the depth of time. And once this whole long series—
names as the early modern equivalent of the twentieth-century's *Annales*
historian's focus on serial documentation—becomes open to the historian,
everything follows as a possible subject of scholarship: mores, subsistence,
cities, migrations. Thus did Robortello identify history, as an inquiry, with
the subjects that had previously been associated with antiquarianism, and as
if this were not clear enough, he offered as an example the one section of an
ancient work of history widely recognized as antiquarian, the so-called Sicilian antiquities at the beginning of book 6 of Thucydides's *Peloponnesian
War.* "Thus," writes Ginzburg, "for Robortello history is synonymous with
antiquarianism." For our question of naming, Robortello went even further: names are the pivot on which his entire argument turns, from history
as a series of events to history as antiquarianism.

How, then, can we understand the presence, even the profusion, of
names in Peiresc's archive, and how, to put it in Croce's terms, are we to
make history out of it—to read the "namescape"?

One use of naming is locating oneself. As we have seen, Peiresc ex-
perimented with his own name. Was he "Nicolas-Claude Fabry de Callas,"
"N. C. Fabry," "N. C. de Peirets," or just plain "Peiresc"? Each of these
names meant something different to him.

Another use of naming is remembering someone else, a function as
old as the oldest human monuments. When Peiresc heard of the dervish
from Aleppo who had a large library, he wrote Father Celestin that "his
name, his country and his admirable qualities ought not be ignored."[14]
This memorial function lies at the heart of antiquarian scholarship; it is
also related to the intergenerational nature of scholarship that Peiresc so
frequently invokes. We need only recall Cyriac of Ancona's boast that his
research could help "wake the dead." Names are almost apotropaic: "may
his name be a blessing" or "may his name be blotted out."

Another use of names is practical. Names delineated networks, provided correspondents with hand-holds, people to whom they could turn
for help. They could also be arrayed in parallel—essential in risky long-

distance communication, when the path of a letter might fail, or a lost shipment needed to be recovered. Goitein's merchant letters do much the same work and also use names as a form of orientation.

Names, moreover, define space. Where we think of maps, Peiresc and his friends navigated by names, indicating the route taken by ship or letter by naming the people it would cross on its way. Peiresc tells correspondents in India they can write to him anywhere along the Provençal coast since the name "Peiresc" was address enough; thus do we see the synonymy of place and name.

Names also define time. The Peiresc archive contains volumes devoted to reconstructing the names and generations of Provençal families, putting names at the center of historical investigation.

But if there is a kind of history that emerges from names, what kind of history is it? Here the graphic form in which Peiresc related to names—his genealogical charts—tells us something very important. His way of charting generations, moving from left to right, seems to have been unique (Figure 14).[15] Scholars of genealogy have focused on the top-down or bottom-up, "arboreal" model, which allows one to draw very clear connections between the present and its justifying, legitimating origins. Peiresc's way of representing family does not do this. But it shows the reality of human history: we cannot, in fact, discern from one generation to the next the "elect" or which path will bear fruit. History is messy, because it is human.

Peiresc's genealogical method seems to have borrowed from the cursive Ramism of Christophe de Savigny's *Tableaux* (1587, 2nd ed. 1619), a visualization of the "Encyclopedia" whose left-to-right analysis privileges *copia* and obscures clear linear descent (Figure 15).[16] Peiresc's adaptation of this structure to the universe of names recognizes the centrality of people and acknowledges the unpredictable nature of history itself. Only when we move away from life does it resolve into clarity; Peiresc resists this temptation.

But even names could be unstable, and not only because our Nicolas Fabri (he also used his baptismal name, "Claude," sometimes) could identify himself as the sieur de Peiresc, sieur de Callas, or baron de Rians. Wolfgang Kaiser has written about the "Solicoffre" of Marseille, merchants and *patrons* who turn up in Peiresc's world (he refers to them always as "Salicoffres"). They were originally the Zollikover of St. Gallen in Switzerland; because of their ties to the English in Tunis, the Spanish described them as Tunisians, while in Livorno they were known as Jews. In Marseille

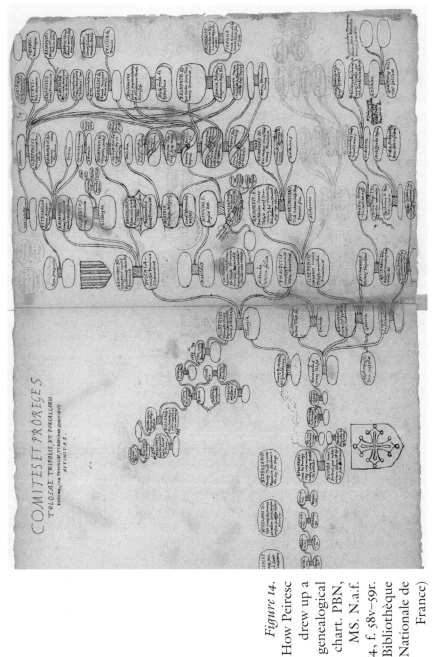

Figure 14. How Peiresc drew up a genealogical chart. PBN, MS. N.a.f. 5174, f. 58v–59r. (Bibliothèque Nationale de France)

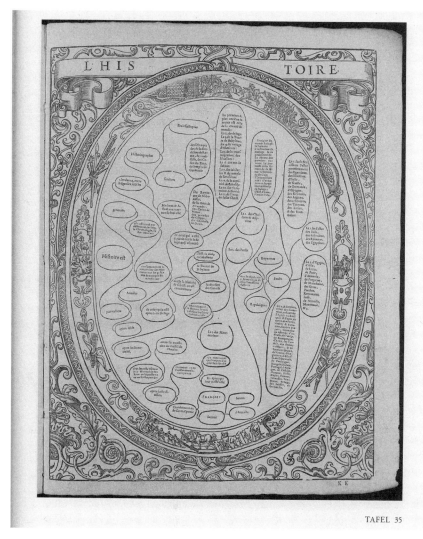

Figure 15. "Histoire," in Christophe de Savigny, *Tableaux accomplis de tous les arts liberaux* (Paris, 1587). (Special Collections, University of Virginia Library)

they might have been crypto-Protestants.[17] Another case: Peiresc asked after "Sherif Mehmet Eltacaoni" in Aleppo. His ungarbled name (and title) was "al-Sayyid al-Taqwā." How many other examples are there of connections that are never made simply because names are lost in transcription? What's in a name? indeed.

Victor Hugo's very late (1874) evocation of the *ancien regime* name-scape helps us understand how men like Peiresc navigated by naming.

> This man is Planchenault, also called Cœur-de-Roi. Show him this knot. He will understand. Then go, whatever way you can, to the woods of Astillé; you will find there a knock-kneed man surnamed Mousqueton, and who shows pity to nobody. You will tell him that I love him, and that he is to stir up his parishes. You will then go to the woods of Couesbon, which is one league from Ploërmel. Make the call of the owl; a man will come, out of a hole; it will be M. Thuault, seneschal of Ploërmel, who has belonged to what is called the Constitution Assembly, but on the good side. Tell him to arm the castle of Couesbon, belonging to the Marquis de Guer, a refugee. Ravines, groves, uneven ground, good place. M. Thuault is an upright man, and a man of sense. Then go to Saint-Guen-les-Toits, and speak to Jean Chouan, who is, in my eyes the real chief. Then go to the woods of Ville-Anglose, where you will see Guitter, called Saint-Martin. Tell him to have an eye or a certain Courmesnil, son-in-law of old Goupil de Préfeln, and who leads the Jacobins of Argentan. Remember all this well. I write nothing because nothing must be written. La Rouarie wrote out a list, but that lost every-thing. Then go to the woods of Rougefeu, where Miélette is, who leaps ravines, balancing himself on a long pole.[18]

Hugo's text was born already a fossil. Already this way of thinking about past people had been smoothed out of existence by the kind of historiography that we associate with the long nineteenth century and its grand and still-influential names of Gibbon, Ranke, Macaulay, and Michelet. It was to get back to the seventeenth century's way of doing history that Michel de Certeau, reflecting on the "historiographical operation" a long generation ago, emphasized that names opened up a rupture or fissure in the narrative smoothening that modern historians effect in their writing. The name could therefore lead us back to the age of curiosity, which he identified as the period "from Peiresc to Leibniz." The name for de Certeau was a reminder that before there was narrative, there were archives, and before there were books, there were documents.[19] As if building on this, Jacques Rancière identifies the development of modern history as an explicit move away from archives and documents toward closed narratives—with a divestiture from names in the pursuit of clarity.[20] But if we go back beyond

Peiresc, and read de Certeau through the lens of Ginzburg's Robortello—
or Grafton's Patrizi—we might add that before there was ancient history
versus the antiquarian, there was a practice of historical research. How to
understand *that* and the period from Peiresc to Leibniz—or Patrizi to
Caylus—is the challenge for a twenty-first century that is separated from it
by the birth of the modern discipline of History.[21]

Perhaps the most careful observer of this premodern world of names
was Proust.[22] "A name," he writes: "that is very often all that remains for
us of an individual."[23] Because Proust recognized that his own personal
history lived in the names he knew, he perceived that others' names could
be vessels for other histories.[24] He entitled the third part of the first volume
of the *Recherche du temps perdu* "Place-Names: The Name" ("Noms de
pays: Le Nom"). Thinking about place names, he reached the same conclusion that de Certeau would reach about personal names: "How much
more individuality still did they assume from being designated by names,
names that were theirs alone, proper names like the names people have.
Words present us with little pictures of things, clear and familiar."[25]

It was Proust's obsessive interest in the aristocracy of his own day that
led him to think about names. But this also makes him an especially keen
guide to the meaning of names in premodern aristocratic Europe. As he
wrote in volume 3, the nobility are like "the learned, the etymologists of
the language, not of words, but of names." This study of names restored
to the aristocrats "their lost poetry."[26] Here we have found the "poetry"
of names that Gentil da Silva told us we would find in the merchant letters of the sixteenth and seventeenth centuries.

This attention to the liquid character of names is exactly the kind of
poetry one finds in Peiresc. Analyzing the conversation at the table of the
Duchesse de Guermantes, Proust noted how names stood for facts, events,
and places, and how they enabled him to wake the dead: "One could say
that history, even mere genealogy, restores life to old stones."[27] Proust was
more confident on this than T. S. Eliot, who thought of the "old stones
that cannot be deciphered"; he seems to warrant Momigliano's aside that
if antiquarianism were to revive anywhere in modern times it would be in
France.[28]

Proust envisioned history as a dense tangle of names, each bearing
a whole complex of associations. "Thus," he wrote, "the empty spaces
of my memory were covered by degrees with names which in arranging,
composing themselves in relation to one another, in linking themselves
to one another by increasingly numerous connexions, resembled those

finished works of art in which there is not one touch that is isolated."[29] Peiresc's abandonment of the clarity of the arborial model for the jungle-like thicket of left-to-right charts seems to illustrate such a vision.[30]

Paying attention to names is another way of acknowledging the centrality of curiosity in the exploration of the past. Proust, again, explored this in terms closer to our experience: the curiosity at work in attending to names and places is like amorous curiosity; "perpetually disappointed, it revives and remains for ever insatiable."[31] And then—brilliantly—as if to reassure those for whom the pursuit of facts about the past and of beauty in the fleshly present seems utterly antithetical, he concludes:

> But in this strange phase of love, an individual person assumes something so profound that the curiosity he now felt awakening in him concerning the smallest occupations of this woman was the same curiosity he had once had about History. And all these things that would have shamed him up to now . . . now seemed to him to be, fully as much as were the deciphering of texts, the weighing of evidence, and the interpretation of old monuments, merely methods of scientific investigation with a real intellectual value and appropriate to a search for truth.[32]

Proust lays bare, through this triangulation from genealogy to research via passion, what Benjamin, in his book on German tragic drama, called "the philosophical foundations of baroque philology." Benjamin's challenge to the philologists of his own time—in what was, perversely, his bid for entry into their guild—was to seek out the subterranean emotional resonances of historical exploration. What Proust shows us is that far from being "dead from the waist down," the passion for research—which he described as the antiquary's passion—is the passion for life itself.

8 ↝

The Problem of Detail

*P*roust signals for us that names are but a special case of a more general problem that we confront in Peiresc's letters: the profusion of detail. The skeptic—Proust casts him as a journalist— would say of all this detail that it was pointless, sure to be forgotten, if not tomorrow, then the day after. And yet, he writes, just across from the same newspaper column, "on page 3 does not the report of the Académie des Inscriptions speak often of a fact, in itself of smaller importance, of a poem of little merit, which dates from the epoch of the Pharaohs and is now known again in its entirety? Is it not, perhaps, just the same in our brief life on earth?"[1] Precisely because a lived life is full of detail, protests against too much detail in historical narration take us directly to the question of the relationship of research to life.[2]

Daniel Morhof, for instance, praising Gassendi's *Life of Peiresc* as the best biography of a nonpublic figure—neither a ruler nor a general—also felt the need to defend such works against what was seen already in the seventeenth century as their chief flaw: a surfeit of detail. Roland Maresius, in his *Epistolarum Philologicarum libri duo* (Paris, 1655), had condemned these biographies as "conglobations" of many details mixed together somewhat indiscriminately. Morhof's reply to Maresius was that all this information was potentially worthwhile and that the more information one provided the reader, the greater the book's potential "wisdom and utility."[3] In the lives of rulers it was understood that little things and "unexpected circumstances" were often telling, indications of some greater significance. "It is for this reason," Morhof concluded, "that I value the Life of the great Peiresc written by Gassendi, which in all parts scatters and branches out, that our man [Maresius] had strongly condemned as a *micrologion*."[4] If Morhof anticipates the chief rationale behind what we now call "microhistory," he might easily have done so on reading the life of a ruler, but he does not: instead, he draws on the life of a scholar, and none other than Peiresc.

Leibniz in the *Nouveaux essais sur l'entendement humain* (1703) also offered a rejoinder to the Maresiuses of the world: "I do not at all dismiss analyzing antiquities down to their smallest trifles, because sometimes the knowledge that critique extracts from them can serve more important things. I agree, for example, that one can write a whole history of clothing and of the art of tailoring from the uniforms of the Hebrew priests."[5] And yet, Leibniz came to feel that the proliferation of detail posed a problem that required some kind of answer.

His answer was the *Monadology* (1714). Its vision of how one monad related to other monads suggested a way in which a discrete event or fact could relate to the totality of events and facts. For Hayden White, "Leibniz could write history in an annalistic form because he believed that the dispersiveness of phenomena was only apparent; in his view, the world was one and continuous among its parts. Accordingly, his conception of the historical process . . . did not require that he distinguish between larger and smaller provinces."[6] Leibniz explains that "this connexion or adaptation of all created things to each and of each to all, means that each simple substance has relations which express all the others, and, consequently, that it is a perpetual living mirror of the universe." Moreover, simple substances can in some instances be acted upon and in others do the acting. Leibniz sees this as the definition of causation: "And one created thing is more perfect than another, in this, that there is found in the more perfect that which serves to explain a priori what takes place in the less perfect, and it is on this account that the former is said to act upon the latter."[7]

For nonclerical historians of the eighteenth century, the explicit theology of the *Monadology* undercut its value. And so the problem of detail remained. Voltaire, famously, used Gassendi the microhistorical biographer as the foil for his notion of what good history should look like: "God preserve me," he prayed, "from devoting three hundred pages to the story of Gassendi!"[8] More thoughtfully, perhaps, Johann Christoph Gatterer, professor of history at Göttingen and a pioneer in historical methodology, argued in 1767 that detail was essential because it was only with all these "facts" that our imagination could then work to reassemble the past—the "What was it like?" that enabled the reader to imagine himself into a lost world. Gatterer sought to forge a connection between erudition and imagination in an age when the novel reengineered the relationship between detail and the persuasiveness of storytelling.[9]

But detail remained a stumbling block into the next generation. Ludwig Wachler (ca. 1800) began his great history of historical erudition by acknowledging that his own "mikrologische Genauigkeit"—

"microscopic precision," though it might not be going too far to translate it as "microhistorical detail"—was not for everyone, but it was necessary for anyone who wanted a comprehensive understanding of historical development.[10] Wachler worried nonetheless. In his comment on the study of ancient monuments, he noted that among the Italians philology frequently led to "a preference for micrology and the often burdensome combination of disparate materials."[11]

One of Wachler's contemporaries, Frederick Rühs, the professor of history at the University of Berlin who taught the course on historical method that influenced every subsequent generation, was also deeply uncomfortable with detail. He sharply distinguished between antiquaries and historians, positing that the "art of history" lay in representing the detail made available by research, not presenting the research itself. In a sketch of the history of history writing in Europe, which included the Reformation-era turn to monuments and the Göttingen circle's work on chronology and geography, France was said to have produced only "critics" who, "if they often lost their way in *Micrologien,* still gave lots of foundational information, such as Ducange, Duchesne, Mabillon, etc."—antiquaries all.[12]

Another of Wachler's contemporaries, Goethe, in his *Materials for a History of Colour Theory,* tried to offer an explicit justification for the large amount of detail he presented to readers. His book was, he wrote, "like a kind of archive," and would function as a "commentary" on what he would later write.[13] Putting all the details forward was a way of acknowledging that embedding them in a narrative would inevitably deform them. He pointed to another biography by Gassendi, that of Epicurus, and held him up as a model writer of history trying to avoid imposing himself on his subject matter. And yet, Goethe was also keenly aware that his book would appear to some to offer far too much, and to others, far too little.[14]

Droysen, too, who more than any German historian in the direct line of descent from Ranke seems to have been aware of the challenges that nonliterary sources posed, also described his problem in terms of microhistory. In the unpublished part of the *Historik,* the handbook on methodology that grew out of his long-running lecture course on the subject, he argued that though there were many kinds of history, not all of them deserved to be written. Just because there were facts and stories did not mean that they could all be turned to a historical purpose: "It would be false to say that we can make out of every investigation of a given empirical occasion something called historical. It is, rather, trivial history [*kleingeschichtlich*]. It is micrology [*Mikrologie*] which sees the big things as small and the small as big."[15] In the end, we would have to conclude that Droysen could not escape from his own categories of analysis.

Friedrich Nietzsche's swingeing attack on antiquarianism may be much better known, but even his denunciation of the "meticulous micrologists" ("peinliche Mikrologen") climbing around "on the pyramids of monumental ages" seems to reflect Droysen's sense of disproportion between scope and subject matter.[16]

And yet, turning the argument ever so slightly around, Nietzsche goes on to say that "the small and limited, the decayed and obsolete receives its dignity and inviolability" from the antiquarian's researches.[17] And so, according to Raymond Geuss, when Nietzsche at the beginning of *On the Genealogy of Morals* (1887) praises "petits faits," or "small facts," he does so because he believes that when one studies them carefully one sees that the historical process is in fact "the historically contingent conjunction of a large number of such *separate* series of processes that *ramify* the further back one goes."[18] And so Alexander Nehemas concluded that for Nietzsche, genealogy "simply *is* history, correctly practiced," just as for Ginzburg's Robortello, history and antiquarianism are "synonymous."[19]

Aby Warburg, like Nietzsche, saw detail as Janus-faced. In his 1909 lectures he worried that Petrarch's interest in archaeological detail—the study of the pieces of the past—could be suffocating. (In 1929 he came back to this fear when he described the ancient world as being "archaeologically sterilized" at the hands of its students.) On the other hand, recapturing the past in its emotional fullness was still an antiquarian project.[20] It is but a short step from here to his famous declaration that God himself "lived in the details."

Walter Benjamin, at exactly the time Warburg was working this out in practice, sent a volume to Warburg in which he offered up a theoretical justification for "micrology." In a single (long) sentence in the "Epistemo-Critical Preface" to *The Origin of German Tragic Drama,* the thirty-three-year-old Benjamin compressed many of the ideas that would later emerge as his "Theses on the Philosophy of History." First, he likened "fragments of thought" to a mosaic's tesserae. Then he pointed not to the relationship of the fragments to one another, but to the invisible underlying scheme of the mosaic. Finally, and counterintuitively, he described the relationship of the visible to the invisible as inverse: "The value of fragments of thought is all the greater the less direct their relationship to the underlying idea, and the brilliance of the representation depends as much on this value as the brilliance of the mosaic does on the quality of the glass paste." Fragments of thought, like ruins of whole buildings or things, are greater the less they are mere illustrations—even though that illustrative value did exist and had to exist. It was this tension that made detail, of thought as of thing, central: "The relationship between the micrological treatment of the work and the proportions of the imagistic and intellectual whole demonstrates that truth-content is only to be grasped through immersion in the most minute details of subject-matter."[21]

With Benjamin, we have come out the other side of the long-running argument: detail is no longer a "problem" but the key to grasping the truth about the past. After Benjamin, we may look to his friend Siegfried Kracauer, who "under the spell of the living Warburg tradition" many decades later picked up this strand in arguing that "the higher the level of generality at which a historian operates, the more historical reality thins out."[22] This is the claim that Ginzburg then presented as an after-the-fact foundation for microhistory.[23]

There is one genre of modern intellectual inquiry in which we accept that there can never be too much detail: the novel. Cervantes, Fielding, and Sterne represent for us an apotheosis of the early modern commitment to detail, even representing their fictional writing as history and including, as in the prologue to *Don Quixote,* an extensive discussion of the meaning of history and of writing from sources. We might well say that the desire to reconstruct the past "as it really was" has been achieved—and *can be achieved*—only in fiction, and was achieved there long before Ranke formulated this as the goal of professional history. For only in the novel is it possible to know what everyone is thinking and doing, an experience of history which, as Ranke understood, was God's alone.

The novel functions by integrating microhistory and macrostructure (it calls the latter "plot").[24] Proust himself, at the end of his very long novel, addressed exactly this point. His first readers, those who read sketches of what would become his book, congratulated him on discovering his truths "with a 'microscope,' " while his detractors complained that he was only "sifting through endless detail."[25] Nabokov's *Pale Fire* represents an even more self-conscious reflection—it comes in the form of commentary, after all—on how much random detail could be heaped up without destroying the possibility of a coherent plot.[26] Braudel, at least as great a writer as he was a historian of the sixteenth century, saw the integration of a mass of detail into a vast canvas as *the* challenge of the new history: to translate "economics into history, that is, into human life."[27] And Ginzburg, another great historian-as-writer, has defended his use of narrative as an analytical tool by reference to the novel.[28] Collingwood is the most explicit in spelling out "the resemblance between the historian and the novelist." For him, it extended through points of method (narrative, description, analysis) and ambition (coherence, persuasiveness) to justification (imagination). As for imagination, Collingwood saw no difference between the scope and skill of the historian and the novelist other than that the historian must tell the truth.[29]

From this perspective, the jagged shape of Peiresc's archive—excerpta, reading notes, memoranda, a few draft essays, jottings after conversations, and thousands of letters—is closer to the experimental novel of the twentieth century than to the grand narratives of the nineteenth century. For in the study of the past it is the act of making a single coherent plot out of fragments that is the fundamental fiction. Peiresc the researcher failed to make all his pieces into a whole—at least this has been the judgment of posterity. But perhaps that failure is what makes his archive so precious to us: it takes us closer to the early seventeenth century than we might have been able to get had he succeeded at turning it all into a single story.

Long ago, Robert Alter made explicit the connection between the way early modern novelists such as Sterne and Diderot and modern ones such as Nabokov called attention to the act and artifice of writing.[30] Historians of the novel might have their own feelings about this argument, but historians of history will surely be struck by the parallel between the ways in which early modern antiquaries (and this trait is shared by their distant modern academic historian cousins) self-consciously alert readers to their presence ("when I was in the Forum in Rome I saw . . . ," "as I have stated above . . . ," "my thesis is . . .") at the expense of narrative illusionism. Both before 1750 and after 1900, one can match the periods when the novel called attention to itself and its mechanics with the prominence of nonnarrative, discontinuous, and predominantly thematic rather than diachronic forms of historical writing.

And it is no accident that this same period between approximately 1750 and 1900 was dominated by the realist novel *and* by grand historical narrative. The heyday of the realist novel with its fictive world-making corresponds exactly to the era of the grand narrative histories: the century from Gibbon to Burckhardt was also the century of Dickens and Hugo. Looking at the writing of history through the lenses provided by fiction, and specifically the various forms imaginative writing can take, may indeed make us aware of other ways of telling a story.[31]

Not every work of historical scholarship has to look the same—that is what studying the history of historical scholarship can show us. Even more, trying to grasp the methods, and maybe the madnesses, too, of seventeenth-century researchers with the tools and expectations of nineteenth-century historical practice makes the whole endeavor more difficult, a bit like trying to eat soup with a fork. Some bits might be caught, but they will be taken out of context *and* we will get no sense of what the whole once was. Of course learning—relearning—how to use a spoon is not so simple. It requires more than the historicism of Wilhelm von Humboldt or of Ranke, because it means acknowledging that the tools and the analytical categories we use are themselves historically conditioned. But the effort of writers and scholars such as Matthiessen, Farge, Schlögel, and Banham to create a literary style that does more for their subject matter than merely historicize it—that instead helps capture it—suggests that getting at the seventeenth century might just be best achieved by entering into the seventeenth century's ways of thinking and writing. Peiresc and his archive, so rich in details of practice and perception, happen to be an excellent resource for this experiment.

Grand narratives will not go away, because storytelling is a cognitive tool. But in our own fragmented time we understand that this tool comes in many sizes and shapes. Microhistorical narratives but also lists and tables can open up whole worlds, even if the worlds so discovered do not fit seamlessly together but are, like Benjamin's tesserae, clearly distinct, and clearly separated by the cement that holds them together.

9 ॐ

The Postal Link

*T*his Mediterranean of Peiresc, as vast as it was, was still vaster because it was connected to a land-based network, the postal web that brought him information from elsewhere in Europe and allowed him, in turn, to play the role of "Prince" of the Republic of Letters, as Marc Fumaroli so felicitously put it.[1] This was how Peiresc shared the news and objects that came in from across the sea. It was the singular genius of Braudel to have realized that "the Mediterranean" extended far to the north, south, east, and west of the inland sea. Recognizing the varied forms of this extension opened up a new vision of history. Yet it would not have seemed new to Peiresc, whose Mediterranean extended to landward contacts and byways.

Communication within the Mediterranean, at least between France and Italy, was conducted as much by land as by sea. In a letter to Marc Antonio Lumaga in Genoa, setting out the conditions of communication just after his return to the South in the fall of 1623, Peiresc explained that the "ordinarii" from Avignon departed on the first Thursday of every month, passing through Aix on the Friday. Because there were often delays at sea, Gaspard Signier had urged that Peiresc use Genoa as a transfer point between Rome and Marseille instead of attempting direct point-to-point maritime contact.[2]

The south of France was indeed singularly well served by crossing communication routes—merchant ships, papal galleys, and overland routes to Italy all converged in Provence. Peiresc benefited greatly from this, as we have seen. But he also realized how important it was to connect all of this to the north, especially via Paris. Gassendi presents Peiresc's role in establishing a regular service between Avignon and Lyon, whence it connected to the Paris *courrier*, as one of his great achievements.[3]

Gassendi's narrative can be compared with a record kept by Peiresc on the deliberations about establishing a regular service between Aix and Lyon. The baron de Tourres, premier consul of Aix, proposed creation of a regular service (hence "Ordinaire") that could take either of two distinct forms: by "express courier" door-to-door and by "a stage rider" who would hand off the mail to the next relay. Peiresc then emphasized the national security value of a working communications net. He cited the recent English attempt on the Île de Ré as the ever-present Protestant menace. Peiresc estimated the cost of the express courier at 3,480 livres per annum and the "Estafette," or stage rider, at 2,160 livres. These included all costs for paper and ink to make the packets and the office for their distribution. The assembly decided on the stage rider option and gave power to the consul to negotiate with M. Fontenay Jacquet the sieur de Fetan, royal councillor and intendant of the king's post at Lyon.[4] A contract was signed on 9 December 1627 between the "procureurs" of Provence on the one hand and the masters of the post of Aix and Lyon on the other. The Lyonnais agreed to effectuate a once-weekly transport of packets and letters between Lyon and Aix, departing Aix every Sunday and Lyon every Wednesday. For this service Provence allocated 2,000 livres per year, to divide equally between Lyon and Aix, with the cost fixed at 2 sous per ounce from Lyon to Aix with an additional 3 sous for the continuation from Lyon to Paris.[5]

This development enabled Peiresc to count on a seven- or eight-day postal travel time to Paris.[6] And while he counted the intendant, Fontenay Jacquet, as one of his collaborators (he handled Peiresc's book purchases and searched for missing shipments), this agreement made Peiresc somewhat independent of personalities.[7] A much smaller but similar achievement was the establishment of an Aix–Toulon "relais," in which Peiresc was also involved. This made the years of his retreat to Belgentier, when Toulon was the closer metropole, less difficult.[8]

Peiresc's exploitation of new regional services, as well as his adaptation of existing local and international communications vectors, is an example of a highly sophisticated practice.[9] His commitment to the post was rewarded: when the ordinaire from Lyon to Aix happened to be delayed, the "maître de la poste" sent a special "estaffette" to deliver letters just to him. But paying attention to Lyon, and getting better service as a result, also required an investment in the local end of the connection. And indeed we find indications of regular contact between Peiresc and M. Cayre, who was master of the post at Aix, though living in Marseille and only occasionally present at Aix.[10]

Even planning for de Thou's trip to the Levant, ca. 1628, we see that Peiresc remained heavily dependent on Lyon. Outlining to Valbelle, lieutenant of the admiralty, the best way to communicate with the Levant, Peiresc suggested sending via Lyon to Venice, where the ambassador could then readdress the package for Constantinople, to which it would travel by ship.[11] Peiresc used this same routing with Marcheville in the 1630s, though sometimes only as a parallel to a preferred seaborne carrier.[12] When there was no shipping, he turned without hesitation to the route from Lyon, utilizing as always M. Lieu, general of the posts, as his respondent. Five weeks was about the time it took for return post from Constantinople.[13] He suggested that correspondence *from* Constantinople could take the same route—by ship to Venice and overland via Lyon.[14]

We will have more to say about Venice later but, for example, in a letter to Gaffarel in Venice in the summer of 1633, Peiresc began, typically, by informing his correspondent that he had received a letter written in Venice on 28 July via the ordinaire of Lyon of 17 August. Peiresc then addressed Gaffarel's complaint that he had not written. One of his household reported that in the "bordereau" he saw, letters had been sent on 4, 19, and 25 July and 9 August, along with another from his cousin which was sent out in a simple envelope.[15]

The link to Italy was crucial. Traffic by sea from Livorno to the Provençal coast was regular. Genoa was a key crossroads. Avignon was especially important because of its papal extraterritoriality. Peiresc made sure to ingratiate himself with the town's messenger staff almost as soon as he took up residence again at Aix. In his log for November 1623, only a month after returning, we find a packet for Rome carried by the ordinaire of Avignon, who is then explicitly identified: "envoyé par Giraud messager ordinaire d'Avignon."[16]

The regular papal courier traveled from Avignon to Genoa and thence down the Tyrrhenian coast to Rome. In 1635, when the ordinaire was delayed, Peiresc wrote to Aycard explaining that, nevertheless, the Avignon courier remained the fastest route. We learn that he was now scheduled to depart from Avignon the first Wednesday of the month, stopping in Aix along the way. Letters reached Genoa in five or six days. But he could be delayed for weeks.[17]

Sometimes the longest delays in getting letters across the sea were generated at home. For instance, when de Gastines had to spend two months at court, the mail piled up in his house.[18] And sometimes there were problems getting the Avignon-based courier to stop at Aix to take on Peiresc's letters. In 1632 Peiresc complained to Jean-Marie Suares, bishop of Vaison and resident in the Barberini household in Rome, that the courier "absolutely refused," even though the addressee was Cardinal Barberini, and even though Peiresc gave half an écu for the bother of going from Avignon via Aix to Genoa. This "young rascal [*frippon*]," he complained, would not accept the letter from the hand of a Capuchin he had sent specially to do this. Peiresc being Peiresc, he did not hesitate to complain to the vice-legate. But to Suares he lamented that if this new status quo held, he would have to send his letters to Avignon a week before the departure of the ordinaire, slowing down the velocity of his network and devaluing it commensurately. Though there were other ways to send letters to both Avignon and Italy, they were less secure and more prone to mishaps.[19]

From Peiresc's correspondence we also learn of a plan to establish a regular route from France to Genoa and, potentially, on to Rome. This was the vision of M. de Lieu, successor of Jacquet, Sr. de Fetan, as intendant of the king's post.[20]

Sometimes, it was easier to send mail to Italy than to somewhere else in Provence. Carpentras, for example, was a place Peiresc could hardly send to conveniently "since the opportunities are so rare from here to Carpentras (where this city has no commerce) that it would have required too long waiting for the passage of knowledgeable people."[21] Nîmes was another city that was hard to reach from Aix; but here Peiresc had an important contact. Their letters help illuminate communication pathways in Provence. To Samuel Petit, his man in Nîmes, Peiresc explained that there were not many "commoditez" to communicate directly between their two cities. However, he continued, "Sr. de Gastines, one of the most celebrated of Marseille's merchants, who has come to see me here, assures me that there is such a good trade between Marseille and Nîmes that every day there are knowledgeable people who come and go from one place to another."[22] Gastines indeed did provide the connection to Petit, using two of his friends who were traveling there: Sr. Artaut, who was a draper, and a Sr. Grimaud. Peiresc added that when the Tarascon fair came to Nîmes, Petit was to inquire from the merchants of Nîmes who traded at Marseille about the cost of letters.[23]

Another way of connecting Aix with Nîmes was via Arles, with which both cities seem to have had better connections. Peiresc tried first via Beaucaire, which with its fair seemed likely, but it offered no better connections. Arles worked and the muleteer of Aix was comfortable going there; indeed, so happy—it seems—was he to work for Peiresc that he even offered to take the box of Arabic books directly to Petit's door. In the meantime, Peiresc noted that he would have the muleteer deliver the box to his relative in Arles, Chavary.[24] A separate but simultaneous letter to

Chavary filled him in on the plan, with his role being either to bring the box to Petit or to await his arrival. Peiresc asked him to open the case in the event customs officers wanted to charge him, and to tell them that it contained old books in Arabic for Petit to translate. (Taking no chances, Peiresc also wrote to the customs official of Nîmes, telling him that the books were being loaned to Petit from his private collection—the common binding in monographed red leather helped make this point—and were not part of a commercial transaction.)[25] In the end, Cousin Chavary brought the box to Nîmes.[26]

The difficulties Peiresc had in connecting with Petit forced from him a detailed presentation of the bureaucrats in charge of the post in that part of France. So now we know, too, that M. Cartier was master of the posts at Avignon who would readdress letters for Peiresc to M. Moreau in Aix, who was intendant and master of the royal couriers in Provence, adding that they were both "among my friends."[27]

10 ✍

The Last Mile (Mule Is King)

*A*s we just saw, Peiresc paid attention even to the smallest detail about how a package came to its recipient. And so, if we ask the question "How did things actually reach Peiresc's door?" we can expect an answer. If the items were small and light, they could be brought by individual visitors. Ship's captains, sailors, and *patrons* often made the short trip from Marseille to Aix with objects and letters. Aycard, in Toulon, could easily send to Belgentier materials arrived from overseas, such as a packet from Constantinople with letters from Galaup de Chasteuil and Théophile Minuti brought to him by a young man of Sixfours who had been scrivener on the barque of Patron Tourtel, also of Sixfours.[1]

Merchants, too, carried things to Peiresc's door. Grange of Marseille, for example, was the courier carrying to him a book from Cyprus that had come first to Danmartin.[2] Tarquet, consul for Syria and based in Marseille, came to Aix to talk to Peiresc, but Peiresc happened not to be there.[3] Sr. Berengier, the Marseille merchant who trafficked in North Africa, was prepared to carry a letter from Peiresc back to Marseille in his "magasin."[4]

Merchants were also, of course, major sources of news about ships come in. Peiresc, in turn, often counted on them to get their hands on his goods faster than might otherwise be the norm.[5]

When Théophile Minuti returned "en Chrestienté" he crossed from Civitavecchia to Marseille, but when passing Toulon he charged some fishermen to send his greetings to Peiresc and to Aycard.[6]

When the goods being communicated were bulkier, as they often were, they had to be carried by animal power, and, as we know already from Braudel, in the mountains of the Mediterranean, the mule was king.[7] Muleteers appear frequently in the Peiresc correspondence, sometimes with a name and sometimes without. In a letter of 1621 to Signier, merchant of Marseille and later Peiresc's merchant-banker there, Peiresc refers to "Lawrence mulletier d'Aix."[8] From Marseille, items often traveled to Aix by mule, even small items.[9] In 1635, the muleteer of Aix was named Pierre Artault.[10]

When Captain Bartolle arrived back in Marseille with objects acquired by Minuti for Peiresc in Egypt, and Peiresc wanted to get them as soon as possible, he tried to lure Bartolle out to Belgentier, suggesting "one has only to take some muleteer who knows the way by Aubagne, Cuges and Signes by which it is only 9 leagues from Marseille to here."[11] In the end, Peiresc decided to send his own lackey to pick up the case.[12] At Cuges, one of the villages on the south side of the range of the Sainte-Baulme, it was the chatelaine herself, Madame de Cuges, who oversaw the relay of books and cases to Peiresc.[13] From another letter to her, it appears that there was a daily departure of muleteers from Cuges to Marseille, and that Peiresc was utilizing it.[14] This would be an example of flexibility in the "system"—chased from his home, and his usual lines of communication, Peiresc reestablished another one centered on Belgentier and Toulon, rather than Aix and Marseille.

When Minuti returned from the Levant amid an outbreak of plague, Peiresc was keen to hustle him to Belgentier, both for Minuti's sake and to facilitate talking with him at greater length. Peiresc outlined a route that was more or less free of plague. He explained that he could not send a driver for him because it was "impossible" to find a person who would take the risk of going to Marseille. But once he made a decision about route, he was to send word via de Gastines, who was then waiting out the plague in Cassis, or Madame de Cuges or Monsieur Icard of Signes. If he left early enough in the morning, and if either Issaultier or Sardre—two *patrons* then in Marseille—gave him a beast, there would be no difficulty in arriving that same day.[15] Peiresc also used his relatives on his friends' behalf, mobilizing his cousin Astier to get letters written by Minuti to his brother-in-law in Barjols who would in turn deliver them to their final destinations.[16]

Two months later, hearing that Patron Alphant had returned from the Levant with a tub of dirt and plants for him, and had, because of the closure of Marseille as a result of plague, unloaded at Sanary just up the coast, Peiresc wrote that he would send a "wagon or some mules" ("charette ou des mulletz") to retrieve it.[17] Peiresc used a mule to send to Joseph Baulme in Marseille a box and letters to be shipped east. By the return mule, Peiresc received his letter. Note that one of Baulme's letters was written the morning of Peiresc's nighttime response, suggesting that the mule trip did not take longer than in the daytime hours.[18] Peiresc used the muleteer of Sisteron, one Melchior Magnan, to send to the merchant

Jean Venture in Marseille a case of books destined for Pierre and Jean Constans in Aleppo, on behalf of Father Celestin.[19]

When Peiresc needed to send a box of illustrated books to Marseille for transshipment to Albert in Egypt (who in turn was to send them on to Vermeil in Ethiopia), he was so pressed by the schedule of the muleteer that he complained to Jean-Baptiste Magy that he did not have time to wrap up the boxes properly.[20]

It seems that every town had its muleteers. We know already about the muleteers of Aix and Sisteron. In a letter to Samuel Petit of Nîmes we learn about those of Nîmes, as well as of the exigencies of mule travel. A book of Sicilian inscriptions sent by Petit came to Peiresc with the illustration missing and a terribly smoky smell. It arrived with the muleteer of Aix, who had picked it up in Marseille from a muleteer of Nîmes named Pierre Boulet. This Boulet told Peiresc that he had left the figure at the inn used by the muleteers—the Sign of the Eagle—with someone named Gregory. The mule had fallen or lain down in water—the ambiguity is in the story told to Peiresc—and the muleteer decided to leave it to dry out. Peiresc recounted to Petit that he immediately sent to the inn but that no account of the illustration was given to him by this Gregory or by Boulet. Peiresc asked Petit to inquire with the Marseille merchants of Nîmes.[21]

When Peiresc was in the country at Belgentier, he was even more dependent on the muleteer since there was no other means of communication and few travelers on the roads. When heavy rains discouraged his muleteer, he was tempted to borrow the one of a "Sr. Chaullan," who was going directly to Marseille.[22] When Vallavez was in Lyon, Peiresc received letters from him via "the muleteer and the horse groom" by "a *voiturin* of Toulon" and a "*messager* of Toulon."[23]

The muleteer could also be a source of information. Jean Bernard, muleteer of Riez, not only brought Peiresc an inscription that was found there; he also provided Peiresc with information. "He said," Peiresc jotted down in his log of outgoing correspondence, that there was wagon traffic between Riez and the Durance where at a particular house—seemingly a ruin—large, fallen stones were being scavenged for building materials.[24]

But sometimes the mule train broke down. Denis Guillemin told Peiresc in April 1629 that a large, inscribed stone incorporated into the Church of the Cordeliers in Riez and earmarked for Peiresc was sent by mule. But the muleteer was so afraid of the weight of "such a big burden on the back of his mule" that Guillemin decided to leave the stone at the nearby home of an acquaintance, whom he asked to hold it until the return of the other muleteers who had stronger mules.[25]

Aside from the muleteers, for delivery to nearby destinations Peiresc often depended on friends. Thus, for example, for Marseille, when Peiresc was writing to Jean-Baptiste Magy, he might send the mail with someone else, such as "M. Pisciolini," telling him to deliver it to a third person, in this case a M. Bovis. It would be his responsibility to see that the letter got to Magy.[26] De Thou's goods, once fished out of the sea, were sent by de Gastines to Peiresc with a "porteur"—later described as a "muletier"—named Claude Roulé. For three boxes, one large, one with a cover, and one with a crocodile, he asked "two quarters of an escu." De Gastines also paid 2 sous for the cost of his lodging.[27] Sometimes, when Peiresc was in a rush, for instance if he feared that a ship would sail before his letters reached it, he would send a man overnight from Aix to Marseille. Leaving at night, one could arrive at Marseille "at the opening of the gate" ("porte ouvrant").[28] On a horse one could even go from Aix to Marseille for lunch and be back by the evening. That is how close they were.[29]

II ֍
Marseille's Merchants

*H*alf a century ago, Franz Bierlaire devoted a fascinating short book to the problem of identifying the anonymous, almost invisible helpers who made Erasmus of Rotterdam a learned celebrity.[1] We have since become much more attentive to the importance of these marginal figures and their role in large-scale narratives.[2] Peiresc's Mediterranean is a "whole world of *patrons* and small-scale merchants," whether Sicilian, Maltese, Corsican, or Marseillais, who functioned as commercial and cultural intermediaries. These men were able to open doors in different lands by speaking different languages to different sorts of people.[3] Wolfgang Kaiser has, in particular, pointed to the leading role taken by Marseille merchants in the late sixteenth century, serving as the "front" for a coalition of Roman and Neapolitan confraternities looking to ransom back Europeans seized and brought to Algiers.[4]

This is the world opened onto by Peiresc's archive. Marseille and its *système portuaire*/portuary complex can be studied through his archive as through no other single contemporary source. We see exposed the human community (merchants, factors, bankers, agents, brokers, officials, captains, mariners, etc.), the built environment (docks, warehouses, offices), and the physical surroundings (harbor, bay, roads). We know little about any of this for the 1620s and 1630s in Marseille.[5] The recent and very welcome burst of scholarship on movement and exchange in the Mediterranean has completely skipped over Marseille. Nor do we have any sense of the merchant society of Marseille at the time, and certainly not of its members as individuals. From the Peiresc archive, however, we can at least make a start at sketching in some of the necessary details toward an understanding of how Marseille functioned as a knowledge community.[6]

Peiresc and his brother were routinely in Marseille. On a visit to Marseille in 1631, for example, Vallavez mentions all those he had seen: Tarquet, the younger Bermond, de Gastines, l'Empereur, Granier, Vias, and Fort.[7] But who were all these people?

A historian wishing to explore the merchant community of Marseille in the first half of the seventeenth century would turn to a limited number of public documents. Surviving notarial records enable us to identify individuals and their parents through lists of marriage.[8] Records of the admiralty present merchants at specific formulaic moments: insuring their departing merchandise, listing their returning merchandise, when some relationship to another merchant was acknowledged or broken, or when things fell apart and legal recourse had to be taken.[9] But with these records—and they happen to be limited for the period from 1620 to 1640—we would know these men only in their commercial function: merchants as economic actors.

Even here, because of the scholarly focus on Marseille in its later years of glory—not coincidentally much better served by the archival record—we know very little of the economic activities of these men as a group. And as for their broader interests? We know almost nothing. The great volumes of merchant letters published by Braudel and the Centre de Recherches Historiques in the 1950s are about business correspondence. Where the personal juts in, as in the ne plus ultra of this genre, the exactly contemporary *Merchant of Prato* (1957), it is just that, an interruption. But rarely, because of who the writers were and—perhaps even more—who the recipients were, do we learn much about the intellectual aptitudes, dispositions, and interests of these merchants. Even Iris Origo's magical portrait of Francesco Maria Datini eludes us somewhat on this score.

Not so in the Peiresc archive. Here, because of the unusual disposition of the letter-writer—a scholar interested in merchants and valuing the intellectual virtues that a successful merchant could bring to his own enterprise—we learn an astonishing amount about the participation of merchants in intellectual projects (see Section 31, "Merchants as Intellectual Collaborators").[10] And because so much of Peiresc's intellectual venture is carried out overseas, these letters also tell us a great deal about commercial life, though, to be sure, they will not tell us everything that a ship carries, only what interests him.

In the Peiresc archive we find a whole other side of the "merchant function," a side that we would in no way have been able to anticipate or divine from those public documents alone. When a ship comes in from Alexandretta or Alexandria and an accounting is given of the goods on board, the letters, books, and crocodiles are never mentioned (just to choose some random examples). From the point of view of the documentary collection system of that time, the activities of Peiresc do not exist.

And yet Peiresc, inversely, does tell us something about economic life. Because of the poor survival and poor preservation of commercial documentation for the early seventeenth century in Marseille and because of Peiresc's dependence on traffic for the movement of his goods, his letters are full of data that, in the absence of a dense public record, present economic historians with valuable information. For example, we possess entry records for the port of Marseille only for the years 1634–1637, and maritime assurance contracts only for 1631–1635. But we have Peiresc's log of outgoing correspondence for the entire period through 1632 and, of course, we have the letters themselves, which can be read and digested for this kind of information.

The first thing that the Peiresc archive tells us for "economic history" is *who* constitutes his network. This account of Peiresc's Mediterranean can also stand as a contribution to the history of Marseille's merchants as people, and to that of their commercial life as much broader than the buying and selling of goods alone. There is only small comparison between Peiresc's Marseille merchants and the great Tuscans of the late Middle Ages and Renaissance, such as Datini, Francesco Sassetti, and Giovanni Rucellai, yet in both cases we find men of wealth prized also for their knowledge of the world.

Let us begin with a sample document, a single letter from Peiresc to Santo Seghezzi in Cairo. Peiresc began by telling him that the letter was coming to him under a cover addressed by Peiresc to Gela, his relative. It came on the barque of François Taxil, which sailed on 17 May and brought letters from Jean-Baptiste Magy. Peiresc explained that he knew from a letter of Seghezzi to Esperit Laurens in Alexandria that the latter had received packages from Peiresc for Jean Magy and Jacques Albert, as well as one for himself. Since all of this went from Marseille to Alexandria in the ship of Captain Laure, and from Alexandria to Cairo under the care of Captain Abeille of La Ciotat, to whom both Laure and Laurens consigned their packages, they all should have been received.[11]

This is an utterly unremarkable letter. But the density of names and the movement of names is the story of the letter. There are thousands of passages like this in Peiresc's letters. These passages ought to remind us of similar ones in the letters of the Cairo Geniza studied by Goitein. As for Marseille, Wolfgang Kaiser's observation that it is "in the sixteenth century, a 'transit city' which attracts visitors and pilgrims, travellers passing through and important people" is equally true for the early seventeenth century.[12]

Who were Peiresc's Marseille contacts? Some were intellectuals. We know the most about them. The rest were commercial actors, and of them we know much, much less. Indeed, as people we know them only from the Peiresc archive. But one thing we do know is that these were personal, not purely profitable or professional relations. Glimpses are usually all we get of this world.

The intellectuals included Charles Cassagnes, Baltasar de Vias, and Antoine de Ruffi. We possess many of the letters to Peiresc written by both Cassagnes and Vias, and most were published in the nineteenth century in Tamizey de Larroque's occasional series of *Les Correspondants de Peiresc*.[13] Cassagnes was one of Marseille's leading doctors, and amid the troubles of the civil wars he was sent to Rome as the city's delegate in negotiations with the pope.[14] In the Peiresc archive, he is mentioned as early as 1609 as doctor to Guillaume du Vair, whose secretary Peiresc was at the time.[15] He later provided Peiresc with an Arabic calendar taken from a captured corsair. He seems to have known enough Arabic to distinguish between its western and eastern hands.[16] He was still active in 1637.[17]

Baltasar de Vias is probably the best-known Marseille culture figure of the first half of the seventeenth century. His neo-Latin poetry was the local voice celebrating the great national figures, such as Henri IV or Louis XIII, and local ones, such as Peiresc.[18] He was also the absentee consul in Algiers, inheriting the title and the revenue stream from his father in 1627.[19] This involved him in questions of trade and communication of a fairly high level—parlement, king, and court (he was eventually named *conseiller d'État* in 1647). Vias provided Peiresc with news about ill-judged renovations at Saint-Victor that destroyed an old tomb, and copies of the inscriptions found there.[20] And his collection of coins from Arab lands made his home the center, for a time, of Europe's study of Islamic numismatics.[21]

Of Antoine de Ruffi, the first historian of Marseille, the Peiresc archive yields less.[22] We know they knew each other, as letters asking Peiresc for help with some documents survive, and also gratefully acknowledging Peiresc's mastery of these source materials.[23] Peiresc, in turn, identified coins presented to him—like the one of King Louis, governor of Sicily and Count of Provence, married to Queen Marie.[24] He explained, in a subsequent letter, that the coins of Marseille were also struck with the name and in the image of the counts of Provence.[25] We have a list of manuscripts in a volume Peiresc sent him in August 1636.[26] None of this help was acknowledged in Ruffi's printed *History of Marseille*.[27] (Peiresc also transmitted letters from Ruffi to his brother, Pierre, who was traveling to Rome in spring 1630.)[28]

High-level government administrators, such as the governor of Provence, Charles de Lorraine the duc de Guise, and the lieutenant of the admiralty, Barthélemy de Valbelle—an appointee of du Vair—appear in Peiresc's circle, but more as colleagues than collaborators. We encounter also lower-level officials, the notaries and clerks who managed the document treasuries that Peiresc drew upon again and again. "Sr. Prat" of Marseille made copies for him of materials in St. Victor; Pierre Astier worked for Peiresc in the archives of Aix; Elzias Arfeuille, royal notary in Arles, attested to the accuracy of dozens of excerpts of medieval charters there.[29] More shadowy still were the translators, whom we know from glancing references to have been based in Marseille, such as Honoré Suffin, Said of Taroudant, and Salomon Casino.[30]

Now we come to the merchants. And here we can introduce some terminological specificity. For in the Peiresc archive we are dealing with a maritime orientation, with merchants who travel extensively or whose agents were permanently based abroad. Shipping and the sea dominate their existence. In a document reporting on the finances of the French merchant community in Alexandria the authors, who were themselves merchants, introduce two specific terms: "Marchands patrons & Mariniers negotians": merchants who were the *patrons,* or owners, of ships, and sailors who were trading on the side.[31] Another document from the consulate of Alexandria refers to the categories of "residents, captains, *patrons,* scriveners, officers, seamen" ("Residantz, cappitaines, patrons, escrivains, officiers, mariniers de vaisseaux").[32] With this terminological precision we are directly on the terrain studied so masterfully by Biagio Salvemini in a series of essays that focus on the meaningfulness of the vocabulary of merchant identification—*marchand, patron, négociant*—in the seventeenth and eighteenth centuries. And though he focuses on the later period, the depth of his work suggests the likelihood of continuity of categories.[33] Peiresc's Marseille provides us a snapshot of a society about to undergo a dramatic transformation.

We can also locate some of these people in space, as well. Robert Ruffi, a notary and grandfather of the future historian of the city, left a precious document that clarifies the urban sociology of later sixteenth-century Marseille: "All the fishermen, the men of the marine, and some of the merchants," as well as "the strangers, come by sea" and those "going to travel to the Levant, Ponant and elsewhere," were said to live in the Quarter of St. Jean, near the outlet of the port to the sea. We know that Peiresc had contacts there as well.[34]

Sometimes this seaborne vocation was pointed more at one location than another: Egypt, say, rather than Syria. Others are specifically *not* identified with a place. Still others were more important for work they did for Peiresc in Marseille.

Louys Vento is associated in Peiresc's archive with a memorandum listing collectors with Near Eastern objects.[35] He was the scion of a great aristocratic trading family, and son of the former vice-consul in Alexandria whose letter from there to the consuls of Marseille in 1607 survives.[36] We also know about him from a letter Peiresc wrote to Vallavez in 1625 in which Vento is identified as the first consul of Marseille, and as "a curious man who has very nice 'singularities' and who completely obliged me on the last visit I made to Marseille, this past Holy Week, having not only shown me his cabinet, but having put at my disposal certain little curiosities of the world."[37]

But far the two most important figures for Peiresc's Marseille-based project were Pierre Fort and Gilles Mass (or Mace) de Gastines. Peiresc described Fort as "one of the most honest citizens of the city and to whom one can consign this affair, and any other even bigger, believing that he will serve you loyally in it."[38] We know, too, that he was respected enough to be chosen *viguier* of Marseille in 1642 and was suggested by the court of the parlement to manage the affairs of a barque put at the disposal of Sanson Napollon for sending to Algiers in 1627.[39] Fort worked closely with de Gastines, and their relationship is evoked in letters to Peiresc's agents overseas. To Guillame d'Espiot in Rome, for example, Peiresc explained that he was forwarding on a letter of Sr. Fort for François Marchand and that all the costs were to be defrayed by de Gastines in Marseille.[40] Beyond this, we know little about him. He is rarely discussed by Peiresc in letters to others, though often mentioned. We possess only two letters from him to Peiresc and two letters to him.[41] Yet in them we get a glimpse of a whole other dimension of Peiresc's life. We discover, for instance, that he sometimes wrote to Fort several times a day.[42] Yet none of these letters survive. In the public archives, Fort appears as an occasional investor in maritime insurance, de Gastines even less.[43]

Peiresc relied on Fort as a receiver and dispatcher. Thus, for example, books that Peiresc was sending to Mallon at Damascus were first sent to Fort in Marseille. He was then to inquire into available shipping to Alexandretta, and to talk to Mallon's kinsman, the apothecary Thibault, to be sure of the correct address. Peiresc also left specific requests for information which he would then record for later use, such as the name of the ship chosen, the name of the captain, the name of the person charged with the packet, and its estimated time of departure. Some of this was needed so as to prepare in time for the sailing; the rest, one suspects, in case of trouble later.[44] When the first of the Samaritan Pentateuchs reached Marseille in the possession of Patron Aurivelier, it was Fort who was to retrieve it and hire a muleteer to get it to Peiresc. When the muleteer was reluctant, it was Fort who offered to accommodate him overnight in his own home.[45] Providing these sorts of services on Peiresc's behalf was how Fort served.

De Gastines is, if anything, an even more mysterious figure. We do not, for instance, ever find his first name being used by Peiresc. There are also only a handful of letters that survive, each very much dealing with practical matters in medias res and none of them revealing much about the man.[46] And yet this was the most fundamental of Peiresc's relationships: de Gastines spent his money for him and handled his port tasks in Marseille. When things arrived addressed to anyone in Peiresc's world, it was de Gastines who took over. When the Maronite Father Michael of Damascus wrote, simply, "Théophile Minuti. Minime. Marseille," it was to de Gastines that the envelope was delivered.[47]

Nor is he a more prominent person in the public archives of Marseille. We find only one mention of a "De Gastines" in the *état civil* in Marseille for the entire seventeenth century: the marriage of our Gilles Mass on 15 September 1643.[48] "Gilles Mace de Gastines" is identified in the long, printed royal declaration of 1648 ending efforts to enforce a 5 percent tax on Marseille merchants in the Levant.[49] Two other documents of this sort, dated 19 March and 2 April 1641, also refer to a "Julles de Gastines" or a "Masse de Gastines."[50] He is present in the merchant record, but it is a lighter impact, at least in what I have seen, than what was made by some of his contemporaries.[51] We find him importing goods—two bales of hides and two containers of wine ("vin de Gomet") from Rome on the tartane of Pierre Gallo in 1636,[52] and exporting them—forty-five barrels of wine—on the barque of Patron Jacques Calmet, also in 1636. This latter was charged to "the account of Lambert & Gastines" as were goods on the boat of Captain Jean Damian returning from Alexandria on 30 July 1636.[53]

Other merchants also appear regularly in Peiresc's archive.

Leonard Danmartin, a "Merchant in bulk living on the shore near the *Place Neuve*," offered to help Peiresc in late 1626. His first commission was to find Peiresc some cheese: about half a dozen of those "little Marzolino or cheeses of Florence in the shape of a bottle" ("petitz Marzolin ou fromages de Florence en forme de bouteille"). To this, Peiresc added an order for some Roquefort from Languedoc.[54]

Danmartin was also a respondent and "particular friend" of Espannet, vice-consul in Cyprus, to whom he wrote on behalf of Peiresc.[55] Peiresc also asked the titular consul of Syria, Viguier in Marseille, to write to Espannet on his behalf.[56] Peiresc asked Danmartin, in reply to an earlier letter of Espannet's, to obtain a list of his finds in Cyprus, and their prices. Peiresc offered to subsidize the cost of this secretarial work and told Danmartin that he was authorized to purchase, without the need for consultation, any book that was not too expensive and was written on parchment in Greek, French, or Latin, or even on old paper if in those languages.[57] In May 1628 Viguier reported receiving a letter from Espannet reporting that he had sent a book to Peiresc from Cyprus to the address of Sr. Danmartin, from whom Viguier promised to retrieve it.[58] The "book" was none other than *Assises of Jerusalem*.[59]

Jean Guez (referred to sometimes in the public record as Jehan Gués) was based in Marseille. He had a brother in Constantinople named Guillaume. The two constituted a major correspondence axis and were key vehicles for the funding of François-Auguste de Thou and Théophile Minuti when traveling.[60]

Giovanni Alvise (or Alviggi) Gela was a relative of Santo Seghezzi in Cairo, of Venetian extraction.[61] He also worked closely with Jean Magy. So, in a letter written from Marseille in February 1637 he passed along the thanks of Magy (he does not say whether the one in Cairo or Marseille) for Peiresc's good wishes upon the birth of his nephew. Being able to do Peiresc's bidding had "brought him unequaled joy" and Gela wished him "quiet for his soul" ("la quiete a lei nel spirito").[62] He provided Peiresc with information about Egyptian weights and measures in 1634, most probably derived from Seghezzi.[63]

Baptiste Tarquet was consul for Syria from the time of Minuti's first expedition onward.[64] When planning it, Peiresc had Tarquet draft a "To Whom It May Concern" letter to accompany Minuti, asking the recipient to give him all possible assistances with accommodation, passage, and whatever acquisitions of "ancient curiosities that M. the Councillor Peiresc wished to recover" ("curiositez anciennes que M. le Conseiller de Peiresc desire de recouvrer"). That the letter was dated "Aix" suggests it was written while Tarquet was visiting Peiresc.[65]

Jean Venture seems chiefly to have handled de Gastines's communications to Aleppo and was bound up either by business or by blood with Jean and Pierre Constans of Aleppo. Peiresc turned to him with questions about specifically Syria-destined or -originated objects. Thus, for example, it was Venture in 1635 who sent on letters from Father Celestin and the merchants Constans and Baltasar Claret in Aleppo to Peiresc. When still looking for a delayed letter from the Capuchin Michelange de Vendôme, Peiresc asked Venture to check with the superior of the Capuchin convent in Marseille. Meanwhile, M. Constans had written that there was on the *St. Victor* under the charge of Captain de l'Ourme a packet of books and another of plants, and Peiresc was worried—it was November—that the plants would not last through a quarantine. He asked Venture to try to extract them from the *Intendantz de la Santé,* where he had already failed. In the meantime, he was drawing up replies for Aleppo to be sent along with Patron Jean Lombardon, and some others for Captain Rigault, if he had not yet departed.[66] Thus were the responsibilities that Peiresc imposed upon one of his Marseille contacts.

Antoine Piscatoris, a merchant plying the Levant route, returned to Marseille in mid-October 1629 with a letter from Minuti for Peiresc. Piscatoris had a legal favor to ask of Peiresc. Peiresc advised formulating his request as a letter which he would then send to M. Fort or M. de Gastines, who, in turn, would convey it to either Judge Chabet at Toulon or Commander de Forbin at Aix.[67] Another Levant merchant, Grange, was also brought in as a witness to Piscatoris's character.[68] Peiresc, in turn, wrote on his behalf not only to Lieutenant de Valbelle, but, in his absence, to de Valbelle's mother, praising the just-back-from-the-Levant merchant.[69]

One addressee, Mallon, in Damascus, had his own respondent in Marseille, the master apothecary Thibault. Thibault transmitted to Peiresc the three packages of coins sent by Mallon, Aymini, and Minuti, as well as a box of curiosities. Peiresc, in turn, offered to obtain for Thibault, with the assistance of their mutual friend (and Thibault's "voysin") Pierre Fort, the drugs that Mallon wanted. In fact, Peiresc even suggested provisioning these drugs on Marseille ships stopping at Toulon for supplies on their way to Sidon—Sidon being, apparently, on the direct route to Damascus.[70] With the outbreak of plague in 1630, Peiresc warned Mallon that the *commis* of Marseille were scattering along the Provençal coast. He suggested that Mallon send duplicates of his letters to Fort and Thibault at Marseille and Aycard and Chabert at Toulon.[71] Thibault delivered to Peiresc letters from Mallon and Aymini. Peiresc explained that the Recollet Father Aymini could bring back any coins that Mallon would purchase for him. Estelle in Sidon, who covered Minuti's purchases, could do the same for him there; in any event, when Tarquet was next in Syria he would reimburse Mallon's expenses.[72] Also in Sidon was Charles Blanc, a merchant who aided Minuti. Minuti himself had most recently written from Sidon saying that Charles Blanc was charged with sending raisins and bananas on the *Grand Henry*.[73] Honoré Marquesi, with whom Peiresc had arranged credit for Aymini, was Blanc's uncle.[74]

Another of those who had assisted Aymini and Blanc in Sidon was the Tuscan baron d'Alegre, sent to Lebanon to negotiate with Fakhr al-Din. Peiresc wrote to the baron d'Alegre in Livorno on his return, extending thanks, both for helping his people and for the information on the gardens of "Facardin."[75] Simultaneously, Peiresc wrote to a French merchant at Livorno named Claude Chastaignier, asking him to recover from the baron d'Alegre some little trees brought in one or two tubs and carried on the same Flemish boat as the baron.[76] This reminds us of Peiresc's preference for northern shipping, as well as of the French network in Italian ports.

The Syrian network is exposed also in its failure. For though a crucial person, de Gastines was not perfect. In a letter to Father Celestin of May 1636 we see Peiresc apologizing for letters and mémoires on eclipse observation that had piled up in Marseille in October and November 1636, and older ones, too, from April and May, "since Sr. de Gastines forgot to tell you in advance of a trip he was taking to Paris."[77] Worse still, when he returned, he found these letters in his "contoir" and made excuses, sending them all to Sr. Venture, who gave them to Lombardon. All were then lost with his ship.[78]

Jean l'Empereur (sometimes Lempereur), who traded at Constantinople, had been appointed consul-general in Jerusalem by Louis XIII on 13 July 1621, arrived in Constantinople in April 1622, and reached Jerusalem on 2 December 1623. He immediately ran into difficulties with the Franciscans and those who accused him of conspiring with Fakhr al-Din. He was deported to Damascus and imprisoned. He was released at the end of October 1624 and left Jerusalem for good on 8 January 1625.[79] He had a large and valuable collection of curiosities and a nephew at Marseille of the same name.[80] Peiresc thanked him for "the curious news" about the gems possessed by his cousin that had come from Georgia, India (Mogor), and Moldavia. Peiresc was pleased to know of his impending return "en Chrestienté," that is, Europe. The passage of an otherwise unidentified M. de la Rivière afforded him the opportunity to write.[81]

Barthélemy Issaultier was a very close collaborator of Peiresc's. He was also, and not atypically, very active in local politics. Vallavez wrote to Peiresc in mid-October 1633 from Marseille that Patron Issaultier had arrived, though leaving his ship in the Isles d'Yeres "to run to the election of the consuls, being of the number of the electors of the city." He brought Peiresc some candied almonds, though he preferred them ripened on the tree.[82] In 1635, when de Gastines was away and preoccupied, it was Issaultier who extracted two cases that had come from Aleppo on the *Ste. Claire* and were stuck in quarantine.[83] He had a relative named Jean whom we discover trading in Italy (Genoa and Venice).[84]

Benoit Pelissier enters the record described as a knight of Marseille ("escuier"), offering his offices to the Fathers Daniel Aymini and Joachin da Goa in the east.[85] A little later he was writing from Aix seeking a meeting with the comte de Marcheville, just then gone on pilgrimage to the sanctuary of the Magadalen on the Sainte Baulme; Peiresc offered to help, and expressed interest in some amethysts Pelissier was selling.[86] In July 1631, on the verge of another trip to Italy, Pelissier paused long enough to report to Peiresc on various artifacts that had just come to him by way of Cairo. There was "a Chinese porcelain god" similar to one owned by Peiresc. Pelissier gave it to M. de Gastines to pass along to Peiresc; in exchange, de Gastines offered Pelissier "the sword that he bore behind his left shoulder," another that was "all gilded," and his bonnet and long robe. De Gastines also gave him a short dagger *(poignard pistolet)* that he said belonged "to the late chief priest of Mecca."[87] Peiresc promised to come to Marseille to look at the Chinese idol, once plague conditions had lifted.[88] To de Gastines, at the same time, Peiresc wrote asking him to communicate his indebtedness to Pelissier.[89]

During Peiresc's extended plague-driven retreat to Belgentier, it was a Toulon-based network that served him, and the "last mile" led there, and not to Aix. The cast of near-anonymous actors also changes. For instance, an otherwise unnamed Berard was responsible for getting a box of Greek medals from Sidon off the boat and into the hands of de Gastines, who got it to Peiresc's lackey.[90]

Michel Tourtel (or Tortel), sieur de Ramatuelle, of Sixfours near Toulon was also a regular traveler to the East. With Marseille closed by plague and Peiresc's network relocated to Toulon, Sixfours became an important alternate for him. In 1633, Tourtel was a *patron,* owning, not "merely" piloting, a craft. He was capable therefore of also serving a banking role, and furnished credit to Jean Magy in Cairo.[91] Peiresc recorded his *armoiries*—reminding us that commerce and aristocracy did not always diverge, even in France.[92] His was a seafaring family: we learn from another document of a brother or cousin who fought four Dutch ships to a standstill in the Bay of All Saints in Brazil in 1634.[93]

Even when disrupted, Peiresc's system kept functioning. The passage through Belgentier of the Portuguese New Christian jewelers Manuel da Costa Casseretz and Fernand Nunes left a trail in Peiresc's archive (see Section 35, "Where Mediterranean Meets Orient"). Peiresc thanked Christofle de Bermond for the care he had taken with Sr. Fernandez "au fonds du Levant," and for the letters Peiresc had addressed to him and da Costa. The maintenance of ties with the Portuguese East, Peiresc commented to Bermond, was a "mark of good faith" that stood out as an exception "that does great shame to the Christians who do not know how to comport themselves as worthily as the infidels."[94]

Just as Peiresc created an informal network of merchants and French Capuchins to do his work in the Levant, when those same Capuchins needed communications they piggybacked upon the merchant backbone. Luguet, d'Armand, Pisctoris, and de Gastines, for example, were explicitly mentioned as possible respondents by Michelange de Nantes, writing to Raphael de Nantes in July 1632, before taking ship to the Levant. Peiresc also gave Robert Contour as the person in Aleppo to whom letters of exchange for the missionaries should be addressed.[95]

Libertat Sacco and Durand were other key figures in Peiresc's Marseille world in the mid-1620s. Durand was a brother-in-law of Pierre Fort, as was the poet Vias.[96] Durand held the office of consul in 1626.[97] What is most telling is a series of very brief notes from them to Peiresc in the summer of 1626. Some of them are not dated but *timed*—"vendredy a quatre heures de soir," "ce dimanche a midy"—suggesting an extreme frequency and regularity of correspondence, just as we have seen with Fort and de Gastines.[98] Contact between these men was so frequent that dates were not needed.

Then there are the almost unknown parts of Peiresc's knowledge community, people like "M. de St. Jacob," who collected from the quayside three cases for Peiresc that had come on the *St. Victor* from Syria. Peiresc recalled his late father, and then asked that special care be taken with the plants that were likely to be uncomfortable with the northern cold (the letter was written in late November). But St. Jacob was only a small cog in a large wheel; Peiresc had actually tapped Issaultier to arrange for delivery.[99] Or Bovis, whom Peiresc met after he was shown a relation about the taking of a whale by an unnamed sacristan and received the latter's permission to send it on to Peiresc.[100] Bovis was one of those invisible figures who held networks together. For example, he writes to Peiresc in March 1637, "I have given your letter to M. Magy, which M. Pisciolini brought to us, and asked to bring it to the man [Jean Magy] to whom he sent for you the little box and the pot of sherbet."[101] In the same way, when the loss of a ship between Livorno and Marseille seriously touched Jean-Baptiste Magy and de Gastines, Bovis felt he could not "dare" to ask for the peach pits Peiresc wanted.[102] He seems also to have been part of the network Peiresc used to get materials to Ruffi, then writing his history of Marseille.[103] Pisciolini was himself a much more significant figure, but he is only mentioned incidentally here, and then once more, in a memorandum on the fruits and vegetables Peiresc wished to acquire from Chios. Pisciolini, scion of an important sixteenth-century Marseille family, was to be the addressee of said items in Marseille.[104]

Artisans also show up, active, in Peiresc's archive. For instance, an otherwise unidentified Gilly, who may have been Dr. Cassagnes's factotum, is thanked for having so well made three lead impressions of an Arabic inscription that they could then be given to Honoré Suffin, royal translator in Marseille, for him to translate.[105] Then there was an Antoine Escouard, master goldsmith of Aix, who weighed out for him on 20 January 1633 the two Greek-inscribed vessels found at Vallauris.[106] A "Maitre Aman," later described in full as "Claude Aman" and an embosser who worked with metal, was sent for from Toulon to repair his ancient silver phiole, which had been dented by those who dug it up.[107] Nor should we view this close relationship to artisans as at all exceptional. For when Peiresc is seeking out just the right kind of leathers, probably for covering his books, he writes that the "craftsmen are among my best friends."[108]

Finally, there are the bare names. Some are listed in an inventory of coin collectors from whom Peiresc made purchases: from "Jacques Palle, goldsmith," a native of Toulouse residing in Marseille on 4 April 1625; from "Gilles, servant of Dr. Cassagne" on 1 September 1625; from "the goldsmith Provins" of Toulon on 1 June 1625; from "Patron Chaillan, these days."[109] From the letters to Vallavez we learn of a "Maitre Giraudon, notaire de Marseille"; a "Sr. Pichenat of Marseille, who knows something of botany"; a "bonne femme de Marseille" named Jannote Fauchiere who is "a lady in waiting of Madame de Bourgoigne"; and the death of "Prost, merchant of Marseille."[110]

But, in particular, two letters of Peiresc to Vallavez, written in 1626 when Vallavez was in Marseille, map entire old continents of relationships, *almost none of which* turn up in Peiresc's other letters. It is a breathtaking—and to the researcher, humbling—demonstration that even with all that we can know about Peiresc and Marseille, there is probably much more that escapes us. On 18 November, Peiresc asked Vallavez, since he was in Marseille, to collect their annual invoice for salt. He also asked him to look for the "Flemish woodworker" near St. Victor; he was well known to a "Sr. Cesari." He asked Vallavez to get from "Gilles, Dr. Cassagnes's man," some sulfur poultices. If "Sandrin" was with him, Vallavez was to buy some sugar "of the sort that he knows is best for our apples, and does not smell at all of saffron." "Danmartin, the merchant grocer" who was Peiresc's host, could do this for him. He lived very near to "Dignoly." Finally, a "M. de Gomerville" had departed from Aix so quickly that not only would he take no money from Peiresc for the books he seems to have provided him, but he deprived him of seeking out a gift for him in Marseille of a "blade" or some such thing. Meanwhile, Peiresc heard from one "Simeonis" that Madame de Gomerville wanted a parakeet or small monkey but could not find one in Marseille. The implication is that Vallavez was to find one.[111] Aside from Danmartin and Gilles, those mentioned in this paragraph are completely unknown to us, even though they seem to have played important and in some cases long-running roles in Peiresc's existence.

A second letter, written two days later, charges Vallavez to see "M. Bernier" and have him examine his ledger to see what Peiresc had most recently sent him to cover the cost of some unidentified bales, so that he might in turn reimburse "M. de Seve" for these, as well as for some advances made in 1624 so that Peiresc could close that account. Afterward, if Vallavez were to go to St. Victor, he was to look for the ancient inscriptions turned up during some recent renovations, according to "the son of Councillor Ollivier." If any were worth being preserved he should talk to "M. Gerente, who was the man for making it happen easily."[112] Again: the everyday world of Peiresc at Marseille comes into view, just for an instant, before receding again into the mist.

This is at the extreme, for some of the more prominent figures combed out of the Peiresc archive against its grain do appear in the commercial archives that survive from the period. Even in its partial state we find, for instance, in a volume of "Acts de Soumission à la jurisdiction de l'Admirauté 1622–29," the familiar names of Gaspar Signier, Pierre Fort, Jehan Baptiste Roubaud, Jehan Allemand, Durand, Charles Blanc, Thomas Vandestraten, Gilles Salicoffres, Jean Pierre Lombardon, Jean Venture, Jehan Caillan, Sanson Napollon, Baptiste Tarquet, Charles Laurens, and Jean Guez, among others—all Peiresc's partners.[113] Another file in the very

Figure 16. Worm-holed record of maritime insurance contracts from Marseille. MAD, 9 B 12. (Archives Départementales, Bouches-du-Rhône)

poorly conserved records of the admiralty contains the declared goods in all ships entering the port of Marseille between 1634 and 1637. This is the only such volume for the entire period between 1615 and 1696.[114] Its first three quarters are entirely illegible, crushed, and resewn by hundreds of wormholes, as beautiful and melancholy as anything depicted by the great sixteenth-century Flemish ruin-masters Postma, Heemskerck, and Cock (Figure 16). But its last, unpaginated, quarter contains unique information on Marseille's trade during this period, information that complements what we find in the Peiresc archive.

Then there is the Archive of the Chambre de Commerce of Marseille. This ancient, private corporation, whose beginnings lie in Peiresc's youth (founded in his eighteenth year, in 1598) was the administrator of the consulates of the Levant and in that sense functioned as more than a quasi-governmental agency. Its archive contains much of the Marseille-based correspondence with the individual merchant-administrators of these thriving but also oppressed bases of operation.[115]

A legal document of 8 January 1648, *Arrest du Conseil d'Estat portant cessation du droict de cinq pour cent qui se levoit sur les Marchandises venantes des Eschelles & pais d'Egypte,* preserved randomly in the Archive of the Chambre de Commerce, could be read as a business history, as a history of French Levantine trade, and as a history of legal disputes among the community of merchants. It narrates in great detail the long story of the merchants' effort to lower the tax burden imposed on them by their own consuls in Egypt to help defray the enormous debts of Ambassador Césy in Constantinople. It is a history of suits and countersuits numerous enough to suggest that the French merchants of Egypt spent as much time litigating as they did trading. The scope of this document is vast, captured in the request of the consuls of La Ciotat for "discovery" that the king gather up all documents concerning the raising of funds in the Échelle of Alexandria from 1628 to 1641, and that extracts be made from the accounts of the consuls, Gabriel Fernoux and heirs, Seghezzi, Philibert and Christophe de Bermond, as well as of all the merchants who directly or indirectly paid duties there.[116] Many of the names we find in Peiresc's merchant correspondence also appear in this document and in parallel materials surviving in the Archive of the Chambre de Commerce of Marseille.

Random facts, not found in the Peiresc archive, are preserved here, as if caught in amber. Jean Magy and Joseph Baulme are among the four plaintiffs bringing suit on behalf of the merchant community against the then-consul, Martichou, who took office in 1641.[117] The widow of his brother, the Marseille-based Jean-Baptiste Magy, is named as Heleine Beau.[118] In 1632, the son of Sanson Napollon, François, paid 500 piastres to René de Morgues.[119] Cesar Lambert was still in business in 1646, with his son Gaspard Lambert.[120] In 1646 Baltasar de Vias was serving as deputy for commerce of the city of Marseille.[121] In 1640 an account was drawn up of the amounts owed by French merchants to Turks, Jews, and Moors in the time of Santo Seghezzi and Christophe de Bermond.[122] In 1640 Jean Magy and Lange Alphant were the deputies of the French nation.[123] A Lambert Constans, perhaps related to the Constans who corresponded with Peiresc from Aleppo, was sued for the return of funds by another merchant in 1645.[124] Gabriel Fernoux, appointed by de Brèves long before, was still remitting substantial sums from the consulate back to de Brèves's heirs, long after his patron's death.[125] Yet it seems that the younger comte de Brèves remained involved in Egyptian affairs, as we learn of a "letter written by the said merchants residing in Cairo to the said lord, comte de Brèves," on 26 August 1646. It seems that de Brèves Jr. was engaged in trying to recover revenues farmed from the consulate of Alexandria.[126] The *Arrest* records the existence of a "certificate of debts" that Santo Seghezzi had engaged the French nation at the time the consulate was taken over by Christofle de Bermond on 1 May 1637—showing us the end point of the tangle that Peiresc had thrown himself into (see Section 33, "Peiresc's Mixing in Cairo's Consular Politics").[127] But as early as 1630 we learn of an "arrest du conseil" issued to mediate between Seghezzi and Philibert de Bermond.[128] A certificate from the "Commis a la chaisne de Marseille" documented the merchandise arriving on the account of Jean-Louis (Peiresc's Giovanni Alviggi, or Luigi) Gela on 4 March 1647.[129] The resignation on 19 November 1647 of the consulate of Cairo and Alexandria by Camille Savary, comte de Brèves, marks the end of an era in Peiresc's Mediterranean, if not of French orientalism more broadly.[130]

Though merchants are equally present in the public and commercial archives as in Peiresc's own, there is one major difference that needs to be remembered. The merchants appear in the public and commercial archives because of their function as merchants: their transactions, their ships, their money. They figure in the Peiresc archive, however, as people, with feelings, thoughts, ambitions, and failings. Looking at them from this perspective, while of course remembering that their trade put them in other places and other circumstances, shines a rare light into the world of merchants.

12 ✑

Marseille's Merchant Families

O ne fact that emerges clearly from surveying the Peiresc archive is how much the business of the Mediterranean was family business. Of course we know this already, whether from the work of Gentil da Silva in the 1950s or Francesca Trivellato in our own decade. The merchant community of Marseille, a part of which is visible through the Peiresc archive, is composed of family businesses. Understanding exactly how they were structured, and what their scope, will require a much more comprehensive tackling of the city's surviving public archives. This is only a beginning, a set of hints to be followed up.[1]

We seem to find family firms in which one (or more) family member stayed home and another went overseas. Thus, for example:

Honoré Aycard was in Toulon. His nephew, Jean Salvator, was in Damascus, where he tended to the sickness of Minuti over two months.[2]

Jean Grange was at Smyrna with his cousin François Grange. Their uncle at Marseille was Baltasar Grange.[3]

L'Empereur in Constantinople had a nephew of the same name at Marseille.[4] In a letter of September 1633 Peiresc acknowledged hearing from the nephew that the uncle was planning to return soon "en Chrestienté."[5] But in a letter of July 1632, Dr. Cassagnes reports on his death, orphaning "many manuscripts and very beautiful things."[6]

De Gastines worked closely with Cesar Lambert, and Peiresc identified Lambert as his brother-in-law ("cognato").[7] We learn from a letter of Peiresc to de Thou that de Gastines also had a brother who would be approaching de Thou for assistance with a legal matter.[8]

Pierre Fort, Peiresc's financier, and Baltasar de Vias, the neo-Latin poet and consul (nonresident) of Algiers, and Durand, consul in the 1620s, were brothers-in-law.[9]

Jean Magy in Egypt and Jean-Baptiste Magy in Marseille were brothers.[10] There is an appreciative reference to Jean Magy being solicited in 1645 by an agent of Chancellor Séguier for some Greek manuscripts.[11]

Jérome de l'Isle in Aleppo had a brother in Marseille.[12] He was also the son-in-law of Sanson Napollon.[13]

Jacques Estelle, vice-consul for Sidon from 1627 to 1634, had a brother named Honoré Estelle, who also traded in Sidon. He followed as vice-consul from 1634 to 1637.[14]

Esperit Laurens, chancellor of the French consulate in Alexandria, was the father-in-law of Joseph Baulme, the apothecary in Marseille.[15]

François Galaup, sieur de Chasteuil, from Aix, became a pilgrim to Mount Lebanon. He was the cousin of Daniel Aymini, the Recollet friar.[16] His brother Jean lived in Aix and was the *procureur-général* in the Cour des Comptes, Aydes et Fiances of Provence. He had been responsible for programming the entry of Louis XIII into Aix in 1622.[17]

François Aurivelier was the nephew of Jacques and Honoré Estelle. He brought Peiresc the Samaritan Triglot that Daniel Aymini purchased.[18]

Honoré Marquesi in Marseille was the uncle of Charles Blanc, in Sidon at least from 1630.[19]

Jean Guez in Marseille had a brother in Constantinople named Guillaume.[20]

Giovanni Alviggi, or Luigi—and sometimes Jean-Louis—Gela in Marseille was the brother-in-law of Santo Seghezzi in Cairo.[21] By 1647 Seghezzi was in business with his son, Alexandre.[22]

Barthélemy Issaultier, who appears sometimes as a shipboard scrivener and sometimes as a *patron*, had a relation, Jean, who was a merchant traveling to Venice and Genoa.[23]

13 ❧
Financing, Disbursing, Reimbursing

*T*he question of financing lies at the heart of Peiresc's Mediterranean, as his extended world, of both people and ideas, could not have functioned without money. We can, therefore, trace the origins of the network back to funding or, conversely, trace the funding through the structuring of the network. Peiresc built his own atop those developed by Marseille's merchant bankers (he used the term "marchand banquier").[1]

Peiresc's first "respondent" at Marseille was Antonio Labbia, who lived and worked near a "M. Dori." By October of 1615, Labbia was deeply involved in managing the shipping from Marseille and points east.[2] Especially interesting is the disclosure that every week there was an overland courier from Venice to Genoa and thence on to Marseille.[3] That Peiresc could be collecting seeds from Cairo as early as 1612, comparing them against verbal descriptions in Prosper Alpino's *De Plantis Aegypti* and then trying to cultivate them in Provence, suggests that they came via Labbia.[4]

The early establishment of his network relied on connections he had made as a student in Venice in 1599–1601. Before 1617, Peiresc was based entirely in Provence; between 1617 and 1623 he spent almost all of his time in Paris, with trips back to Provence during court recesses. At this stage his archive outlines the two main routes from the Mediterranean (Italy): overland via the post through Lyon or by sea through Marseille. For the latter, he named a "M. Servian" as an agent.[5] For the former, in 1616, we find Peiresc advising Labbia to write to his "friends of Padua" by way of the Venetian merchant "who responds to Signori Curio Franciotti and Aurigo Burlamachi [*sic*] of Lyon"—the Burlamacchi being a respected Lucchese banking family who had long maintained an outpost in Lyon to support their business in silks.[6]

When Peiresc lived in Paris between 1617 and 1623, the importance of a Marseille-based communications system was not an issue. From Paris, Lyon was the natural through-point for any communication to the south. After Peiresc returned to Provence in the fall of 1623, however, this situation changed.

Labbia was soon replaced by Gaspard Signier, a merchant-banker through whose own network Peiresc sent his letters.[7] Peiresc explained to his friend, the poet John Barclay in Rome, that Signier was a "very honest man" with a corresponding agent at Livorno so that he could organize whatever was necessary at Marseille and have it done at Livorno, from whence "fallouques ou fregattes" departed regularly for Marseille.[8] Livorno was another transit point: seeking to send a chest to Barclay, Signier noted to Peiresc that he would send it to Livorno in the absence of a direct passage between Marseille and Rome.[9] First mention of credit being furnished by Signier is in November 1623, only a month or so after Peiresc returned to Aix.[10] We have few letters written by Peiresc to Signier; one, from 1621, sent with a package carried by "Lawrence mulletier d'Aix," asked him to utilize one of the tartanes of Martigues that regularly sailed from Marseille to Rome to carry a message to the ambassador's secretary, the marquis de Leure.[11] Livorno, Martigues—Peiresc locates his own operation within an existing Mediterranean network by sea as well as land.

In this early stage of his Mediterraneanism, Peiresc already had a Roman agent, Pierre Eschinard, whom he may have met through Signier. Eschinard was told to address mail to Signier, to Vias, or to Peiresc's own father, M. de Callas.[12] Similarly, Eschinard would be reimbursed by Signier via M. Robin, M. de Soeur, Lumaga of Genoa, or another of his choice.[13] Each of these names helps broaden our understanding of the texture of communication and commerce. With Eschinard, Peiresc offered to pay the "freight" charge ("freyste") of Marseille and reimburse at either Lyon or Rome.[14]

In Genoa, Marc Antonio and Ottavio Lumaga managed a banking operation with nodes at Lyon and Paris. A letter from Peiresc to Marc Antonio Lumaga from just after his return to Provence in 1623 identifies Signier as his respondent in Marseille, and makes clear that it is Signier who would pay all the related costs of any transshipment of letters and packages.[15] The next month's letter shows Peiresc working the kinks out of his new system. He asked Lumaga to send a slip acknowledging receipt of Peiresc's packages; since he received none for the one he intended for Rome, he asked Lumaga to inquire after it from "the captains, the messengers of Nice" ("delle capitani li messagieri di Nizza"). He also asked Lumaga to forward a small shipment to the Signori Pianca in Venice. They would, in turn, be sending him a box of books. All Lumaga's costs on these, he explained, could be drawn against Signier.[16] Signier himself made contact with the Lumaga branch in Paris ("Lumaga et Mascrany") and

expressed his good will at their future collaboration.[17] The debts were accumulated by Lumaga at Lyon, and Peiresc paid them through Signier at
Marseille.[18]

It is worth noting that Genoa was the gateway to Italy (northern as
well as southern) for Provençaux like Peiresc.[19] Thus, Gaspar Signier's account reached to Venice, as well, where Peiresc charged Gasparo Molino
and Francesco Rosa with shipping him books ordered for him by Lorenzo
Pignoria or Paulo Gualdo. These books were to go by way of Livorno and
the Pandolfini family, who would get them to Aix and Peiresc.[20] A hiccup
in this process provides us with evidence: in a letter of January 1626 Peiresc
tells Molino and Rosa that he had given Signier permission to reactivate
a standing order for books from Venice that his factor in Venice had inadvertently closed.[21] And we possess the accompanying note from Signier
announcing that he was putting 30–40 scudi at the account of Signori
Ribiano and Estariat.[22] Thus we know that Signier had a Venetian correspondent. On the other hand, when setting up a standing order for
Pignoria in July 1626, Peiresc used the bookseller Horatio Pianca as the
local respondent.[23]

In April 1626 Peiresc reported to Vallavez that Signier was so ill that
his doctor had urged him to leave Marseille, with its bad air, and relocate
to Aix. He "seemed to me a skeleton, and filled me with pity. It was,"
Peiresc concluded, "the pain of his wife's death which brought this sickness upon him." A month later, Peiresc reported that Signier returned to
Marseille, his condition unchanged.[24] He did not die immediately, but he
did soon die, for in a letter to Lumaga of 29 October 1627, acknowledging
the reception of books from Sr. du Bouilan in Venice via Lumaga in
Genoa, Peiresc announced the reshaping of his system. From henceforth,
in Marseille in place of the deceased Signier, he asked Lumaga to address
correspondence to "Messrs. Mary, Douaille and Fraisse, or alternately to
Messrs. Cesar Lambert and de Gastines," whichever would be easier.[25]

Geraud Mary, Jean Douaille, and François Fraisse were also bankers,
with branches in Lyon and Marseille, though perhaps with greater commodity in Lyon than in the Mediterranean, thus explaining Peiresc's limited use of them once his Mediterranean operation got going.[26] They also
had credit in Toulouse.[27] They were being used in correspondence with
the Genoese Lumaga in 1628.[28] In fact, we possess the text of a letter of
credit written by Fraisse in Marseille to Lumaga in Paris, advancing 150
livres of credit to M. Dupuy "and in his absence to M. Tavernier," on the
account of either Vallavez or Peiresc and payable "sur les messrs. de

Lyon."[29] One of Peiresc's earlier Roman contacts was M. Marchand. We possess the copy of a letter of exchange written by Mary, Douaille, and Fraisse to Pettau, banker "at the court" in Rome for Marchand on the account of Peiresc. This seems to try to regularize an earlier transaction where debt was contracted at Lyon to be reimbursed there from a Sr. Didier of Marseille.[30]

With Lyon's key place in the road net came the necessity of some financial clearing function. Lyon may have been a second-best for Peiresc, but in addition to its role vis-à-vis Italy, it also faced north. Thus, as late as 1636, when some plates from Antwerp went astray, Peiresc asked M. Plaignard, "Marchant Libraire a Lyon chez M. Coffin," to search among the colony of Antwerp merchants.[31]

It was with Peiresc's own turn to the Levant that we can date the ascendency of de Gastines. Peiresc described him to his friends as "of the most honest men in Marseille and one of the most obliging" ("de plus honnestes gents a Marseille et des plus obligeants") and as a "fort cordial" friend.[32] Peiresc continued, for a while longer, to draw upon the firm of Mary, Douaille, and Fraisse for recommendations and credit on behalf of Théophile Minuti in advance of the latter's first expedition to the Levant, in March 1629.[33]

De Gastines often worked in partnership with Cesar Lambert. As early as 1627, we find Peiresc telling Aubery in Rome that Lambert would handle reimbursements, along with the "droit de remise," or commission.[34] Lambert himself, in Marseille, explained to Guillaume d'Espiot, a French merchant in Rome who was *his* agent on the spot, that he would "by way of Lyon and Livorno" furnish him with 50 écus for Louis Aubery.[35] In 1628, Lambert and de Gastines seem to have worked together on Peiresc's behalf to furnish funds to a widow of the late prior of Lignage in Paris.[36] De Gastines also seems to have been connected with Jean-Baptiste Magy. Both were investors in a ship that foundered between Livorno and Marseille.[37] And Peiresc describes him as having a "grand commerce" with Malta.[38]

A letter of 1629 to a Roman correspondent seems to announce a new centrality for de Gastines. He is described as "a very obliging person who would be happy to be able to serve you, not only during your stay at Marseille but also during the one you could take at Rome, if you use him."[39] Nearly every single letter Peiresc wrote to Mediterranean contacts in the decade 1628–1637 mentions his name, usually in the key role of addressee, reimburser, or fixer.

It was in 1629 that Peiresc noted that reimbursement for freight and port expenses would henceforth be handled by Mssrs. "Gastines and Fort."[40] In June of that year, de Gastines was named as the "addressee" in Marseille for Roman correspondence directed to Peiresc.[41]

In 1630, writing to Marchand in Rome, Peiresc explained that he had authorized de Gastines, then relocated to Cassis because of the closure of Marseille, to reimburse him by way of his respondent, "M. d'Espiotz." As the system shifted in Marseille, from Signier to Mary, Douaille, and Fraisse, and then to de Gastines, the respondents overseas changed as well. This same letter shows us something else about the mature Roman system, namely, that while bills were paid by d'Espiot, they first had to be approved. Louis de Bonnaire was named here as the chief authorizer, and in his absence Christophe Dupuy or others.[42] Aubery, in Rome, noted that d'Espiot laid out money that he had received from Marchand and de Gastines but expected to be reimbursed from him (Aubery).[43]

With the expedition of Minuti, de Gastines comes into his own. In the last landward letter Peiresc was able to send to the Minim before sailing, he wrote that de Gastines would provide letters for Lambert and Fernoux, both in Egypt. Peiresc recommended against depending on either M. Fraisse or M. Salicoffres because they did not have any connection with Flemish shipping. It seems that it was precisely de Gastines's readiness to use northern shipping that won him a place with Peiresc (see Section 17, "Northerners in the Mediterranean").[44]

De Gastines did many things for Peiresc. When Peiresc was in a rush, and time was short, he was comfortable sending his letters to de Gastines and letting him figure out where to send them.[45] But when de Gastines was away, as he was sometimes, his deputies were not as on top of things. Thus, when he went away in April 1635, it turned out that his deputies fell far behind and two letters to Aleppo may have gotten lost in the shuffle.[46] De Gastines was also made responsible for covering Peiresc's account in Paris with the Dupuy brothers, a regular and demanding role given their importance for Peiresc as a source of news, books, and manuscripts.[47]

When de Thou's materials finally came ashore at Marseille, including a "round" box and a crocodile, Gastines managed the disembarkation and delivery to Peiresc by way of a porter. He was the one who handled all the local arrangements: he negotiated a price of two quarters of an écu, which Peiresc was to pay on delivery; he paid two for the carrying of the box and the crocodile to the lodging of the muleteer; and he handled the port fees and the "passport" for Captain Roubaud.[48]

The relationship between Peiresc and de Gastines had to do with more than money. We might expect the merchant to have enjoyed the status his connection with the great man bestowed upon him. And there were practical advantages. As with his other correspondents, Peiresc did not hesitate to use his political connections where they could be useful. In the case of de Gastines, this involved intervening with F. A. de Thou on behalf of de Gastines's brother, on an unidentified matter "which is so precious to him, and so important" ("qui luy est si cher et si importante").[49]

What was the relationship between de Gastines and the Dutch trading firm of Ruts and Martin that Peiresc also used (discussed in Section 17)? We have seen that the Flemings began to take over the route to Aleppo in the 1630s and even provided some backup banking functions to Peiresc.[50] It still seems, however, that de Gastines remained the chief banker, with money being remitted to Ruts and Martin for whatever assistance they provided at their overseas operations, whether in the Levant or in Genoa, their main western Mediterranean outpost.[51]

(Of course, there were other moneymen in town. Jacques Gaffarel, for instance, living in Venice, had sent marbles back to Marseille to the address of a "Sr. Giraudon.")[52]

This was the financing at the Marseille end of the network. But the correspondence is also full of details about the movement of monies at the Levantine termini. Indeed, the letters to the merchants in the Levant give a real sense of the practical underpinnings—the very conditions of possibility—for Peiresc's scholarship, especially as it was necessarily in the hands of others. More than the diplomats, it was the merchants who defined the horizons of possibility in the Near East. When, for example, a group of Jesuits on their way to Ethiopia were seized in Egypt, the French consul in Cairo, Gabriel Fernoux, was powerless. He had to borrow money at high rates of interest (2,500 piastres borrowed at 24 percent "from the Jews," and 3,000 at 20 percent) and still would not have been able to pay the ransom had it not been for a 1,000 piastre interest-free gift from Cesar Lambert, Peiresc's friend and de Gastines's partner.[53]

When Minuti set off on his first expedition, Peiresc had to establish a system of exchange. For he operated in a world of livres and écus, while his colleagues in the Levant paid in piastres. Hence the importance of what he articulated in a later letter to Father Celestin at Aleppo. If the expense incurred was 80 piasters, it would be covered in Marseille as 80 écus "because to reimburse the indemnity here it is necessary to return an écu for a piastre." Moreover, Peiresc always offered to pay the change, travel cost, and maritime profit ("change, nolis et profits maritimes"). What are these? And how much did they cost? What can we deduce, working backward, were the profits captains expected when they plied the Levant route?

By the end of October 1629, Peiresc had learned from Minuti, in a letter carried by Captain Bartholin, from Tarquet, and from Piscatoris, newly arrived in Marseille, that Minuti had already left Sidon, whence he had written his letter, en route to Damiette in Egypt. Peiresc offered to reimburse Tarquet's vice-consul in Sidon, Estelle, who had fronted Minuti 45 piastres for a book—in fact, a Samaritan Pentateuch—which was en route to Marseille on a different ship, the *Grand Henry*. Peiresc asked Tarquet if he knew what route it would be taking on its return voyage and how long this might take. Minuti had also mentioned another boat, captained by Patron Cornillon of Cassis, who was bringing Peiresc letters from Jerusalem.[54]

When Minuti was passing through Sidon, he gave to Charles Blanc the Samaritan Pentateuch he had purchased in Damascus. Peiresc wrote to Blanc asking him to keep it from moisture and send it by an assured way to Marseille either "to M. de Gastines, who looks after my affairs" ("a M. de Gastines, qui a soing de mes affaires"), or to M. Tarquet. Marquesi, who as Blanc's uncle was the natural recipient, was too frequently absent from the city and thus not to be preferred. Peiresc also authorized Blanc's extending up to 20 écus further credit to Aymini for the purchase of a more complete version of the Pentateuch. Peiresc promised to reimburse Blanc for the capital plus the "changes" and "profits maritimes" which, presumably, Blanc would have had to make over at the time of departure to the ship's captain, or the ship's captain to the port authorities. On top of that, Peiresc offered to make up to Blanc what the money he had laid out on these books might have brought in if spent on other merchandise.[55]

On the same day that he wrote to Blanc in Sidon, Peiresc wrote also to Estelle, the consul there. This letter effectively recapitulated what had been written in the parallel letter, adding only an explicit request that if Aymini needed additional funding then he was to provide it, up to 20 écus. In conclusion, Peiresc mentioned having written also to the French Capuchins in Sidon—an early reference to the mission established by Gilles de Loches before his relocation to Egypt.[56] A year later, Estelle had still not been reimbursed, not for this first purchase, nor for a second one made later by Meynier in Damascus.

Reimbursement for Aymini's Samaritan Triglot allows us to follow the financial trail, and the practice of reimbursement from Marseille all the way to the Échelles of the Levant. It ran right through Pierre Fort. Estelle in Sidon provided the initial outlay of money, received the object, and then handed it off to François Aurivelier, his nephew, to bring it back to France.[57] Learning of this, Peiresc directed a long letter to Aurivelier—a first letter, of the sort that Peiresc wrote to bring a new correspondent completely up to speed with his practices. He asked him to give the book to M. Fort, "who will give you a public receipt from me, if you would like" ("qui vous en fera une quittance publique si vous voulez de ma part"). Peiresc was also prepared to write out something in his own hand. Fort would then reimburse any monies paid out, either for the recovery of the book there or for anything else. Estelle had written on 10 December saying that Aymini paid out 31 piastres to a Venetian who seized the book and that Minuti gave Aymini 30 of these piastres out of the 50 that had been furnished by Estelle to Minuti and which Fort paid out to Baptiste Tarquet on Estelle's wishes. If there were any additional charges, Aurivelier was to pay and Fort was to reimburse. In the postscript, Peiresc added that after writing he had decided to send "express" to M. Fort to cover any remaining costs.[58]

The problem Peiresc faced was that Estelle's nephew, Aurivelier, who brought the book, did not want to accept anything. This resistance elicited explicit commentary from Peiresc. He insisted that Tarquet and the others involved take the *charges maritimes* "in the proportion of profits taken on the other monies employed on goods." He noted that Cesar Lambert, who gave Minuti 30 piastres at Cairo, did not object to accepting reimbursement at a rate of 30 percent "and that pleased me, so I will employ him even more freely another time." This was the rate that he was proposing for those involved in the Sidon group—Estelle himself, Aurivelier his nephew, Mallon in Damascus, and Charles le Blanc in Sidon.[59]

To Tarquet, too, he insisted on full payment, again using the example of Lambert: "but on condition that you will *accept the nautical charges as did Mr Cesar Lambert, who knows my humor and whom I will use happily in the future, with less regret, and I would remain no less indebted to you in this.*" He was not to make any resistance to being reimbursed, "since without a doubt it was necessary there to add some supplement to redeem it from a Venetian who had cut into my market."[60]

We have been paying attention to the geography of Peiresc's financial network. One of its interesting features—in exact parallel to his intellectual network and to wider economic trends in the Mediterranean—is the disappearance of Venice. Venice was not a city in which Peiresc had a direct agent, which means Venice was not a city in which the Marseille merchants felt a need to have a branch. This tells us something important about Marseille's Mediterranean map but also of the lessened role for Venice in a Mediterranean commercial system weighted toward the Levant—and thus a turning point in the history of both Venice and the Mediterranean. So, in 1633, by which time Peiresc's system is fully developed, when Peiresc asked Jacques Gaffarel to do some shopping in Venice, he explained that reimbursement would be effected either through a Genoese merchant, Horatio Tridi, or through the Genoese firm of Lumaga based in Lyon. The French consul in Venice would serve as the local respondent, the "piggybacking" failsafe employed by Peiresc elsewhere in the Mediterranean where he lacked Marseille merchant contacts.[61]

What did all this cost Peiresc? We have seen already that he was happy to pay a 30 percent premium on goods loaded at Sidon. In a letter to Danmartin we learn that 20 percent was the charge put on goods taken in Cyprus.[62] The same figure of 20 percent comes up in a letter to Jean-Baptiste Magy, where Peiresc gives it as the "change"—or exchange rate commission—stipulated by his brother in Egypt.[63] In Rome, d'Espiot had been content with a 27 percent rate on the exchange when others were paying up to 35 percent—and Peiresc greatly lauded his "honnêteté" for this.[64] D'Espiot came to serve an important role as paymaster not only for Peiresc but for those of his friends who needed an address for funds while passing through Rome, such as Gabriel Naudé and M. d'Arène.[65] We know that Peiresc also reimbursed d'Espiot at a rate of 22 percent.[66] Cesar Lambert, who gave Minuti 30 piastres at Cairo, pegged the reimbursement rate at 30 percent.[67] The cost of the money loaned to Minuti, in Egypt, through Lambert, and in Sidon through Estelle, was also estimated at a 30 percent "change maritime."[68] But in Sicily, on the coast at Siracusa, the going rate was 50 percent![69]

A letter from Guillaume Guez in Constantinople was received for Peiresc by Aycard in Toulon. Peiresc knew that 50 piastres had been promised there to Minuti. In addition to reimbursing the 50 piastres, Peiresc would pay any additional "changes & proffitz maritimes." Peiresc added a stock phrase whose precision sheds light on the typical practice: "proportional to what the same sum could have brought in profit to the merchant who had furnished it if it had been employed for goods on that same ship." Peiresc estimated this at 20 to 30 percent, which, as we have seen, reflected the varied rates charged across the eastern Mediterranean.[70] In other words, however much he was invested in the moral economy, Peiresc understood that there was a commercial one that had to be satisfied too.

With Minuti and Aymini in the Levant, the need for a secure financial backbone was imperative, and Peiresc relied on Fort to provide it. Because of this, we know that an import profit of around 20 to 30 percent could be expected.[71] That Peiresc's generosity seems not to have made him a mark for frauds testifies to the high respect in which he was held, his good judgment of people, and good luck.[72] Eliyahu Ashtor has calculated profit margins in the Venetian trade of the fifteenth century; they are not substantially different from what we can read out of the Peiresc archive for the seventeenth.[73]

These costs were of course initially incurred by the captains, and it is to them that the reimbursement effort was primarily oriented. Peiresc's key agents on the ground in Marseille were the ones who had to take care of this, Jean-Baptiste Magy, Hugh Mace de Gastines, and Pierre Fort. In 1634, it was Magy who was charged with paying the freight charge for the polacre of Captain Courtez and the vaisseau *St. Esprit* of Captain Audibert.[74]

There were also insurance costs. Peiresc chastised Honoré Marquesi, the Marseille-based agent for Charles Blanc in Sidon, for taking a 30 percent "commission" for "insurance" ("prendre les seuretez") without actually spending it on insurance.[75] This still rankled a year later when, in a letter to Jérôme de l'Isle in Aleppo, after thanking him for the help he provided Daniel Aymini, and the love he had shown de Gastines and himself, Peiresc added that he had reimbursed his brother as requested, with the charges and maritime profits. He wanted to make sure that the whole process in Aleppo was in his hands, not like when Marquesi "let it get lost at sea for failing to take out a similar insurance as I had charged him to do when taking it from his relative Charles Blanc."[76] Peiresc had de Gastines cover the payment to de l'Isle, and thanked him for making sure that duplicates were sent with another ship, and insured, in case the first one came to ruin—learning from the recent, painful past.[77]

When the expense was incurred far away by a distant agent, as was the case with Peiresc's Levantine contacts, the transaction had to go through various parties. The evolution of this system began in 1629 with Minuti and Aymini shopping for manuscripts and coins in Lebanon and Syria. In a letter to Tarquet, consul for Syria but resident in Marseille, Peiresc acknowledged the help he was receiving from Estelle and Blanc in Sidon, and Meynier in Damascus. Aymini had proved especially talented and so had been charged by Peiresc "to seek out some additions to what I have received," and to facilitate this he had asked Estelle to furnish all his necessities up to 20 écus. In the meantime, he was sending an additional 101 livres toward maintaining his capital of 45 piastres.[78]

At Sidon, Estelle and Tarquet were key figures. In 1631, Peiresc was still telling Tarquet to pass along to him all charges and "profits maritimes"—as was done in the past with Estelle.[79] A little later, and a little farther up the coast, at Alexandretta-Aleppo, Pierre and Jean Constans were the financial contacts. It was they who advanced money to Father Celestin and were reimbursed "according to your orders to M. J. Venture by way of M. Lambert and de Gastines." To this Peiresc added another 200 livres to cover capital as well as "charges ou profits maritimes." Venture was unwilling to accept this additional money, but Peiresc insisted that he take it "in the commission on the exchange rate and on the recuperation of the goods, conforming to the profit that it would bring on merchandise carried on the same ship." In other words, Peiresc wanted his goods to be charged at the same rate as the profit that could have accrued to the captain had the space been occupied by other items. Why? We see here one of the secrets of Peiresc's success. In order to encourage merchants to make place for his manuscripts and other small items, he wanted to make sure that they would be compensated at the highest possible rate by treating his items as if they were profit-generating at the highest possible level.[80]

With Peiresc forced to Belgentier because of plague and urban revolt in Aix, and the dispersal of Marseille merchants along the coast because of the port's closure, much of Peiresc's business was handled through Toulon. And perhaps the financing there was less well-provisioned than at Marseille. So, in a letter of July 1630 Peiresc turned to a M. Truillet to mediate a discussion of a debt owed at Lyon to Sr. Nicolas Pichery. Pichery had married the sister of Peter-Paul Rubens in 1627, and was based at Marseille between 1628 and 1630. He handled Peiresc's communications with Rubens and also with the Netherlands. Through his other brother-in-law he provided banking services to Peiresc after his return to Antwerp in 1630.[81] Peiresc had thought that the debt in question might have been reimbursed already at Lyon by one René Bais when Vallavez was passing through the previous month. In any event, Peiresc was furnishing Truillet with 15 Spanish pistoles out of which Truillet was to take the 115 livres and 4 sous that he was owed and use the rest to cover the transport to Belgentier of the plants that had come from the East. All of this seems to suggest that some Levantine debts were collected or charged to Lyon firms despite all the shipping going back and forth on the coast.[82]

The clearing-house function of Peiresc and Marseille, and the general question of north-south relations, comes through clearly, again, in the situation of Father Celestin, for he, too, was being subsidized at long range, in his case by his brother Jacob Golius at Leiden. These letters of exchange, like regular familial correspondence, were sent to Peiresc for dispatch. Peiresc then turned to Venture, who seemed to have the best "commoditez" for Alexandretta (the port of Aleppo). Peiresc, in this case, announced that he had received from Golius a letter of exchange for his brother for the sum of 50 piastres payable by Sr. Antoine Piscatoris. Peiresc asked Venture to take the letter of exchange countersigned by him and collect the sum from Piscatoris. Or, he could send the countersigned letter to Aleppo and clear the cash there. In an afterthought, Peiresc decided on this option.[83]

The complications reflect the details of doing long-range financial transfers through layers of absent partners. Peiresc had the letter from Golius copied into his register of outgoing correspondence, perhaps as a record, which while addressed to him employs Spanish pieces of eight as the unit of exchange. It was drawn on the account of David Willehem at The Hague.[84] Interestingly, Peiresc also monetizes in pieces of eight in a letter to Jean Magy in Cairo at just this same time, adding that he hoped that Magy would not be hurt by rising currency costs.[85] This might make us wonder at the impact of war between Spain and France on the Spanish piece of eight as the global reserve currency.

The letter of exchange from Golius evoked complex feelings in Peiresc. He wrote the brother, Father Celestin, a long letter about it in May 1636: "When I paid out at Marseille the first *deniers* that you received from Mssrs. Constans on my recommendation, I had not at all imagined being paid back, but felt it a singular pleasure to render you this little service. . . . I was so ashamed to receive another letter from M. Golius your brother of last November with a letter of exchange for Marseille for the reimbursement of the 50 piastres that you have had." Peiresc did not want to present the letter, or to seek repayment of that amount. But Celestin was insistent, and Peiresc did not want to antagonize Professor Golius either. His solution was elegant: he sent the letter to Venture, who drew down the funds, satisfying the sender, but then Peiresc had Venture put the monies at the disposal of Constans in Aleppo for *future* use on Celestin's behalf.[86] In short, Peiresc managed never to take the money after all. This generosity was part of how he did business, as it was—aside from everything else—a way of establishing long-term psychological dependence as well as financial indebtedness. It was only when this caused difficulty for the

Golius brothers, and therefore threatened the long-term goal Peiresc was seeking, that he shifted gears.

The Aleppo account, by the later 1630s, seems to have gone through the Dutch firm of Niklaes Ruts, who would be depicted so magnificently by Rembrandt, and Durand, or David, Martin (both names are used).[87] When the bill came from Aleppo, Peiresc directed that it be paid by the Dutch to his Marseille clearing agent (Ruts and Martin to Venture).[88] De Gastines and Fort seem not to have been active in this sphere.[89]

Ruts and Martin also provide us with access to the question of where Peiresc got his money from, both metaphorically and literally. Metaphorically, the monies that subsidized his Mediterranean operation came from the revenues of his abbey at Guîtres, on the right bank of the Gironde, between Fronsac and Libourne. Literally, they came from his agent in Bordeaux to his bankers in Marseille. The first evidence of this money trail may be from early 1624.[90] In 1625, Peiresc was valuing Guîtres at 2,000 livres annually, based on its old status—though reaching this figure still depended upon Peiresc's recuperating the revenue lost with the lands that slipped away with the destruction of the abbey's titles during the civil wars of religion in the later sixteenth century.[91]

From here, already, we can see the outline of the plan that Peiresc would hatch, and then implement, over the next decade. It also explains the resistance to these efforts that he encountered from his neighbor, the Cardinal de Sourdis, so much so that Peiresc appealed directly to his acquaintance, Pope Urban VIII, to command the recalcitrant cardinal to play better. A brief of 22 February 1625 and another of 5 April 1625 ordered the cardinal to comply. Sourdis, undeterred, in 1627 offered informally to pension Peiresc at 2,000 livres annually, paid to whomever he named in Marseille, if Peiresc would relinquish the abbey to him. By 1633, the "offer" price—this time coming from Peiresc's new neighbor, the duc de Fronsac—also known as Cardinal Richelieu—had gone up to 2,500 or even 3,000 livres, suggesting that the real value was even higher.[92]

Traces of the dependence of Peiresc the universal scholar on Peiresc the *abbé commendataire* are scattered through the correspondence. In Bordeaux, Dennis Guillemin, Peiresc's factotum and the prior of Roumoulles, a village in Provence near Riez, superintended the monks' managing of the abbey. He was the one who ensured that money was collected and sent south.[93] In April 1626, Peiresc sent a letter to Fraisse—of the firm Mary, Douaille, and Fraisse—"with the *lettre de change* of Bordeaux."[94] In January 1627, Peiresc's log records a letter sent to Fraisse "pour les

1200 l.t. [livres tournois] avec lettre de change."[95] In 1628, Peiresc records sending to Fraisse "the three *lettres de change* of Bordeaux for paying out, etc."[96]

More elaborately, in 1629, Peiresc wrote to Guez in Marseille saying that he had just received from Bordeaux a "lettre d'advis" addressed to Guez along with a *lettre de change* for 1,000 livres addressed to him by the Marseille merchant Jean Meynard, who was based in Bordeaux.[97] The money came in and was already allocated. Simultaneously, Peiresc wrote directly to Meynard, thanking him for taking care of the purchases made by M. Lombard, and conveying to him the package for the "R.P. Carmelite" and two letters of credit ("lettres d'advis"), one for his neighbor M. Guez and the other for M. Fraisse. Peiresc requested that Guez accept the payment and keep the funds until he received an order charged against it ("la garder jusques a ce que vous ayez l'ordre de ce qu'il en faudroit faire"). In other words, Peiresc is advancing him the money in expectation of upcoming charges. If we look to the date, April 1629, and realize that it was just then that Peiresc was outfitting the Minim Father Théophile Minuti for his first trip to the Levant, we realize what those charges might be. This money transfer could have been anticipating all the many expenses that Minuti would accrue in the upcoming months, at a great distance.

The second letter of exchange, made out to Sr. Fraisse, was for 1,500 livres, out of which were to be immediately deducted debts to de Gastines of 158 livres and Burgues of Toulon (otherwise unknown) of 75 livres as well as some small expenses ("de quelque chosette") of his own and of his brother. The rest was to remain with Fraisse, with some portion of it being eventually sent on to Paris.[98] Into the copybook Peiresc had transcribed the letter of exchange from Bordeaux, from one Pierre Taillevant for M. Guez. The money was being transferred for Peiresc from a M. de Guassier "bourgeois & marchand" of Bordeaux to M. Guez, "bourgeois & marchand" of Marseille. Peiresc, in his own hand, wrote that "you"—meaning Guez—could furnish the monies to Meynard at his earliest convenience.[99]

By 1632, the whole system had been reoriented around de Gastines. This is made clear in a brief but revealing letter from Peiresc to d'Espiot in Rome. He began by thanking d'Espiot for providing Louis de Bonnaire and Gabriel Naudé in Rome with money to buy *tchotchkes* ("certains petites curiositez") but also to sct up the reimbursement of costs and exchange "according to the events that could present themselves from time to time," whether organized by Peiresc or by Sr. Marchand *expedition-naire,* "to whom I sometimes give commissions for my friends as well." Turning to the question of d'Espiot's own reimbursement, Peiresc noted that he had passed to de Gastines a 519-livre bill for his affairs, apart from another for 1,500 livres that he had already put into his hands "from the farmers of my abbey of Guîtres" ("par les fermiez de mon abbaye de Guistres").[100] A year later, in 1633, Peiresc sent a cover letter to Guez that accompanied more "lettres d'advis," or "letters of notification," received from Bordeaux containing sums earmarked for Guez out of funds that came in for Peiresc: "We have assigned Sr. Tallevant to take it out for you from the account of my brother Valavez as from mine." With these "lettres d'advis" Guez could then turn at his convenience to de Gastines, who would furnish him with *lettres de change.* Peiresc concluded by asking Jean Guez to pay out from this sum a smaller amount owed to Fort for purchases already made and which was included in that *lettre de change.*[101] When Minuti arrived in Constantinople in 1633 he carried a letter for Guez's brother, Guillaume, asking him to provide a line of credit up to 100 écus by "drawing on a *lettre de change* against me or M. de Gastines of Marseille."[102]

As usual, it is a breakdown in a system that enables us to reconstruct its ideal form. Thus, in April 1636, Peiresc apologized to Jean-Baptiste Magy for a delayed repayment, but since Christmas, he writes, "my agent in Bordeaux" was unable to get a letter of exchange to Marseille. Peiresc had, therefore, just then asked Messrs. Ruts and Martin, the Dutch firm with wide *commodité* on the Syro-Lebanese coast, to have one of their English merchant friends come from there with the money to pay Magy "and others of the Levant." Peiresc acidly observes that "there are none but these English who trade between Bordeaux and Marseille."[103] Ruts and Martin were still paying off Magy's account in June.[104] Their importance in Marseille, for Peiresc, extends also to their *internal* French connections.

A side point about Bordeaux and its resources: if we can say that the money that fed Peiresc's oriental studies came from Guîtres, we can also say that the success of this venture depended on his ability not only to continue increasing its revenue through reuniting to the abbey lands that had drifted into the possession of others, but of warding off his increasingly incessant neighbor, Armand Jean du Plessis, Duke of Fronsac, and Cardinal de Richelieu. From a letter of 1635, we see Peiresc aggrieved at what he saw as the cardinal's groundless challenge to the legitimacy of the church's lands and his acute awareness of the peril a too-straightforward opposition could land him in: "not having grounds to throw in doubt the pretentions of His Eminence, despite the little they have of substance, without committing a great crime."[105]

When packets for Peiresc arrived in Marseille, Peiresc charged the recipient to give them to M. Fort, who would provide a receipt for the item and pay off debts incurred at any point in the process up to then. In the case of the Samaritan Triglot purchased by Aymini, we can follow the transaction. It began with the news: Estelle wrote him that Aymini paid out 31 piastres to the Venetian who possessed the book and that Minuti gave Aymini 30 piastres to this effect out of the 50 that had been furnished by Estelle to Minuti and which Sr. Fort paid out to Baptiste Tarquet in Marseille on Estelle's wishes. Peiresc noted that if the new parchment leaves that were commissioned to fill in gaps would cost an additional 5 or 6 piastres on top of the 30, "I imagine that this would be the extra that you might pay out. Whatever it is, M. Fort will indemnify you." Peiresc added that he would send a procuration to M. Fort to have a discharge of debts and quittance drawn up.[106] Fort was also the receiving address for Minuti's letters from the Levant.[107]

Similarly, when Mallon, the French surgeon at Damascus, needed medicines from his contact in Marseille, the master apothecary Thibault, it was Fort who was commissioned by Peiresc to locate and provide them.[108] Two years later, Fort was still going between Thibault and Mallon on behalf of Peiresc. In a letter to the apothecary of January 1632, Peiresc informed him that he had given Fort an order for M. l'Archier to furnish Mallon with 30 or 40 écus but that l'Archier had never made the short trip from Alexandretta to Aleppo, leaving Mallon without funds and at the risk of having his books seized by creditors.[109] We see how even carefully laid plans, such as Peiresc's, could be foiled by a single break in the chain of responsibility.

There are very few letters directly to Fort, given how omnipresent he was for Peiresc. A rare example from January 1631 ranged over some basic issues, suggesting their typicality. Peiresc began by saying that he would be sending from Aix a small bundle of books destined for Mallon in Damascus in response to a request. He asked Fort to confirm with Thibault that everything was in order with Mallon's request. Peiresc then asked Fort to find out if any ships were departing imminently for Alexandretta, as well as the name of the ship that was eventually chosen, the name of the captain, and the name of the person charged with the packet. Finally,

Peiresc wanted Fort to let him know as soon as there was solid information about the ship's departure schedule so that he could supply all the other letters and goods to accompany it "just in time."[110] A rare surviving letter *from* Fort dated 1 February 1630 mentions four letters from Peiresc, two each on 28 and 30 January.[111] A letter from Fort of the previous day, 31 January 1630, mentions receiving three letters from Peiresc at the same time.[112] These suggest a huge volume of correspondence—as with de Gastines—almost no trace of which has survived, as if intentionally excluded from preservation on account of its uninteresting, everyday nature. But blame cannot be cast on those who preserved the archive; the person who made it seems to have shared the same value system. For these many quotidian letters to Fort and de Gastines were generally not included by Peiresc in his log of outgoing correspondence.[113]

Similarly, when Peiresc was trying to manage the research trip of the Minim Father Jean François to Barcelona in 1629, he turned to Fort. We possess a letter from Fort, dated 27 May 1629, announcing that a "Sr. Salvy Rocafort" was now authorized to advance Jean François 20 écus on Peiresc's order, and was sending this with a "troop" of Minim fathers who were going to Barcelona.[114] This Rocafort was one of Fort's agents in Barcelona, and thus someone who could provide not only money but other sorts of material support.[115]

Fort handled other sensitive matters as well. He was the vector for a shipment to Peiresc of "preservatifs," one of which for demonstration's sake was covered in satin, provided and fabricated by an otherwise unidentified "Marengo." The term in the eighteenth century referred to a kind of air filter for use during plague. The fact that this letter was sent in August 1629, just as plague was breaking out across Provence, and that Peiresc was asking for a large number and Marengo was offering them for "your friends in Aix," points to the plague.[116] (This same Marengo also brought Peiresc a copy made by Lucas Holstenius of Robert Cotton's "Pisan Portulan.")[117]

Fort played a major role in managing all reimbursements, but he was not the only one. Captains, because they moved between coasts, were especially valuable agents in this process. The captain often had to lay out the money, and so Peiresc was at pains to guarantee at least a "no loss" situation. Thus, writing to Captain Carrayre in 1633, Peiresc thanked him for bringing a book purchased by Minuti. Peiresc had arranged for de Gastines to pay the "nolis"—the freight charge—from Sidon to Marseille, but also, and here we see Peiresc thinking of his long-term needs, from

Cyprus, which must have been his previous port of call, to Sidon. Moreover, Minuti mentioned that he had spent 43 piastres on Peiresc's service; if these had been furnished by the captain or by anyone of his acquaintance, Peiresc wanted to resupply it immediately.[118]

Finally, just to give a sense of comparative pricing, if the costs of supporting an overseas expedition for the one day from Aleppo to Mount Casius was near on 100 piastres, an "idol" in black marble from Egypt came with a cost of 400 piastres.[119] And the cost of supporting a traveler in the field was even greater. Galaup-Chasteuil was bankrolled by his brother, who paid out 2,400 livres, and his mother, who provided 200 livres for immediate necessities. For his part, Peiresc had provided a letter of credit for 600 livres in August 1635 in case he wished to return home, and another 150 livres for immediate necessities.[120]

Finally, Marseille was where not only Peiresc's oriental studies were funded but also his domestic accounts. A letter to Vallavez of July 1626 shows us Peiresc selling salt and wheat at Marseille for thousands of livres (the asking price is 5,000 to 7,000). Peiresc was the one handling the negotiations, and they seem to have gone through a totally different network of names.[121]

14 ✣
Sanson Napollon

O ne of the most interesting of those Marseille people was Sanson Napollon, the person whom the young Braudel first encountered in Algiers and who connected him to the Peiresc archive.

Napollon was a Corsican-born Marseille merchant. To this extent he resembled many of those otherwise unknown Marseillais who appear on the stage of the Peiresc archive. (Antoine Berengier, for example, who handled part of Peiresc's correspondence with North Africa, was also Corsican by birth.)[1] But Napollon assumed a series of diplomatic roles as well, moving on a more public platform, and so we can see him through other archival prisms as well. He served in a variety of diplomatic roles in the decade after de Brèves's departure from the East. We find him first in Aleppo in 1615, where he was serving as consul. He reports there on the movement of Ottoman armies and internal Ottoman politics—insofar as they were accessible to him—and on the costs of doing business in the East.[2] In the early 1620s he was sent back to the Levant by the Crown to inspect and advise on the better management of the French consulates in the Levant, which were suffering during the ambassadorial "reign" of the controversial and spendthrift comte de Césy, especially that of Aleppo.[3] For this work he was ennobled in 1623.[4] He was then appointed consul in Smyrna.[5] He arrived there in January 1624, only to find the Dutch already present and collaborating with the Armenians.[6] By March he was in Constantinople meeting with the ambassador and other officials, such as Gédoyn, then traveling as a special envoy.[7] He was still there in the middle of May.[8] By 10 June he was back in Smyrna, and we find him there at the end of July as well.[9] Peiresc's archive preserves excerpts of a letter from Napollon written from Cape Sunion, in Greece, on 4 September 1624.[10] At some point in 1624, while in Smyrna, Napollon purchased for Peiresc what later become known as the "Arundel Marbles" when he was jailed by the local authorities, and Sir William Petty repurchased the stones for his master and spirited them out of the country.[11]

Napollon seems also to have been in Aleppo during this period.[12] But this visit may have stepped on the toes of other French officials on the site, if the words of the then-consul Gédoyn stand for more than just selfish reflection: "I find myself greatly scandalized by the enterprise of that Napollon."[13]

By April 1625 Napollon was given charge of negotiations with Algiers by Cardinal Richelieu and was heading from one end of the Mediterranean to the other.[14] A set of formal "Instructions" to Sanson Napollon for negotiating the peace with Algiers is dated 16 February 1626.[15] By January 1627 he was in Algiers. We know this, among other things, because he copied down some ancient inscriptions there and sent them to Peiresc in Aix.[16] When Napollon was away, Jean Gazille lived in his home and managed his mailbox.[17] From this period, and this vector, we can trace the various documents on Algiers that are found in the Carpentras volume on the Regency of Algiers—the one from which Braudel pulled those paltry seven documents so many years ago because he did not understand where to look.

Peiresc and Marseille friends such as Vias saw Napollon as an ally in the perpetuation of the de Brèves "interest."[18] De Brèves was actually appointed by Louis XIII to collect the funds donated by the coastal towns of Provence for the redemption of their captives and to give the money to Napollon.[19] Yet the latter's role as "special emissary" also roiled the local waters, since the interests of Marseille were not always identical with those of Paris and, even if they were, people were sensitive to local rights and privileges being trampled on, whatever the good intention or cause. Thus, when Napollon needed a ship to travel to Algiers, Peiresc told him that the court was willing to loan him one, so long as the charge would be picked up by someone else, or if the barque could also carry some cargo to help defray its cost. Peiresc suggested Pierre Fort as a supporter of Napollon's who would be glad to help and whose relation to Vias—they were brothers-in-law—linked him to the de Brèves party.[20] Madame de Brèves was selling scarlet cloth in Algiers because there was no market for it in Marseille, and while Napollon managed the import-export, Fort was the "garde de cette affaire."[21] Fort was also named by the court of the parlement to outfit the barque being put at the disposal of Napollon for his negotiations in Algiers in 1627.[22]

Peiresc's archive preserves a copy of the peace agreement Napollon negotiated, as well as his report on the month he spent in Algiers completing the negotiations.[23] Peiresc also retained copies of letters sent to Napollon by Mustafa, captain general of the galleys of Algiers, and by Sidi Amoda, first secretary of the divan and militia of Algiers.[24] An additional letter to Napollon from Bechar Bassa of Tunis found its way, perhaps via Peiresc, to the Dupuy brothers in Paris.[25]

Napollon had a clear personal interest in peace: as governor of the newly reestablished Bastion de France he would reap the profits on any wheat exported from there. Indeed, in this same dossier in Carpentras there is a list of wheat exports from Bastion to Italy, showing monthly shipments in the first four months of 1629, that is, immediately after the signing of peace.[26] Shipping to Italy maximized profits for Napollon, but it drove up costs in Provence, and this put Napollon and the consuls of Marseille on a collision course. The continuing attacks by the corsairs, even after Napollon's peace treaty, and the hostility in Marseille to the way new wheat imports from the Regency of Algiers cut in on old profit streams, kept Napollon on the defensive.

After the treaty-signing in September 1628, Napollon took possession of Bastion de France as its governor. His "Discours du Bastion de France" and "Le Budget de Sanson Napollon" were both published in *Bastion de France*.[27] And though he moved back and forth between North Africa, Marseille, and Paris trying to secure support for the French position in North Africa, and for the commerce of Bastion de France—which often ran contrary to the vested interests of Marseille's merchants—Napollon remained its governor until his death in battle in 1633.[28] Bastion de France was itself destroyed not long after, in 1637, and 317 Corsicans were sent to the galleys.[29]

15 ❧
Naturalizing Merchants

*T*hinking about Peiresc's operations, one has to wonder about the means he used to mobilize so many different people to act as his agents, exercising his authority at a distance. He had many tools at his disposal. Money, of course, was one of them. He spent it carefully, but always generously. He also provided assistance and, perhaps still more important, access to those in positions of authority. Thus, in the case of Antoine Piscatoris, Peiresc was not bashful in applying directly to the mother of Valbelle, the lieutenant of the admiralty, to have his legal case favorably adjudicated.[1] He offered the same support to de Gastines. Minuti asked him to intervene in the legal case of Jérôme de l'Isle, and then de l'Isle added his own request.[2] And at the end of a letter filling him in on the state of Napollon's negotiations in Algiers, his man in Marseille, Antoine Gazille, was not bashful about asking Peiresc to help him with a legal case involving the widow of his late cousin.[3]

But one feels that for many of the merchants he worked with, merely being asked by an aristocrat, scholar, and celebrity of Peiresc's eminence was inducement enough. In an economy of status, working with Peiresc meant a lot. We have seen this operating in many aspects of Peiresc's activities, as, for instance, with the Jewish correspondents of Salomon Azubi in little towns in the Comtat Venaissin who were eager to share their finds with the great man and occupy even the smallest part of his world.[4]

But one of the tools at Peiresc's disposal that we might not otherwise have anticipated had to do with his very good political ties. Beginning early in his career, Peiresc took to using his access to the high judiciary to secure papers of naturalization on behalf of his foreign-born contacts. It is a mark of the Mediterraneanism of the Marseille trade that many of its players were not born French. Helping with their citizenship secured for him a deep sense of loyalty that he could then rely on.

Eschinard in Rome was naturalized thanks to Peiresc.[5]

Sanson Napollon had already been honored for his services to France. Peiresc helped arrange for a passport for Madame Napollon and for Gazille, Napollon's assistant.[6]

Through the elder M. le Tenneur, Peiresc obtained letters of naturalization for Claude Menestrier, one of his Roman agents, and for Sacco and Durand, merchants and consuls of Marseille.[7]

Peiresc also worked through his brother at court to obtain a passport for one of his regular collaborators among the Marseille merchants, Barthélemy Issaultier.[8]

The long arm of Peiresc reached also to Rome: in 1636 he intervened with his agent Marchand to seek letters of naturalization from the pope for one François Taxil, a native of Entrevaulx near Peyresq in the Alps of Provence. Taxil is elsewhere described as a ship's captain.[9]

The information we possess about the naturalization of Peiresc's two chief Egyptian agents, Santo Seghezzi and Jean Magy, is more extensive. In a letter to Gela, Seghezzi's brother-in-law in Marseille, Peiresc asked if he could see an "extract" from Seghezzi's letters of naturalization to make it easier for him to intervene and resolve whatever difficulties there might be. He suggests that Seghezzi make a brief return to France to speed the process. He did not have any information about the "particulières habitudes" of M. Boilliau—perhaps the person who made the decision on citizenship?—but he could try to find out through his friends at court.[10] When Peiresc charged Magy with giving Seghezzi a series of instructions "and to communicate to him only and confidentially all my mémoires and instructions," he added, "and it is necessary to extract whatever you could by way of said Sr. Santo, because he is declared completely French, and assures me of so much good will."[11]

Peiresc worked for his friends. A note from 21 January 1634 to Jean-Baptiste Magy in Marseille lapidarily begins, "I have written about it to M. the Lieutenant for the affair that you desire, and have written to my brother to recommend it further with enthusiasm."[12] This seems to refer to his effort to arrange at court for Jean Magy's wife and their oldest child to obtain letters of naturalization.

Documentation for this in Peiresc's archive allows us to reconstruct his actions and the biography of those involved. First indications of this affair are found in a letter fragment to Jean Magy dated 14 July 1633: "I wrote to Court for the naturalization of Mademoiselle Magy."[13] On the very next day Magy wrote back thanking him on behalf "of my wife and my little Egyptian" ("mon petit Egissien").[14] Proceedings seem to have reached a decisive stage in the summer of 1635. Peiresc wrote to Secretary of State Villeauxclercs in July of 1635. Peiresc described Magy as a "poor boy who has more good will and probity than means" and who had served the merchants of Marseille in Egypt for many years without acquiring any means ("sans pouvoir acquerir guieres de facilitez").[15] He had taken up with a Pole who had been seized from her cradle by the Tatars and then sold to the Turks, who resold her to Egypt for 60 or 80 piastres. She— Anne Belle—and Magy had a boy in 1631 and married in 1632 in Marseille. Magy wished now to naturalize the child. Essentially, Magy was asking to be treated like any French person who, while on His Majesty's service outside France, gave birth to a child. In addition, because they lacked means, Magy asked that the cost of the "seal," or the notarial solemnization of the decree, be waived on their behalf. Peiresc added his voice to the request, explaining that "he is employed in that far land to recover for me some old manuscript books which I pay rather dearly for but for which, nevertheless, I am very satisfied and content." Peiresc asked, in conclusion, that the letters of naturalization be addressed to the Cours des Comptes, Aydes et Finances of Provence in which he served.[16]

After this letter, Peiresc left Vallavez, then at court, to handle things from the inside.[17] Peiresc explained to Mrs. Magy that in the absence of her husband they had to obtain a declaration by Agostin Magy, his father (and her father-in-law), stating that she had no debts through marriage, that she had no other means or property but her own industry, and that her son was still a minor and also with no means of inheriting anything. This, along with depositions from himself and Minuti, would be sufficient.[18] A second letter, however, a week later, adds some extremely valuable information. Peiresc explains that the attestation should note that when Jean Magy and Anne Belle were married she had no property at all because she had been a slave of the Turks. Peiresc suggested sending also an extract from their marriage contract, if there was one. Benoit Pelissier would serve as the third character witness.[19] The letters of naturalization were finally registered by the Chambre des Comptes in October 1635.[20]

This story of Marseille and its foreign-born merchants pieced together from the Peiresc archive corresponds exactly to the picture of naturalization in sixteenth-century Aix and Marseille pieced together for us out of other archives by Gabriel Audisio. For him, Marseille is "the most 'foreign' city of Provence," with a non-French population that is heavily Italian but also drawn from other Mediterranean littorals and as far east as Greece. Most of these foreigners, he finds, are in commercial, artisanal, and maritime occupations (and there is likely overlap between the first and third categories).[21] But Peiresc and his names are nowhere to be found.

16 ⁊

North Africans in Marseille

North Africans were a regular presence in Marseille. Wolfgang Kaiscr has pointed to the existence of Muslim domestics, mostly from North Africa.[1] Naval warfare brought in others. A letter from de Brèves to the consuls of Marseille in 1617 was carried by ten Turks for whom de Brèves had obtained a royal passport and who were on their way home.[2] In a letter to John Barclay in 1619, Peiresc notes that a group of "Turks come from Algiers" were recently hauled in by the governor of Provence, M. de Guise, and on their knees begged for mercy and pardon for their anti-French deeds.[3] Only a year later, rumors of a Marseille ship that had been seized, its crew mostly killed, and the ship scuttled led to a lynching. Forty-five members of an Algerian embassy, as well as galley slaves, were killed.[4] A similar bloody manhunt occurred in 1627.[5] In that same year, just to show that it was not all hostility, Peiresc wrote to Pelletier, the treasurer-general of France, of the arrival of three Turkish galleys from Algiers. They came to salute Marseille and return Marseillais slaves whom they had taken, all on account of the captain of their galleys having being saved from a wreck by the French and set at liberty. They claimed that they wished to repatriate even more slaves in the event that France would agree to the terms being negotiated by Napollon.[6] In 1628, Peiresc mentions a "Turkish *Capigy* who is at Marseille."[7] In all this we see Peiresc using "Turk" and "North African" interchangeably, though perhaps also precisely.

From Toulon in 1627, Vallavez reported to Peiresc the presence of a lone "Granadin"—the term used for a Morisco expelled from Spain to North Africa in 1609—who was a potter (he planned to place an order with him).[8] Dr. Cassagnes in 1620 reported on the presence of many Turks, or Turkish-speaking North African galley-slaves, prisoner in Marseille. In 1633 he reported on additional ones.[9] These captives sometimes came with texts: one of these, a calendar and almanac, was sent from Cassagnes to Peiresc and on to Gabriel Sionite in Paris for translation help.[10] And of course there was Sayet, the Berber from Morocco who joined Napollon's retinue in Algiers, probably in early 1627, and was put to work by Peiresc translating his Islamic coins in a study group with Salomon Casino, the Greek-born Jew who joined Napollon's service in Smyrna or Constantinople, and Baltasar de Vias.[11]

In 1630, Peiresc thanked the merchant Antoine Berengier, who did a large volume of trade with North Africa, for some marble fragments for which he was as grateful as if they were "antiques." Peiresc conjectured that they might refer to some Genoese sent to Tabarka or Corsica. The *armoiries* and the eagle seemed to him to point to a Genoese provenance.[12]

With merchants traveling back and forth, news from Algiers was always plentiful on the docks in Marseille. In August 1633, Peiresc informed the secretary of state in Paris of a rebellion in Algiers between the ruling Turks and the locals who, abetted by Moriscos arrived from Spain, tried to torch the city. The rebellion was put down with a loss of eight thousand lives and special destruction wreaked on the Moriscos.[13]

Peiresc saw the population of North Africans, most of them slaves, as potential sources of information. We know from a letter to Mersenne of July 1634 that Peiresc listened to a galley-slave sing and, upon asking, discovered that he had learned the song in North Africa from black Moors. If the music could "not be expressed easily in our notes," and reflected "a taste different from our usage in some manner," it was nevertheless "full of grace." It was Peiresc himself—"ce fut moy"—who went to Marseille and worked with a local musician to transcribe the song into musical notation. He wrote in Latin letters all the syllables of the Turkish, in the form most approaching the pronunciation of the unfortunate gallerian. Peiresc's conclusion on this encounter was clear: "These people there are not so rude and so barbarous as one would build them up, and they like harmony when they can play it, whether with the voice or with instruments."[14]

17 ⚘

Northerners in the Mediterranean

Napollon was born in Corsica, lived in and became a citizen of Marseille, and died in North Africa. Many other of Peiresc's Marseille contacts also came from elsewhere. One of the most dramatic of Fernand Braudel's pinpoint visions of change—in a book generally dedicated to anesthetizing it upon a table—was the "Northern Invasion," the discovery of the Dutch and English penetration of the Mediterranean at the beginning of the seventeenth century.[1] This parallels the *translatio studii* that was so noted by contemporaries.[2] Dutch and English diplomats in Constantinople were present from the beginning of the seventeenth century and were immediately perceived as meddlesome threats by the French, encroaching on a nearly century-old *Entente* between France and the Ottomans. Along with the Venetians, the Dutch and English are seen in the correspondence as conspiring "to ruin our nation's business in order to raise up theirs the more."[3]

The Dutch and English are also present in Peiresc's Mediterranean. When Sir Henry Spelman's son travels in France, he visits Marseille and reports to Peiresc's brother, Vallavez, of the "ressentiment" of the English who live there.[4] A document dated to 1621–1623 and emanating from Algiers lists the number of Western prizes broken down by nation. The single largest number, more than double the next highest, is Dutch. Assuming that all ships were more or less equally vulnerable, deviations would have to represent a much higher volume of shipping. (If we follow Peiresc's assumption that Dutch shipping was much less vulnerable than French, then there would have to be even more Dutch ships in circulation.)[5] All this would seem to confirm arguments about intensified Dutch penetration of the Mediterranean during the Twelve Years' Truce (1609–1621) such that by 1620 they had seized a large part of the trade.

The same Seguiran Report of 1633 that documents the powerful role of Marseille merchants in the Levant trade also documents a number of northern ships in Mediterranean ports. For instance, it locates three Flemish ships with cargo of "lead, coal and herring" for Marseille that planned to return to Toulon to fill up on oil and salt. Three English ships of 200 tons—no tonnage was given for Dutch ships—were reported as arriving carrying only silver with which to buy olives, soap, and capers. Records of ships arriving in Marseille show that from one Dutch ship arriving in 1612, the number rose to four in 1613, nine in 1628, and seven in 1636.[6] Careful examination of surviving admiralty court records in Marseille would surely provide additional examples.

Seguiran also interviewed Flemish and English consuls at Toulon: "It was told to us that every year there landed at Toulon 15 or 20, and sometimes 30, Flemish ships usually carrying herring, hake, a kind of coal used on ships, fat, lead and other similar things." About the same number came from England, Ireland, or Newfoundland with salted fish, lead, pewter, cowhide, and white herring, and returned with olives, capers, almonds, salt, and rice, "which they bring from Genoa. He asked and they told of the usual customs duties."[7] Seguiran's report also pays attention to trade goods and the Turkish *avanies*, or various shakedown taxes and bribes, as well as tonnage, size, and number. (Peiresc used the Turkish term to describe the attempt by others to get him to overpay for services in the Republic of Letters.)[8]

Peiresc also collected—we do not know exactly when—a Dutch treatise of 1607 "touching on the navigation, traffic, fisheries, commerce and other things appropriate to the North Sea, the Ocean and the Indies where His Majesty's rebels live and trade."[9] This manuscript, on which Pierre Dupuy noted that a lot had since changed and which Hugo Grotius corrected in the margins, begins with pages on the different fisheries, but *does not* include a separate section on the Mediterranean. There was discussion of Spain and Italy, but nothing on Marseille. In the section devoted to India there is mention of a Dutch factory at Aleppo, but there is nothing on Egypt. At this moment in time, and for the author of this treatise, it seems that the Mediterranean as such did not exist as a separate, recognizable interest.

The correspondence gives us a very different view of Dutch presence than we might get in Braudel's depiction of Dutch convoys penetrating the sea at its western orifice and thrusting through to its eastern limit: the famous *Staatsvart*.[10] Peiresc was paying close attention: even a sole "Dutch or English ship"—and the absence of precision is itself telling— sailing to Aigues-Mortes in 1621 was worthy of note, as in a letter from Vallavez to Peiresc, or a "Flemish" ship loading oil at Toulon.[11] The shipwreck of a Dutch ship some years before 1627 led Peiresc to draw up a brief on the laws and customs in such cases.[12] Peiresc had brought to him a copy of part of the treaty between Cardinal Richelieu and a group of Dutch entrepreneurs "for the establishment of big commerce."[13] De Thou also was paying attention: when his weather-plagued trip from Venice to Constantinople deposited him at Crete, far behind schedule, he switched to a Dutch ship that was going to Constantinople.[14] And it was on English ships coming from Venice that Peiresc (and Marseille) received the rumor of Marcheville's death sentence and his ransoming for 100,000 piastres by the European diplomatic community there.[15]

Reality was much more complicated, as related in a letter from Aycard to Peiresc of 1634. Aycard told of a stone-cutter from Lucca named Antonio Leivan, who had stopped in Toulon on his way back from Beziers, where he had bought some jasper-like stones. He needed money, so Aycard loaned him 50 écus, and Leivan left the pieces on deposit until he could return from a planned trip to Genoa. In the meantime, a Dutch captain arrived and purchased the stones. Leivan had left his address at Genoa with an apothecary named Nicoloso Friedany. Later, Aycard found out that Leivan was at Lucca and had become a merchant in wood for making barrels. His nephew had taken over the business at Beziers.[16] The very ordinariness of the presence of the Dutchman in this typical Mediterranean picture of movement and filiation is the point of the letter.

We have already met the Dutch merchant bank based in Marseille, Ruts and Martin.[17] In a letter to his Genoese correspondent Pietro Maria Boerio, Peiresc had Ruts and Martin drawing an order of 8 écus for the account of William Vandestraten.[18] In a letter of June 1637 we see Peiresc working with two different reimbursement streams: his own banker, de Gastines, and the Dutch connection of Ruts and Martin in Marseille and Vandestraten in Genoa. There was also a Vandestraten in Marseille, Thomas.[19] The presence of the Dutch in these western Mediterranean ports suggests a different dimension of the *Staatsvart*—not just the occasional flotilla but a permanent presence.[20]

Nicolas Pichery (or Piquery), Rubens's brother-in-law, opens up still another angle on the question of Peiresc and the Netherlanders. For Rubens and Peiresc to have exchanged letters "per la via di Marsiglia" suggests that there was direct shipping between the South and the North.[21] We know, too, that in 1625 Peiresc could write of "waiting very impatiently" for the "Dutch and Norman" ships—the latter no doubt those of Saint-Malo—suggesting some kind of regularity.[22] When Peiresc asked Rubens if he could help obtain an example of Cornelius Drebbel's perpetual motion machine, he explained also that Rubens ought to send something by ship, taking advantage of the regular traffic to Marseille. "On account of the glass," Peiresc wrote, "I believe it will be easiest to send it by way of sea, on the ships that come from Holland to Marseille, addressed to Sr. Gaspar Signier, who is charged to pay the port fees and securely bring the package to Aix."[23] (Signier, as we have seen, was Peiresc's banker at the time.) Rubens agreed that "there was not lacking in Antwerp the most secure communication with Marseille."[24]

Peiresc named names, telling us even more about the Dutch community in Marseille. We learn this way of two men, Baltasar Boyer and Abraham Stayar, who were the local agents of Guillaume van Steenwinckel of Amsterdam.[25] It was this network—Dutch, not Flemish—that Peiresc hoped to activate in order to get Drebbel's machine from Rubens. The Dutch merchants described Peiresc, in turn, as a "person of great merit and for whom we very much desire to be able to render some kind of appropriate service." Peiresc wanted "to group together some little boxes or other things that he sent by way of Amsterdam."[26] And Peiresc for his part was sure that any monies laid out in Amsterdam could easily be reimbursed by way of mutual contacts in Marseille.[27] In this context, we learn of a man named Guillaume (Guillelmo) Lancelot, or Nancelot, who was based in Marseille but in 1627 was responsible for a Dutch ship loading goods in Toulon and then sailing directly to Antwerp. Peiresc put a package on this ship.[28] And we know that Rubens on at least one occasion sent his letters to Peiresc by way of this Lancelot of Marseille.[29]

War, of course, played a major role in this narrative. The outbreak of hostilities between France and Spain in 1635 severed communications with the Spanish Netherlands and complicated them with the United Provinces. Pichery, for example, advised Peiresc to send his letters to one Abraham Garnier at Middelburg in the United Provinces, rather than to Spanish-controlled Antwerp. Peiresc explained to a friend—this was in 1635—that "from that side, their letters go more freely than from ours, and possibly without going through so many formalities."[30]

At sea, however, the outbreak of war between the Catholic powers was an opportunity for the Dutch. To Loménie in 1634, Peiresc reported a rumor that 136 Dutch ships had passed the straits and were heading to attack Barcelona.[31] To Petit, a year later, he reported that the king had hired thirty Dutch ships to fight Spain.[32]

But before open warfare, there had been Dutch privateers in the Mediterranean. One of the most famous of these was Simon Danser (originally Zymen Danseker).[33] The gunners on his ship, Peiresc wrote to

Malherbe in 1609, "were all Flemings," and Danser himself was not averse to massacring the Turks he worked for and holding others to ransom for Dutch prisoners.[34]

A fascinating, and dominant, inflection of the theme of northerners in the Mediterranean was Peiresc's constant harping on the moral weakness of the Provençaux compared to the Dutch and English. Whereas these latter would stand and fight off the corsairs, the Provençaux would flee or strike sails.[35] (De Thou was more charitable; given the slightness of the French ships compared to the English, their only hope when challenged lay "in speed and flight.")[36] The problems with the Provençaux were threefold: they did not know how to fight at sea (or would not, which amounted to the same thing); they waited to be fully loaded rather than sail back with an empty hold (thus slowing down communication); and they did not know how to travel in a convoy like the northerners. On the other hand, when there were only Provençal ships nearby, Peiresc did not advise missing the present opportunity.[37] This on at least one occasion led to recriminations when the choice of the present opportunity (Provençal shipping) conflicted with the general maxim (use northerners) and led to the loss of the ship and its cargo to corsairs (see Section 29, "Ransoming").[38]

Peiresc drew the consequences of his judgment, sending his letters to Egypt as often as possible on the English ships hired out by Lambert and de Gastines.[39] In turn, he repeatedly urged his agents in Egypt to use northern shipping. Thus, he asked Jean-Baptiste Magy in Marseille to second his own request to his brother in Egypt to consign his Arabic Gospels to Durbec (perhaps Durbeck?), captain of the English ship financed by de Gastines.[40] The ship made Marseille by the beginning of August, and Peiresc explicitly expressed satisfaction with the English captain: "Because although I had no knowledge of them at all, and their humor seems so rude and brusque, they are wanted much more than ours because they know better how to fight and contest for their honor, their faculties and their life." The Provençaux, by contrast, "are not so careful or so protective."[41] For the future, Peiresc urged Magy to use English or Dutch shipping on the account of Seghezzi—suggesting that the Venetian had better "commodity" with the northerners. Again Peiresc justified this in terms of the moral difference between the northern and southern sailors: "Because those men are more hardy and combative than ours and, God willing, will not fail to acquit themselves as loyally in the least, if God wills to bless our goods and innocent wishes in this regard."[42]

He would not have been surprised to learn that when de Thou was becalmed at Kefalonia, he saw an English privateer bringing in two French prizes.[43] And when the ships of Captains Baille and Beaussier were lost in the same year, it made Peiresc insist the more on the value of choosing "a Dutch ship."[44]

We find several instances of Marseille merchants relying, as often as possible, on English shipping. We know that de Gastines used English shipping.[45] So did Gela.[46] In fact, a document in the Archives of the Chambre de Commerce records the accounts "of all those who have loaded French merchandise on English and Dutch ships."[47] We can, therefore, conclude that the practice was fairly widespread. Interestingly, though, the French consul in Tunis, Lange Martin, reports in February 1628 that the Dutch and English loaded cargo onto French ships in Alexandria and Alexandretta.[48] Nevertheless, noting that the Dutch and English ships "are big and well armed," everyone wanted to use them for shipping goods, and not the smaller ships of the French and Italians.[49]

And if Peiresc was urging the use of English shipping, he was also thinking that it might go better with his Mediterranean contacts if they looked and sounded English too. Writing to Minuti, he announced, "I do not at all believe that you will be able to come to a good end as you are. It will be necessary almost, if you can, to disguise and transform into an Englishman instead of a Frenchman in order to extract the cordial and confidential recommendation—which you will as little know how to do, as to play the minister rather than the priest or monk."[50]

If English ships seemed the northerners more likely found in Egypt, it is the Dutch who seemed to predominate in Aleppo. When Aycard's nephew Salvator returned from Syria, he took a Flemish navire to Genoa, where he switched to a barque of La Ciotat for the last leg.[51] When contemplating the return to France of Galaup-Chasteuil in 1635, Peiresc suggested that he would return in a few months "on a Dutch fleet which is going to that country, capable of destroying the Turkish and the Spanish armies together."[52] Writing to the merchant Constans in Aleppo, Peiresc noted that he received the latter's previous letter on the Flemish *Galleon Bleu*. For the future he urged that letters be sent on Dutch or English ships when they were going directly to Marseille.

The outbreak of war with Spain in 1635 created conditions of instability, which made recurrence to northern shipping even more desirable. In August of that year, Peiresc wrote to Constans on "a Dutch ship which Messrs. Ruts and Martin sent to the Levant." If he had anything to send back, Peiresc recommended that he send it "by this means rather than by any other during this war with Spain."[53]

Ruts and Martin also seem to have helped connect Peiresc to the network of Dutch captains. Thus, Peiresc asked Jean-Baptiste Magy in Marseille to inform Ruts and Martin that he needed to go to Arles, "so that if the Dutch captain wants to come to this city [Aix], they should know that I will be absent from it and could be away three or four days."[54]

In addition to using the shipping commodity provided by Ruts and Martin, Peiresc used their banking services as well. As we have seen, Peiresc generally relied on the contacts of de Gastines and Lambert.[55] While de Gastines had "correspondants" in Aleppo, it seems that on the Syro-Lebanese coast, at least by the mid-1630s, Peiresc was relying more heavily on Ruts and Martin.[56] We can see this in a letter of inquiry to an unnamed figure in Sidon whom Peiresc wanted to help support Galaup-Chasteuil, which spells out both that it was the confidence that Peiresc had in the friendship of Ruts and Martin that led him to write in the first instance, and that it was through Ruts and Martin that reimbursement could be expected.[57]

When Peiresc was trying to persuade Galaup-Chasteuil to return home to Provence, he urged him to travel on one of the Flemish ships that came to the Levant on the account of Ruts and Martin "just as I would choose it for myself if I were in your place" ("come je la choisirois pour moy mesme si j'estoit en votre place"). But even if he did not want to travel on one of their ships, Peiresc assured him that they could help in other ways.[58] Peiresc even arranged for Ruts and Martin to forward to Galaup a stipend from Galaup's family.[59]

Ruts and Martin had also established themselves in maritime France. As we have seen, when Peiresc's agent in Bordeaux was held up and thus could not communicate the rent money from the abbey of Guîtres to Peiresc's regular banker, Peiresc turned to Ruts and Martin. They had an English friend who was able to come from Bordeaux to Marseille with the money. Peiresc declared that "there are only these English who traffic between Bordeaux and Marseille."[60] In a parallel letter to Guillemin, Peiresc insisted that no one could more conveniently assist him with remittances "than the English merchants who have their *correspondance* at Marseille." They always had lots of cash around for the purchase of wine, Peiresc explained, and so could convert letters of credit into ready money.[61] Two months later Guillemin was still looking for a way to send money to Peiresc; it had been held up because Peiresc was trying to avoid paying the usual delivery charge ("droit de remise"). He reports being told by a "marchand flamand" at Marseille that he would look to find this through some English who were the only ones who saw their way to dropping this fee.[62] In the end, it seems the transaction was effected by Ruts and Martin at a low rate.[63]

But the historical persistence of the English presence in Bordeaux also had maritime consequences. When Peiresc wanted to get some marble from Toulouse, he proposed that it be sent downriver to Bordeaux, where it could then be loaded onto the English ships "which come to Marseille."[64]

It is possible, also, that Peiresc's turn to Ruts and Martin reflects the application of his own principles. In a letter to de Thou of May 1635, Peiresc complained about the pusillanimity of the French compared to the Dutch and English. Noting how a recent attempt by corsairs to take a "Flemish" ship was repelled, he added, "It is the truth that it almost only applies to them and to the English to sail [there], because the others so little know how to defend themselves and I think that now one must hire the English and Flemish to trade in the Levant."[65] In other words, the Provençal captains did not realize that their behavior was driving French merchants to hire out English and French ships to trade in the Levant, "just as M. de Gastines did a few months ago, who happily hired an English ship which despite the plague in Alexandria arrived safely at Livorno, thank God." On his example, Sr. Gela was doing the same, hiring another English or Dutch ship for the voyage to Alexandria.[66] An extract from material prepared by Christofle Bermond, French consul in Egypt and dated 1639, gives the names of ten merchants based in Cairo who had hired out Dutch or English ships, including Jean Magy, and then it gives the captains' names, the dates of the sailing, and the value of the cargo. All date from 1635 and later—just that moment when we have seen the dramatic uptick in the volume and intensity of Peiresc's Levantine operation.[67]

Perhaps the most telling demonstration of the importance of frequency and speed for communications rather than heft is illustrated by the correspondence of Jacob Golius, the great Arabist at Leiden, with his brother Pierre, who as the Discalced Carmelite Celestin of St. Lidwine had moved to Aleppo. When they exchanged letters, they sent them to Peiresc, who then arranged for either outbound placement on a Provençal ship leaving Marseille or onward forwarding by land to Leiden.[68]

Sometimes, as we learn in a letter of Peiresc's from August 1635, this correspondence was hindered by quarantine rules, where a dousing in vinegar was common practice. But this, in turn, led Peiresc to delineate the path by which he would try to forward them on: to M. de Lieu, "maistre des couriers du roy," at Lyon and then on to Nicolas Pichery, his banker at Antwerp and the brother-in-law of the painter Peter-Paul Rubens. Another letter was addressed directly to Amsterdam, but without indicating its intermediate path. In conclusion, Peiresc noted that his letter was being carried on a ship organized by Ruts and Martin, "who are my good friends." Better to send with them "than by our French ships which do not fight well at sea and do not know how to preserve themselves like the Dutch, and especially during the war with Spain."[69]

But we should not imagine that this was a perfect system. In a letter to Father Celestin of May 1636, we see Peiresc apologizing for the letters he had written and the mémoires on eclipse observation he had prepared, which had piled up in October and November 1636—and even older ones, too, from April and May—which de Gastines had simply forgotten to send before leaving for Paris.[70] Worse still, when de Gastines returned, he found these letters in his "contoir" and sent them all to Sr. Venture, who did a high volume of trade with Aleppo. Sr. Venture, in turn, gave them to Patron Lombardon, and all were then lost with the sinking of the *St. Nicolas*. Worst of all was that this included a packet from Jacob Golius which had come to Peiresc in November 1635 and was sent on along with the books Celestin had asked of Peiresc, including Giggeius's Arabic dictionary. Peiresc was especially sad about this loss, "seeing so miserably interrupted the commerce which I had hoped could be shared between you and your brother more certainly and commodiously than by another way." First, there was the loss of the letter or packet to Golius because of poor handling of the purification in Marseille, and now that of the package from him because of shipwreck. Hard as he had tried, these were the "accidents that are hardly avoidable. Because Sr. Venture thought to have chosen the most assured of all the ships which were leaving in the fleet with Lombardon, and almost as if under his [personal] protection, and nevertheless . . ."[71]

Contact with Golius was all the more precious to Peiresc because made so precarious by war. If Pichery in Antwerp had suggested Peiresc write to him via Middelburg in the United Provinces, even finding a ship ready to sail from Marseille to Holland could prove vexing.[72] Indeed, for nearly all of 1636, Peiresc wrote in November to Golius, "the Marseillais had not sent any ship to that coast, which put them in great pain."[73] At almost the exact same time, the professor's brother in Aleppo was also complaining that no ships from Marseille had come to Syria.[74]

The loss of his Hexaglot Psalter in 1635 (see Section 29, "Ransoming") brought out a potential conflict for Peiresc and his people in Egypt. On the one hand, Peiresc urged them to use the first ship that presented itself as ready to depart in order to speed communication. On the other, he urged them to use Dutch and English shipping whenever possible. Responding to Peiresc's complaint about his having sent the book on a Provençal ship, Jean Magy pointed to this seeming contradiction, "and, what is more, Father Agathange gave me the courage to do it with the reason that in the port there was no other ship, and because of the plague that was at the time in the land no hope for the coming of others, and your order was that as soon as there would be something ready, to send it to you, which we have done."[75] Peiresc responded to this by reminding him that he had himself mentioned sending it on the English ship but that Father Agathange persuaded him "against your own sentiment to hazard by this means here the volume of the Four Evangelists, and nevertheless I had begged you by the same English to send it to me with them." Baille—the Provençal captain—had already shown himself unfortunate in losing a bale of books to the Nile on his way there, which should have disqualified him from further service altogether.[76]

This was how Peiresc sorted out the contradiction—what he was most explicit about was to be followed, and using English shipping was something he was always explicit about.

A month later, and with the earthiness that he so often dropped into with friends, Peiresc thanked Jean Magy for sending the letters of St. Paul on the "Flemish navire where it will not run the same risk as the Marseille barques, like wet chickens which lose their heads at the first shot of a cannon."[77]

Among the means tried by Peiresc to track down his lost Hexaglot Psalter was writing to the scrivener, Sr. Faysan, for information. "I have had such a hard time extracting from him this letter," Peiresc writes. "That is how unhelpful and irresponsible these people are, having found a lot more honesty in the English who seemed to you so rude." And yet, it was they who made the effort to bring him letters from Livorno and to look for the volume of the Evangelists.[78]

Was fear also linked to superstition? In other words, might there be a quasi-Weberian "deep" cause for the cowardice of the Provençaux? When seeking Egyptian mummies, Peiresc asked the Marseillais *patrons* to use Flemish shipping because, unlike the Provençaux, the Dutch and English were not afraid of mummies.[79] Apparently, the Provençal sailors believed that carrying any dead body on board, not only a mummy, would cause the ship to break open, while the English and Dutch entertained no such fantasies. Peiresc was, therefore, pleased that de Thou had himself seen mummies in a "grotto" in Egypt: "It has been a long time that these superstitions of our mariners have prevented me from bringing over a whole and well-conserved one, as I had hoped." Peiresc was sure that sooner or later de Thou would find a Fleming who would transport one for him, "because they laugh at all these scruples."[80] When planning for Minuti's trip, and his possible acquisition of a mummy, Peiresc wrote to the Marseille ship owner of Swiss heritage, Salicoffres (or Zollikoffer), with whom he had not yet been in touch, boldly asking his help to bring from Egypt a well-conserved and entire mummy "by means of your Flemish navires whose pilots and captains are not as scrupulous as our Provençaux," assuming it could be had at a reasonable price, which he thought not unlikely.[81] Elsewhere he wrote that "these English do not have as many scruples as the Provençaux about carrying it on their ships."[82] Fascinating for its glimpse into the culture of mariners, it also documents the increasing reliance by Marseille merchants on English shipping.

Writing to Fernoux, the vice-consul in Cairo in that same year 1629, Peiresc added that if Dutch ships were not as frequent visitors to Egypt as the English, the English would serve just as well.[83] Peiresc's report on the volume of trade is as interesting as the insight it offers into his own preferences: he preferred the Dutch, but the English were the more common. In the end, Peiresc got his mummy on a Provençal ship, *Notre Dame de la Consolation*, and it was carried by its scrivener, a Marseille merchant, Barthélemy Issaultier.[84]

18 ❧
Ship's Captains and *Patrons*

A particular feature of Peiresc's intellectual life, compared with his many contemporaries in the Republic of Letters, was the depth and extent of his interaction with the maritime merchant class. The last two decades of the history of scholarship has made clear the role of printers and print houses in the production of knowledge in early modern Europe.[1] But the relationship of scholars to the merchant class in general, and to the *patrons,* the traveling maritime merchants in particular, has been almost completely left aside.[2] Without their help, Peiresc would not be Peiresc.

Peiresc was equally involved with the captains who sailed the ships fitted out by the *patrons.* Just as he worked with merchants as equals, Peiresc wrote to the captains directly; they visited him at Aix, and he shared with them his ideas, plans, and projects. They were in many cases his partners. And from his archive we can establish a list of the captains who worked many of the Mediterranean routes, especially to those ports heavily frequented by Peiresc, such as Constantinople, Alexandretta, Sidon, Alexandria, Tunis, and Algiers.

Peiresc's archive is full of names of captains, *patrons,* and their ships, far in excess of what we can learn in published material.[3] It is richer than the Seguiran Report, prepared by Peiresc's brother-in-law for Cardinal Richelieu in 1633, which gives an enumeration of captains and ships, ordered by the ports from which they sailed, and richer on this question than even the Archives of the Chambre de Commerce of Marseille.[4]

A tabular rendering of these three paragraphs is presented as Appendix C.

19 ✲

Tasks Entrusted to Captains

*P*eiresc worked closely with captains. He kept track of their move-ments, invited them to his home, and corresponded with them about his projects. For instance, the polacre of Captain Roubaud set off for Alexandria in early September 1628.[1] It was on a return trip with de Thou's Egyptian objects when his ship sank in early summer 1629.[2] When Roubaud finally reached Marseille with items from the shipwreck, Peiresc devoted a letter to explaining how to restore them. He under-stood that the material was not in great condition, having been in the sea for eight days. Interestingly, Peiresc feared less the immersion than the damage produced by the air once the items were fished out of the water.[3] He explained to Captain Roubaud that he needed to get the objects as soon as possible and asked that de Thou's coffer be given to the lieu-tenant of the admiralty Valbelle or, even better, to de Gastines, who would pay the relevant charges.[4]

The haste proved wise. By August, Peiresc had received the objects and could report on the preliminary restoration work he had performed. The old vellum book had held up very well, while other materials, espe-cially the papers, were completely lost, the pages being stuck together. The medals were in good shape, having emerged from their immersion so shiny that the unversed would have thought them modern objects. Peiresc sug-gested that a possible remedy would be to plunge them into sweet water—or oil—immediately after taking them out of the salt water, and then drying them completely. All this, he concluded in another letter to Captain Rou-baud, was for the next time, in case malign fortune struck again.[5] Even more interesting, all this information is contained in a letter that was a *response* to one written to Peiresc by Roubaud. In other words, Peiresc's thoughts about objects' conservation were developed in a dialogue with a ship's captain and were then directed to that same ship's captain.

In another instance, Théophile Minuti specified that Captain Bartolle was to hand deliver to Peiresc the two cats he had acquired for him in Damascus.[6] Hearing that Captain Bartolle was passing through Toulon on the way to Marseille, Peiresc wrote to thank him for the help he provided Minuti on Minuti's passage and visit to the Holy Land. Some of this involved particular care for those cats. Peiresc offered to entertain Bartolle at his country estate at his convenience, knowing that the captain would be busy upon arrival with the unloading and organization of the cargo ("par la configuration de voz marchandises"). Still, Peiresc wanted to get his things as fast as possible, and he proposed various ways to do this.[7]

Peiresc also learned from Captain Bartolle about current shipping in Marseille. Bartolle informed him of the impending arrival of the navire *Grand Henry* on which Peiresc was expecting to find books, dried fruits, and plant grafts. Peiresc asked specifically if Bartolle knew when the ship had left the Levant, what route it had taken, and when he expected it to reach Marseille.[8] Or, writing to Gela in May 1634, Peiresc asked not only about his own goods but also more generally of the ships and the captains, and their estimated sailing time to Cairo.[9] He also collected information in letters that were sent to others in his network. Thus, he copied out a letter from l'Empereur in Constantinople, who reported to de Thou that one of his old friends, Captain Chaban, was going to the Black Sea with seventeen galleys, *galliotes,* and brigantines. He would be coasting from Sinope.[10] Synthesizing all this information, Peiresc was in a position to inform friends, such as Samuel Petit of Nîmes, that there were ten or twelve Marseille ships near or in Egyptian harbors in mid-1634.[11] He could also write with a knowledge of what shipping was planned for the future, as in a letter to Jean Magy in Egypt that noted that he would expatiate on a particular point in his next letter, which would be on a ship arriving in several weeks.[12] Under these circumstances, when he did not receive anything from Egypt for more than four months, he grew concerned.[13]

Peiresc's mental map of Mediterranean communication links extended far beyond the shores of the sea. When a boat loaded with letters for Egypt stayed in Marseille for over a month, Peiresc fretted that he would miss the caravan that left Egypt for Ethiopia around Easter time—and thus spoil his attempt to make contact quickly with Zacharie Vermeil at the emperor's court there.[14]

One reads these passages and can envision Peiresc plotting the courses of ships on a giant map of the Mediterranean, an "as if" Churchill in an "as if" war room. We can say with certainty that Peiresc's constant search for information about shipping on the move in the Mediterranean was not a form of train-spotting. It was, on the contrary, extremely practical, since having a sense of where everything was meant that in the event he needed to ransom an object that was lost, or quickly orient toward a particular person or object, he would know which "assets" were nearby.

Captains could, and did, provide information on natural phenomena.[15] And, like merchants, they were in a position to collect—and thus, in a republic of learned conversation, to discuss. One Captain "Beau," for example, possessed two gold coins of Alexander the Great.[16]

A mariner's experience of travel could itself yield knowledge, even in unfortunate circumstances. One, Anthoine Armand of Martigues, the son of Patron Jannot Armand, called Troupillon, and just returned from slavery in Algiers, translated for Peiresc an Arabic calendar captured from a corsairing ship. Armand had been taken at age ten and sold to one "Assenb Belluc" Basha, a member of the governing divan of Algiers, for 75 piastres. He had been forcibly converted to Islam and circumcised two months after his capture. He was later put to sea and made to serve as a scrivener. His knowledge of Arabic was seized upon by Peiresc. But what he could not do was translate the parts of the calendar that Peiresc called Persian—this knowledge went beyond his Mediterranean curriculum.[17]

20 ✑

Port Practices: Packaging—Plague—Quarantine

*P*eiresc's familiarity with port practices in the Mediterranean emerges clearly from his letters. These extend from details of how best to package his objects to understanding administrative guidelines to knowing how to circumvent them for his own benefit.

When preparing Théophile Minuti for his first voyage to the Levant, in 1629, Peiresc drew up a series of mémoires. They conclude with information about how to pack and ship:

> It will be necessary to properly pack the lot, and to enclose it in some well-marked box, bundle or little box, addressed to the Lord of Peiresc, with an envelope on top addressed to M. de Valbelle, Royal Councillor and Lieutenant General in the Admiralty, at Marseille, to have it held for the said Lord of Peiresc, and to recommend the box or little box, or bundle, to Sr. Estelle, Consul at Sidon, or to other consuls of the French nation who are found in those places to which one would want to send the said bundles, together, to the ships captains who are charged to carry them.[1]

Similarly, in a mémoire on citrus fruits from Crete, Peiresc continued seamlessly from their description into details of packing. Several plants, he noted, could be put together in "good barrels or half 'tuns'" with space enough to include soil from their *terroir*. The plants were not to be moved in winter, and had to be shielded from the sun and spray by a carefully positioned canvas "pavilion or tent."[2]

But it is the oubreak of plague, and the exigencies of quarantine regulation, that made good packaging a priority. In fact, bureaucratic intervention to establish a sanitary regime in Marseille dates to 1622, just prior to Peiresc's return to Aix, and we have seen that Peiresc used the back of a "bill of health" on which to record the path to him of the Samaritans' letter to Scaliger.[3]

The outbreak of plague in Marseille in 1630 had an instant and huge impact on shipping. Because of his exposure to risk—plants and animals would have been especially vulnerable to prolonged delay in reaching him—Peiresc was constantly engaged in finding ways around the rules. From these letters we learn much about the way the port functioned in the early seventeenth century.[4]

The return of Théophile Minuti from the Levant in April 1630, during the height of the plague, put Peiresc in a difficult situation. Peiresc expected Minuti to disembark at Cassis, where the Marseille merchants had relocated, and promised that de Gastines would take care of the procedures. If he disembarked at Toulon, Peiresc promised a welcome from his friend, the lieutenant of the admiralty, Valbelle. Peiresc thought this might be more convenient because of quarantine roadblocks between Cassis and Toulon, which lay on the route to Peiresc's country home at Belgentier. Peiresc also thought it best to avoid the purification regime for books, antiquities, and mummies, which involved dousing everything with vinegar: "It would be good to leave them in their original packaging and to get a certificate from the Intendants of Commerce and the consuls and Intendants of Health of Cassis since they were not unpacked, so that in burning the [outer] envelopes we will be done with all these formalities."[5]

That mémoire on citrus fruits from Crete paid special attention to how the plants were to be shipped. Packaging appears as a theme in the letters. From Constantinople, Minuti specified that he was sending two boxes put into a leather sack and sealed with his cachet.[6] From Egypt he received objects in a *caffas*. This was a kind of packaging unique to Egypt. A blue canvas sack was enclosed in a square cage of palm branches, which was then covered by cowhide or by a combination of cowhide and canvas.[7]

One of the more detailed—and roundabout—of Peiresc's Mediterranean itineraries was also all about the packaging. In 1630, Peiresc explained to Pierre Dupuy that he had a plan to retrieve a package currently with Jacques Godefroy in Geneva and send it to him in Paris. He would ask Godefroy to "pack and seal [it] on top with the lead ball of the Republic of Geneva and attach to it a certificate of said packaging and sealing." It would then be sent downstream to Lyon without being unpacked, and then by way of the Rhône to Marseille where, because of the plague, it would go with all other goods to the quarantine in the Isles of Marseille under the care of the intendants of the *Santé*. Peiresc would claim it from there and then send it on to Paris.[8]

From the plain sense, and between the lines, it is clear that Peiresc counted on the help of local health officials to circumvent their own procedures. But as we learn from an immediately subsequent letter to Minuti and a second to François-Auguste de Thou, despite Peiresc's efforts these materials were brought to Marseille, where they were caught up in the quarantine regime.[9] In the end, Peiresc urged Minuti to come to him, but mapped out a route that would avoid passing through Aubagne, La Ciotat, Castellet, Lerins, or any place where plague was found. It would be much better to go in the direction of La Cadière to the home of Valbelle, lieutenant of the admiralty, where the Minim Jean François had retired, or to Signes. Although it was only nine leagues from Marseille to Belgentier by the straight road via Signes, Cuges, and Aubagne—Minuti's route would be longer because more roundabout to avoid plague hotspots—it was "impossible" to find a person who would take the risk of going to Marseille. Minuti was advised either to bring all of his belongings from the Levant or to leave them "without worry" with Barthélemy Issaultier, who would take care of them as if his own merchandise.[10]

We find many instances in the correspondence of Peiresc using his connections to cut through the quarantine regime.[11] Thus, from a letter to the Dupuy brothers we learn that Peiresc managed to obtain permission from the Bureau de la Santé of Toulon to remove the boxes of Minuti and de Thou from the regular quarantine to the farmhouse of one of the previous consuls, who did this favor for Peiresc. And then, once there, Peiresc sent one of his men to open them in the presence of the intendants of the Santé. As soon as they were authorized, Peiresc planned to send them on to Marseille.[12] In this context we can understand his complaint, in a 1632 letter to Aycard, about what he believed to be the too-rigorous application of the quarantine to the craft of Captain Raysson just returned from Constantinople.[13] The very next day, the Bureau de la Santé met and decided to allow him into the harbor immediately, "as much for his person as for what was loaded on his ship and to excuse himself [based on] the freedom of trade from Constantinople." Raysson, it turns out, was from Toulon, but all the investors in his ship were from Marseille.[14]

One of the reasons Peiresc was so keen to get his goods out of quarantine is that things seem often to have gotten lost there. He wrote to Jean-Baptiste Magy in Marseille that he had been brought a letter from Magy's brother Jean in Egypt dated 15 March that had been passed through vinegar and found, discarded, in the Bureau de la Santé.[15] We know that Peiresc tried to extract two cases of plants and books which had come from Aleppo to Marseille on the navire *Ste. Claire* in mid-November. Peiresc feared for the plants and worked on the intendants to release them. He would have succeeded, he wrote ("ils ne feroient pas tant de difficulté"), but for the death of a sailor on the *Ste. Claire,* which led to a more rigorous implementation of the existing regulations.[16]

There was also a whole cast of characters involved in the quarantine regime. Thus, we learn of a M. de St. Jacob in Marseille, whom Peiresc thanked for taking good care of his three cases unloaded from the *St. Victor* with plants, books, and things from Egypt. Peiresc shared his recollections of St. Jacob's father, and then, worried about his plants suffering from the cold, suggested that they wash the wooden case with vinegar—and then release them to Issaultier.[17] Simultaneously, Peiresc approached Viguier, the consul just back from Syria, and asked him to assist Issaultier in getting the plants out of quarantine.[18]

Under the impact of plague, Peiresc's contacts scattered. His merchant-banker, de Gastines, retired to Vallon de Jonquet, then north of Toulon, now swallowed up by its northern expansion and surviving only as a street name. Barthélemy Issaultier, scrivener on the ship that returned Minuti from the Levant, had retired to a *bastide* in the country owned by one Jean Roux. Valbelle had gone to his farm at La Cadière. M. Marquesi, the uncle of Charles Blanc, was nowhere to be found when Peiresc wanted to reimburse the items purchased by Blanc. The letter was addressed to M. Marquesi, "at the port where he may be" ("la port ou il sera").[19]

The commerce the merchants represented also relocated. Marseille's merchants moved first to Cassis, but when Cassis became infected there was talk of a further relocation to Sixfours. In a letter to de Thou of 5 June 1630, we find Peiresc writing that while Aix seemed just out of danger, Marseille appeared to be descending into a "grosse furie."[20] In another letter to de Thou of 17 June, Peiresc informed him that the plague had since spread to Cassis: about seven or eight days earlier, all the Marseillais who had relocated there had decided to flee. All the ships in the harbor, and indeed in all the harbors up the coast to Sixfours, had put to sea.[21] But this drew the opposition of merchants at Toulon, who were loath to allow for so much competition so close to home. In the meantime, most of the Cassis fleet shifted just one harbor over to La Ciotat.[22]

Indeed, during the plague outbreak, Toulon became a major scene of activity. Moreover, Peiresc had himself left Aix for his country seat at Belgentier, which was in the same physical relationship to Toulon as Aix was to Marseille. The key figure at Toulon was Honoré Aycard, who was described to de Thou as having "very good connections throughout Italy and Constantinople and along almost all the Mediterranean coasts."[23]

Peiresc's correspondence with him was extended and deep. It was almost exclusively through Aycard, for example, that Peiresc communicated with d'Arcos in Tunis, a correspondence that flourished precisely during this period.

When he wanted to send additional letters to Jacques de Vendôme, the Franciscan Guardian of Nazareth who had sailed from Cassis for Sidon, he sent materials on to a Toulon merchant he knew, named Truillet, who had "connections" ("habitudes") all along the coast. In a letter of June 1630, Peiresc alerted him to the impending arrival of letters for Jacques de Vendôme and a group of five or six comrades, to be passed on to Daniel Aymini, also a Recollet, in Sidon. There were also other letters for his plague-scattered Marseille diaspora (Tarquet, Gastines, and Bermond are specifically mentioned), as well as of the ship of Patron Alphant with his plants from the Levant. As Peiresc feared for the plants' well-being under the merciless summer sun, he had also written to friends at Sixfours (Tourtel and Vicard, the town's Viguier) to put them on alert.[24] It turns out—more details of how Mediterranean tramping worked—that while the tub of plants originated in Sidon and had come to Livorno on a ship carrying the returning Tuscan baron d'Alegre, it had there been put onto the Provençal ship of Patron Alphant.[25] Peiresc feared that the plants would not survive forty more days on a ship, and so was working preemptively to ensure that they were not unloaded at Cassis, where the port was apparently overwhelmed by the transplanted Marseille bureaucracy.[26]

After all this effort, the plants were nevertheless discharged at Cassis, on the very day when plague broke, and just after Jacques de Vendôme's ship had set sail.[27] In a letter to de Thou, Peiresc explained that de Gastines was stuck in La Ciotat and Bermond the Younger in Sixfours. The plants therefore had to remain at Cassis at the height of summer, and were sure to sicken with little attention.[28] In the meantime, all shipping in the harbor had cleared out.[29]

The plants may have been stuck in quarantine, but a letter that was sent on the boat of the baron d'Alegre from the grand commander of Malta (M. de Venterol) had to be answered. The contact was Ruffi of Avignon, now residing in Vauriaz.[30] Peiresc was concerned about the plants.[31] He managed to discover from Antoine Truillet in Toulon that the plants were left by Patron Alphant with one Mazerac, in the quarantine at Port-Miou—apparently this *calanque,* isolated from the rest of Cassis by the peninsula of the Roches Blanches, was where the quarantine was located. Peiresc asked him to make sure the plants were not exposed directly to the sun and had "only a little watering, well moderated" ("un peu d'arrousage bien moderé seulement").[32] Somehow, in the end, Mazerac managed to get the plants to Toulon.[33]

As for the letters intended for Jacques de Vendôme and Aymini, they never did catch up with their ship, but were carried a few days later by Pierre Tourtel of Sixfours—illustrating the advantage to Peiresc of the high frequency of Provençal traffic to the Levant, if in smaller ships piloted by more skittish captains, so that even in time of plague something might be moving.[34]

Peiresc also advised his correspondents in the Levant of this change in situation. In a letter to Estelle in Sidon of February 1630, he urged him to avoid Marseille. As his name was known all along the coast, any letter arriving there would find its way to him. Other names who could serve as possible destinations were de Gastines and Fort, formerly of Marseille, and Aycard and the judge Pierre Chabert at Toullon, "and all other judges and officers on the coast of this country where ships could land and unload."[35] As Toulon became his central port, Peiresc added the merchant Truillet as another possible respondent there.[36]

Peiresc sat out the plague in Belgentier. Despite all his provisions we can discern a clear and sharp drop in his correspondence during this period. In a letter of August 1631 we learn why. Contact with Marseille had been broken for some time. And communication along the coast had been disrupted. Only special travelers—"des gents d'honneur"—were traveling, and they were coming through Toulon. But even then, just in the past days, a barque sailing to Genoa had returned, forbidden from landing there on account of the Italians' fear of plague.[37] The Italians, Peiresc wrote, had published a list of the Provençal ports and commercial installations still free from quarantine.[38]

There was for Peiresc a small silver lining to all this. With Marseille closed, nearly all commerce was funneled to Toulon at just the time when Peiresc was living only a scant few kilometers away. As Peiresc explained in a contemporary letter to de Thou, "this contemptible place is now become the great postal highway, on the routes for the ambassadors of Rome, Constantinople (and if I would dare say), the Indies."[39]

21 ❧
Setting Sail

S etting sail was always complex. Travelers and sailors would often board ships and then wait for the wind to shift. Sometimes this meant that Peiresc would be able to send follow-up letters, adding further requests or repeating additional words of worry. What all of this represents is a desire to be in contact up to the last minute, as if every minute on this side of the sea mattered so much because once it had passed, so very many hours, days, weeks, or even months would have to go by before contact could be reestablished. In the writing we see desire—the desire to remain close, accentuated by the knowledge that letter-writer and recipient would soon be far apart.

For example, Peiresc prepared three letters on 14 December 1628 to be sent out on a ship sailing to Sidon and the Levant, to Estelle and the nameless Capuchin we know to be de Loches. But when the ship did not leave, Peiresc hurriedly drafted another letter to send on to de Thou. It did not add anything much, just a few pieces of information from Paris, as if an excuse to justify the new communication as informational rather than purely emotional.[1]

And then there was the departure of Théophile Minuti for the Levant in the spring of 1629. He was present in Marseille from the beginning of April 1629, received Peiresc's package of letters of recommendation on 14 May, and was still receiving letters from Peiresc in early June. During this time, Peiresc kept writing to him, adding always more and more information. The same pattern was repeated with Nunes and da Costa—they visited him at Belgentier in mid-July 1630, and Peiresc was still writing to them in mid-August and forwarding to them letters he had received for them in the meantime.[2]

But there was one fundamental condition imposed by Peiresc's location on the inland end of the Marseille-Aix axis, namely, that the "last minute" communication had to be written hours earlier. Thus, for example, a letter to Théophile Minuti in Constantinople written on 22–23 August 1632 had to be written sometime between the evening before, when Peiresc received word from the *patron,* sieur de Ramatuelle, that his ship, the *Ste. Anne,* was to sail at 10:00 the next morning, and that next morning.[3]

One fact about sailing that can be clearly asserted on the basis of Peiresc's archive is that there was no season "closed" to sailing. Ships left for long and short hauls at all times of year. Looking only at the log of Peiresc's outgoing mail, we find no appreciable difference in departures across the year. For the period it covers (1623–1632), we find letters explicitly marked with Levantine destinations, such as "Egypt," "Syria," or "Cyprus," departing every month of the year except January, March, April, and August. Certainly there are periods when ships do not leave Marseille and Toulon, but external factors such as war or financial limitations are likelier explanations than climate. Nor does evidence in the correspondence of the subsequent period (1632–1637) show any change to this pattern. As many letters left in February as in May, in December as in July (see Chart B.10 in Appendix B).

22 ✌

Merchant Routes

*I*n his magnificent book on the early medieval Mediterranean, Michael McCormick discerned several constantly used tracks across the sea, which he described as "trunk routes."[1] Reading across the Peiresc correspondence, we can discern something similar for the seventeenth century. We know that Peiresc thought seriously about roads, for it was he who proposed to Nicolas Bergier to publish the first study of road-making and road networks of the Roman Empire.[2]

Already in 1609, writing to Malherbe about a naval sweep for corsairs along the North African coast, Peiresc referred to the fleet taking "the African route" ("la routte d'Affrique").[3] Much later, when trying to organize the shipment of letters to de Thou, Guez in Marseille, knowing de Thou's general plan to proceed from Constantinople to the Holy Land and then Egypt, sent the letters directly to his brother in Constantinople, who then forwarded them to Alexandria, "because that is the regular route from Constantinople" ("la routte ordinaire de Constantinople").[4] There was also "la voye ordinaire de Marseille."[5] Of course, sometimes the roads were closed and there was no traffic to Marseille, not even from the heavily trafficked ports of Egypt.[6]

Within the Mediterranean, Peiresc's routes largely overlapped with those of Marseille. Where there seems to have been most divergence is with westward-bound shipping. While Peiresc had almost no correspondence with Spain and nothing regular with Spaniards—Peiresc wrote to a French expatriate, Antoine Novel, in San Lucar de Barrameda; to a noble Fleming, Lucas Torrius, in Madrid; and to a visiting French cleric, Jean François of the Minims, in Barcelona—there was fairly regular shipping from Marseille to Barcelona and Alicante, and also out to the Canary Islands.[7] We can catch a glimpse of this wider world in a mémoire Peiresc prepared for Michel Tourtel, sieur de Ramatuelle, in case he was going to the Canary Islands. Peiresc asked for canaries—of course—but also the seeds of melons, potatoes *(batatas)*, unnamed herbs that were supposed to be excellent, pits of peaches, prunes, almonds, dates, and seeds from oranges and citrons, apples, and pears. Above all, Peiresc was interested in those plants of the Indies that were being acclimatized there.[8]

The regular routes cut across the sea. Reporting to the French ambassador to Venice, M. de la Tuillerie, on the expulsion of Spanish invaders from the Isles de Lerins in 1637, Peiresc described a route from Spain to Italy that went straight across the Gulf of Lyon to Sardinia. It was "like a canal."[9] Writing to Rubens, in 1629, he referred to the Spanish galleys that made no landfall "in our seas, but go straight [far canale] from Sardinia to Majorca."[10] Peiresc's language was the same as that used by his merchant-banker de Gastines. Explaining to Peiresc the strange-seeming itinerary of F. A. de Thou, de Gastines wrote that the galley he had boarded at Malta went directly to Barcelona, "having made the canal without stopping at Rome."[11] This language, "ayant fait canal sans toucher a X," however odd it might sound to our ears, was actually the opposite: a commonplace technical term that enters the Peiresc correspondence, and Peiresc's own language, directly from the world of commerce. Maritime insurance documents from exactly this period use this phrase within descriptions of the route specified of the ship being insured. For instance, a contract of 31 March 1633 specifies that on the ship's return from Italy it "makes a canal without stopping at Monaco or Nice."[12]

Thus, while cabotage was the venerable Mediterranean norm, longer-distance direct routes also existed. When François Galaup left for Constantinople with Ambassador de Marcheville, they went directly from Marseille to Malta and from there due east to their first port of call in the Aegean, at Cythera.[13] Coming from Venice, de Thou changed from Venetian to Dutch shipping at Crete.

The Aegean and eastern Mediterranean had their own patterns. For Marcheville, Minuti, and Galaup, Chios—"the most beautiful and the most abundant in fruits of all the archipelago"—was a staging point. They stopped there en route to Constantinople, and Galaup later stopped there on his way from Constantinople to Sidon.[14] When Minuti and Aycard's nephew Salvator departed Constantinople on a Greek-crewed Turkish merchantman, they headed to Rhodes, another of these points where routes crossed. From Rhodes they traveled to Sidon on a barque of the type named "sambaquier," which was propelled by wind and oar.[15] Galaup followed the same route.[16]

For ships heading west, Malta was a key rendezvous. From there, some ships proceeded directly to the western Mediterranean, while others went to Italy; we see this on Marcheville's return from the East.[17] The impor-

Figure 17. Illustration of Isles de Lerins. CBI, MS. 1860, f. 337r. (Bibliothèque Inguimbertine, Musées et Bibliothèques de Carpentras)

tance, even centrality, of Malta was acknowledged as a given by Peiresc when he referred to "the Malta caravan." The context is also clear: the same western Mediterranean that Braudel referred to as "the desert of the sea" was in the early seventeenth century actually borrowing the terms of desert travel. Peiresc himself repeatedly used the term "caravan" to refer to maritime traffic.[18]

Knowing that there were routes and that the routes normally took a certain amount of time enabled Peiresc to monitor traffic. Having heard from Captain Bartolle that there were goods coming to him on the *Grand Henry* sailing out of Sidon, he asked Tarquet if he knew what route it would likely be taking back to Marseille.[19] And when, for instance, he had not heard anything of the polacre *Ste. Anne,* which had departed Alexandria three months earlier, he complained that it had given him a blow to the head ("m'a dato gran martello in testa"). This was only mitigated somewhat by the fact that he had heard that it had passed near Messina and that a polacre—perhaps this one?—had just arrived at Livorno.[20]

Following Peiresc's conversations, we see that he used this knowledge of shipping patterns to help anticipate trouble, or at least to know when trouble was brewing. Islands, such as Rhodes, Cyprus, and Malta and even smaller ones such as the Isles de Lerins off the coast of Provence, were focal points for him. He understood that those who controlled them were "Maîtres de la Mer."[21]

The Isles de Lerins—St. Honoré and St. Marguerite—stand just off-shore between Cannes and Antibes, and just west of Villefranche (Nice) and the frontier of Spanish-controlled Italy. Like the Isles d'Hyères off Toulon and the Isles de Frioul in the Bay of Marseille, these small archipelagoes protected the harbor traffic. The Seguiran Report warned of the consequences of neglecting the strategic importance of the Provençal coast, but this is exactly what persisted until, in September 1635, the Spanish seized and began fortifying the Isles de Lerins. The extensive attention Peiresc devoted to the French attempts—initially botched, eventually successful—to retake the islands fills many of his letters to Paris during that time, especially to the Dupuy brothers and to Secretary of State Lo-ménie. Peiresc gathered documents in order to make a "fidèle relation."[22] This "contemporary history" coincides with careful work he had commissioned on the economic situation of the Benedictine Abbey on St. Honoré in the Lerins archipelago.[23] The detailed watercolor of the abbey's buildings on the island of St. Honoré in the volume Peiresc devoted to his monastic research likely also dates from this period (Figure 17).[24]

23 ✑

Mapping the Mediterranean

*D*ense shipping routes and intense patterns of mobility across a large but land-bound body of water describe a mediterranean.[1] Peiresc's letters themselves trace these routes and measure them. But mapping was for him more than a metaphor. In March 1610—immediately after Peiresc heard of Galileo's telescopic observations from Lorenzo Pignoria in Venice, and just as the *Siderius Nuncius* became available—Peiresc wrote to Jodocus Hondius, the great Dutch Calvinist cartographer.[2] The actual letter was penned by Peiresc's chief helper, his brother Palamède, the sieur de Vallavez. The latter had, we learn from this letter, visited Hondius in Amsterdam the previous summer, and was now wondering aloud whether his brother—Peiresc—could recommend to the great printer and cartographer a map of Provence for the Dutchman to print, and at the scale desired by Peiresc ("de la taille qu'il vous l'envoyerà").[3]

Hondius may or may not have received this letter, for we only possess a reply to a letter of Peiresc's written more than a year later, on 7 August 1611—itself now missing—that Hondius wrote on 26 August, or immediately upon receipt. Hondius expressed his gratitude for their offer of a better map of Provence which he very much wished to include in the next edition of his atlas, with suitable acknowledgment of their help. He proposed a phrasing emphasizing their "singulière affection à la Géographie."[4]

With his reply to this letter, Peiresc took over the correspondence. He suggested that the proposed map of Provence contain longitude as well as latitude. The latter, it was known, could easily be deduced from a measurement of the height of the polestar or sun at the solstice. The former, however, as Ptolemy had himself noted, could also be resolved by observation, but only by comparative simultaneous observation. In 1611, writing to Hondius, Peiresc offered the Atlantic islands as a possible extra-European coordinate for this project

> so that joining their distance to the point where we are in this country,
> I could assert without fear at how many degrees of longitude we are

situated, and draw from it by the difference of place where we are
with every other place on earth the true degree of longitude belonging to it. And because there is no nation in the world that
makes such important and illustrious navigations as yours, I would
well desire to know if there is being prepared any kind of voyage
where would be employed persons knowledgeable enough in geography and capable of reporting to us two or three true observations
of the height of the polestar at the Azores, and another thing which
is not more difficult to learn than the polar height, together with
some similar measurement taken at the Cape of Good Hope and in
some other signal places on earth. Because I could make for them
mémoires and instructions to this effect which would render the research much easier for them, and in exchange you could assure them
that for all the places from which they report the observations that I
request, I could determine for them the true degree of longitude.[5]

In this very important letter, Peiresc recognizes the Dutch prominence
in international shipping as a potential tool for science. Foreshadowing
his later practice, Peiresc offers to prepare memoranda and instructions
in order to standardize observational practice. He also presents himself
as possessing the key to determining longitude, a contemporary "holy
grail." He even suggests—cannily—that the establishment of longitude
would require nothing more than taking the distance from here to there,
adding the height of the pole, "and another thing that is no more difficult to measure than the height of the pole."

Peiresc neglected to tell Hondius exactly what this other method was.
But if we pay attention to the date of this letter, the end of October 1611,
we can read between the lines, for it was at exactly this time that Peiresc
began to formulate a parallel plan. Relying on neither a commercial nor a
diplomatic network, but on his own circle of friends, and focused now
not on the distant Atlantic islands but the nearby Mediterranean islands
and French Échelles, Peiresc arranged to send an observer whom he had
trained in his own protocols, Jean Lombard, by ship to Tripoli in Lebanon via Malta and Cyprus. Lombard was to note the positions of Jupiter
and its moons while Peiresc would observe them at the same time. Peiresc
seems to have realized with Galileo that the movements and changing con-
figurations of these satellites could serve as a celestial "clock." Knowing
the latitude—which was easily determined by taking a reading of the height
of the sun at noontime—the time and the distance between the two points,

it was relatively simple to calculate longitude, since it was known that the earth's rotation moved one degree of longitude every four minutes.[6]

Lombard left Marseille for Malta on 30 December 1611.[7] The route was due south by the compass, and he arrived in Malta very quickly: on 5 January 1612. The archival record includes Peiresc's note that it was "extracted from a letter of Lombard's of 8 January, from Malta." In this letter, Lombard explained that though there was constant cloud cover he did try two or three times to take the height of the sun, which he could not easily do. He also tried to take the declination but, again, without "assuredness." On 11 January the ship departed for Tripoli, from which they set sail in return on 18 May. Lombard's measurements of the height of the sun and the declination, and the height of the pole, are given for Tripoli and Cyprus, which they reached two days later, on 20 May.[8]

Lombard's "Observationes Melitenses" follow Peiresc's pattern of representing Jupiter by a large circle, and its four moons, clearly labeled as Catha[rine], Maria, C[osmus] Ma[jor], and C[osmus] mi[nor]—using Galileo's Medicean names—represented by stars (Figure 18). Estimates of diameters of distance are indicated by dots. The page's verso reveals it was sent as a letter to Peiresc, probably accompanying another of 8 January. Here Lombard writes, "I have made you 3 observations which I am sending."[9] The content of the letter, describing his attempts to make observations despite the cloudy weather, repeats what had been given in the appended narrative descriptions. Lombard is not much for local color, but in the final sentence of the letter he does describe Malta as "a very strong city, as much as could be, and possessing good ports, and full of people who give themselves only to the lubricity of the world."[10]

We also possess Lombard's running narrative as well as his schematic descriptions. For that first week in Malta it includes one additional observation, for Monday 9 January at 5:30 a.m. Its tone is matter of fact, its detail sparse, and its mood skeptical. Observation was also made on board ship—again not inspiring in him much confidence in its accuracy.[11] Other pages contain similarly businesslike descriptions of observations made 4 through 17 February "en Tripoly de Suryie," every so often indicating where observation was impossible because of cloudy conditions (e.g., "Dimanche [12 February]").[12] The final set of measurements was that of 18 May, upon setting out on the return leg from Tripoli for Cyprus.[13]

These pages must have accompanied Lombard back to Provence. He was himself no adventurer, as he explained in the first letter he wrote to Peiresc from overseas: "And I assure you that it greatly displeased me to

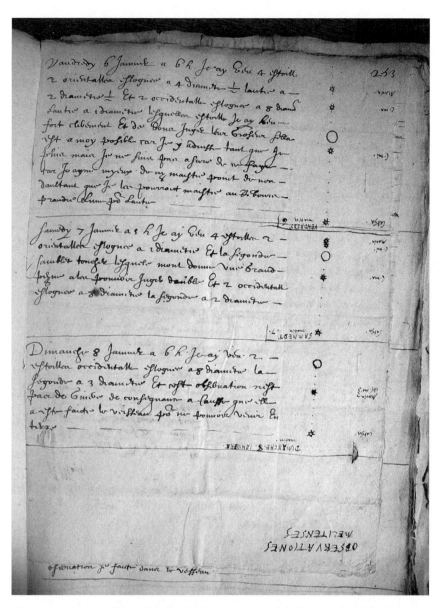

Figure 18. Page of Lombard's "Observationes Melitenses." CBI, MS. 1803, f. 254r. (Bibliothèque Inguimbertine, Musées et Bibliothèques de Carpentras)

navigate by sea, and if God graces me to return to our house, the sea will never again have me as its subject."[14]

The Lombard project sheds light on a crucial episode in the history of astronomy, of scientific expeditions, and of Mediterranean-wide science. But it also points to the deeply intertwined relationship between astronomy, geography, and maritime commerce: a mapping of the Jovian world that is at the same time a mapping of the Mediterranean and the contemporary Mediterranean world (tracing the route Marseille-Malta-Cyprus-Tripoli).[15]

This comparative Mediterranean scientific project of 1612 grew directly out of Peiresc's correspondence with Hondius about making a better map of Provence.[16] Peiresc's next mapping project was his involvement in 1633 in the Seguiran Report (discussed in Section 3, "Marseille and the French Mediterranean"), which focused exclusively on the coastline of Provence.

In 1635, Peiresc attempted something much more complex: a comparative observation of the lunar eclipse of August 1635 (the eclipsed moon made for a more observable clockface than the rapidly moving, and only telescopically visible, moons of Jupiter, though there remained the problem of accurate measuring of local time) to be performed all around the Mediterranean, from Provence to Italy to Syria to Egypt to Tunis, by merchants and missionaries as well as learned folk, and with a goal of reforming maps of the sea.[17]

The letters Peiresc wrote to his many correspondents first to solicit their willingness to participate in the project and then to instruct them on experimental protocol provide fascinating evidence for how astronomy was done in the early seventeenth century. A representative example, for its fullness of detail as well as its general shape, is a letter of 17 May 1635 sent to Father Agathange de Vendôme in Cairo.[18] To standardize and improve practice, Peiresc had Gassendi prepare a "how-to" memorandum, which traveled with two other Capuchins who passed through Aix on their way to Sidon in spring 1636.[19]

The final report on the eclipse observations was drawn up early in 1636 and took the form of a summary written by Gassendi for Peiresc. A second, parallel, but more detailed text was prepared as a letter to Elie Diodati.[20] A third version is preserved in Gassendi's astronomical diary, the *Commentarii de Rebus Caelestibus*.[21] In the version of Gassendi's text written in his own hand to Peiresc, the "great man and great friend" ("Per-illustri, ac per-amico"), Gassendi tersely summarized the results by place, beginning with Aleppo and Cairo—perhaps a nod in the direction of Peiresc's passion, perhaps because of the significance of at least the

Aleppo data—and then following with the European stations at Naples, Rome, Digne, Aix, and Paris.[22] There was some comment on the quality of the observations (neither the Jesuits in Rome and Quebec nor the professor in Naples nor the Capuchins in the Levant were competent; only the readings from Aix, Digne, Paris, and Aleppo were reliable).[23]

The printed version of the letter begins "ALEPI in Syria," emphasizing the importance of the Aleppo observation—which did, indeed, contribute the key data point—and the context, clarifying the significance of the Mediterranean-wide project. In his much longer letter to Diodati, Gassendi began by noting that Peiresc had obtained these reports from his contacts in the Orient, who held him in veneration.[24] Gassendi understood the implications of this research. First, Paris was farther to the west of Aix and Digne than had been thought. Second, the distance between Marseille-Aix and the Levant was less than was displayed by "all the tables and geographical charts" by a whole hour of arc, or 15°, something that the great astronomer declared "astonishing, and worthy of being noted" ("quod mirabile sane est, et adnotatione dignum").[25]

In June 1636 Peiresc and Gassendi performed an extraordinary experiment at Marseille, reproducing as best they could one performed there nearly two thousand years earlier, during the time of Alexander the Great, by the cosmographer Pytheas. Using a gnomon erected on the roof of the College of the Oratorians, partially demolished at Peiresc's request in order to provide an adequate platform—and does this not again underline Peiresc's clout in Marseille?—they turned the building into an observatory in order to determine the height of the sun on the longest day of the year.[26] The experiment was undertaken at the behest of Godefroy Wendelin (1580–1667), the Marseillais astronomer who had moved to Belgium.[27]

Peiresc saw the solstice observation and the previous year's eclipse observation as linked. In the upper margin of his excerpted copy of Gassendi's letter to Wendelin describing the experiment, he summarized its content as follows: "*1636*. July. Father GASSENDI to GODEFROY WENDELIN CONCERNING THE SOLSTICE OF MARSEILLE and THE LUNAR ECLIPSE [of] 28 August 1635, from which is proved the error in geographical tables of more or less 300 leagues between Marseille and Alexandretta."[28] When writing to Jacques Dupuy in Paris, Peiresc joined to these experimental results "the instructions derived from it by the most experienced mariners concerning navigation in the Mediterranean."[29]

This is the especially fascinating point to consider: Peiresc's familiarity with the "experience of mariners." In a discussion elsewhere of Mediterranean currents, for example, Peiresc noted the east-west flow from the Isles St. Pierre to Marseille, "and that the Marseillais mariners insist on giving a quarter [of wind] to the right, excusing themselves according to their routine."[30] (He also, occasionally, relayed for us their very words, such as the matelots' term for waterspouts: *siaillons*.)[31] He seems to have felt that the experience of mariners made them the best judges of the new experimental data.[32]

The "most experienced mariners" had for years coped with the discrepancy between cartographic theory and reality through practice, "for which they could never understand the cause and reason." With these new observational results, however, Peiresc wrote to Jacques Dupuy in Paris, "by reducing the space [of the sea], there was nothing so easy to understand, as you will see when we send you the result of his observation, and of the comparison of it with all the others."[33] To Thomas d'Arcos in Tunis, Peiresc described those "very most expert mariners of Marseille . . . and those themselves who made marine charts" as being "rapturous and almost beside themselves" to discover the reason for their practice. Peiresc explained that this would all be made clear in the enclosed diagram he had copied out from a letter of Gassendi's to Wendelin on the subject.[34] This no doubt refers to the one printed in the 1658 Gassendi *Opera Omnia* (Figure 19).[35] The point is that Peiresc was in contact with mariners and saw an intellectual problem to be solved in the gap between their practice and the governing theory.[36]

Another thing that stunned the sailors and cartographers was that the foundation of this reform rested upon observations done in Aleppo by a merchant named Balthasar: either Balthasar Claret or Balthasar Fabre (Peiresc uses both names somewhat interchangeably but more often Claret).[37] A few more observations done at that same place by even slightly better-trained observers could, Peiresc mused, result in much more precise results—and thus even more precise maps.[38] As he explained in a letter to Fabre of May 1636, this error had always been corrected in practice by mariners, "thinking it nevertheless—it seemed to them—to be in error when they gave a quarter [of wind] to the left on their course from Malta to Crete, and two quarters, in the same direction, from Crete to Cyprus. And practicing on their return the same proportion of declining to the left without their being able to give or to understand any reason for it." But now theory had come to the aid of practice. The eclipse "opened the

ad Solstitialem vmbram. 535

ftantia fit maior minutis illis 18. quàm à
Keplero fupponatur. Ex quo efficitur , vt
cùm vniuerfa peccetur in conftituenda diftantia , fiue differentia longitudinis inter
Maffiliam , & loca illa ad extremum mare
Mediterraneum conftituta, potiffima erroris
pars ex Campania vfque,& Sicilia,ac Melite
prorfum fit nata.

Poffem id tibi confirmare ex eo , quòd
cùm nuper verfaremur Maffiliæ , Nautas va-
rios rogauimus , vt omni chartarum præiu-
dicio depofito, recenferent ipfi quid itineris
inter proxima quæque loca interiici exifti-
marent, prout fulcantes Mediterraneum ob-
feruaffent fæpius eorum interualla cum ipfis
chartis non cohærere. Siquidem id euici-
mus,vt ex 2700. milliaribus,quæ inter Maffiliam & Alexandriam Syriæ , feu Alexan-
dreettam vulgò numerantur,cenfuerint 500.
detrahenda effe (plura haud-dubiè detractu-
ri, fi femel præoccupationem potuerint am-
pliùs exuere)& minimam quidem partem ex
Maffilia in Meliten , maiorem ex Melite in
Cretam, & maximam ex Creta in Cyprum,
ipfamque Alexandriam. Sed rem totam pla-
cet potiùs confirmare ex folutione Proble-
matis , quod noftratum ingenia fruftrà huc-
vfque vexauerat (ac forté etiam exterorum
quando quotquor Nautæ hoc mare frequen-
tant , id ferè proponunt quibufcumque nô-
runt curam effe Mathefeos) fcilicet hæc fo-
lutio referuata videbatur agnitæ ex illa Ecli-
pfi contractionis diftantiæ , quam hactenus
Nautæ ex chartis fupponant.

Problema fic habet, *Qui fiat , vt Nautæ,
poftquàm fuperarunt Sardiniam , & Africæ
oram, aut faltem vicinas faluarium Infulas , ac
potiffimùm ex quo præterierunt Meliten , de-
beant, vt in Cretam appellant, non rectâ via in-
fiftere , fed deflectere ad lævam , fiue verfus Boream, vnâ quartâ, vt vocant, venti, fiue ½. to-
tiu circinu, prout Pixide Nautica , feu Ma-
gnetica indicatur : ac duabus etiam quartis, feu
dimidio venti, vt ex Cretâ vfque fuperata, per-
ueniant in Cyprum; & ex Cypro tandem at-
tingant Alexandriam. Qui etiam fiat , vt redeundo , non poffint in Cyprum & Cretam de-
duci , nifi venti dimidio ; neque in Meliten nifi
quartâ venti à rectâ via deflectentes , atque id
quidem femper ad lævam , hoc eft , iam verfus
Auftrum , cùm opertet iam ad dextram , feu
verfu Boream deflectere.* Ac ferè quidem ipfi

Nautæ trahi fefe à Terra dicunt , fed nempe
non confiderant, cùm duæ funt naues , quæ
inuicem fibi altera eundo , altera redeundo
occurrunt, tam debere vnam quàm aliam in
eandem partem attrahi , licet non poffit ab
eadem Terra vtraque nauis recedere, nifi, vt
altera ad lævam, ita altera ad dextram flecta-
tur. Sunt , qui caufam coniiciant in motum
Maris proprium , ac illum præfertim,qui ex
Ponto vfque per Ægeum imprimitur : fed
ij tamen fe ab ea difficultate non expediunt,
quorfum etiam fiat redeundo verfus lævam
deflexio ; quoniam eo cafu error curfus à
motu inductus non corrigeretur , fed du-
plicatus proueheretur. Sunt , qui caufan-
tur ventorum lineas cum chartis malè co-
hærentes ; fed , vt præteream cætera , nihil
poteft hoc facere ad duplicatam deflexio-
nem. Sunt , qui caufam fubeffe putent in
ipfa acu Magneticâ , illiufque variatione,
quæ, quòd verfus ortum increfcat, deflexio-
nem illam faciat neceffariam. Verùm docet
nos experientia variationem Magneticam
non obfequi legibus fecundùm Gilberti pla-
cita præfcriptis,& maximè quidem,cùm nobis Anglia orientalioribus ea magnopere
decrefcat. Vt prætermittam variationem,
quæ obferuata Alexandriæ , aut mediis locis
dicitur , non effe eorum graduum , quos
eiufmodi exigit deflexio. Ad fummum hæc
omnia meræ coniecturæ, & vt breue faciam,
nihil hactenus quod hunc nodum foluat
videtur prolatum. Ipfi an videamus faci-
liùs ex contractâ diftantia rem expedire , tu
iudex efto.

Sunto A Melite, B Creta ; vera diftantia,
feu rectum iter , & ventus , quo ex Melite
tenditur in Cretam , eft linea A B. Verùm
Nautæ chartis fidentes Cretam non putant
adeò propinquam , fed eam arbitrantur
iacere in C, atque idcircò rectam viam , feu
ventum , ex Melite in Cretam ducentem
effe ipfam lineam A C. Porrò , quia docuit
experientia incedentibus per lineam A C
euenire , vt poftquam tantùm confectum
eft viæ , quantum reuera eft neceffe, vt per-
ueniatur in Cretam , reperiatur nauis non
in B , fed potiùs in D, verfus Africam , toto
interuallo B D. Eapropter huic malo vt
occurreret , cogitauit cum deflexione
verfus lævam incedere , & loco venti A C.
vfurpare quartam ab ipfo , videlicet lineam

A B. Quæ ea ipfa eft , quam fequi opor-
tuit. Sic redeundo vera diftantia , rectâ via,
germanus ventus , quo ex Creta venien-
dum eft in Meliten , eft linea B A. Non putant id Nautæ , qui Meliten habent longè
diftantiorem , nempe non in A , fed in E.
Vnde & viam rectam , feu ventum illeinc
huc ducentem exiftimant lineam B E. At

quia experiundo edocti funt fore , vt fi illâ
incederent , poftquam emenfi effent itet ad
Meliten vfque neceffarium , non iam effent
in Melite , feu in ipfo A , fed potiùs in F, feu
verfus Siciliam, toto interuallo A F. Idcircò,
ne id eueniret , incedendum conftituerunt
cum deflexione rurfus in lævam , & loco
venti B E vfurpare quartam ab ipfo , videlicet lineam

SSs 3 licet

way to understanding this truth hitherto unknown for so many centuries." Peiresc added that all it took "was a man who had had the curiosity
to observe an eclipse in that land at the same time as one was observed in
this." It was by this means that "now maps could be corrected so that
without giving these quarters and double quarters of wind to the left one
could actually follow the routes given on the maps."[39]

This episode is reported at great length by Gassendi in the *Vita*. Indeed, the description of the "problem" is taken word-for-word from that
letter to Wendelin referred to by Peiresc—clearly intended by both of them
to be a canonical account:

Finally, he would have me expound that problem, which till that time had tormented all Navigators and Mathemati[ci]ans, to find out the exposition thereof. The Problem was this; How comes it to passe, that Navigators, after they have passed Sardinia, and the Coast of Africa, or at least have saluted the neighbouring islands, and especially after they have passed Malta, to the end they may come unto Crete, they must not keep right on, but turn to the left hand, or to the North, one point of the wind, or the two and thirtieth part of the Compasse; and two points or half a wind, that they may passe from Crete to Cyprus, and from Cyprus to Alexandria in Syria? And how comes it to passe, that in returning, they cannot sail to Cyprus or Crete, unless they turn aside half a wind out of the right way, and that always to the left hand, which is now to the South, whereas they should rather incline to the right hand, or to the North?

Finally understanding why this was so, Gassendi writes, "Peireskius called together a company of Seafaring men and so expounded the Problem that they were amazed" and agreed that of the 2,700 miles generally accepted to separate Marseille from Alexandretta, at least 500 could be sliced off.[40] To Holstenius Peiresc gave the more moderate—and accurate— number of 200 or 300 leagues (or about 100 miles.)[41] We might have thought Gassendi's description of a meeting between the scholar and the sailors unlikely—had we not the parallel account in the letters, and all the surrounding evidence of their close working relationship.

Having figured this out, Peiresc immediately sought to immerse himself in the best contemporary Mediterranean navigational literature, as if himself to gauge the potential resonance of the results.[42] In fact, the cartographic problem highlighted by Peiresc and Gassendi had been solved more than a half-century *earlier,* though the method they used would not become standard until a half-century *later.* Bernardo Baroncelli explained in a portulan of the 1560s that Cyprus was generally located 100 miles too far to the north.[43] Correcting the distortion was, however, not only a matter of shortening the distance between Cyprus and Africa but also of rotating the entire axis of the sea clockwise by something like 8°, moving the eastern Mediterranean basin and Black Sea to the south. An atlas executed in 1586 by Antonio Millo presented a corrected Mediterranean, with Gibraltar, Crete, and Cyprus almost perfectly aligned, with the former at 36° N and the two islands at 35°. We then find a similar correction, though by different degrees, in the charts of Willem Barents (1595), Bartolomeo

Crescenzio (1596, but published in 1602), Gerolamo Costo (before 1605), Giovanni Francesco Monno (1613), and Joan Oliva (Messina, 1614, and Livorno, 1618).[44] But mariners were slower to adopt these changes.

In addition, Marseille was among the last cartographic centers to make this correction at all.[45] The Marseille school of portulan-making was driven by a few personalities. The Oliva family, which came from Messina, then Naples, installed itself in Marseille at the beginning of the seventeenth century. Charlat Ambrosin worked in Marseille as a pilot before producing the *Atlas de la Méditerranée* of five charts with the goal of assisting those sailing to the Levant. Then there was Augustin Roussin, who published the *Atlas Provençal de la Méditerrannée* in 1633 with three charts. It has been argued that with Roussin, Ambrosin, and Oliva "disappeared the last generation of cartographer-artists and cartographer-mariners, who combined a bit of science and a lot of art. The next generation of 'geographers' would be that of the scholars: astronomer-voyagers."[46] The work of Maretz in 1633 and Peiresc in 1635 marks this very turn, but was completely lost. Cassini and his student Guillaume de l'Isle (1675–1726) were the ones who got the credit for reducing the length of the Mediterranean in the *Encyclopédie*'s article on the "Mediterranean Sea."[47]

At the very same time Peiresc pursued these broad comparative campaigns, he also worked much more locally, through individuals, and with texts. Thomas d'Arcos in Tunis sent him a map of Africa, now lost. Peiresc, in turn, shared with him his conjectures about the continuity of mountain ranges on the northern and southern shores of the sea. But the mountains were also connected to the water. The Mediterranean Sea itself, he writes, was aligned from west to east from the Straits of Gibraltar to the Holy Land. The same was true for the Black and Adriatic Seas (though he notes that the latter declined a bit to the south). Nor was the Red Sea, Peiresc added, so very differently aligned. "And," he concluded, "I think that the majority of the mountains that border all these great seas follow the same alignment, almost, and particularly those of your map of Africa."[48]

D'Arcos also provided Peiresc with a whole series of maps of the North African coast and of Tunis in particular.[49] First, there is a portolan-like projection (south on top) of "Part of the Barbary Coast" ("Coste d'une partie de la barbarie") and the southern tips of Sardinia and Minorca (Figure 20). The capes, bays, and promontories are numbered and identified by both their "vulgar" and "modern" names. More spectacular are a series of sketches and then finished drawings of the site of Carthage,

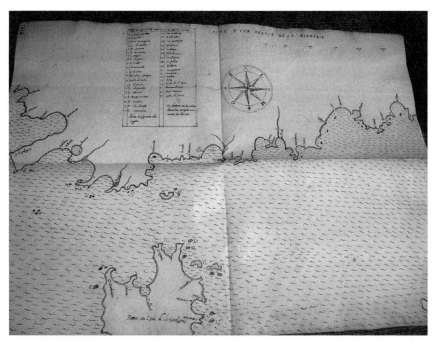

Figure 20. "Part of the Barbary Coast" ("Coste d'une partie de la barbarie"). CBI, MS. 1831, ff. 417v–418r. (Bibliothèque Inguimbertine, Musées et Bibliothèques de Carpentras)

some general and some in detail (Figure 21).[50] The finished ones are in the same hand as the map of the North African coast and include the same indexing technology (letters on the map and a boxed guide fit into an empty corner). There are also pencil sketches and pen-and-ink drawings. On one we can see Peiresc drawing in the names of sites based on his knowledge of the relevant ancient texts (Figure 22).[51] On another we can see Peiresc explicitly comparing the maps on the grounds of fidelity.[52] The next step was, of course, to compare the maps with the texts. Peiresc's conclusion was that "there are some difficulties in accommodating the statements of the ancient authors with the plan of Carthage which was made according to the present state."[53]

If we examine the two indexed maps, we find references not only to physical phenomena—mountains, gardens—but also to human constructions and historical products, whether acqueducts, Moorish palaces, Spanish fortresses, or local villages. There is even a note on flora: "the

Figure 21. D'Arcos's map of site of Carthage. CBI, MS. 1831, f. 428r.
(Bibliothèque Inguimbertine, Musées et Bibliothèques de Carpentras)

trees which surround Tunis are almost all olive trees."[54] This information
could only have come from on-site observation. In fact, Peiresc received
a four-page memo, which he then passed on to the brothers Dupuy, describing this landscape in detail, with measurements.[55]

The project of confronting knowledge from books with the witness
of the eye (Peiresc's "tesmoin oculaire") is at the leading edge of new scientific thinking in the 1620s and 1630s. We see "autopsy in action" in the
Mediterranean basin in a letter to Henri de Valois of 6 November 1633.
Peiresc explained that he was sending a sketch of the Gulf of Smyrna and
its ports as remembered by sailors recently returned from there. He had
also commissioned someone on-site to portray it "more precisely" ("plus
exactement") and to pay attention to its physical surroundings of mountains and hillsides descending into the sea. Why? To see if a physical description would "show more or less the proportion of the distances, *and
symmetry*" with a sketch that he had of a vase to which "Aristide" (Aelius
Aristides (117–181?) had once compared it.[56] What Peiresc did next was less
usual: he turned to contemporary artisanal practice to understand better
the ancient description.

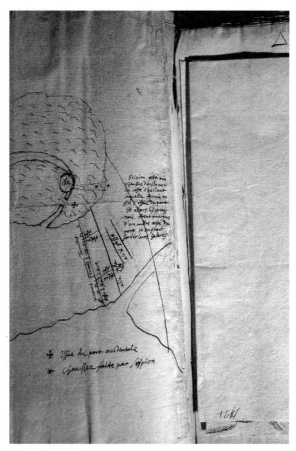

Figure 22.
Peiresc annotating
map of Carthage.
CBI, MS. 1831,
f. 430v. (Bibliothèque
Inguimbertine,
Musées et
Bibliothèques de
Carpentras)

The ready recourse to an artisanal reference to make an observation about a physical space is not so very different from his recourse to mariners and captains to evaluate cartographic data. Actual making, actual practice, came readily to mind for Peiresc: "This squares very well with what the goldsmiths and other artisans call *goderons,* on the circumference of a plate or small basin, and [I] suppose that the one and the other Greek and Latin word are taken in their proper meaning of sources of streams and rivers, most of them coming from different veins and then surging up." These springs circle the headwaters of a river and make "the image of diverse little ports or semicircles full of water and the same figure of those bowls with *goderons.*" So, in one instance, we see Peiresc as if in an experiment trying to reproduce an ancient judgment that a particular place resembled a material artifact by reference to artisanal making, and to the natural process that would have produced the parallel to a man-made product.[57] And then, in a final twist, Peiresc compared this landscape with that around the Argens Valley near St. Maximin that he knew so well. Unexplained is whether the contemporary artisanal practice is understood as *preserving* an ancient meaning or whether it simply and coincidentally illustrates it.

In conclusion, Peiresc turned back to Aristides's word, "phiale" or "cup"—from which comes the modern term "vial" or "phial"—which he thought made clear that the reference was to an inlet of the sea, as opposed to the bay of Smyrna, which was rounder.[58] This brought Peiresc back to contemporary French and the question of whether the language in use reflected this understanding: "And though we commonly call in French a *godet* what the ancients called *poculum,* I do not know if the word *goderon* does not make some allusion to this or is a diminutive of godet, as if many little godets, or goderons put together, would make a great goderon'd godet, or else surrounded by goderons or by little godets."[59] Peiresc sought further help from a gilded leather bowl that had come from Constantinople in this shape. He was sure that similar ones could be found in many Parisian cabinets of curiosities "where you could, when they are full of water, take pleasure in seeing the great conformity that they have with a great port surrounded by many little ports." The Montmorency collection had one in this shape made of agate which, he adds, had recently been sold to some goldsmiths for the whopping sum of 500 or 600 écus.[60] This seamless merging of philology, archaeology, and contemporary artisanal practice demonstrates what a philology of things might look like long before Boeckh in mid-nineteenth-century Berlin made *Sachphilologie* the philologist's claim to world domination.

Peiresc's commitments to the contemporary Mediterranean and to precise forms of visual description come together in a proposal he made in 1637 to Henri-Auguste de Loménie, comte de Brienne, the secretary of state and son of Antoine de Loménie, sieur de La Villeauxclercs, also once secretary of state. Peiresc begins by recalling the decision to bring "the poor, late Callot"—Jacques Callot—to the siege of La Rochelle in 1628 in order to have him record the events.[61] It was this that had given him the idea of suggesting that Claude Mellan be employed by the Crown in the same capacity. Mellan was a superior draftsman and engraver who had visited with Peiresc on his way to and from a twelve-year residence in Rome, and on his way back stayed long enough to make the sketch for

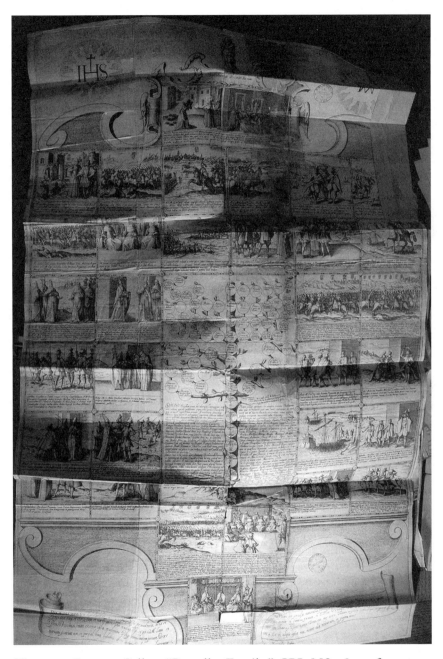

Figure 23. Jacques Callot, "Porcellet Family." CBI, MS. 1844, f. 420ter. (Bibliothèque Inguimbertine, Musées et Bibliothèques de Carpentras)

Figure 24.
Jacques Callot, detail
of Porcellet family.
CBI, MS. 1844.
(Bibliothèque
Inguimbertine,
Musées et
Bibliothèques de
Carpentras)

his well-known print of Peiresc as well as his even more important prints of three phases of the moon.[62] Now, with the Isles de Lerins occupied by the Spanish and menacing the French coast, Peiresc suggested that the king commission Mellan to have him make "a great big map of the surface of the Isles de Lerins with all the works, both the enemy's and ours, and all the naval dispositions, both ours and the enemy's."[63]

If Callot provided Peiresc with the model for Mellan, he also gave him another, different vision of Mediterranean mapping. For in Peiresc's archive, undisturbed for hundreds of years—and unnoticed by its catalogers—lies the second extant print of a broadside history of a medieval Provençal family, the Porcellets, executed by Callot sometime around 1616 (Figure 23).[64] Theirs was a story, once upon a time, of Mediterranean mobility, from ninth-century Spain to Provence, to Outremer with the Crusaders and to southern Italy with the Angevins, before settling in Lorraine. Callot maps this human Mediterranean visually, with vignettes from this spatial genealogy—thirty-two of them (Figure 24). But just as extraordinarily, these images sit atop captions detailing the archival sources illustrated by the artist. This is the Mediterranean mapped twice over—through the movement of past people and through their persisting archival presence.[65]

24 ✑
Sicily

Sicily, as Goethe observed, "points me towards Asia and Africa, and it is no trivial thing to stand in person on the remarkable spot that has been the focus of so much of the world's history."[1] Sicily, in the center of the Mediterranean, also lies at the center of Peiresc's interest in the relations between water, earth, wind, and fire. It was Europe's primeval treasure house. He had wanted to go there himself on his Italian trip and would urge the same on others, like Lucas Holstenius.

Peiresc was a careful reader of Cluverius's *Sicilia Antiqua* and was delighted to be sent relations on Sicily by Cassiano dal Pozzo.[2] And so, when his Roman antiquities buyer, Claude Menestrier, turned from Sicilian amber to giants' bones and a mountain full of teeth, Peiresc was ready to follow.[3] He was even willing to cover the costs of Menestrier's voyage to Sicily in the unlikely event (or so he thought) that Cardinal Barberini would refuse to subsidize it.[4] This brought him back to Vincenzo Mirabella y Alagona's *Dichiarazioni della pianta dell'antiche Siracuse* (1613), which reported on giant skeletons found there, and thence to Tunisia, where his own correspondent, Thomas d'Arcos, had come across giant remains six or seven years before.

It remained necessary, Peiresc thought, to investigate "the forms and quality of the ivory fossils and other things mentioned that could be found buried together, in order to make a more certain conjecture if these were teeth of an elephant, hippopotamus or of another marine monster." Nor would it surprise him if the fossils reported found on Malta also proved to be marine monsters or other large creatures.[5]

Peiresc explained himself in a long letter of 21 March 1635 to Pierre Bourdelot in Rome that was intended as a guide for Doctor La Ferrière from Lyon, who was traveling to Italy in the suite of Peiresc's friend, the archbishop of Lyon. Peiresc was happy to have been introduced to La Ferrière by Pierre's uncle, Jean. Peiresc wanted to know as much as possible about the giant bones found in Sicily, but also about the "fabric" or structure in which they were found, as well as the nature of the surroundings. He asked specifically about the possible use of caves as human dwellings, or any other signs of human construction, as well as the possible presence of other sorts of bones or shells still immured in the nearby rockface. More precisely, Peiresc wanted La Ferrière, a medical doctor after all, to affirm that the bone or bones he found were indeed of human origin. His own experience had led him to suggest the possibility of a large fish or whale—something that could be corroborated by the presence of even the least "petrification" that could be found there, whether of shells, snails, or other marine fossils. The uncertainty and obscurity of these matters demanded such attention to detail. Other objects of study would be the fossil mountain that he had heard about, as well as the salt mountains and Aetna and all that was "vomited up from these sources of oil" ("est vomi de ses souces de petroglia"), and finally the many-colored amber found in various places.[6]

Fossils and Mediterranean mountains led Peiresc to some of his most acute theoretical observations. La Ferrière had planned to visit Sicily as part of a research trip that involved also a visit to study the petrifications at Aquasparta.[7] If he were to find marine petrifications, he was to note the situation and positioning, and whether the nearby woods were "in the same bed of rock or terrain like a level or otherwise higher or lower than the vein where the wood trunks were." This is the language of stratigraphy, which transformed antiquarianism into archaeology over the course of the eighteenth and nineteenth centuries. Peiresc used "beds" ("couches") throughout this discussion of fossils.[8]

Peiresc struggled to explain the convergent volcanic activity in 1631 at Vesuvius, Aetna, and the Ethiopian Mount Sem (likely the Semien Mountains, whose tallest peak is Ras Dashen, 4,550 meters). What Peiresc had not yet been able to explain sufficiently to himself was the ability of the fire to emerge from so deep beneath the ground, as it had to, "because it raised up islands in the midst of the sea, and opened up mouths of fire in their midst as is recounted of some islands found in the sea of Naples as well as that of Greece." Peiresc thought there had to be some connection to Aetna and Vesuvius which "would seem to imply I do not know what kind of necessary correspondence of the one to the other beneath the surface of the water, because in it one finds the fiery islands of Vulcan and Stromboli."[9]

The heated water came from fires deep within the earth, he wrote, "as it has been verified at the baths of Pozzuolo at the place at which opened a mouth of subterranean fire during the time of Pope Paul III, whose slag formed a very high mountain in 24 hours, which I viewed up to the summit where there remained a form of a great theater or caldera ["chauderon"] whose mouth was closed up by the collapse of the earth on either side which the rains carried down into it."[10]

The peak of Tenerife in the Canary Islands, which was held to be one of the highest mountains in the world, seemed also to have been formed in the middle of the ocean by the same process. Its crater remained open, though no longer on fire.[11] In the northern lands, Peiresc continued, and in the midst of the ocean, there were still "burning mountains" much more marvelous still, as well as others that had ceased to erupt. There were said to be additional ones in America, while some in Greece were no longer visible—in the same way that the fires of Sodom and Gomorrah had left no trace.

Turning back to the Levant, Peiresc noted that there were the hot springs on one side of the Red Sea in the city of Medina and on the other at a-Tor. It was said that near to Mecca in these last years a pestiferous subterranean wind killed a number of people and camels. There could be some link, he speculated, with the eruption of Mount Sem on the other side of the Red Sea "if the material which feeds these subterranean fires is deep enough under the ground to have some connection from one place to the other beneath the Red Sea, just like it seems there is between Aetna and Vesuvius and other places around Pozzuolo, as well as with Vulcan and Stromboli."[12] Even though over time the eruptions seemed to cease and the canals to their craters seemed clogged, "I do not think, however, that they stopped within because one sees it lit up from time to time."

Again, it was Pozzuolo, which Peiresc had visited on his Italian trip, that served now, three decades later, as a point of reference. Just as the Monte Novo had not erupted since its opening had closed up, though the fires still burned deep inside its cone—the smoke issuing forth nearby, at Solfatara and Fumarola—"and I indeed think that the passage or communication from the one of these places to the other could be blocked up and closed, for some time, by earthquakes and rockslides as could the mouths" and then open once again, even far out in the sea, "whatever difficulty we have in conceiving of this" ("quelque difficulté que nous ayons à le conceptvoir"). This fire "was capable of raising mountains and new islands, where exhalations of subterranean fire burning beneath the sea opened up. It has pushed up similar mountains or elevations within the depths of the sea between Sicily and Syria which did not arrive at such a height as to appear above the surface of the waves and opening up like the others."[13]

Drawing on his knowledge of the winds, Peiresc suggested that the Scirocco was "capable of impressing some kind of movement of compression in the deepest entrails of these burning furnaces" with the effect of stoking and augmenting the fires in the submarine cones.[14] Mariners, according to Peiresc—again documenting his close contacts with them—had no more certain signs than these, "so they say," and it was likely upon the basis of similar experiences that was founded the ancient fable of the rule of Aeolus. Because of the relationship between these burning mountains and the appearance of winds, the one was used to predict the other.[15]

Peiresc then speculated that the existence of subterranean connections beneath the Mediterranean could explain similar but widely spread physical phenomena: "if it were possible to suppose an underground connection as well between Mount Aetna and those of Greece and Palestine which burned or produced hot springs, and with those others along the Red Sea, supposing also that these fires, being based on bituminous and oily materials, form a crust or a kind of pocket or furrow capable of supporting the sea water and preventing it from entering these burning caverns."[16] Peiresc went on to consider what role the Mediterranean Sea itself might play as a geological agent, with the waters being given direction by the winds, and their weight compressing and propelling the subterranean fires.[17]

The role of the wind as a propellant and as the proximate cause of the fire via its impact on water led Peiresc to remind his reader that if Stevinus's wind-driven sled could travel fourteen leagues in an hour, the Scirocco could travel very quickly indeed from Syria to Sicily. It would be preceded by the fire, whose movements were even faster and whose course, aided by the convexity of the earth, was shorter.

Peiresc allowed that his reader might mock these "feverish reveries," but he recalled to Philippe Fortin de la Hoguette that during Vesuvius's eruption the sea at Naples retreated and left galleys and large barques high and dry. Peiresc thought that the loud, thunderous noises coming from the earth could have opened up some kind of fissures in the roots of the mountain into which the bay drained. "Who knows," Peiresc concluded, whether the similarly burning or boiling liquids spit up by the mountain through diverse fissures on its sides, and which formed torrents "that ravaged the surroundings, did not come from waters swallowed in that way, like redirected rivers."[18]

Around this same time Peiresc would seem to have drawn up a concise mémoire, untitled, that covers precisely the points made at greater length in this letter.[19] He began with a discussion of the hot spring ("La fontaine ardante") of Dauphiné that was cool when low, but whose rising waters brought up the heat. Peiresc turned to the Scirocco "that blows in Sicily" and moves the smoke and fumes of Aetna and Vulcan two or three days' distance away. Peiresc discussed the possibility of "subterranean caverns that could communicate beneath the Mediterranean Sea" and connect, for example, Sodom and Gomorrah with "Aetna and these other burning mountains." Then Peiresc turned to the question of wind velocity, drawing on Stevinus's wind-driven ice sled as an experiment in nearly friction-free wind speed (fourteen leagues in two hours; in the letter to La Hoguette he gave it as fourteen leagues *per* hour), in order to suggest how fast the liquefied fire compressed by the wind-driven waters could possibly travel beneath the surface of the sea. Next, Peiresc discussed the "sac," or channel, through which the magma (not his word) traveled, and the properties of its crust. Finally, Peiresc discussed the relationship between seismic activity and the fracturing of sea beds—both sucking in water and stoking the burning liquid at the heart of the mountain. The example of Vesuvius and the Bay of Naples stood at the center of the discussion.

Peiresc never stopped thinking about volcanoes. The regular eruption of Aetna offered continuing possibilities for close ocular observation—albeit by a surrogate. Peiresc received a letter written from Malta in 1636 that described a tour of Sicily and, in particular, a terrifyingly close examination of Aetna:

> I approached it with horror and admiration and can assure you that that which the ears heard of the terrestrial Phlegeton does not begin to express that which the eyes saw. The matter that flows is like a liquefied metal that flows from the furnace to make a piece of iron; very red and blazing and which hardened little by little in the measure that it grew distant from its source. It is a mixture of iron, lead, earth, salt and sulfur. I was curious to approach within four fingers of the iron, to toss stones at it, and plunge some piece of wood into it, which caught fire quickly, and nevertheless it was distant from the source of the fire by about two leagues—being a little above "le grand Chesne" or "la belle quercia" (which you could see on the plan that I have sent).[20]

Figure 25. Antoine Leal's drawing of Aetna erupting. PBN, MS. Dupuy 488, f. 173. (Bibliothèque Nationale de France)

The map that accompanied Antoine Leal's letter has survived—down to the larger-than-scale figures praying at a makeshift altar surrounded on three sides by lava fields, though whether this met Peiresc's standard of detail as outlined in the letter to Cassiano is unlikely (Figure 25).

Gassendi's characterization of Peiresc's volcanology is succinct, and startling. Gassendi gives Peiresc credit for theorizing the existence of what we would call a "Ring of Fire":

> Whereupon he discoursed largely touching Channels under ground, by which not onely waters, but fires also might passe from place to place: and consequently Vesuvius might communicate the fire to Aetna, and Aetna to Syria, Syria to Arabia Foelix, Arabia Foelix to the Country bordering upon the Red Sea, in which stands the Mountain Semus aforesaid: whether a long row of arched Rocks do make the Channel, or whether the fire it self breaking in at the chinks do make it self way, and create channels, pitching the same so with a bituminous suffumigation, that it keeps out the Seawater which goes

over it. And that fires under ground do make themselves way, may be known by the Mountain Pouzzoles in the time of Pope Paul III, and others at other times made by the eruption of fire.[21]

Aware of the constantly changing face of the earth, Peiresc was able to imagine an entire history of change projecting backward beyond the memory and record of man. Like Montaigne, who saw the working of wild rivers in the Dordogne or the ocean at the Médoc and came to understand Plato on Atlantis and the separation of Sicily from Italy, Peiresc looked at the natural history of Sicily and saw the history of time.[22] Hooke's "Discourse of Earthquakes" of 1688 is the direct descendant of Peiresc's work on the Mediterranean of the 1630s, in a likely case of parallel development, though the possibility of knowledge transfer via the Hartlib circle cannot be completely ruled out.[23] It was this very question of the origin of volcanic mountains that led Hooke to the convergence between the study of natural and human antiquities.[24]

25 ॐ
People in Motion

eiresc's Mediterranean was mapped by the shipping routes and remade through conversations with sailors about the results of eclipse observations. But Peiresc also charted it by mapping people moving through space. In his world, the fact of mobility was itself unremarkable; what was deemed noteworthy was the biography of those individuals in motion. The mémoires he drew up identifying key figures in Syria, Egypt, Chios, and Sicily suggest the value he placed on these people, precisely because of their very mobility. These memoranda also offer us a window into his overseas network. The brief biographies reveal for us a certain commonality: born in one place but now in a second or third or fourth. Peiresc's archive brings together for us a gallery of Mediterranean "types" of the sort that Horden and Purcell alert us to in *The Corrupting Sea,* that Claudia Moatti and Wolfgang Kaiser have focused on in a recent series of volumes, and that Nathalie Rothman saw from her Venetian observatory.[1] Behind them stands the even farther-reaching reassessment of mobility: in earlier history, Michael McCormick's *Origins of the European Economy* (2001); in prehistory, Barry Cunliffe's *Europe between the Oceans* (2008); and today, Karl Schlögel's *Planet der Nomaden* (2006).

When Father Minuti left Marseille for the Levant in June 1629, he carried with him a series of memos. Some were shopping lists, but one focused on people.[2] This memo was entitled by Peiresc "Instructions Sent to the Reverend Father Théophile Minuti on His Going on Pilgrimage to Jerusalem with the Plan to See the Levant and Egypt, and the Books and Other Curiosities That He Wishes to Have for Sr de Peiresc His Servant."[3] This lists the people to address in different places and what to ask of them. In Sidon, he was directed to Estelle the vice-consul; in Jerusalem to M. l'Empereur (he was by then in his "exile" in Istanbul); in Egypt to Fernoux and Lambert; in Cyprus, if time allowed, to Espannet. The memo was itself dated 14 May 1629—and then sent off with all the letters that were to accompany the departing Minuti, who was by then in Marseille waiting only for a favorable wind.

Another of the lists drawn up by Peiresc sometime before July 1633 came from information about Cairo shared with him by Jean Magy and Cesar Lambert. It mentions a Recollet Father "Genie de Sainctes," who was the vicar of the French consul but was now back in Paris. He was said to "hate" the Maronites and Greeks who lived in the Venetian quarter and from whom he learned Arabic. He possessed a number of manuscript books. The Coptic Christians, or "Nassarans," were described as among the greatest writers in the land and as having an unsurpassed quantity of books. They were not as "traitorous" as the Greeks. The memo then identified particular individuals: "Sr. Domenico l'hoste" from Marseille managed Lambert's household and bought Peiresc his mummy;[4] "M. le Gris," a doctor, was "very curious" and had a fine collection of porcelain;[5] "Stephano da Petra," from Messina or Reggio, was also "very curious" and possessed the two marble mummy covers that came to Marseille. "Sr. Albert"—probably the Marseille merchant Jacques—was so rich as to lack nothing at his house. "Giacomo d'Alvyse," of Messina, possessed many curiosities from the Red Sea, and was called "the master of mummies" ("le maitre des Mommyes") on account of his loaning money to the black Africans who, in exchange, made everything available to him as soon as their caravans reached Cairo. Then there was "Sr. Bertier," the jeweler from Lyon, who was also "very curious." He had strange serpents and other animals, and provided Lambert with most of his vases. There was "Simon de Dime" ("Simone Dimo"), the Venetian vice-consul at Rosetta. He was so "very open and generous" ("fort Franc et genereux") that despite being "the most curious person in Cairo" ("le plus curieux du Cayre") he gave away his acquisitions too freely.[6] Note that Peiresc uses "curious" to mean a person interested in a serious way in many things—in exactly the sense in which he would describe himself as "curious."

A second list was drawn up based on conversations with Jean Magy, probably in early July 1633 when he visited Peiresc in Aix. It lists all the people Magy saw in his twenty years in Egypt, including passing luminaries such as Pietro della Valle and Tomasso di Novarra but also a range of unknowns, only a few of whom, thanks to Peiresc, have crossed back from oblivion's shore. These included the following:

"Vermeil of Montpellier, who makes artificial emeralds and medals" (Sr Vermeil de Monpellier, qui faisoit des esmeraudes & medailles artificielles) and who had just departed for Ethiopia

"Jacques Albert, Marseille merchant, who has the most credit in Cairo, in the absence of Jean Magy, from whom this Albert has returned the commission" (Jaques Albert marchand de Marseille qui a le plus de credit au Cayre, en absence du Sr Jean Magy, lequel Albert a r'envoye la commission)

"Joseph Baulme, apothecary at Marseille, for the recovery of some books" (Joseph Baulme Droguiste à Marseille pour le recouvrement des quelques livres)

"A Spanish Franciscan who has become Jewish and is named Abraham Gayt, who has given up the faith on account of doctrine, and seems to have dreamed to return to Rome, having taken letters of recommendation to that effect" (Un Cordelier espagnol qui s'est faict Juif et nommé ABRAAM GAYT qui a grande creance entr'eux pour la doctrine et sembloit avoir songé de retourner à Rome ayant prins lettres de recommandation pour cet effect)

"A Spaniard of importance whom the King of Spain sent to Hormuz who wears glasses all the time" (Un Espagnol d'importance que le Roy d'Espagne envoyoit a Ormus qui portoit des lunettes continuellement)

"A Coptic bishop who is one of the principal heads of the Church of the land, and of Saint-Macarius" (Un evesque Cophte qui est des principaux chefs de l'eglise du pais et de Saint-Macaire)

"A Turk, or *Cavagy* [probably "capigy"] who has a number of books in Arabic and other oriental languages, both for the history of Egypt and the land of Yemen as of others more ancient" (Un Turc, ou *cavagy*, qui a quantité des livres en Arabe et aultres langues orientales, tant de l'histoire d'entre l'Egypte et le Pays de l'Hiemen que aultres plus anciennes)

"Sir Bobaquer Soala, Damascus merchant, of the most curious of Cairo, with correspondence to the Indies, Yemen, Abyssinia, Aleppo" ("Sieur Bobaquer Soala, marchand damasquin, des plus curieux du Cayre qui a correspondance aux Indes, Hiémen, Abyssinie, Alep")

"The Andalusian Doctor named AQUIN MUSTAPHA, who passed through here and saw Mr du Vair before the expulsion of the Moriscos" (Le medecin d'Andalusie . . . nommé AQUIN

MUSTAPHA, lequel passa icy et vit Mr du Vair avant l'expulsion des Morisques).

Others mentioned here are the "Vignon," "Doctor le Gris" and "L'Hoste," Lambert's agent.[7]

The third document of this sort seems to come from the period before 1631, since it locates the Capuchin Gilles de Loches at Sidon. Santo Seghezzi is identified as a philo-French Venetian who lived in Cairo but had a brother-in-law named Gela who lived in Marseille. "This Seguetti [*sic*] had such good connections in Egypt that he is more powerful than the Basha and can easily recover, and at a better price than any other, all that there is that is curious, and particularly *books*." After Seghezzi, the memo turns to Bertier, the jeweler from Lyon, who was very curious and "had a *number of mummies* and a kind of *little rabbit*." Bertier also had many medals and knew how to get them. Turning from Cairo to Sidon, the memo notes that "one had to address *M. Payen of Marseille,* whose brother is at Marseille the *patron* of a polacre, and who trades with Damascus and is very curious." If he were not there, "M. Truc" would answer for him. For Cyprus, the memo lists the Dutch consul Daniel Westenaing.[8] The identity of Seghezzi himself is the subject of still another, and seemingly prior, mémoire in which Peiresc asks the otherwise unidentified "Anthoine Scava" if Seghezzi, the brother-in-law of Gela, was still in Egypt.[9]

That there are three such memoranda identifying people in Egypt obviously reflects Magy's presence and Magy's importance for Peiresc. That he could note such a range of *other* visiting Westerners suggests that Egypt had become a destination. That so many of the names are Arabs or Turks suggests the existence of a society in which they could meet. What we desperately lack, however, is identification of these people from the standpoint of the local archives.

Peiresc also prepared similar, if briefer, memoranda for other island emporia. For example, we have a document from 1636 describing key contacts on Chios. This was derived from Capuchins returning from the East and debriefed by Peiresc in 1636.[10] It identifies three Capuchin fathers, Evangeliste from near Reims; Bernard of Paris, then Superior at Smyrna; and Stephano Giustiniano, of Chios. The former were both "curious in mathematics," while the latter had been a slave of the Turks along with some English who had been fishing for cod in Russia.[11] Another memo, undated, asks the recipient for information about the Grimaldi who lived in Chios and vicinity: their status and how long they lived there.[12] For Sicily, the memo focuses on a variety of local figures. First mentioned was a *"Prince de Botera"*—probably Giuseppe Branciforte V, prince of Butera—who lived at Castelvetrano, twenty-five miles from Palermo, and had the richest antiquities cabinet in Sicily. Peiresc then singled out a "Don Joseph de Balsamo" of Messina, who was in Spain at the date of the memo's composition, arguing for the need for a separate viceroy and parlement for Sicily, and a "Jacques Zagry," merchant of Palermo, who sold Bordeaux wines, was very courteous, and traded diamonds. Peiresc thought him the right person to sell the giant bones found there. Last on the list was *"Giacomo Maringo bookseller of Palermo,"* who possessed many medals and other curiosities.[13]

These mémoires give us some sense of the people on the move one might find in these ports of call. Before we turn to the Marseillais and Provençaux who peopled the Levantine ports, we should first stop to note just how many other sorts of people turn up in the Peiresc correspondence in places other than where we might have expected them based on their birth.

Jews, like Peiresc's friend Salomon Azubi, could reside in Provence but came from elsewhere in the Mediterranean and often ended up elsewhere in the Mediterranean. Azubi, for example, was born in Sofia and ended up in Livorno. Peiresc also understood that there was a connection between their Mediterraneanism and their history. Telling Gaffarel about his astronomical tables, he noted, "I also believed that Spain was full of Jews, whatever inquisition persecuted them there, and that is why I do not find it strange" that tables made in Spain survived in a Hebrew translation.[14] Then there is the reference in a letter to Wilhelm Schikard to "a Levantine Jew from Safad" whom he was expecting in Aix. The Jew understood Arabic and Hebrew, and Peiresc was hoping for help with a Samaritan-script, Arabic-language genealogy of Mohammed.[15] This almost certainly refers to Giovanni Battista Iona (1588–1668), a Jew from Safed who moved to Cairo, where he converted to Christianity and became an Arabist and professor of Hebrew at Pisa after 1634.[16] "Ioannes Baptista Iona Galilaeus" contributed the Hebrew poem to the memorial volume dedicated to Peiresc, *Monumentum Romanum*.[17]

Moriscos are also present. Aycard in Toulon, for example, was supplied with chameleons by a "Grenadan returned from Tunis"—a Moor from Granada, dislocated with the expulsion of the Moriscos by Philip IV in 1609. This "Grenadan" or "Grenatin" was not simply a courier, as he also discussed with Aycard some characteristics of the chameleon. There was a tragic side to this intercultural conversation, too. Aycard notes that this Morisco had come to Provence in the first place to look for his father.[18] Interestingly, d'Arcos, who had converted to Islam and taken the name of Osman, played an important role for the Moriscos in Tunis. Aycard described him as their "oracle." The chameleons he sent Peiresc were actually regifted; he had originally received them in gratitude from these Grenadans. Recounting, presumably, what he picked up from his Morisco courier, Aycard informed Peiresc that they caught the chameleons in spring, underground, where they laid their eggs, and that they lived in trees in the summer. D'Arcos had a dozen or so which he kept in summer on the orange trees in the interior courtyard of his lodging. He never kept them in cages.[19]

The chameleons are interesting for Peiresc's natural history.[20] But perhaps, even more, their transmission served as an occasion to open a window onto the world of the Moriscos in Tunisia.[21] In the margins of Aycard's letter of 2 November, Peiresc jotted down some notes on the condition of these Grenadans: "*Mustapha de Cardennas,* who is called *King of Andalus,* or the Grenadans who left Spain, lives at *Bourombaille,* a country house which he built 6 leagues from Tunis, and the Grenadans have built a village there to be near him in a good number. His father was treasurer of the last kings in Spain and foreseeing the expulsion of the Grenadans had sent his goods out of the kingdom with his son, in advance, to Toulouse." This information came from one "Jacques Vallent" of Martigues, who had been a slave for four years at Bourombaille. He had found chameleons there while preparing the fields to sow wheat.[22] Peiresc at around this time referred to "our Grenadin" in a letter to Mersenne as being an elegant Latin speaker who had gone on a brief visit to Damascus and who he thought could help translate an Arabic musical text.[23] Mersenne, in his reply, remained skeptical, arguing that while the sound was pleasant, he wondered if the Turkish slave had not learned the music from a Frenchman. The Grenadan could shed much light on the subject, he concluded.[24]

Natural historical information, such as the sea's currents, also came to Peiresc from people on the move. Ship's captains, merchants, and captives all supplied him with eyewitness accounts of North African coastal currents, which were incorporated into his "Relation on the Perpetual Current of the Sea and Ocean in the Mediterranean" ("Relation de la courante de la mer perpetuelle de l'ocean dans la Mediterranée"). One of his sources, the chevalier de Montmeian, had been a slave for three years in North Africa. He reported that in the estuary of the river that served as the outlet of the port of Bizerte in Tunisia, the tidal flux was so great that it could easily leave boats high and dry. He had learned this from galley slaves and many others who had lived in that port. Montmeian had seen nothing like it, Peiresc noted, in the mouth of La Goulette, or in the lagoon of Tunis, or at Carthage.[25] This phenomenon was confirmed for the other end of the sea by Captain Gilles of the *Dauphin,* who had spent six months at anchor with Ambassador Marcheville in the port of Constantinople. A Provençal doctor living in San Lucar de Barrameda downstream from Seville reported something similar for oceanic tides.[26] Capuchins in Chios even told him that the current was actually visible.[27] Patron Paschal said it was "specially" evident in the straits between Corsica and Elba.[28]

This research on tides casts a very clear light on what is so distinctive about Peiresc: on the one hand, a close attention to observation and an almost ethnographic approach to the observation of nature drawing on a wide range of personal contacts and, on the other, an attempt to connect it to theory. Thus, writing to Jean-Jacques Bouchard in 1631, then on his way to Italy, Peiresc urged him to visit with Galileo and learn everything that he can, *"and particularly concerning the book on the flux and reflux of the sea."*[29] Indeed, in April 1635 Peiresc would himself write to Galileo, reporting a six-hour cycle of high to low tide. This, he noted, might not please Galileo, who had argued for a single twelve-hour daily period.[30]

Even more remarkable is the way Peiresc made the natural history of the Mediterranean an important instrument for navigating contemporary events. Writing to his brother-in-law, Henri de Seguiran, and Richelieu's lieutenant in charge of maritime affairs in Provence, Peiresc reported on the Spanish attempt to fortify the Isles of Lerins, which they had just seized. They were building a causeway to connect the islands of Sainte-Marguerite and Saint-Honnorat. Only "high seas" ("les grand mers") could set back this building project, and particularly the Scirocco, which could drive the "natural current from east to west." As for the "Mer du Mistral," there lacked enough open water between the coast and the islands to build up sufficient height and force to damage the causeway. Nor could the Labech, from the southwest, do much damage because it was broken by the point of the island.[31] The nature of the sea, in this presentation, fit perfectly into the world of high politics, not just of mariners, adventurers, and antiquarians.

The eruption of Vesuvius, we know, was tracked in "Relations" that flowed in from around the Mediterranean.[32] Aycard relates, for example, a conversation he had with a "Jurat" from Palermo who had come to Naples and thence via Livorno to Toulon, and was passing on in his felucca to Spain. He reported to Aycard that there was no change to the regular aspect of Stromboli and Vulcano, which he passed on his outbound voyage from Palermo, and that these together were mere sparks compared to what was coming out of Vesuvius. Aycard notes that this comparison was not made in any of Peiresc's other relations on the eruption.[33] Important information about the contemporary eruption of Mount Sem in Ethiopia and fires in Arabia came to Peiresc from Magy, but was sourced to the Ragusan-born Mehmet Basha of Suakin, and the Damascene merchant, bibliophile, and Cairo resident Bobaquer Soala.[34]

Not disaster but normal need also put people in motion. Armenian merchants are scarce in Provence before 1640.[35] Olivier Raveux's careful investigations have identified a group of Armenian merchants in Paris in 1625, escorted there from Marseille by the royal physician, as well as the death of a Persian—perhaps an Armenian from New Julfa?—in Aix in 1638.[36] Seguiran's secret annex, "La Côte Maritime de Provence," preserved in Peiresc's archive, devotes a section to the Armenians who had come to Provence seeking justice against the Marseille merchants who had absconded with their money when abandoning their part of the silk trade in Aleppo. It places the Armenians in Marseille in the second decade of the seventeenth century and in Toulon, confidently, after 1622, at the expense of the locals.[37] Peiresc identified the presence in Aix of an Armenian come from Venice, where he lived near San Zacharia on the Riva degli Schiavoni. On 23 February 1612, "Angelo Michele Suriano, Armenian merchant, dressed in the Armenian style with a fur-lined cloak and a black beard," had sold him eighty-five gems.[38]

In January 1633, Peiresc asked Aycard if the three Ligurian merchants, Domenico Maiolo, Benedetto Gnieco, and Domenico del Monte, who usually passed through at that time of year with citrus fruits and jasmine, had yet appeared.[39] Peiresc met them in 1625 when they had planted some orange trees at Belgentier—they were in Toulon with oranges intended for the queen mother, Marie de' Médicis.[40] Peiresc's relationship with them seems to have moved well beyond that of vendor and customer. In 1625, when Maiolo, Gnieco, and Del Monte were being harassed by the duc de Guise, their goods seized and their persons threatened with arrest, it was Peiresc who intervened personally with the president of the parlement on their behalf and who invited the two merchants to his home, where they were found "at table with me" ("a table avec moy").[41] In February 1627 the Ligurians passed through Aix again, and Peiresc noted in his log that he had purchased seventy-four oranges and six jasmine plants for 60 livres.[42] By the end of the 1620s, Peiresc's commercial and personal relationship with the citrus sellers blossomed into an intellectual one.[43] In December 1630 he composed a memorandum, "On the Citrus or Oranges That Could Be Recovered from Crete and Possibly from Reggio and Naples." The Ligurians were his likely source. Peiresc discussed a shipment of very unusual lemons which came from the village of Canea on Crete (the modern Chania; then the Venetian administrative seat on the island) to Antonio Pisani, "General of the Galleys," in March 1624 and then asked for some for himself, including local Cretan species called "Perette," "Spadafuori," and "Lanzapsada."[44]

In February 1630, Peiresc wrote to the Ligurians at Toulon, and, perhaps on their way home, they carried a letter of his from Aix back to Toulon in May.[45] They were again in Aix in February 1631 and brought oranges as a gift to a correspondent of Peiresc's in Lyon.[46] In Marseille, Peiresc later saw the merchandise and put in an order for a dozen Chinese orange trees and a half dozen of his yellow jasmines.[47] These oranges were also prizes—the jeweler Alvares in Paris, who helped Peiresc understand the world of precious and semiprecious stones, "in exchange" asked for some oranges and citrons "even though I had ordered them from Lisbon, but I hold those of Provence are better."[48] In January 1633, Benedetto Gnieco came to see him in Aix while Domenico Maiolo remained in Marseille making a delivery; Gnieco was then going on to Lyon, Paris, and Flanders. Peiresc sent them with items to deliver in Paris.[49] In a letter of 5 December 1634 to M. Villeauxclercs, we find Peiresc explaining that Domenico Majolo, from the riviera of Genoa, who regularly brought oranges to France, wanted to bring in fifteen or sixteen bales to sell in Holland and the Low Countries. Each bale had about forty or fifty oranges. He wanted to go via Lyon and Lorraine and Franche-Comté and desired a passport from the Crown in order to transit France without mistreatment. Peiresc offered that the passport could be sent either to him or to the French consul Sabran at Genoa. Narvio (modern-day Nervi), whence Maiolo hailed, was only two miles from Genoa. The plan gave Peiresc an opportunity to voice his support for the idea of toll-free movement, if not exactly free communication: "Simple transit is very favorable to commerce throughout Europe, and I would be quite certain that this good man would not abuse it at all."[50] Peiresc used his chief Genoese correspondent at that moment, Pier Maria Boerio, to accompany a packet for Domenico Maiolo in December 1634.[51] The matter of the oranges and the passport remains in the correspondence of Peiresc and Villeauxclercs through February 1635.[52] What should we think about a scholar intervening on behalf of a foreign itinerant citrus merchant with the secretary of state of France?[53]

People were also set in motion by harsher realities. Maronites fled the civil war in Lebanon set in motion by Emir Fakhr-al-Din and his suppression by Ottoman forces. Sergio Gamerio Reiskalla first appears in Peiresc's correspondence in a letter to Galaup (in Lebanon) of August 1633. He was in Aix teaching Denis the Capuchin Arabic in exchange for Hebrew lessons, while waiting for assistance from his distant relative Gabriel Sionite, then professor of Syriac at the Collège Royale in Paris (who was, typically, not extending himself overmuch), or from his uncle Giorgio Amira, the newly elected Lebanese patriarch, then in Rome.[54] De Loches reported that when he had been in Aleppo, nine years before, Gamerio had left for Paris to find Sionite and then studied at Orléans before returning to Lebanon.[55] Gamerio stayed with Peiresc for a while, and then relocated to the house of Galaup-Chasteuil's brother, also in Aix. Gamerio had tried to explain to Peiresc exactly how he and Sionite were related; they were, apparently, cousins germain—Sionite's mother was the sister of his grandfather Sergio.[56] Peiresc described him as very modest ("d'humeur fort modeste") and said that he was content to teach Arabic and Syriac to the children of Procureur-Général Chasteuil in exchange for the service done him by his brother in Lebanon.[57] Gamerio seems still to have been in Aix in October when Peiresc invited Piscatoris to visit with him.[58] He then seems to have gone to Paris, from whence he wrote to Peiresc in February 1636.[59]

Peiresc tells François Luillier that Gamerio communicated a great deal of information about Mount Lebanon in general, and Fakhr al-Din in particular. He possessed a real knowledge of Arabic and Syriac, which Peiresc thought could be useful for assisting Sionite, and he carried letters of recommendation from the French consul in Cyprus and the patriarch Amira. Peiresc was trying to shift him to Paris.[60] (Gamerio's predicament seems much worse in Peiresc's letter to La Ferrière from that same summer of 1635, where he is described as just washed up in Marseille, his letter of introduction from Amira destroyed by vinegar in the purification process.)[61]

A little later, in October 1634, Peiresc was entertaining Moyse de Giacomo, said to be the brother of Gabriel Sionite. Sr. Moyse had been
robbed along the way, so that when he arrived in Marseille from Livorno
he had no money, only a letter of recommendation to Peiresc from Jacques
Gaffarel. It was on the basis of this "letter of credit" that the *patron* of the
ship had taken him on board. Peiresc paid off the *patron* and provided him
with money and necessities for the onward journey to Paris. But—and this
is why Peiresc was writing to the ambassador in Venice, whence Gaffarel
had written—the bale of Arabic books that Gaffarel mentioned having
sent Peiresc by sea had not arrived yet. Peiresc asked the ambassador, no
task apparently too trivial, to look into the recent shipments to Marseille.
If the package was still in Venice, Peiresc asked that it be sent to the address of de Gastines of Marseille, whether by the consul of the Marseillais in Venice or by someone else.[62] In a simultaneous letter to Gaffarel,
Peiresc added a few facts: that the Maronite had left Venice in June and
been stranded for some time in Tuscany after being robbed. He now regretted not following Gaffarel's prudent advice to doff his "Turkesque"
clothing. As for the missing books, Peiresc was concerned that Gaffarel
had sent the material via the Lumaga in Lyon, but without naming an
addressee in Marseille.[63]

Things with Moyse de Giacomo did not get better. Peiresc did eventually send him on to Paris with Ruffi, the notary and *greffier* of Avignon,
whom he described as "of the friends of our house" ("des amys de notre
maison"), and with recommendations to his friends, though he warned
Jacques Dupuy that he lacked industry.[64] To Gaffarel, now in Paris, Peiresc
complained of his lack of aptitude for scholarship, having seen him lounge
around his own house ("je ne l'ay point veu jaloux de l'estude ains dans
une feneantise"). Peiresc did not think Sionite would be able to make much
of him, himself not having "more humanity, which I have learned on other
occasions."[65] A final letter to Gaffarel, from late January 1635, showed the
whole story unraveled. The Maronite had brought suit against Gaffarel
for the loss of his books. Peiresc was stunned, and blamed himself for "believing so easily in the story about his books." Of course, in the meantime, he had reimbursed neither Peiresc for his portuary expenses nor Ruffi
for the travel costs from Avignon to Paris. He had talked of helping Sionite
on his edition of the Bible, but with Sionite's laziness this was unlikely.
Peiresc doubted that he would ever repass Aix, "after all these flimsy little
maneuvers he has employed."[66]

A third Maronite passing through Provence is also named by Peiresc. Writing to Antoine Piscatoris in October 1635, Peiresc explained that he had received Piscatoris's letter by the hand of "votre Rabias Maronite." Peiresc invited him to stay in Aix, but he wished only to see the other Maronite in Aix, lodged at the Procureur-Général Chasteuil—none other than Sergio Gamerio. Peiresc wrote that Rabias seemed nice enough but was not of a scholarly disposition.[67]

There is an interesting twist to this story, taking us from the Lebanon to the Baltic. Writing to Jerome de Dorne in Lübeck, Peiresc lamented that they had not been able to meet when he had been passing through Provence, "in the absence of which, having learned that in the chaos of the purification process of merchandise recently arrived from the Levant there were some strange petrifications and stones which were said to belong to you, I had the curiosity to ask to see them, which was very courteously extended to me, in good faith." (Note: Peiresc is essentially saying that he took advantage of his position and contacts to snoop around in someone else's package!) He noted the difference between these petrifications and those that he was more familiar with from Provence.[68]

All of this made him keener to know whence these pieces came. "Judging well," he continued, "these were for the most part collected on the shores of some sea, whether the Red or another more distant, or from some river which flows along metal-rich mountains, or able to form stones of the hardness, weight and color of the present ones." He would ask the bearer of Dorne's letter, Leonard Danmartin, for further information.[69]

It was Danmartin who had made Dorne's materials available to him. But it was from Danmartin's nephew that Peiresc learned that the petrifications did not come from Egypt, where Danmartin's son was resident—we begin to glimpse here some of the texture of these extended merchant families, with the father at home in the city bureaucracy managing the quarantine, one nephew engaged in the business, and a son overseas—but rather from Sidon where it happened that Sr. Dorne had connections to the captain of a navire sailing for Livorno.[70]

Writing to the Marseille-based Danmartin, Peiresc reports that a couple of people from the Levant were visiting with him who reported having seen on the road from Beirut to Tripoli mountains all carved with stones of this nature.[71] Peiresc is more precise in a second letter. He writes that "there is found here a Maronite"—Gamerio—to whom he showed the objects, and who assured him "that on the road from Tripoli to Beirut he had seen stones whose nature very much approached many of yours."[72]

But the story did not stop there. From Maronites, it then turned to Turks. For, Peiresc continued, a Turk "who is also in this city," and who had often traveled to Mecca and navigated the Red Sea—this is "Mattouk Chiassan"—confirmed that he had seen nothing like this on those shores. This inclined Peiresc to accept the Maronite's claim, overcoming his own initial inclination, but he still wished to hear Danmartin's thoughts.[73]

This "Chiassan" was in the possession of Nicolas Crouset, a relative of Sr. Audifredy of Marseille. Audifredy and Crouset were both merchants who sailed the routes to the Levant.[74] Chiassan was said to have been in Yemen. How they got hold of Chiassan and under what terms—free or slave—are unclear.[75] By 1635 he seems to have been based in Aix.[76] Peiresc even calls him "mon Turc."[77] In a letter to Mersenne he describes him as "very intelligent" and says that he had been to Persia. Peiresc employed "a Provençal to aid him and serve the translation of what would not be so intelligible for us in the discourse of this Turk."[78]

On another matter, the Arabic inscriptions on a silver bowl, Peiresc again contrasted the judgments of Gamerio and Chiassan. He told Mersenne that he put "notre Turc" to work and that he disagreed with the judgment of "a Maronite that we have here."[79] The varied human talent mobilized to work on this translation project in 1635 seems to follow a pattern visible in the study of Islamic coins by Said of Taroudant, Salomon Casino, Baltasar Vias, and Peiresc in 1627–1628.[80] Maronites, Marseille merchants, and Turks who travel: this is the cosmopolitan world of a Mediterranean port city.

There are other Maronites, too, who have only walk-on roles. There is "this valiant Maronite Captain who became so celebrated in the service of the poor Emir Facardin" with whom Jacques de Vendôme happened to travel from Lebanon to Malta.[81] Thomas d'Arcos, in Tunis, reported on the visit of Abraham Ecchelensis, then already esteemed for his mastery of oriental languages, in the context of negotiations for the redemption of slaves.[82] Giorgio Amira, the prelate of Mount Lebanon, appears in Peiresc's world at a distance—Peiresc's letters to Cardinal Barberini seek a pension on his behalf for services Amira provided to Europeans like Galaup-Chasteuil, who studied with him at Ehden in the mountains of northern Lebanon.[83] And even after Peiresc died, his "system" kept working, tracking visitors. In April 1638, Gilles de Loches reported to Vallavez that he had heard from Antoine Piscatoris, the merchant, of a Persian who had been in Paris and was now living in Marseille, who was said to know seven or eight languages.[84]

With Peiresc firing up the project for the large-scale recovery of Coptic and Arabic books in the mid-1630s, the pressure was on the translator. For some time, in Egypt, the translator was Giovanni Molino, also known as "Giorgio the Armenian," who knew a great deal and worked steadily for the Venetians.[85] Through his Egyptian network, Peiresc sent and received letters from Molino, who participated in the Mediterranean-wide eclipse observation that Peiresc organized in August 1635. Cassien de Nantes, who passed his observations back to Peiresc, thought he did it very precisely, "but, absent the instruments, he could not notate the measurements that you asked for."[86] Peiresc asked him to take the height of the sun at midday whenever he happened next to pass through Alexandria.[87]

Indeed, Peiresc became frustrated when he could not get someone's name or identity. He complained to Magy in 1635 "about that German recommended by the Sr. de la Croix whom you did not identify by name, nor the particular land he came from. Which would not have been unhelpful."[88]

One of the fascinating "rediscoveries" that can be tracked through Peiresc's Mediterranean correspondence is that of the person referred to in Magy's summer 1633 mémoire as the Andalusian doctor Aquin Mustapha, who had met with du Vair in Aix long before—"before the expulsion of the Moriscos."[89] Immediately afterward we find Peiresc writing out a long letter to "Sr. dottore medico d'Andalusia."[90] Peiresc began by recalling their happy conversation with du Vair many years before, when the "Andalusian doctor" was en route to Constantinople. Now that Magy had remade the connection, Peiresc hoped to enter into correspondence.

Peiresc offered to put his library at the doctor's disposal to aid in his studies, and in exchange—Peiresc actually writes "in scambio"—asks for his help with the acquisitions plan managed by Magy and Minuti. In particular, though, Peiresc wanted news and information. He specifically asked for information about the earthquakes of the previous year in Cairo, and the fire visible from Suakin at the Ethiopian border at the time when Vesuvius was erupting at Naples. Peiresc then aired his theory of a ring of fire that somehow connected the eruptions in Italy, Sicily, and Ethiopia, later fully developed in a letter to Cassiano dal Pozzo.[91]

But the main theme of the letter concerned Peiresc's quest for knowledge of ancient weights and measures. He asked if the doctor would supply him with a relation on the weights and measures used in Egypt, "particularly among the doctors." He especially wanted to know whether the Egyptian measure of "Artaba" was the same as the one commonly called "Ardeb." Peiresc's respect for the empirical aptitude of medical doctors in general, and for this one Muslim in particular, is evident.

Behind Peiresc's query lay the belief that the ancient Greek and then Roman measures were conserved scrupulously among the Muslims. Comparison could resolve many unsolved problems and contradictions among the ancient authors.[92] In a long postscript, Peiresc related that he had heard that in "the mosque" of Cairo some large and ornamented ancient vases were preserved. He wanted them sketched with precise measurements. Above all, though, he wanted to know the volume of liquid they held, measured by the "Ardeb." Peiresc wanted to be able to compare these with Greek and Roman measures. The larger context is Peiresc's long-term project on ancient weights and measures, for which he had "examined with greater exactitude than was ever done until now all the principal authorities in ancient Greek and Latin writers on this subject."[93]

People passed through port cities like Marseille on their way to some place else. Missionaries and diplomats, like merchants, constituted whole classes of people on the move: from Peiresc's beloved Capuchins, to de Brèves and Marcheville, to Magy and many others. Sometimes, it is only a bare, eccentric reference that casts light on what must have been utterly commonplace. For instance, in a letter to Cardinal Barberini about affairs in the Ottoman Empire, Peiresc writes that a Jesuit recently passing through Marseille who had been in India reported on how the Indians extracted the "silk" threads from inside a cucumber-like plant that Peiresc had heard about from his Mecca-Cairo-based correspondents.[94] But who the Jesuit was, we never learn.

26 ঞ

Ottoman Empire News

*W*ith people moved news. On the docks, when the sailors disembarked, the news was unloaded at the same time. For instance, in 1610 Peiresc writes to Malherbe that "an *information* is made at Marseille on the report of all the mariners who have come from Spain."[1]

The information Peiresc collected on the Ottoman Empire mixed politics and religion, both internal and external. For example, an extract from a *consulta* of the Propaganda Fide in Rome dated 13 November 1627 responds to news that the Greek patriarch in Constantinople, the celebrated and infamous Cyril Lucar, was sending children to Holland to be instructed in Calvinism.[2] A letter to Secretary of State d'Herbault of August 1627 informs him of the arrival eight days earlier of an English ship carrying twenty-five or thirty small cases of Greek characters for printing the heretical works of the patriarch Lucar. The Protestants' goal in pouring oil on the fire was to render the Greek and Roman churches utterly incompatible. Peiresc notes how remarkable it is that the Ottomans allowed entry to the printing press given that they did not permit any of their own books to be printed.[3]

Another, anonymous, report from March 1628 details the arrest of the Jesuits in Constantinople and their expulsion to Chios—and complains that Christians had lived in liberty in Galata since the Ottoman conquest but that the Jesuits were ruining this through their actions.[4] A "Relation veritable de la vie & de la mort de Nassouf Bassa 1613" was not only preserved by Peiresc but transmitted to the Cabinet Dupuy, where it was kept in a volume entirely devoted to news from the Ottoman Empire.[5] A copy of a letter from Constantinople reporting the news to the Duke of Guise found its way into the Peiresc archive.[6] So did unsourced relations.[7]

We should not therefore be surprised to find that as the traffic of the Ottoman world flowed into metropolitan Provence—and to Peiresc—in ever-greater quantity, the volume of news increased commensurately. Peiresc's archive preserves information in many forms. Typical is a scrap measuring maybe 2" × 8" dated Toulon, 17 April 1632, reporting, "A vessel arriving at Marseille having left Smyrna 4 March reports that this past February at Constantinople the Janissaries mutinied." Peiresc's judgment was that the Ottoman Empire was wracked by constant disobedience and ever-impending civil war. The notice concludes with the report of the arrival of a ship at Marseille loaded with grain.[8]

And then there were the letters written to him by his friends, and for his taste. Minuti's letters, for example, were full of nonstop reportage. From Sidon in September 1632 he told Peiresc of his trip from Constantinople to Rhodes and then on to Sidon in the company of badly equipped Turkish galleys. This included a forced twenty-day rest stop in Rhodes because no ship was allowed to depart while the Ottoman navy was in port. During this time the admiral was deposed and forced to return to Constantinople and await execution. Emir Fakhr al-Din ("Facardin") had raised an army to fight the emir of Nablus, but in the end they reconciled. In the meantime, the prince of Sidon wished to deliver his country "into the hands of our king"—only to discover that "the Christian princes turn a deaf ear to him."[9] Minuti in November wrote to Peiresc of the revolt of Facardin, who had united all the lands from Mount Lebanon to Aleppo; that the people of Damascus were in rebellion against their basha; that there was rebellion also in Anatolia; that the grand seigneur demanded that the Jesuits leave; that the French ambassador sheltered them in his embassy; that after being spurned by the French, Facardin turned to Tuscany for support; that the Grand Duke of Tuscany sent five vaisseaux with infantry to Cyprus to secure a possible bolt-hole for Facardin, but they were repelled; that Ambassador Marcheville sent his maître d'hôtel to the Échelles to impose a 2 percent tax to defray his debts and he was now in Aleppo. The ambassador in the meantime borrowed another 10,000 piastres and so owed more than 40,000. All this time, Césy was held in Constantinople with a debt of 350,000 piastres. A duty of 3 percent could pay off the capital, though not the interest. All this flowed out of one letter.[10]

Cesy's debts were notorious. They were a huge drag on commerce, since they had to be defrayed out of the earnings of French merchants. Their impact on French Levantine policy was enormous. A manuscript volume in the Dupuy collection tells the story of this debt. Many in the Archive of the Chambre de Commerce of Marseille document its effects.[11] And when the next French ambassador, Marcheville, was expelled, some of his retinue were able to sail home (on the navire *Dauphin*), while others were kept at Constantinople as quasi-hostages.[12] Their debts were still the subject of legal disputes between the Chambre de Commerce of Marseille and some individual Marseille merchants that went all the way to court and continued as late as 1666.[13]

Jean l'Empereur, a Marseille merchant based in Constantinople, wrote in 1634 to François-Auguste de Thou, whom he had hosted on the latter's trip several years earlier, with a similar omnibus account. He reported news of the sultan's mustering the army in the west, at Adrianople, perhaps intending designs on Poland, while from Aleppo, but months earlier, there was word that the Vizir planned to march east to Diyarbekir. A copy of this letter found its way to Peiresc, probably from the writer's Marseille-bound brother, possibly from the recipient in Paris.[14] The same l'Empereur, later that month of May 1634, passed along news from Captain Chaban, "one of my [l'Empereur's] old friends," who was en route to Sinope when he learned of thirty or forty Russian barques raiding the Black Sea coast in the vicinity of Varna (Bulgaria).[15]

The rise and fall of Fakhr al-Din runs right through Peiresc's letters from the Levant.[16] Minuti, from Damascus in April 1633, wrote of his mortal illness, then recovery and preparations for war, menaced as he was by a Turkish army on land and sea. The struggle between the Turks and the Persians had for the moment immobilized them both.[17] Minuti, just before leaving Sidon for Aleppo on 1 September 1633, reported on the arrival in port of forty galleys under the command of the "captain Basha" to mark the surrender by Fakhr al-Din of the castles of Sidon and Beirut, even as two other Ottoman *capigy* arrived to proclaim that Fakhr al-Din would retain his function as provincial governor.[18]

From Aleppo, before returning to Constantinople late in 1633, Minuti reported on the breakdown of the ceasefire: Fakhr al-Din refused to surrender the castle of Beirut and called his son Ali, the emir of Safed, to join him. His army of 15,000 men and 5,000 horses were met at Banias by a detachment of the emir of Damascus. Ali was felled by a musket shot and chose death rather than exemplary punishment in Damascus. At the news, Fakhr al-Din retired from the field into a fortress to mourn his loss. "You can well imagine," Minuti concluded, "that all his beautiful land is lost and is at present almost all in the hands of the Turk who will have soon ruined it." Consequently "the commerce of Sidon is also ruined." All the Franciscans and Capuchins were fleeing Lebanon, and also Jerusalem, because its basha was executed by the victorious ruler of Damascus for having supported Fakhr al-Din, and the replacement was no friend of the fathers. Even in Aleppo, though here at the instigation of the Venetians, the reaction against the monks was sharp: the *cadi* ordered the conversion into mosques of the buildings of the Capuchins, Jesuits, and Discalced Carmelites. By the end of 1633 it was clear to Peiresc that the land of Fakhr al-Din was now "prey for those Bashas."[19]

With Minuti back in Europe, it was the merchants in Aleppo and Sidon, de l'Isle and Allemand, who took to informing Peiresc of goings on in the Levant. De l'Isle reported on the campaign against Facardin's castles, the meeting in the desert of the armies, the movements of the captain basha from Tripoli to Cyprus and then back to Constantinople.[20] He reported on the very courteous treatment of the captive Fakhr al-Din by the victorious basha of Damascus, who had brought him there along with his treasures to await the sultan's decision. Word that Fakhr al-Din would remain master of the land was balanced by his knowledge that life and death lay in the sultan's hand. A postscript, dated 29 January 1635, announced the beginning of summary executions and Fakhr al-Din's transfer to Constantinople.[21]

Fallout from Fakhr al-Din's defeat was also registered across Peiresc's necklace of listening posts. From the Chouf Mountains east of Beirut came word in January of attacks by the Druse. From Sidon in April Peiresc learned of the dissipation of Fakhr al-Din's allies.[22] The repercussions even reached Aix. In a letter to Aycard of October 1635, Peiresc reported entertaining at Aix the Maronite Rabias, who brought Peiresc a letter from the Marseille merchant Piscatoris, conveying news that Sr. Guillaume Audifredy of Marseille had heard from Malta of the retirement to Rome of the famous Maronite leader Sheikh "Abeneder," who had been "the heart, soul, and counse" of Fakhr al-Din, along with his entire family.[23] The death of Fakhr al-Din he reported on the basis of news from Rome "which was confirmed to us from Cyprus, Sidon and Smyrna."[24] Peiresc, in turn, retailed all this information to high government officials, such as Loménie de Brienne, just then become secretary of state. His newsletters always include phrases such as "from the Levant one writes," "from Damascus one writes," "from Constantinople I learned," or ships "arrived with news."[25]

The embassy of Henri de Gournay, comte de Marcheville, was a colossal failure, but it did generate a lot of news. While Peiresc initially hoped for a rich intellectual harvest, all it left was more debt to weigh down Marseille's merchants.[26] Through the words and eyes of other members of the French legation and merchant community in Constantinople, however, we can get a real sense of what people there thought was happening. An unsigned relation from Constantinople of 17 December 1631, for example, described Marcheville's first audience with the sultan: his arrival at the Topkapi Palace, the festive meal served and eaten before the audience, the ritual of the encounter, and the reasons behind the enmity between Marcheville and the captain general of the Turkish galleys.[27] We know, for instance, that Marcheville's secretary, Sr. Fortet, stopped at Aix on his way back to Paris, no doubt briefing Peiresc on affairs at the other court. He also brought with him a book "composed by a Mehmet Emin son of Sadredin, and translated from Turkish into Italian by a Jew" which was made at the commandment of one of the first ministers of the sultan and discussed all the different sects of Muslims held heretical.[28]

Peiresc's relations with the embassy were so close that a letter of Minuti's from Constantinople was countersigned by the ambassador himself and was received by the hand of his secretary, M. Jacques d'Angusse.[29] And as affairs in Constantinople spiraled toward their ruin, it was directly from d'Angusse that Peiresc learned of the various plans that were circulating to liquidate the French debt.[30] Letters from Guillaume Montolieu, a merchant and chancellor of the embassy, to Peiresc, Guez, and de Gastines give details of the Turkish harassment of Western ambassadors, an attack on the French ambassador's home, and imprisonment of merchants such as himself as hostages for the outstanding French debt.[31] In April 1634, Peiresc explained that news of Marcheville's death sentence and its commutation had arrived in Marseille in a letter from Livorno of 20 March, which was itself drawing on information communicated by an English ship that had left Constantinople on 5 February and had just arrived in Marseille.[32]

In May 1634, Jean Guez, whose brother, Guillaume, worked in Constantinople, explained to Peiresc that he had not yet had the chance to draw up the relation of the troubles in Constantinople that he had promised, so that he was now sending the original, unredacted materials that he had received from his brother.[33] The contents of a letter from Jean l'Empereur in Constantinople to de Thou from May 1634 reporting on the crisis in diplomatic relations that led to the expulsion of Marcheville also found its way into Peiresc's archive.[34] Two letters from Montolieu reported in detail—from prison—on the Ottoman persecution of Marcheville, and another, written to Guez in Marseille, completed this narration.[35] Montolieu also wrote directly to de Gastines, his "cher amy," complaining of the bad treatment he had received from the ambassador and asking de Gastines to pass along the letter to the commander Forbin and the general of the galleys.[36]

Letters arrived in and moved through all the Provençal ports, making Peiresc's broad contacts especially valuable. In one instance, Peiresc thanked Honoré Aycard, in Toulon, for passing on to him a letter from Aleppo. In exchange, Peiresc was sending Aycard a copy of a letter to him from Minuti, who had written from Constantinople *about the murder of Ambassador Marcheville*—this was the state of the rumor mill at the end of March 1634. Peiresc explained, and the detail is, as always, valuable, that the letter had been brought to him on the polacre of Captain Michel Guigo, who had just arrived in quarantine in the Isles of Marseille, after being similarly held at his prior stop, at Civitavecchia. Officials of the sanitary regime ("Intendants de la Santé") took the further precaution of dousing his letters in vinegar.[37]

It was from Livorno that Peiresc received the latest rumor of Ottoman anti-French persecution, writing to de Thou in August 1635 that "all the facilities of the French in Constantinople have been seized once again for the debts of Césy." This foretold the "total ruin of French commerce not only in Constantinople but throughout the Levant," especially of Marseille.[38] From Italy, Peiresc heard of a renegade who fled Constantinople with his family for Algiers. His galley was seized by the Tuscans—presumably the Medici-founded Knights of St. Stephen—and was estimated at between 200,000 and 500,000 écus' worth. There was also a rumor that galleys of Malta—the Knights of St. John—had seized Tripoli in North Africa, but Peiresc noted that "this is not very certain."[39]

In fact, though, Peiresc's Marseille was no more central than Minuti's Sidon when it came to news. For news, like the current and shipping, did not flow but circulated. Sitting in Sidon, in March 1633, Minuti was able to write to Malta and to Constantinople to complain about the Provençal corsairs who had stolen his belongings. By the end of the summer he could report to Peiresc that Ambassador de Marcheville had written to Malta on his behalf and that the grand master in Malta had confiscated all the stolen goods aboard the offending barque.[40]

Finally, as in S. D. Goitein's vision of a medieval trading zone "from Spain to India," the seventeenth-century Red Sea world, opening out as it did to the Indian Ocean, was at the same time bound up with the Mediterranean system, not least because united to it by both the Ottoman sword and the intrepid European trader. Drawing on letters received from Cairo, themselves based on reports from the caravan from Mecca, Peiresc was able to report to de Thou in Paris on a rebellion against the provincial governor of Yemen who was besieged in Moucal (Mocha) until by a ruse he managed to assassinate the leader of the rebellion. Levies were being raised in Egypt to send across the Red Sea to quell the rebellion.[41] A few months later, bringing de Thou up to date on the ongoing rebellion, Peiresc introduced a new factor, adding that the English "had well and truly ruined the trade that was established in the Red Sea."[42]

"Writing now from Cairo"—with this Peiresc introduced a letter to Cardinal Francesco Barberini that reports on the rebellion of Ahmet Basha, the conqueror of the rebel Fakhr al-Din, and then moves on to a detailed account of the anti-Turkish rebellion in Yemen.[43] As an outpost on the farther east, Cairo was a better listening post for provincial news than was Constantinople.

27 ॐ
Time and Timings

*T*he same letters that informed—and sometimes misinformed—
Peiresc of all that was happening in the wider world also convey
crucial information about the reality of communicating across
space. We can read Peiresc's correspondence much as Braudel read Sanu-
do's, Scatudo the Jesuits', and Petitjean Ragusa's: as a record of how long
it took to know what was happening elsewhere in the biosphere.[1] Many
of Peiresc's letters include information about the length of various sea passages. The sea was fast. Praising the connectedness of Guillaume d'Espiot,
de Gastines's man in Rome, Peiresc explained to Holstenius that he had
daily possibilities for sending all sorts of packages to Marseille directly, or
by way of correspondents in Livorno and Genoa. Without this maritime
highway, Peiresc warned, "whole years would slip away from you."[2] His
correspondents also thought about speed, and correlated it with tonnage:
the bigger the ship, the slower the traveling. Hence Théophile Minuti, in
Constantinople, chose to send a load of goods to Peiresc by way of a polacre rather than a vaisseau, even though it was going via Ancona, because
"I do not think it as good for sailing as the polacre."[3] And yet, travel times
in 1630 were not always faster than those calculated by Franco Melis from
information in the Datini archives circa 1400.[4]

Details of timing can be extracted from many of Peiresc's letters. He
received word from mariners returning from Constantinople of the murder
of Ambassador Marcheville. Peiresc conveyed this false report to de Thou
in a letter written on 29 March 1634. The "murder" was said to have taken
place on 28 January 1634. News of it came to Peiresc in letters carried on
the polacre of Captain Michel Guigo dated "Smyrna 4 February." Peiresc
explained that the letters traveled from Constantinople to Chios by
caïque, a ketch-like ship, in four days, and then from Chios to Smyrna.
The polacre eventually arrived at Civitavecchia, from which the letters were
sent on 20 March![5]

Other examples are the following: From the Levant coast, the Samaritan Triglot left Sidon not long after 10 December 1629 and arrived safe
and sound at Marseille on 27 January 1630.[6] To Aycard, in November 1632,

Peiresc reported that a ship had just reached Marseille after having departed from Sidon thirty days before. (Especially interesting for our understanding of Peiresc is that he also noted that this ship brought news of
a second one that had planned to leave Sidon within fifteen days after the
first departed—Peiresc was always thinking ahead.)[7] A book sent to Peiresc
by Mallon in Aleppo was recorded as leaving by 1 November 1632, and it
reached Marseille not long before 31 March 1633. (Peiresc had the book
itself in hand by around 2–3 April 1633.)[8] But the navire *Ste. Anne,* carrying
a Coptic grammar and lexicon, was in transit between 3 November
and 12 May![9] Letters written by Father Celestin in Aleppo on 29 September
and 2 October reached Peiresc around 22 November 1635.[10] On 24 April
1633, Peiresc was pleased to be able to inform Marcheville in Constantinople that he had learned that the *St. Esprit* of Patron Lombardon had
left Sidon in mid-March and was expected at any moment. Five weeks,
therefore, seemed an unremarkable time, neither overly long nor surprisingly swift.[11]

De Thou's direct crossing from Alexandria to Siracusa in ten days,
by contrast, seemed so fast as to be considered especially noteworthy by
Peiresc. But Peiresc also recorded the more typical remainder of de Thou's
route, which took him to Malta, where he was stranded for three weeks,
and thence by galley to Palermo and from there via Trapani to Sardinia.
This last leg took only twenty-four hours. From there he proceeded to
Mallorca and Barcelona. The trip back to Marseille from there required
four or five days and merited no comment.[12] But in a stormy time, Peiresc
reports to de Thou, the way from Malta to Marseille took twenty-nine
days.[13] De Thou, for his part, stated as a reasonable expectation that with
decent weather a ship could reach Marseille from Sidon in a fortnight,
although 1,000 leagues distant.[14] At the outside, Father Celestin responded only in late January 1636 to a letter that his brother Jacob Golius
sent to him on 22 May 1635.[15]

Minuti's first voyage to the Levant took him twenty-five days at most,
with his ship making no stops between Marseille and Sidon.[16] On his
second trip, Galaup, Minuti, and Marcheville left Marseille and reached
Malta in seven days, and in three more days reached Cythera off the southeastern Peloponnese.[17] In the correspondence of the Capuchins we find
an even more startling travel time, an astonishingly rapid passage of fifteen days from Marseille to Sidon, which included a two-and-a-half-day
stop at Malta.[18] On the other hand, in this same dossier we learn of a forty-

three-day trip from Sidon to Damiette instead of the usual six, because of a pirate-provoked evasion to Cyprus.[19] In the eighteenth century, thirty to forty days were not uncommon for the route from Marseille to Alexandria.[20] And in the sixteenth and the nineteenth centuries, it was more or less the same: Denis Possot took forty-five days from Venice to Jaffa, and Jerome Maurand fifty days from Constantinople back to Marseille.[21] Chateaubriand's ship took forty-two days to travel from Alexandria to Tunis.[22] A forty-odd-day trip from Marseille seems about standard, which included time spent in Malta and taking evasive action against corsairs.[23]

It was to Peiresc a fact worth noting when the bishop of Montpellier was able in his felucca to pass from Livorno to Toulon in twenty-four hours, suggesting that it typically took longer.[24] On the one hand, de Thou writes that his very short trip from Marseille to Genoa took seven days! He called this coastal tramping "a real ladies' sightseeing trip" ("une vraie navigation des dames").[25] On the other hand, a German traveler, Pierre Hartzwick, apologizes for not stopping at Belgentier, explaining that Cardinal de Bagni, in whose suite he was traveling, had gone from Toulon to Civitavecchia in six days.[26] This would have been by papal galley, used by the regular service that went back and forth between Rome and Avignon every month. But Minuti also made it from Rome to Marseille in "only" six days, with one spent at Genoa.[27] And with Marcheville's departure from Marseille on 20 July 1631 in favorable weather, he could be expected to reach Malta in four or five days![28] North Africa was generally two weeks away—a bit too long, as it turned out, for some of the chameleons sent to Peiresc from Tunis.[29] Barcelona was just a few days away: close enough for the French to live in fear of a surprise descent.[30]

When boats did not come, time itself seemed to slow down. Peiresc wrote to Jean Magy in January 1635 that he had been waiting the whole month for the arrival of the navire *Ste. Anne* "with more impatience than do the Jews for their Messiah."[31] Commerce with the Levant, we perceive, had become regularized enough that even small interruptions were noted, and perhaps experienced, as ominous. Thus, we learn in a letter of Peiresc to Gilles de Loches that while Captain François Laure was ready to depart for Egypt at the beginning of March, he hesitated because of the ten navires that had gone there, none had as yet returned, "which makes one fear some new extortion [*avanie*] of those barbarians."[32] Indeed, no ship was to depart from Marseille for the Levant between early March and mid-November 1634.[33] From Constantinople Peiresc learned that in the chaos of Marcheville's expulsion nine French navires were seized by the Turks against the debts of Césy, who had been restored to his position as French ambassador.[34]

The discussion of time and shipping could even be the subject of a letter. For example, writing to Minuti on 9 January 1634, Peiresc began by explaining that he had written fifteen days earlier by way of Venice, only to realize that one of his servants had failed to include "the mémoire on music" that Mersenne wanted clarified. It was now being sent with this letter. A ship had just come in from Constantinople, having departed on 21 November—too soon for Minuti to have reached the city by caravan from Aleppo. Then, at the other end of his world, in Paris, on 30 December, he had learned of the deposition of Cyril Lucar. But that most recent ship from Constantinople, which departed on 21 November, brought no such tidings. Could someone in Paris have received the news in the month between the departure of a ship from Constantinople on the 21st and the arrival of a letter in Paris just before year's end? Peiresc doubted it, and thus doubted the veracity of the Parisian "information." Only an express courier could have brought this news that fast, and he was unsure one had been employed.[35] We see how Peiresc used his knowledge of the practicalities of Mediterranean communication as a tool with which to evaluate the reliability of documentary evidence.

At both ends of the Mediterranean, roads of sea and land met. At his end, Peiresc frequently compared the likely journey times from Italy over the Alps and via Lyon with the coastal route from Genoa.[36] And at the Levantine end, the sea-land interchange connected Marseille to the caravan cities of Asia.[37] In February 1633, Peiresc wrote to Aycard that he had received a letter from Minuti sent from Sidon with the news that Aycard's nephew, Jean Salvator, had stayed behind in Damascus to wait for the caravan from India.[38] Minuti wrote from Damascus that the caravan from India and Baghdad was held up by the Arabs two days' journey away and was composed of 3,400 camels. This, however, was nothing compared with the Mecca caravan, which was to depart from Damascus in eight days; it was composed of fifty thousand people, or that from Cairo to Mecca, which was even bigger and was departing around the same time.[39] Writing to Aycard in December 1633, Peiresc relayed details of Minuti's preparation for the caravan trip from Aleppo to Constantinople. The trip was scheduled to take around forty days, and the foodstuffs cost 27 piastres and filled an entire duffel bag ("besace").[40] The late departure of a ship from Marseille bound for Cairo (the polacre St. François of Captain François

Laure) vexed Peiresc because it risked missing the connection to the caravan that left Egypt for Ethiopia around Easter time.[41]

We possess a precious document, probably derived by Peiresc from conversation with the diamond merchants Manuel Da Costa Casseretz and Fernand Nuñes in Belgentier in 1630. It reflects their experience in going by caravan from the eastern Mediterranean deep into southwestern and southern Asia:

> From *Aleppo* to Basra by the desert in 33 days[42]
>
> From *Basra* by sea to Muscat in 7 days
>
> From *Muscat to Hormuz* by sea in about a day
>
> From *Muscat to Goa* takes about 15 days
>
> From Goa one goes to *Surat,* which is the port of Mogor [*sic*], or to *Gaya,* which is less commercial
>
> From Gaya to *Lahore* there is 8 or 10 days on the way. From Surat less.[43]

Another set of measurements of time and space came from Magy in Cairo. He had explained that the journey from Cairo to Mecca took thirty-five days, traveling day and night, and from Mecca to San'a, the capital of Yemen, forty days, and another forty days from there to Moucal (Mocha), the port of Yemen.[44]

Even from places like Goa, on the farthest edge of the European world, the mail still traveled. The jeweler Alvares in Paris received by 12 June 1633 a letter from his brother-in-law in Goa written on 5 April 1632.[45] This seems exceptionally slow compared with letters sent from the Casseretz brothers at Goa on 8 February, transshipped from Lisbon on 11 July and reaching Alvares in Paris the third week of August, all in the same year of 1633.[46]

If we wonder at the huge amounts of time involved in these correspondences with the Far East and how people like Peiresc managed it, the answer is "patience." As Peiresc explained to Alvares by way of absolving him forever of any need to apologize for not writing sooner, "as I have the patience to wait for years on end for news of the Indies, I can wait no less for news of my friends, when their affairs can permit them to remember me." He had to practice this on himself, too, since because of his physical infirmities, and his responsibilities at the parlement, he "often had to defer for weeks and entire months that which I would much more want to do the next day."[47]

And yet, beyond space and time, Peiresc always returned to people. His sense of how far was too far was defined by the presence of Provençaux. Writing to Minuti in 1633, Peiresc feared for his traveling farther east, "the farther one goes away from the familiar lands where reaches the commerce of the Provençaux."[48] (Minuti had, in fact, represented to Peiresc the relative familiarity of Jerusalem by his unexpected encounter with two Provençal sailors in the Church of the Holy Sepulchre.)[49] Similarly, writing to de Loches, Peiresc warned him not to venture too far west. He urged de Loches to make Africa, not America, the arena for his missionary-ethnographical work, for in America he would be dependent on the Spanish, "their commerce there being much more frequent than ours could be." Africa, by contrast, was almost home: "where it falls to us only to get a foothold, if we want, and to maintain a very frequent and very comfortable commerce with it."[50]

28 ॐ
Corsairs

*T*he great threat posed on the water came from corsairs. The first part of the seventeenth century, with the arrival of "peace" in the Mediterranean between Christians and Turks, saw a dramatic upsurge in corsairing activity. Recent scholarship has been alive to the many dimensions of this "dirty war of peace," the *guerre de course*.[1] But where Braudel, and those who followed him, saw corsairing as a form of war, it is equally accurate to see it as a form of trade: more violent, perhaps, than others, and surely less respecting of certain laws, but definitely a commerce.

Because Peiresc's letters, friends, and goods traveled by ship, and with great frequency, he was especially exposed to risk. Indeed, shipwrecks and hijacking were a constant threat. When ships sank they took their goods with them down to the bottom of the sea. Sometimes, as in the case of de Thou's crocodile, the goods could be recovered and even restored.[2] When ships were taken by corsairs, they and their crews and cargoes could sometimes also be ransomed back.

The corsairs were a problem across the Mediterranean. From Tripoli in Lebanon in 1623, Peiresc learned of two French ships and their crews that were held hostage by the basha himself, who was apparently notorious for such tactics.[3] But it was the relationship between Provence and the regency of Algiers that was almost entirely shaped by the corsairs, including the counter-corsairing expeditions undertaken either formally or informally.[4] Peiresc's relationship with Sanson Napollon, as well as his proximity to the coast, put him at the center of this diplomatic, economic, and social problem. Napollon's shuttle diplomacy with Algiers, which resulted in the treaty of 1628 and the redemption of a good number of captives, is amply recorded in the volume at Carpentras devoted to "Turcs. Maritime" (MS. 1777) and its counterpart in the collection of the Dupuy brothers, largely compiled from Peiresc materials.[5]

During those negotiations of 1627–1628, Peiresc informed Secretary of State Loménie that the corsairs returned a French slave in order to make the point that French sailors should not abandon ship at the mere sight of the corsairs, because the "express commandment" of the divan was "to treat favorably and protect," with a prohibition on harm, any of the French.[6] This was a propaganda move no different than the governor of Provence, Charles of Lorraine, Duke of Guise, staging the repentance of the Moors on the Marseille quays a few years earlier. It is also worth noting the commonplace observation, made here from the enemy's perspective, that flight was the French response to the sight of corsair vessels, as this corroborates Peiresc's own view of their behavior.

Algiers was the capital of *la course*. Aubery, in 1629, about to leave Rome to avoid the summer heat, told Peiresc that he would be going by horseback to Venice because "the roads of Lombardy and the sea" were so perilous. The corsairs of Algiers and Tunis brazenly patrolled just off the coast of Civitavecchia, and only the day before three barques had been captured and led off to Barbary.[7] In December 1633, Peiresc reported, again to Loménie, on the arrival in Marseille of an Armenian come from Algiers who had been taken prisoner in the capture of the *St. Lazare*. He provided information about its seizure, noting the decision of the captain to try to negotiate with the corsairs rather than fight them. The ship itself was carrying goods worth around 70,000 écus, a huge sum by Marseille standards, and it led to a cascading chain of bankruptcies that spread all the way to Lyon.[8] In mid-June 1637, just days before his death, Peiresc was still passing along the latest from Marseille that the corsairs of Bizerte and Algiers were creating a joint squadron of fourteen or fifteen galleys and galliotes with Sardinia as the target.[9]

Where Peiresc's own shipping seems to have suffered most was in the east. We have fragmentary information in a letter of Peiresc's to Gilles de Loches of December 1633 reporting an incident that occurred in the very harbor of Alexandria. A Provençal ship trying to leave the harbor was pursued by a corsair, but so close into shore that Mustafa Bey, the ruler of Alexandria, gave orders to fire on the corsairs, providing the ship with all the opportunity it needed to escape.[10] Even being in port posed risks. Early in 1634 there were "10 or 12 navires of Marseille" in the harbor of Alexandria from which only one had returned to Marseille, leading Peiresc to fear they were being held hostage.[11] Another version of the story recurred a year later in a way that put both de Gastines and Peiresc in "great alarm." In the port of Alexandria, seven Provençal navires found themselves alongside corsair ships. Peiresc's view of what this meant was clear and dark: "If these disorders are not repaired it will be necessary to abandon the whole trade with the Levant."[12]

There were also Christian corsairs, most famously the Knights of St. Stephen based in Livorno, and those of St. John at Malta. Around these more formal units circulated a larger riffraff of adventurers, idealists, and opportunists. They sometimes discriminated not only between Christian and Muslim shipping but between Christian and Muslim crewmembers. Thus, François Galaup reports that on Rhodes he took ship with a Greek caïque going from Salonica to Sidon with a load of iron. The merchants on board had made a deal with the captain not to take any Jews or Turks "because on this route there was found only the corsairs of the Occident [Christians] who often save the Christians." If they found Jews or Turks on board "everything on the vessel would be in peril." Galaup left the Jews on Rhodes and changed ships.[13] The galleys of Marseille also preyed on Muslim shipping. One of Peiresc's small treasures, a calendar and almanac produced in North Africa, came to him via Dr. Cassagnes, who had acquired it as booty from Turkish shipping that had been attacked at the Straits of Gibraltar.[14]

Indeed, the best-documented story of corsairing in the Peiresc archive involves Christian corsairs from the west—in fact, from Provence. Théophile Minuti's boat was captured off Cyprus by a barque of Martigues armed at Malta and crewed by twenty-five Provençaux, a Venetian, and a Maltese. After three weeks of living rough in the woods with the other passengers, all Greeks and Maronites, they were rescued by Turks. Minuti paid close enough attention to his captors to be able to provide Peiresc with important clues as to the perpetrators. The *patron* from Martigues had departed Provence with 6,000 piastres and "a plan to come to the Levant and to trade according to the usual customs" ("avec dessain de venir en Levant et negocier sellon la coustume ordinaire"). But passing Malta he was asked by a Savoyard knight named Castellonovo to arm the barque as a corsair "to which the said Martegan consented," and gave over his money to the Savoyard. Minuti also identified one of the Provençal mariners as a native of Frejus, tall and thin ("homme maigre et de belle taille"), who bore a leg wound from a musket shot fired two days before from a Turkish *caramürssel*. Minuti hoped that with all this information it would be possible to identify these criminals and put some teeth behind his threat: "I promised that said Martegan that he would pay, but he mocked me."[15] A month later, Minuti noted that while the Martegan used a barque, his partner, or "wingman" ("sa conserve"), whom Minuti explains he did not see, was a "vaisseau" whose *patron* was "Castello Novo Nissart"—the one who had prompted the corsairing exploit. Minuti also wrote to Marcheville in Constantinople and to Malta to alert them to this attack and to the identities of the perpetrators.[16]

This event echoed through Peiresc's correspondence. He described the Provençaux pirates as "more inhuman than the Turks" ("plus inhumaines que les Turcz"). He promised Minuti to do everything he could to track down the perpetrators and to retrieve the goods, or their value, both for the love of him and for the interest of the proprietor Sr. Allemand. Peiresc promised to write to the grand master of the Knights of the Hospital in Malta by way of the premier president, by way of the commander of the galleys Fourbin, and possibly by way of the marshal de Vitry, governor of Provence since 1631. He had not yet been able to determine the name of the captain or whence he hailed, though he thought this could be easily ascertained. He addressed a query to another captain from Martigues, Pierre de Vaulx, and was waiting for his reply. He hoped to make it an exemplary case. Captain Carrayre in the meantime advanced Minuti 43 piastres on Cyprus to enable him to buy clothes, food, and transport.[17]

To Jean Louis Allemand, who was shipping caps of some sort ("bonnetz") back to France, Peiresc affirmed that he "would employ all my credit for you," whether in Malta or in Provence. If those corsairs returned, "I assure you that they will be received there as they merit." What Peiresc needed to know was "their names, qualities and origins or residence."[18]

A still more elaborate account is found in a letter to Honoré Aycard, also of 7 June 1633. Peiresc reports, matter-of-factly, that Minuti "was robbed by a barque of Martigues, armed for war, flying a Maltese flag with only 27 people: a Venetian, a Maltese and the rest Provençaux, whose captain was, it is said, from La Ciotat, or from Martigues, but without him [Minuti] having been able to learn his name. He was on a barque fully loaded with Christian mariners, Greeks and Maronites, and they were all stripped and left naked, in only their shirts, without being able to obtain from his thieves anything other than his breviary and my mémoires." Minuti, gentle soul that he was, was hurt by "this inhumanity," and if Peiresc could discover the name of this captain he would bring him to justice ("je tascherois de luy en faire fare la raison").[19] Later in June, Peiresc wrote to Aycard that Minuti complained about being robbed by a sailor from Frejus named Mienas [sic?] who was on the navire of the knight Castelnuovo of Nice, who acknowledged the theft to M. Lombard, but said that he had excepted Father Minuti the "Provençal" and left him with sixteen bottles of oil, as well as his valise and papers. Peiresc hoped Aycard could shed some light on the whole episode.[20]

The fullest version of the Minuti story is told by Peiresc in a letter to Gaffarel of November 1633. Peiresc had by now heard the good deeds performed by the French ambassador to Venice for those twenty Provençaux who had been taken prisoner by the Savoyard and then captured and thus liberated by Venetian galleys off of Crete. As it happened, those twenty were "quite unworthy of this grace," as they and their captain had previously cruelly used a group of Greek and Maronite Christians who were on a caïque from Sidon to Cyprus when they were seized off of Cape St. Andrea. They were robbed, as was the Minim Minuti—"whom you possibly know as he is well known throughout the Levant," Peiresc adds—who was despoiled of everything but his breviary and "a small notebook of mémoires that he had of me," notwithstanding his protestations of common *patria*. Minuti was also carrying a case of red hats which was consigned to him on the account of Jean Louis Allemand of Marseille for delivery to a Venetian merchant at the salt pans of Cyprus. But those "crooks" ("Canailles") were so "denatured and unpitying" that the Turks could not have been more barbaric: they left the passengers without their clothes, in a place with no food and water. For three weeks they ate nothing but mushrooms and anything else that could be scavenged off the land, while their greatest difficulty was in looking for water. Finally, in fact, they were aided by a passing Turkish ship which, seeing their despair, picked them up and transported them to a more salubrious spot on the island from which they could find assistance and in the meantime shared out their food and drink. From there, Minuti caught a ship back to Constantinople, where he passed a few months, again in the retinue of Marcheville, and then returned to Sidon and the Holy Land on Peiresc's scholarly service—as if nothing ever happened. Peiresc concluded by asking Gaffarel to see if he could find out the name of that Venetian merchant in Cyprus who was to receive Allemand's bonnets so that he could reimburse him for the lost value and so clear Father Minuti's account.[21]

Peiresc was able to report all this back to Minuti, including the disheartening news that the French ambassador to Venice had secured the release of the Provençal sailors whom the Savoyard had taken prisoner. The ambassador had made demonstrations about their making good the theft of Allemand's bonnets.[22]

Minuti's experience makes for a fascinating microhistory. But it is also a small piece of "big" history, for by the end of the seventeenth century, the export of bonnets to Smyrna alone counted for a full fifth of all the manufactured goods the French sold there. It was the Greeks, Armenians, and others who covered their heads who made this market. Cyprus would have been no different. Jean-Louis Allemand, whose name comes to us from out of the past, must have blazed this trail.[23]

29 ❧
Ransoming

*I*n all this archive of achievement, the most common sentiment, in fact, is loss. In Peiresc's merchant correspondence, this threat is always present. Some losses were to nature, such as shipwreck, and others to men, such as corsairs. Victims could, however, sometimes be ransomed back. This is a subject about which the historical literature has exploded in the past decade.[1]

Ransoming captives was a central component in the negotiations between France and the corsairs of Algiers. Sadok Boubaker has noted that there were three types of ransomings: collective, individual, and by exchange. In Napollon's treaty of 1628, money was raised in Provence for the liberation—at a price—of French captives in Algiers.[2] This was collective ransoming.

Peiresc himself engaged in the ransoming of individuals. He set out to raise funds from "la Redemption de Marseille"—the Trinitarians—on behalf of a family friend of Aycard's (though acknowledging that the sum was insufficient).[3] The nephew of one of his better friends had been taken and made prisoner in Tunis; Peiresc wrote to his correspondent there asking him to do "whatever would be possible for you" on behalf of "the poor boy."[4] The presence of Sanson Napollon in Algiers made him an obvious address for special requests, but the ransoming of captives was also central to the peace process of 1628. It was only when a local name was not on the list of those to be redeemed that Peiresc swung into action.[5] But, even then, he understood that the high ransom meant that in order to redeem the greatest number of Christian slaves with a fixed amount of money, men like Louis Apvril might come last.[6]

The story of Lange Roustan is the most elaborated of these tales of redemption in the Peiresc archive. In a letter to d'Arcos of 14 January 1635, Peiresc described Lange as "the youngest child of someone who was the nurse in our house at Belgentier, and thus whose whole family had always had a certain dependence on us and ours." Lange followed his cousin, Saulueree Roustan, down to the sea and wound up a slave in Tunis. The father was dead and the family lacked money for a ransom. Lange was just fifteen or sixteen years old, and his owner's name was "Murat the Greek" ("Morato Greco"), suggesting that he too was of European origins. Peiresc asked d'Arcos to see if the ransom could be reduced.[7] By the end of March, Peiresc could inform d'Arcos that a delegation of the Trinitarians of Marseille was heading to Tunis with money for the redemption of captives and wished to include Lange Roustan among them—if the ransom could be reduced.[8] Peiresc also proceeded with a parallel plea to the merchant Berengier, who had regular commercial contact with Tunis and who had been sent to redeem captives in Tripoli in 1629, in the wake of Napollon's negotiated deal with Algiers.[9] The silence of the mission made him concerned that something had gone amiss.[10] We do not know what happened to the poor boy, and Peiresc died not long after writing this letter.

The redemption of captives was a major part of the treaty concluded by Napollon with the divan of Algiers in 1628. At a time when the city's population is estimated, no doubt much too high, at around 120,000, with approximately 25,000 Christian captives, Napollon's success was in bringing 130 French prisoners back with him to Marseille that October.[11] We have a list of their names, and of those whose hometown is identified, 13 were from Marseille, 5 from Cassis, 4 from La Ciotat, 5 from Sixfours, 4 from Tollon, and 9 from Martigues. This perfectly mirrors what we find in the Seguiran Report: the dominance of Marseille and the disproportionately heavy toll extracted from Martigues shipping.[12] Napollon even provided the ransom sums paid out by the individual Provençal ports. Again the dominance of Marseille is easily gauged; of the total of 79,983 livres, Marseille contributed 72,000.[13]

In Peiresc's copy of Napollon's own report on the negotiation, we learn much about the workings of the divan of Algiers and the politics of piracy. We read that there was a faction in the divan that was dependent on the duties from prizes—just then at 13 percent, bringing in 26,000 livres the previous year—and was thus unlikely to enforce a cessation of predation.[14]

But people were not the only thing that got ransomed in Peiresc's Mediterranean. Books were also lost and sought. And Peiresc's hunting after his books helps us realize that the "geography of ransoming" can be extracted from his archive, too, as it has, recently, from the public ones.

A ship captured on the way from Alexandria might be sold at Rhodes, or Chios, or if taken farther out to sea, at Tunis or Livorno.[15] Following Peiresc following a lost object is, then, yet another form of mapping. The seizure of the barque St. André, for instance, led Peiresc to seek the advice of captains. Peiresc wanted to know the corsair captain's age, hometown, and ethnic origins since it was said that he understood something of the books on board, which were of Eastern, not Roman Catholic, Christianity.[16] Having learned that the barque was seized near Rhodes—taken by three galleys from Algiers and two from Rhodes—Peiresc asked Seghezzi to draw upon his eastern Mediterranean connections, and also that of his relative Gela.[17] This is where Peiresc's almost obsessive desire to know the whereabouts of Marseille's shipping, even the boats that were not carrying his goods, paid off, for it meant that in a situation like this Peiresc could quickly set people into action. Indeed, in this case he knew within two weeks that the corsair captain was named Osman, that he had been employed as a scribe in the customs house at Algiers, and that he had kept the books destined for Peiresc. But Peiresc had also heard that a sailor who had helped sell the barque at Rhodes remembered having seen the books in the hands of one of Osman's slaves. Peiresc urged that this matelot be identified and then interrogated as to the name, age, and country of that slave.[18]

But by far the best illustration of Peiresc's North African system, shedding light on his Mediterranean system as a whole, came about in the last years of his life and was triggered by the loss of a single manuscript book, a polyglot Psalter. Gassendi, for his part, tells us briefly about its loss in his account of the year 1637. Others, writing much later, tell us about its recovery.[19] What occurred between loss and recovery has not thus far been told.

The Psalter is first mentioned by Father Agathange in a letter of 18 March 1634, which describes it as a book of Psalms in Coptic, Arabic, Greek, Armenian, Ethiopic, and Syriac. The superior of the convent was willing to give it to him, even though it was the property of the church. "I persuaded them to ask for something else which they needed for their church. They asked us for a silver chalice, with a little silver plate which could work for them instead of a paten." Agathange hoped that Peiresc could arrange for the chalice. But Peiresc had an ulterior motive: "Beyond that it is for the church and the service of God, who knows well how to compensate what is done for Him, I hope that we can draw from this convent a number of good old books."[20] Agathange also gave Peiresc specific instructions as to the desired chalice's shape and appearance.[21]

In May 1635, Peiresc told de Thou that he had been given hope for a polyglot book—he said "octaple"—"which would really dazzle the eyes of those most refined in the matter of books."[22] Peiresc asked Jean-Baptiste

Magy in May 1635 whether he had yet received from his brother in Cairo the mémoire "of what he had furnished on my account for the purchase of that said book, and other things."[23] Agathange informed Peiresc on 25 July 1635 that the manuscript contained the Psalms in Coptic, Armenian, Ethiopic, Arabic, and Chaldaic (Aramaic), that it was from the monastery of Saint-Macaire, and that it was going to be put on the ship of Captain Baille.[24]

In early August 1635, while he was organizing the Mediterranean-wide eclipse observation scheduled for the end of the month, Peiresc asked Jean-Baptiste Magy in Marseille whether there was a ship readying to sail for Alexandria because he was having made a silver chalice for sending there, and that it would miss the immediately departing barque.[25] Peiresc confirmed this in the accompanying letter to Jean Magy in Cairo in which he also noted—interestingly—that he knew the whole story only from Magy's letters of 15 and 20 March, not from anything written to him directly by Agathange.[26] By early September the chalice was ready, and Peiresc was planning to have Father Théophile Minuti come to Marseille and find a ship ready to depart for Alexandria.[27] It turned out that three boats were departing, and Peiresc left it up to Jean-Baptiste Magy and Gela to decide whether to send the chalice with Pierre Caillon, with Crouset, or with Chabert.[28] To Agathange de Vendôme, Peiresc talked about the importance of sending the Psalter with English shipping, "because the English do not get frightened, like our Provençaux. And I do not think I would ever have received anything from that country if the good manners of the captains of our navires did not have the habit of taking from the corsairs they encountered as the corsairs had taken from them."[29]

A week later it was all done. Peiresc explained to Magy in Cairo that he had sent the silver chalice and paten to Father Agathange for the use of the fathers of St. Macaire in the swap for the polyglot book "which you have made me rejoice from so far away." Minuti had brought the cup from Aix to Marseille and witnessed Jean-Baptiste Magy consigning it to Captain Pierre Caillon, who left on the *Ste. Magdeleine*.[30]

Only two weeks later, Peiresc's joy turned to gloom. The barque of Patron Baille, with the book that he described as "the most precious that I could have expected from the Levant" ("le plus precieux que je pouvois attendre du Levant"), was taken by corsairs (he had received the news from Patron Lombard, himself just arrived from Egypt).[31] Peiresc was mortified that Magy had disobeyed his explicit instructions to send the book with an English or Dutch ship. "Because we knew already that this Captain Baille had so little courage," he protested, "that instead of preparing to fight the corsairs he abandoned his barque to them near Malta."[32] Typically, he even dared to go to sea in a boat that had already sunk once in the Nile. "And if you had followed the letter of my instructions," Peiresc rounded on Magy, in a very rare expression of anger, "that I expressly made, you would not have sent this volume of the Psalter as soon as the agreement was concluded concerning the chalice, which you could have done by the English *vaisseau*.[33]

But even in his desolation, Peiresc immediately focused on practical measures. To Jean-Baptiste Magy he asked for whatever information he had picked up about the seizure, but also about the news he had heard that the corsair was himself later captured by the galleys of Tuscany or Malta.[34] On the same day, Peiresc wrote to Gela with even more bad news. In addition to the loss of the Psalter, there was news of a barque from Marseille shipwrecked near Malta and Peiresc feared, by rough calculation of time and space, that it might have been that of Patron Caillon, carrying the chalice. But again Peiresc focused on facts and practicalities. Having heard that it was a Livornese ship that had seized the corsair who had captured Baille and the book, Peiresc asked Gela to find out the name of the corsair, the name of the Livornese ship and its commander, the place and time of its capture as well as that of Baille, and where the corsair was now "so that I could write and try every means possible to regain my book."[35] These are, as we have seen, Peiresc's standard questions, but they presumed the existence of an entire information network into which merchants could tap as needed. And this was need.

Peiresc's campaign to track down the precious volume involved sending letters to contacts all along the Barbary Coast. To Pion, the vice-consul in Algiers, Peiresc wrote that the barque of Patron Etienne Beaussier (carrying the letters of St. Paul in Arabic, the prophecies of Jeremiah in Coptic, and an astronomical text in Arabic) was seized by corsairs of Algiers and, specifically, by an apothecary in arms, while that of Patron Baille was taken near Malta without anyone knowing yet whether it was being brought to Tunis, Algiers, or Tripoli.[36] Peiresc wrote to Thomas d'Arcos in Tunis on the same day, 30 September 1635. He informed him of his loss of three books with Beaussier, and another with the barque of Baille, abandoned to the corsairs near Malta. He tersely related to d'Arcos the story of the Hexaglot Psalter in case it was taken by "your corsairs" and the information could assist d'Arcos in ransoming it. Although the book only cost him 8 piastres to buy (compared to 31 for the Samaritan Triglot) he would gladly pay 20 to redeem it. It was also traveling with a box of curiosities from the Red Sea and a large sea chest, and he would make a good deal for the rest if he could get the book. As for the corsairs who seized the ship of Patron Beaussier, they were, Peiresc wrote, surely from Algiers.[37]

Peiresc soon learned that the barque of Patron Baille had been taken to Tripoli in Libya. His first response was to find out from within his merchant contacts if any of them had reliable agents there. After discovering that Claude Luguet had such a correspondent, Peiresc wrote directly to Antoine Bayon, a Provençal merchant living in Tripoli.[38] The volume, he had heard, remained with the scrivener, Sr. Faysan. Peiresc was willing to pay 20 écus (or piastres) for it. Peiresc stressed how useless the book was for the Turks. He did not think that these corsairs would take their prize as far as Tripoli because they were from Algiers and had already gone to Rhodes, where they could have sold a good part of the ship. But they might not have cared about the books; they might even have tossed them into the sea "as the corsairs often do, who have nothing to do with books." But he had heard from one of the crew who had escaped at Rhodes that one of the corsairs who had been an apothecary at Algiers had kept all the books and papers to use for folding up spices. Peiresc was explicit about why he offered all this information, most just hearsay: "I give you all these indices to aid you in following the trail."[39]

Peiresc wrote again to Luguet for Bayon the next week, after learning that there was a ship heading to Malta, from which there was more likely contact with Tripoli.[40] The sailing of the *Dauphin* afforded Peiresc an opportunity to write again to Bayon. He began by denouncing the disgraceful abandonment of the polacre of Baille to a measly barque "which was not strong enough to attack that polacre." He then explained that he had asked Luguet to recommend to Bayon the task of recovering the book. He had learned from Captain Beau, who was at the market where the goods on Baille's ship were sold off, "that they were sold en bloc to a Corsican merchant who frequented Livorno, but that the basha of Tripoli had retained the chest of the scrivener, who was Sr. Faysan, who assured me that my book was in that chest, that it was bound in pale red leather, about a pan and a half long and a pan and a quarter wide, and about a quarter of the height—about 4 fingers worth." In an interesting twist, Peiresc recalled seeing letters from the basha of Tripoli, "if I am not mistaken," who desired improved relations with Marseille and had on this account written to the parlement—which afforded Peiresc the opportunity to offer his small intervention in this case, if it could help liberate his captive book.[41]

To Gela, Peiresc told a slightly different tale. The whole lot was sold at Tripoli to "a certain Captain Beau" from Marseille, and then to a Livorno merchant who outbid Beau by 1,000 piastres. It was then taken to Livorno by Captain "Angelo," or Langy Castor, of Toulon. But where the papers were, at this point, he did not know.[42] In a letter to Magy in Egypt sent the same day, Peiresc added that Patron Baille and Captain Beau were currently in jail in Marseille.[43] Beau, just to complicate things, had two years earlier been respected enough to have been sent by the consuls of Marseille to Tripoli in Libya with plenipotentiary powers to redeem Captain Jehan Maille and Patron Bonanie and their ships from the corsairs.[44]

In mid-October 1635, Peiresc wrote again to Bayon, informing him that he had just heard that in their desire to ensure that they had everything, the authorities in Tripoli searched for the ship's manifest in the scrivener's chest, that of M. Faysan, in which his book had been kept. It was now certain that it was in the possession of the basha and he, Bayon, was authorized to repurchase it.

Peiresc added that he had seen some letters written by the basha to the authorities of Marseille and to the parlement, of which he was a member, and if there was a will to seek "the liberty of commerce" he would certainly lend his support.[45] He was now more explicit about his own role. A person of good will was needed to work on Barbary's behalf, to help renew the treaty negotiated by Napollon: "To which I would serve with a good heart out of the inclination I have to serve the public and promote the liberty and safety of commerce which will go to ruin if it is not soon remedied. Those who lived by their corsairing would lose money, but would be better off not running any risks for the payment of the big duties that they would get from free trade at home."[46]

Aside from those who lived by their corsairing, who would lose money, the others "would find themselves much better off without any doubt whatsoever, paying the higher duties that will come with free trade." That Peiresc was willing to put himself forward as a political intermediary with the basha of Tripoli to convince him of where his advantage lay—all for a manuscript—is astonishing. Peiresc seems to have understood also that the economic issue was whether legal duties on a higher volume of trade— because of peace—would be greater than the extorted amounts taken by the divan from the corsairs' sales.[47] In fact, correspondence between the basha and the consuls of Marseille exists—it is in French and stamped with the basha's cartouche, suggesting either that the basha possessed some French or that he had his own translator—so Peiresc was not simply making this up.[48]

Almost casually, in this same letter, Peiresc informed Bayon that a merchant in Livorno named Sr. Jean Masseau bought the whole prize, and may therefore have aquired his other items, including those "curiosities of the Red Sea." Peiresc offered to reimburse Bayon his costs at Marseille, Hyères, Livorno, Malta, or even Tripoli. Since this would be done using merchant-bankers, it also maps the wider Provençal network.[49]

At the very same time, Peiresc was writing to the ship's scrivener Faysan, who had remained in Marseille but then apparently gone back to Egypt, asking him to write to Antoine Bayon in Tripoli and find out what had actually happened.[50] To Luguet—still on 18 October—Peiresc expressed his optimism that at the sale in Tripoli to Jean Masseau of Livorno the effort to verify all the goods had led to the chest containing the ship's documents and that this, now, was in the possession of Bayon. And even if it was not, but still with the basha, Peiresc was confident it could be easily recovered.[51] Peiresc identified le Beau as the Marseille merchant doing business with Tripoli, whose "commercaire" Bayon was, and wrote urging him to use his influence on Bayon. Peiresc also pumped him for all the details of the ship's seizure and its subsequent fate.[52]

Peiresc's letter seems to have crossed with le Beau's of 19 October, which Peiresc acknowledged on 24 October. Peiresc thanked him for his help, and specially requested him to make a duplicate of his request to Bayon for the book so that if the *Dauphin* passed by Malta without leaving his letters, or if they went astray, Peiresc's book would not fall into other hands from which it could be extracted only with greater difficulty—which is of course exactly what happened.[53]

Peiresc's next move was to interrogate Faysan in order to find out exactly what might have happened.[54] In a letter to Jean Magy we learn that Faysan had been a prisoner of the basha in Tripoli. That the latter had descended from the Genoese family of the Giustiniani of Chios—because, in other words, he was a renegade—gave Peiresc hope that if the book remained in Tripoli he would be able to ransom it back.[55]

It is amazing that within one month of learning of the seizure of the manuscript Peiresc had succeeded in localizing it and developing a plan for its ransom. He was able to do this because of an elaborate information network that spanned the commercial sea. We see this in an exactly contemporary letter to a Marseille merchant not directly involved in this loss. Peiresc asked Piscatoris several questions, all trivial, and yet each aimed at a data point that could contribute to unraveling the much bigger riddle. First, Peiresc wanted the name "and quality" of the friend Piscatoris said had written already to Malta about the book, and who was a friend of the basha. Second, he needed the name of the Flemish slave who was taken with the barque of Beaussier and dragged back to Algiers. Lastly, he desired the name of the man who went there to ransom the Danish slaves—all in case there was some small fact here that could be turned to good use.[56]

To Lombard, a notary from Sixfours, Peiresc wrote with another set of questions. He wanted to know the route that the corsair might have taken with the prize boat when he left Rhodes, where he might have retreated, and what correspondences he might have had "whether with Tripoli or Alexandria, or indeed with Algiers or Tunis; of what age he is; of what country and what profession he had taken up, because it is said that he understood something of my books, which nevertheless are mostly for Christians, though not Catholic Christians."[57] Peiresc here too was looking for little clues to help him figure out how to track down these materials.

By the end of the year, Peiresc's hopes had diminished. In a letter to Magy of Christmas Eve, Peiresc explained that though he had written to Tripoli he had few expectations, even as he had tried and failed at Algiers to locate the Letters of St. Paul lost with Beaussier. "These corsairs are hardly capable of reason" ("Ces corsaires ne sont gueres cappables de raison") was his conclusion. As for Baille, still in prison in Marseille, Peiresc pledged to keep helping him, "for the love of you and your brother," and of Joseph Baulme and his relative Jacques Albert.[58]

Peiresc's disgust with the cowardice of the Provençaux was stoked by their utter fecklessness. Apparently, Baille had not even tried to preserve his own personal goods, which Peiresc's bundle would have resembled, and which corsairs typically released back without a ransom. Even if they had asked for one, it could have been pledged on their behalf by the person exercising the role of French consul at Rhodes. Apparently, Baille did not even care enough for himself to do this.[59]

News seems to have traveled slowly from Tripoli, much slower than from farther away. Peiresc's archive preserves a letter from Bayon in Marseille to his brother in Tripoli dated 26 August 1636, responding to one of 12 October 1635, itself written in response to Peiresc's initial flurry of letters, which only reached Marseille that very month! Bayon in Marseille was ready to provide Bayon in Tripoli with whatever funds were needed to ransom the book, though, typical of the North African correspondence of the time, the bulk of the letter dealt with the question of ransoming hostages.[60] As it turns out, four of Peiresc's letters—of 30 September 1635, 14 October 1635, 17 October 1635, and 7 April 1636—reached Bayon in Tripoli on 19 August 1636. He responded by proclaiming his desire to help Peiresc and his pleasure that Peiresc's misfortune had at least brought him into the employ "of a person of your sort and your merit."[61]

Bayon finally got the book. Having received Peiresc's letters, he knew to look for the captain of the corsair ship and was told that the book had been handed over to the basha upon arrival in Tripoli, thinking that it was a precious object. Bayon then returned to the basha and extended Peiresc's greeting and request. The basha kissed Peiresc's hands in greeting, and said that he was sad only to be able to demonstrate his affection in nothing more significant than retrieving a missing book. It had already passed through various hands, but the basha commanded that it be returned. As for the other curiosities—the box of Red Sea items, for example, these had been sent to the Duke of Florence by a Livornese merchant resident in Tunis. Bayon promised to send the book within the month by the hand of his cousin. He had also communicated Peiresc's offer to help further commercial ties between Tripoli and Marseille. The basha had demurred, saying that a separate peace would be impossible while France and Spain were at war—and opening a window, for us, onto the savvy diplomatic skills of the corsair chieftains.[62]

In December 1636 Peiresc was still hanging on news from Tripoli.[63] He announced himself willing to intervene in the affairs of the Bayon family if that would help.[64] It seemed to him that a happy end was in sight and that his friends had finally found and ransomed back his Psalter.[65]

Peiresc waited for the book. But when it eventually arrived, in April 1637, he experienced a devastating disappointment. The package had been sent in November 1636. When he opened it, he saw immediately that the volume inside was too small. When he unwrapped the book itself he was shocked: it was none other than a Latin-Arabic grammar and dictionary printed in Holland! While it was true that he had never received an accurate description of it since the accompanying letters disappeared with the book, he thought based on his knowledge of Ottoman books that it would have been written on large-format glossy paper, not vellum, though he admitted he had not been given this information, and that it would be bound in the Ottoman style which, he notes, was also called Greek, and which Peiresc defined as "without threads on the back in the manner of the Levantines, who use a thicker leather than we do, and without any backing." None of this applied to the book he had been sent. But it was now too late to bother with such an accurate description; the book no doubt "must have gone through too many risks and possibly passed through too many hands to be able to follow the trail."[66]

Nevertheless, Peiresc—at least in this letter—pointed the finger at those who cozened Bayon, rather than at Bayon (though in the accompanying letter to Bayon's brother in Marseille Peiresc does note that some of the obvious visible features, such as the use of Latin and Arabic, ought surely to have appeared incompatible with his description of it as "a Psalter in different languages and different characters").[67] They were besmirching the reputation of the basha, who now appeared as someone capable of deceiving in trade. If it were possible to trace the book ("de le suyvre de main en main"), it would be a great debt that Peiresc would honor. He was now willing to pay even more than the 20 piastres or écus he had offered before.[68]

What happened? The book must have been sold. Either the Livornese ship that acquired the other items belonging to Peiresc also took the manuscript and then sold it off—or gave it as a gift—elsewhere; or Bayon himself, when learning of the high price that Peiresc put on it, sought a higher bidder; or the manuscript never reached Tripoli but embarked on an independent trajectory that brought it to Malta. What Bayon's role was in this story cannot be ascertained. Could he have been unable to distinguish between a printed book, albeit with columns in two languages, and an ancient manuscript with five columns of very unusual-looking languages? Does this point yet again to the limitations of a merchant collaborator? Or does its extremity suggest another explanation altogether? This degree of negligence does not square with the attentiveness with which Bayon answers Peiresc's query in his surviving letter of September 1636.

Where Peiresc's story of the loss of the manuscript joins the better-known one of its recovery is in late spring 1637. Peiresc learned that Holstenius would be going to Sicily and Malta with Phillip Landgrave of Hesse (Darmstadt). Peiresc proposed that Holstenius visit libraries where he was sure to find things. Peiresc focused his attention on Holstenius and not on his traveling partner, Athanasius Kircher, whom he knew well and of whom he here observed that "he has a very different genius and there amuses himself with very different research than M. Holstenius." Peiresc wrote that he expected great things, since the abbeys and monasteries of

Figure 26. The "Hexaglot Psalter." MS. Barberini-Orientalia 2, ff. 16v–17r. (©2015 Biblioteca Apostolica Vaticana)

Sicily were full of Greek manuscripts that could no longer be found in Greece. "I imagine," he continued, "that M. Holstenius will extract more than in the Vatican, and with greater freedom."[69] (To Henri Dormalius, Peiresc emphasized that it was Kircher who was accompanying the Landgrave, and the importance of seeing Aetna and Vesuvius, and measuring the height of the pole and sun, and laying hands on Arabic texts.)[70]

While Peiresc lay dying in Aix in June 1637, the young Landgrave landed in Malta with Holstenius and Kircher in his suite. We do not actually know how the Psalter came into his hands, but the Abbé Tisserant suggested to the grand master of Malta, Jean Paul Lacaris de Castellar, that he offer it as a gift to Cardinal Barberini, the protector of their order.[71] At the end of a ciphered letter from the inquisitor at Malta, the future Alexander VII, Fabio Chigi, to Cardinal Francesco Barberini of 19 September 1637, Chigi writes in passing, "The Grand Master sends to Your Eminence by his 'Master of Pages' a book in many languages which Sr. Holstenius ought to have had a look at."[72] On 29 September, Holstenius, already back in Naples, wrote to Francesco Barberini, repeating that "the

Psalter in five languages" was being brought to Rome by a servant of the grand master.[73] Unfortunately we have no letter surviving from Holstenius between 17 June (just after his arrival at Malta) and 17 August (when he passes Messina).[74] The book figures today as Barberini-Orientalia MS. 2 in the Vatican Library—Oriental MS. 1 being the Samaritan Pentateuch given by Peiresc to Barberini as a posthumous bequest (Figure 26).

30 &

End Points

*A*t this distance in time from Peiresc and the seventeenth century, we might feel that his Mediterranean correspondence network had something of the exotic about it. But by the early seventeenth century, as we see very clearly through the Peiresc archive, Mediterranean communications had become so regularized, despite the corsairs, despite the seeming fragility of its institutions, that Peiresc could instead treat it as something common. Could *count on* its regularity. This revision of our sensibility comes from being inside Peiresc's world.

Yet there was danger, and so Peiresc provided these correspondents with instructions about how best to reach him. Multiple pathways to Marseille were recommended "lest that if by one way it is lost, one would not be deprived of it, but could have it as well by another way."[1]

When Théophile Minuti was in Constantinople, Peiresc asked him to write directly to him, "adding there on the side some recommendation at Marseille to M. de Valbelle and M. de Gastines and at Toulon to M. Aycard and Captain Tourtel."[2] Writing to l'Empereur in Constantinople in 1634, Peiresc named M. Lieu, chief of the royal post, as his poste-restante at Lyon, and de Gastines and Valbelle at Marseille.[3]

A more elaborate version of this mapping is found on the concluding page of a long "Memoire pour les Indes" drawn up for Fernand Nuñes and Manuel de Costa Casseretz, who were going to Goa. To make sure letters reached him, Peiresc advised:

> Address the letters to Marseille, Toulon, and all other places of the maritime coast of Provence, to the Lieutenants, Seneschal, the Admiralty and other judges, and officers of the King, to hold them for the said Sr. de Peiresc.
>
> Address the original envelopes to the French consuls established in Aleppo, Sidon, Smyrna and Cairo, as elsewhere. To hold them for Provence for the said Sr. de Peiresc.

Likewise, if the occasion presents itself, to the French consuls established at Lisbon, Seville, Valencia, Barcelona, and all other ports
of the Spanish coast, to hold them for Marseille.[4]

Even short-distance communication within the Levant was fraught
with risk. Writing for Minuti on the eve of his departure on 1629, Peiresc
reminded him that if he were in Syria it would be best to send his shipments back to Provence via Sidon rather than send the originals overland
to Egypt "in order not to expose them to other dangers which are rather
frequent throughout these oriental lands."[5]

By 1635, when François-Auguste de Thou was planning a return to
Constantinople at the head of a French embassy, Peiresc's network was
established. Peiresc offered to put it at de Thou's disposal, and reflected
on its shape. It existed "not only at the biggest stopping points, but at
the more isolated and less frequented places."[6]

It was de Thou's first trip that catalyzed Peiresc's Mediterranean network. As it unfolded, we see Peiresc scrambling to secure adequate communications. In February 1628 he wrote to Valbelle, lieutenant of the admiralty, asking to renew the earlier favor he had performed in asking M.
Servian to deliver letters of recommendation to the Levant.[7] Valbelle himself provided letters of recommendation—marking the web for us—to
the consuls of Alexandria, Aleppo, and Sidon, and to the French merchant
Guez, who lived in Galata and had a brother at Marseille. Viguier, the
consul of Syria, similarly provided letters for the consuls of Alexandretta,
Aleppo, and Sidon, and the president of the parlement baron d'Oppède
did the same for the consuls of Alexandria, Aleppo, Sidon, and Chios.
Peiresc even hoped to obtain a letter, courtesy of Sanson Napollon's intervention, from a Turkish *capigy* then in Marseille.[8]

Because of the nature of travel, and Peiresc's ambition to have correspondence ready at the destination when his travelers, like de Thou, first
arrived, Peiresc's letter-writing draws a map. Thus, to de Thou on 6 September 1628, Peiresc reported receiving his letter from Galata of 2 July
via Guez, who added his own of 24 July. Meanwhile, Peiresc sent on the
package from the Dupuy brothers in Paris to Marseille, as instructed. Guez
of Marseille wrote to him on 4 September, saying that he had placed Dupuy's package on the polacre of Captain Roubaud, sailing for Alexandria,
where the letter would be left for Jacques Albert.[9]

Peiresc's practice seems to have been to make the respondent of
whatever ship was next sailing his respondent, whether or not they had

previously been in contact, and then to charge them with distributing his letters as specified. Thus, in January 1633 we find Peiresc writing to Honoré Sabatier in Constantinople—not one of his regular correspondents— following up a package sent to him the previous August by the boat of Tourtel of Sixfours. This included letters for Minuti, Marcheville, l'Empereur, and Guez. Peiresc's expectation was that they would be forwarded on as appropriate. It was the silence that ensued that made him follow up with Sabatier and make evident to posterity the "system" that had been employed five months earlier.[10] Eventually, Peiresc heard back from Sabatier, learning that Minuti received at Sidon the letters sent to him at Constantinople by the ship *Ste. Anne*. But there was nothing sent by return voyage—only much later did he receive letters from Sabatier, l'Empereur, Guez (all of 18 May), and Marcheville (of 8 July). Having clarified what was in the pipeline, Peiresc went on to press Sabatier for an order of cats "because I really like that kind of animal."[11]

"The sea," T. S. Eliot wrote, "is the land's edge also." The cities of the Levant and Asia Minor were the end points of Peiresc's network, and at the same time, from an Ottoman or Arab or Persian perspective, the gates of a whole continental world. We know relatively little of individual lives in those cities during this period. Nelly Hanna's work on early seventeenth-century Cairo and Daniel Goffman's on early seventeenth-century Izmir stand out.[12] But of Aleppo, Sidon, Tripoli, and even Damascus, we know too little. And in general, most of what we know comes from court documents and other public records. The perspective of the Peiresc archive, or even that of the Chambre de Commerce of Marseille, is of an intense focus on individuals and their stories. As much as one would want to see these people through Ottoman eyes, and to be able to tell their story from both directions, we will have to content ourselves for the present with the hope of inspiring such work in the future.

Rome

"In this miserable country we have no access to books and other singularities that can be found elsewhere. But all the same, the commerce of Rome and the Levant lets us enjoy sometimes of the one and the other things far from the most common." This was how Peiresc, with his usual excessive modesty, introduced a discussion of his treasures from the Levant to a correspondent in Augsburg. It is the linkage of Rome and the Levant that marks the path for us to follow.[13]

Writing from Rome, Aubery could only express astonishment at the number of people with whom Peiresc stayed in contact by each ordinaire.[14] Much of Peiresc's activity centered on Rome, probably more than on any city outside France. At Rome, his earliest merchant contact was Pierre Eschinard (the beginning of their surviving correspondence dates to 1616).[15] Eschinard held the title of *banquier-expéditionnaire du Roi,* which made him responsible for the movement to and from Rome of all goods concerning royal patronage, under the authority of the French ambassadors at the Roman Curia.[16] Peiresc, typically, piggybacked on this official position, instructing Eschinard to ship to his own business partners in Paris, or to one "François Marchant Libraire" on the rue St. Jacques.[17] Communications to Marseille were received by Conseiller Labbia.[18] From Paris, the route from Rome via Lyon was the "droict chemin," though Peiresc nevertheless requested that Andrea Brugiotti, the bookseller in Rome, send his books directly to Marseille.[19]

As Peiresc's maritime persona came into focus, his contacts in Rome became more central. In 1626, Aubery informed him that he had regular "commoditez" by barque to Marseille so that "when you will have the desire to bring anything from here, give me the commission."[20]

Maritime funding extended to Rome, as well. When Peiresc activated François Marchand, based in Rome in 1635—assuming he is not the same person already mentioned in 1616—in order to get his brother-in-law Seguiran's son into the Knights of Malta, Peiresc asked him to draw funds from Sr. d'Espiot to be reimbursed at Marseille by Lambert and de Gastines.[21] Similarly, Aubery received reimbursements directly from Lambert, but also from d'Espiot: "The said Lambert wrote here to his friend that he give to me on occasions what I will ask for on your account."[22] By the middle of 1627, we can point to the "maturation" of Peiresc's Roman system. In June, Aubery wrote that he would no longer be transmitting correspondence via Sr. Marchand "because he only writes from time to time and by way of Avignon"—presumably as opposed to very regularly and by way of Marseille.[23]

D'Espiot—otherwise unknown—figures centrally in an account of Peiresc's Roman system that we find in letters to Galaup de Chasteuil and Jacques de Vendôme, both in Syria. To the former, seeking support for Giorgio Amira in Rome, Peiresc explained, "And by means of Sr. Guillaume d'Espiot, respondent at Rome of Sr. de Gastines of Marseille, there will be good means to deliver throughout the Levant all that we could obtain for him from our Holiness the Pope and his Eminences the

Cardinals of the Congregation of the Propaganda Fide for which I will work as hard as I can."[24] And writing to Jacques de Vendôme at the same time, Peiresc was even more explicit. If money were involved, "I would consign it to Rome in the hands of Guillaume d'Espiots [sic], merchant, for transmitting it to the Levant by way of the correspondence and access he has with M. de Gastines, the relative of M. de l'Isle of Sidon, to whom he will send it, or to M. Tarquet the consul, or to any other."[25] D'Espiot, Peiresc explained elsewhere to Holstenius, had daily possibilities for sending all sorts of packages to Marseille directly, or by way of correspondents in Livorno and Genoa.[26]

The movement of the "alzaron," a gazelle-like animal come from Africa and sent by Peiresc as a gift to Cardinal Barberini, was another event that exposes Peiresc's web. We have the memo that de Gastines prepared for Patron Pascal in Marseille. Pascal was to take the animal on the barque of Patron Dalle to Aegidio Rossi, customs official, at Civitavecchia. In case of trouble there, they were to contact Sr. Marchese Malatesta, the governor, or his lieutenant. In Rome, the addressee was Suares the bishop of Vaison, or Cassiano dal Pozzo for Barberini. (And Patron Paschal was to return with books and boxes of goods.)[27] Peiresc in parallel wrote to Rossi. He asked that any correspondence be directed to my "amico particolare" de Gastines at Marseille. He no longer had as much commodity for direct passage from Marseille to Rome, as he was burdened down by many obligations ("si trova charicato di tante facende"). He asked that Rossi's reply be sent to Genoa, to Andrea Spinola, "General of the Post," confirming the precariousness of direct communication between Provence and southern Italy at this time.[28] Given the earlier role of d'Espiot, one suspects a falling out between him and de Gastines, his departure from Rome, or his death. Rossi responded immediately, and favorably. Peiresc thanked him for accepting "l'offerta fattale della mia servitu."[29] Peiresc also made a point of writing directly to Marchese Malatesta, the governor of Civitavecchia, explaining that this gift animal was being carried to Cardinal Francesco Barberini in a barque of Patron Dalle, under the care of Patron Paschal, whose own barque could go no farther than Civitavecchia. Dalle's barque was then to take the animal to Fiumicino, so as to avoid having to disturb it by dis- and reembarkation. It was necessary to obtain the governor's permission for a ship to go all the way to Fiumicino, hence this letter.[30] Rossi himself confirmed Paschal's passage with the animal on to Rome.[31] And, later, when Patron Paschal's barque was taken by corsairs and then dumped at Civitavecchia, Peiresc wrote on his behalf directly to Cardinal Francesco Barberini seeking its restitution.[32]

Genoa

Genoa was another key city for Peiresc, in many ways much more important for his system than was Venice. With the dominance just then of Marseille in the Levant, the role of Venice had diminished, and Genoa was not only the first destination to the east of any ship sailing out of Marseille, it was also the way across the isthmus to Milan and Venice and through them to the trans-Alpine world. All this made Genoa a key relay station for Peiresc's Italian correspondence. The city remains very much underrated in our cognitive geography of the cultural Mediterranean.[33]

Setting forth his network to Eschinard in 1627, Peiresc explained that mail for him could be sent to the "General des postes de Genoa," who would connect them to the ordinary and extraordinary couriers who had to pass through there.[34] His two Genoese addressees were the Lumaga brothers and Girolamo Spinola.[35]

Peiresc worked from the beginning with the Lumaga brothers, Marc Antonio and Ottavio. In a letter of December 1623, just after returning to Provence, Peiresc "officially" asked if they would mind receiving packages sent from Rome for him, and then forwarding them on to Signier in Marseille, as in fact they had been doing.[36] In 1633 Peiresc could refer to Antonio as "ce venerable veillard" and lament that for all the years they worked together he had never laid eyes on him.

Another interesting role played by the Lumaga brothers and Genoa was vis-à-vis the traditional economic centers of southern Germany. When Henri de Valois wanted to open contact with a correspondent in Augsburg, he asked Peiresc, and Peiresc turned to these cosmopolitan Genoese for assistance.[37] It worked—Peiresc copied into his register of outgoing correspondence the text of the letter from Sr. Phillip Hainhofer, the librarian at Augsburg, to Bartolomeo Lumaga in Lyon.[38] Peiresc's plan was to write to Augsburg via Genoa and Venice.[39] This southern German vocation was another value of the Genoese link.

The second key destination in Peiresc's Genoese hub was Girolamo Spinola, "General of the Posts." Peiresc often used him as a mailing address, and gave his name to correspondents.[40] When speed was of the essence, Peiresc would tell Roman agents such as Eschinard to send to

Spinola for transshipment to Marseille, rather than wait for the papal galleys.[41] A third Genoese middleman was Orazio Tridi, who "has every day many convenient opportunities from Genoa to Marseille, where he usually writes to M. de Gastines."[42] A fourth, and still more unknown, is Stefano Mercante, who is identified as "General of the Posts" in early 1631 and is described by Peiresc as "an *honnête homme* among my friends."[43] Then there is Pier Maria Boerio, to whom Peiresc addressed twenty-one letters between 1634 and 1637.[44]

But Peiresc also wrote frequently between 1633 and 1637 to the baron de Sabran, scion of a Provençal family, who was the French consul in Genoa. He served the same function as contact person and postbox.[45] Most of the letters written to him are concerned with communication and its discontents.[46]

Most of all, Genoa was a communications hub on the way to Rome. In order to get mail to Rome, Peiresc could opt to send it via Lyon (the traditional route); with the papal ordinaire, who went by land and sea; or by merchant ship. The ship was fastest, in clement weather, the ordinary secure, and the route from Lyon the most regular.[47] Genoa was the stopping point for all of them.

A fascinating letter to Suares, the bishop of Vaison, and one of Peiresc's creatures in the Barberini household, offers access to the texture behind the raw details of postal communication between Provence and Italy at that time. Peiresc explained that he would prefer that all the letters coming from the Barberini household—and in September 1633, at the time of the letter's writing, these would include those written by Cardinal Barberini himself, Cassiano dal Pozzo, Lucas Holstenius, Giovanni Battista Doni, Jean-Jacques Bouchard, and, of course, Suares—be stuffed into one envelope, cacheted with the cardinal's seal, and sent to Spinola in Genoa. Peiresc had just now spoken with M. du Lieu, "Intendant des Courriers du Roy à Lyon," who had charge also over those couriers sent to Genoa. These would take the package from Spinola in Genoa and bring it to him in Aix, "by means of a certain gratification which I ordinarily provide to the couriers, both in going and coming, whether my packets are big or small." In other words, Peiresc tipped heavily or, more critically, Peiresc engaged in bribing the couriers, with official connivance, to make a slight deviation from their official route on his behalf. This way, he concluded, there was more of a chance that their correspondence would be free of regular delays (the exceptional ones by definition being unavoidable). The papal couriers were less reliable because they were less punctilious about covering all the costs.[48] In other words, the Curia did not pay enough or promptly. If, however, Suares found that it was too difficult to organize the secretariat of the cardinal to manage the correspondence in a systematic fashion, Peiresc noted that he had an offer from Sabran, the French consul in Genoa, to handle the correspondence. He preferred—what he said was that he "thought" it was easier—for his friends in the cardinal's entourage to send things through his secretariat.[49]

Sometimes, Genoa's position also made it the site of particular inquiries. In December 1634, Peiresc reported that the September courier from Rome to Avignon, Francesco Clot alias Merindole, got sick at Pisa, and was hospitalized there from 9 to 25 September. He died on the road from Pisa to Genoa. Peiresc wanted Boerio to try to find out what happened to his objects by asking around whether "on the shores of the sea, or of the land" ("cosi della riviera del mare, come di terra").[50]

Through Genoa, more than through Provence, in fact, Peiresc gained access to a wider Europe. The Provençaux may have spread themselves like sparrows across the Mediterranean, but it was the Genoese who had the vaster and older continental European network. For instance, it was through Genoa that Peiresc gained an agent in Kraków whom he sought to program, long-distance, to hunt for fossils on his behalf. The possibility of piggybacking on a permanent Genoese connection to Kraków was especially attractive.[51]

Genoa was also Spanish Italy, and after 1635, an enemy territory. Thus, while physically close to Provence, it had become difficult to reach. In a letter to a "Father Maximilian," Peiresc outlined different communication paths. There was the over-mountain route from Pignerol southwest of Turin down to Cannes. There was the route from Pignerol to Lyon, addressed to M. du Lieu, "maître des courriers du Roy." And there was the route from Pignerol to Genoa, at the address of Sabran. Sabran, in turn, would place any letter with the next papal ordinary to Avignon. If the letter happened to arrive while the messenger was still there, Peiresc thought the response could reach him in fifteen days.[52]

Finally, Peiresc was very interested in Genoese history in its own right. At root, this connected to his deep engagement with the social history of Provence, and his operating principle of a western Mediterranean *koinē* that stretched from Barcelona through Marseille to Genoa.[53] Genoese authors, especially historians, were of particular interest.[54] And sometimes Genoa was just the best way to access Milanese publishers and libraries, as in Peiresc's quest for Giggeius's four-volume Arabic-Latin dictionary.[55]

Venice

Finally, and perhaps most obviously, one passed through Genoa on the way from Marseille to Venice.[56] Now, the case of Venice is among the most interesting to be illuminated by the Peiresc archive. We know that the Venetian position in Mediterranean trade at the time was shrinking and under pressure. In the Levant, the Marseillais had usurped their primacy for a short time, and the Dutch and English were increasingly present. Within the Italian peninsula, the decades after the Interdict Crisis were for stock-taking, and were perhaps lonely ones for Venice. War in the Alps, war in the Adriatic, war in the eastern Mediterranean—all of these strained the city's resources. And intellectually, the city's position as a roundtable for discussion was being slowly skimmed off by Amsterdam and London.

That Genoa bulks larger for Peiresc than Venice shows us how, in the small scale and from the perspective of a single individual, we can ask questions about very big changes. The view from within Peiresc's archive may corroborate the findings of historians, may challenge them, or may be silent about them, but it is in the "game of scales" that we can move closer to better understanding.

This shift within Peiresc's own world occurs for the following reasons. If in 1600 he lived in Padua and circulated in the intellectual world made by Sarpi, Pinelli, and Galileo, by the 1620s and 1630s intellectually interesting things are happening on the western side of the Italian peninsula, in Florence and Rome. Peiresc's Mediterranean policy, in turn, did not need to depend on Venice because of the dynamism of Marseille's trade across the Mediterranean.

In 1600, when Peiresc lived in Padua, the Venetian book trade was a central attraction of the city. And, as elsewhere in Europe, because of booksellers' familiarity with expediting, they often served both as purveyors and as poste restante for itinerant *érudits*. Writing to Marcus Welser from Padua in 1601, Peiresc identified Giovanni Battista Ciotti as a "bookseller of Venice" who obtained for him books from the Frankfurt fair.[57] A letter of Peiresc's from 1604 to Ciotti reveals that Peiresc had left books with Ciotti, along with his belongings, under the name of his tutor, the Bernese Paul Fonvives. Peiresc had wanted these sent to him care of his father in Aix, but as Ciotti had found this difficult, Peiresc instead asked that they be released to his friend Lorenzo Pignoria. Ciotti apparently refused until he received written permission from Fonvives himself. Peiresc asked that Ciotti include with the goods released to Pignoria also a catalog of his shop ("l'indice de'libri della sua bottega").[58] A full ten years later Ciotti had still not sent the books! Peiresc asked again that they be given to Pignoria, but adds that if Ciotti liked them so much he would be prepared to take equivalents, or to let Pignoria choose from a list—perhaps one that Peiresc drew up for Pignoria in that same year.[59]

However regular the connections might have been between Paris and Venice, there were always problems. For example, in 1616, from Paris, we have a letter from Peiresc to Pignoria explaining that books sent from Venice to him might have been switched inadvertently in Lyon by the "maestro delle poste."[60] In addition to Ciotti, Peiresc also worked with Bartolo Abbioso at the Rialto, a colleague of the bookseller's. He was instructed to send materials for Provence to Gasparo de Molin and Francesco Rossi, who would reimburse as appropriate.[61]

Venice is surprisingly inactive in Peiresc's mature Mediterranean web. When Jacques Gaffarel was working there in 1633, Peiresc asked him to ask the French consul in Venice (P. Vedon) to send mail to Genoa at the address of Horatio Tridi.[62] Reimbursement was arranged to be paid through M. de Rossi in Lyon, as if to suggest that the Marseille-based systems did not have connections in Venice.[63] And the Venetian connection via Lyon was hostage to war in the Grisons.[64]

In fact, when Peiresc needed a direct contact to Venice, he worked through a Marseille merchant family. Thus, in 1634, when Gaffarel finished his project of drawing and preparing models of the vases in the treasury of San Marco, Peiresc instructed him to utilize the services of Antonio Seghezzi, brother of Santo Seghezzi in Cairo and thus brother-in-law of Gela in Marseille. They were to send the items to their respondents in Livorno or Genoa, who would then send the package on to Marseille.[65] In 1635, Peiresc asked Gela to ask his brother-in-law Seghezzi in Cairo, and his family in Venice, to look into the business of Benoit Pelissier, which he wanted paid off on his account, either through Lyon or Marseille. Peiresc also asked for the names of those Venetian relatives in order to employ them directly for shipping books to him at Marseille.[66] The path taken by books marks a real trail: books from Antonio Seghezzi in Venice on the order of Fortunio Liceti (then at Padova) were sent to Gela in Marseille, whence they came to Aix for Peiresc, who then sent them on to Paris.[67] And when Peiresc needed to wind up the affairs of Pelissier, who had been murdered en route to Venice in 1636, he turned back to Gela. He suggested pursuing "the via del mare" if there was "commodità" from Marseille, but if not, to use the way through Livorno and Genoa. Because of the war, he wrote, commerce with France was not free "in those regions of Calabria and Napoli" that were under Spanish control.[68] The first letter directly from Peiresc to Antonio Seghezzi seems to have been

written in February 1637. (We know this because Peiresc begins by identifying himself as a servant of "your brother" Santo Seghezzi, and "your
relative" Giovanni Alvigi Gela.) He thanks him for the past service of
sending those books from Padua—the work on that must therefore have
been done entirely by Gela without Peiresc's direct involvement. But it
was especially his help with "Benedetto Pelisserio" for which Peiresc was
most grateful. At the same time, Peiresc mentions a new project: a Giovanni
Issaultier of Marseille would be making his way to Venice "per via di terra
ferma," through Livorno, Bologna, and Ferrara, and was commissioned
to purchase books and vases. Peiresc had therefore asked Gela to write to
his Seghezzi relatives to help with purchases up to 50 scudi on Peiresc's
behalf.[69]

The death of Benoit Pelissier also sheds light on the state of Peiresc's
Venetian contacts. Peiresc wanted to write to a Venetian respondent to
look for his goods—but he had none. Gaffarel had already departed for
Paris, so Peiresc turned to the French ambassador himself. This suggests
that at this time he had no native Venetian contacts.[70] Peiresc concluded
his letter of April 1637 to the French ambassador in Venice by musing on
how the personae of his Venetian network had changed over the years: "I
do not know any of the *curieux* in that land since I lost my old acquain-
tances the Procurator Federigo Contarini and Giovanni Mocenigo the
Lame, who had the richest cabinets in my time, more than 30 years ago,
and very often took pleasure in sending their precious rarities to show me,
even to here."[71]

A measure not of Peiresc's estrangement from Venice but of Venetian marginality in the Mediterranean (or of the centrality of Provence,
of Peiresc's sense of its centrality, of his need to offer something in exchange for the favors he needed from others, or, finally, of the isolation
of the French diplomatic corps and the ambassador in particular) is that
it is Peiresc in Aix who informs the French ambassador in Venice of the
fate of Fakhr al-Din in Lebanon. He adds to the information contained
in the written relation from Constantinople what he had heard about Fakhr
al-Din's mother being a witch, from a "Turc que nous avons icy naturel
d'Alep"—a reference to Mattouk Chiassan.[72]

Malta

Malta was a staging post on the east-west trunk route, registering the com-
ings and goings of others. And many of them were from Marseille.[73]
Peiresc, never one to miss an opportunity to make a contact, made sure

to acknowledge the sender of a packet that was charged by the baron d'Alegre from Malta. Peiresc identifies his intermediary as M. Ruffi of Avignon.[74] Having withstood the siege of 1565, Malta remained a stick in the corsairs' craw. Aubery reported to Peiresc in 1627 of a planned uprising of slaves on the island that was coordinated with a descent of corsair galleys. Only inclement weather interrupted the plan and led to its exposure and the punishment of the ringleaders.[75]

Jacques de Vendôme, Guardian of Nazareth, moved back and forth between Italy and the Levant, and Malta was a regular stop for him. In 1635 he was in Italy, meeting with the pope and Cardinal Barberini about the affairs of Lebanon before rejoining his household at Malta and returning to Lebanon. An earlier letter from Malta, his point of arrival, was carried by Captain Etienne Beaussier—the same Beaussier whose ship would be seized by corsairs. Father Jacques referred to a close escape, noting that they had reached Malta "by the grace of God," and explained that Peiresc could hear the details directly from Beaussier, who was carrying the letter.[76] Jacques de Vendôme was still in Malta in March of 1636. He noted to Peiresc that he sent letters to Galaup's brother, the procureur-général, by way of M. Bonpar on the vaisseau of Etienne Beaussier, whose relative ("parent") he was. But he had not received a reply. This letter was being carried by Guillaume Audifredy.[77] The Capuchin Agathange de Vendôme also spent time on Malta—"beaucoup de temps," he tells Peiresc—with the knight Monsieur Labbi, "who is reputed to know a lot about mathematics and astronomy."[78]

Constantinople

Constantinople was a key node in Peiresc's Mediterranean, as it was the political capital of the Ottoman Empire (Figure 27). But because of the weakness of Ottoman central government faced with the breadth of the empire, and because of the high volume of French trade with the provinces, the imperial capital less determined than impacted upon outcomes in Sidon or Cairo. Moreover, in Constantinople the drama of the French ambassador hung like a dark cloud over the merchant community. Even the statistics on the weight of trade from the Seguiran Report show the relative unimportance of Constantinople. There we see that while fifteen vaisseaux or barques sailed to Alexandria with a cargo worth 900,000 livres tournois (l.t.), and eight vaissaux or barques went to Sidon with goods valued at 480,000 l.t., and a whopping twenty polacres, vaisseaux, and barques set off for Alexandretta, the port of Aleppo, with 2,400,000 l.t.

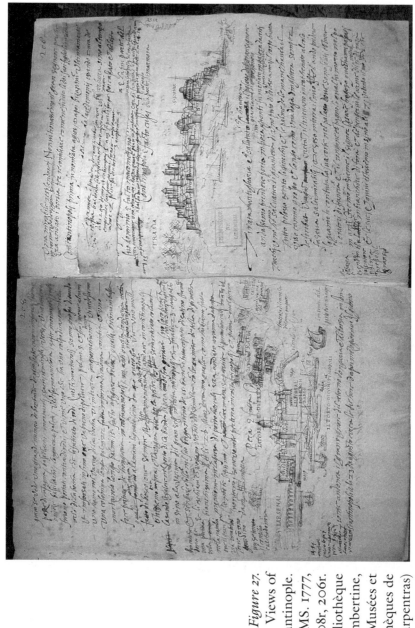

Figure 27. Views of Constantinople. CBI, MS. 1777, ff. 208r, 206r. (Bibliothèque Inguimbertine, Musées et Bibliothèques de Carpentras)

worth of merchandise, only ten vaisseaux with a cargo of 300,000 l.t. went to Constantinople.[79]

When de Thou headed to Constantinople in 1628, Peiresc turned to Guillaume Guez in the European quarter of Galata to furnish him with credit. Presumably the reimbursement was made through his brother, Jean Guez of Marseille. But correspondence from the Constantinopolitan brother was directed to the French ambassador in Venice, "who is a very good friend" ("qui est fort de mes amis"). At that time, Peiresc's connections via Venice must have seemed, at least to his mind, more rapid as well as more secure than his directly from Marseille. To and from Venice, communication generally traveled overland via Lyon and thence to Aix.[80]

The appointment of Henri de Gournay, comte de Marcheville, as French ambassador to the Sublime Porte offered Peiresc the exciting possibility of crafting an entire team to advance learning. Peiresc wrote to Marcheville, "Your stay in Constantinople will attract there the greatest men in Europe and will give you a means of restoring good letters. I am sorry that I cannot count on good health over such a long voyage because nothing else could restrain me from such an opportunity if only to serve your person and men of letters."[81] Peiresc envisioned his embassy as the occasion for a scientific mission, continuing the practice established by the expedition of Minuti in 1629. He initially hoped that Gassendi and Holstenius would be able to accompany the ambassador. When neither could go, his choice fell on two local friends, Minuti again and the local aristocrat—soon to become the "Hermit of Mount Lebanon"—François Galaup, sieur de Chasteuil. Peiresc's dream has been the focus of a recent essay by Alastair Hamilton.[82]

The passage of the ambassador led to a flurry of writing. Marcheville traveled with Minuti and l'Empereur of Marseille. Peiresc, for his part, wrote to the Constantinopolitan l'Empereur "activating" him. Minuti had never made it there on his previous trip, and Peiresc felt he had to renew his request for Minuti to see l'Empereur's collection of rarities and medals. Peiresc also asked for assistance for Galaup, who was making his maiden voyage.[83] Similarly, when the traveling priest "Gaugeric de Marquaiz" was going to Constantinople and the Holy Land, Peiresc wrote on his behalf to Gela and Sabatier for them to activate their contacts there.[84]

From a letter Peiresc wrote to Minuti on the eve of Minuti's second departure, we can see just how much Peiresc depended on these merchants. In addition to alerting l'Empercur and Guez to Minuti's needs, Peiresc made Michel Tourtel, sieur de Ramatuelle, especially responsible for Minuti.

Peiresc explained to Minuti that he would be housed well and that ships arrived there frequently and "the way to Marseille will always furnish what you need and will give you your news." And when Minuti was ready to visit the sites in the Levant, "we will refresh the suitable orders there as best as we can for your contentment."[85] Marcheville, as the ambassador, was the point of address for Peiresc, as he explained to Minuti in August 1632: all the letters to Peiresc's correspondents in Constantinople would be sent under the cover of one to the ambassador.[86]

After their arrival in Constantinople, it was through letters that Peiresc was able to fill in the rest of the story. Minuti reported on the warm reception he received from Patron Sabatier, who accommodated them while the ambassador was rebuilding the embassy. The ambassador also included Galaup in his retinue for the first audience he had with the sultan.[87] Galaup eventually left for Lebanon and Marcheville became swallowed up by politics; though he looked for items worthy of Peiresc, he found none. In this, the ambassador sounds like any other ship's captain, missionary, or fellow scholar: wishing to serve Peiresc but not always able to find anything that he thought would sufficiently appeal to the great scholar.[88]

Smyrna

Peiresc seems to have had only two correspondents in Smyrna subsequent to the return of Napollon to France in the mid-1620s, Jean and François Grange. Their uncle, Baltasar Grange, was a more long-standing correspondent of Peiresc's. The younger Grange had found and sent on to Peiresc twelve copper coins from the time of Constantine. Peiresc was giving eleven of them away because they were not worth keeping.[89] Grange also worked to find chameleons for Peiresc.[90] And it was one of them who likely provided information on the shape of the harbor of Smyrna.[91]

Cyprus

On 30 October 1627 Peiresc sent a letter to Espannet at Cyprus.[92] Peiresc was looking for medieval manuscripts. Specifically, he was hunting for versions of the maritime legal code, the *Libre del Consolat* and the late Crusader *Assises of Jerusalem*.[93] In November he sent three more letters to Espannet inquiring about these manuscripts, and also to Viguier and Danmartin.[94] The arrival of the *Assises* from Cyprus is signaled in block letters for 13 December 1627—that is, before his letters of November could have been received.[95]

Théophile Minuti spent the winter of 1633 manuscript-hunting on Cyprus. He was not favored in the least by the consul, who was himself consumed by poverty. In fact, Minuti wrote that lacking bread, the consul had to subsist on what Minuti gave him. He had no servant and was clothed like a beggar ("comme un gu") so that there was no visible difference between him and a mariner (this says a lot about the appearance of mariners, too). Minuti marveled that Viguier, the consul residing in Marseille, abided such dishonor to France. By contrast, the Dutch consul Van Steenwinkel was "a very good man" ("fort honneste homme") and allowed Minuti to plant anemone bulbs in his garden with the promise that he would pull up the flowers in July and send them to Peiresc.[96]

Sidon

For the first part of the seventeenth century, the French were the only foreigners resident in Sidon.[97] The consul occupied a highly ornate house originally built by Emir Fakhr al-Din for his wives. The French merchants lived either by the shore or inland in the wealthier neighborhood.[98] The brothers Jacques and Honoré Estelle held the position of vice-consul between themselves from 1627 until at least 1637. Baptiste Tarquet, the consul, also traveled there.[99] Two Capuchins arrived in 1626, among them Gilles de Loches, later Peiresc's collaborator.[100] Peiresc worked closely with them in advance of Minuti's first voyage. The second voyage led to Galaup-Chasteuil residing in Lebanon by May 1633. We find him sending letters back from Mount Lebanon recommending to Peiresc's attention Giorgio Amira, a Maronite bishop, and provoking Marcheville to wonder at his absence and silence.[101] Jacques de Vendôme, a Franciscan and Guardian of Nazareth, was a neighbor and acquaintance of Galaup's in Lebanon. Moving back and forth between the coasts of the Mediterranean, Jacques de Vendôme provided a constant communication circuit. Peiresc preserved letters written by him from Mount Lebanon and from Malta; from other correspondence we know of periods of residence in Rome and visits to Provence. A first letter, from Ehden in Mount Lebanon dated 15 June 1633, mentions an earlier one, written during Lent and sent from Sidon with Captain Danin to accompany one of Galaup's. Father Jacques was trying to gin up support for Amira. Galaup, he writes, was already very competent in Syriac and was making progress in Arabic.[102] Daniel Aymini and Mallon, the surgeon from Damascus, were also answered out of Sidon. Mallon had sent Peiresc a box full of medals and other curiosities, and

Aymini the Samaritan Triglot. The reimbursements came through Sidon, via Estelle. Charles Blanc, in Sidon, also sent a package to Peiresc (though it was lost and it transpired that his uncle Marquesi in Marseille had failed to purchase the insurance he said he had, to Peiresc's lasting regret).[103] Jerôme de l'Isle was another Sidon-based merchant who helped Aymini, and Peiresc assured him that reimbursement would be more secure than with Blanc and Marquesi.[104] Minuti was especially complimentary about Tarquet, writing to Peiresc, "I have found more courtesy in the person of M. the Consul Tarquet than I have in M. the Ambassador"—not out of malice so much as poverty: "I left him so poor that he had not another [pot] for boiling his soup."[105]

Damascus

Meynier, a merchant from Languedoc, lived in Damascus. He supported Minuti and Aymini during their visits. He conducted them through the town, showing them the sights. It was he who first connected them with the Maronite Father Michael in whose library they found a Bible written in Samaritan, Hebrew, and Syriac, but all in Samaritan characters. Meynier intervened decisively with Father Michael to win the book. And it was Meynier who supervised the payment and preparation of the copy for transfer—missing leaves were to be filled in for a small additional price (the whole cost 30 piastres and an additional 4 or 5 were required for the new work).[106]

In his letter to him, Peiresc treats Meynier as an equal, spelling out to him exactly what he wanted and what his concerns were, trusting to Meynier's judgment. As the Triglot had gaps, Peiresc wished to have any lacunae marked in the book, in order to facilitate recopying. The Maronite (Michael) was doing the recopying. Peiresc asked Meynier to find out if he worked at a moderate price, and if he had other things for sale. For Meynier's information—he was the one on site, after all—Peiresc noted that he would be interested in buying whatever was in the Samaritan script but principally what touches "their history, their calendar and their rules and way of living (in their sects)." Peiresc also wanted to have a catalog made of Michael's library, and was willing to tempt him with some "chosette" from his own collection or elsewhere in France. Any expenses Meynier incurred would be compensated "in the field" ("sur le champ") by Estelle. The sense of responsibility and empowerment of the merchant expressed by Peiresc is noteworthy.[107]

From Sidon, Minuti had traveled to Damascus in October 1632. His letter to Peiresc begins with the items he had bought there and was sending back to Provence. The list included fifteen boxes of large grapes *(panse)* of Damascus adding up to two quintals, two vests of a squirrel-like fur to keep Peiresc warm, a Bible in Arabic with all the incipits in Samaritan characters, an Arabic-Samaritan book, six damascened daggers with sheaths of agate, one damascened sword, three Indian bed-covering cloths, a piece of silk described as "Anacarate"—probably what we call "nacarat," a shade of pale red or orange, the term itself coming into French from Arabic—and twenty-odd coins and medals, four or five of which seemed to match Peiresc's sketches.[108] Meynier had still not accepted the reimbursement offered him by Peiresc for his work in 1629. Minuti had come to insist he take it, as did Jerôme de l'Isle. He had thus far refused, Minuti reported, even though "he is rather poor and has a great deal of hardship just to live."[109]

Resident in Damascus was Aycard's nephew, Jean Salvator. Apparently, he found life there fine enough, especially since aside from a lone Jewish surgeon, he found no other doctor—presumably this means "European"— in the whole city, despite its grandeur, wealth, and huge population.[110] Before departing for Cyprus in winter 1633, Minuti charged him with picking through the caravan from India that was to arrive in March for goods to ship back to Peiresc.[111] Back in April 1633, Minuti received medical treatment from Salvator for a rheumatism-like condition he contracted while living rough in Cyprus.[112] Minuti seems to have been ill for a part of the late spring and summer, since he acknowledges that during these two months Salvator cared for him "more even than if I had been his own brother."[113] While he was gone, Salvator had bought some ancient coins, including two little Samaritan ones that Peiresc had "strongly recommended." One of these had three small flowers and the other a mitre-like object. Salvator had purchased them at the price of gold ("achatees au poys de l'or"), which he would not have done, Minuti hastened to add, if his uncle of Toulon had not intended them as a gift for Peiresc.[114] By the summer of 1634 Salvator was dead, described elliptically by Allemand as "wanting to take up another profession than his own, has gone to see the other world by a very perilous jump."[115]

Aleppo

At the beginning of this period, there were about fifteen Marseille merchants based in Aleppo.[116] It is probable that the box of ancient coins and medals Mallon sent Peiresc via Daniel Aymini and Théophile Minuti was acquired in Aleppo.[117] The surgeon Mallon, who had been in Damascus, had in the meantime left and gone to Sidon. We possess a long letter that Peiresc wrote to him in February 1630. Peiresc dismisses, gently, the proffered rhinoceros horn, saying that he could get them easily in Holland, and cheaper. He was more upset about the Samaritan books that Mallon had let get away. Peiresc urged him to see if it were possible to discover who had purchased them, if they had left the country, whether they could be bought back, and if so at what price. Peiresc also spelled out exactly what kind of texts he wanted—and this *is* interesting for us: "principally I would want of their chronologies and histories and of their religion, and calendars even when they are written on parchment and are old, even if I am not of the opinion that you should neglect everything that is written on paper." Peiresc also wanted Mallon to continue purchasing coins and medals. To this end he explained that he had furnished Minuti with casts of different coins with which "you could recognize enough, just about, the manner of those on which my curiosity falls."[118] Again we see not only Peiresc's willingness to rely on a nonscholarly respondent but how he tried to prepare Mallon to make the decision to buy or not to buy and to do so through material paradigms.

Peiresc had Pierre Fort arrange additional credit for Mallon through Captain Naudin l'Archier. L'Archier, who was a relative of Fort's, was going to Aleppo.[119] We even have the copy of a letter from Mallon in Aleppo to l'Archier in Alexandretta saying that he had heard from Peiresc that Pierre Fort had consigned a packet of books to him (l'Archier) for delivery. Mallon proposed that they be given to a "M. Franege" or his colleague "to bring them with the caravan" ("pour le conduire avec la caravane"), but l'Archier never made the short trip from Alexandretta.[120] This made Peiresc fear that his books, then in Mallon's possession, might be seized by creditors.[121] So precarious was the state of merchants in the Levant.

Eventually, Peiresc received from Mallon the fifty copper coins in two boxes, along with a letter telling of Mallon's three separate attempts in the past year to write to Peiresc via other people. Peiresc complained—and this tells us a lot about his mentality—that Mallon had omitted the single most important thing, the names of those he charged with the letters, preventing Peiresc from even trying to track down the missing communications.[122] Mallon, in turn, had difficulty in reaching Peiresc—three separate letters seemed to him to have gone astray—and his source of medals, the one called "maître," had died, and all his goods were being inventoried.[123]

By the end of the period, Peiresc was deeply involved in supporting Father Celestin through the merchants Constans and Venture. Their collaboration, and that of the chancellor of the consulat, Claret, supported astronomical observation and book purchasing in particular (see Section 6, "Writing to the Levant, 1627–1637").

Cairo

When Peiresc's interest in the Levant picks up strength in 1627, we know exactly who constituted the French merchant community in Cairo. A report on an assembly of the "Nation" in the house of the consulate in Cairo on 25 January 1627, preserved in the Archive of the Chambre de Commerce of Marseille, records the names of those assembled.[124] There are fourteen so enumerated, two of whom are identified as "captains" and therefore likely only visiting Cairo. Of the other twelve, three are closely connected to Peiresc: Cesar Lambert, Jacques Albert, and Jean Magy.[125] A similar list, from the Alexandrian consulate, included none of Peiresc's friends, suggesting the relative importance to him of Cairo.[126]

As Peiresc's involvement intensified, Magy came to the fore.[127] Their closeness enabled Peiresc to treat him as a deputy; sometimes Peiresc used Magy as a destination for top-security information that was to be provided to others later, and sometimes he expected Magy to give verbal instructions in his name to Seghezzi.[128] Peiresc described him as having lived in Cairo for two decades.[129] But Michel de Tourtel, the sieur de Ramatuelle, in a letter of mid-July 1633, wrote, "I am very pleased by the contentment you receive from the resolution M. Magy has taken to go and reside in Cairo." Tourtel promised to keep a line of credit open to Magy.[130] Two years later, Tourtel was still handling Magy's reimbursement.[131]

Peiresc used Magy as the handler and paymaster of "specialists," like the Capuchin book-hunters in Wadi Natrun. In a letter of 15 September 1634 Peiresc charged him with managing the swap of a chasuble for an Arabic volume of canons of church councils, and to draw on his *lettre de change* for payment with "intherestz maritimes, ou changes." He specifically named Gela (in Marseille), Ramatuelle (who seems to have gone back and forth), and Seghezzi (in Cairo) as individuals who could hand over the requisite cash.[132]

Magy was the person responsible for packaging up the items to be shipped back to Peiresc. So, in April 1634 we learn from a letter Peiresc wrote to Magy's Marseille-based brother that he had just received from

Cairo "a container filled with many curiosities, a case holding two trees, and aside from this a book in 'moresque,' a porcelain figure and a pot of sorbet." Within the container there were many "packets, sachets or goblets, full of different seeds, pieces of weights and measures, a copper kettle or heater, a lantern, 7 *massons* [*sic*], 12 buffalo tongues—which I do not know what it is—[a kind of marine crab, the *Plagusia*], and a box holding almost 35 medals, 32 idols and other little things."[133] Peiresc wanted additional weights and asked for them in a later letter, but he also wanted Magy to write out and send to him the Arabic letters engraved on the reverse, and the animals with their interpretations.[134] When Magy returned to Provence for a visit in July 1633, he brought back with him gifts for Peiresc and his niece. Those for Peiresc included the fruit of a Baobab tree, a fine piece of Indian cloth said to be "worthy of your cabinet," some "arcquifoux," or archisoul, for spreading around the eyes (perhaps *kohl*), and two vests. They had been bought in Surat by a merchant who brought them back to Cairo. Their lining was from a *baubille*, a bird with a large beak common in Egypt. It was cleaned with grains of lime. The men's and women's versions were entirely different; the men's, for instance, had a different lining and could last up to fifty years.[135]

Animals also came to Peiresc from Magy. He sent a crocodile skin, which Peiresc intended to send to Paris as a gift, probably for de Thou. The crocodile seems likely to have been intended to accompany the African animal ("dafasa") that Seghezzi had acquired and sent on to Gela. This was part of his lobbying campaign on behalf of Seghezzi's retention of the consulship of Egypt. Peiresc asked Jean-Baptiste Magy, his brother's Marseillais respondent, to supervise conservation of the crocodile.[136]

But Magy also sent information, putting his empirical experience into writing. It makes sense that Magy, who had to orchestrate Peiresc's payment schedule, knew and could communicate to Peiresc the cost of money in Cairo. He identified for Peiresc the copper *Fourle*, the silver *Medin*, the gold *Cherif*, the even bigger gold *Medical* of Morocco, and the "*Kiz* or Pouch," giving their convertibility into French or Venetian coinage, explaining their origin—the *Cherif*, for instance, was minted in Cairo as in Constantinople—and the precise, current rate of exchange in Marseille (4 livres tournois and 13 *sequins*, "a peu prez," at Marseille for the *Cherif* and 5 francs for the *Medical*, though that, Magy writes, was "some years ago") and in Cairo (the *Kiz*, which contained 25,000 *Medins* or 800 piastres, with the piastre paid out in Cairo in *Medins* at either the old rate, or the new).[137] Magy also tells Peiresc that the caravan from sub-Saharan Africa (the "caravan d'Acrouri") used only shells for currency, that the white ones came from "Muchal" (Mocha), the red ones from the Red Sea, and that these exchanged in Cairo at 70 piastres for an "Ardeb" of white shells and 6 for the red.[138]

The longest entry discussed the resemblance of current oriental utensils to ancient ones. Peiresc introduced the memo by identifying him as "Jean Magy of Marseille, who has been for a long time in Egypt, up to 20-odd years, says he has seen there diverse vases and utensils in common usage, of a form very similar or close to those of the ancients, among others."[139] Magy's familiarity with the contemporary examples of ancient forms, and Peiresc's confidence in him, are registered in another document, describing bronze artifacts belonging to Claude Menestrier in Rome. Peiresc adds the comment, "M. Magy of Marseille, returned from Egypt, being at Aix 30 June 1633, recognized the ancient fragments of diverse instruments, vases and machines as similar to those which the Turks still use."[140] The ancient tripod, in particular, seemed to live on in the Ottoman East.[141] Perhaps the most exceptional document to derive from the visit's discussion of Turkish vases is actually the record of a conversation, as opposed to a literary preparation. (In this it most resembles the memoranda produced by Peiresc during his study sessions with the Rabbi of Carpentras, Salomon Azubi.)[142] The document contains drawings of six bowls and pots, along with their names in Arabic (transliterated) and an explanation of their use (e.g., "for drinking water"). The document is indexed "VASCULA ARABUM/AEGYPTIORUM" and is captioned "from a Moor in Cairo, reported by Sr. Jean Magy, son of Agostin of Marseille, 29 July 1633, at Aix."[143]

Magy knew all of this because he had, to some extent, gone native. We know that he married a woman in Cairo. We know also that he socialized with Cairene merchants. He was at the home of the "Cavagy Salaboussati" for the earthquake he associated with the eruption of Mount Sem in Ethiopia. This was his way of rendering *khawadja sala bussuti*, or "rich merchant trading in textiles." Similarly, he learned of the great fire at Mecca from a Rajab Chaoux and a Cavagy Bubaquer Suala. "Chaoux" was a rendering of *Gawish*, or member of one of the seven militias of Ottoman Egypt, and "Bubaquer" was "Abu Bakhr."[144] Similarly, the long report on the practices and dwellings of the Jews of Cairo offers the kind of ethnography only an embedded foreigner could have provided.[145]

In Peiresc's letter to Magy of 10 August 1635, we catch a reference to another Frenchman based in Cairo, François Daniel, here described as Magy's agent *(commis)*.[146] But Minuti, writing in 1633, reported that all the French merchants and the consul had moved to Alexandria to avoid the cost of Cairo, leaving there only a "M. Vignon" to assist him in need.[147]

Having a fine network of correspondents did not guarantee that letters were actually delivered. We know of a letter of Peiresc's to Father Thomas de Saint-Calain that was sent to Magy in Egypt, who then either neglected to pass it on or thought better of it. Father Thomas came to Egypt, saw Egypt, and left Egypt. The letter followed him home to Paris.[148]

A document preserved in the Archives of the Chambre de Commerce of Marseille and dated March 1638, only a year after Peiresc's death, presents a snapshot of the community of Provençal merchants in Egypt. The vice-consul in Alexandria was Esperit Laurens, and Christofle de Bermond was consul in Cairo. Jacques de Vendôme was listed as chaplain of the French nation in Alexandria.[149] Magy was in Cairo. We last see him in 1656 complaining to the consuls of Marseille about the Bermond regime in Cairo.[150]

North Africa

Peiresc knew a great deal about North Africa.[151] By the 1630s he could insinuate himself into an established Marseille–Toulon–North Africa network which included Berengier of Marseille, who owned a barque; the *patron* Jean Lomiert, who brought Peiresc his Alzaron; de Gastines, of course, at the receiving end in Marseille; Aycard in Toulon; and Thomas d'Arcos in Tunis.[152] Napollon was the central figure in Algiers, itself by far the most important North African actor from a Marseille-based perspective. He and Peiresc worked very closely together, going back to Smyrna in 1624, when, as we have seen, Napollon purchased for Peiresc what posterity knows as the Arundel marbles. Jean Gazille minded Napollon's house when he was away in Algiers, and was the respondent for cross-Mediterranean communication.[153] Peiresc's relationship to Napollon brought him into close documentary proximity with the regency of Algiers and its maritime projections.[154]

Of Tunis, the general consensus is that knowledge of the French merchant community before 1660 is "fragmentary."[155] Hence the tremendous importance of the correspondence of Peiresc with the captured humanist-turned-renegade Thomas d'Arcos. Even before the arrival of d'Arcos, Peiresc was working through the Marseille network, in this case Berengier and Danmartin, to order jasmines.[156]

But even before returning to Provence, we find Peiresc in contact with Provençaux who were regular visitors to North Africa. In 1620, for example, Peiresc received a letter from a fellow Aixois reporting that some time before, a friend of his from Marseille had gone to Tunis and, hearing reports of Latin and other inscriptions being found in the environment, set out to copy them. He was told that other places on the Barbary Coast were rich in ancient Roman inscriptions. Here, as elsewhere in Peiresc's Mediterranean, a commercial opening created an opportunity for the study of antiquities and peoples.[157]

But with the presence there of d'Arcos from around 1630, Peiresc gained a crucial correspondent. D'Arcos was a native of Rouen and resident in Cagliari. He had been a secretary to the Cardinal de Joyeuse. He was taken prisoner by the corsairs and brought to Tunis, where he soon converted to Islam. He seems to have had some regrets, but did not, so far as we know, pervert. He appointed his wife, Mariana d'Arcos y Valentin, to recover outstanding debts owed him.[158]

From him, as we have seen, Peiresc gained information about ancient Carthage, contemporary foodways, natural history, and sub-Saharan Africans.[159] For d'Arcos, too, it seems, the correspondence offered an important lifeline, and not only because of the Bandol wines Peiresc had Aycard ship him from Toulon. In March 1633, for instance, we find Peiresc sending d'Arcos a Koran—he had in the meantime converted and taken the name Osman, though Peiresc treated this as entirely insincere—but acknowledging the limitations of Bibliander's translation, and also Erpenius's fragment on the Joseph story in the Koran, of which he thought much more highly.[160] Another renegade who came to Peiresc's attention through Tunis, and therefore through Arcos, was identified as being from Ferrara, though he now lived in the region bordering Libya and Egypt. He had, according to d'Arcos, made many trips to the area of the Niger River and seen many apes.[161]

Peiresc had no contacts in Tripoli but relied entirely on the Marseille merchant community. Tripoli was the smallest of the Barbary regencies and the least frequented by Provençal shipping.[162] Nevertheless, when trying to track down his missing Polyglot Psalter, Peiresc was able, within a relatively short time, to establish a correspondence with the Marseille merchant Bayon in Tripoli (see Section 29, "Ransoming").

Spain

Peiresc had no correspondents in Spain who were natives. What encounters he had with Spain depended on the visits of French or Italian colleagues. Spain came to Peiresc mostly in the form of ships tramping between Spanish Catalonia and Spanish Italy (whose border effectively began at Villefranche [Nice]). Thus, in 1626, Peiresc was notified of the arrival of eight galleys from Naples en route to Spain. The consul Durand informed Peiresc in case he wished to use them to carry any communication to Spain.[163] Similarly, when Cardinal Francesco Barberini took up his mission as legate to Spain, he passed through the Provençal ports and afforded Peiresc a precious opportunity to visit with his entourage but also to communicate with Spain. On board one of the cardinal's ships in 1626 at the border post of Tour de Bouc, Peiresc wrote to the Flemish noble in Madrid, Lucas Torrius, recommending to him Doni and Aubery; to them he explained that costs would be reimbursed by either Gaspard Signier in Marseille or Raymond Masse—probably one of Signier's respondents—at Valencia.[164] Peiresc offered his hope for renewed freedom of communication. Any copying of manuscripts done on his behalf, he concluded, would be reimbursed by Masse.[165] Torrius was able to reply, and Peiresc, exceptionally, to answer back. Typically, much of the reply was about the mechanics of replying, and this usefully conveys the place of Spain in the Republic of Letters. Peiresc writes that he was going to reply via Paris, but learning that the merchants of Marseille were going to send someone to Spain to protest against some injustice done them in Sicily, he took advantage of this means.[166]

The only other correspondent Peiresc had in Spain was also non-Spanish: Antoine Novel, a Provençal doctor based in S. Lucar de Barrameda near Seville. Peiresc had asked about currents in the Straits of Gibraltar. In a long letter of 10 December 1633, Dr. Novel reported on the strength of an "Oceanic" (Atlantic) current capable of driving a ship before it even into the teeth of a strong wind. Reports from Spanish mariners sailing to and from North Africa who had to correct for this strong west-to-east current corroborated those sailing from ocean to sea and back.[167]

Interestingly, Peiresc's dearth of correspondents in Spain and his seeming inability to insinuate himself into an existing Marseille merchant network, as he did in Italy and the Levant, would suggest that there was little contact between Marseille and Spain. Yet there was a large volume of Spanish or Spanish-bound shipping, both incoming and outgoing. There was more than twice as much traffic in this direction than to the next-most-trafficked destination, Genoa; three times as much as was Levant-bound; and ten times more than to Rome.[168] This vantage point, then, suggests that Peiresc's Marseille connections represent but one distinct grouping within the larger community of maritime traders and that as much as this seems to constitute an entire world, it remained but one of Marseille's many Mediterraneans.

Lisbon

Peiresc had no direct contact with Portugal. Writing in July 1633 to Henriqué Alvares, the Portuguese jeweler then based in Paris, Peiresc asked if it were possible to learn of his "correspondances" in Lisbon, "because I know no person in that land, and the Marseillais have very little regular correspondence there." If any Marseille merchants were to go there, having a contact would facilitate their "recovering with my money [the] plants and fruits of the Indies."[169] Peiresc was more optimistic in a letter to Menestrier when he wrote that in the hunt for Indian chestnuts he would have "some merchant of Marseille" write to Lisbon.[170] Indeed, along with his letter to the merchant and ship's captain Michel Tourtel, Peiresc forwarded one other of his for Genoa and a second, from Lisbon, that would be sent by his brother.[171] Meanwhile, a mémoire "of the *Agrumi* or Oranges that could be recovered from Portugal" testifies to Peiresc's planning for the faint possibility that he would be able to establish a contact there who could satisfy his love of citrus fruits.[172]

Alvares, in his reply the next month, noted that he had many correspondents at Lisbon, but he thought that the person who would best be able to serve Peiresc in everything was Duarte Dios de Olivarez. At Seville, he recommended Diego Cardotto, and promised to write to both immediately.[173] In his next letter, Alvares wrote that they had already been put on notice that "seeing something of your command to serve you in all," and specifying this to include "all kinds of rarities and curiosities natural and ancient."[174] Peiresc, in turn, thanked Alvares for sharing these Iberian connections and for news of the India merchants Manuel da Costa and Nunes.[175] In a later letter, Peiresc said he would write to Lisbon by the next Marseille ship that went in that direction.[176]

31 ∼
Merchants as Intellectual Partners

*T*he subject of scholars collaborating with merchants who were not in the printing trade has barely been broached.[1] Historians of ideas, and even of scholarly practice, have tended not to focus on merchants, while economic historians for their part have rarely been interested in merchants as intellectual figures, even where their accomplishments as, say, vehicles for transmission have been widely acknowledged. Even the most forward-thinking engagement with the life of merchants as expressed in their letters, the volumes published in the 1950s by the VIe Section of the École Pratique des Hautes Études in the book series *Affaires et gens d'affaires,* does not shed any light on what we might call the *érudit*-merchant interface. Nor is there anything in Origo's Datini that shows any participation in learned inquiries. The literate Florentine merchants of the Renaissance studied so carefully by Vittore Branca and Christian Bec, who wrote so much, do not seem to record their intellectual collaborations with scholars.[2] Making the *Mercator sapiens* was the goal of Caspar Barlaeus when he inaugurated the Athenaeum Illustre of Amsterdam in January 1632; the implication must be that he did not yet exist.[3] Nor has the most recent turn toward artisanal knowledge by students of early modern art and science recuperated the likely role of merchants as intellectual collaborators; they are still present only insofar as they *support* scientific and artistic production by providing materials, collecting, or creating a context.[4]

The merchants of Marseille may not have been writers, but that surely can no longer be taken as the sole index of intellectuality. Nor may they have left portraits of themselves, whether in pigment or stone, like the Sassetti, Rucellai, and Strozzi of Florence. But their participation in Peiresc's intellectual life, like their collecting practices in the East, enables us to glimpse their initiative and ambition. It gives us, in the end, just what we find in Renaissance Florence: individuals.[5]

In the parallel universe of business history, we would see these Marseille merchants buying, selling, and suing. Indeed, the contemporary historical documentation, whether of the admiralty court in Marseille, insurance contracts, cargo declarations, or public disputes between consuls in Marseille and those in the Levant, could be used to build a picture of the merchant community of Marseille. But only certain aspects of merchant life would be recorded and captured in these sorts of sources. And how different this is from the picture of merchants as intellectual actors that we find in the Peiresc archive![6]

For these names were more than "respondents": not mere post boxes, but collaborators and even partners capable of entering into a project and adapting general principles to local particularities. Peiresc's close involvement with merchants, which seems so unusual to us and is absolutely synonymous with his Mediterraneanism *tout court*, offers a deep reflection of his personality. We might even wonder at how much of what we take to be characteristic of Peiresc's intellectual posture is indebted to the merchants, as opposed to seeing the merchants as benefiting from his attention. But this question we can reserve for later.

(That all this might seem surprising or novel speaks volumes about our contemporary expectations of the relationship between scholarship and the world of affairs. There must have been many others, like Peiresc, who worked between the head and the hand, the book and the tool, but their papers have not survived, have not been found, or have not been properly studied.)

At the foundation of Peiresc's relationship with merchants lay respect. We might say that he was showing them respect "merely" by engaging with them intellectually. But the real respect in the relationship is evident in the fact that not only would he disagree with them—we might expect this—but he felt the need to justify his disagreements. Thus, when Peiresc informed Gela in January 1636 that he had received the objects sent by Gela's brother-in-law Seghezzi, he shared his thoughts about one of the objects, a terra cotta head of a woman whose antiquity Seghezzi had identified with that of a mummy he sent. Peiresc demurred, saying that it was more than four hundred or five hundred years later than the mummy, a judgment that he made based on his assessment of the woman's costume.[7]

Next lay a shared commitment to curiosity. No piece of antiquity was too insignificant for Peiresc. He stressed to Seghezzi that for his project the virtue most needed was curiosity: "And if this attempt is to succeed, it will be necessary to have great curiosity to gather up all the other ancient objects that are found around the mummies, above all the books that are included sometimes in boxes, and the pedestals of wooden figures."[8] The interesting point is that by addressing this to Seghezzi, a merchant, Peiresc was implying that Seghezzi had the necessary curiosity to succeed. And he was right. After enumerating the four objects he was sending off at the end of September 1635, Seghezzi wrote that they "were all things *of little value but of some curiosity,* being so old."[9]

Peiresc had many friends in the highest of circles, but he recognized that he could be more effective sometimes working through a purely merchant channel. Thus, when Peiresc wanted a particular coin of the emperor Hadrian, he asked Henriqué Alvares in Paris to write to his correspondents in Flanders to find the object. "I would normally have written to Rubens or Roccox for help on this," Peiresc wrote, "but as the commerce of merchants is freer than others', it will be easier now for you to reach the goal than me."[10]

This freedom of communication was something that Peiresc the scholar shared with his friends the merchants. The language he used joined together "commerce," "correspondence," and "communication," in different combinations. In a memo on travel to the Red Sea and Indian Ocean, he described his priorities in terms of "le commerce et la correspondance" and "correspondance et communication."[11] Discussing with Gaffarel the danger posed by overzealous bureaucracies, he emphasized that learning had a need for a "correspondance et communication" free from "the intervention of so many interpreters and superfluous people."[12] Escaping the plague by moving to the countryside left him feeling as if mired "in the sands of Libya," "in the middle of a desert," cut off "from all commerce and communication."[13] The Genoese attempt to damage the economy of Lyon was conducted through a blockade of Marseille shipping because of the perceived "communication et commerce" of the two cities.[14] Peiresc hoped that a rumored rapprochement between the sultan and the disgraced French ambassador de Marcheville could salvage the "liberté du commerce" on which depended his own trade in books.[15] The outbreak of war between France and Spain at the opposite end of the Mediterranean had interrupted, Peiresc wrote, "public liberty of commerce" ("la liberté publique de commerce").[16] And his own communication system, he wrote to Samuel Petit in 1634, was even more sensitive to disruption than that of the merchants because vulnerable even to the rumor, not just the reality, of war.[17] Father Celestin, in Aleppo, writing to his brother in Leiden, in a copy preserved by Peiresc, explained that wars interrupted "not only the negotiations of merchants but the commerce of letters."[18]

Of course, there were obvious practical reasons for Peiresc to work closely with merchants; four can suffice here. First of all, the merchants were on the spot, and Peiresc was not. When he wanted a book on the court of Savoy that could not be found in Nice or Genoa, he sought it at Turin "par correspondants des marchands de Lyon."[19] When he wanted a report on an underground grotto near Kraków, he wrote to one Genoese agent, to pass on to another, Horatio Tridi, who was based in Kraków.[20]

Second, merchants were good at accounting. When Peiresc was seeking evidence in higher tax revenues of past unions between the Archbishopric of Aix and other nearby churches, such as the abbey of Silvacane, it made sense for him to ask a merchant to go through records of tax returns.[21] The upkeep of his personal network required financing and banking facilities. He needed merchants for this.

Third, merchants got things done. Peiresc valued this as well. This emerges most clearly perhaps in a letter to Robert Contour, a Marseille merchant based in Aleppo. Peiresc looked to him to govern the missionaries there; they were enthusiastic collaborators, but there was a need to "throw some sense into these good fathers" ("jetter sens a cez bons peres"). Morever, while they often had book learning, they sometimes lacked practical skills, as Peiresc had discovered on other occasions "when it was necessary to do things in practice which seemed easy in theory."[22] Peiresc relied on the merchants to show common sense. Writing to another merchant in Aleppo, Sr. Constans, Peiresc explicitly asked him to "break up the party" the next time there was the danger of any action that would expose the participants to extortion and persecution.[23]

Fourth, merchants had access to all kinds of objects. When Peiresc planned to host the cardinal of Lyon, formerly archbishop of Aix and the brother of the Cardinal-Duke de Richelieu, for dinner the next day, he inquired of his friend Gela whether he had access to any caviar. Peiresc explained that he had gotten a lot ("gran quantità") from Venice on other occasions, and since Gela's relatives were based in Venice, if he could lay hands on any that was fresh and tasty ("che fosse ben recente & ben saporito") it would be a huge favor. Peiresc asked for one or two pounds! But, he repeated, he needed a lot and since it was for the cardinal it had to be fresh "and not rancid."[24] Gela sent five pounds of caviar, and Peiresc was pleased to report that his brother, who was present at the meal, told him "how much it was enjoyed" by the cardinal.[25] On another occasion, a year or so later, Peiresc asked this same Gela for Murano glassware for a person of importance and a week later received a box "of beautiful glasses of Murano."[26]

As a corollary, merchants also knew where to look. In a memorandum on Parisian antiquities collections, Peiresc noted that goldsmiths and jewelers should be consulted because they knew where to find things, *and* they knew where to find the things that had been melted down and remade into other things, as weights and measures had been remade into cups "in the current style."[27] "Famous druggists and apothecaries" often also had important objects which they used "to ennoble their shop windows."[28] Goldsmiths and jewelers straddle the line separating the artisan from the merchant; while we have been focusing on the latter in this study, it is by acknowledging Peiresc's familiar relations with the makers of objects that we perceive the depth of his comfort with the world of the practical.[29]

Place also mattered. Marseille's deep engagement with the Levant meant that there were merchants to whom Peiresc could turn when he wanted help with Arabic. It was a merchant who translated the Arabic inscriptions on a copper vase that had first been transcribed by the Aleppo native Mattouk Chiassan, the "Turc natural d'Alep" mentioned in a letter to the French ambassador to Venice in July 1635.[30] In another, Peiresc writes to Petit that he will have an Arabic text copied out by a merchant who has a good Arabic hand.[31] After Peiresc thanks Doctor Cassagnes's factotum, Gilly, for making three lead impressions so well done "I esteem hardly less than the originals," he asks him to show the Arabic plaque to M. Suffrin—Honoré Suffin, royal translator in Marseille—and to have him translate it "on my piece of paper."[32]

Marseille's merchants learned Arabic in the East, and they also collected.[33] Louys de Vento, scion of the great aristocratic trading family, had a beautiful vase ("Letertiarus ou de Triens") which "had been brought from Egypt to Marseille by one of Vento's ancestors who had been consul in Alexandria."[34] With Minuti ready to go, Peiresc wrote to the Marseillais Jean l'Empereur in Constantinople, saying that Minuti was carrying a letter from his cousin in Marseille. He wanted l'Empereur's assistance and protection for Minuti, but even more, the opportunity for Minuti to see his collection. Peiresc wanted Minuti to weigh and record specific items which could then be used for "a small work I have on my hands."[35] Peiresc also asked l'Empereur to look out for a Flemish missionary, "Gaugeric de Marquaiz" (Marquez?) who knew how to paint and whom he had charged to depict as carefully as possible the obelisk in the hippodrome. Peiresc already had "a rather exact portrait" of its four sides along with their hieroglyphics. What he wanted this time was a depiction of the *inside* of the obelisk. Peiresc went into some detail about the figures he wanted copied, in case the missionary could not or would not do it and l'Empereur had to find a replacement. Most important for purposes of identification were the portraits of the figures on the base.[36]

Merchants also served as scouts for Peiresc, even close to home, acting on what they knew were his interest in historical and natural antiquities. Benoit Pelissier, for example, traveling along the coast to Frejus, notified a "M. Maupin" who was working on its fortifications that if he came across any old thing ("quelque chose d'antique") he was to hold on to it for Peiresc. Another merchant, Baltasar Grange, drew an ancient altar found in Toulouse and copied out its inscription.[37]

Let us begin with Peiresc's study of ancient vases. The prototype was work he specified for a collection he personally knew very well, that of St. Denis.[38] On this model, he formulated a plan to measure the famed vases of Italy.[39] He mobilized scholarly circles in Venice, Rome, and Florence. But in Genoa he worked through merchant actors as well. Most of his attention was focused on public collections, as he believed that old churches were repositories of ancient vases, and of the most precious sorts— again, modeled on what he knew of St. Denis.[40]

Writing to Giulio Pallavicino in Genoa, Peiresc asked if there were any Genoese vases to be included—based on his own researches, Peiresc did not expect to find any.[41] Boerio in Genoa was urged to seek out permission to measure an emerald basin ("catino") as had been done in the cabinet of the Grand Duke of Tuscany and in the treasury of San Marco. Peiresc did not want Genoa left out of his "discourse on the most celebrated ancient vases in Italy."[42] This letter was brought to Genoa by the Marseille merchant Jean Issaultier, who was also carrying a pewter vase approximately the same size as the one to be measured, in order to facilitate the work.[43] Both Boerio and Issaultier were expected to do some of the heavy lifting in this project. Another letter to Gaffarel recalled that once upon a time Peiresc used his personal relationship with Federigo Contarini, procurator of San Marco, to gain access to the vases in its treasury: "He had control over the keys for communicating very particular things so that I could have him open the silver chest in which was the Gospel of St. Mark made by a goldsmith, and make other experiments no more difficult than those I am asking for now." Unfortuately, he currently lacked this kind of clout. But in exchange, Peiresc advised Gaffarel to seek out prized objects among the "merchants, goldsmiths or jewelers." These, he thought, would be less likely to resist Gaffarel's attempts to pour millet or water into their ancient vases than would the clerical and political hierarchy.[44]

Henri de Gournay might have been the comte de Marcheville, but insofar as he was a nonscholar stationed overseas but connected to Peiresc he, too, like the merchants of Marseille, could be converted into an agent of scholarship. In April 1633 Peiresc brought him into this same project on vases. Peiresc began with an overview of what he wanted to achieve, and how he was going about finding things. He had a "fantasy," he wrote, of making a little treatise on ancient weights and measures and vases. Accumulating more examples could resolve some of the problems that individual pieces posed. For this reason he asked "if in that land there were found ancient bronze vases, especially those highly worked and enriched with ornaments." The element of beauty was not, or so it seems, important from an aesthetic point of view, but because Peiresc believed it signaled that the pieces' makers intended some significance. Then he gave Marcheville his tasks. He started with the "what" before turning to the "how":

> If you can find a way of seeing, amidst the jewels of the Grand Seigneur, the vases that he must have of Agate and other precious stones, this would well merit making a bit of a relation and a portrait if it were possible, and if it were possible to make a measurement of the contents of the vase there would be much to discuss. It would only be necessary to fill them with water or any other kind of liquid or indeed with millet or some other little grain, and then to measure the same liquid or grain in another vase of whatever sort, and to compare them and to adjust a bit to the exact contents of the water that would have filled the ancient vase in precious stone, and then to send me the model used, whether of tin or pewter or other material, on which I could make an examination of the capacity or measure of the ancient one.

Peiresc was not insensible to the exterior of the vessel, or to the possible significance of that exterior: "There are sometimes found very old vases that are heavily ornamented silver with figures and writing whose manner is very different from modern silver vessels." If "it were possible and easy to make a cast in order to better appreciate the manner of the figures and other works and ornaments," it would be highly appreciated. Peiresc added, in conclusion, that Marcheville was not to exclude ancient plates and spoons of silver, as well as copper and precious stones, where even their copies could aid us "in our researches."[45]

The last link in this erudite project that relied upon nonscholarly agents overseas called upon a nonscholar closer to home. Peiresc engaged the jeweler-goldsmith Henriqué Alvares to help him study these vases. In a letter of November 1633, Alvares spoke of the "model of the Agate which I sent you the measure of." He had also sought measures, at Peiresc's request it seems, from some of his noble customers. The vase itself was still awaited, but as soon as it came, Alvares wrote, "I will cast the model perfectly, as you commanded, in tin. The same as the one I have received from Venice."[46]

We may be able to date Peiresc's interest in this kind of comparative project to even earlier. In a letter to Minuti of August 1632, Peiresc asked him for the name used for a particular kind of vessel sent from Constantinople, so as to distinguish it from one in the collection of Cesar Lambert. Lambert, before his return to Cairo the previous week, had told Peiresc that in Cairo this kind of vase was called "Bredaques"—which name seemed to Peiresc so bizarre that it made him want to learn all the names used for this type of vase.[47]

Cesar Lambert was the source for many mémoires on Egyptian material culture. In Peiresc's dossier on weights and measures, we find a memorandum comparing Arabic and Indian weights in use in contemporary Cairo—Peiresc makes a point of dating the memo to Lambert's return from Cairo in August 1632.[48] There is also a third mémoire listing different kinds of Indian gems Lambert had acquired in Egypt and brought to him at Belgentier.[49]

On 19 October 1632, the *patron* Crouset came to visit Peiresc and brought with him the Turk from Aleppo Mattouk Chiassan. Peiresc's notes on their conversation together are indexed under the title "VASCULA ALABASTRINA EX IEMENIA." In four columns (Figure 28), he represents the shape of the object, its names in Arabic and Turkish, and its function. In connected prose, Peiresc noted their material and their origin—they were of Bezoar found in Yemen.[50]

Peiresc must have pursued this question with Thomas d'Arcos in Tunis, for in his letter of 30 June 1633, d'Arcos explained that he would send a separate paper on weights and measures "with the catalog of plates and vases that one uses in this land." More particularly on vases, he noted that there was nothing appropriate for Peiresc's good taste because "of the rusticity" of the place, but to satisfy his obligation he was sending six bowls

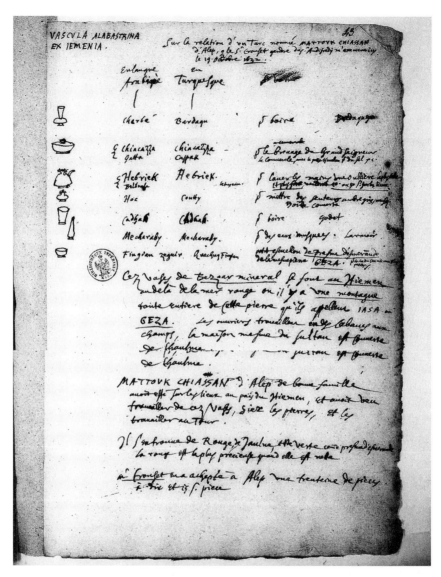

Figure 28. Drawings of vessels. PBN, MS. F.fr. 9532, f. 43r.
(Bibliothèque Nationale de France)

"used for drinking the *cavé* which came from Constantinople, and some little ones which came from Yemen."[51] A month later, the summary of a conversation with Jean Magy of 29 July 1633 about vessels used in Cairo records his mention that some came from "the land of Adam or Heden in Arabia Felix, where they are what the people use for drinking the 'cinnamon water' which they drink in large quantities in that land."[52] Might that "eau de canelle" consumed in such prodigious quantities in Yemen have been coffee? *Cavé* certainly was. The first coffee beans are said to have reached Marseille only at the end of the 1650s, perhaps via Tunis, but it seems from here that they were preceded by the material culture of coffee.[53]

But the main points of the conversation with Magy concerned the utensils and vases he had come across during his twenty-odd years in Egypt. The memo summarizing their conversation contains drawings of six bowls and pots, along with their names in Arabic (transliterated) and an explanation of their use (e.g., "pour boire de l'eau"). The document is indexed "VASCULA ARABUM/AEGYPTIORUM" and is captioned "Ex Moresque du Cayre/au rapport du Sr. Jean Magy filz d'Agostin de Marseille/ le 29 Juillet *1633* a Aix."[54] Peiresc even introduced the question of vases right into the title of a memo: "Jean MAGY . . . said he had seen there different kinds of vases and instruments in common use, in form quite similar to or approaching that of the ancients, among others." Magy adds information on how "the women use this instrument a lot" for heating and cooking.[55] Nor did Peiresc leave the question of ancients and moderns at the level of speculation only, for he actually measured "the modern Arabic tripod" in use in the Levant, and brought back by Magy, with an ancient cotyle he possessed.[56] He even sought to integrate "modern Arabic" measures into a glossary of measures "from Egypt, Italy, France and the Orient" that he prepared at Aix on 22 July 1633.[57]

Peiresc must have kept thinking and talking about this with his merchant friends from Marseille. As if in reply to an inquiry that has been lost, Cesar Lambert wrote to Peiresc in November 1634. A copy preserved in the latter's dossier on weights and measures discusses precisely the system of weights in Egypt and elsewhere in the Levant. Peiresc calls it a "relation." Lambert reviews the different local weights and measures and comments on how they vary—or how what they are called varies—across the Ottoman Empire. There was the "Grand Picq" and then the ordinary ones in use by merchants in the different cities of the empire. There was also one used by the "Francs," which stands in for the French "and others who trade there." Lambert then gives divisions of the picq, including the "Turquesque" and the "Moresque." This latter was in use in Cairo.[58] Lambert added that he had asked the old vice-consul, Gabriel Fernoux, for some help but that the latter said he did not have enough experience with these matters.[59] When Peiresc discovered a chapter on weights and measures in an epitome of Coptic grammar, he immediately wrote back to Father Cassien de Nantes seeking more information of the same sort and to see if any of those terms were still in use.[60]

It was also possible, he thought, that some diversity was a function of the instrument used to establish the measure itself. This clearly came from his own mania about weights and measures: "One must see if all these differences do not proceed from some manner of measuring the compounds in the vases, or the measures which produce this diversity of weights, like the difference of wine from oil, or honey or wheat or other foodstuffs, whether liquid or dry, and capable of being measured."[61]

Peiresc then turned directly to Egypt, and the most recent addition to his équipe, Santo Seghezzi. The question began elsewhere—with the Nilometer. Peiresc wanted "an exact portrait" ("ritratto fedele") of the marble column in the Nile that displayed the water's height, with all of its measuring marks.[62] But, Peiresc continued, since he understood that on that site there was a mosque, he wanted Seghezzi to see if it did not house any large, ancient, marble vases. If there were, he wanted them measured, too. Either water or oil could be used.[63]

Mummies were also high-priority objects. Because most of the obvious places—caves and open grottoes—had already been rifled through, to find a mummy one had to seek out "some virgin grotto" where one could find not only mummies "but their clothes, ornaments for idols, vases, books, and other things."[64] In a later letter to Seghezzi, the need to articulate the general problem so that the merchant on the ground could make the right decisions led Peiresc to put his book learning to practical use. He proposed that since the ancients buried in necropolises, if one could figure out the pattern, or at least find one part of it, it might be possible to find a body. Peiresc drew an example of an ancient burial plan; he must have insisted on its importance, because his amanuensis copied the illustration along with the text of the letter (Figure 29). He intended this as a blueprint for the excavators.[65]

Climate also played a role. Objects survived in Egypt, he wrote, which were not found anywhere else in the world because of the especially dry climate. In the unexplored caves in which mummies could be found, there

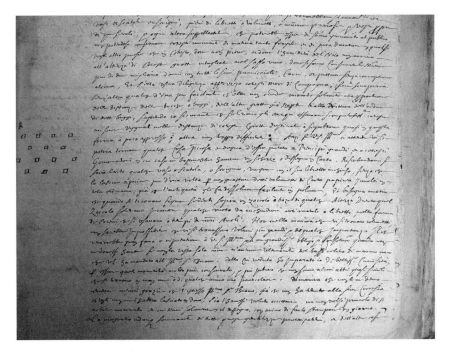

Figure 29. Peiresc's drawing of excavation plan for mummies. Peiresc to Seghezzi, 25 April 1636, CBI, MS. 1874, f. 423r. (Bibliothèque Inguimbertine, Musées et Bibliothèques de Carpentras)

lay a whole realm of material culture, "in which will surely be found," Peiresc wrote,

> vases and boxes and treasure chests full of books or little volumes and precious mummies, and other remains of those centuries, and every other accessory that could be of the highest benefit to the public, for such monuments of material so fragile and perishable could not survive in any other land than this one, where it does not rain and where the humidity of the Nile does not reach the heights of those grottoes cut into the living rock where the mummies were preserved for more than 2000 years with all their wrappings, foods and pictures and without any degradation at all.[66]

Mummies, in some sense, stood between human and natural history.[67] Peiresc regularly drew on merchants for other services in natural history.

When Peiresc heard from Baltasar Grange in Marseille that his nephews, Jean Grange and (his cousin) François Grange, were going to Smyrna in 1635, he prepared for them a mémoire on chameleons. Peiresc had received two shipments from d'Arcos in Tunis, though none were able to survive the winter in Provence. Having heard that they were found in large numbers also in Smyrna, Peiresc provided these merchants with information about their shape, color, and practices. He thought they could be had cheaply, as well.[68]

Peiresc suggested sending the chameleons with the "Dafasa," the large African antelope known as *Oryx besia,* that was going from Egypt to Paris as a gift from Seghezzi to de Thou. Peiresc also left extremely careful instructions for the depiction of this animal. He was prepared to send a painter from Aix, or to have Gela find one in Marseille, to "paint the head alone, separately, at the true size and with the true length of the horns, and the proportion of the front and back and the distance of the horns from each other." Peiresc also wanted measurements taken so that they could be compared with the depiction, "doubting that the painter" would represent it at exactly life size.[69] The picture survives today in a private collection.[70]

To M. Pion, a member of the merchant community who had been made vice-consul at Algiers, Peiresc addressed a series of inquiries about Mediterranean currents and mountains. These followed the precise questions laid out in an earlier letter to d'Arcos. In particular, Peiresc wanted to know whether the mountains were oriented from east to west or west to east, whether these chains were more broken on their northern- or southern-facing sides, more precipitous on the one than on the other, contained banks or veins of different kinds of stones, and were parallel or skewed. What makes this letter so precious, however, is that Peiresc had the copyist reproduce in the file copy of the letter the drawings that Peiresc must have made in the holograph (Figure 30). And so, from the two relevant perspectives, we see Peiresc illustrating exactly what he meant. In the first drawing, looking as if from the north, we see the slope of the mountain rising up gradually from the east, the jagged ridge line, and then the broken, sharply declining western face. In the lower drawing, as if looking from the west, we see the sharp northern rock face and then the gentle sloping away from the ridgeline to the south. The dotted lines represent the "banks or veins" of rock mentioned in the letter.[71] But this was not only an imagined drawing. Looking east to the Montagne Saint-Victoire from Aix, he would have seen something that looked exactly like

Figure 30. Marginal sketch of the mountains of the Mediterranean. CBI, MS. 1874, f. 391. (Bibliothèque Inguimbertine, Musées et Bibliothèques de Carpentras)

this, as I did from the A8 motorway one afternoon, returning from a day in the Peiresc archive in Carpentras (Figure 31).

By far the most elaborate and significant natural scientific project Peiresc put into the hands of merchants was the eclipse observation that he organized for late August 1635. Jean and Pierre Constans, in Aleppo, were the respondents for Father Celestin de Ste. Lidwine, and so it was to them that Peiresc sent two telescopes and some money. Nor did Peiresc hide from Constans the purpose of it all: "to learn the true situatedness of this land on the terrestrial globe."[72] Another Aleppo-based Marseille merchant, Robert Contour, was made responsible for the Capuchin Father Michelange de Nantes. He had observed the eclipse from his lodgings in the city. Peiresc asked Contour to help make sure that a relation be made "of what he had observed, with all of its circumstances and more the original, or original summary, than one which was cleaned up"—that is, with more details left out.[73] In other words, Peiresc was counting on

Figure 31. Montagne Saint-Victoire from the west. (Photo, author)

the merchant to review the observational data and make sense of them for him—and, potentially, for posterity.

Nor did Peiresc feel that the big picture was too big for a merchant: with the Capuchin's observations, he explained to Contour, it would be possible to make the comparison with those made at the same time in Egypt, Lebanon, Tunis, Rome, Padua, Naples, Florence, Paris, Holland, Germany, and elsewhere, "which will give us means to establish on a map the true distances of one place to another." In Aleppo, Father Celestin had made observations, as had Baltasar Claret, but Peiresc hoped for "something better, if he is willing."[74]

As it turned out, Claret's observation was precise enough to stand comparison with the findings of Peiresc and Gassendi in Aix. What does it mean that it was made by a merchant, the chancellor of the French consulate? That Claret was an apothecary suggests that some of the manipulation of precision instruments could have been part of his training.[75] It certainly suggests that Peiresc's confidence in him, and in the capacity of merchants to take on intellectual projects of high complexity, was well placed.

But just these kinds of elaborate, long-distance projects also pointed up the limits of Peiresc's reliance on merchants. Peiresc acknowledged these himself. In a letter to the astronomer Wendelin in May 1636, Peiresc announced the success of the previous year's eclipse observation for reforming maps of the Mediterranean.[76] Peiresc was keen to organize more observations like the one he did with Gassendi in Marseille, both in Constantinople and elsewhere in the Levant. Peiresc was sorry to have to report that he had not progressed further toward this goal because of "the great interruption of Marseille's commerce in those parts" ("la grande interruption du commerce de Marseille en cez quartiers là"). But even with its rebound there remained the limits imposed by the human material: "There are found so few people capable of making observations exact enough to base important conclusions upon it."[77] Peiresc tried to overcome this by formulating mémoires, as in the one developed by Gassendi for sending to Sidon, but also by writing letters containing specific instructions.[78] For example, Peiresc wrote specially to Giovanni Molino, "the Armenian," who worked as a translator for the Venetian consul in Egypt, explaining how to measure the height of the sun in Alexandria. Peiresc also wanted to see exactly how the observation was taken: he asked Molino to send him his astrolabe, along with "a detailed relation," "in order to judge whether it [the observation] was such that one could have confidence in it."[79]

Practices could be methodized, even if accurate implementation could not. But a big part of Peiresc's intellectual activity relied on knowledge acquired in the field, whether we term this "artisanal" or "connoisseurial." To communicate this, in relatively narrow compass, meant communicating basic principles and counting on a discriminating judgment to apply generality to particularity. We can follow Peiresc doing this with Charles Mallon, a surgeon based in Damascus. Mallon had purchased for Peiresc sixty-six copper coins, which he had sent back to Peiresc with a letter of 20 September 1630. In exchange, Mallon wanted some books on surgery that Peiresc hunted down in the shops of Avignon, Aix, and Marseille. About the coins, though, Peiresc had some concerns.[80] Because of this, he wanted to see whatever it was that Mallon was preparing to buy, before he bought. Peiresc first suggested a scheme whereby he made a "pot de vin" available to the customs agents in order for the objects to be exported to Provence for viewing, but after some reflection he suggested an alternative: relying on Mallon's trained judgment ("selon la cognoissance que vous en avez prinse").

Peiresc wanted Greek or Samaritan coins. Mallon knew what both sets of characters looked like (this indicates either a certain degree of priming by Peiresc or prior exposure by Mallon). To further aid Mallon, Peiresc oriented him to the type of crown depicted on these coins. This was a subject about which Peiresc had thought long and hard.[81] Heads crowned by a simple circlet ("ruban") were likely the best to keep. Material was another point of reference, as was size: large medals in fine silver were to be sought. If the figure represented on the coin was an emperor, he would be crowned with either laurels or solar rays. Finally, if after all this Mallon remained uncertain, he was to make impressions and send them to Peiresc.[82]

This is a typical example of the confident way in which Peiresc used his contacts, playing to the strengths of the individuals—Mallon as a doctor could be counted on to have both a background in ancient letters and a refined empirical sensibility. Yet even here there were limits. At the end of a long and detailed letter to Minuti in Constantinople, in which Peiresc laid out his thinking about where Minuti was most likely to find the ancient weights and measures he desired, he came around to plants. Here, however, Peiresc was much less optimistic about Minuti's ability to help him: "This is a trade so subject to fraud that I would not give you a commission in it since you have not been able to acquire enough of the practice and knowledge [*pratique et connoissance*] that is needed to dare to tackle plants."[83]

What Peiresc did share with these merchants was a feeling which is more or less accessible to us, of living in a world of loss, or of the constant threat of loss. "Where Fortune intends us to make landfall, I know not, in view of the upheavals and the changes amid which we now find ourselves"—that is how Francesco Sassetti saw himself in 1488.[84] How to proceed from there was what John Donne sought in the lines, "We doe those shadowes tread / and to brave clearnesse all things are reduc'd."[85] This was also Peiresc's *Tempus Edax Rerum*. We rarely hear a merchant's voice trying to solve for this condition. When Jean-Louis Allemand sat down at the end of 1634 to catch up with his friend Minuti, by then safely back in Europe, the melancholy lurks very close to the surface. And then it breaks through: "I pray God give my spirit rest. Made unquiet by the gout that I have been given since the first of the year that in one month will be revolved, but more so by seeing that my fortune is more reduced than me. I would very much want to be indifferent, but I am but rarely in this posture, as my philosophy has not yet strengthened me enough." "Your commandments," he concluded, "render me worthy of your memory, which I value above all the things of the world."[86]

Let us here pick up a thread, left hanging earlier. Having explored the different dimensions of Peiresc's work with the merchants of Marseille, the almost key-in-lock way in which his interests and their abilities fit together, could we not imagine this section with a slightly different title, not one emphasizing the way merchants fit into Peiresc's world, but the way Peiresc fit into theirs? "The scholar as practical man" or "the scholar as agent" could even serve for the book as a whole.

But were we to persist a bit longer with this serious game, we would come upon the answer to another important question. Once we can imagine Peiresc in the merchants' Marseille, and it must be an act of imagination since we do not have any parallel in the commercial world to his archive in which we can see him from their perspective, then we can also try to imagine not the merchants learning from the scholar, but the scholar learning from the merchants. We see what the merchants might have learned from Peiresc. But what did Peiresc learn from them? From his erudite world we possess documents of collaboration, like the pages on which Peiresc and the rabbi of Carpentras recorded their insights into rabbinic texts, each in his own unmistakable hand. We do not have anything exactly like this from the practical world Peiresc also inhabited.

But let us pause a moment. Where did Peiresc learn about insurance premiums and *lettres d'échange*? About working around quarantine regulations? About how captains loaded their ships? Surely not as a young man with the Jesuits in Avignon, or as a youth studying law at Padua and Montpellier, and not at court with his neostoic mentor du Vair and his friend the poet Malherbe. No, this is knowledge he could only have learned from those who did it, day after day, on the quayside in Marseille and in the taverns and counting rooms that lay behind it. And what of the very watchwords by which he lived as a hero of the Republic of Letters? "Commerce," "communication," and "correspondence" were part of the discourse of merchants, not professors.

We have become attentive as never before to the shifting, and maybe mirage-like, frontier between the practitioners and the book-learned in early modern Europe, and in any number of fields. Might we now imagine that a certain kind of scholarship, embodied by Peiresc, could also straddle the practical and the theoretical? That how the past was studied, or nature anatomized, could have been shaped by everyday exchanges with other people for whom observation and description, precision and practicality, credibility and conjecture were also part of their tool-kits?

32

Before *Statistik*

*U*nlike his older contemporary, King Phillip II of Spain, who possessed an imperial bureaucracy, or his younger one, Athanasius Kircher, who exploited the infrastructure of the Jesuit order, Peiresc had to build his own system. Perhaps nowhere is this more spectacularly on view than in his attempt to persuade Cardinal Francesco Barberini, in his role as prefect of the Congregation of the Propaganda Fide, to use the French Capuchins—already part of Peiresc's équipe—to establish a mission to Ethiopia.[1]

At the heart of his information architecture was the memorandum, which began, "One would want to know . . ." ("On desireroit sçavoir . . ."). Frequently this took the form of a questionnaire. Sometimes these questions found their way into letters sent off to individuals, and sometimes they remained for Peiresc's own use. The questionnaire was itself a form that emerged from the Spanish imperial chancery and was used, famously, to find out about the geography of Spanish America.[2] The literature on "relazioni" that developed in Italy converged with that of the questionnaire in focusing on real conditions, whether of government, economy, religion, or war. If José Acosta might have been a familiar name to Peiresc, Giovanni Botero certainly was, and Ulisse Aldrovandi was an early correspondent. Peiresc's study of non-European societies is a reflection of their successful model of inquiry.[3]

In Peiresc's Mediterranean system, merchants above all, but also missionaries, were the ones providing him with relations. Merchants were often best placed to provide the kind of intelligence reports we associate with diplomats. Careful attention to bureaucracies, to fiscal regimes, and to military power was necessary in order to function commercially *in partibus infedelibus*. From Algiers, long before Napollon entered the scene, Peiresc had received from another merchant, Guillermi, a very interesting document that was an analysis of the population, military, and government of Algiers. It belongs to a genre of political analysis that typified the age of *raison d'état*. The document began with population. There were about 200,000 inhabitants before a recent onset of plague. The census that followed enumerated 30,000 Turks, 97,000 Moors, 10,000 Jews, and about 20,000 slaves—suggesting that about 50,000 people had died. The author then turned to the number and organization of soldiers and sailors, to galleys, to the Western prizes taken, and to the names of the Provençal barques taken, all of which were copied onto a roll held by the French vice-consul in Algiers.[4] The *relazione* takes its place amid a series of similar presentations of Algiers to a European audience.[5]

A dozen years later, much more sophisticated political-economic-geographical relations on the current state of Egypt came to Peiresc from the Marseille merchants Cesar Lambert, Jacques Albert, and Santo Seghezzi. These documents should be seen as an extension of the intense curiosity of Peiresc and his merchant friends about the economic position of Egypt.[6] For instance, Jean Magy prepared for Peiresc an entire mémoire on the sub-Saharan caravan trade ("entre l'Aethiopie et le Maroc"). After discussing the nature of their currency (cowrie shells), Magy explains that with their gold the traders buy 500,000 or 600,000 écus' worth of goods in Cairo—this would be an astonishing amount if it were accurate, which we cannot be sure of, as it is more than five times the volume of Marseille's entire Levantine trade at the time—including Italian silks, corals, paper, lead, pewter, copper, and quicksilver.[7] Magy adds that "Maugarbins" (Maghrebis) from around Tunis often joined this caravan, as did the Ethiopians, who brought gold powder. The gold powder came from negotiations with barbarous peoples along the way, and they also brought with them elephant teeth and ostrich feathers. Magy gives an ethnographer's account of the wordless negotiating process used among these peoples, who did not speak each others' languages, as well as their commercial good faith.[8]

In June 1635, Peiresc reported to de Thou of the arrival in Marseille of Sr. Portal from Egypt (via Livorno) on the *Ste. Anne*. Portal was the "parent" or close relative of Jacques Albert, then in Egypt, and he bore two letters from him, as well as the copy of a "mémoire that he composed on the state of the provinces of Egypt." Albert said he acquired this information with difficulty "from those who frequent the public places where were kept the acts and legal registers of the Sultan," and which came at a cost in caresses and persistence.[9] It was in the postscript of his letter to Albert of February 1634 that Peiresc introduced the question of the mémoire. Apparently, Albert had kept a journal with essays. Peiresc wanted a copy and, to sweeten the pot, mentioned that it would not be for him only, but for others, just as he had done already with a mémoire on the same subject drawn up by Cesar Lambert.[10]

Peiresc wrote again in October informing de Thou that he was awaiting a letter from Albert in Cairo and "a very particular relation of the lands of Egypt." He had just recently recovered another very precise and succinct relation.[11] It is likely that this earlier one—indeed, terse by comparison—was Lambert's, which dates from sometime after 1627 but before 1631. Peiresc would eventually receive a third, from Seghezzi, on the "Revenues of Egypt."[12]

Lambert's mémoire was labeled by Peiresc "The Relation of Cesar Lambert of Marseille of the Remarkable Things He Saw in the Years 1627–31 in Cairo, Alexandria, and Other Cities of Egypt."[13] It takes the form of a cultural geography. Lambert began with the citadel of Cairo, and the way in which its internal organization reflected the shape of the basha's government. This then led him into discussion of some of those subgroups, such as the janissaries. Down from the castle one entered the town, and Lambert described the marketplace. He noted that direct trade with the Indies had dwindled, so that it was now the Europeans who were importing cinnamon, ginger, and pepper, "which makes trading in Cairo so miserable, and as a consequence, the city less flourishing."[14] Still available were wools, leathers, and textiles, many coming from Yemen or Ethiopia (f. 216v). Foodstuffs were in abundance, and people had distinct ways of consuming them (f. 217v). The discussion of domestic space and decoration, and then of clothing (f. 218v), although not extensive (one page) brings us right up against Goitein's account of daily life in Cairo found in volume 4 of *A Mediterranean Society* (1983). In addition, Lambert pays attention to the decoration of the palace, with "antiques" and objects of gold, silver, and precious stones warranting special mention (f. 220r). Lambert followed with a long description of the wells, cisterns, and irrigation system that served the castle and surrounding gardens (ff. 220v–221r). He offers a long discussion of the ceremonies surrounding the official beginning of the Nile's inundation, as well as a survey of the fruits and vegetables grown in its fertilized soil (f. 222r).

There is a brief description of the monasteries of Wadi Natrun (f. 224v) and of the lands along the Nile, rich with villages and economic activity (ff. 225r–v). Two leagues from Cairo stood the place called "Matalie," where Mary and Joseph were said to have halted with the baby Jesus. Lambert gives a long description of the site and its buildings, well (replete with inscriptions in Hebrew characters), and lush plantings (ff. 226r–v). Lambert follows the itinerary of the Holy Family to a house in Old Cairo ("Fustat") where they rested, to the very room and floor upon which Jesus reposed, then marked by a cross. The place was well tended by the Copts, who at the time became the subject of their own extended description (f. 228r). No visit to Egypt could have been complete, even then, without a trip to see the Pyramids (ff. 228r–229r). Lambert also entered one of the "imperfect" pyramids along the Nile and describes the funerary chamber (f. 230v). The route to the Red Sea from Cairo allows Lambert to mention the departure of the Children of Israel under Moses (f. 232r) and the "rare and remarkable things in infinite number" of the Red Sea (f. 232v). The mémoire concludes with Lambert's description of a visit to Alexandria (ff. 233r–236). Because of its many associations with classical and Christian history, this part of the relation more resembles the genre of *mirabilia*.

Lambert's relation draws on two venerable traditions: the traveler's account and the pilgrim's. To it he adds a contemporary sensitivity to the natural world and its human economic role.

This side is emphasized still more in Jacques Albert's "Memoire ample de l'estate de l'AEgypte" (1634). Albert's mémoire began by identifying the officials of government, the basha or "viceroy," and his subordinates, the *Beglabey* and heads of the *Sangiat,* or guard.[15] After describing their authority, he gave their salary in currency and as measured in grain. The work and structure of the divan is discussed next. Then come the caravans—the number of camels (1,500), speed (thirty-six or thirty-eight days to Mecca), the number of soldiers who accompanied the treasury (500) and their various names. Albert then turns to the number and disposition of Egypt's garrison, paying special attention to the names, ranks, and authority of different subordinate officers. A tabular division of the militia into cavalry and foot, then subdivided by units, is followed by a discussion and enumeration of castles, especially in the area of Alexandria and Cairo. From there, Albert turns to different administrative units, and from governors and governorships to customs districts and customs collectors. The first tax "farm," Bouar, handled all the merchandise from Mecca, Mocha, and India. The second, including Alexandria and Rosetta, had to make heavy payments of 30 bourses to the basha, 220 to the sultan, and around 12,000 piastres' worth of silk fabrics and wools for the basha's army.[16] The farm of Damiette, which made similar payments to sultan, basha, and soldiers, drew its revenue from the "entry of merchandise from Turkey, such as grains, oils, soaps, almonds, as well as other goods come from Gaza, Sidon and Damascus, all of which are levied at 10%." Meanwhile, caïques from Turkey and Cyprus brought rice and legumes, though, Albert notes, the duty on these was negligible.[17] The farm of Burlis brought in its revenue from dates and fish, these latter of which were salted and shipped to Crete and from there to the rest of Greece.[18] And so on. Albert's mémoire, with its careful attention to fiscal-administrative matters, moves into a very different world than Lambert's.

This new political-economic focus is fully realized in the third mémoire, Santo Seghezzi's "Revenue of Egypt."[19] Right from the start Seghezzi signals its sharper edge: it is no longer a "relation" and no longer a coherent narrative. The document moves from region to region, and subregion to subregion. Seghezzi identifies the form of government and its dependency, and he indicates the nature of its economic life. Thus, for example, the document begins with "Sayt" or Said, "a great big place, where in other times resided the Bascha of Constantinople. At present it is governed by a Sangiat of Cairo sent by the Bascha who governs through the same council as Cairo. He has under him 14 governors for the 14 little provinces, and when the Nile rises it returns all kinds of wheat without end."[20] The aforesaid governors "are absolute and there is no appeal beyond them, neither for peoples' life, nor for their goods."[21] Each region, save Sayt, was composed of 360 villages, though over time some had decayed or been replaced. Seghezzi then listed the rents of twenty different governorships, as well as the taxes imposed on *dhimmi*, Jewish and Christian nonbelievers, women and children under the age of sixteen, on smoking, and on various legal documents. He also provided an account of the customs income from different areas, such as Alexandria, Rosetta, and Damiette, as well as the amounts brought in on different objects (foods, skins, horses, and the dead). Rights, such as bearing arms, were also taxed. Seghezzi even provides a conversion into French money of account (25,000 silver "Maidins" of Egypt came to around 700 French écus).[22] Then there was taxation in kind; the amount of wheat handed over to the government in lieu of tax from six governorships is given, along with the observation that this reflected an absence of silver. Most interestingly, there is also an explanation of the unit of volumetric measurement employed: "A *Reddebe*, which is the measure of wheat in Egypt, comes in France to a weight of about 300 pounds."[23]

From revenues, Seghezzi turned to expenses. He first listed the "emoluments" given by the basha to the different provincial governors, measured in "purses" ("bourses"). He then gave the amounts extracted by the customs officers at different customs houses, and proceeded down to the various local bureaucrats, all of whom received something, including translators, scribes, justiciers, and the intendants of finance.[24] An additional cost was a per capita payment made to the family of each deceased soldier. On the other hand, whenever a landowner died, the tenancy returned to the king or basha to redistribute for additional profit. Of anyone whose goods were seized, a part could be gleaned by the basha. But as these revenues were uncertain, Seghezzi kept them out of the account. The cost of various ambassadors and embassies is given—to Mecca and to Constantinople, both in monies (bourses) and in amounts of wheat. Imams of various Cairo mosques were also subsidized out of the public purse, and Seghezzi gives the amounts.[25]

By the later eighteenth century, a term was invented for just this kind of analysis. *Statistik,* as we know it from its brief heyday, was a synchronic form that combined information from political economy, ethnography, and geography. Its leading theorist, Ludwig August von Schlözer, a professor at Göttingen, described it as "history standing still" (and history as "statistik in motion"). Looking at Schlözer and his colleague Johann Christoph Gatterer from the perspective of early modern antiquarianism demonstrates a clear family resemblance.[26] Peiresc and his merchant friends, in turn, show something of the path from the Spanish imperial questionnaires to political economy.[27]

33 ⌘

Peiresc's Mixing in Cairo's Consular Politics

$\mathcal{G}$ overnance in the Échelles was always a problem. Sanson Napollon first worked for Peiresc during his special appointment by the king to sort out the consulates of the Levant in the middle of the 1620s. The trips of Picardière, Gédoin (equally Gédoyn) "le Turc," and Deshayes, likewise, all had more or less official, reforming dimensions.[1] The structural problem of having merchants govern themselves and, on top of that, represent the French nation to the local powers could not be resolved.

The situation in Egypt had a direct impact on Peiresc's life. For while the conflict between Savary de Brèves and the consuls of Marseille over the vice-consulate in Alexandria in 1624–1626 did not draw in Peiresc, that between Philibert de Bermond and Santo Seghezzi over the consulate of Cairo in 1634–1635 very much did.[2] This, too, was set in motion by a de Brèves, this time the son, Camille Savary, who obtained royal approval for his plan to withdraw authority from Philibert de Bermond and replace him as consul with Santo Seghezzi.[3] (In June 1633, Peiresc was still referring to Bermond as "Consul des français en Egypte Alexandrie.")[4]

When Peiresc first mentions Seghezzi, he tells de Thou that although he did not know him personally, he had heard only good words about him from the Levant, save from the family of the ousted consul, Bermond.[5] Seghezzi's advent did indeed ruffle feathers in the close-knit community of French-born merchants, many of whom viewed their posting as a cash-raising opportunity. Seghezzi's brother-in-law, Alvise Luigi Gela, was based at Marseille, and Peiresc wrote him soon after—in Italian, so there would be no harm done—urging him to advise Seghezzi to reconcile with Jacques Albert, who had many powerful friends at court. Again, here, Peiresc demonstrates both a very granular local knowledge of the merchant community in Egypt and a sense of how these local divisions mapped onto those at the volatile French court.[6]

The controversy between the former (Philibert de Bermond) and current (Seghezzi) holders of the consulate also brought out splits in the merchant community in Marseille, with Bermond initially marshaling much greater support.[7] Moreover, Peiresc explained that Albert, who was his friend and who had done good work for him over the years, had turned against Seghezzi and assumed that their long friendship would silence Peiresc. Instead, Peiresc asserted his "customary freedom" ("franchise accoustumée") to tell de Thou the truth: Albert was not good at managing the immense difficulties of operating in a place like Egypt, where his credit was "nothing" compared with that of Seghezzi. Indeed, while it seemed that Albert's credit—and Peiresc used it both literally and figuratively—was declining, Seghezzi's was on the increase.[8] Peiresc was explicit about Seghezzi's personal behavior; he comported himself with "an economy and moderation" that never failed. Moreover, having embraced France—there had been some misunderstandings between him and Venice—Seghezzi espoused its interests more readily than all others. Just as France was happy to employ the "arms and sword" of the king of Sweden against Austria and to fund the Dutch in order to harm the Spanish, there was no harm in hiring a Venetian "in order to oppose Turkish barbary and the bad behavior of the French." It was Seghezzi who stood between the collapse of the French position in Egypt and the triumph of the Dutch ("& si vous n'ouvrirez pas la porte aux Flamantz & aultres nations"). Finally, Peiresc, concluded, it would be a mistake to ignore Seghezzi's practice in favor of his place of birth. It was "a very dangerous counsel, and without reason," to assume that his origin trumped "the interests of France, which are more attached to the correspondence of the French merchants than to the formality of origins."[9]

Surveying other French consulates across the Mediterranean, Peiresc found a Venetian representing France in Venice and a Genoese in Chios, and until recently a Genoese had done the same in Genoa. Moreover, he continued, those Marseille merchants lined up behind Bermond were unrepresentative of those who actually traded with the Levant and knew about commercial conditions there.[10]

Jean Magy also wrote to Peiresc on Seghezzi's behalf. He thought the accusations were lies—"A thousand things, all false"—and that Seghezzi had been a friend of the religious at all times, and "rendered signal services" on their behalf. The charges had to come from Bermond and his circle alone, "because from here, no one who is a merchant made any complaints against him." It was a "canaille" whose end "would be the total ruin of our nation in this country." If Seghezzi had taken a strong stand at all against the missionaries, it was in telling them "to act moderately" and for their own benefit, "because the Turks, Moors, Greeks, Jews and Copts are murmuring against them, and giving him advice to safeguard them from ill."[11]

Bermond headed back to France in December 1634 to plead his case.[12] Seghezzi, stuck in Egypt, had to use his words. To the consuls of Marseille in September 1634, Seghezzi addressed a long letter explaining how precarious the situation in Egypt currently was. During the twenty-three months of Bermond's consulship, he writes, Bermond had extracted 23,000 piastres from the merchant community to defray debts and communal costs, but the debts of the community as a whole had mounted to 40,000 piastres. Meanwhile, Seghezzi had been given no authority to access the accounts of the French nation, and the creditors were demanding a 36 percent commission on money transactions. Seghezzi wanted to institute a 5 percent charge to be used to pay off these mounting debts, which he thought could be accomplished in two years. Still, the overall situation *was* bad. Customs officers in Alexandria routinely overestimated the value of cargoes by more than 50 percent in order to be able to extract extra-high duties. In Rosetta, corruption was so endemic that no one wanted to trade there. On land, several of the French had taken to renting taverns, not realizing that the death of any Turk there in a drunken brawl—and Seghezzi presents this without comment as if a normal occurrence—would result in disastrous punishment for the French community as a whole ("ce qui seroit pour ruyner & exterminer la nation"). Meanwhile, the baker who provided bread for the French in Alexandria charged 25 piastres a year—Seghezzi implies price-gouging—and the butcher who provisioned the ships charged 1½ piastres for what was not worth more than 1.[13]

Reading these details of merchant costs, one realizes that under such hostile conditions there had to have been profits being made or no one would have endured it all. In a follow-up letter, referring to Bermond, Seghezzi proclaimed that "it is not my nature and, on the contrary, it is to do good to those who have done me ill."[14] In this letter he adds one more name to our collection: Pierre Mercurin, whom he identifies as "my agent in Alexandria."[15] The report of two members of the merchant community who were finally able to inspect the books of the consulate concluded that Bermond owed the merchant community 2,633 piastres, 16 medins.[16] In December 1634, Seghezzi summarized the situation in Egypt and noted that he had convoked two merchants to serve as his deputies and liaison with the merchants, and these were Antoine Mazarat, one of the two authors of the October report on Bermond's debts, and none other than Jean Magy.[17] By early in 1635, Seghezzi's position seems to have worsened, as his letter to the consuls of Marseille contains an explicit rebuttal of the "calumnies" being spread about by the Bermond faction.[18] Of course, Bermond for his part complained right from the start about "the malice and wickedness of those that wished to calumniate me."[19]

As the Seghezzi-Bermond controversy unfolded, Peiresc used it to build an archive. When Gabriel Fernoux, de Brèves's long-standing vice-consular appointment in Alexandria, passed through Provence on his way to court, Peiresc asked him to prepare for de Thou "a little memorial or instruction on the present state of the affairs of business in the Levant."[20]

The initial legal decision favored Bermond.[21] But Peiresc was not much deterred and, in any event, this was only the first act of a longer ballet. Peiresc preserved a series of letters from Seghezzi directly to de Thou. These targeted the latter's interest in oriental antiquities. In September's letter, Seghezzi promised to seek in the cabinet of curiosities of a friend, as well as in his own, for an appropriate object to send de Thou.[22] In the end, Seghezzi chose an "idol" from his own collection to send on an English ship. But along with this news of a forthcoming gift, he took the liberty of informing de Thou of the pressures he was under from a cruel and unrelenting basha on the one hand, and the machinations of Jacques Albert "with 2 or 3 of his supporters" on the other. Finally, Seghezzi was sending as an additional gift an animal presented to him by the "Basha of Labech," who had originally intended it for the sultan. Some thought it related to the unicorn. Seghezzi's wish was for it to be presented to the king. At the end of the letter, Seghezzi got around to reminding de Thou that once upon a time he had asked de Brèves *"to obtain for me some formal letters patent of the King or Council carrying such orders sufficient to contain our merchants in their obligations."*[23]

The next stage in the controversy involved the French merchants of Egypt sending a delegate to France. Jacques d'Altoviti, representing the Seghezzi faction, passed through Aix on his way to Paris.[24] Peiresc announced d'Altoviti's forthcoming visit in a letter to de Thou of April 1636 and pronounced him "so well informed" of Egyptian affairs that he could answer any question. Peiresc warned of the threat to French commerce that would ensue if the king and his council did not turn their attention to goings on in Egypt. Decades earlier, facing a similar crisis, de Brèves—again appearing as the figurehead of the Mediterraneanist faction to which Peiresc was recruiting de Thou—had acted decisively and saved his position as well as France's.[25] Letters from Seghezzi to de Thou were

sent via Peiresc, along with one addressed to Peiresc that apologized for
the gifts all being intended for Paris, and gratefully acknowledging his
assistance. Seghezzi promised to send some "bella anticaglia, ò libro."
But "time and opportunity" were needed ("tempo e commodità").[26] The
idol arrived in Marseille by year's end.[27] Seghezzi also informed Peiresc
that Bermond had bribed the basha to extort money from him, and accused him unfairly of pocketing customs revenues. Especially interesting
was Seghezzi's observation that the superior of the Capuchins had joined
Albert, "mon cnncmi," in spreading false rumors of his hostility to them.
Machinations among the missionary orders seem to have been endemic in
the European expatriate communities of the Levant.[28]

By the end of 1635 Christophe de Bermond had replaced Seghezzi,
and in a letter to the consuls of Marseille announced that the account books
of the French nation had been officially handed over to him by Seghezzi.
De Bermond, in turn, denounced Seghezzi's "abusif" practices which were
"contrary to the forms" of long standing.[29] De Bermond had triumphed.
His position was confirmed by the king for four more years in late 1636.[30]
But only in 1637 did Seghezzi actually stand aside for Philibert's brother,
Christophe de Bermond. Seghezzi remained in Cairo, where he became
known as a leading dealer in antiquities.[31]

In Oslo, at the Sixth Congress of the Historical Sciences, Marc Bloch
delivered one of his most famous lectures, outlining why a comparative
medieval history was important and how it could be done.[32] A side trip,
afterward, to Stockholm with Henri Pirenne generated an even more important formulation, at least for us here. Having just arrived, Bloch tells
us, Pirenne turned to him and asked, " 'What shall we go to see first? It
seems that there is a new city hall here. Let us start there.' Then, as if to
ward off my surprise, he added: 'If I were an antiquarian, I would have
eyes only for old things, but I am a historian. Therefore, I love life.' "[33]
For Bloch, who loved life a great deal—his bookplate showed a man
pressing grapes into wine—the difference between history and antiquarianism was between being committed to the here and now and of
somehow being absent from this world.[34] A couple of centuries earlier, this
difference was figured in terms of *Ancients versus Moderns*. By now, after
following Peiresc through the details of his negotiations, interventions,
and manipulations of the consular politics of Cairo, it is clear that either
Bloch's definition of the difference between historian and antiquarian is
false—antiquarians could also care deeply about the present, and could
believe that their work served it—or Peiresc was no antiquarian.

34 ᧕
Peiresc and Travel

*P*eiresc was committed to travel as a form of learning. We know that he himself traveled abroad, to Italy in 1599–1602 and to the Low Countries and England in 1606–1607. His library was full of travel books.[1] And he sponsored their publication, too: the Latin translation of al-Idrisi's *Geographia Nubiensis* and Van Schouten's *Relation Exacte* were published with his patronage. He brought in Nicolas Bergeron, who had already made order out of François Pyrard *(Voyage contenant sa navigation aux Indes orientales, Maldives, Moluques et Brésil, depuis 1601 jusqu'à 1611)* and Jean Mocquet *(Voyages en Afrique, Asie, Indes orientales et occidentales)* to edit, arrange, and publish the travels of the Marseillais Vincent Blanc.[2] From Bergeron he learned of the publication of *Purchas His Pilgrimes* and its arrival in France.[3] Peiresc had excerpts of Purchas and its table of contents copied out for him. His plan was to organize a translation.[4] Peiresc's archive contains many travel accounts in manuscript form. These include autograph copies of Jérôme Maurand's *Itinerario e viaggio dell'armata navale di Barbarosa sino in Levante* [after 1544] and the *Discours du voyage faict en Levant par le sieur de Beaulieu de Pairsac, par le commandement du feu roy Henry le Grand* [1608–1610], as well as the relation of the "Voyage which was made by land from Paris to China by the sieur de Feine de Montferran" ("Voyage qui a esté faict par terre de Paris jusques à la Chine par le sieur de Feine de Montferran") and another to Persia, simply indexed as "*1598:* Voyage to Persia."[5] Of the farther east, Peiresc preserved a copy of a letter written by Augustin de Beaulieu from Bantam in 1617.[6]

The 1598 voyage to Persia includes what is probably one of the earliest, if not the earliest, recorded mention of the great trilingual set of inscriptions carved into the mountainside at Bisitun. There was a "mountain of living rock on which are seen many figures of men and beasts with Greek inscriptions." Time did not allow for more detailed investigation, and Montferran thought it an image of the Ascension—not so surprising given the presence of the winged Persian deity.[7] Peiresc himself later refers to the site in a letter of 1628 to Pierre Dupuy. A "Le Tenneur," who was the son of the "greffier" of the council—likely of Aix or Marseille—who was his "bon voisin et ancien amy," had returned from Persia, where he had seen "a mountain all engraved and figured with great Histories in relief, using the stone itself, all of a piece on the side of the mountain, which is a very rare and very marvelous work."[8]

Another text, describing a pilgrimage to Jerusalem ("VOYAGE DU Sr. RAIMONDIN/EN HIERUSALEM") contains much information about the Holy Land and its environs but also about the Westerners one encountered on such a trip—and many of these, it turns out, were Provençaux in Peiresc's wider circle.[9] For instance, heading south from Aleppo on the way to Damascus, Raimondin met Jean l'Empereur—the Marseille merchant and consul general in Jerusalem after 1621—and turned off to look at many ancient ruins, perhaps the late antique villages of the lime-stone massif discussed by Chris Wickham.[10] At Jenin, in the Samarian highlands, the group received a message from Sanson Napollon, then consul in Aleppo, containing a letter from the grand vizier commanding their good treatment. Back in Tripoli, the group dined with M. Aguil-lonqui of Marseille, French consul at Tripoli—and later to become an-other of Peiresc's correspondents.[11]

Finally, of course, Peiresc personally planned and outfitted the two expeditions of Théophile Minuti. Minuti's letters were fully attentive to practical details of travel, as if aware of Peiresc's precise preferences. After describing being robbed by corsairs and dumped on a Cypriot beach, Minuti enumerated all the things taken from him in the hope of legal res-titution. But this also gives us a rare window into what kinds of things people took with them on a voyage. Minuti's gear consisted, he writes, of "a coverlet, a cape like those of Marseille, a pair of boots, three pairs of shoes, a hat, an undershirt, a Turkish-style robe, a cloak, 10 handkerchiefs, 3 hoods in the Minim's color, my medicines, which consist of theriac, a concoction of hyacinthe and water . . . and other things needed for my trip."[12] Similarly, when preparing to depart Aleppo by caravan to Con-stantinople, Minuti gave an account of what he was taking to eat for his forty days in the desert: biscuit, wine, oil, *eau de vie,* vinegar, salt, lentils, beans, rice, and *bottarga,* as well as bedsheets, a cape, "and lots of other things."[13] Describing Minuti's departure to Peiresc, Jérôme de l'Isle added to the list, as if in amazement, "a little bit of onion biscuit, a vegetable pilau, with a little pot ("pignatte") for making his soup." "I do not know how this good man can live traveling in this land," he continued, "without eating meat or at least butter and eggs." Still, with all this limited fare,

Minuti "is in very good health and appearance, with his long beard that comes down almost to his belt." Travel was costly, though; the mount alone, de l'Isle tells us, cost 27 piastres—more than half the cost of Peiresc's famed Samaritan Triglot.[14]

Peiresc the historian of travel was also Peiresc the promoter of travel and the conceptualizer of travel as a form of research. His work fills a gap that Joan-Pau Rubiés has discovered in the French cultural history of travel. Between Montaigne and Descartes, Rubiés writes, the French "reception" of travel and its literature was channeled into epistemic debates and away from the *Ars Apodemica* itself. Against this backdrop, Peiresc's own commitment to gathering and publishing travel literature, as well as his own consistent formulation of "instructions for travelers," seems much closer to Rubiés's English model. (This may also help explain why there was such a profound English reception of Peiresc and a comparative French neglect of him.)[15] It was in his harnessing of Marseille's commercial dynamism to his own intellectual curiosity that Peiresc was able to accomplish so much.

35 ✌

Where Mediterranean Meets Orient: Ethiopia, India, Yemen

*D*e Brèves in 1619 thought it was time to redescribe the arena of France's maritime world from the Levant to the Mediterranean: "the seas of the Levant or, to say it better, the Mediterranean Sea."[1] But Peiresc's Mediterranean reached out, via Egypt, to touch an Orient bordered by the Ethiopian highlands, the Malabar Coast, and the Yemeni seas.[2] Looking out to this farthest Mediterranean, the Mediterranean that Braudel taught us to see, actually helps us perceive features, perhaps otherwise less visible features, of the smaller, inland Mediterranean.

At this limit, then, we turn back to some of our major themes, to the role of commercial actors in learned projects, to the very personal character of Peiresc's nearly worldwide web, to the ambition and diffusion of the Marseillais in the early seventeenth century, and above all, of course, to Peiresc's curiosity, which was not contained by distance or dispirited by the intractableness of human nature.

Merchants, mariners, and missionaries; dockworkers, lackeys, and muleteers; consuls, governors and local bureaucrats—they fill Peiresc's Mediterranean. But jewelers and goldsmiths need to be included in this story as the great unsung heroes of early modern long-distance cultural communication.[3] Adam Smith's observation in book 3 of *The Wealth of Nations* that the "unnatural and retrograde order" through which Europe emerged from the ruins of the Roman Empire came by way of the pursuit of beauteous "baubles and gee-gaws" leads us directly to this discussion. But while the tendency in recent decades has been to shift away from the heroic tale of long-distance trade toward the unglamorous but more local trade, the kind of coastal tramping that for Mediterranean histories is synonymous with "cabotage," what we see here is that the two are consistent with one another. The most distant trade routes in Peiresc's Mediterranean, those to India, Yemen, and Ethiopia, were all conducted stepwise, just like the day-in-and-day-out trade of Marseille with Genoa and Civitavecchia, or Barcelona and Chios. The difference is only one of the number of steps and the scale of the final voyage. India, Yemen, and Ethiopia may have been farther away, but they were all steps out from Cairo, and Cairo just happened to be at the end of a whole other series of short steps from Marseille. In Peiresc's Mediterranean, even at its farthest extent, all trade was local.

Why were there so many jewelers and goldsmiths on the move? They must have been in search of rich commissions and rich materials with which to work. Some echo of this French goldsmithing of the seventeenth century has survived in the al-Sabah collection in Kuwait.[4] The bigger answer has to do with an intensifying global market in which consumption in one corner drew in producers from another. The very high-end work represented by the French—by the early seventeenth century already seemingly dominant in this part of the luxury trade—might explain their relatively easy success with the great oriental potentates.

Almost a century ago, Charles de la Roncière suggested that the jewelers preceded the missionaries as agents of French influence in the Near East.[5] Looking through the lens of Peiresc's archive, we see Bertier in Cairo, Vermeil in Ethiopia, Herryard in Lahore, Jaloux traveling to the Deccan, Cassertz and Da Costa going back and forth to Goa, and Pelissier planning his enterprise in Yemen. We even possess a letter of Peiresc's to the bishop of Mans, from the last months of his life, commending to him a Sr. Bouttier de la Val, who had gone to Italy "to make himself more expert and more worthy of recommendation, in his art of goldsmithing and diamond-setting, where he has become so excellent that he has received preference everywhere he has stayed, above all the other goldsmiths of his vocation." De la Val had taken a wife in Genoa from the family of the leading goldsmith there. For leaving the country, his family was trying to disinherit them. Peiresc made the point that he should not be punished, since he was just like those other subjects of the king who had traveled outside the kingdom and resided "not only in Christendom, but in deepest Barbary and the Levant" ("non seulement en chrestienté mais jusques dans le plus profond de la Barberie & du Levant"). One hears in Peiresc's justification of de la Val the experience of all these other jeweler-travelers.[6]

Not long after he returned to the south in 1623, Peiresc told Pierre Bergeron that he had a friend in Marseille who had made a trip to Mogor and the Deccan.[7] Three years later Peiresc wrote again to Bergeron. The unnamed traveler was again heading east to the Indies. He had just now written from Aleppo saying that he had done some translating for the visiting François-Auguste de Thou, and was going directly to the Deccan via Persia in order to draw up his memo on site—a memo about whether diamonds could be found. "He is a very well informed man, and very truthful," Peiresc concluded, "a fact that gives me high hopes for his work."[8]

Mixed in among Peiresc's notes on Islamic coins in Marseille collections is the name "Nicolas Jaloux." On 4 April 1626 we learn that Peiresc "purchased for 6 Suzidas of Nicolas Jaloux de la Verdière, worker in precious stones, who took a trip to the Indies, Babylon, Hormuz, Goa and the Kingdoms of the Deccan and Golganda [sic], from which he brought back the rubies that he sold me; the rulers there are Mahometans but the people for the most part are idolators of serpents, cows and other animals, like the Egyptians."[9] Peiresc notes that one of these stones had come "from the Kingdom of Golgonda [sic], a tributary of Mogor, in the year 1622."[10] Peiresc added three subsequent entries to this memo on the reverse, dated "1626 7 Decembris" and "1627 22 Martii."[11] The third and last note, at the bottom of the page, puts Jaloux in motion: "He had to leave for another voyage to Persia the 20th August 1627 on the barque of Patron Viguier, relative of the Consul of Aleppo."[12] Peiresc wrote to him there on 30 October 1627 "in the envelope of Isoard his brother-in-law."[13] He was in Aleppo by November, and wrote from there to Peiresc.[14] In his letter of 10 November, Jaloux passed along news of the state of the country, "fort mizerable" and racked by war. He reported that he planned to depart within two months for Persia and then India.[15]

Peiresc made a stab at contacting Jaloux in July 1630, when he addressed a letter to the "gem-merchant presently traveling toward Persia and the East Indies" ("Marchand Lapidaire estant de present en voyage vers la Perse & les Indes Orientales"). Peiresc passed along news of his good health, despite the return of plague in Provence. He was relieved to read in Jaloux's most recent letter, from Aleppo, that he had had a favorable meeting with de Thou's former translator, who was prepared to accompany him to Persia. From there, Peiresc did not doubt that he would be able to pass on to India and the Deccan kingdom. He hoped Jaloux would acquire for him "the particular information" he desired concerning the nature and production of diamonds, about which he wanted a relation.[16] There was no reply to this letter, and by 1633 Peiresc had received news of his death.[17]

Jaloux was from Marseille. Augustin Herryard was from Bayonne.[18] Peiresc must have been fascinated with Herryard because he collected copies of letters written by him to others. In 1609 Herryard decided "to voyage to the Oriental monarchies, and not finding in Egypt, Arabia, Mesopotamia, Babylonia or Persia anything worthy of a king, I passed beyond to that King of the Indies commonly known as the Grand Mogor, or Mughal."[19] Herryard had arrived in India in 1612 in a party of Frenchmen, all of whom died. He entered the service of the king and rose up in the service of the king to make for him a royal throne full of gold and silver and involving "many other inventions, like cutting a diamond of 100 *guilats*" in ten days. Herryard asked his Constantinopolitan respondent to make a copy of the letter and send it to a M. Castauiac, a "merchant jeweler" ("marchant Jeolier") at the Place du Pales in Bordeaux. The letter was signed Augustin "Houaremand, which name the King has given me. In Persian it means inventor of the arts."[20] Indeed, in a later letter Herryard ended by saying that he was now serving the king as engineer in a time of civil wars.[21] His inventions included an armored chariot that shot arrows and burned those who approached it.[22]

The last document from Herryard in Peiresc's archive is the copy of a letter that he wrote seven years later—and they must have seemed despairingly long, if we remember that in 1625 Herryard was already aching to leave—explaining that he had finally received permission to depart. His wife and child were in Agra, and in seven days he hoped to be in Goa. Peiresc labeled the letter "Relation du pais des Indes ou du Mogor," and indeed it presents information about Shah Jahangir's family, and about the mineral wealth of Golconda ("the King of Goulouconda [*sic*] has thirteen diamond mines" ("terre fort riche en or, et le Roy de Goulouconda a 13 mines de diamantz"), or about the throne he was just then making for the king at Agra.[23]

Finally, Herryard had heard—but how?—that the servant of his friend Jacques Peyron-Selly was residing in Basra for six months. Herryard believed that his correspondent, Bermon, had received his letters, and that he had given an account of the goods that had been shipped on his master's account. In other words, while working as a jeweler for the Mogul king, Herryard had found a way to export Indian products on his own, through Peyron-Selly, who must have been another wandering Frenchman in the East. The accounting given in the letter ran to 200 rupies, 1,000 "pataques" of goods that he had taken away, while acknowledging that Peyron-Sally ("son maistre") had lost 20,000 rupees' worth of goods coming from "Mechelipatan" in Pegou, or Burma.[24] Just a few years later, when Tavernier was visiting Agra, "Augustin de Bordeaux" was still very much a living memory.[25]

We cannot be sure how Herryard's letters came to Peiresc. But we do know that the one letter Peiresc wrote to Herryard he sent via the jeweler Henriqué Alvares in Paris, and it is likely that Herryard's letters came to him from the same source. Alvares was, for Peiresc, the point of entry into a whole network of jewelers and goldsmiths with operations in India. He had a brother named Fernand Nunes (also called Guillaume Corner) from Hamfort in Holland. He was married to the sister of a man named Manuel da Costa Casseretz. Manuel, in turn, had a brother named Gaspar da Costa Casseretz. These family ties were summarized by Peiresc in an undated memo, probably prepared in 1630 when Fernand Nunes and Manuel da Costa visited Peiresc at Belgentier, likely at the direction of Alvares.[26] They arrived on 16 July and left on 19 July carrying letters for Jaloux, Herryard, and Gaspar da Costa.[27] While there is no mention of this fact in the Peiresc archive, that of the Inquisition in Lisbon reveals that they were a family of Portuguese New Christians.[28]

A second letter triggered by their passage was to the brother already in India. Addressed to Gaspar da Costa in Goa (and in his absence to Francisco Tinoco de Carvallo, and in his absence to Ruy Lopes da Silva), Peiresc, after the requisite preliminary pledges of service, asked for information about the kinds of places in which diamonds, rubies, and other precious gems were found. In order to reach him, Peiresc suggested that they write to the French consuls in Aleppo, Sidon, and anywhere else in the Levant, all of whom would be able to communicate with him. An alternative would be to address communications to the king's officers at Marseille, Toulon, or anywhere else on the Provençal coast, with whom he also had easy connections; or in turn to Paris, addressed to M. Dupuy or M. de Thou.[29] The third letter occasioned by their passage was to M. Jaloux, the jeweler from Marseille. This would be Peiresc's last attempt to reach him before learning of Jaloux's death in India.[30]

Immediately after their departure, perhaps as an afterthought, Peiresc dashed off a brief letter to Fernand Nunes and Manuel da Costa—described here as "Marchands Lapidaires"—asking them to seek out in the Levant, Holy Land, or Persia some Jew or Christian "or other" who knew something about mathematics and astronomy. If such people could be found, Peiresc would then establish a correspondence with them and ask them to make astronomical observations of solar or lunar eclipses. This marks a step toward the comparative eclipse observation of August 1635.[31]

Nunes and da Costa must still have been in port in mid-August 1630, because Peiresc was still writing to them and forwarding a letter from

6 August, responding to the letters they had written him at Peiresc's in mid-July. He reminded them of his desire for some small precious stones and some account of the physical environment—the landscape and soil—in which they had been found. The letter was accompanied by one to the captain bearing them eastward, Bermond the Younger of Ollioules, a town near Toulon.[32]

When they eventually left for the Levant and India, they carried with them a "Memoire pour les Indes" that Peiresc had drawn up for them.[33] Peiresc began by noting their willingness to carry letters to Gaspar da Costa in Goa, to Augustin Herryard at the Mogul court, and to Jaloux, if and where they crossed his path. Peiresc then turned to content, and focused almost entirely on diamonds, precious gems, and where they were found. He would pay for an impression in lead, plaster, or sulfur, especially for the best workmanship. He would also take an impression of any large ancient gold medals.

As Peiresc turned from natural history to human culture, his mémoire became a guide to acquisitions—and thus a reflection of his own priorities. If there were weights for sale, he would take them, especially those in Samaritan characters, but not in Greek, Latin, or Arabic, presumably because he already possessed many of these. He was not interested in copper coins with inscriptions in Latin and Arabic but he was very interested in those written in Greek or Samaritan characters, "which resemble them a bit" ("ou qui les ressemblent à peu prez").[34]

From the ancient cities of Persia and India, whose ruins Peiresc had heard so much about, he hoped they could "make some sketch of the most beautiful structures, figures and low reliefs that can still be seen there, and above all inscriptions that could be there, whether in Greek or barbarous [languages]." He ended with an explanation of how to make sketches of inscriptions. Later he instructed Thomas d'Arcos in Tunis and Zacharie Vermeil in Ethiopia to make squeezes, and not to trust the eye to capture the shapes of strange scripts.[35]

The memo then turned back to natural history and, in particular, to shells and fossils. Were there any there "like those in Europe," he wondered? If there were other kinds of petrification, especially coral, he would be delighted to have them. If there were large, living shelled animals in the "seas of India," he would like to have a drawing or sketch of them. He then ran through a list of specific creatures of which he wanted documentation, if they existed there.[36] He concluded with questions about plants and bezoar stones.

By December 1630, Peiresc had gotten news of Nunes and da Costa's arrival in the Levant. He wrote to Christofle de Bermond, thanking him for the care he had taken in conveying his letter to Nunes "to the deepest East" ("au fondz du levant"). He was glad for the news of them that he brought back from there. Peiresc was pleased to learn also of "the conservation of commerce amidst war, which is a mark of good faith that ought to give great shame to Christians who do not know how to comport themselves with as much dignity as the infidels."[37]

The most extensive of the connections between Peiresc and the jeweler-goldsmiths, and the most long-standing, was with Henriqué Alvares. Letters to him begin in May 1633, but Peiresc had known of him much earlier, referring to him in July 1630 as the "celebre Alvarez de Paris."[38] In the first surviving letter, Peiresc reminded Alvares of the note he had received from him in 1630, which he had immediately passed on to Nunes and da Costa, and the thank-you note he had subsequently received for performing this service. From his contacts, Peiresc wrote, he had heard that Nunes had remained briefly in Aleppo while da Costa proceeded directly to Goa. He had also just received news of Augustin Herryard, "rather fresh given the distance of the place," which he wanted to pass along, though he assumed that Alvares had better communication with him. Peiresc wished to hear any news at all that Alvares might have of their common friends.[39]

Alvares replied on 12 June that Peiresc's letter filled him with joy and gratitude for the courtesy shown to his brother-in-law. He had himself just received letters from Goa dated 5 April saying that all were well. Having learned of Nunes's "great skill" ("grand pratique"), the king of the Deccan took him into his service. Meanwhile, Manuel da Costa was ready to depart for "the Manillas, which is in Japan and of China" (*"les manilles* qui *est en Japon e della a la Chine"* [*sic*]), referring, it would seem, to the Philippines. He had conveyed news of a clash between Dutch and Portuguese ships, along with information about the wars of the "Grand Mogor." Alvares passed along information about an increase in the price of diamonds on account of "the difficulties caused by the Chinese beginning to take pleasure in the joys of diamonds" (*"rencheris a cause que les chinoies commancent a prandre plesir aux joeux de diamants"*) and the corresponding impact on supply (*"tous les diamants de la europe ne seront pas assez a envoir de dela"*). Via the Portuguese carracks, Alvares explained, he was always receiving "particular relations" from all the lands up to China.

He ended by thanking Peiresc, in turn, for news about Herryard, "whom I knew very well at Lahore and knew his parents at Bayonne."[40]

Peiresc was pleased with all this news from the world of *converso* jewelers, wishing Nunes well and da Costa luck with his travels to Manila and China. Their successful arrival reawakened in him the desire for some rock samples—as he had spelled out years earlier in the "Memoire" he prepared for the two travelers.[41] Peiresc then followed up on the autobiographical information that Alvares let slip in his letter—that he knew Herryard in Europe ("en Chrestienté") and at Lahore; and that Alvares had received his information via the Portuguese carraques. This caught Peiresc's eye. Given the limited contacts of Marseille's merchants with Spain and Portugal, Peiresc was especially keen to have access to Alvares's contacts in Lisbon: "If it was possible to learn of your correspondents in Lisbon where it seems there are some, I would very much want to know them, to take some addresses for me when on occasion the barques of Marseille might go there to recover for my money, plants and fruits from the Indies." In a reflection of how much latitude he was comfortable assigning to the mercantile intelligence, Peiresc noted that when these plants and fruits came to Europe fresh ("fraiz"), it would be useful to him if someone could "check the taste and conserve the seed of those that could be domesticated, whether in vases or clay pots." At the moment, he added, "I do not know anyone in that country, and the Marseillais have very little established contacts there though once they did, so that the mariners on their barques cannot fulfill their commissions as comfortably as those of the country, having neither the addresses nor the credit that is sometimes needed for this."[42]

With this letter, one new subject—India—becomes intertwined with an older one—ancient weights and measures, and in particular liquid measures, of the sort that fed Peiresc's quest for vases. In Alvares's letter to Peiresc of 22 August, he replies to Peiresc's questions about specific vases in Paris; he explained that he could not get for him rubies in the rough and commented on letters that he had received that very week from the Casseretz brothers at Goa, sent on 8 February, and transshipped from Lisbon on 11 July. They wrote that Herryard and his family were at Goa, where Herryard was involved in negotiating a truce between the English and the Portuguese. Manuel da Costa was given the charge of "councillor" by his father, who wanted him nearby and would therefore be returning to Europe. Fernand Nunes was "in the greatest authority in the Deccan," and it was said in Goa that he was "entirely governing that land."[43] In his reply of October 1633, Peiresc thanked Alvares for the news of da Costa and Nunes and for sharing his Iberian connections.[44] In a letter of 28 November, Peiresc said he would write to them by the next Marseille ship that went in that direction.[45]

This Indian initiative might have tempted Peiresc. There is some indication that he might have proposed, or hoped, that Minuti, on his second mission in the Levant in 1633, would himself continue on to India, but it came to nothing in the end. In a letter to Aycard from October 1633, Peiresc adds, as a postscript, "it was necessary that the voyage to India be canceled since, on the contrary, Father Théophile was on the point of leaving in order to return [home]."[46] And yet the idea of an Indian expedition persisted. In a letter to Aycard of 1634, Peiresc welcomed the return of the brother of his late nephew Salvator, who had been in Damascus, with either a real emerald or some kind of bezoar. But then Peiresc added that if he would consent to a voyage to the Indies, "give me your approval, as I would write to my friends that I have there, both French and Portuguese."[47]

From Jean Magy, in July 1633, Peiresc learned of Zacharie Vermeil, a goldsmith from Montepellier, and likely a Protestant, who had wandered on to Ethiopia. "Sr. VERMEIL of Montpellier, a Gascon," Peiresc noted, "who makes emeralds and artificial medals, has gone off to Ethiopia, where he is a favorite of the Emperor." In February 1634 Peiresc sent Vermeil one of his most extraordinary letters, an example of his letter-writing and gift-giving art at its highest.[48] Nevertheless, his questions for Vermeil, packed into that long and exemplary letter, focused on the antiquities of Ethiopia rather than its mineral wealth. History, in particular the Christian history of Ethiopia, was what most interested him. For precious and semiprecious gems, and for jewelers and goldsmiths as swashbuckling pioneers, we need to turn to a third geographical zone, Yemen.

We might think of Yemen as far from the Mediterranean, though S. D. Goitein long ago and Roxani Margariti more recently have shown us that Yemen was closely connected through Cairo to the Mediterranean's trading network, even as it sat athwart the sea lanes of the Indian Ocean that joined East Africa to India.[49] More surprising still is how present Yemen was to Marseille's merchants in the age of Peiresc.

In March 1626, a few Marseille merchants gathered to talk about Persia, prompted by a letter from Peiresc and his gift of Louis Deshayes de Cormenin's *Voyage en Perse*.[50] In his reply of 20 March, Gaspar Signier,

Peiresc's banker, lamented the general condition of the Marseille trade. He explained how he, Vias, and Durand, all friends of Peiresc—the former, like his father, consul of Algiers and the latter a consul of Marseille—had been talking about the way commerce had been managed. Signier bemoaned the interventions of those who knew nothing and did not understand how weakened the city's trade had become:

> That a company of 300,000 écus would be small and yet one does not know how to make one of 10,000. Because you must know that our vaisseaux going to the Levant, which bring 400,000 écus today, are content to bring back 15 or 20,000 at the most. . . . Our nation is the worst of all, impatient and incapable of staying in the place and furthermore the English are now erecting a barrier and go to load their silks at Hormuz and then in a few days a vaisseau comes to London with 600,000 bales, and in the state we are in, none of our vessels can carry 30, and yet on other occasions one alone could have carried 15,000. I think that the late M. Viaz and Durand would say the same.[51]

What is interesting here is not only the insider's sense of things, and the precise numbers he provides, but also his recognition that it was the English who were now posing the major challenge to the Provençaux by loading silks at Hormuz, bypassing the Levantine emporia of Alexandria and Aleppo, and then shipping huge quantities back to England in their heavy merchant ships. That the merchants of Marseille were speaking the language of state-centered economics long before Colbert is not surprising.[52]

We have Vias's thoughts on this subject because we possess the letter he wrote to Peiresc summarizing the discussion. The three had discussed together an idea of Deshayes de Cormenin, who had been sent to the East by Louis XIII in 1621, that Marseille should conduct direct negotiations with the king of Persia. Shah Abbas had restricted the export of Iranian silks in 1619, drying up the Aleppo trade and pushing the French into Sidon and Tripoli, where they bought cheaper Lebanese raw silk.[53] The prominent Marseille merchants with whom he talked about this did not think it could work. There was simply not enough money in Marseille to drive the trade—he thought at a minimum one million écus were needed annually to buy the Persian silks directly, not to mention the costs of ferrying them by caravan to Aleppo and the other Levantine ports. Moreover, the

caravans were now organized by the Persians, Jews, Turks, and Armenians, who knew how to control costs, "which would be impossible for
the French," so that it would cost three times as much. But the single
biggest problem was the poverty of Marseille, whose whole Levant trade
now did not go beyond 80,000 or at the most 100,000 écus, and whose
single richest merchant did not put more than 8,000 or 10,000 écus into
the trade on an annual basis. Nor would the Persians be interested, Vias
thought, in an exclusive deal with Marseille, since everyone wanted their
silks and the Dutch and English most recently had even started coming
to Hormuz to get it. He had spoken with "M. Boër, secretary and archi-
vist at the Hôtel de Ville," who showed him a thick dossier of royal letters to Marseille outlining the powers ("qualités") of the first president of
the parlement, and of the consuls. Vias concluded that Signier and Durand would write to Peiresc directly and that, in any event, they were more
experienced in trade.[54] These letters document not only a strategic discussion of trade, but put Peiresc right in the center of it alongside merchants and government officials.

The English changed the game by extending the Mediterranean to
Hormuz. The initial Marseille response was to think of Persia. But once
the Mediterranean had been stretched eastward, Yemen was the next step.
A year after this conversation, a letter from Gabriel Fernoux in Cairo to
the premier president d'Oppède at Aix, a copy of which must have been
passed to Peiresc, who in turn sent it on to the cabinet Dupuy, began with
a description of Yemen and its place at the hinge of the Indian Ocean–
Mediterranean trade. It was "situated at the entry to the Red Sea, across
from Ethiopia, where all the ships dock that come from the Indies charged
with spices and other goods of high value, from which the ministers of
the Sultan extract a great revenue from the duties that they have established in Yemen, in a place called Moca [al-Mokka; Mocha, or Peiresc's
"Moucal"], which is on the sea." All this revenue had just been lost because of a rebellion that had broken out in protest at the rapaciousness of
the rulers—taking money from the rich and withholding it from the soldiers' pay.[55] Lacking galleys or ships of any kind capable of ferrying
troops across the Red Sea, or the necessary supplies, all the Ottomans could
do was to send a new basha armed with sweet talk. Fernoux thought this
unlikely to succeed at restoring Ottoman control.[56]

By the spring of 1629 Peiresc was soaking up news about Yemen, and
already viewed it as a place of significance.[57] The Peiresc archive reflects

this focus on the Red Sea theater, the mirror-image, from the other end of the Mediterranean, of its recognized importance in Cairo as a source of wealth, beginning circa 1600 and continuing into the eighteenth century.[58] At the end of 1629, in the intemperate postscript to his deeply hurt-sounding letter to de Thou, Peiresc signaled as among the highlights of his collection—he was then explicitly trying to evoke in de Thou a sense of how much he had missed by not bothering to visit him—petrifications of shells, plants, and marine fruits "of which many are so strange and so remarkable, that one recognizes there plants that are only found in the depths of the Red Sea, and great shells or snails similar to those of mother-of-pearl that are fished for along with oriental pearls, from which the Chinese make such beautiful drinking cups, and what is more there are marine fruits so curious and also so bizarre that one could hardly conceive."[59]

At the mouth of the Red Sea was Yemen.[60] Peiresc's several memoranda on the state of Yemen reflect its connectedness to Cairo and the Mediterranean as they synthesize face-to-face conversations with excerpts from letters. In the very first of these Peiresc focused on the alabaster vases (stones, again) that came from Yemen. "VASCULA ALABASTRINA EX IEMENIA" was the filing title. He draws seven different vessels in the left margin (the shape of the objects and the ductus is the same as in the later memorandum of Magy, suggesting Peiresc's hand), with the Arabic and Turkish names in parallel columns, and the identification of function in the fourth column, on the right side of the page.

The explanation, extracted from the conversation between them, is as follows: "These vases"—Peiresc's old interest—"of *mineral Bezoar* are made *in Yemen* on the other side of the Red Sea where there is *a mountain* entirely of this stone which they call IASA or *GEZA*. The Laborers work in small huts in the fields; even the house of the Sultan is covered in rushes."[61] Peiresc identifies his source as "MATTOUK CHIASSAN of Aleppo, from a good family; he had been to the sites in Yemen and had seen those vases being worked, the stones being cut, and their being worked in the round."[62] To Jacques Gaffarel, Peiresc wrote that the Bezoar vases were brought to Cairo from Mocha and that according to the merchant community, the mines were not far from there.[63]

Less than a year later, Jean Magy came to see Peiresc upon his return from Egypt. In the note summarizing their talk on 7 July 1633, Magy wrote, "You will know that at Moucal Camson Basha was killed, and the Grand Seigneur lost the whole country of Yemen."[64] The document "VASCULA

ARABUM/AEGYPTIORUM," which analyzed vases in Cairo, derived from another conversation with Magy, as it was captioned "from a Moor of Cairo, in the report of Jean Magy son of Agostin of Marseille" and dated Aix, 29 July 1633.[65] But the discussion of vases seems to have led directly to a discussion of Yemen, since we find below the drawings of objects Magy's report on the caravan connections to Yemen (via Mecca, it took forty days), its system of government, names of government officials, and the trade goods that came from there.[66]

In "Aden, or Heden," the Magy mémoire continues, people live for two hundred years—hence the name Arabia Felix. It was ruled by a prince who was called "Chiacharab" (shaykh al-'arab?), and who was richer than the others, and it bordered Persia, with the sea between them. The prince rebelled against the sultan, paying his militia in foodstuffs and places in paradise, "of which he claimed to have the disposition in his role as Sherrif, descended from the race of Mohammed." He had seized the village of Senam (Sa'na?), where the basha resided. From politics, Peiresc turned to the land's natural products, such as incense, myrrh, aloes, *nux vomica*, and "the coffee which the Moors call Ben." In Arabic *bunn* refers to unground coffee beans. From his sources, Peiresc had arrived at a fairly accurate description of a drink that would not appear in Europe for another decade.[67]

We know from a letter that Peiresc wrote to Magy of 17 May 1635 that he had written another mémoire on "the present state of the land of Yemen and of the pieces coming from the land of Abais to Suakin, on which there was much to discover." We know that Magy communicated news of Yemen and Ethiopia to his brother of Marseille, who then passed it along to Peiresc.[68] In May 1636 Peiresc was thanking Magy for "the news of Yemen" and "that of the caravan of Dacroy, about which I would very much want to have a very detailed relation."[69]

Egypt was like the edge of Europe, from which reports on the wild East and South—Yemen and Ethiopia—were sent back.[70] Peiresc makes this point in the postscript of a letter to Jacques Albert in February 1634, distinguishing Egypt, for which he was able to collect real statistical information, from "the other lands more distant and more completely strange." These were the lands "of the caravans that go from Cairo, whether in the direction of Africa or the Abbysinians, or the direction of Moucal or Arabia or the Indies." If Albert's friends could provide any solid account of these, "I would take great pleasure in seeing all of them" ("je prendray grand plaisir d'en voir toutes").[71]

With everything that we know of Peiresc, it is no surprise that his closest connection to Yemen came through a relationship to a Marseille-based jeweler. Peiresc seem to have come into contact with Benoit Pelissier through a letter of Pelissier's written on 12 April 1631 and sent via de Gastines. Peiresc's reply of 25 April thanked Pelissier for the good will shown to two clerics, one of whom was Daniel Aymini, and hoped for a future relationship—making clear that they had none as of yet.[72] In June of 1631, Peiresc was advising Pelissier to arrange a meeting with Marcheville, then in Marseille before setting sail to Constantinople. Peiresc thought that "all those who mixed in trade had a right and obligation to go and greet him." Peiresc would have made the presentation himself, he said, but for the ill health that prevented him from undertaking even a short trip.[73] By later in the month the meeting had still not occurred, and so with Pelissier in Aix, and Marcheville making a pilgrimage to the shrine of the Magdalen on the Sainte Baulme, Peiresc suggested that Pelissier go there to meet him.[74]

In July 1631, Pelissier informed Peiresc that he was departing again for Italy and wanted letters of recommendation from him. He reported to Peiresc on his receipt, from Cairo, of a Chinese god made of porcelain like one he had seen at Peiresc's. He passed it on to de Gastines on condition that he would give it to Peiresc. He also gave de Gastines the sword he wore on his left shoulder in exchange for a gilded one, and a bonnet and long robe in exchange for a "revolver with bayonet" ("poignard pistolet") that had originally belonged to the "grand Prieur" of Mecca. The Chinese deity had captivated him: "As for *this dervish and Chinese saint*, it is perfectly well made and has something of piety and religion about it that one knows not how to say." He could not easily understand it, "thinking to myself that had it been buried, it would have so drawn my senses to its contemplation that I would be an idolator for more than an hour."[75] Peiresc was charmed by these objects, but responded warily to Pelissier's romantic response to the "Chinese dervish or santon." "[You found it] so capable of moving you to piety," Peiresc replied, "by contemplation of its cold and devoted bearing. But I do not know how it could be compatible with the sacred you are armed with." He concluded by saying that he would come to look at it the next time he was free to come to Marseille (Figure 32).[76]

Peiresc's relations with Pelissier between 1631 and 1635 are undocumented. But by winter of 1634–1635 a plan had evolved to send Pelissier to the Red Sea. A memorandum that Peiresc preserved in his dossier on

Figure 32. The Chinese idol. Paris, Res. Est, Aa 54, f. 37. (Bibliothèque Nationale de France)

"Turcs: Voyages" outlines this project and provides us with some precious biographical details about Pelissier. "Instructions pour le Sr Benoict Pelissier allant au Moucal" is presented from Peiresc's point of view (and in his words) as if for submission to court. De Thou was the likely recipient, with the hope that he could arrange the necessary bureaucratic support for the project.

From this memorandum we learn that Pelissier was a native of Aix who now resided in Marseille, from which he had made many trips to the Levant. He wanted permission to establish himself at some place in the East where there was not already an official French presence. Two possibilities lay on the Turkish Aegean coast: on the island of Kos near Rhodes, and the port of Bodrum on the mainland nearby.

But the main thrust was to establish an outpost at Mocha on the Red Sea. To this, the memo devoted four long paragraphs. The site offered a means of tapping into the luxury trade not just of Yemen ("Arabia Felix") but also of the Indies and Ethiopia. It was from Mocha that the wealth of the Indies came to Cairo, whence it was exported to the rest of Europe. Because the current French consul in Egypt was Seghezzi—underlining the importance to Peiresc of the conflict over the consulate—who was said to have greater credibility ("plus de creance") than any other consul in the East, it was now possible to establish "le commerce et la correspondence" between a French Cairo and a French Mocha. Because of Pelissier's good will and disposition, he would be able to link to Goa and other Indian ports, "the contact being quite ordinary from Goa to Mocha, and from Mocha to Suez or to Mecca, just as the regular caravans also go from Cairo to Suez and Mecca." Ethiopia was also easily reached across the Red Sea, and because of the presence there of Vermeil, who would certainly prefer to be in contact with Europe ("Chrestienté") via France than through Portugal and Spain, an outpost in Mocha would give France preferential access to the Ethiopian trade as well.[77]

Peiresc thought carefully about these issues and discussed them in his correspondence from this period. In December 1634, writing to his brother-in-law Henri de Seguiran about Seghezzi, he mentioned among his valuable contributions the ability to reestablish French commerce in the Levant as he had already established "correspondence at Monquas [Moucal], which is almost at the mouth of the Red Sea where all the East Indies embark." The Turks were now in control of the city and its hinterland. "I will one day make you a relation with projects," Peiresc concludes.[78]

Pelissier traveled to Paris in February 1635. It was for this occasion that Peiresc drew up the memorandum about establishing an outpost in Mocha. He also drafted a series of letters to interested Parisian parties. To Villeauxclercs, the secretary of state, Peiresc explained that Pelissier had traveled a great deal in the Levant and was looking now for some official support or employment, or an official title of "lapidaire" or "Joyellier." This would empower him overseas in his negotiations without running afoul of the local goldsmiths and jewelers who had their own rights and privileges.[79] Peiresc's wish was duly fulfilled by the secretary of state.[80]

To de Thou, Peiresc wrote that Pelissier was seeking support at court for his establishment at some place where he imagined being able to create commerce. The key was to exempt Pelissier from the overall authority of neighboring French consuls, who would either try to undermine any competition or to skim off its profits. Pelissier was petitioning Cardinal Richelieu and those in charge of commerce to establish him at Mocha where he could link up the trade of Ethiopia and the Indies. Peiresc suggested that

there was a value to the public of opening up a commercial channel outside of the Spanish and Portuguese and that Santo Seghezzi, then consul
in Egypt, would be a valuable assistant because of his knowledge and familiarity with the region.[81]

A week later, Peiresc wrote again to de Thou. In case de Thou had
somehow forgotten, Peiresc wanted to remind him of Pelissier's proposition to go to Mocha, to which the commerce of Aden had been transferred and from whence many merchants from Goa, Callicut, and beyond
embarked, and also from Ethiopia on the other side of the Red Sea. It
was by this means that goods from the Orient came to Cairo. "If this was
reestablished," Peiresc wrote, "as seems not so difficult, the commerce will
be much shortened and well ordered with the French merchants of Goa
and Mogor, and the consulate of Cairo will be worth more." It would be
difficult, he wrote, to find someone better equipped for a project of this
sort. He concluded that whatever start-up costs were involved could be
covered by the king or the young M. de Brèves—de Brèves senior still
casting a long shadow over the French Mediterranean.[82]

Peiresc wrote to his friend Alvares to inform him of Pelissier's plan
and to solicit, insofar as it was useful, his support and that of the merchant community, since on it ultimately hung the success or failure of Pelissier's venture:

> Knowing the customs and correspondences you have in the East In-
> dies, and having learned of the plan of Sr. Benoit Pelissier of this
> city of Aix to go and live in the city of Moucal, which is on the coast
> of Arabia Felix very near to Aden on the other side of the mouth of
> the Red Sea where the commerce and shipping are so frequent . . .
> you could possibly find it worthwhile to hold some kind of corre-
> spondence with him, to share news of your friends in those lands of
> the Indies by that way, which is the shortest, since from Mocca to
> Mecca by way of Suez and Cairo, the commerce is very frequent,
> and from Cairo to Marseille even more so. He has traveled in the
> Levant and made a particular trade in all kinds of stones and other
> things that could in some way fall to your taste. That is why I be-
> lieved that you would not find it disagreeable that he make some
> offer to you of his service, and that he would find from you a good
> welcome.[83]

In August 1635, Pelissier wrote to Peiresc that he was going to visit
"my colleague M. Jacob Vermeil, brother of the one who is found in Ethi-

opia." Ironically, this other Vermeil was then living at Bastion de France, Napollon's old home. Pelissier decided to go visit him in the hope of persuading Vermeil to accompany him to the Red Sea. Pelissier hoped that the possibility of seeing his brother again would clinch the deal. But one more amazing coincidence is in store for us: Pelissier explained to Peiresc that he had independently been charged by Alvares to buy coral for him when at Bastion, though the commission itself had been— apologetically—rescinded when the outbreak of war with Spain led to the cancellation of many orders.[84] What we are seeing here is the outline of an entire community of long-distance traders in semiprecious stones and gems.

Also in August 1635, Peiresc wrote to Magy asking for news of "Suaquin," the port of Egypt on the Red Sea, "or of Mouqual."[85] In October, Pelissier was visiting chez Peiresc and provided the third testimonial in the naturalization process on behalf of Jean Magy's wife and son.[86] In November, Peiresc was writing to M. de la Tuillerie, the French ambassador in Venice, to notify him that Pelissier was going to Venice for a "difficult contention" with someone there and needed protection.[87] At the same time, Peiresc wrote to Gela asking him to write to his Seghezzi in-law there to intervene on behalf of Pelissier in a "negotiation" he had there involving money left in deposit for him.[88]

The next letter to de la Tuillerie, of 17 June 1636, reported the sad news that Pelissier had been attacked, was wounded, and died at Livorno. He had passed along this information in a previous letter which he presumed had gone astray.[89] In February 1637, Peiresc was reporting him murdered in Venice. He was still trying to locate the goods Pelissier had amassed in Venice but that had been stranded there and lost with his death.[90]

Pelissier could have become one of those shadowy figures, like Peyron-Sally, who established private import-export businesses based on now-untraceable contacts in far-off lands, taking great uninsurable risks in hope of uncountable profits. Or he could have become a government-backed official, a small-scale Sanson Napollon, who used connections and geography to turn commercial advantage into a political bridgehead for France.[91] His success would have earned a place alongside the extraordinary goldsmith-jeweler-adventurers who sought out the rarest luxuries of the East and in so doing built bridges for those who followed. But instead, Pelissier disappeared from history, lost to everyone except Peiresc, with his amazing archive. With the disappearance of this archive, in turn, the entire story of Marseille's quest for the distant Mediterranean also slipped beneath the horizon.

36 ๛

At the Still Point

ate in the summer of 1624, his first since returning from Paris,
Peiresc traveled the short distance from Belgentier to Toulon,
hired a small ship and crew, and went fishing for coral "in the
sea of La Ciotat, by Bandol, to the south of Caudalon [the rock of Can-
delon, 23 km to the north], at a mile and a half out to sea and 3 miles
from Bandol." The plot is from notes made by Peiresc of a conversation
with a coral fisherman, Jean Caulne of La Ciotat, likely the person who
took him out on the water.[1] Gassendi, basing himself on these notes, described in detail the process, the instruments used, what was fished up,
and how Peiresc studied the objects.[2] On 6 September Peiresc sent a box
containing a piece of coral—perhaps a souvenir of this expedition—to
one of his Roman correspondents.[3] A few years later, to another Roman
agent, Jean-Marie Suares, the bishop of Vaison-la-Romaine, Peiresc reflected on this experience: "In the past, I had the pleasure of going in
person to see this fishery, where I observed a thousand little singularities
of nature that I really regret not having recorded in writing while of fresh
memory as it warranted, the authors not having treated this material as
exactly as I could have done."[4]

It is a precious image, this, of the forty-four-year-old but already rather
frail Nicolas Fabri bobbing about on a flat September sea while the rough-
and-tumble fishermen deployed a large wooden or metal rake, which
they dragged along the sea floor as he watched closely and plied them with
questions. He, of course, could not have known it, but he was at a turning
point in his life. Though among the most cosmopolitan of his countrymen,
and sharing so many interests with colleagues living in Italy, the Low
Countries, and England, the man we know as Peiresc was profoundly
marked by what would happen next: thirteen years immured in the Aix-
Belgentier-Marseille triangle. These were years working closely with men
like Gassendi, who would represent him and his commitment to observation and experience to a world uninterested in the old dogmas of Aristotle or the newer ones of Descartes. But these were also years spent
working closely with nearly anonymous ordinary people like Jean Caulne

of La Ciotat, the coral fisherman. As we have come to accept that there were many Montaignes, not only the writer in his tower, so, too, there were many Peirescs: not only the austere humanist, the judge, courtier, political operator, and traveler but also the friend and companion of fishermen, merchants, and mariners.

The Peiresc on the water was the Peiresc who was always engaged with people, regardless of their status; who was interested in nature, in techniques, in change, in continuity, in matter, and in ideas. We see him here in close and comfortable communication with fishermen and artisans, just as elsewhere his projects were bound up with "merchant bankers," "merchant *patrons*," and "sailor-businessmen." And, above all and always, we see his love of research: his characteristic attentiveness to detailed observation, the awareness of the necessity of archival preservation, and the sense of serious play. These have made possible the tour we have taken of Peiresc's Mediterranean, in the company of all these merchants, mariners, and missionaries.

And what might Peiresc have been thinking of while bobbing on the sea? Beyond what I have related in the previous paragraphs, or in the previous hundreds of pages, we cannot be sure: about whether Fronton le Duc would ever return to England the *Cotton Genesis* that Peiresc had borrowed on his behalf; about whether the young scion of the de Thou family would grow up to be his father's son; about whether Richelieu would maintain or even tighten his grip on Louis XIII; about whether the war in Europe would spill over into the Protestant towns of southern France; about whether being a parlementaire would take too much time away from his scholarship; about the health of his father, which was just then beginning its decline. Or he might have been thinking about the underwater archaeological expedition undertaken by Leon Battista Alberti and Flavio Biondo in 1447 on Lake Nemi, southeast of Rome, which turned up Roman imperial ships and maritime apparatus, and wondering whether in the future someone would liken his coral-fishing expedition, raking up artifacts from the sea floor, to their antiquities-fishing expedition of nearly two centuries earlier.[5] Perhaps he even wondered about his own posterity, and whether he had made the right choice in forswearing family and children. Indeed, almost endless are the thoughts that we could imagine running through Peiresc's head, association after association, as he stared out onto the sparkling face of the deep that September day.

As much insight as we have into Peiresc from the vastness of his surviving archive—probably more than we know about any other scholar of his age—there is still a limit to how far we can pursue the reconstruction of his very thoughts. For unlike Montaigne, Peiresc did not make it his project to reflect on his life in writing, or draw together its many different threads. It is here, therefore, at the land's edge, that the antiquarian and the novelist, who have walked alongside one another all this way, must finally part company. Only the novelist can go further, and make something more of this moment upon the sea.[6]

APPENDIX A
Peiresc in History, 1637–1932

APPENDIX B
Peiresc's Letters to the Levant, 1627–1637, Analyzed

APPENDIX C
Patrons *and Captains*

✄

Abbreviations
Notes
Acknowledgments
Index

Peiresc in History, 1637–1932

*T*o begin with, Peiresc's presence is marked in the publications of local *érudits* just after his death.[1] Although the scholars of international repute to whom he was closely bound, such as those in the Cabinet Dupuy and the Barberini Circle, memorialized his passing with published expressions of grief, it was only Pierre Gassendi's deeply sympathetic biography of 1641, reprinted in the Netherlands in 1651 and 1655, that attempted to survey his work.[2] Indeed, despite all the protested devotion of friends, when Peiresc's wastrel nephew, Claude de Rians, put his working papers up for sale in 1646, and one of those friends, Gabriel Naudé, came shopping on behalf of his employer, Cardinal Mazarin, he made no effort to acquire Peiresc's personal papers. Alas, there was no one in France at the time like Samuel Hartlib: as early as 1634 he argued for collecting the working papers of scholars.[3]

In fact, it was Hartlib who, after Gassendi, was most responsible for Peiresc's posterity. He organized the translation of the *Vita Peireskii* into English as the *Mirrour of True Nobility and Gentility* (1657). The book was dedicated to John Evelyn, who was set up as "the only man I ever heard of in England whose *Peireskean Vertues,* did challenge this Dedication."[4] A generation later, deep into the "Scientific Revolution," Peiresc remained the polestar by which the English virtuosi were navigating. Writing to Evelyn himself after the death of Robert Boyle, Samuel Pepys exclaimed, "Pray let Dr Gale, Mr Newton, and my selfe have the favour of your company to day, forasmuch as (Mr Boyle being gone) wee shall want your helpe in thinking of a man in England fitt to bee sett up after him for our Peireskius."[5]

One volume of Peiresc's papers was soon after purchased by the family of the same Galaup-Chasteuil who had been Peiresc's collaborator at Aix and then correspondent in Lebanon. Seven, and perhaps as many as ten, were acquired by "Sibon," a local *parlementaire,* and others by another Aixois, the apothecary Toussaint Lauthier. The rest of the archive attracted no interest and was allowed to decay (and perhaps was destroyed through negligent handling). It was saved from eventual destruction by the family piety of Louis Thomassin de Mazaugues, who had married Peiresc's grand-niece (Vallavez's granddaughter) in 1676. He gathered up what had remained in the family, and he sought to reacquire materials that Rians had sold off. Indeed it was he who chose for a motto "Tempus Edax Rerum"—Time the Devourer of All Things—making the act of recovering the past a personal goal. Peiresc was part of his public persona: in the collection made of letters sent to him we find one from Pierre Bayle thanking him for bringing to his attention the details of the Peiresc papers, and for his "patience and diligence" in serving the Republic of Letters.[6] Mazaugues died in 1712, but his heirs continued in his footsteps. By 1739, when Montfaucon recataloged the Peiresc papers, the Mazaugues family held eighty-three volumes, and in the next four years they acquired twenty-one more volumes. This material, amplified by some further small acquisitions, was eventually purchased by the bishop of Carpentras, Dom Malachie d'Inguimbert, in 1745. They form the "Collection Peiresc" of the current Bibliothèque Inguimbertine of Carpentras.[7] The Sibon materials were acquired by Michel Bégon (for whom the *begonia* is named) in 1688 and entered the Royal Library's collection in 1770 as Fonds français 9530, 9531, 9532, 9533, and 9534 and MSS. Latin 8957, 8958, and 9340.[8]

Because Peiresc's papers were not published, only those who had the sufficient motivation and skill to go to Provence and read the papers could know him. Others—the vast majority—had to rely on Gassendi's *Life of Peiresc*. Spon and Montfaucon belong to the former, Mabillon to the latter.[9]

Charles Patin, the great medalist, purchased one thousand of Peiresc's Greek coins and said that Peiresc was the only one of his time who could make sense of their inscriptions.[10] In his 1692 guide to the Cabinet of Sainte-Genviève, its keeper, Père du Molinet, published the core of Peiresc's material as something like a treatise on the Roman *as*. In fact, Antoine Schnapper has suggested that study of weights and measures in France in the seventeenth and eighteenth centuries was almost entirely based on Peiresc's researches.[11] The papers of du Cange in the Bibliothèque de l'Arsenal show careful attention to Peiresc's corpus—they include, for example, a copy of the catalog of his papers made for the Dupuy brothers.[12]

Leibniz seems to have relied solely on Gassendi for his knowledge of Peiresc.[13] Yet he was especially devoted to Peiresc, commenting often in his letters on the need for publication of the correspondence.[14] This derived in part from his sympathetic understanding of the antiquaries' achievement in establishing the category of "historical evidence."[15] But it also reflected his own sense of Peiresc's significance. Through the glass of Gassendi he saw that Peiresc was a great student of the Mediterranean, and offered him one of posterity's biggest compliments: "Aristoteles et Peireskius credunt . . ."—"Aristotle and Peiresc believe . . ."[16] Of the encyclopedists, Morhof, as we have seen, was highly impressed by Gassendi's *Life,* Gravevius waited expectantly for the publication of his letters, and Peiresc's collection of objects was carefully communicated in Neickel's *Museographia.*[17] A plan to publish some of the letters written to Peiresc by famous people was fairly well elaborated by the end of the seventeenth century, but it never came to be.[18] And yet, already Peiresc had become a watchword of sorts; Bishop Huet brought his example alongside those of Pythagoras and Socrates to demonstrate that one did not have to publish to be thought worthy.[19]

To the English antiquaries of the eighteenth century, Peiresc stood for "experience and practice" in "unriddling" antique objects, as against the "rules" implemented by Mabillon and Montfaucon.[20] But to the comte de Caylus, who featured objects from Peiresc's collection throughout his *Recueil des Antiquités,* as well as to Johan Joachim Winckelmann, who carefully read through the original copies of Peiresc's Roman letters in the collection of Cardinal Albani, whose librarian he was, Peiresc was a living presence.[21] Stories from Gassendi's *Vita* appear in *Tristram Shandy* and in Samuel Johnson, though the latter referred to him as "Pieresk."[22] To the enlightened of Europe, Peiresc appeared as one of their own: he was paired with Captain Cook as the subject of a prize essay competition proposed by the Academy of Marseille in 1783.[23]

The "Renaissance of Peiresc" began at the end of the eighteenth century in France and built on this, leading to the erection of monuments to him, both in stone and in print.[24] In Italy he was the subject of Ennio Quirino Visconti's attention for his commitment to high-quality reproduction of artifacts, and in Goethe's Weimar circle he was hailed as the "first archaeologist."[25] But at the very same moment, Ludwig Wachler, who knew much about antiquarianism in seventeenth-century France in general and about the work of Peiresc's friends in particular, did not mention Peiresc at all in his history of historical learning.[26] In England, D'Israeli very astutely celebrated him as the best example of "those eminent men of letters, who were not authors," thereby creating a category that could save Peiresc from the oblivion to which he was consigned by earlier historians of scholarship, like Wachler, for not having published.[27] By midcentury, enough momentum seems to have built up, at least in the South, to lead to a revival of the plan to publish Peiresc's papers (not the "letters" per se). It was, apparently, a casualty of the Revolution of 1848.[28] Another generation would go by before Peiresc would sufficiently intrigue the man of letters Philippe Tamizey de Larroque. It was he who launched the modern study of Peiresc in 1879, announcing a publishing project that was to print the letters of Peiresc.[29]

In 1880, Karl Bernhard Stark published his *Handbuch der Archäologie der Kunst* (1880), which Arnaldo Momigliano proclaimed in 1950 as the closest thing that existed to a history of antiquarianism.[30] The key figure in Stark's historical account was Peiresc. Stark hails him as "the great Peiresc," "one of the most universal men of modern times, the first archaeological critic, important more through his letters and personal communication than through writings. In him was united for the first time in Europe the breakthrough of the coming study of nature with literary erudition and sensibility for art." And Stark noted, too, that Peiresc lived—and still lived—under an unlucky star, an *Unstern* that affected also his manuscript *Nachlass,* "which even today is still not fully exploited."[31] We could say that a measure of how right Stark *got* the antiquarian tradition is just how precisely he *got* the importance of Peiresc. By comparison, Stark devotes a paragraph to Kircher, a paragraph to Maffei, a long paragraph to Cassiano dal Pozzo—which was surely unusual at the time, given that Lumbroso had published his *Notizie* only five years earlier—and *five pages to Peiresc alone.* This was more than he allotted to anyone else before Winckelmann (thirteen pages) and his century (Goethe received seven pages). Stark's survey of Peiresc's life is as detailed as anything published between Gassendi's *Vita* of 1641 and Henri Leclerq's biographical entry in the *Dictionaire d'archéologie chrétien et de liturgie* (1939).[32]

It would be hard to summarize Peiresc's achievement more succinctly than did Stark:

> The great and enduring importance of this man for archaeology lies, first of all, in his universal scientific position, that universal history along with ethnography and geography was the goal for the study of monuments; just like the prejudice-free, empirical and experimental study of nature, he considered a sharp, comparing, proof-driven observation of the object as a necessary condition of these studies.[33]

Ever perceptive, Stark recognized that comparison drove Peiresc's studies.[34]

Tamizey de Larroque began publishing Peiresc's letters with the Imprimerie Nationale in 1888, and he continued through 1898.[35] But a house fire destroyed his transcriptions and left this publishing process a damaged torso, with only seven of the proposed ten volumes of French letters eventually appearing.

Yet in that same year, Henri Berr, the innovative French historical theorist, wrote a book about Peiresc's best friend, Pierre Gassendi.[36] Berr described himself as among the "friends of Gassendi and Peiresc."[37] He began as a historian of philosophy, but between founding the *Revue de synthèse historique* in 1900 and the Centre de Synthèse in 1925 he emerged as one of the most interesting historical thinkers in Europe. If we no longer think of him in the same breath as Aby Warburg, that is our mistake. Like Warburg he was a philosopher of history, an institution-builder on the periphery of the academy operating across disciplinary frontiers, and a Jew. He published Henri Pirenne and Karl Lamprecht, and was the Parisian *patron* of Lucien Febvre and Marc Bloch, commissioning the former to write *La Terre et l'évolution humaine* for his book series, and the latter to write about the Île-de-France.[38]

For Berr, Peiresc and Tamizey de Larroque came to serve as a touchstone for reflection on the differences between the analysis—we might say "positivism"—of the *érudit* and the synthesis that he believed defined the historian. Berr's conclusion, in fact following Bacon, Leibniz, and Goethe, was that the preparation of source materials was not opposed to history but rather was the foundation of history—a *Hilfswissenschaft* in all but name.[39] Yet Berr, whose historical vision tended toward the complex collaborative research projects that he inspired in Paris in the 1930s and who is now viewed as the forefather of the *Annales,* also saw that the antiquaries' study of material evidence played the key role in exploding the subject of history from politics to social, economic, and intellectual life.[40] It was through Berr's notion of *synthèse* that "comparison" moved from being a subject fit for Durkheim to one fit for Bloch.[41]

With this, we return to Braudel and the Mediterranean. In 1930, just as Braudel was beginning his association with the "Société Bastion de France," he met Berr at a historical congress in Algiers.[42] On one level, Braudel's *Mediterranean* is the great expression of Berr's vision of *synthèse*. It introduces the notion of different kinds of time, to build, as Berr thought Tamizey and Peiresc did not, a work of narrative integration atop a broad factual base. Of course, as many critics from Bailyn to Hexter to McNeil have noted, the parts do not cohere and "Braudel, in effect, found himself with a collection of learned, delightful chapters on his hands, each fascinating in itself but only slenderly connected with what went before or followed after."[43]

Thus, even as the book's rhetoric—and its supporters—proclaimed a new kind of history, overcoming the narrow categories of people and events, the book itself *performs* like the old antiquarian literature. The point about the persistence of the antiquarian amid the modern-seeming self-presentation was made, gently, by Georges Huppert in the *Festschrift* for Braudel. That *The Mediterranean* could seem so novel was "in large part due to our ignorance of the history of antiquarian studies."[44] Precisely this tension—*our* tension—between narrative and research in *The Mediterranean* was singled out by Paul Ricoeur and Jacques Rancière in the last decades of the twentieth century as the paradigmatic example of the limits of writing in historical scholarship.[45] The book you have just finished reading is an attempt to go beyond those limits.

When Braudel met Peiresc in Algiers in 1932, he had already shifted his field of vision from Phillip II to the Mediterranean, from men to matter. That "choosing the Mediterranean," as Braudel later described it, did not mean having to give up on people was something he was unable then to see.[46] Whether he was "defeated" by the Peiresc archive or simply not interested in what it offered, we cannot say. What we can say is that discovering that this is not an either/or opens up new opportunities for the future of writing history.

APPENDIX B ↝

Peiresc's Letters to the Levant, 1627–1637, Analyzed

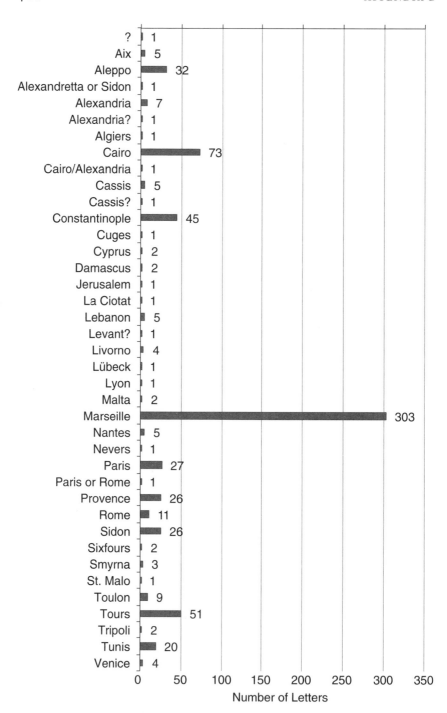

Chart B.1. Letters per location

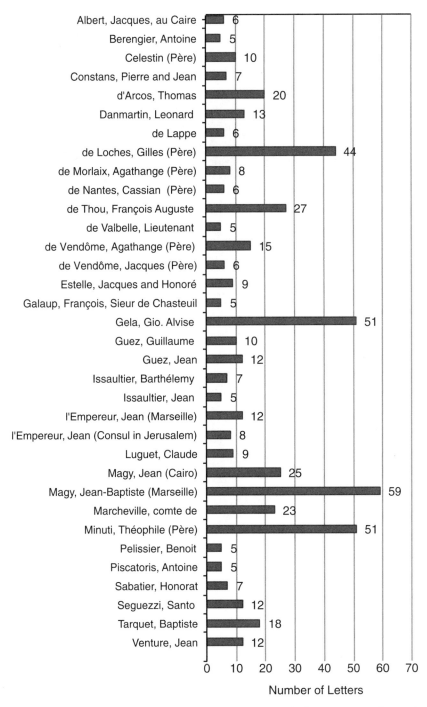

Chart B.2. Letters per recipient (recipients with four or more letters)

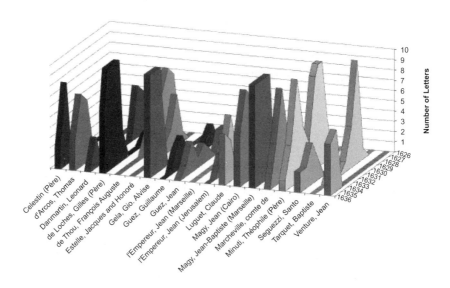

Chart B.3. Letters per recipient per year (top twenty recipients)

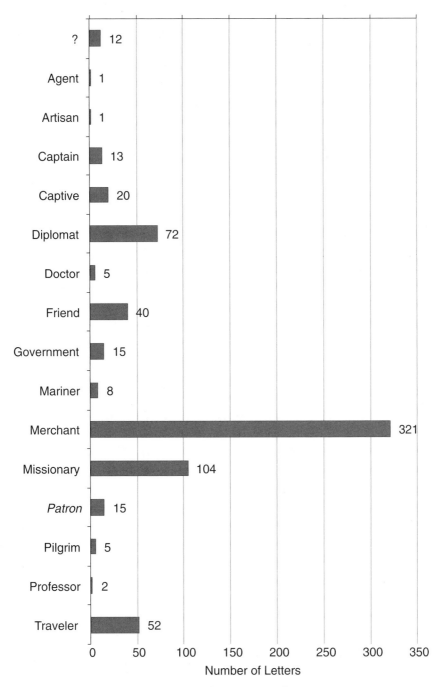

Chart B.4. Letters per profession

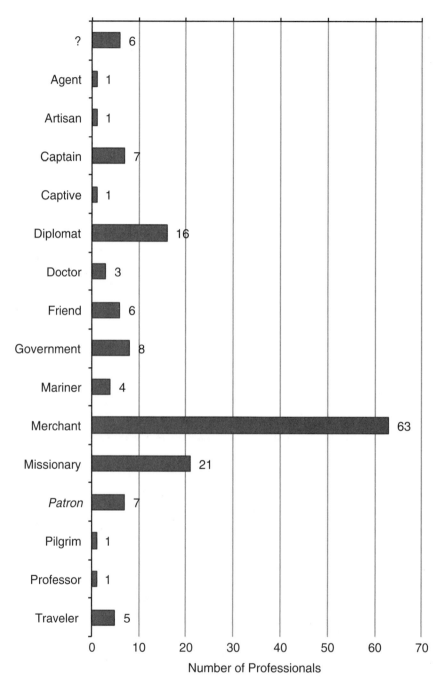

Chart B.5. Recipients by profession

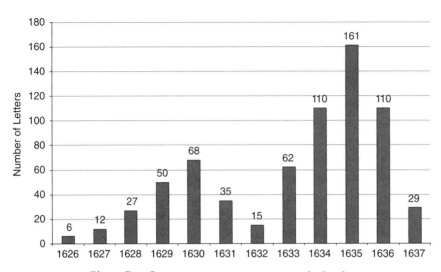

Chart B.6. Letters overseas per year, 1626–1637
(CBI and other relevant manuscript volumes)

Table B.1 Letters Overseas by Year

Location	1627	1628	1629	1630	1631
Aleppo					2
Alexandretta or Sidon		1			
Alexandria		2	1		
Alexandria?		1			
Algiers					
Cairo					
Cairo/Alexandria					
Constantinople		3	1		2
Cyprus	1				
Damascus			1	1	
Jerusalem			1		
Lebanon					
Levant?			1		
Malta				2	
Sidon		2	7	5	2
Smyrna					
Tripoli					
Tunis					
Total	1	9	12	8	6

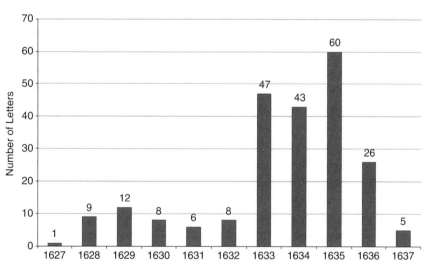

Chart B.7. Letters overseas per year, 1627–1637
(CBI MS 1874 and 1876 only)

1632	1633	1634	1635	1636	1637	Total
1	2		20	7		32
						1
	1	3				7
						1
			1			1
	13	17	28	14	1	73
		1				1
6	17	16				45
			1			2
						2
						1
1	4					5
						1
						2
	8		1	1		26
	1			1	1	3
			2			2
	1	6	7	3	3	20
8	47	43	60	26	5	225

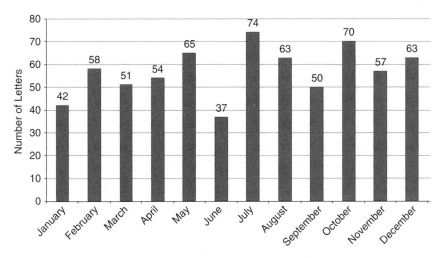

Chart B.8. Letters per month, aggregated, 1627–1637
(CBI MS 1874 and 1876 only)

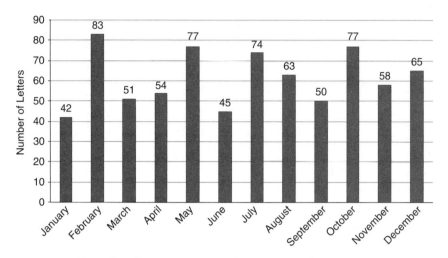

Chart B.9. Letters per month, aggregated, 1627–1637
(CBI and other relevant manuscript volumes)

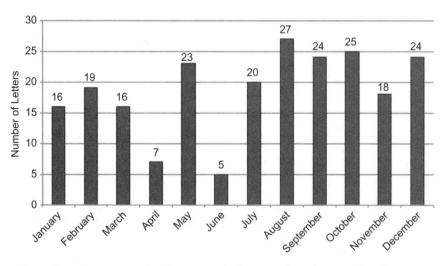

Chart B.10. Letters to the Levant only by month, aggregated, 1627–1637

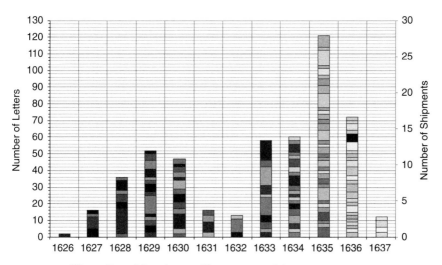

Chart B.11. Numbers of letters per shipment per year,
1626–1637 (grayscale indicates the relative size of each
shipment by number of letters)

APPENDIX C ༚

Patrons and Captains

Patron	Captain	Ship Name	Passenger	Type of Ship
	Abeille (of La Ciotat)		Same goods as Laure-Abeille	
	Aguez			Navire
Alphant			Plants for Peiresc	Polacre
		Amsloys	Montolieu (with letter from Peiresc to Marcheville)	
	Jehan Audibert de Sixfours			
	Gabriel Audibert			

Sailing from	Sailing to	Date	Source
Alexandria	Egypt		From Alexandria to Cairo the goods were put on the boat of Captain Abeille of La Ciotat. Sailed to Egypt from Marseille. Peiresc to Esperit Laurens, 15 September 1634, CBI, MS. 1874, f. 355v.
	Sidon		Peiresc to Jean-Baptiste Magy, 1 May 1634, CBI, MS. 1874, f. 339v.
Livorno	Cassis		Arrived on the day plague broke out in the town. Peiresc to Vallavez, 20 June 1630, CBI, MS. 1821, f. 468r. This letter is not published in *Lettres de Peiresc*, 6.
Marseille	Constantinople		Peiresc to Marcheville, 24 April 1633, CBI, MS. 1874, f. 604v.
			MACC, J 731, #2, unfoliated. In the attestation dated 5 February 1634 and produced by the consul Philibert de Bermond and Mary Laugeiret, deputy of the consuls of Marseille, in support of his consulship, we read the names of other captains.
			MACC, J 731, #2, unfoliated. In the attestation dated 5 February 1634 and produced by the consul Philibert de Bermond and Mary Laugeiret, deputy of the consuls of Marseille, in support of his consulship, we read the names of other captains.

Patron	Captain	Ship Name	Passenger	Type of Ship
Baille				Polacre
Evangeliste Bartolle		St. Louis		Polacre
	Bartolle	Mont Carmel	Carrying Minuti to Levant	Barque
Etienne Beaussier of Sixfours				
	Beau (of Marseille)			
Hugon Bermond of La Ciotat				
Maricy Brest			Brought oranges to Peiresc	
Caiolh [Pierre Cailhou?]			Leonard Challon	

Sailing from	Sailing to	Date	Source
			Peiresc to Gela, 27 February 1635, CBI, MS. 1874, f. 365v.
Alexandria		February 1633	MACC, J 745 unfoliated, Procuration made by Vincenzo Giglio, 22 June 1632.
Levant	Marseille	3 June 1629	Peiresc to Bartolle, 3 June 1629, CBI, MS. 1876, f. 356r.
			Peiresc to Aycard, 9 November 1635, CBI, MS. 1871, f. 56r. That Beaussier was from Sixfours: Peiresc to Gela, 4 September 1635, CBI, MS. 1874, f. 386v; Jacques de Vendôme to Peiresc, 22 November 1635, PBN, MS. F.fr. 9542, ff. 164r.
			Peiersc to Gela, 10 October 1635, CBI, MS. 1874, f. 393v.
Marseille?	Alexandria	May 1635	In May 1635, Jean-Baptiste Magy informed Peiresc that Patron Leonard Challon of Marseille and Hugon Bermond of La Ciotat were both preparing to depart for Alexandria. Peiresc to Magy, 28 October 1635, CBI, MS. 1874, f. 395v.
Liguria	Provence		Fraisse to Peiresc, 24 February 1627, CBI, MS. 1878, f. 551r.
Egypt	Marseille	Spring 1636	Peiresc to Magy, 24 December 1635; Peiresc to Jean-Baptiste Magy, 5 April 1636, CBI, MS. 1874, f. 413r.

Patron	Captain	Ship Name	Passenger	Type of Ship
	Pierre Caillon [Cailhou?]			
	Anthoine Carbonet			
	Carraye		Cat (sent by Minuti to Peiresc)	
	Carraye			
Caulet		St. Esprit		Vaisseau

Sailing from	Sailing to	Date	Source
Marseille		1635	Peiresc to Magy, 12 September 1635, CBI, MS. 1874, f. 386v. Peiresc to Venture, 24 October 1635, CBI, MS. 1874, f. 393bis r. We know that on one of his trips to Egypt he touched at Malta en route (Peiresc to Magy, 24 December 1635, CBI, MS. 1874, f. 413r).
			MACC, J 731, #2, unfoliated. In the attestation dated 5 February 1634 and produced by the consul Philibert de Bermond and Mary Laugeiret, deputy of the consuls of Marseille, in support of his consulship, we read the names of other captains.
Sidon			Peiresc to Aycard, 7 June 1633, CBI, MS. 1871, f. 32v; Peiresc to Minuti, 7 June 1633, CBI, MS. 1876, f. 827v. Unfortunately the cat fell into the sea and was lost.
Sidon		1633	Peiresc to Captain Carraye, 5 June 1633, CBI, MS. 1876, f. 827r.
Aleppo		February 1616	MACC, J 866, Napollon to Consuls of Marseille, 6 February 1616.

Patron	Captain	Ship Name	Passenger	Type of Ship
Leonard Challon (of Marseille)		Galleon Bleu		
	Challon			
Cornillon of Cassis				
	Anthoine Courtes (of Marseille)			
	Courtez			Polacre
	Nicolas Crouset	St. Hierosme		Polacre
	Crouset			Polacre

Sailing from	Sailing to	Date	Source
Marseille	Alexandria	May 1635	In May 1635, Jean-Baptiste Magy informed Peiresc that Patron Leonard Challon of Marseille and Hugon Bermond of La Ciotat were both preparing to depart for Alexandria. Peiresc to Magy, 28 October 1635, CBI, MS. 1874, f. 395v.
Alexandria	Marseille	February 1635	Agathange de Vendôme to Peiresc, 8 February 1635, PBN, MS. F.fr. 9543, f. 255r.
			Peiresc to Bartolle, 6 November 1629, CBI, MS. 1876, f. 360v.
			MACC, J 731, #2, unfoliated. In the attestation dated 5 February 1634 and produced by the consul Philibert de Bermond and Mary Laugeiret, deputy of the consuls of Marseille, in support of his consulship, we read the names of other captains.
Cairo			Peiresc to Aycard, 3 May 1634, CBI, MS. 1871, f. 42v; Peiresc to Jean-Baptiste Magy, 1 May 1634, CBI, MS. 1874, f. 339v.
	Egyptian route		Peiresc to Gela, 4 September 1635, CBI, MS. 1874, f. 386v; MACC, J 745, unfoliated.
Egypt			Peiresc to Magy, 15 September 1634, CBI, MS. 1874, f. 354v; Peiresc to Gela, 4 September 1635, CBI, MS. 1874, f. 386v.

Patron	Captain	Ship Name	Passenger	Type of Ship
Claude Danin				Navire
Jean Dauman		*St. Victor*		Polacre
Jean [Dauman/ Douman] or Doumas		*St. Barthélemy*		Polacre
		Dauphin	Aymini, Marcheville	

Sailing from	Sailing to	Date	Source
Sidon	Marseille		About Sidon: Peiresc to Jacques de Vendôme, 12 May 1633, CBI, MS. 1876, f. 826r; Jacques de Vendôme to Peiresc, 15 June 1633, PBN, MS. F.fr. 9542, f. 162r; Peiresc to Aycard, 11 May 1633, CBI, MS. 1871, f. 31r. In a letter to Aycard of 20 April 1634, Peiresc refers to both a "barque" and "vaisseau" of Captain Danin (CBI, MS. 1871, f. 42r). About the navire: Peiresc to Jean-Baptiste Magy, 1 May 1634, CBI, MS. 1874, f. 339v.
Egypt		1635	Peiresc to Magy, 24 December 1635, CBI, MS. 1874, f. 413r.
	Levant	Late December 1635	Peiresc to Gela, 24 December 1635, CBI, MS. 1874, f. 407bis r; Peiresc to Magy, 8 October 1636, CBI, MS. 1874, f. 431r.
Constanti-nople	Malta, then Marseille (without Marcheville)	1631, 1634	The *Dauphin* brought Daniel Aymini back from the Levant in March 1631. Peiresc to Aymini, [March 1631], CBI, MS. 1876, f. 811v. The *Dauphin* also brought Marcheville back to Europe. Peiresc to l'Empereur [Constantinople], 24 December 1633, CBI, MS. 1874, f. 323v. Peiresc to de Loches, 22 July 1634, *Correspondence de Peiresc*, 73 [= CBI, MS. 1874, f. 348v]. The *Dauphin* continued on to Marseille, but without Marcheville.

Patron	*Captain*	*Ship Name*	*Passenger*	*Type of Ship*
	de l'Ourme			
	Antoine de Lueby of Cassis		Letters of Magy, Cassien de Nantes, Giovanni Molino l'Armeno	
	Pierre Denans			
Lazarin de Pont				Barque
			De Thou's Egyptian objects	
	P. Dol			
	Drago "Ingelse"			

Sailing from	Sailing to	Date	Source
	Alexandretta		Peiresc to de l'Ourme, 22 November 1635, CBI, MS. 1874, f. 403r.
			Peiresc to Jean-Baptiste Magy, 1 November 1636, CBI, MS. 1874, f. 431v; Peiresc to Magy, 2 November 1636, CBI, MS. 1874, f. 432v.
			MACC, J 731, #2, unfoliated. In the attestation dated 5 February 1634 and produced by the consul Philibert de Bermond and Mary Laugeiret, deputy of the consuls of Marseille, in support of his consulship, we read the names of other captains.
Civitavecchia (Rome)	Marseille	1627	Aubery to Peiresc, 6 March 1627, PBN, MS. F.fr. 9542, f. 226v; Peiresc to Aubray, 1 April 1627, CBI, MS. 1871, f. 466v.
		1629	Ship sank. Peiresc to Lieutenant de Valbelle, 27 May 1629, CBI, MS. 1876, f. 356r.
			Peiresc to Venture, 24 October 1635, CBI, MS. 1874, f. 393bis v; Peiresc to Golius, 8 May 1636, *Peiresc: Lettres à Saumaise*, 262.
	Egyptian route		Peiresc to Aquin Mustapha, 14 July 1633, CBI, MS. 1876, f. 830r.

Patron	Captain	Ship Name	Passenger	Type of Ship
	Michael Durbec (English)			Navire
Sr. d'Espiot				Navire
Eymar	Lebau	St. Christophle		Vaisseau
	Anthoine Fabre de la Cieutat			
Faulconier				
Faulconier				Vaisseau
Ferand				
Guillaume Gaultier		St. Nicolas		
Guillaume Gaultier				Vaisseau Anglois

Sailing from	Sailing to	Date	Source
		1635	Leased out by Gastines. Peiresc to Jean-Baptiste Magy, 13 May 1635, CBI, MS. 1874, f. 368r.
Cairo		1634	Sr. d'Espiot was a major figure for Peiresc in Rome, "controlled" a navire. Peiresc to Aycard, 3 May 1634, CBI, MS. 1871, f. 42v.
	Alexandretta (Aleppo) route		MACC, From Olivier, 18 January 1631, MACC, J 891, #4, unfoliated.
			MACC, J 731, #2, unfoliated. In the attestation dated 5 February 1634 and produced by the consul Philibert de Bermond and Mary Laugeiret, deputy of the consuls of Marseille, in support of his consulship, we read the names of other captains.
Rome		1634	Peiresc to Menestrier, 9 February 1634, *Lettres de Peiresc,* 5:685.
Marseille			CBI, MS. 1775, f. 24r.
	Tunis	1635, 1636	Peiresc to Aycard, 20 September 1635, CBI, MS. 1871, f. 53v; Peiresc to [Jean-Baptiste] Magy, 22 July 1636, CBI, MS. 1874, f. 420v.
Civitavecchia		1637	Peiresc to Holstenius, 7 May 1637, *Lettres de Peiresc,* 5:479; Peiresc to Menestrier, 4 May 1636, *Lettres de Peiresc,* 5:799.
			CBI, MS. 1775, f. 23v.

Patron	*Captain*	*Ship Name*	*Passenger*	*Type of Ship*
Grimaud				
	Phelip Giremonde			
	Ambrose Guache			
	Nicholas Guigo[u]			Vaisseau of Marseille
	Nicholas Guigo[u]			Polacre
	Nicholas Guigou			

Sailing from	Sailing to	Date	Source
Levant	Toulon	1630	Peiresc to baron d'Aligre, 21 June 1630, *Lettres de Peiresc*, 7:20, [= CBI, MS. 1871, f. 271r].
			MACC, J 731, #2, unfoliated. In the attestation dated 5 February 1634 and produced by the consul Philibert de Bermond and Mary Laugeiret, deputy of the consuls of Marseille, in support of his consulship, we read the names of other captains.
			MACC, J 731, #2, unfoliated. In the attestation dated 5 February 1634 and produced by the consul Philibert de Bermond and Mary Laugeiret, deputy of the consuls of Marseille, in support of his consulship, we read the names of other captains.
			CBI, MS. 1775, f. 24r.
	Marseille	1634	Peiresc to Aycard, 29 March 1634, CBI, MS. 1871, f. 41v.
			MACC, MS. J 731, #2, unfoliated. In the attestation dated 5 February 1634 and produced by the consul Philibert de Bermond and Mary Laugeiret, deputy of the consuls of Marseille, in support of his consulship, we read the names of other captains.

Patron	Captain	Ship Name	Passenger	Type of Ship
			Pierre Heure (of La Ciotat)	
Issaultier				Vaisseau
			Barthélemy Issaultier (scrivener)	Polacre
François Laure	François Laure	St. Lazare		Polacre
	Laure		Same goods as Laure-Abeille	
	Laurent	Dauphin		

Sailing from	Sailing to	Date	Source
	Alexandria	1630	MACC, Unidentified to unidentified, 12 May 1630, Cairo, Arch. Chamb. Comm., J 891, #1, unfoliated.
	Sidon	1633	Peiresc to Magy, 14 July 1633, CBI, MS. 1874, f. 313r.
			Peiresc to Issaultier, 23 April 1630, CBI, MS. 1876, f. 799v.
	Egypt	March 1634	Peiresc to Albert, 2 March 1634, CBI, MS. 1874, f. 331r; Peiresc to Laurens "Capp.ne de la polacre," 2 March 1634, CBI, MS. 1874, f. 331v; Peiresc to Baulme, 2 March 1634, CBI, MS. 1874, f. 331v.
Marseille	Alexandria		From Alexandria to Cairo the goods were put on the boat of Captain Abeille of La Ciotat. Sailed to Egypt from Marseille. Peiresc to Esperit Laurens, 15 September 1634, CBI, MS. 1874, f. 355v.
Levant		1630	Peiresc to Minuti, 22 August 1632, CBI, MS. 1876, f. 818v.

Patron	Captain	Ship Name	Passenger	Type of Ship
	Laurent			
		Le Grand Henry	Balthazar Grimaud of Toulon brought letters	
		Le Grand Henry		
Liotaud			Minuti	Polacre
Liotaud				
Lombard				Polacre

Sailing from	Sailing to	Date	Source
			Captain Maillet was charged by Daniel Aymini in Sidon to inform Peiresc that he would be sending coins and antiquities with Jean Berard on the *St. Hierosme/Gerosme* of Captain Laurent. Peiresc to Minuti, 8–13 October 1630, CBI, MS. 1876, f. 808r; Peiresc to Jean Berard "venu de Levant sur le navire St. Gerosme du Capp.ne Laurent a Marseille ou a la Ciottat," 8 October 1630, CBI, MS. 1876, f. 808r.
Sidon		1630	Peiresc to Grimaud, 23 April 1630, CBI, MS. 1876, f. 799v.
Sidon	Marseille	Late 1629	The ship carried the book bought by Aymini and left by Estelle with Sr. Aurivelier, to secrete in the meantime among the registers of the Chancellery. Peiresc to Tarquet, 27 January 1630, CBI, MS. 1876, f. 792v.
Alexandria		1630	Peiresc to Aymini, 20 February 1630, CBI, MS. 1876, f. 796v.
			Peiresc to Bonnaire, 9 February 1624, CBI, MS. 1872, f. 149v.
	Egypt		Peiresc to Jean-Baptiste Magy, 7 December 1634, CBI, MS. 1874, f. 357r.

Patron	Captain	Ship Name	Passenger	Type of Ship
Lombardon	Audibert	St. Esprit		Vaisseau
Lombardon		Notre Dame de la Consolation (based in Marseille)	Sauvinge (scrivener, took a box sent from Mallon of Damascus)	Navire
Lombardon				"Navire ou polacre"
	Jean Maille (de Marseille) François Mailhet			Vaisseau

Sailing from	Sailing to	Date	Source
Alexandretta	Marseille	October 1635	Peiresc to Aycard, 3 May 1634, CBI, MS. 1871, f. 42v; Peiresc to Jean-Baptiste Magy, 1 May 1634, CBI, MS. 1874, f. 339v. Elsewhere the *St. Esprit* is described as "le navire St Esprit de Patron Lombardon." Peiresc to Marcheville, 24 April 1633, CBI, MS. 1874, f. 604v. Peiresc to Venture, 9 November 1635, CBI, MS. 1874, f. 395v.
			Peiresc to Sauvinge, 10 December 1630, CBI, MS. 1876, f. 810r.
Marseille	Alexandria	November 1635	Peiresc to Golius, 8 May 1636, *Lettres à Claude Saumaise*, 261. The ship was taken by corsairs near Malta not long after setting out from Marseille. It contained a packet from Jacob Golius for his brother, Father Celestin, in Aleppo, as well as Giggaeus's Arabic dictionary for Father Celestin.
			CBI, MS. 1775, f. 24r.
			MACC, J 731, #2, unfoliated. In the attestation dated 5 February 1634 and produced by the consul Philibert de Bermond and Mary Laugeiret, deputy of the consuls of Marseille, in support of his consulship, we read the names of other captains.

Patron	Captain	Ship Name	Passenger	Type of Ship
	François Mailhet			Navire
Marquet				
	Jaulmet Martin			
	Jaulmet Martin	Ste. Marguerite		Polacre
	Elzias Martinencq	Ste. Anne		Vaisseau

ı

Sailing from	Sailing to	Date	Source
			Peiresc to Magy, 26 May 1635, CBI, MS. 1874, f. 372r.
	Tunis	1634	Peiresc to Aycard, 5 August 1634, CBI, MS. 1871, f. 45r.
			MACC, J 731, #2, unfoliated. In the attestation dated 5 February 1634 and produced by the consul Philibert de Bermond and Mary Laugeiret, deputy of the consuls of Marseille, in support of his consulship, we read the names of other captains.
			A document from Cairo dated 24 October 1634, and reporting on a meeting of the French merchants in Cairo critical of the consulate of Philibert de Bermond and supporting Seghezzi lists Martinencq, Martin, Martuche. MACC, J 550, #1, unfoliated.
	Alexandria		A document from Cairo dated 24 October 1634, and reporting on a meeting of the French merchants in Cairo critical of the consulate of Philibert de Bermond and supporting Seghezzi lists Martinencq, Martin, Martuhe. MACC, J 550, #1, unfoliated; J 550, piece 4, report of Antoine Mazarat and Jean Fargues.

Patron	Captain	Ship Name	Passenger	Type of Ship
	Antoine Martuche	Ste. Barbe		Barque
	Meynard, Issaultier			
Paschal			Alzaron	
	Paul?	St. Laurence		Vaisseau
	Jean-Louis Pebrier	St. Louis		Vaisseau
	Honnoré Porquier			

Sailing from	Sailing to	Date	Source
Alexandria		October 1634	MACC, J 550, piece 4, report of Antoine Mazarat and Jean Fargues. A document from Cairo dated 24 October 1634, and reporting on a meeting of the French merchants in Cairo critical of the consulate of Philibert de Bermond and supporting Seghezzi lists Martinencq, Martin, Martuhe. MACC, J 550, #1, unfoliated.
Marseille			Peiresc to Aycard, 11 June 1633, CBI, MS. 1871, f. 33r.
	Tunis, Rome	1634	Brought the Alzaron from Tunis accompanied it to Rome. Peiresc to Aycard, 19 August 1634 and 26 August 1634, CBI, MS. 1871, f. 45v.
	Aleppo	1623, 1624	Viguier to Consuls of Marseille, 8 March 1623, MACC, J 889; Delestrade to Consuls of Marseille, 5 February 1634, J 892; from Olivier, 28 Februray 1631, MACC, J 891, #5.
Alexandria			MACC, J 745 unfoliated, Procuration pour Cap. Jacques Roguet à François Martin.
			MACC, J 731, #2, unfoliated. In the attestation dated 5 February 1634 and produced by the consul Philibert de Bermond and Mary Laugeiret, deputy of the consuls of Marseille, in support of his consulship, we read the names of other captains.

Patron	Captain	Ship Name	Passenger	Type of Ship
	Pierre Quiellet			
	Raysson	St. Hierosme		
	Raysson			Vaisseau
	Reynaud			
	Charles Roubaud			Polacre
	François Roux			

Sailing from	Sailing to	Date	Source
			MACC, J 731, #2, unfoliated. In the attestation dated 5 February 1634 and produced by the consul Philibert de Bermond and Mary Laugeiret, deputy of the consuls of Marseille, in support of his consulship, we read the names of other captains.
Constanti-nople		1632	Peiresc to Minuti, 22 August 1632, CBI, MS. 1876, f. 818v.
Constanti-nople		Spring 1632	Minuti to Peiresc, 14 April 1632, ABM, MS. 207 (1025), 251. Detained in the Isles de Marseille for quarantine. Peiresc to Aycard, 6 August 1632, CBI, MS. 1871, f. 16r.
Marseille	Alexandria	Late 1635	Peiresc to Celestin, 18 October 1635, CBI, MS. 1874, f. 393bis v.
	Alexandria	Early September 1628	Peiresc to de Thou, [6 September 1628], CBI, MS. 1876, f. 371r; MACC, J 745, unfoliated.
			MACC, J 731, #2, unfoliated. In the attestation dated 5 February 1634 and produced by the consul Philibert de Bermond and Mary Laugeiret, deputy of the consuls of Marseille, in support of his consulship, we read the names of other captains.

Patron	Captain	Ship Name	Passenger	Type of Ship
	Jean Raynaud dict Betton		Goods of Minuti	
	Sarde	Mont Carmel		
	Raymond Sardre (of Marseille)		Minuti	
		St. André		Polacre
		St. André	Issaultier (with letter from Minuti for Peiresc)	
		St. André		Barque
		Ste. Claire		Navire
		St. François		Polacre

Sailing from	Sailing to	Date	Source
	Levant		Raynaud was from Ollioules, near Toulon. Thomas de Mayo of Messina had rented him the boat that he used for anti-Turkish corsairing. Peiresc to [Minuti?], 11 October 1633, CBI, MS. 1874, f. 314r.
Livorno	Marseille		Peiresc to Minuti, 23 April 1630, CBI, MS. 1876, ff. 800r–v.
Levant		1630	Peiresc to Sardre, 23 April 1630, CBI, MS. 1876, f. 799v.
		1638	MACC, J 893, Bermond to consuls of Marseille, 14 August 1638.
Sidon		1631	Peiresc to Issaultier, 18 October 1632, CBI, MS. 1876, f. 825r.
			MACC, J 745.
		1633	Taken by corsairs of Tunis and Algiers in 1633 with a loss of more than 150,000 écus. Peiresc to Gaffarel, 13 November 1633, CBI, MS. 1873, f. 407v.
Levant			Peiresc to Aycard, 18 March 1634, CBI, MS. 1871, f. 41v; Peiresc to Magy, 12 March 1634, CBI, MS. 1874, f. 332v.

Patron	Captain	Ship Name	Passenger	Type of Ship
		St. François		Vaisscau
		St. François de Paul		Vaisseau
		St. Victor		Navire
		St. Victor		Vaisseau
	Michel Tourtel, sieur de Ramatuelle	Ste. Anne		
	Michel Tourtel, sieur de Ramatuelle			

Sailing from	Sailing to	Date	Source
Sidon			Peiresc to Aycard, 20 November 1632, CBI, MS. 1871, f. 17v; Peiresc to Aycard, 17 October 1632, *Lettres de Peiresc*, 7:285 [= CBI, MS. 1871, f. 21v].
Aleppo		February 1616	MACC, J 866, Napollon to Consuls of Marseille, 6 February 1616.
Alexandretta	Marseille?	November 1635	Peiresc to Celestin, 22 November 1635, CBI, MS. 1874, f. 399r.
Aleppo		February 1616	MACC, J 866, Napollon to Consuls of Marseille, 6 February 1616.
	Levant		Peiresc to Procureur-General Chasteuil, 3 June 1632, CBI, MS. 1873, f. 443v; Peiresc to Aycard, 23 August 1632, CBI, MS. 1871, f. 17v; Peiresc to Magy, 9 May 1635, CBI, MS. 1873, f. 46v; Peiresc to l'Empereur in Constantinople, 22 August 1632, CBI, MS. 1873, f. 199v; Peiresc to Gela, 6 March 1635, CBI, MS. 1874, f. 367r; Peiresc to Minuti in Constantinople, 23 August 1632, CBI, MS. 1876, f. 820r.
	Constantinople	1632	Carrying mail to and from Ambassador Henri de Gournay, comte de Marcheville. Peiresc to Marcheville, 22 August 1632, CBI, MS. 1874, f. 602v; 12 January 1633, CBI, MS. 1874, f. 603r.

Patron	Captain	Ship Name	Passenger	Type of Ship
	Truillet (of Toulon)			
François Taxil				
				Navire
				Vaisseau

Sailing from	Sailing to	Date	Source
		1633	Peiresc to Minuti, 7 June 1633, CBI, MS. 1876, f. 827v.
Marseille	Egypt	March 1634	Peiresc to Magy, 15 September 1634, CBI, MS. 1874, f. 331v.
Constanti-nople	Marseille	6 November 1632	Peiresc to Aycard, 6 November 1632, CBI, MS. 1871, f. 23v.
			The *St. Esprit*, commanded by Jean Maille, was visited on 7 December 1632 in Marseille port and found to be carrying cargo not found on the mani-fest—i.e., smuggling. Nor did Maille, or a Flemish ship just leaving, carry a passport from Cardinal Richelieu. CBI, MS. 1775, f. 23r.
Alexandretta	Marseille?	November 1635	Peiresc to Venture, 14 November 1635, CBI, MS. 1874, f. 397v; Peiresc to Celestin, 22 No-vember 1635, CBI, MS. 1874, f. 399r.
Sidon		January 1630	Peiresc to Tarquet, 27 January 1630, CBI, MS. 1876, f. 792v.

Abbreviations

ABM	Aix-en-Provence, Bibliothèque Méjanes
BAV, MS. Barb.-Lat.	Bibliotheca Apostolica Vaticana, MS Barberini-Latina
CBI	Carpentras, Bibliothèque Inguimbertine
MACC	Marseille, Archive Chambre de Commerce
MAD	Marseille, Archives Départementales des Bouches-du-Rhône
PBN, Ms. Dupuy	Paris, Bibliothèque Nationale, MS. Dupuy
PBN, MS. F.fr.	Paris, Bibliothèque Nationale, MS. Fonds français
PBN, MS. Lat.	Paris, Bibliothèque Nationale, MS. Latin
PBN, MS. N.a.f.	Paris, Bibliothèque Nationale, MS. Nouvelles acquisitions françaises

Frequent references are made to the following printed works:

Correspondance de Peiresc	*Correspondance de Peiresc avec plusieurs missionnaires et religieux de l'ordre des Capucins 1631–1637,* ed. P. Apollinaire de Valence (Paris: Alphonse Picard, 1891)
Gassendi, *Mirrour*	Pierre Gassendi, trans., *The Mirrour of True Nobility and Gentility* (Haverford, PA: Infinity, 2003 [London, 1657])
Lettres à Claude Saumaise	Peiresc, *Lettres à Claude Saumaise et à son entourage (1620–1637),* ed. Agnès Bresson (Florence: Leo S. Olschki, 1992)

447

Lettres de Peiresc	*Lettres de Peiresc,* ed. Philippe Tamizey de Larroque, 7 vols. (Paris: Imprimerie Nationale, 1888–1898)
Mersenne Correspondance	*Correspondance du P. Marin Mersenne religieux minime,* ed. Paul Tannery, Cornélis de Waard, and René Pintard, 17 vols. (Paris: Éditions du C.N.R.S., 1933–1988)
Vita Peireskii	Pierre Gassendi, *Viri Illustris Nicolai Claudii Fabricii de Peiresc Senatoris Aquisextentis Vita* = *Opera Omnia,* 6 vols. (Lyon, 1658), vol. 5

Notes

Introduction

1. Van Dyck's visit to Peiresc is recorded in *La Vie, les ouvrages et les élèves de Van Dyck: Manuscrit inédit des Archives du Louvre par un auteur anonyme,* ed. Erik Larsen (Brussels: Académie Royale de Belgique, 1975), 62. There is no parallel supporting evidence for this encounter and good reason to suspect it as wishful thinking. I am deeply grateful to Bert Watteeuw, research assistant at the Rubenianum in Antwerp, for this reference and for his discussion of this point.

2. For Van Dyck's depiction of Peiresc, see Joneath Spicer, "Anthony van Dyck's Iconography: An Overview of Its Preparation," in *Van Dyck 350,* ed. Susan J. Barnes and Arthur K. Wheelock Jr. (Washington, DC: National Gallery of Art, 1994), 327–364. For Mellan and Peiresc, see David Jaffé, "Mellan and Peiresc," *Print Quarterly* 7 (1990): 168–175.

3. "Certo che questo personaggio possede in tutte le professioni quanto ciascuno nella sua propria, ne posso imaginarmi come una anima sola tot functionibus diversis possit sufficere." Rubens to Pierre Dupuy, 22 June 1628, in *Correspondance de Rubens et documents épistolaires concernant sa vie et ses oeuvres,* ed. Charles Louis Ruelens and Max Rooses, 6 vols. (Antwerp: Veuve de Backer, 1887–1909), 4:435.

4. The phrase is Marc Fumaroli's: *Nicolas-Claude Fabri de Peiresc, Prince de la République des Lettres* (Brussels: [Association Pro-Peyresq], 1993). For the biography, see Peter N. Miller, *Peiresc's Europe: Learning and Virtue in the Seventeenth Century* (New Haven, CT: Yale University Press, 2000). For a comprehensive bibliography, see http://peiresc.wikis.bgc.bard.edu/peiresc-bibliography.

5. Jean-Jacques Bouchard, ed., *Monumentum Romanum Nicolao Claudio Fabricio Perescio . . . Doctrinae Virtutisque Causa Factum* (Rome, 1638).

6. Henri Pirenne quoted in Marc Bloch, *The Historian's Craft* (New York: Random House, 1953), 42.

7. See Miller, *Peiresc's Europe,* 33. More generally see A. D. Nuttall, *Dead from the Waist Down: Scholars and Scholarship in Literature and the Popular Imagination* (New Haven, CT: Yale University Press, 2003).

8. Arnaldo Momigliano, "Ancient History and the Antiquarian" [1950], in *Contributo alla storia degli studi classici* (Rome: Edizioni di Storia e Letteratura, 1955), 67–106; Momigliano, *The Classical Foundations of Modern Historiography* (Berkeley: University of California Press, 1990), 54.

9. "*L'Angeiographie* est une étude vaste & épineuse, qui explique les poids, les vases & les mesures, les instrumens pour l'agriculture & pour le domestique, ce qui appartenoit aux jeux, aux vetemens, à la navigation, & mille autres choses dont

l'examen ne se peut pas commodement rapporter aux Sciences precedentes; & qu'on croit pouvoir comprendre sous le nom d'*Angeia,* quoy qu'il ne soit pas assez general." Jacob Spon, *Réponse a la critique publiée par M. Guillet, sur le Voyage de Grece de Iacob Spon* (Lyon, 1679), 70. The full impact of Peiresc on the history of scholarship and, in particular, on the history of studying the past through objects is presented in Appendix A in this book.

10. Connors's bibliography is no longer accessible but may return; Richard Bradley, *The Past in Prehistoric Societies* (London: Routledge, 2002); *World Antiquarianism: Comparative Perspectives,* ed. Alain Schnapp with Lothar von Falkenhausen, Peter N. Miller, and Tim Murray (Los Angeles: Getty Publications, 2013); *Antiquarianism and Intellectual Life in Early Modern Europe and China, 1500–1800,* ed. Peter N. Miller and François Louis (Ann Arbor: University of Michigan Press, 2012); *Was There Antiquarianism in the Islamic World?,* a workshop at the Wissenschaftskolleg zu Berlin, 30 May 2013, organized by Martin Mulsow and Peter N. Miller.

11. On this claim, see *Momigliano and Antiquarianism: Foundations of the Modern Cultural Sciences,* ed. Peter N. Miller (Toronto: University of Toronto Press, 2007). In the opening paragraph of the Sather Lecture devoted to antiquarianism, Momigliano began by saying that if the antiquary came back to life in the twentieth century it might be as the director of an institute for art history or anthropology (Momigliano, *Classical Foundations of Modern Historiography,* 53).

12. Making this connection is the purpose of a companion project, *An Intellectual History of Material Culture* (Ithaca, NY: Cornell University Press, forthcoming).

13. Peiresc to Pierre Dupuy, all in 1627: *Lettres de Peiresc,* 1:228 (16 May); 1:236 (16 May); 1:293 (17 July); 1:296 (17 July; 2 references); 1:317 (2 August); 1:426 (16 November).

14. Momigliano, *Classical Foundations of Modern Historiography,* 56–57.

15. See, for instance, *"Historia": Empiricism and Erudition in Early Modern Europe,* ed. Gianna Pomata and Nancy Siraisi (Cambridge, MA: MIT Press, 2005); Nancy Siraisi, *History, Medicine, and the Traditions of Renaissance Learning* (Ann Arbor: University of Michigan Press, 2007).

16. *Histories of Scientific Observation,* ed. Lorraine Daston and Elizabeth Lunbeck (Chicago: University of Chicago Press, 2011); Joan-Pau Rubiés, "From Antiquarianism to Philosophical History: India, China, and the World History of Religion in European Thought (1600–1770)," in Miller and Louis, *Antiquarianism and Intellectual Life in Early Modern Europe and China,* 313–367.

17. See Peter N. Miller, "Peiresc in the Parisian Jewel House," in *Artificii Occulti: Knowledge and Discernment in the Artistic and Scientific Cultures of Early Modern Europe (16th–17th Centuries),* ed. Sven Dupré and Christine Göttler (Farnham, UK: Ashgate, forthcoming).

18. Hooke makes the comparison in his "Discourse of Earthquakes," in *Posthumous Works of Robert Hooke,* ed. Richard Waller (New York: Johnson Reprint Corp., 1969 [1705]), 321; for Hooke in this light, see Jim Bennet, Michael Cooper, Michael Hunter, and Lisa Jardine, *London's Leonardo: The Life and Work of Robert Hooke* (Oxford: Oxford University Press, 2003). More broadly

see Craig Ashley Hanson, *The English Virtuoso: Art, Medicine, and Antiquarianism in the Age of Empiricism* (Chicago: University of Chicago Press, 2009).

19. Anthony Grafton and I have been going back and forth for almost two decades on precisely this question of "narrow" versus "broader" interpretations of the antiquary. See Grafton, *What Was History? The Art of History in Early Modern Europe* (Cambridge: Cambridge University Press, 2007), esp. 125–141; and Grafton, "What Was the Antiquary? The Case of the Maurists," delivered at the Italian Academy at Columbia University, 18 April 2014; Peter N. Miller, "Description Terminable and Interminable: Looking at the Past, Nature and Peoples in Peiresc's Archive," in Pomata and Siraisi, *"Historia,"* 355–397; and Miller, "A Tentative Morphology of European Antiquarianism, 1500–2000," in Schnapp et al., *World Antiquarianism,* 67–87.

20. Michael Shanks, *The Archaeological Imagination* (Walnut Creek, CA: Left Coast Press, 2012).

21. Taking the seven published volumes of *Lettres de Peiresc* as a sample and having made a word-searchable version, I have found Peiresc using the noun form "recherche(s)"—research as a thing—78 times; the verb form "rechercher" (including "faire recherche")—research as an activity—37 times. For comparison's sake, the less specific verb "chercher" is used more than three times as often (131 times).

22. On these terms, see Louis Antoine Olivier, " 'Curieux,' Amateurs, and Connoisseurs: Laymen and the Fine Arts in the Ancien Regime" (PhD diss., Johns Hopkins University, 1976). A comparison of the terms "curieux," "curiosité," "érudit," "érudition," and "antiquaire" across a sample of Peiresc correspondence (the seven printed volumes of 1888–1898) shows the following:

	Vol. 1	Vol. 2	Vol. 3	Vol. 4	Vol. 5	Vol. 6	Vol. 7
curieux	80	74	59	7	9	33	40
curiosité	56	52	31	17	4	10	47
érudit	0	0	0	0	0	0	0
érudition	1	1	2	2	1	0	5
antiquaire	1	0	0	0	0	1	2

23. "Nous avons veu icy le Sr de la Rivière venu sur le mesme navire qui a esté huict mois avec luy en Constantinople durant tous cez dezordres dont il nous fit hier une si ample relation qu'il fauldroit un grand libvre & non une simple lettre pour la vous desduire." Peiresc to Loménie, 25 July 1634, CBI, MS. 1874, f. 193r.

24. See Peter N. Miller, *Peiresc's Orient: Antiquarianism as Cultural History in the Seventeenth Century* (Farnham, UK: Ashgate, 2012).

25. See Miller, *Peiresc's Europe,* esp. ch. 1, "Free Mind and Friend"; Peter N. Miller, "Friendship and Conversation in Seventeenth-Century Venice," *Journal of Modern History* 73 (2001): 1–31.

26. Peiresc to Vallavez, 21 April 1626, *Lettres de Peiresc,* 6:501.

27. See Peter N. Miller, "Peiresc and the First Natural History of the Mediterranean," in *Sintflut und Gedächtnis,* ed. Jan Assmann and Martin Mulsow

(Paderborn: Wilhelm Fink Verlag, 2006), 167–198; Peter N. Miller, *Peiresc's "History of Provence": Antiquarianism and the Discovery of a Medieval Mediterranean,* Transactions of the American Philosophical Society 101, 3 (Philadelphia: American Philosophical Society, 2011).

28. Pierre Gassendi, *Viri Illustris Nicolai Claudii Fabricii de Peiresc Senatoris Aquisextiensis Vita* in *Opera Omnia,* 6 vols. (Lyon, 1658), 5:337; Gassendi, *Mirrour,* bk. 6, 277, quoted in Miller, *Peiresc's "History of Provence,"* 13.

29. "Le fruittier est passé; mon pere luy fit rescription sur le rentier de Beaugentier, lequel le paya aussy tost et vint hier apporter à mon pere les 27 escus de reste de la rente de Pasques, avec des fruicts du Prieur qui ne vauldroient pas l'envoyer à Paris, et des marcottes que nous envoyerons avec celles de Marseille et avec les figuiers." Peiresc to Vallavez, 3 February 1625, *Lettres de Peiresc,* 6:98.

30. While no one I stopped and asked about Peiresc knew who he was, the town drunk, playing chess in the shade of the church after midday, correctly described him as a great scholar, though exaggerated (charmingly) in referring to the painting as commemorating Louis XIV's coming to see him.

31. M. Fauris de Saint-Vincens, *Monument consacré à la mémoire de Peiresc* (n.p.: A. Henricq, 1802); M. Fauris de Saint-Vincens, *Correspondance inédite de Peiresc avec Jérôme Aléandre, etc.* (Paris: Porthmann, 1819); G. Matthew Adkins, "The Renaissance of Peiresc: Aubin-Louis Millin and the Postrevolutionary Republic of Letters," *Isis* 99 (2008): 675–700; Jacques Ferrier, "Monuments consacrés à la mémoire de Peiresc," *L'Été Peiresc. Fioretti II Nouveaux Mélanges,* ed. Jacques Ferrier (Avignon: Aubanel, 1988), 31–36.

32. "Le bruict de l'abolition que Monseigneur le Cardinal de Lyon a obtenüe pour cette ville-là faict esperer la grace toute entiere, non seulement pour Lyon, mais pour touts les peuples voisins qui y peuvent participier, et principallement pour ceux de nostre coste, qui y ont leurs plus importantes correspondances. Les choses de la marine nous sont si à coeur." Peiresc to François-Auguste de Thou, 20 March 1633, *Lettres de Peiresc,* 2:467.

33. Peiresc to Berengier "a Marseille au cartier de St Jehan prez la fontane," CBI, MS. 1876, f. 808v. Jean l'Empereur lived at the Place Vivaux (to l'Empereur, 19 September 1626, CBI, MS. 1873, f. 197r); Giovanni Gela lived near "S. Jaume de l'Espagne" (CBI, MS. 1864, f. 257r). The *Civitates Orbis Terrarum* began publishing in 1572, but Marseille was depicted in vol. 2, published in 1574. A corrected image was published the following year, probably taken from François Belleforest, *La Cosmographie Universelle de tout le monde* (Paris, 1575). On this see Guenièvre Fournier-Antonini, *Barcelone, Gênes et Marseille: Cartographie et Images (XVIe–XIXe siècle)* (Turnhout: Brepols, 2012), 663–664.

34. Walter Benjamin, "Marseille," in *Reflections* (New York: Schocken Books, 1978), 132, originally in the *Neue Schweizer Rundschau* 22 (1929): 291–295.

35. "On m'a tenu en telle desbauche ou faineantise durant cez derniers moys, hors de certaines chetives occupations necessaires, qu'on ne m'a poinct laissé reprendre les livres de la marine; mais je n'ay laissé pourtant d'en rechercher des exemplaires meilleurs que les miens. . . . Je pensois aller fouiller dans les archives de Marseille, mais je n'ay peu trouver ce temps a mon grand regret. Je

n'en pers pas pourtant encores l'esperance et attends encor responce d'autres endroicts, car pour l'amour de moy des officiers de Marseille ont escript jusques à Barcelonne mesmes sur ce subject." Peiresc to Pierre Dupuy, 19 September 1627, *Lettres de Peiresc*, 1:369.

36. Gassendi, *Mirrour*, bk. 6, 191.

37. On the practice of using loose pages as opposed to a notebook—defended strongly by Boyle and Hooke—see Richard Yeo, *Notebooks, English Virtuosi, and Early Modern Science* (Chicago: University of Chicago Press, 2014), 173. For the idea of the archive as a body I am indebted to Marco Wimmer, *Archivkörper: Eine Geschichte historischer Einbildungskraft* (Konstanz: Konstanz University Press, 2012).

38. For a study of his books and library, see Agnès Bresson, "Les livres et les manuscrits d'un 'chercheur': La place de la bibliothèque dans le cabinet de Peiresc," *Bulletin du bibliophile* 2 (2007): 280–310; Jean-Marie Arnoult, "Les Livres de Peiresc dans les bibliothèques parisiennes (Bibliothèque Nationale, Bibliothèque Mazarine, Imprimerie Nationale)," *Revue française de l'histoire du livre* 24 (1979): 591–609; Jean-Marie Arnoult, "Catalogue du Fonds Peiresc de la Bibliothèque Municipale de Chalons-sur-Marne," *Mémoires de la Société d'agriculture, commerce, sciences et arts de la Marine* (1975): 1–110; Edith Bayle, Agnès Bresson, and Jean-Francois Maillard, *La Bibliothèque de Peiresc: Philosophie* (Paris: Éditions du Centre National de la Recherche Scientifique, 1990). For Peiresc's coins and cabinet, see Antoine Schnapper, *Le Géant, la licorne, la tulipe: Collections françaises au XVIIe siècle* (Paris: Flammarion, 1988), 140, 151; note also the references in the index (p. 408); David Jaffé, "Peiresc—Wissenschaftlicher Betrieb in einem Raritäten-Kabinett," in *Macrocosmos in Microcosmo: Die Welt in der Stube: Zur Geschichte des Sammelns 1450 bis 1800*, ed. Andreas Grote (Opladen: Leske+Budrich, 1994), 301–322; David Jaffé, "Towards a Reconstruction of Peiresc's Rarities Cabinet," in Ferrier, *L'Été Peiresc*, 143–149; for his art objects, see Agnès Bresson, "Peiresc et le commerce des antiquités à Rome," *Gazette des Beaux-Arts* 85 (1975): 61–72; David Jaffé, "The Barberini Circle: Some Exchanges between Peiresc, Rubens, and Their Contemporaries," *Journal of the History of Collections* 1 (1989): 119–147.

39. For this collections history I, and all those who study Peiresc, are deeply indebted to the work of Francis W. Gravit, especially *The Peiresc Papers* [= University of Michigan Contributions in Modern Philology 14] (Ann Arbor: University of Michigan Press, 1950).

40. Variation in numbers between the printed seventeenth-century catalog and the present reflects preservation issues: some volumes have been recombined while others have been broken up; some were scattered and others lost. But the overall shape remains clear.

41. On Peiresc's archive, see Miller, *Peiresc's "History of Provence,"* 14–18.

42. Miller, *Peiresc's "History of Provence,"* 38n9.

43. In 1993 Stallybrass founded the seminar on the History of Material Texts and has been the moving force behind the "Material Texts" series published by the University of Pennsylvania Press since 2001. For what it might mean to be the author of an archive, see Miller, *Peiresc's "History of Provence,"* 16–18.

44. Ben Kafka, *The Demon of Writing: Powers and Failures of Paperwork* (New York: Zone Books, 2012); Lisa Gitelman, *Paper Knowledge: Toward a Media History of Documents* (Durham, NC: Duke University Press, 2014).

45. Miller, *Peiresc's Europe*, 98.

46. "J'ay receu trois vostres en mesme temps ce matin environ neuf heures." Fort to Peiresc, 31 January 1630, PBN, MS. F.fr. 9540, f. 162r.

47. Fort to Peiresc, 1 February 1630, PBN, MS. F.fr. 9540, f. 160r.

48. See Paula Findlen, ed., *Early Modern Things: Objects and Their Histories* (London: Routledge, 2013); and Pamela Smith, Amy R. W. Meyers, and Harold J. Cook, eds., *Ways of Making and Knowing* (Ann Arbor: University of Michigan Press, 2013).

49. Gassendi, *Mirrour,* bk. 6, 197–198.

50. For Peiresc's one "book," see Peter N. Miller, "The Ancient Constitution and the Genealogist: Momigliano, Pocock, and Peiresc's *Origines Murensis Monasterii* (1618)," *Republics of Letters: A Journal for the Study of Knowledge, Politics, and the Arts* 1, no. 1 (May 1, 2009), http://arcade.stanford.edu/rofl/ancient-constitution-and-genealogist-momigliano-pocock-and-peiresc%E2%80%99s-origines-murensis.

51. Nothing like the study of the Toulouse-based Marseille-trading merchant Pierre Gloton exists for any of Peiresc's merchant contacts. See Gaëlle Lapeyrie, "De la boutique au comptoir: La trajectoire d'un négociant toulousain en textile, entre traditions et nouveautés (vers 1600–1620)," *Rives méditerranéennes* 29 (2008): 79–105.

52. "Et puis avois demeuré longtemps sans en recevoir aulcunes, quand l'homme que Mr d'Agut avoit envoyé exprez à Lyon rompit la glace, et m'en r'apporta une du 19 novembre toute pucelle sans estre passée au vinaigre, laquelle fut bientost suyvie de cinq autres, du 9, 16, 23, 30 octobre et 6 novembre qui vindrent quasi en mesme temps bien que par diverses voyes, les unes du costé de Marseille, les aultres du costé de Sallon, et les deux plus vielles, et neantmoings les plus tardives, du costé d'Aix, où elles m'estoient allé chercher a contre temps, lesquelles furent suyvies de prez de deux aultres du 4 et 18 decembre, venües pareillement l'une par Marseille et l'aultre par Sallon, avec lesquelles nous eusmes de si beaux livres et si curieux papiers, et si bonne part des nouvelles du monde, qu'il nous sembla, aprez une longue absence, estre tout d'un coup retournez au milieu du Louvre, et de l'academie, bien qu'en effect nous en fussions si esloignez, et quasi confinez au milieu d'un desert." Peiresc to Dupuy, 17 January 1630, *Lettres de Peiresc*, 2:214.

53. Fernand Braudel, "Avant propos," in *Lettres de négociants marseillais: Les Frères Hermite (1570–1612),* Affaires et gens d'affaires 3, ed. Micheline Baulant (Paris: Armand Colin, 1953), v.

54. José Gentil da Silva, *Stratégie des Affaires à Lisbonne entre 1595 et 1607: Lettres marchandes des Rodrigues d'Evora et Veiga,* Affaires et gens d'affaires 9 (Paris: Armand Colin, 1956), xi, 9. Marc Bloch, in his wartime memoir, had warned historians against feeling "ashamed" of the poetry in historical research. Marc Bloch, *The Historian's Craft* (Garden City, NY: Vantage, 1950), 8. Contemporary scholarship has not advanced much beyond the Braudellian paradigm; for

example, V. Parello, ed., *La correspondance dans le monde méditerranéen (XVIe–XXe siècle): Pratiques sociales et représentations culturelles; Actes du colloque international, 26 et 27 avril 2007 IREC–Université de Montpellier III* (Perpignan: Presses Universitaires de Perpignan, 2008).

55. "Leur intérêt, si je ne me trompe, est de nous introduire au coeur des pratiques et réalités de la vie quotidienne des marchands: ces réalités, par elles-mêmes ou du fait de leur répétition, dépassent souvent le détail simplement anecdotique." Braudel, "Avant propos," v.

56. Iris Origo, *The Merchant of Prato: Daily Life in a Medieval Italian City* (Harmondsworth, UK: Penguin, 1957).

57. Burckhardt to Albert Brenner, 24 May 1856; Burckhardt to Willibald Beyschlag, 14 June 1842, quoted in Sabine Loriga, *Le petit x: De la biographie à l'histoire* (Paris: Éditions du Seuil, 2010), 201, 203.

58. This theme is discussed fully in Miller, *Peiresc's Europe,* ch. 5, with full bibliography.

59. Friedrich Nietzsche, *Encyclopädie der klassichen Philologie,* in *Nietzsche Werke,* pt. 2, vol. 3, ed. Fritz Bornmann and Mario Carpitella (Berlin: Walter de Gruyter, 1993), 343, 349.

60. "Mon nom est assez cogneu par toute la coste de ceste province afin que les navires ou barques surquoy vous les chargent abordantz aux autres ports que Marseille je puisse recouvrer ce qui sera à moy sans les faire passer par Marseille." Peiresc to Estelle, 25 February 1630, CBI, MS. 1876, f. 797v.

61. Nicholas Purcell, "Tide, Beach, and Backwash: The Place of Maritime Histories," in *The Sea: Thalassography and Historiography,* ed. Peter N. Miller (Ann Arbor: University of Michigan Press, 2013), 84–108.

62. Walter Benjamin, *The Origin of German Tragic Drama,* trans. John Osborne (London: Verso, 1985), 41.

63. Francis Bacon, *The Advancement of Learning* (London, 1605), 2:5; Jean Besly to Pierre Dupuy, 3 September 1633, quoted in Olivier Poncet, "Cercles savants et pratique généalogique en France (fin XVIe siècle–milieu du XVIIe siècle," in *L'Opération généalogique: Cultures et pratiques européennes, XVe–XVIIe siècle,* ed. Olivier Rouchon (Rennes: Presses Universitaires de Rennes, 2014), 125.

64. Peter Matthiessen, *Far Tortuga: A Novel* (New York: Vintage Books, 1975); Arlette Farge, *Vivre dans la rue à Paris au XVIIIe siècle* (Paris: Gallimard, 1979); Karl Schlögel, *Moscow 1937* (Cambridge: Polity Press, 2012 [2008]); Reyner Banham, *Los Angeles: The Architecture of Four Ecologies* (Berkeley: University of California Press, 2009 [1971]). Banham and Schlögel explicitly discuss the relation of structure to subject matter (*Los Angeles,* 18; *Moscow,* 9).

65. Walter Benjamin, "On the Concept of History," theses 2 and 3, in *Selected Writings,* vol. 4, ed. Howard Eiland and Michael W. Jennings (Cambridge, MA: Harvard University Press, 2003), 390.

66. Mark Salber Phillips, *Society and Sentiment: Genres of Historical Writing in Britain, 1740–1820* (Princeton, NJ: Princeton University Press, 2000).

67. See György Lukács, "Narrate or Describe? A Preliminary Discussion of Naturalism and Formalism," in *Writer and Critic: And Other* Essays, ed. Arthur Kahn (Lincoln, NE: Iuniverse, 2005 [1970]), 110–146. Lukács, of course,

would never have thought of writing about antiquarianism, but his discussion of the role of research and narration does exactly parallel our contrast between antiquaries and historians, making his observations on Zola's research-mindedness, for example, tell for the question of writing antiquarianism.

68. Gassendi, *Mirrour*, bk. 6, 193.

69. See Pierre Nora, "Introduction," in "La Culture du passé" (special issue), *Le Débat* 177 (November–December 2013): 5. In the same number, see also the contributions of Regis Debray, "Un temps intemporel," 31, and Gil Bartholeyns, "Loin de l'Histoire," 119.

70. *The Poetical Works of Byron* (Boston: Houghton Mifflin, 1975), canto 4, lxxxi, 67.

71. The point is made in a letter to Gottfried Kinkel in 1842, quoted in Felix Gilbert, "Jacob Burckhardt's Student Years: The Road to Cultural History," *Journal of the History of Ideas* 47 (1986): 249.

72. Mersenne's dedication to Peiresc of one part of his *Harmonie Universelle* [= Mersenne to Peiresc, 20 April 1635,] *Mersenne Correspondance*, 5:135.

73. R. G. Collingwood, *The Idea of History* (Oxford: Oxford University Press, 1956 [1946]), Epilegomena, §1, ii, 212 (the archaeologist as exemplar); §2, 243–246 (imagination and the novel); §3, iv, 258 (turn to nonliterary sources); §3, viii, 269 (centrality of the question); §3, x, 281 (questions and evidence); §4, 283 (reenactment as history). The quotation is at §1, ii, 212. Momigliano did include Collingwood's "Human Nature and Human History" (*Proceedings of the British Academy* 22 [1936]), later published as Epilegomena §1, in a list of readings on "Storicismo" (Pisa, Momigliano Archive, N-b 1). I am grateful to Professor Roberto di Donato for making possible access to the archive.

74. Claudia Wedepohl, "Introduction" to Aby Warburg, "From the Arsenal to the Laboratory," *West 86th* 19 (2012): 108.

75. "Peu de gens devineront combien il a fallu etre triste pour entreprendre de res-susciter Carthage!" Flaubert to Ernest Feydeau, 29–30 November 1859, in Gustave Flaubert, *Correspondance*, vol. 4: *1854–1861* (Paris: Conard, 1926–1933), 348. Benjamin cites this in thesis 7 of his *Theses on the Philosophy of History*, but omits the words "to undertake."

1. Prologue

1. This material on Bastion de France is found in PBN, MS. F.fr. 16164.

2. *Bastion de France* 7 (1932): 342. "Nous sommes heureux d'annoncer à nos lecteurs que nous avons découvert, après bien des recherches, un véritable trésor documentaire à la Bibliothèque Inguimbertine de Carpentras."

3. These include letters from Napollon to the premier president of the Parlement de Provence, written from Smyrna on 4 September 1624; captain-general of Algiers to the duc de Guise, 29 May 1628; divan of Algiers to Napollon, 1 February 1629 (all from the volume on Turcica, CBI, MS. 1777); from Peiresc to Vias and Napollon on 13 April 1626, Napollon to Peiresc on 18 April 1626 (from CBI, MS. 1876); and a list of slaves redeemed by Napollon in Algiers (CBI, MS. 1777).

4. "Nous espérions trouver dans les minutes et copies de la correspondance de

Peiresc des documents importants; notre attente a été quelque peu déçue . . .
Nous aurions été fort en peine de déchiffrer le texte, dont la graphique est par-
ticulièrement 'rebutante' " (*Bastion de France* 8 [1932]: 359).

5. The "Discours du Bastion de France" was published in *Bastion de France* I (1929):
7–11, with a note "Au Lecteur": "C'est à Sanson Napollon lui-même que nous
empruntons la glorieuse préface de notre modeste Bulletin. Voice le texte complet
et jusqu'à présent inédit de son admirable 'Discours' qui est conservé à la Bibliothèque Nationale sous le no. 16164 des manuscrits français. Nous en avons fait
prendre une photographie par M. Lécuyer, spécialiste des travaux de ce genre. Mr
Braudel, professeur au Lycée d'Alger et très dévoué secrétaire général de notre
Comité, a bien voulu se charger de la difficile lecture du manuscrit. A part très peu
de mots, vraiment indéchiffrables, M. Braudel a parfaitement interprété ce document. Notre Comité lui adresse ses plus chaleureux remerciements." This text is
partially quoted in Jacques Ferrier ("Une Symphonie algérienne: Lettres inédites
de Peiresc à Sanson Napollon," in *L'Été Peiresc. Fioretti II Nouveaux Mélanges,* ed.
Jacques Ferrier [Avignon: Aubanel, 1988], 250), who confuses the date of publication of Napollon's *Discorso* with that of the Peiresc material (1932 rather than
1929). Ferrier brings no evidence to support his assertion that Braudel was the one
who presented the Peiresc materials. Perhaps he simply had this on personal tradition. Nevertheless, the fact remains that Braudel was an active member of this society, was then working on North Africa in the early seventeenth century, and had
published the earlier Napollon materials. He was someone who could well have
been given this task as well.

6. Aubery to Peiresc, 4 June 1627, PBN, MS. F.fr. 9542, f. 240r. "Pour *le papier*
selon la grandeur que desires on en trouveroit en le faisant rogner de mesure mais
s'est de gros papier asses vilain de sorte que pour l'avoir fin & beau il fauldra se
server du mesme dont est escript ceste lettre."

7. He saw letters as a way of telling time (Fernand Braudel, *The Mediterranean
and the Mediterranean World in the Age of Phillip II,* trans. Siân Reynolds
[New York: Harper and Row, 1972], 366–367) and of reconstituting space
(Braudel, "Avant-propos," in Étienne Trocmé and Marcel Delafosse, *Le Com-
merce Rochelais de la fin du XVe siècle au début du XVIIIe* [Paris: Armand
Colin, 1952], i).

8. For a discussion of Goitein in the context of *Affaires et gens d'affaires,* see
Peter N. Miller, "Two Men in a Boat: The Braudel-Goitein 'Correspondence'
and the Beginning of Thalassography," in *The Sea: Thalassography and Historiography,* ed. Peter N. Miller (Ann Arbor: University of Michigan Press, 2013),
27–59.

9. A very good example of this kind of sensitive treatment of commercial letters is
Jessica Goldberg, *Trade and Institutions in the Medieval Mediterranean: The
Geniza Merchants and Their Business World* (Cambridge: Cambridge University
Press, 2012). For recognition that archives and the quantification of microhistorical narratives—which new work on the Geniza like this represents—are at the
center of what is new in history, see Christophe Granger, "Ouverture," in *À quoi
pensent les historiens? Faire de l'histoire au XXIe siècle,* ed. Granger (Paris: Éditions Autrement, 2013), 15.

10. See Peter N. Miller, "*From Spain to India* becomes *A Mediterranean Society: The Braudel-Goitein 'Correspondence,' Part II," Mitteilungen des Kunsthistorisches Institut 55* (2013): 112–135. I am grateful to Marina Rustow for alerting me to this dimension of Goitein's thought. The phrase is Siegfried Kracauer's (see *Briefwechsel: 1941–66,* ed. Volker Breidecker [Hamburg: Akademie Verlag, 1996]).

2. Marseille-Aix

1. Louis Bergasse, *Histoire du commerce de Marseille,* vol. 4: *1599–1660* (Paris: Plon, 1954). There is a brief discussion in Romano Canosa, *Storia del Mediterraneo nel Seicento* (Roma: Sapere 2000, 1997), 226–230.

2. Fernand Braudel, *The Mediterranean and the Mediterranean World in the Age of Phillip II,* 2nd ed. (Boston: Harper and Row, 1972), 220, 310–311, 335, 361, 627. Nor is the treatment any different in the 1955 "Remarques sur la Méditerranée au XVIIe siècle," *Autour de la Méditerranée,* ed. Roselyne de Ayala and Paule Braudel, pref. M. Aymard (Paris: Éditions de Fallois, 1996), 539–564. There is no single essay devoted to Marseille in Braudel's Mediterranean oeuvre.

3. Paul Masson, *Histoire du commerce français dans le Levant au XVIIe siècle* (Paris: Hachette, 1896). But note Masson's anti-Semitism: "Ces Juifs"—those who farmed taxes for the sultan—"grands ennemis de notre nation, et poussés par leur cupidité, employaient toutes les ressources de leur esprit inventif à imager de nouveaux profits" (75; also 491). Clarence Dana Rouillard, *The Turk in French History, Thought, and Literature (1520–1660)* (Paris: Boivin, 1973 [1940]), builds upon Masson, but argues for the minimal impact of the commercial encounter on cultural representations (159). This thesis seems unsustainable.

4. "On ne s'étonnera pas en tête d'une telle publication de l'absence d'une bibliographie des ouvrages et des sources consultés." *Lettres de négociants marseillais: Les Frères Hermite (1570–1612),* ed. Micheline Baulant, avant-propos Fernand Braudel, Affaires et Gens d'Affaires 3 (Paris: Armand Colin, 1953).

5. There is nothing at all for the seventeenth century akin to Charles Carrière, *Négociants marseillais au XVIIIe siècle,* 2 vols. (Marseille: Institut Historique de Provence, 1973). marseille is not present in Francesca Trivellato, "Merchants' Letters across Geographical and Social Boundaries," in *Correspondence and Cultural Exchange in Europe, 1400–1700,* ed. Francisco Bethencourt and Florike Egmond (Cambridge: Cambridge University Press, 2006), 80–103. Jean-Pierre Farganel, "Les marchands français dans l'Orient méditerranéen aux XVIIe et XVIIIe siècles: La présence française dans les Echelles du Levant (1650–1789)" (PhD diss., Paris I, 1992), is devoted to the later period, as are his articles based on it, for example, "Les Consuls pivots de l'organisation de la navigation commerciale et des stations navales au Levant aux XVIIe & XVIIIe siècles," in *Stations navales et navigations organisées en Méditerranée,* ed. André Leroy and Christiane Villain-Gandossi (Ollioules: Éditions de la Nerthe, 2004), 81–102.

6. For the Middle Ages, see, for example, S. T. Loseby, "Marseille and the Pirenne Thesis, I: Gregory of Tours, the Merovingian Kings and 'Un Grand Port,'" in *The Sixth Century: Production, Distribution, and Demand,* ed. Richard Hodges and William Bowden (Leiden: Brill, 1998), 203–229; Loseby, "Marseille and

the Pirenne Thesis II: 'Ville morte,'" in *The Long Eighth Century: Production, Distribution and Demand*, ed. Inge Lyse Hansen and Chris Wickham (Leiden: Brill, 2000), 167–193; Charles-Emmanuel Dufourcq, *La Vie quotidienne dans les ports méditerranéens au moyen age: Provence-Languedoc-Catalane* (Paris: Hachette, 1975); Thierry Pécout, ed., *Marseille au moyen age, entre Provence et Méditerranée: Les Horizons d'une ville portuaire* (Marseille: Desiris, 2011). For the eighteenth century, see K. Fukasawa, "Marseille, Porte du Levant, un essai de comparaison," *Actes du 50e congres d'études régionales de la fédération historique du Sud-Ouest tenu à Bordeaux le 25–26 et 27 Avril 1997*, vol. 2: *Bordeaux porte océane, carrefour européen* (Bordeaux: Publications de la Fédération Historique du Sud-Ouest, 1999), 581–593; Biagio Salvemini and Maria Antonietta Visceglia, "Pour une histoire des rapports économiques entre Marseille et le Sud de l'Italie au XVIIIe et au début du XIXe siècle: Flux marchands, articulations territoriales, choix politiques," *Provence historique* 177 (1994): 321–365; Patrick Boulanger, *Marseille, marché international de l'huile d'olive: Un produit et des hommes de 1725 à 1825* (Marseille: Institut Historique de Provence, 1996). Despite the title, Junko Thérèse Takeda, *Between Crown and Commerce: Marseille and the Early Modern Mediterranean* (Baltimore: Johns Hopkins University Press, 2011) focuses almost entirely on the second half of the seventeenth century and the eighteenth century. Michel Morineau did study the first part of the seventeenth century, but only to make precise that while there was a "decline" in Marseille's fortunes, shipping was less affected than previously thought ("Flots de commerce et trafics français en méditerranée au XVIIe siècle [jusqu'en 1669]," *XVIIe siècle* 86 [1970]: 86–87, 135–172).

7. Wolfgang Kaiser, *Marseille im Bürgerkrieg: Sozialgefüge, Religionskonflikt und Faktionskämpfe von 1559–1596* (Göttingen: Vandenhoeck and Ruprecht, 1991).

8. There is nothing for Marseille at all comparable to the ambition of Jacques Bernard, *Navires et gens de mer à Bordeaux (vers 1400–vers 1550)*, Ports-Routes-Trafics 22 (Paris: S.E.V.P.E.N., 1968): "L'objet de ce travail est avant tout la marine de l'époque" (3). There is not even a general overview of Marseille in the seventeenth century along the lines of Françoise Hildesheimer, *La Vie à Nice au XVIIe siècle* (Paris: Publisud, 1987). Michel Fontenay, rewriting and combining essays of 1994 and 2006, still dismisses Marseille's early seventeenth-century significance in a sentence, and when he is forced to return to it, he manages to wriggle away after a paragraph (Michel Fontenay, *La Méditerranée entre la Croix et le Croissant: Navigation, commerce, course et piraterie [XVIe–XIXe siècle]* [Paris: Classiques Garnier, 2012], 157, 163). Nor is there any discussion of Marseille in the most comprehensive recent *tour d'horizon*, *La Recherche internationale en histoire maritime: Essai d'évaluation* [= *Revue d'histoire maritime* 10–11] (Paris: Presse de l'Université Paris-Sorbonne, 2010).

9. On movement between the cities, see Wolfgang Kaiser, "La Gestation d'un crime: Le contexte religieux et social du meurtre de Frédéric Bagueneau, évêque de Marseille (26 September 1603)," in *Mélanges Michel Vovelle: Volume aixois* (Aix: Publication de l'Université de Provence, 1997), 287–296.

10. An inadequate and superficial exception is Paul Amargier, "Peiresc et Marseille," in *Les Fiortti du Quadricentaire e Fabri de Peiresc*, ed. Jacques Ferrier

(Avignon: Aubanel, 1981), 97–103; also Sidney Aufrère, *La Momie et la tempête: Nicolas-Claude Fabri de Peiresc et la "curiosité Égyptienne" en Provence au début du XVIIe siècle* (Avignon: Éditions A. Barthélemy, 1990), 68.

11. A page of inscriptions and drawings of funerary monuments from St. Victor of Marseille survives in Peiresc's early hand, but there is no explicit date (PBN, MS. Lat. 8958, f. 80r). The sketch of an ancient sculpture found in a private house in Marseille is dated "1614" (f. 41). There is an entire dossier of inscriptions from Marseille, and drawings of ancient sculpture in Marseille (PBN, MS. Lat. 6012, ff. 92r–111r).

12. In his log of outgoing correspondence for the years 1624–1632, Peiresc noted "VOYAGE A MARSEILLE" in September 1626, January 1627, and June 1629, PBN, MS. N.a.f. 5169, ff. 21r, 22r, 22v, 41v). He writes to Vallavez from—or about to leave for—Marseille in March 1625, August 1626, and September 1628 (*Lettres de Peiresc*, 6:139, 597, 619). There were likely many other trips. For example, letters to Aubray and an otherwise unidentified "Madame Maon" were both dated "a Marseille 30 December 1636" (CBI, MS. 1871, f. 435r).

13. The melons were requested from a M. Barthélemy, who owned a shop in Marseille, "La Vigne de la Souque." Peiresc had purchased melons from him the previous year as well (Peiresc to Barthélemy, 7 August 1635, CBI, MS. 1874, f. 380v; Peiresc to Jean-Baptiste Magy, 7 August 1635, CBI, MS. 1874, f. 381r).

14. Peiresc to Vallavez, [late May?] 1626, *Lettres de Peiresc*, 6:543.

15. Peiresc to Vallavez, 18 November 1626, *Lettres de Peiresc*, 6:601; Peiresc to Rubens, 31 March 1627, PBN, MS. N.a.f. 5172, f. 139r.

16. In 1627 he hunted there for information on marine law (Peiresc to Dupuy, 17 July 1627, *Lettres de Peiresc*, 1:296); in 1631 he had a colleague do research for him on the medieval city (Peiresc to Granier, 7 June 1631, CBI, MS. 1873, f. 580v); and in 1632 he made notes on Marseille's weights and measures (PBN, MS. F.fr. 9532, ff. 36r, 37r).

17. Peiresc sought the assistance of M. Bond, "Secretaire et Archivaire en la maison de ville de Marseille," with the consuls on behalf of an acquaintance seeking to do "la recherche de quelques plantes curieuses dans les montagnes" (18 April 1634, CBI, MS. 1871, f. 566r).

18. CBI, MS. 1882, ff. 411–414v; Christofle Bermond to Philibert de Bermond, 13 May 1633, CBI, MS. 1874, f. 310r. Peiresc explained to Guillemin that the acclaim was greater than of anyone else in living memory. Peiresc to Guillemin, 2 May 1633, *Lettres de Peiresc*, 6:154. The log of outgoing correspondence places Vallavez in Marseille in October and December 1626 (PBN, MS. N.a.f. 5169, f. 22r, 22v) while Peiresc's letters to Vallavez find him there in 18–21 November 1626 (6:601–606) and May 1633 (29 May 1633, *Lettres de Peiresc*, 6:638). Peiresc to Minuti, 28 October 1633, refers to Vallavez as being in Marseille (CBI, MS. 1874, f. 317v).

19. CBI, MS. 1882, ff. 415–417v.

20. Peiresc to Vallavez, 4 January 1625, *Lettres de Peiresc*, 6:61; and Peiresc to Vallavez, 24 June 1626, *Lettres de Peiresc*, 6:560.

21. Peiresc to Vallavez, [early 1626], *Lettres de Peiresc*, 6:352. "Restent maintenant les affaires de Marseille où personne ne peult plus vivre avec la liberté accoustumée

parceque Mr de Guise veult qu'ils facent ce qui luy plaict et non aultre chose et si quelqu'un contredict il est menassé et jusques aux consuls mesmes." This letter, like others of this period (e.g., 7 December 1625, 6:328), is in cipher.

22. Peiresc to Jacques Dupuy, *Lettres de Peiresc,* 3:523. "Mais s'il passe jusques à Marseille la premiere veüe de la mer sera capable de luy oster le regret du deffault de juste subject pour le reste de son voyage."

23. Peiresc to Pierre Dupuy, 15 December 1629, *Lettres de Peiresc,* 2:268. The same expression is also in Peiresc to [Dupuy], 9 January 1634, *Lettres de Peiresc,* 3:10.

24. Peiresc to de Thou, 20 March 1633, *Lettres de Peiresc,* 2:467.

3. Marseille and the French Mediterranean

1. Peiresc to Holstenius, 30 December 1627, *Lettres de Peiresc,* 5:263.

2. Fernand Braudel, "Remarques sur la Méditerranée au XVIIe siècle" [1955], in Braudel, *Autour de la Méditerranée,* ed. Roselyne de Ayala and Paule Braudel, pref. M. Aymard (Paris: Éditions de Fallois, 1996), 563. Braudel was not at all interested in Marseille, and his Mediterranean was entirely divided between Spain and Venice. The question of the "decline" of Marseille has been a point of debate going back to the seventeenth century.

3. Michael McCormick, *The Origins of the European Economy: Communications and Commerce AD 300–900* (Cambridge: Cambridge University Press, 2001).

4. Molly Greene suggests the usefulness of this reimagining in "Beyond the Northern Invasion: The Mediterranean in the Seventeenth Century," *Past and Present* 174 (2002): 54. The only work I have found explicitly devoted to the "French Mediterranean," Jean-Claude Izzo and Thierry Fabre, *La Méditerranée française: Les Représentations de la Méditerranée* (Paris: Maisonneuve & Larose, 2000), is entirely focused on the post-Napoleonic period and makes little pretense of original scholarship.

5. Jacques Revel, "Au XVIIe siècle: Le déclin de la Méditerranée?," in *La France et la Méditerranée: Vingt-sept siècles d'interdépendence,* ed. Irad Malkin (Leiden: Brill, 1990), 357.

6. It is a sure sign of the condition of "the field" that the published biography of de Brèves dates from 1904 (J. B. Derost, *Francois Savary, comte de Brèves* [Marcigny: J. B. Derost, 1904]) and the only modern study is partial, and has not been published (Isabelle Petitclerc, *François Savary de Brèves, ambassadeur de Henry IV à Constantinople [1585–1605]: Diplomatie française dans l'Empire ottoman et recherche orientaliste* [PhD diss., Paris IV, 1988; Lille: Atelier National de Reproduction des Thèses, 1989]). I have found some of his letters (PBN, MS. Dupuy 812, ff. 98–280); PBN, MS. Dupuy 194, 180–194; MACC, J 129, J 1862. On de Brèves, see A. Hamilton, "The Study of Islam in Early Modern Europe," *Archiv für Religionsgeschichte* 3 (2001): 179. A handful of references to Peiresc are found in Charles de la Roncière, *Histoire de la Marine française,* vol. 4: *En quête d'un empire colonial* (Paris: Plon, 1910).

7. Viorel Panaite, "A French Ambassador in Istanbul and His Turkish Manuscript on Western Merchants in the Ottoman Mediterranean (Late 16th and Early 17th Centuries)," *Revue des études sud-est européennes* 42 (2004): 122.

8. Still the best book on the French ambassadors in Constantinople is Gérard Tongas, *Les Relations de la France avec l'empire Ottoman durant la première moitié du XVIIe siècle et l'ambassade à Constantinople de Philippe de Harlay, comte de Césy (1619–1640)* (Toulouse: F. Boisseau, 1942).

9. *Relation des Voyages de Monsieur de Brèves, tant en Grece, Terre Saincte et Aegypte, qu'aux Royaumes de Tunis & Arger* (Paris: Nicolas Gasse, 1630).

10. MADD, 9 B 1+², f. 439, dated 23 July 1609. For the most recent study of the system of consulates in the Levant, see Géraud Poumarède, "Naissance d'une institution royale: Les Consuls de la nation française en Levant et en Barbarie aux XVIe et XVIIe siècles," *Annuaire-Bulletin de la Société de l'histoire de France* 2002 (Paris: Société de l'Histoire de France, 2003), 67–128.

11. Most recently on this, see Bernard Heyberger, ed., *Orientalisme, science et controverse: Abraham Ecchellensis (1605–1664)* (Turnhout: Brepols, 2010).

12. Henri Omont, "Projet d'un Collège oriental à Paris au début du règne de Louis XIII," *Bulletin de la Société de Paris et de l'Île de France* 22 (1895): 123–127.

13. De Brèves to Puysieux, 12 May 1619, MACC, J 1862, unpaginated. "Les subiectz du Roy trafficans par les mers de Levant ou pour mieux dire sur la mer mediterranée."

14. Generally, histories of the Mediterranean begin in the 1820s, with Ranke's history of the clash between the Turkish and Spanish Empires, and the French and German "scientific" discovery of the Mediterranean (Daniel Nordman, "La Méditerranée dans la pensée géographique française [vers. 1800–vers. 1950]," in *From the Mediterranean to the China Sea: Miscellaneous Notes,* ed. Claude Guillot, Denys Lombard, and Roderich Ptak [Wiesbaden: Harrassowitz Verlag, 1998], 1–20; *L'Invention scientifique de la Méditerranée: Égypte, Morée, Algérie,* ed. Marie-Noëlle Bourget et al. [Paris: École des Hautes Études en Sciences Sociales, 1998]).

15. Peiresc to Malherbe, 25 November 1606, CBI, MS. 1874, f. 456r. "Il raconte des merveilles de ces pays orientaux."

16. CBI, MS. 1794, f. 230v.

17. De Brèves to Consuls of Marseille, 21 January 1617, MACC, J 1862, unpaginated.

18. I present Peiresc as an heir of de Brèves; Alastair Hamilton and Francis Richard present Du Ryer, in parallel, as another heir: *André Du Ryer and Oriental Studies in Seventeenth-Century France* (Oxford: Oxford University Press, 2004).

19. CBI, MS. 1777, ff. 7r–8v. On the flyleaf Peiresc labeled the document as "Coppie d'un petit advertissement, et succintes instructions des interests qu'a le Roy d'entretenir l'alliance avec le Turc, dressé par M. de Brèves" (f. 8v).

20. For du Vair and Marseille, see Wolfgang Kaiser, "Guillaume du Vair et la pacification de la Provence," in *Guillaume du Vair: Parlementaire et écrivain (1556–1621),* ed. Bruno Petey-Girard and Alexandre Tarrête (Geneva: Droz, 2005), 109–122.

21. CBI, MS. 1777, ff. 7r–v.

22. De Brèves to Consuls of Marseille, 29 January 1617, MACC, J 1862, unpaginated.

23. "Je pris liberté de vous représenter l'avantage que Dieu nous a donné sur tous les Princes de l'Europe, non seulement en puissance pour la vous server, mais

pour agrandir votre domination, par la facilité, que l'assiette de votre Conté de Provence vous en donné, riche comme il est de bons et grands ports, et d'un nombre infiny d'excellens mariniers." CBI, MS. 1789, f. 34r.

24. "Pour luy en oster les moyens il fust que Votre Majesté pense a bon escient aux affaires de la Mer . . . d'autant qu'il n'a acces ny communiquation avec l'Italie que par ceste voye la." CBI, MS. 1789, f. 35r.

25. Aubery in Rome wrote to Peiresc that he would do everything in his power to discourage de Thou from his "fantaisie *s'aller promener en Levant*" and that he was awaiting letters from M. de Brèves on the subject (Aubery to Peiresc, 30 July 1627, PBN MS. F.fr. 9542, f. 243v).

26. See H.-D. [Henri-Delmas] de Grammont, *Relations entre la France & la régence d'Alger au XVIIe siècle: Deuxième partie; La Mission de Sanson Napollon (1628–1633)* (Algiers: Adolphe Jourdan, 1880).

27. De Brèves to Consuls of Marseille, 9 November 1627, MACC, J 1862, unpaginated; Peiresc to Napollon, 13 November 1627, CBI, MS. 1873, f. 363r: he reported receiving from his cousin Guittard in Paris a packet containing letters for Napollon from de Brèves.

28. "Les voyages que le sieur Sanson Napollon a faicte en Constantinople, a Tunis et Alger vous sont assez Cogneu, son soing est louable: Il a reduit ce me semble ceux d'Alger en assez bonne tenue voir la gloire et l'audace de cete milice." De Brèves to Consuls of Marseille, 1 October 1627, MACC, J 1862, unpaginated.

29. De Brèves to Consuls of Marseille, 31 December 1627, MACC, J 1862, unpaginated; de Brèves to Consuls of Marseille, 14 January 1628.

30. Peiresc to Gazille, 13 March 1628, CBI, MS. 1873, f. 464v.

31. Peiresc to Napollon, 13 November 1627, CBI, MS. 1873, f. 363r.

32. Peiresc to Napollon, 6 February 1628, CBI, MS. 1876, f. 367r. Peiresc explained that he would then send all the various letters to Smyrna, on de Thou's route from Venice.

33. Peiresc to Fernoux, 9 March 1629, CBI, MS. 1873, f. 364r. Peiresc identified Fernoux in a letter to Madame de Brèves as "ancien serviteur de votre maison" (Peiresc to Madame de Brèves, 5 June 1630, CBI, MS. 1874, f. 71r). On "Fernoux"—how he signed his name—see Sydney Aufrère, *La Momie et la tempête: Nicolas-Claude Fabri de Peiresc et la "curiosité Égyptienne" en Provence au début du XVIIe siècle* (Avignon: Éditions A. Barthélemy, 1990), 99. Six letters from Peiresc to Madame de Brèves of March–April 1628 move immediately from condolences to the question of securing her son's hold on the abbey of Montmajour (CBI, MS. 1874, ff. 66r–71r). This crisis began unfolding before de Brèves's death, with Peiresc occupying the position of power and de Brèves in the role of supplicant (de Brèves to Peiresc, 10 February 1628, PBN, MS. F.fr. 9542, f. 64r).

34. Peiresc to Gazille, 16 May 1629, CBI, MS. 1873, f. 468r: "Au reste Madame de Brèves est en peine de certaines pieces de scarlate que le Sr du Troncay devoit porter en Alger comme vous savez, lesquelles sont demeurez inutiles a Marseille. Si vous pouvez trouver moyen de les faire employer ou en debiter en sorte qu'elle demeurat satisfaite de ce coté là vous l'obligeriez grandement. Parlez en un peu je vous prie avec Mr Fort qui a garde de cette affaire et me donnez avis et votre sentence sur ce sujet."

35. Peiresc to de Thou, 13 February 1635, CBI, MS. 1877, f. 426v. "Cet homme est assez industrieux & a d'honnestes garantz de ceste ville. Difficillement trouvera on des personnes de meilleure condition qui voulussent s'aller exposer de la sorte. C'est pourquoy je pense qu'il ne le fault pas negliger, & quand mesmes il en cousteroit quelque chose pour le commencement soit au roy ou a Mr de Brèves possible la despense n'en seroit pas toute perdüe."

36. Peiresc to Dupuy, 17 January 1630, *Lettres de Peiresc*, 2:230.

37. Peiresc to Moreau, 6 December 1634, CBI, MS. 1874, f. 773v. "Ce que le peché original de notre commune naissance en un sie chetif lieu, & un pais si sterile et si voysin de la Barbarie (qui n'en est separaré que par un canal de mer)." On the trope of the sterility of Marseille and its hinterland, see Wolfgang Kaiser, "Une aristocratie urbaine entre la plume et l'épée: Les 'nobles marchands' de Marseille, XVIe–XVIIe siècles," in *Le Second Ordre: L'Idéal nobiliaire; Hommage à Ellery Schalk* (Paris: Presses de l'Université de Paris-Sorbonne, 1999), 164–165.

38. Peiresc to Hainhofer, 17 October 1633, quoted in Bresson, "Peiresc et le cercle humaniste d'Augsbourg," *Sciences et Techniques en Perspective*, 2nd ser. 9 (2005): 240.

39. Peiresc to Dupuy, 19 September 1627, *Lettres de Peiresc*, 1:369.

40. Peter N. Miller, *Peiresc's "History of Provence": Antiquarianism and the Discovery of a Medieval Mediterranean*, Transactions of the American Philosophical Society 101, 3 (Philadelphia: American Philosophical Society, 2011), 38–42, 45–47.

41. Peiresc to Dupuy, 19 September 1627, *Lettres de Peiresc*, 1:369.

42. Peiresc to Dupuy, 17 July 1627, *Lettres de Peiresc*, 1:296. "Il fault que j'aille faire un petit tour à Marseille. J'iray voir dans les archives de l'hostel de ville s'il n'y auroit rien de curieux sur ce subject, Dieu aydant, et en feray de touts costez toute la plus exacte recherche que je pourray, pour l'amour de vous."

43. Peiresc to Dupuy, 2 August 1617, *Lettres de Peiresc*, 1:317.

44. CBI, MS. 1775, f. 174r. "Edit du Commerce," also titled "Edit du Roy pour l'establissment du commerce general en France Par Mer & Par Terre Levant, Ponant, & Voyages de long Cours."

45. CBI, MS. 1775, ff. 174r–v.

46. CBI, MS. 1775, f. 179r.

47. CBI, MS. 1775, f. 226.

48. CBI, MS. 1775, f. 232r. "Les advantages et commoditez que le Roy d'Espagne recevra *de l'Admirauté de Seville*."

49. CBI, MS. 1873, f. 684r.

50. "Je me resjouys grandement avec vous du bon visage que vous dictes avoir receu du Roy et de Mr le Cardinal et de la favorable audiance qu'ilz vous ont donnée concernant le restablissement du commerce de noz mers." Peiresc to Aubespine, 11 August 1627, CBI, MS. 1871, f. 410r [*Lettres de Peiresc*, 7:250–251].

51. Peiresc to Richelieu, 24 July 1628, CBI, MS. 1875, f. 486v.

52. Peiresc to Richelieu, 20 March 1633, CBI, MS. 1875, f. 495r; Peiresc to Villeaux-clercs, 20 March 1633, CBI, MS. 1876, f. 623r.

53. For example, Peiresc to Richelieu, 8 November 1635, CBI, MS. 1875, ff. 511r–v.

54. CBI, MS. 493, f. 119r.

55. CBI, MS. 493, ff. 248r, 251r.

56. Peiresc to Aycard, 4 June 1635, CBI, MS. 1871, f. 52r. Much of the same material is then retailed to de Thou in a letter of 15 October 1635 (CBI, MS. 1876, f. 380v).

57. For example, Peiresc to Loménie, 18 April 1634 and 15 August 1634, CBI, MS. 1874, ff. 190r, 193v.

58. Peiresc to Sabran, 8 November 1635, CBI, MS. 1876, f. 12v. "Qu'ils ont gardé si longuement a la barbe du Roy de Perse et de toute sa puissance et des autres pareil places qu'ils ont occupées sur les bords de la barbarie et des Indes."

59. Peiresc to de Thou, 20 February 1635, CBI, MS. 1877, f. 427v. "Si la France n'avoit pas maintenant d'ailleurs les aultres plus grandes affaires qu'elle à sur les bras on se pourroit embarquer sur la confiance que recognoissant l'importance de celles du Levant on y prevoyeroit comme il fault." In this same letter Peiresc noted that M. de Marcheville "m'a dict icy qu'il à esté des années entieres sans avoir aulcunes responces formelles aux affaires plus pressantes de son Ambassade."

60. Though they are generally ignored in the existing literature on early modern merchants. See, for example, *Commercial Networks in the Early Modern World,* ed. Diogo Ramada Curto and Anthony Molho (Florence: EUI, 2002); *Trading Cultures: The Worlds of Western Merchants*, ed. Jeremy Adelman and Stephen Aron (Turnhout: Brepols, 2003); *Cultures et formations négociantes dans l'Europe moderne,* ed. Franco Angiolini and Daniel Roche (Paris: EHESS, 1995).

61. Peiresc to de Thou, 25 April 1629, CBI, MS. 1876, f. 354v. Seghezzi is discussed in Aufrère, *La Momie et la tempête*, 91–96; Oleg V. Volkoff, *À la recherche de manuscrits en Égypte,* Recheches d'archéologie, de philologie et d'histoire, vol. 30 (Cairo: Institut Français d'Archéologie Orientale, 1974), 81–82.

62. Peiresc to Seghezzi, 6 December 1634, CBI, MS. 1874, f. 358r. "Commercio non solamente in Egitto, ma molto piu oltre come era stato altre volte, cosi nell'Affrica, et nell'Etiopie, come nell'Arabia & sino all'India ch'havevano tanta prattica nel Moucal, & altri luoghi del Mar Rosso."

63. Peiresc to Seguiran, 9 December 1634, CBI, MS. 1876, f. 163v. "Non des nobles de la Republique ains de ceux qui sont subjects . . . restablir le commerce qui s'en alloit ruiné tout a plat en ce pais la."

64. Peiresc to Gela, 6 March 1635, CBI, MS. 1874, f. 367r: "Ciò che m'haveva piu mosso a questo pensato va fondato su l'opinion da me presa, che Mr de Brèves come piu interezzato d'ogni altro, potessi parlare à nome dell'Ill.mo Sr Segezzi, si come quelli che facevano instanza contraria per il Sr Bermondo, sotto bene-placito però dell'uno & dell'altro."

65. Peiresc to de Thou, 20 March 1633, CBI, MS. 1877, f. 307v. "Les choses de la marine vous sont si à coeur que je ne doubte nullement que vous ne vous em-ployerez volontiers en ceste occasion comme je vous en supplie."

66. Peiresc to de Thou, 5 December 1634, CBI, MS. 1877, f. 408v: "Qu'il ne fault pas trouver estrange ce que mande le Sr Santo et pense que le bonne heure Monsr de Brèves c'est advisé de l'employer en l'exercice de ce consuls car tout le commerce s'en alloit aultant et plus ruiné de ce coste là qu'en Constanti-nople vous avés cogneu la personage sur les lieux et scavés mieux que tout aultre je m'asseure ce qu'on en peult attendre croyant vu que n'aura pas esté sans votre conseil, que Monsr de Brèves a traité avec luy."

67. Peiresc to de Thou, 27 April 1635, CBI, MS. 1877, f. 440v: "Mr de Brèves, eust ce consulat appres avoir supplanté un Venitien qui l'avoit possedé plus de dix ans dont vous pourres avoir apprins sur les lieux les tenants et aboutissans, pour dire qu'il n'y avoit rien de nouveau, quant un autre Venitien l'auroit."

68. I am grateful to Jerome Delatour for sharing with me information about the career of François-Auguste de Thou.

69. Peiresc repeatedly urged him to drop this plan, for example, Peiresc to de Thou, 15 January 1635, CBI, MS. 1877, f. 419v.

70. Interestingly, Peiresc emphasized the importance of linguistic competence because it would free him from the "ordinary betrayals" ("trahisons ordinaires") of the translators. Peiresc to de Thou, 30 January 1635, CBI, MS. 1877, f. 422v.

71. Peiresc to de Thou, undated, probably late February or early March 1635, CBI, MS. 1877, f. 431r.

72. Peiresc to de Thou, 14 March 1635, CBI, MS. 1877, f.432v. "Encores que plusieurs se persuadent qu'il aye d'aussi grandz desseins a s'y faire employer qu'avoit eu feu M. de Brèves."

73. Peiresc to de Thou, 8 May 1635, CBI, MS. 1877, f. 446r.

74. Peiresc's long account of the Duke of Guise's review of the strategic situation in the western Mediterranean focuses on the shipping capacity available in Spain, Genoa, Naples, and Sicily. CBI, MS. 1826, f. 292r.

75. Peiresc to Loménie, 20 December 1632, CBI, MS. 1874, f. 174r. As early as January 1628 Peiresc knew of Richelieu's plan to suppress the office of admiral and claim its powers to himself (Peiresc to Dupuy, 22 January 1628, *Lettres de Peiresc*, 1:505).

76. MAD, 9 B 2, f. 252r, dated 24 September 1632. Seguiran succeeded his father as premier president of the Cour des Comptes, Aides et Finances of Provence.

77. For the sum, see MAD, B 9 2, f. 252r. For Peiresc's work on behalf of Seguiran, see Peiresc to le Grand, 5 May 1628, CBI, MS. 1873, f. 560r, seeking a letter from the king or from the "secretaire du Cabinet" on behalf of Raymond (le Grand was a "Conseiller du Roy" and "Recepveur General de ses Finances en la generalité de Paris"). In exchange—for this is how things worked in Peiresc's France—he obtained from his Roman contacts a letter on the subject of the priory desired by le Grand's son (Peiresc to le Grand, 19 May 1628, CBI, MS. 1873, f. 560r). From beyond the grave it was Peiresc who secured the transfer to the Seguiran clan of his abbey at Guîtres.

78. Peiresc to Gassendi, 18 November 1632, *Lettres de Peiresc*, 4:265.

79. The presentation copy is PBN, MS. F.fr. 24169, ff. 1–80. It is printed in *Correspondance de Henri d'Escoubleau de Sourdis. . . . Augmentée des ordres, instructions et lettres de Louis XIII* par Eugène Sue, 3 vols. (Paris: Crapelet, 1889), 3: 223–319.

80. CBI, MS. 1775, ff. 80r–99r, printed in Peiresc, *Histoire abrégée de Provence & autres textes*, ed. Jacques Ferrier and Michel Feuillas (Avignon: Aubanel, 1982), pp. 290–316. I discuss the Mediterranean context for the Seguiran Report in Section 23, "Mapping the Mediterranean."

81. "Côtes maritimes de Provence," printed in Peiresc, *Histoire abrégée de Provence*, 301: "Et ce fut lors que commença la richesse et opulence de leur ville."

82. This information is presented in tabular form in Michel Fontenay, *La Méditer-ranée entre la Croix et le Croissant: Navigation, commerce, course et piraterie (XVIe–XIXe siècle)* (Paris: Classiques Garnier, 2012), 162. Fontenay gives the last figure as 1.5 million piastres, but we know that the exchange rate was three livres for the écu and approximately one écu for the piastre.

83. The presentation copy of the report, PBN, MS. F.fr. 24169, matches what is found in CBI, MS. 1775, ff. 1–75, while adding two more pages (f. 81 lists seats of the admiralty for Provence and f. 82 the differential taxation of Marseille vs. other admiralty seats). The "Côte Maritime de Provence" is not included for presentation.

84. "Cela a procédé de ce que le luxe étant devenu plus grand qu'il n'avait jamais été, les soies ont été de requête et les Marseillais s'étant attachés à cette espèce de marchandise y ont trouvé un grand profit." Peiresc, *Histoire abrégée de Provence*, 302–303.

85. De Thou to Dupuy, 5 August 1628, PBN, MS. Dupuy 703, f. 140r. "J'irai d'ici droit a Smyrne d'ou je vous manderai de mes nouvelles car ily a tousjours des vaisseaux pour Marseille."

86. Louis Deshayes de Courmenin, *Voyage du Levant fait par le commandement du roy en l'année 1621 par le sieur D.C.* (Paris, 1629, 2nd ed.), 457, quoted in Paul Masson, *Histoire du commerce français dans le Levant au XVIIe siècle* (Paris: Hachette, 1896), 478. "Outre cela les mariniers de Marseille sont si adroits et ont une telle pratique de la Méditerranée qu'ils y sont en pareille considération que les Hollandais sur l'Océan." On Deshayes, see René Pillorget, "Louis De-shayes de Courmenin et l'orient Musulman (1621–1626)," *Cahiers de l'Association internationale des études françaises* 27 (1975): 65–81.

87. Peregrine Horden and Nicholas Purcell, *Corrupting Sea: A Study of Mediterra-nean History,* (Oxford: Blackwell Publishers, 2000), p. 144: "Our aim, by con-trast, has been to replace the almost mystical attachment of French geograph-ical historians to the concept of routes with a notion of shifting webs of casual, local, small-scale contacts radiating from slightly different centres in different ages but constant in their economic and social effect—with something nearer, in fact, to Braudel's own formulation: 'the whole Mediterranean consists of movement in space' (1972a, 277). We hope thereby to undercut the dualism of existing approaches to Mediterranean trade, which are founded on a clear dis-tinction between the world of 'high commerce,' *la grande navigation*, and small coastwise movements. Insistence on this dualism (we believe) makes the sophistication of the one end of the spectrum harder to explain, and dis-tracts attention from the humbler movements at the other end, although these are a fundamental ingredient in the social and economic history of the Mediterranean."

88. Blanc to Peiresc, 5 March 1630, PBN, MS. F.fr. 9542, f. 29r.

89. We know that in 1620 Maretz worked with Lombard, whom Peiresc had gotten the appointment as "Controleur des batiments royaux et oeuvres publiques," to represent the city of Aix in a property dispute with the Augustinians. Aix, Arch. municipale DD 35, 733 cited in Myriem Foncin and Monique de la Roncière, "Jacques Maretz et la cartographie des côtes de Provence au XVIIe siècle,"

Actes du Quatre-vingt-dixième Congrès National des Sociétés Savants. Nice 1965 (Section de Géographie) (PBN, 1966), 10. For discussion of the Maretz map in the context of contemporary French cartography, see David Buisseret, "Monarchs, Ministers, and Maps in France before the Accession of Louis XIV," in *Monarchs, Ministers, and Maps: The Emergence of Cartography as a Tool of Government in Early Modern Europe,* ed. David Buisseret (Chicago: University of Chicago Press, 1992), 115–116.

90. For the identification of ship types, see A. Jal, *Glossaire Nautique: Répertoire polyglotte de termes de marine anciens et modernes* (Paris: Firmin Didot Frères, 1848).

91. Peiresc to de Thou, 14 May 1635, CBI, MS. 1877, f. 449r. We know that Fernoux planned to depart from Alexandria in September 1632 (Fernoux to Consuls of Marseille, 26 August 1632, MACC, J 574, unpaginated) but we do not know whether he met with Peiresc on this visit or on a subsequent one or whether Fernoux remained in France.

4. Contingency

1. PBN, MS. Lat. 9340, f. 93r. "Lettres Samaritaines originelles escriptes à feu Scaliger (qu'il nomme Sullarin Afarnachi ou Franchi) lieu de AZA, par ELEAZAR Grand Prebstre des Samaritains l'an 998, le 6 [ou Vendredy] 20 mensis Seba, c'est Januarii, du regne des enfans d'Ismael filz d'Agar, ou Du Regne des Ismaelites Agerus, qui est le Turques et revient a l'an de Christ *1590* au calcul de Scaliger."

2. Peiresc to Scaliger, 15 February 1606, in *Epistres françaises des personages illustres et doctes à Joseph-Juste de la Scala,* ed. Jacques de Reves (Harderwijk, 1624), 142. Pierre Hostagier was part of an elite Marseille merchant family. I thank Wolfgang Kaiser for this information.

3. Gassendi, *Mirrour,* 94.

4. For all these examples and for a broader discussion, see Peter N. Miller, *Peiresc's Orient: Antiquarianism as Cultural History in the Seventeenth Century* (Farnham, UK: Ashgate, 2012).

5. "Tombees ez mains du feu Sr Genebard et puis de feu Mr Pol [*sic*] Hurault Archevesque d'Aix et finalement du Sr. Billon qui les avoit baillees à M. Galaup de qui je les y ay eües. En Aoust 1629." PBN, MS. Lat. 9340, f. 9.

6. I have found only one reference to Genebrard, as a printer of Hebrew manuscripts, in a letter of Peiresc to Petit, 19 March 1633, CBI, MS. 1875, f. 258r.

7. They are PBN, MS. Samaritan 11.

8. PBN, MS. Lat. 9340, ff. 95–103. The Hebrew and Samaritan versions are in the hand of Salomon Azubi, the rabbi of Carpentras. The Latin translation is in Peiresc's hand, which suggests he might have done it from the Hebrew translation or while working with Azubi. On their study sessions, see Miller, *Peiresc's Orient,* ch. 6. We know also, however, that Peiresc worked with François de Galaup, sieur de Chasteuil, on these letters. See Galaup to Peiresc, [late November 1629], in *Les Correspondants de Peiresc,* 2 vols. (Geneva: Slatkine, 1972), 2:310. Peiresc was still working on the letters a year later (Galaup to Peiresc, 2 October

1630, PBN, MS. Lat. 9340, f. 77r). Chasteuil's comparison of the Hebrew and Samaritan versions of Genesis is found in PBN, MS. Lat. 9340, ff. 70r–75v.

9. PBN, MS. Lat. 9340, ff. 93r–v.

10. Peiresc to Roubaud, 1 August 1629, CBI, MS. 1876, f. 357v: "J'admire la fortune de cez pauvres hardes d'estre passée par la mercy de la mer par celle des voleurs."

5. Peiresc's Letters

1. Paul Dibon, "Communication in the Republic of Letters of the 17th Century," *Res Publica Litterarum* 1 (1978): 45–55; Henk Nellen, "La Correspondance savante au XVIIe siècle," *XVIIe siècle* 178 (1993): 87–98; Marc Fumaroli, "Venise et la République des Lettres au XVIe siècle," in *Crisi e rinnovamenti nell'autunno del Rinascimento a Venezia,* ed. Vittore Branca and Carlo Ossola (Florence: Leo S. Olschki Editore, 1991), 348–358; Hans Bots and Françoise Waquet, *La République des Lettres* (Paris: Bélin, 1997); *Commercium Litterarium: La Communication dans la République des Lettres/Forms of Communication in the Republic of Letters 1600–1750,* ed. Hans Bots and Françoise Waquet (Amsterdam: APA-Holland University Press, 1994); *Les grand intermédiaires culturels de la République des Lettres: Études de réseaux de correspondances du XVIe au XVIIIe siècles,* ed. Christiane Berkvens-Stevelink, Hans Bots, and Jens Häseler (Paris: Honoré Champion, 2005); Dirk van Miert, ed., *Communicating Observations in Early Modern Letters (1500–1675): Epistolography and Epistemology in the Age of the Scientific Revolution* (London: Warburg Institute, 2013), 4–6.

2. Francisco Bethencourt and Florike Egmond, "Introduction," in *Correspondence and Cultural Exchange in Europe, 1400–1700,* ed. Francisco Bethencourt and Florike Egmond (Cambridge: Cambridge University Press, 2007), 1–4.

3. See, for example, Jean Boutier, Sandro Landi, and Olivier Rouchon, eds., *La Politique par correspondance: Les Usages politiques de la lettre en Italie (XIVe–XVIIIe siècle)* (Rennes: Presses Universitaires de Rennes, 2009); Johann Petitjean, *L'Intelligence des choses: Une histoire de l'information entre Italie et Méditerranée (XVIe–XVIIe siècles)* (Rome: École Française de Rome, 2013).

4. Exemplary are Francesca Trivellato, *The Familiarity of Strangers: The Sephardic Diaspora, Livorno, and Cross-Cultural Trade in the Early Modern Periods* (New Haven, CT: Yale University Press, 2009); David Hancock, *Oceans of Wine: Madeira and the Emergence of American Trade and Taste* (New Haven, CT: Yale University Press, 2009); and Jessica Goldberg, *Trade and Institutions in the Medieval Mediterranean: The Geniza Merchants and Their Business World* (Cambridge: Cambridge University Press, 2012), esp. ch. 2.

5. The classic article is Marc Fumaroli, "Genèse de l'épistolographie classique: Rhétorique humaniste de la lettre, de Pétrarque à Juste Lipse," *Revue d'histoire littéraire de la France* 78 (1978): 887–905.

6. *Lettres de négociants marseillais: Les Frères Hermite (1570–1612),* ed. Micheline Baulant, avant-propos Fernand Braudel (Paris: Armand Colin, 1953). On merchant letters and their genre, see Trivellato, *Familiarity of Strangers,* ch. 7; Trivellato, "Merchants' Letters across Geographical and Social Boundaries,"

in *Correspondence and Cultural Exchange in Europe, 1400–1700,* ed. Francisco Bethencourt and Florike Egmond (Cambridge: Cambridge University Press, 2007), 80–103.

7. A full-scale comparative structural analysis of scholars' and merchants' letters would be worthwhile, and thanks to the work of the generations of the 1950s and 2000s it can be done easily and at a high level. Goldberg's careful analysis of the eleventh-century Geniza merchants' letters by content, network, and geography shows the *longue durée* of these merchant epistolary practices (Goldberg, *Trade and Institutions,* esp. chs. 7, 9).

8. The manuscript has been the subject of Serge Maupouet, *Le Registre des correspondants de Peiresc, ou le réseau épistolaire et relationnel, européen et méditerranéen d'un humaniste aixois dans la troisième décennie du dix-septième siècle,* 4 vols. (Mémoire de Maitrise, Université de Paris XII—Val de Marne, Faculté des Lettres—Departement d'Histoire, 1996). These figures are his. I thank Françoise Waquet for making this available to me.

9. I mean this, of course, only metaphorically, for a *geniza* is a garbage dump, while an archive is a retrieval system. It is as a tribute to the documentary worlds recovered through the Cairo Geniza that I make this comparison.

10. Robert Mandrou was perhaps the first to see Peiresc as modeling for the early seventeenth century what Erasmus does for the earlier sixteenth. See Mandrou, *From Humanism to Science 1480–1700* (Atlantic Highlands, NJ: Humanities Press, 1979 [1973]; Marc Fumaroli, *Peiresc: Prince de la République des Lettres* (Brussels: Pro Peyresq, 1992); Bethencourt and Egmond, "Introduction," 1–4; *Les grands intermédiaires culturels de la République des Lettres: Études de réseaux de correspondances du XVIe au XVIIIe siècles,* ed. Christiane Berkvens-Stevelinck, Hans Bots, and Jens Häseler (Paris: Honoré Champion, 2005), 103–126; Françoise Waquet and Hans Bots, *La République des Lettres* (Paris: Bélin, 1997). The phrase is Michel de Certeau's (*The Writing of History* [New York: Columbia University Press, 1988], 74).

11. Jean Boutier, "Étienne Baluze et l'Europe savante à l'âge classique," in *Étienne Baluze, 1630–1718: Érudition et pouvoirs dans l'Europe classique,* ed. Boutier (Limoges: Presses Universitaires de Limoges, 2008), 291.

12. The batches of correspondence were compiled by first grouping together any set of letters written on the same day, or, when relevant, within two days. For instance, in January of 1635, Peiresc wrote four letters on the 5th and two on the 6th, and these were grouped together as a likely unit. This list was refined and supplemented by information from PBN, MS. N.a.f. 5169, which specifies the relationship between persons in some of the constellations, and identifies letters not seen in the other manuscripts. If we look at 3–4 June 1629, for example, only two letters (Capt. Bartolle and Minuti) are found in the 1876 manuscript, while N.a.f. 5169 shows that Capt. Bartolle was to pass on a letter to Minuti, along with two other letters (to the vice-legate for Zenobis by way of Fort), and that all these letters would be conveyed initially by de Gastines. I want to thank my research assistant, Antonia Behan, for her work on this material in particular.

13. Peiresc to Sabatier, 12 January 1633, CBI, MS. 1876, ff. 825r–v.

14. The word "portuary" is a calque from French, and has become more common in the recent scholarly focus on ports and maritime life in the Mediterranean. See, for instance, A. Guimerà and D. Romero, eds., *Puertos y sistemas portuarios (siglo XVI–XX)* (Madrid: Puertos del Estado, 1996); S. Fettah, "Temps et espaces des trafics portuaires en Méditerrannée: Le cas du port franc du Livourne (XVIIe–XIXe siècles)," *Richerche storiche* (1998): 243–273; Gilbert Buti, "Ville maritime sans port, ports éphémères et poussière portuaire: Le golfe de Fréjus aux XVIIe et XVIIIe siècles," *Rives méditerranéennes* 35 (2010), special issue, "Les petits ports": 11–27.

6. Writing to the Levant, 1626–1637

1. There is no adequate standard treatment of the man. An old edition of his travel letters exists, *Revue retrospective,* 2e ser. 3 (1835), 351–408; 4 (1836), 5–72, 184–224, 338–397; 6 (1836), 62–97, 207–244. A new comprehensive edition of his letters is being prepared by Jérôme Delatour. For biographical reflections based on new research, see Delatour, "Jacques-Auguste II de Thou, ou l'impossible héritage," in *Jacques-Auguste de Thou (1553–1617): Écriture et condition robine,* ed. Frank Lestringant (Paris: Presses Paris Sorbonne, 2007), 175–209; " 'Les Armes en main et les larmes aux yeux': Le Procès de Cinq-Mars et de Thou (1642)," in *Les Procès politiques (XIVᵉ–XVIIᵉ siècles),* ed. Yves-Marie Bercé (Rome: École Française de Rome, 2007), 351–393.

2. Peiresc to Dupuy, 8 November 1626, CBI, MS. 1877, f. 18v.

3. Peiresc to Bonnaire, 8 January 1627, CBI, MS. 1872, f. 195r. Peiresc identifies Galaup as "votre parent" (Peiresc to Aymini, 25 April 1631, CBI, MS. 1876, f. 813r). For full biographical data, see Gaspard Augeri, *Le Provençal solitaire au Mont Liban, ou La Vie de Monsieur François de Galaup, sieur de Chasteuil* (Aix, 1658); Jean de La Roque, *Voyage de Syrie et du Mont-Liban,* Voyageurs d'Orient I, ed. Jean Raymond (Beirut: Editions Dar Lahad Khater B.P., 1981).

4. Peiresc to Bonnaire, 8 January 1627, CBI, MS. 1872, f. 195r. "Qui a cognaissance des langues orientales lequel pourroit faire des belles observations en ce pais la."

5. Peiresc to de Thou, 30 April 1627, CBI, MS. 1876, f. 364r.

6. De Thou to Peiresc, [ ] May 1627, PBN, MS. N.a.f. 3283, f. 66. "Quand vos comendemens m'en feront naistre les moiens." De Thou also apologized for having nothing much to say, explaining, "Nous sommes en un lieu qui produit aussi peu de nouvelles que le vostre & ou l'ordre est si bon que les changemens qui avient ne sont que naturels & par consequent ne servent apporter de 'alteration a l'estat.' "

7. Peiresc to de Thou, 22 August 1627, CBI, MS. 1876, ff. 365r-v. "Mais quand je pensois a cette peste & a cette barbarie qui est si incompatible avec toute sorte de bonne curiosité il me falloit bien changer d'advice."

8. Peiresc to Bonnaire, 26 August 1627, CBI, MS. 1872, f. 197r. Peiresc was still pushing Bonnaire to obtain the requisite documents for Aymini two months later (Peiresc to Bonnaire, 27 October 1627, CBI, MS. 1872, f. 197v).

9. Peiresc to de Thou, 28 October 1627, CBI, MS. 1876, f. 366r.

10. Peiresc to Dupuy, 2 December 1627, CBI, MS. 1877, f. 99r; Peiresc to de Thou, 2 December 1627, CBI, MS. 1876, f. 366v.

11. Peiresc to Bonnaire, 31 December 1627 and 6 January 1628, CBI, MS. 1872, ff. 197v and 198r.

12. Peiresc to Camerarius, 30 November 1627, CBI, MS. 1873, f. 21r.

13. His letter to Dupuy of 6 January 1628 was written from Venice. PBN, MS. Naf. 5173, f. 40r.

14. PBN, MS. N.a.f. 5169, f. 30v.

15. Peiresc to de Thou, 12 February 1628, CBI, MS. 1876, f. 367v.

16. Peiresc to de Thou, 12 February 1628, CBI, MS. 1876, f. 367v.

17. Peiresc to Valbelle, 7 February 1628, CBI, MS. 1876, f. 367r; Peiresc to Napollon, 6 February 1628, CBI, MS. 1876, f. 367r. Peiresc also wrote directly to Viguier, consul of Syria, on de Thou's behalf (Peiresc to Viguier, 7 February 1628, CBI, MS. 1876, f. 367r).

18. Peiresc to de Thou, 19 February 1628, CBI, MS. 1876, f. 368v.

19. Peiresc to de Thou, 12 February 1628, CBI, MS. 1876, f. 368r: "Si vous rencontrez des livres MS en Caracteres Samaritains soit en cette langue la ou en vray hebraique ne les laissez pas eschapper[.] Feu Mr de la Scala en faisoit tres grand cas & si vous trouvez des medailles chargées aussy de Characteres Samaritains et phoeniciene ou punique soit en cuivre ou en argent quelque ressemblance qu'il y en ait entr'elles ne les laissez non plus eschapper facilement (hors de ce siecle si ordinaire que vous aurez veu fort souvent je m'asseure qui a un Calice d'un costé & une petite branche de l'autre) sur tout si vous en trouviez d'un escript de la sorte elles meriteroient d'estre bien payée."

20. For Peiresc and the Samaritans, see Peter N. Miller, *Peiresc's Orient: Antiquarianism as Cultural History in the Seventeenth Century* (Farnham, UK: Ashgate, 2012), chs. 4 and 5.

21. De Thou to Dupuy, 28 May 1628, PBN, MS. N.a.f. 5173, f. 42.

22. De Thou to Dupuy, 28 May 1628, PBN, MS. Dupuy 703, ff. 124v–125v.

23. Peiresc to Jean Guez [in Marseille], 1 August 1628, CBI, MS. 1876, f. 368v. After arriving in Constantinople, de Thou described Guillaume Guez as "un tres galant homme, & qui le porte plus hault que le marchand ordinaire (il est de la religion)." De Thou to Pierre Dupuy, 28 May 1628, PBN, MS. Dupuy 703, f. 125v.

24. Peiresc to de Thou, 4 August 1628, CBI, MS. 1876, f. 369r.

25. Peiresc to de Thou [undated, but likely August or September 1628], CBI, MS. 1876, f. 370v. "Il n'y auroit pas de mal de vous enquerir s'il s'en trouveroit quelque chose de pardela. Et si en aucune contrée de l'Aegypte et de l'Ethiopie il y reste aulcunes vestiges et reliques de la langue Aegyptienne antique bien que corrompue, comme est l'Italienne du Latin, la vulgaire grecque du vieulx Grec, et celles des Basques, Bas Bretons & Walons, de l'ancienne Gauloise ou Bretonne, car on est maintenant en ceste curiosité tant dans Rome que dans Paris."

26. Peiresc to Guez, 20 September 1628, CBI, MS. 1876, f. 371r.

27. Peiresc to de Thou, [6 September] 1628, CBI, MS. 1876, f. 371r.

28. Peiresc to Guez [in Marseille], 6 September 1628, CBI, MS. 1876, f. 372r. This likely refers to a Jean Aubert.

29. Peiresc to de Thou, 14 December 1628, CBI, MS. 1876, f. 372v. "Principalement ceste histoire sarracinesque si celle est autre que celle qu'il nous à donner Erpenius depuis quelque annees."

30. See Miller, *Peiresc's Orient,* ch. 3.

31. Peiresc to Estelle, 14 December 1628, CBI, MS. 1876, f. 373v.

32. On him, see the new biography by T. J. Gorton, *Renaissance Emir: A Druze Warlord at the Court of the Medici* (London: Quartet Books, 2013). I am grateful to Noel Malcolm for providing me with this reference.

33. Peiresc to [de Loches], 14 December 1628, CBI, MS. 1876, f. 374r. "& principalement leurs chroniques s'il vous en pourroit tomber en main & quelque vocabulaire & grammaire s'il s'en pourroit rencontre comme aussy des livres agiptiens des Jacobites ou Alcuptes qui ont leur Pentateuqe in leur langue avec des traductions arabiques dont on se promettoit bien de fruict . . . tant que vous pourriez, les inscriptions que vous trouverez gravez sur des marbres ou autres pierres en quelque langue que ce peusse estre soit grecque ou latine ou phoenicien." This last point referred to the medieval "Assises of Jerusalem." See Peter N. Miller, *Peiresc's "History of Provence": Antiquarianism and the Discovery of a Medieval Mediterranean,* Transactions of the American Philosophical Society 101, 3 (Philadelphia: American Philosophical Society, 2011), 45–47.

34. Peiresc to Guez [in Marseille], 25 December 1628, CBI, MS. 1876, f. 375r.

35. Peiresc to d'Avaux, 6 January 1629, in *Peiresc: Lettres à divers; Supplément au tome VII de l'édition Tamizey de Larroque et Errata,* ed. Raymond Lebègue with Agnès Bresson (Paris: CNRS, 1985), 82 [= CBI, MS. 1871, f. 398r].

36. Peiresc to R. P. Jean François Provincial des Minimes en Provence à Marseille, 14 February 1629, CBI, MS. 1876, f. 375r.

37. Peiresc to Tarquet, 14 February 1629, CBI, MS. 1876, f. 375v.

38. Peiresc to l'Empereur, 14 February 1629, CBI, MS. 1876, f. 375v. "Des belles curiosities que vous avez recueillir mesme en matiere des medailles antiques grecques & Syriacques. Et si tant est que vous en ayez de celles qui se trouves escriptes en Caracteres Samaritains de quelque metail & grandeur qu'elles soient."

39. Peiresc to l'Empereur en Hierusalem, 14 February 1629, CBI, MS. 1876, f. 376r: "Que s'il se trouver là quelque orphevre ou autre ouvrier qui en sceust faire du empreinte moulleure de plomb en sable, ou en plastre, mon obligation en seroit bien plus grande, car i'y pourrois voir la vraye figure du caractere plus fidellement que si on les desseigner a la plume attendu qu'il est malaisé de les portraire assez fidelement por empescher les equivoques de l'un à l'autre."

40. Peiresc to l'Empereur, 19 September 1633, CBI, MS. 1876, f. 831r. "Ces pierres de George, du Mogor & Moldavie."

41. Peiresc to RP Jean Francois, 26 February 1629, CBI, MS. 1876, f. 376r.

42. Peiresc to Minuti, 26 February 1629, CBI, MS. 1876, f. 376r. "Par ce qu'il est trop malaisé de rediger par escript tout ce que je vous pourrois dire." The memoranda are discussed in Miller, *Peiresc's Orient,* ch. 3.

43. Peiresc to Tarquet, 26 February 1629, and Peiresc to l'Empereur, 26 February 1629, CBI, MS. 1876, f. 376r.

44. Peiresc to Fernoux, 9 March 1629, CBI, MS. 1873, f. 364r. "Et particulierement en la recherche qu'il desire faire de quelques livres s'il en peu rencontre en langue Samaritaine et Aegyptienne parmy les familles qui sont au Caire (et dict on) et de Samaritaines et de Coptites, ensemble de quelque autres sortes d'antiquailles s'il en peu trouver."

45. Peiresc to Lambert, 9 March 1629, CBI, MS. 1873, f. 364v.

46. Peiresc to Mary, Douaille, Fraisse, 9 March 1629, CBI, MS. 1876, f. 158r: "Ce mot sera pour vous prie d'escripre un mot de recommendation en AEgypte a voz correspondantz en faveur du R. P. Théophile Minuti des minimes avec un peu de credit a fin d'y estre secours de ce qu'il pourroit avoir affaire[s] pour luy ou pour employer à quelques singularitez de ma curiosité en quoy vous m'obligerez beaucoup."

47. Peiresc to Salicoffres, 9 March 1629, CBI, MS. 1876, f. 158r.

48. Peiresc to de Gastines, 9 March 1629, CBI, MS. 1873, f. 364v.

49. Copy of letter by Tarquet, 10 March 1629, CBI, MS. 1876, f. 158r.

50. Peiresc to de Thou, 2 March 1629, CBI, MS. 1876, f. 376v.

51. Peiresc to d'Avaulx, 17 March 1629, CBI, MS. 1871, ff. 398v–399r.

52. Peiresc to Guez, 4 April 1629, CBI, MS. 1876, f. 376v; Mssrs Change a Guez pour Peiresc, CBI, MS. 1876, f. 376v.

53. Peiresc to Meynard, 4 April 1629, CBI, MS. 1876, ff. 376v–377r.

54. PBN, MS. N.a.f. 5169, f. 39v, 4 April 1629. All of this will be discussed in Section 13 in terms of finance; here we see how it came into being as part of Peiresc's response to the challenge of a full-scale expedition.

55. Rumor of this came to Peiresc from Rome, though in garbled form. Aubery reported that de Thou had reached Ragusa, but he had done so after a shipwreck that had claimed the life of a valet and traveling partner (Aubery to Peiresc, "12 ou 19" January 1629, PBN, MS. F.fr. 9542, f. 248r).

56. Peiresc to Tarquet, 7 April 1629, CBI, MS. 1876, f. 377r.

57. Peiresc to d'Avaulx, 16 April 1629, CBI, MS. 1871, f. 398v.

58. Mathieu Passarius to Minuti, 21 April 1629, CBI, MS. 1876, f. 377v.

59. Peiresc to Minuti, 28 April 1629, CBI, MS. 1876, ff. 377v–378r.

60. Peiresc to de Thou à Rome, 25 April 1629, CBI, MS. 1876, ff. 354r–355v; referring to Aubery to Peiresc, 21 April 1629, PBN, MS. F.fr. 9542, f. 250r.

61. Peiresc to de Thou, 25 April 1629, CBI, MS. 1876, f. 354r: "Nous apprismes depuis la verité de ce qui s'estoit passé en ce pretenduz naufrage par lettre escripte de Satalie par le consul a Mr de Cesy qui furent envoyé a Paris, ce que Mr Dupuy me fut la faveur de m'envoyer icy l'originellement. Ce qui me faict louer dieu du plus proffond de mon coeur de vous avoir preservé de tels dangers, comme je faict aussy celluy de Nazareth que ne vient d'apprendre presentment mais ce n'a pas esté sans trembler de ffrois [sic] en la consideration de si grandz perilz que je prendz pour manquer infallibillité que dieu vous reserve a d'aussy grandz employs que merite voz sureminantes virtuz & qualitez si recommandable & si rare en ce siecle." Interestingly, Minuti and his party were also attacked at just this point as well. That de Thou had used a firearm in self-defense had so angered the basha of Nablus that the convent of St. Salvator in Jerusalem was forced to pay a 100 piastre fine. Minuti to Peiresc, 29 August 1629, PBN, MS. F.fr. 9542, f. 3r.

62. Aubery to Peiresc, 5 May 1629, PBN, MS. F.fr. 9542, f. 252r. Aubery notes that he had just received letters from Malta from which he learned nothing more of de Thou. By mid-May, Aubery had received a letter from a friend on Malta of 10 April that made no mention of De Thou's arrival, leading him to think that the Siracusan host was wrong about de Thou's departure for Malta. Aubery to Peiresc, 12 May 1629, PBN, MS. F.fr. 9542, f. 254v.

63. Peiresc to Aubery, 1 June 1629, CBI, MS. 1871, f. 507v.

64. Peiresc to Estelle, 13 May 1629, and Peiresc to Guez [in Constantinople], 14 May 1629, CBI, MS. 1876, f. 355r.

65. Peiresc to Spagnet [Espannet], 14 May 1629, CBI, MS. 1876, f. 617r. Espannet, in Cyprus, had himself become a key part of Peiresc's Mediterranean network in 1627 when employed by Peiresc in the search for Crusader-era manuscripts. See Miller, *Peiresc's "History of Provence."*

66. Peiresc to Tarquet, 15 May 1629, CBI, MS. 1876, f. 355v.

67. These materials are discussed in Miller, *Peiresc's Orient,* ch. 4.

68. Peiresc to Minuti, 14 May 1629, CBI, MS. 1876, f. 355v. "Ceste petite jalousie ne faisant tort à personne, ne scauroit estre blasmable, & le temps vous fera cognoistre qui est meilleur d'en user ainsy qu'aultrement."

69. Peiresc to Valbelle, 27 May 1629, CBI, MS. 1876, f. 356r.

70. Peiresc to Bartolle, 3 June 1629, CBI, MS. 1876, f. 356r.

71. Peiresc to Minuti, 3 June 1629, CBI, MS. 1876, f. 356r. "Il n'y aura pas de danger que vous luy fussiez voir mes memoires instructions & empreintes concernant les recherches qui se peuvent faire en ce païs là."

72. As recorded in PBN, MS. N.a.f. 5169, f. 41r.

73. Minuti to Peiresc, 20 July 1629, PBN, MS. F.fr. 9542, f. 1r.

74. On 15 June at night Peiresc received a letter from de Thou written that morning in Marseille (Peiresc to d'Avaulx, 16 June 1629, CBI, MS. 1871, f. 399r).

75. Peiresc to Dupuy, 30 June 1629, CBI, MS. 1877, f. 201v. To fill up the packet, Peiresc sent along a book of Sicilian inscriptions sent him by de Thou which Peiresc thought would make a fine pair with the *Marmora Arundelliana* (1628), published by his friend Selden.

76. De Thou to Dupuy, 29 July 1629, PBN MS. Dupuy 730, f. 169r: "Les raisons qui m'ont induit a ce faire, que j'ay bien au long representées a M. de Peiresc, & lesquelles je m'asseure qu'il vous aura mandées, je vous dirai de plus qu'après un voiage d'un an & demi, plein de difficultez & de hasards j'ay voulu gouster le repos de quelque mois sans estre ambarrassé [*sic*] d'affaires domestiques." For Peiresc's perplexity, see Peiresc to Dupuy, 7 July 1629, *Lettres de Peiresc,* 2:125–126.

77. De Thou to Peiresc, 4 December 1629, PBN, MS. F. fr. 9537, ff. 326–330v.

78. I am again grateful to Jérôme Delatour for his assistance with de Thou material and for discussing this episode with me.

79. Peiresc to de Thou, 3 July 1629, CBI, MS. 1876, f. 356r.

80. Peiresc to Tarquet, 23 July 1629, CBI, MS. 1876, f. 356v.

81. Peiresc to Captain Roubaud, 26 July 1629, CBI, MS. 1876, f. 356v.

82. Peiresc to Valbelle, 26 July 1629, CBI, MS. 1876, f. 357r.

83. Peiresc to Captain Roubaud, 1 August 1629, CBI, MS. 1876, ff. 357r–357v. "Pourroit frotter d'un peu d'huile pour corriger la salleure de l'eau marine."

84. Peiresc to de Thou, 28 July 1629, CBI, MS. 1876, f. 358r.

85. Peiresc to Aubery, 24 August 1629, CBI, MS. 1871, f. 511r. "Je ne m'estonne pas si vous avez tant faict l'amour a cet Alcoran." Aubery himself had a copy of the Latin translation, but Peiresc thought it bore little relation to the Arabic. For help, one had to check with the Dutch Arabists. Peiresc to Aubery, 7 November 1629, CBI, MS. 1871, f. 517r. By 1633 Peiresc had acquired his own Koran and no longer needed Aubery to supply him with one (Peiresc to Guillemin, 24 January 1633, *Lettres de Peiresc*, 5:110). The scarcity of Korans in Rome, attested in a later letter of Kicher's, might explain Aubery's ardor (Kircher to Peiresc, 3 December 1636, PBN, MS. F.fr. 9538, f. 236v: "If only the Koran were not so sternly prohibited here in Rome").

86. Minuti to Peiresc, 20 July 1629, PBN, MS. F.fr. 9542, f. 1r. "Et pendant mon sejour a Seyde je me suis enquesté de tout ce qu'est dans mes memoires et principalement *des Juifs* pour des livres Samaritains lesquels ils *n'ont point. Ils m'ont promis neantmoins que a mon arrivee a Seyde je pourrey recouvrer quelque chose* d'autant qu'ilz *ont escrit a Damas a leurs confreres* pour avoir quelque chose de curieux. J'ey desja recouvert des mains des [*sic*] mes amys que j'ey trouvé en ce pays quelques medailles lesquelles je vous envoyerey avec quelques autres que je doibs recouvrer quand je serey sorti du St. Sepulchre. *J'ey passé a la Napoulouse* qu'est l'entree de la Samarie ou est le pais de la Samaritaine. *Je ne peus pas parler a ces Juifs a cause que j'y arrivay un samedy jour de leur feste*, mais ayant parlé *en ceste ville a un Juif medecin* du couvent de St Salvatour lequel faira tout son possible de me faire recouvrer des medailles et desdictz livres ... *qu'il escrira aux Juifs de la dite Napoulouse* pour men faire avoir."

87. Minuti to Peiresc, 20 July 1629, PBN, MS. F.fr. 9542, f. 1v. "Si nostre bon roy (auquel Dieu donne longue et heureuse vie) *venoit en ce pays avec seulement vingt mille hommes se feroit maistre de toute la Palestine. Le prince Mirfacardin qu'est a Seyde* homme vieux luy *fourniroit volontiers douze mille chevaux* et il voudroit qu'il print lenvye au dit roy d'y venir." For Peiresc's thinking about the Crusades, see Miller, *Peiresc's "History of Provence,"* 45–53, 80–85. For the long memory of the French Orient, see Peter N. Miller, "Making the Paris Polyglot Bible: Humanism and Orientalism in the Early Seventeenth Century," in *Die europäische Gelehrtenrepublik im Zeitalter des Konfessionalismus/The European Republic of Letters in the Age of Confessionalism*, ed. H. Jaumann (Wiesbaden: Harrassowitz, 2001), 79–83.

88. Minuti to Peiresc, 29 August 1629, PBN, MS. F.fr. 9542, f. 3r: "Et par ce que *la caisse* que je vous envoye par le capitaine Bartolle estoit d'un *costé vuide je l'ey remplie tout a fait du cotton fin de Damas*. Madame vostre belle soeur s'en pourra servir pour son mesnage, en cas quelle l'aye pour agreable."

89. Peiresc to Piscatoris, 3 November 1629, CBI, MS. 1876, f. 359r. The letter was actually written on 29 August, from Damascus.

90. Peiresc to Piscatoris, 3 November 1629, CBI, MS. 1876, f. 359r.

91. Peiresc to Granier, 6 November 1629, CBI, MS. 1876, f. 359v. For the son's visit to the seminary, see Peiresc to Granier, 28 February 1628, CBI, MS. 1873, f. 580r. Either he or another son later held the post of "Assessor" of the city of Marseille; Peiresc used him to obtain copies of material in the archives of the Hôtel de Ville

useful for an inquiry of his on Marseille ca. 1200. Peiresc to Granier, 7 June 1631, CBI, MS. 1873, f. 580v. For Peiresc's close relations with the Benedictines, see Peter N. Miller, "Peiresc and the Benedictines of Saint-Maur: Further Thoughts on the Ethics of the Historian," in *Europäische Geschichtskulturen um 1700 zwischen Gelehrsamkeit, Politik und Konfession*, ed. Thomas Wallnig, Ines Peper, Thomas Stockinger, and Patrick Fiska (Berlin: De Gruyter, 2012), 361–378.

92. Peiresc to Madame la Lieutenant de Valbelle, 6 November 1629, CBI, MS. 1876, f. 359v; Peiresc to "l'Advocat Berardy, commis de Mr le Lieutenant de l'Admirauté a Marseille," 6 November 1629, CBI, MS. 1876, f. 359v.

93. Peiresc to Piscatoris, [6 November 1629], CBI, MS. 1876, f. 359v.

94. Peiresc to Captain Bartolle, 6 November 1629, CBI, MS. 1876, f. 360r.

95. But note that in the log of outgoing correspondence (PBN, MS. N.a.f. 5169, f. 43r), the date given for these is 16 November. If we look in the copybook, however, we see that these are all dated the 7th and that there is a *second* group of letters, not recorded in the log, that are dated 16 November. These were also destined for Syria and include another four letters (to Aymini, Blanc, Meynier, and Estelle).

96. Peiresc to Tarquet, 7 November 1629, CBI, MS. 1876, ff. 360v–361r. The inscriptions may be those in PBN, MS. Lat. 8957, f. 157r.

97. Peiresc to Minuti the "Greffier de Bras," 13 November 1629, CBI, MS. 1876, f. 361r.

98. Aymini to Peiresc, 2 September 1629, PBN, MS. F.fr. 9540, ff. 116r–v.

99. Blanc to Peiresc, 2 September 1629, PBN, MS. F.fr. 9542, f. 28r.

100. Peiresc to Aymini, 16 November 1629, CBI, MS. 1876, f. 361v.

101. Aymini to Galaup Chasteuil, 2 September 1629, ABM, MS. 201 (1019), 580–581.

102. He is now the subject of a study by Bruno Marty. I thank him for bringing this to my attention.

103. Peiresc to Tarquet, 1 August 1629, CBI, MS. 1876, f. 357v.

104. Peiresc to Galaup, 17 August 1629, CBI, MS. 1873, f. 433r. Tarquet found a ship, and Peiresc conveyed the information to Galaup in a letter of 10 November 1629, CBI, MS. 1873, f. 434v.

105. Peiresc to Galaup, 8 August 1629, CBI, MS. 1873, f. 433r.

106. Peiresc to Galaup, 18 October 1629, CBI, MS. 1873, f. 433v.

107. Peiresc to Aymini, 16 November 1629, CBI, MS. 1876, f. 361v.

108. Peiresc to Aymini, 16 November 1629, CBI, MS. 1876, ff. 361v–362r. "Il fault que vous feriez cognoissance avec quelques des ces prebtres Samaritaines & le flatter le plus que vous pourrez pour en tirer cela & tous les autres livres que vous pourriez avoir en ceste langue, principalement tout ce qui se trouvera concernant l'histoire Ste. ou profane, et les reglement soulz lesquelz vivent ceux de cette secte, sur tout ce qui concerne leurs calandries et solemnitez & s'ilz ont rien de l'Astronomie, en leur langue n'en laissez rien eschapper. Vous cognoissiez bien je m'asseure leurs caracters a peu prez, ou le[s] pourrez aprendre facilement, pour retenir tout ce qui vous tombera en main de ce caracteres."

109. Peiresc to Aymini, 16 November 1629, CBI, MS. 1876, f. 362v. "Si on fouilloit la terre aux environs de Hierusalem et de la Samaria quoy [qu'on] qui se trouve ne peu quasi estre que de bonne garde & recepte."

110. Peiresc to Aymini, 16 November 1629, CBI, MS. 1876, f. 361v. "Je scay pourtant que les Juifz en font grand cas entr'eulx. Je me suis resolu de l'envoyer a fin de vous en servir si l'occasion s'en presenter, pour acquerir l'amitiée de quelqu'un de ces Juifz de pardela qui ont quantité d'autres medailles, et qui par ceste gratification se pourroit plus facilement laisser persuader a vous despartir de siennes pour de l'argent principalement de celles qui sont escriptes en caracteres Samaritaines dont ilz sont coustumierement plus jaloux que des autres."

111. Of course the masterwork on this subject is Anthony Grafton, *A Study in the History of Classical Scholarship*, vol. 2 (Oxford: Oxford-Warburg Studies, 1994).

112. Peiresc to Aymini, 16 November 1629, CBI, MS. 1876, f. 789r. "Il faudroit que vous prinssiez [*sic*] la peine de les vous faire interpreter et descripre vous mesme l'interpretation telle que vous la pourrez avoir en langage franc vulgaire ou autre au mieux que faire le pourra, et pour cet effect quand aurez coppie bien transcripte, de ses Kalendriers pourrez couldre des feuiletez blancz entre deux dans lesquels vous escripvez ce que pourrez faire deschiffrer sans rien barbouiller, sur les extraictz authentiques en ces langues la."

113. For Peiresc's debt to Scaliger, see Miller, *Peiresc's Orient*, chs. 4–5.

114. Peiresc to Aymini, 16 November 1629, CBI, MS. 1876, f. 789r. This is the continuation of the letter that began on f. 361v. "Si pouvez avoir pareillement des Kalendriers des Turcz & des persanes et autres sectes noz Chrestiennes, & en tirer l'interpretation il ne les faudra pas negliger. Et si faire ce peu choisissez de beau fort papier de damas d'une mesme grandeur surquoy vous ferez transcripre lesdit Kalendriers chacun en cahier à part pour les pouvoir aprez ranger a ma fantaisie comme aussy les Alphabetz de chaque sorte."

115. Notarial records indicate that there was a Pierre Meynier who was married on 3 October 1614 and a Jean Meynier who was married on 20 January 1619. These are the only Meyniers married between 1580 and 1640 (MAD, 201 E 64 and 201 E 65). Géraud Poumarède identifies a Jacques Meynier in the Sidon trade who gave a receipt to Jacques Estelle for two bales of cloth sent to Estelle by the merchant Claude Luguet. (Géraud Pourmarède, "Naissance d'une institution royale: Les Consuls de la nation française en Levant et en Barbarie aux XVIe et XVIIe siècles," in *Annuaire-Bulletin de la Société de l'histoire de France: Année 2001* [Paris: Honoré Champion, 2003], 110n309.)

116. Peiresc to Blanc, 16 November 1629, CBI, MS. 1876, f. 363r.

117. Peiresc to Meynier, 16 November 1629, CBI, MS. 1876, f. 363v.

118. Peiresc to Estelle, 16 November 1629, CBI, MS. 1876, f. 363v.

119. Peiresc to Galaup-Chasteuil, 10 November 1629, CBI, MS. 1873, f. 434v. "D'un Caloyera grandement curieux ou ils m'achepterent un pentateuch Samaritain en trois langues Arabique, Samaritain & hebraique le tout escript en Caracteres Samaritains. Mais ils n'a me l'ont pas envoyé le reservantz à une autre navire."

120. Peiresc to Galaup-Chasteuil, 10 November 1629, CBI, MS. 1873, f. 435r. "Mais vous este si versé en ces langues orientaulx que vous y entendrez toute chose a

demy mot quand vous verrez." "Je, les confereray l'une par l'autre a une autre coppie que j'en ay reteneir."

121. Peiresc to Galaup-Chasteuil, 15 November 1629, CBI, MS. 1873, f. 435v. "L'un petit in 4-o escript qu'en viel papier de damas couvrez de bois et assez bien conservé pour faire croire qu'il soit complet. C'est celuy dont le P. Aymini me parle dans sa lettre."

122. Peiresc to Galaup-Chasteuil, 15 November 1629, CBI, MS. 1873, f. 435v. "Y ayant un regret des chapitres ou concordance comme je crois tout en teste du volume, ou il y a des peintures de vieux Chrestiens de l'annonciation resurrection et autres qui monstrent d'estre de cinqu a six cents ans d'antiquité a mon juge-ment & selon la cognoissance que j'ay prinse du MSS grecz & Latins de mesme siecle. Mais je crains bien que comme la fin y manque il y ayt aussy d'autres tres grandes imperfections, et deffectuositez car le volume ayant esté mal endossé, les cahiers ont esté deschirez par le fondz et puis recousez fort grossement." Generally on the humanist language of dating, see Silvia Rizzo, *Il lessico filo-logico degli umanisti* (Rome: Edizioni di Storia e Letteratura, 1973), 147–161.

123. Peiresc to Tarquet, 18 November 1629, CBI, MS. 1876, f. 789v. "Je donne com-mission de rechercher quelques supplementz de ceux que j'ay receuz s'il est possible d'en trouver."

124. Peiresc to Tarquet, 18 November 1629, CBI, MS. 1876, f. 789v; Peiresc to Jacques de Vendôme, 18 November 1629, CBI, MS. 1876, f. 790r.

125. Peiresc to Grotius, 20 November 1629, PBN, N.a.f. 5172, f. 75v, quoted in *Lettres à Claude Saumaise*, 223n96.

126. Peiresc to Galaup-Chasteuil, 3 December 1629, CBI, MS. 1873, f. 436v. "Au reste je pense que vous scavez l'edition qui se refaict a Paris de la grande Bible Royalle d'Anvers, avec de grandes meliorations & editions, je seray bien ayse d'apprendre de vous si vous jugeriez que ces exemplaires du nouveau testament Syriaque y peussent estre utiles car lors que vous y auriez passé vostre fantaisie on verroit de les y faire tenir & les contribuer au public pour l'honneur de la France & des lettres."

127. Peiresc to Tarquet, 17 December 1629, CBI, MS. 1876, f. 790v.

128. Peiresc to Estelle, 17 December 1629, CBI, MS. 1876, f. 791r.

129. Peiresc to de Thou, 12 December 1629, CBI, MS. 1876, f. 792r. "Aussy ay ie [*sic*] bien de la peine à prendre en patience un si grande mortification que celle que vous m'avez donné a ce coup et vous supplie de vouloir pardonnera un homme sensible quand il est touché si avant s'il luy en eschapper de ressenti-ment que je ne scaurois estouffier."

130. Peiresc to de Thou, 12 December 1629, CBI, MS. 1876, ff. 791v–792r.

131. Peiresc to Gela, 26 April 1636, CBI, MS. 1874, f. 414r.

132. Peiresc to Magy, 27 July 1636, CBI, MS. 1874, f. 422r. "Il est vray que Mr votre frere trouva un homme qui l'accommoda fort bien avec de la fleur de Lavande. Quand on veut accommoder de cez animaux pour les conserver il fauldroit au lieu de sel commun se servir de sel nitre, ou sel pestre dont on faict la pouldre à canon, et le faire dissoudre dans l'eau pour farcier de ceste eau la teste & toutes les concavitez y contenües. Car cela deffend fort de la corruption & puanteur."

133. Peiresc to de Thou, 12 December 1629, CBI, MS. 1876, f. 792r.

134. Peiresc to de Thou, 12 December 1629, CBI, MS. 1876, f. 792v. "Un pauvre fraticelle a qui j'avois donné quelque chosette pour son voyage de Terre S.te qui y rencontra le P. Daniel Aymini que vous y avez veu et à qui j'avois procuré l'obedience en ce pais là comme a luy, et s'estantz joints ensemble. Ils s'en allent fouiller en tant de lieux sur le memoire de cest libvres qu'ils attrapprent en fin ceste piece là."

135. Peiresc to de Thou, 12 December 1629, CBI, MS. 1876, f. 827r. "Apres avoir signé ma lettre, un peu de relique d'esprit de vengeance (innocente pour tant) ma faict reprendre la plume pour ne point obmettre comme j'avois voulu faire un peu de vanteur cappable de donner quelque petit regret, à quiconque n'auroit pas de repugnance aux curiositez de la nature & l'antiquité." Because apart from two letters now preserved in PBN, MS. Dupuy 717, the letters from Peiresc to de Thou have disappeared, we cannot be sure de Thou ever read these harsh words from his disappointed mentor. I thank Jérôme Delatour for clarifying the fate of Peiresc's letters to de Thou. On the tripod, see now Anthony Ossa-Richardson, "Nicolas Peiresc and the Delphic Tripod in the Republic of Letters," *Journal of the Warburg and Courtauld* 74 (2011): 263–279.

136. Estelle to Peiresc, 10 December 1629, CBI, MS. 1876, f. 793r.

137. Peiresc to Tarquet, 27 January 1630, CBI, MS. 1876, f. 792v.

138. Peiresc to Aurivelier, 27 January 1630, CBI, MS. 1876, f. 793r. "Je m'imagine que ce sera le surplus que vous aurez possible fraye quoyque c'en soit M. Fort vous baillera votre indempnité."

139. Peiresc to Aurivelier, 28 January 1630, CBI, MS. 1876, f. 793v.

140. Peiresc to Aurivelier, 2 February 1630, CBI, MS. 1876, f. 793v. There were also supposed to be "marcottes de vigne ou maillots de raison" and some trees for grafting on the *Grand Henry,* but Aurivelier had said nothing about it.

141. Peiresc to Thibault "maitre Apoticaire en la ville de Marseille," 13 February 1630, CBI, MS. 1876, f. 793v.

142. Peiresc to de Thou, 22 February 1630, CBI, MS. 1876, f. 794v.

143. Peiresc to Mallon, 20 February 1630, CBI, MS. 1876, ff. 794v–795r. Mallon's numismatic acquisitions, mostly of Greek coins, are recorded in the inventory of Peiresc's coin collection, CBI, MS. 1869, ff. 39r, 50r, 53r.

144. Peiresc to Aymini, 20 February 1630, CBI, MS. 1876, f. 795v.

145. Peiresc to Aymini, 20 February 1630, CBI, MS. 1876, f. 796r. "Et possible que cela eust esté mis a demi execution sans que ce Venitien courut sur mon marché & l'encherit de quelque chose de plus en l'estat qu'il a esté bien a propos de le retirer tel que vous avez peu et de me l'envoyer. . . . Car de ceste langue la, je fais cas de tout ce qui se peu avoir a prix moderé principalement des livres de chronologie et d'histoire."

146. Peiresc to Aymini, 20 February 1630, CBI, MS. 1876, f. 796v.

147. Peiresc to Estelle, 20 or 25 February 1630, CBI, MS. 1876, ff. 796v–797r; 798r.

148. Peiresc to Minuti, 3 March 1630, CBI, MS. 1876, f. 798r. "Les à fripponnez & qu'il les à mieux aymé donner à quelque autre pour moy." For the identification of the *figues d'Adam,* see Sidney Aufrère, *La Momie et la tempête: Nicolas-*

Claude Fabri de Peiresc et la "curiosité Égyptienne" en Provence au début du XVIIe siècle (Avignon: Éditions A. Barthélemy, 1990), 180, 349.

149. Peiresc to Minuti, 3 March 1630, CBI, MS. 1876, f. 798v. "Un Cretan Venitien avoir courut sur ma marché et pendant l'absence du Sr Meynier qui estoit aller au village, avoit acheté de un maronite mon pauvre pentateuque Samaritain moyenent 31 piastres au mesme estat que vous l'aviez ne m'asseurer laissé je veux dire avec les mesmes imperfections et quelques petits supplements en des petits feulletz & morceaux de papier de diverses escriptures que je ne avois prins presumer estre grand chose qui vaille c'est pourquoy je ne m'estonner pas que ce Maronite ayt en tant de peine de se resoudre a les faire transcrire au net en parchemin comme il vous avoit promis et ne trouver pas estrange qu'il ayt compté les 31 piastres de ce Venitien pour se redimer du soing de ceste escripture qui n'estoit pas aysée a radjuster bien proprement et a bien eu de la peine a le retirer des mains de ce Venitien tel qu'il est le Sr Estelle et ledit P. Daniel Aymini n'ayant pas peu faict de l'arracher de ses mains."

150. Peiresc to Minuti, 3 March 1630, CBI, MS. 1876, f. 798v.

151. Peiresc to Bonnaire, 3 March 1630, CBI, MS. 1876, f. 799r.

152. Peiresc to Minuti, 4 March 1630, CBI, MS. 1876, f. 799r. "De peur de m'engager a les luy envoyer par ce que ce qui va une fois a Rome en ces matieres la, n'en sort pas facilement."

153. Aymini to Peiresc, 5 March 1630, PBN, MS. F.fr. 9540, ff. 119r–120r. P. Paolo Carali, *Fakhr al-Din II Prencipe del Libano e la Corte di Toscana 1605–1635,* 2 vols. (Roma: Reale Accademia d'Italia 1936-XIV), vol. 1: *Introduzione storica-documenti europei e documenti orientali tradotti;* Michel Chebli, *Fakhreddine II Maan, Prince du Liban (1572–1635)* (Beirut: Publications de l'Université Libanaise, 1984).

154. Blanc to Peiresc, 5 March 1630, PBN, MS. F.fr. 9542, f. 29r.

155. Peiresc to Captain Balthazar Grimaud, 13 April 1630, CBI, MS. 1876, f. 799v; Peiresc to Captain Raymond Sardre, 13 April 1630, CBI, MS. 1876, f. 799v.

156. Peiresc to Issaultier, 13 April 1630, CBI, MS. 1876, f. 799v.

157. Peiresc to Minuti, 14 April 1630, CBI, MS. 1876, f. 800r.

158. Peiresc to Minuti, 23 April 1630, CBI, MS. 1876, ff. 800r–v.

159. Peiresc to Minuti, 23 April 1630, CBI, MS. 1876, f. 801r.

160. Peiresc to de Thou, 29 April 1630, CBI, MS. 1876, f. 801v.

161. Peiresc to le baron d'Alegre, 14 May 1630, CBI, MS. 1876, f. 801v.

162. Peiresc to Claude Chastagnier, marchand françois a Ligourne, 17 May 1630, CBI, MS. 1876, ff. 802r–v; Peiresc to Claude Petit a Toullon, 17 May 1630, CBI, MS. 1876, f. 802v.

163. Peiresc to Honoré Tourtel a Sixfours, 16 June 1630, CBI, MS. 1876, f. 803v; Peiresc to Truillet, 16 June 1630, CBI, MS. 1876, f. 803v; Peiresc to Vicard et l'Abbé de St. Victor a Sixfours, 16 June 1630, and Peiresc to Alfant [*sic*], 16 June 1630, CBI, MS. 1876, f. 804r.

164. Peiresc to de Thou, 5 June 1630, CBI, MS. 1876, f. 802v.

165. Peiresc to Jacques de Vendôme, 11 June 1630, CBI, MS. 1876, f. 803r.

166. Peiresc to M. Truillet a Toulon, 11 June 1630, CBI, MS. 1876, f. 803r.

167. Peiresc to de Thou, 17 June 1630, CBI, MS. 1876, ff. 805r–v. "Je tiens que ces livres Arabes et Cophtes pourroient estre bien utiles au public et si nous eussions eu des gentz versez en cez langues nous y eussions volontiers faict travailler tandis que vous estiez hors de chez vous et hors des moyens de vous en servir et d'y employer en voz amis qui s'en peussent dignement acquitter et de faict j'estime que ceste bible Arabique viendra bien a point a l'edition que faict Mr le Jay qui avoit tant desire d'en avoir quelque exemplaires de Rome. Et pour les livres Cophtes si on à trouvé quelque moyen de les laver & d'en reparee les feulletz. Je crois asseurement qu'ils ne seroient pas inutiles." For the Paris Polyglot Bible, see Miller, "Making the Paris Polyglot Bible: Humanism and Orientalism in the Early Seventeenth Century," in *Die europäische Gelehrtenrepublik im Zeitalter des Konfessionalismus/The European Republic of Letters in the Age of Confessionalism*, ed. H. Jaumann (Wiesbaden: Harrassowitz, 2001), 59–86.

168. Peiresc to Marchand, 24 June 1630, CBI, MS. 1874, f. 566r. "Un indult visitandi sepulchrum dominicum aliaque transmarina loca et ibi quandiu voluerit commorari libere et licite. En vertu duquel il y est allé et y a faict des observations tres excellentes pour les O.[bservan]tins. Je voudrois bein a present qu'il y retournast pour mon compte s'il est possible come je le pense . . . [et] d'asseurer de ma part ceux ausquelz il pourra escheoir que ce voyage n'est point de ceux que font communement les relligieux et qu'il en reuscira du fruict pour le bien du croiance de dieu & veneration de cez lieu Saintes et pour autres choses concernant les antiquitez de l'eglise."

169. Peiresc to Barberini, 24 June 1630, Rome, B.A.V., MS. Barb.-Lat. 6503, f. 26r.

170. PBN, MS. N.a.f. 5169, f. 45v, 26 July 1630, "MON RETOUR de Tollon avec Mr de COMTE DE MARCHEVILLE Ambassadeur en Constantinople"; Peiresc to de Thou, 26 July 1630, CBI, MS. 1876, ff. 807r–v.

171. Peiresc to Minuti, 5 August 1630, and Peiresc to Minuti, 13 August 1630, CBI, MS. 1876, f. 807v.

172. Peiresc to de Thou, 26 July 1630, CBI, MS. 1876, f. 807v. "De sorte que ce chetif lieu cy est maintenant devenu le grand chemin des postes, ou des routtes pour les Ambassadeurs de Rome, de Constantinople, (et si je l'osois dire) des Indes, qui est trez autre chose que le simple chemin de la cour."

173. Peiresc to Galaup, 26 September 1630, CBI, MS. 1873, f. 439r.

174. Peiresc to Jean Berard, 8 October 1630, CBI, MS. 1876, f. 808r; Peiresc to Minuti, 8 October 1630, CBI, MS. 1876, ff. 808r–v; Peiresc to Minuti, 13 October 1630, CBI, MS. 1876, f. 808v; Peiresc to Minuti [end of October or early November], CBI, MS. 1876, f. 808v.

175. Peiresc to Minuti, 13 October 1630, CBI, MS. 1876, f. 808v.

176. Peiresc to Issaultier, 8 October 1630, CBI, MS. 1876, f. 808r.

177. Peiresc to Issaultier, 18 October 1630, CBI, MS. 1876, f. 808v, writes that he hopes to have the cases brought back by the one who brings this letter to Marseille ("le present porteur").

178. Father Michael to Minuti, 1 September 1635, PBN, MS. F.fr. 9543, f. 121v. "Io concedo la salute al P. Fra Teofilo; di più a P. la bugia e vergogna. V.P. piglio a me il biblia arabica, e li capitoli in lingua Samaritana et dixit mihi che mandargli a me in cammia di essa un alora stambata, et havese fatto il patto mele

tre mese di tempo hora passato tre anni, e non venne nessuna nova da voi, si non volete mandare il libro, mandate il prezzo suo 20 piastre di rialo, come si hanno daro li altri, e ne manco volsi venderlo overo mandare a me il mio libro presto sensa altro."

179. Aymini to Peiresc, 2 September 1630, Aix, Bibl. Méjanes, MS. 201 (1019), 582–583. "J'espere d'estre [si] tost appelé en Hierusalem pour y voir les solemnités de Noel et de Pasques, ou ie vous supplie d'adresser les vostres avec prieres qu'elles me soient envoyés a la part ou ie l'e[crit]. C'est dans le St Sepulchre ou i'espere mestre en execution vos premier memoires par la commodité de toutes les nations qui y sont dedans." Lebègue omitted this paragraph in his "correction" of the defects in Tamizey de Larroque's edition of the letter (*Supplement au tome VII*, 84). Perhaps this is a common problem among students of Peiresc: Sonja Brentjes levels the same accusations at Sidney Aufrère's *La Mômie et la tempête* even as she herself publishes a preprint full of errors in a collection devoted to already published works without including references to any other secondary literature!

180. Doni to Peiresc, 7 December 1631, PBN, MS. F.fr. 9540, f. 171v.

181. Peiresc to Marquesi, 2 November 1630, CBI, MS. 1876, f. 809v, saying that he was coming to receive Aymini's letters of 2 and 20 September.

182. Peiresc to Tarquet, 20 November 1630, CBI, MS. 1876, f. 809v.

183. Peiresc to Minuti, 10 December 1630, CBI, MS. 1876, f. 809v.

184. Peiresc to Sauvine, 20 December 1630, CBI, MS. 1876, f. 810r.

185. Peiresc to Bermond, 20 December 1630, CBI, MS. 1876, f. 810r.

186. Peiresc to Fort, 23 January 1631, CBI, MS. 1876, f. 810v.

187. Peiresc to Mallon, 17 February 1631, CBI, MS. 1876, f. 810v; CBI, MS 1869, f. 39r.

188. Peiresc to Mallon, 20 February 1631, CBI, MS. 1876, ff. 810v–811r.

189. Mallon to l'Archier, 25 April 1631, CBI, MS. 1876, f. 816v.

190. Peiresc to Mallon, 12 August 1632, CBI, MS. 1876, f. 818r. This possibly refers to Jacques du Lorens, a contemporary lawyer and poetic satirist.

191. Peiresc to Beaumont, 5 April 1633, CBI, MS. 1876, f. 825v.

192. Peiresc to Galaup-Chasteuil, [between October 1630 and March 1631], CBI, MS. 1873, f. 439v. On the embassy, see Alastair Hamilton, " 'To Divest the East of All Its Manuscripts and All Its Rarities': The Unfortunate Embassy of Henri Gournay de Marcheville," in *The Republic of Letters in the Levant* [= Intersections. Leiden Yearbook for Early Modern Studies], ed. Alastair Hamilton, Maurits H. van den Boogert, and Bart Westerweel (Leiden: Brill, 2005), 123–150.

193. Peiresc to Minuti, 3 March 1631, CBI, MS. 1876, f. 811v.

194. Peiresc to Aymini, [30 March 1631], CBI, MS. 1876, f. 811v.

195. Peiresc to Minuti, 1 April 1631, CBI, MS. 1876, f. 812r.

196. Peiresc to Minuti, 6 April 1631, CBI, MS. 1876, f. 812r.

197. Peiresc to Minuti, 13 April 1631, CBI, MS. 1876, f. 812v.

198. Peiresc to Pelissier, 25 April 1631, CBI, MS. 1876, f. 812v. For this identification, see Peiresc to "Mr le RP Joachin de Goa Recollet de l'ordre des Recolletz," 21 July 1631, CBI, MS. 1876, f. 815v.

199. Peiresc to Aymini, 25 April 1631, CBI, MS. 1876, f. 813r. Peiresc also wrote to Joachin da Goa on the same day, CBI, MS. 1876, f. 813r.
200. PBN, MS. N.a.f. 5169, f. 46v. This wine was sent via Aycard in Toulon; we know from elsewhere that the wine Aycard provided d'Arcos was from Cassis and Bandol. Peiresc to Aycard, 14 February 1634, CBI, MS. 1871, f. 40v.
201. Peiresc to Minuti, 4 June 1631, CBI, MS. 1876, f. 813v.
202. Peiresc to Pelissier, 5 June 1631, and Peiresc to Pelissier, 24 June 1631, CBI, MS. 1876, f. 813v.
203. Peiresc to Pelissier, 1 July 1631, CBI, MS. 1876, f. 814r.
204. Peiresc to l'Empereur [in Constantinople], 10 July 1631, CBI, MS. 1876, f. 814r.
205. Peiresc to Guez [in Constantinople], 10 July 1631, CBI, MS. 1876, f. 814r. Peiresc follows up these points in a letter to Guez of Marseille, also 10 July 1631, CBI, MS. 1876, f. 814v.
206. Peiresc to Minuti, 11 July 1631, CBI, MS. 1876, f. 814v. "Memoires, instructions & empreintes que vous aviez eues des l'autre fois avec quelque petite addition, et des nouvelles lettres que je joignez."
207. Peiresc to Tarquet, 16 July 1631, CBI, MS. 1876, f. 815r.
208. Peiresc to Estelle, 16 July 1631, CBI, MS. 1876, f. 815r.
209. Peiresc to de l'Isle, 16 July 1631, CBI, MS. 1876, f. 815r.
210. Peiresc to de Thou, 26 December 1631, CBI, MS. 1876, ff. 816v–817r. "& autres grandes fabriques toutes de marbre."
211. François Galaup, sieur de Chasteuil, to Jean Galaup, 29 October 1631, in *Les Correspondants de Peiresc*, 2 vols. (Geneva: Slatkine, 1972), 2:329–332. For the place of Chios on the trunk route between Alexandria and Istanbul, see Daniel Panzac, *Commerce et navigation dans l'empire Ottoman à XVIIIe siècle* (Istanbul: Les Éditions Isis, 1996), 1–24; for its seventeenth-century decline at the expense of Izmir, see Edhem Eldem, Daniel Goffman, and Bruce Masters, *The Ottoman City between East and West: Aleppo, Izmir, and Istanbul* (Cambridge: Cambridge University Press, 1999), 92.
212. Peiresc to Fort, 29 March 1632, and Peiresc to Thibault, 29 March 1632, CBI, MS. 1876, f. 817v.
213. Peiresc to Thibault, 4 January 1632, CBI, MS. 1876, ff. 817r–v.
214. Peiresc to Guez, 29 March 1632, CBI, MS. 1876, f. 818r.
215. Peiresc to Aycard, 6 August 1632, CBI, MS. 1871, f. 16r.
216. Peiresc to Aycard, 14 August 1632, CBI, MS. 1871, f. 17v.
217. Peiresc to Minuti, 22 August 1632, CBI, MS. 1876, f. 818v.
218. Peiresc to Minuti, 22 August 1632, CBI, MS. 1876, f. 819v. "C'estoit de se bois dont les anciennes romaines faisoient leur *tables rondes cytrines*."
219. Peiresc to Minuti, 22 August 1632, CBI, MS. 1876, f. 820r.
220. Peiresc to Guez, 22 August 1632, CBI, MS. 1876, f. 820v.
221. Peiresc to Minuti, 23 August 1632, CBI, MS. 1876, ff. 821r–v; Peiresc to Sabatier, 23 August 1632, CBI, MS. 1876, ff. 824r–v.
222. Peiresc to Minuti, 23 August 1632, CBI, MS. 1876, f. 822v. "Il en vient quantité du costé des Indes & des turcques s'en servent pour y boire de l'eau de vie. J'en ay autrefois veu ung assortiment d'une demye douzaine qui s'enchassoient ou enboistoient l'une dans l'autre quazy comme les escus des poids de mark de laton

jaune qui se font en Allemagne et qui sont en usage partout la Crest[ienté]."
Also Peiresc to Jacques Dupuy, 8 August 1632, *Lettres de Peiresc*, 2:328.

223. Peiresc to Minuti, 23 August 1632, CBI, MS. 1876, f. 822v. "Car j'aime beaucoup mieux de ceux qui viennent tous faitz [du] costé de Indes ou ses peuples
sont grandement exacts et scrupuleux pour y observer une certaine mesure &
proportion les unes aux autres pour laquelle seule je pretendz de m'en servir et
non pour autre chose a quoy ses lapidaires ou graveurs de Constantinople ne
voudrois pas peut estre s'asujettir. C'est pourquoy je vous prie de faire un peu
de recherche parmy les lapidaires les plus riches et mieux assortiz de Constantinople de tous les vazes de pierres fines que vous y pourrez treuver faitz en
forme d'escuellon ou de godet a boire et si on vous le veut prester a [se] que
vous en puissiez mesurer la contenanse par le moyen de se modelle."

224. For Peiresc and the world of artisans, see Peter N. Miller, "Peiresc in the Parisian Jewel House," in *Artificii Occulti: Knowledge and Discernment in the Artistic and Scientific Cultures of Early Modern Europe (16th–17th Centuries)*, ed.
Sven Dupré and Christine Göttler (Farnham, UK: Ashgate, forthcoming).

225. Peiresc to Minuti, 23 August 1632, CBI, MS. 1876, f. 823r. "Je voudrois que
vous vous peussiez enquerir de noms particulieres qui se donnent communement a toutes ses sortes de vases selon la diversité de leur contenanse plus ou
moins grandes de quoy vous serez esclaircy possible plus tost chez ses vendeurs
d['']eau de vie qu'en tous autre lieu ou chez les droguistes et apoticaires qui
vendent les liqueures plus precieuses ou bien chez ceux qui ont la charge publique de faire ou de jester et de contemarquer par auctorité des magistratz
toutes le mesures de particulieres affin que le jouent bien esgalles les unes aux
autres."

226. Peiresc to Minuti, 23 August 1632, CBI, MS. 1876, ff. 823r–v. "Le nom de
toutes les mesures de quoy on se sert de pardela sinon du vin au moins de l[']
eau de vie et autre liqueur qu'il leur est loisible de boire. voire mesme de celle
de l[']huille car des autres vases faitz a plaisir et qui n'ont pas de mesures certaines je ne m'en sousie pas autrement. Mais si avés le noms turquesques ou ara-
besque de ses diferentes mesures qui sont encor en usage de pardela vous trouvez
moyen de joindre le nom en grec."

227. Peiresc to Minuti, 23 August 1632, CBI, MS. 1876, f. 823v.

228. Peiresc to Minuti, 23 August 1632, CBI, MS. 1876, ff. 823r, 823v. "Et que vous
visitez souvant les vieux fracgmentz de cuivre que bronze qu'ils ont acous-
tumez de fondre bronze y rencontrerez une infinitez de belles choses fort es-
travagante & fort digne d'estre conservez que vous pourez avoir pour peu de
chose, pardessus la valeur du meta[ille]."

229. Peiresc to Minuti, 23 August 1632, CBI, MS. 1876, f. 824r. "N'ayant pas faire difficulté d'entrer dans une de ses boutiques & d'en faire porter deux grande cor-
beilles de fragments de vieux bronze."

230. Peiresc to Minuti, 23 August 1632, CBI, MS. 1876, ff. 823 r–v. "Mais si avez le
noms turquesques ou arabesques de ses differentes mesures qui sont encor en
usage de pardela vous trouvez moyen de joindre le nom en grec vulgaire des
mesmes mesures et l'interpretation que voz truchements pouroient faire tant
de l'un que de l'autre en langage franc se seroit acomply mon souhait."

231. Minuti to Peiresc, 7 September 1632, PBN, MS. F.fr. 9542, f. 5r.

232. Marcheville to Peiresc, 16 September 1632, PBN, MS. F.fr. 9542, f. 165r. "Ou ma charge me donne quelque commerce."

233. Peiresc to Aycard, 5 October 1632, CBI, MS. 1871, f. 21r. "L'armee navalle du grand Seigneur avoit lors nestoyé ces costes là."

234. Peiresc to Aycard, 5 October 1632, CBI, MS. 1871, f. 21r; Aycard to Peiresc, 12 October 1632, CBI, MS. 1871, f. 22r.

235. Peiresc to Aycard, 17 October 1632, *Lettres de Peiresc*, 7:285 [= CBI, MS. 1871, f. 22r].

236. Peiresc to Eyssantier [Issaultier], 18 October 1632, CBI, MS. 1876, f. 825r.

237. Peiresc to Guez, 18 October 1632, CBI, MS. 1876, f. 825r.

238. Peiresc to Aycard, 24 October 1632, CBI, MS. 1871, f. 22v. ("Le tout est renfermé dans les balles des marchandises du sieur Yssaultier qui sont encore en quarantine.") Peiresc to Aycard, 1 November 1632, CBI, MS. 1871, f. 23r.

239. Peiresc to Aycard, 1 November 1632, CBI, MS. 1871, f. 22v.

240. Minuti to Peiresc, 5 November 1632, PBN, MS. F.fr. 9542, f. 9r.

241. Peiresc to Aycard, 6 November 1632, CBI, MS. 1871, f. 23v.

242. Peiresc to Aycard, 5 February 1633, CBI, MS. 1871, f. 27r.

243. Peiresc to Sabatier, 12 January 1633, CBI, MS. 1876, ff. 825r–v. The summarizing in his letters of those previously sent or received no doubt was a form of mnemo-technique but it also enabled him to leaf back through his copies to reconstruct the current history.

244. Peiresc to Guez, 12 January 1633, CBI, MS. 1876, f. 825v.

245. PBN, MS. Lat. 8957, ff. 152–153.

246. Minuti to Peiresc, 15 March 1633, PBN, MS. F.fr. 9542, fols. 11r–12v.

247. Minuti to Peiresc, 15 March 1633, PBN, MS. F.fr. 9542, fols. 11r–12v.

248. Minuti to Peiresc, 10 April 1633, PBN, MS. F.fr. 9542, f. 13r. "Mais par ce que durant nostre voyage de Cipre a Saide j'avois fait boire le gardien de la dit[e] polacre de ce bon vin cypriote afin qu'il eut en particulier soin de nos caisses, en mesme temps qu'il eut rangé son fait dans le vesseau il *plassa les dittes caisses dans l'estine et par consequent elles ce sont bien conservees* Dieu en sont loüé."

249. Minuti to Peiresc, 10 April 1633, PBN, MS. F.fr. 9542, f. 13r. "*Je serois bien ayse de l'accompagner porveu que ledit sieur Aycard donne son consentement audit sieur neveu,* car pour y aller tout seul je n'ose pas d'entreprendre un tel voyage."

250. Minuti to Peiresc, 5 November 1632, PBN, MS. F.fr. 9542, f. 9r.

251. Minuti to Peiresc, 10 April 1633, PBN, MS. F.fr. 9542, f. 13v. "*Cependant je vous prie de me faire sçavoir vostre resolution autrement je prendray le chemin du Caire* que je sçay par coeur et dela en Provence."

252. Minuti to Peiresc, 18 April 1633, PBN, MS. F.fr. 9542, f. 15r.

253. Peiresc to Marcheville, 24 April 1633, CBI, MS. 1874, f. 604r.

254. Peiresc to Marcheville, 24 April 1633, CBI, MS. 1874, f. 604v.

255. Mersenne to Peiresc, 1 May 1633, *Mersenne Correspondance*, 3:393.

256. Peiresc to Mersenne, 6 September 1633, *Mersenne Correspondance*, 3:474. Peiresc had also made inquiries at Tunis. Peiresc to Aycard, 5 April 1633, CBI, MS. 1871, f. 30r. The engravings are found today tipped into the end of PBN, MS. F.fr. 9531.

257. Peiresc to Vendôme, 12 May 1633, CBI, MS. 1876, f. 826r: "Les deputez que la ville de Marseille envoye en Constantinople ne furent voile que huict ou dix jours devant la venir du Capp. d'Avin si voz lettres fussent venües a temps. Je les eusse faict charger de recommander a Mr le Comte de Marcheville tous les interestz de votre ordre." Peiresc also pledged to write immediately to the consuls of Marseille to mobilize the "Corps de ville de Marseille pour luy rendre vos interests plus considerables."

258. Peiresc to Captain Carrayre, 5 June 1633, CBI, MS. 1876, f. 827r; Peiresc to Minuti, 7 June 1633, CBI, MS. 1876, f. 827v.

259. Peiresc to Minuti, 7 June 1633, CBI, MS. 1876, f. 827v.

260. Peiresc to Minuti, 7 June 1633, CBI, MS. 1876, f. 828r. For Peiresc's study of the Constantinople Polyglot Bible, see Miller, *Peiresc's Orient*, 216–217.

261. See, for example, Hugh Trevor-Roper, "The Church of England and the Greek Church in the Time of Charles I," in Trevor-Roper, *From Counter-Reformation to Glorious Revolution* (Chicago: University of Chicago Press, 1992), 83–112.

262. Peiresc to Minuti, 7 June 1633, CBI, MS. 1876, f. 828r. For Peiresc's views on polyglot scholarship, see Miller, *Peiresc's Orient*, chs. 4–5.

263. Peiresc to Minuti, 7 June 1633, CBI, MS. 1876, f. 828r.

264. Peiresc to Minuti, 7 June 1633, CBI, MS. 1876, f. 827v. "Et de ceste marchandise de perse de damas et de cez estoffes quoy que mon frere vous ayt dict au contraire, par ce que c'est aultant dependu à mon humeur, et dont on ne scait guieres de gré de pardecà, et mon frere ne laisse aprez le soing de payer le tout. Or je plains bien l'argent a cest sorte de Marchandise aultant comme au contraire: je le tiens bien employer aux livres antiques et autres curiositez d'ou il se peut apprendre quelque chose et sur tout a ce qui peut estre de votre entretien et de voz commoditez particuliaires. A quoy je tiendray tousiours tres bien employer tout ce qui j'y pourray contribuer. Je dis cela a cause de la grosse balle de perse de damas et de la piece de soye Nacarac que vous nous envoyastes à votre arrivée a Seyde dont nous ne nous sommes pas tant prevalus comme de la seule petite boitte de medailles et encores plus des deux livres."

265. Peiresc to Aycard, 7 June 1633, CBI, MS. 1871, f. 32r.

266. Others Peiresc knew made the trip to Persia. A brother of the famous Parisian engraver Melchior Tavernier visited with Peiresc on his way back from Persia and related what he had seen. Peiresc to Cassiano, 5 February 1637, *Lettres à Cassiano dal Pozzo* (Clermont-Ferrand: Adosa, 1989), 263.

267. Peiresc to Allemand, 7 June 1633, CBI, MS. 1876, f. 828v.

268. Peiresc to Tarquet, 7 June 1633, CBI, MS. 1876, f. 829r.

269. Peiresc to Bermond in Egypt, 7 June 1633, CBI, MS. 1876, f. 829r.

270. Peiresc to Bermond in Egypt, 14 July 1633, CBI, MS. 1876, f. 829v.

271. Mr de Bermond a Sr de Bermond son frere consul des francois en Aegypte en Alexandrie, 13 May [July] 1633, CBI, MS. 1874, f. 310bis r.

272. Peiresc to Aycard, 4 July 1633, CBI, MS. 1871, f. 34v. "J'ay gouverné un marchand de Marseille nommé le Sr Magy . . . qui à esté 10 ans au Cayre."

273. All this is in Miller, *Peiresc's Orient,* ch. 6.

274. CBI, MS. 1864, f. 264r.

275. CBI, MS. 1777, f. 374r: "1633. 7 Juill. IEAN MAGY avec le memoire des livres & graines/pour le ROY D'AETHIOPIE" = Aix, Bib. Mejanes MS. 207 (1025), 3.
276. Peiresc to Magy, 16 July 1633, CBI, MS. 1874, f. 310bis v.
277. CBI, MS. 1864, f. 256r.
278. Peiresc to "Sr dottore medico d'Andalusia" [Mustafa Aquin], 14 July 1633, CBI, MS. 1876, ff. 829v–830r.
279. Peiresc to Magy, 9 October 1636, CBI, MS. 1874, f. 431v.
280. Peiresc to Vignon, 14 July 1633; Peiresc to le Gris, 14 July 1633, CBI, MS. 1874, f. 311v; Peiresc to [. . .] l'hoste, 14 July 1633, CBI, MS. 1874, f. 311r.
281. Peiresc to le Gris, 14 July 1632, CBI, MS. 1874, f. 312r. "Et vous supplie de les vouloir ayder pour l'amour de moy pour en veriffier l'examen, et y adjouster les noms tant des poids que des mesures selon les differentes denominations des diverses nations qui habitent en ces contrées la ou qui y frequentent, et quand il y abborde des marchandz des Indes ou de l'Aethiopie, ou de la Nubie & autres lieux plus reculez de notre commerce. Je vous prie de les faire interroger soigneusement par les Truchementz s'ilz ont des poidz & mesures semblables a ceux du Cayre ou bien plus ou moins grandz ou plus ou moins foibles, et les noms qu'ilz leur donnent que je vous supplie vouloir recueillir pour l'amour de moy. Et non seulement cela, mais aussy les noms des vases de toute sorte, selon la diversité de leur usaige & de leur forme avec l'Etymologie quand elle se pourra rendre, et en toutes langues vulgaires en cez pais la ou circonvoisins."
282. Peiresc to Bertier, 14 July 1633, CBI, MS. 1874, f. 312v. On Bertier, see Aufrère, *La Momie et la tempête*, 100–103.
283. Peiresc to Dimo, 14 July 1633, CBI, MS. 1874, f. 312v; Periesc to Alvyse, 14 July 1633, CBI, MS. 1874, f. 312v.
284. Peiresc to Alvyse, 14 July 1633, CBI, MS. 1874, f. 312v. "Insieme le curiosità che si cavano dal Mar Rosso. Et ch'ella haveva fatto una grande & nobile raccolta di tutta questa singolarità così della natura come del'antiquita, che le da una gran fama nell'Euro[pa?]/ancora. . . . Et son sicuro che nel mar rosso si devono trovar[ono]/ . . . et che meriterebbono ch'un par suo si volesse un giorno dar la brigga,/ . . . posta a solazzo per fare pescare di cotestì founghi & altri frutti maritimi/."
285. Peiresc to Ramatuelle, 14 July 1633, CBI, MS. 310bis v. "Car ie ne fais pas voluntiers la manche plus grande que le bras."
286. "Il fault suyvre mes petites commissions le plus punctuellement que vous pourrez et ne vous pas charger de marchandise hors de mes instructions principalement quand cest de valleur considerable de quoy j'ay esté contraint de faire des reproches au RP Minuti qui m'a envoyé des fourreures de vestes de peau de menu vair qui se gastent ceans faulte de valez qui ayent soing de les mettre à l'air quand il faudroit et des pieces entieres d'estoffes de soye qui ne se sont pas rencontrées a notre usage et des balles de bustes des pault dont nous nous serions bien passez dont le prix d'achept eust esté beaucoup mieux employé en livres ou anticailles ou autres choses du contenu en cez[?] memoires." Peiresc to [Magy], 15 July 1633, CBI, MS. 1874, f. 310r.
287. Minuti to Peiresc, 26 August 1633, PBN, MS. F.fr. 9542, ff. 19r–v.
288. Peiresc to Guez [Constantinople], 19 September 1633, CBI, MS. 1876, ff. 881r–v.

289. Peiresc to l'Empereur, 19 September 1633, CBI, MS. 1876, f. 831r.
290. Peiresc to Sabatier, 20 September 1633, CBI, MS. 1876, f. 832v.
291. Peiresc to Aycard, 2 October 1633, CBI, MS. 1871, f. 36r.
292. Peiresc to Minuti, undated [14 July 1633], CBI, MS. 1874, f. 310v.
293. Peiresc to [Minuti], 11 October 1633, CBI, MS. 1874, f. 314r.
294. Peiresc to [Minuti], 11 October 1633, CBI, MS. 1874, f. 314r. "Le Sr Tomaso de Mayo, marchant de Messine qui avoit baillé la barque audit Betton avec 250 pieces de huict pour aller chargé de vin sachant sa piratterie l'alla attendre à Malthe & luy osta sa barque." I have conferred on this with Jérôme Delatour and Jean Boutier but the reading remains unclear.
295. Peiresc to [Minuti], 11 October 1633, CBI, MS. 1874, f. 314r.
296. Peiresc to [Minuti], 11 October 1633, CBI, MS. 1874, f. 314v. The mémoires are in PBN, MS. Lat. 9340, ff. 111r–113r; that for Minuti alone at ff. 112v–113r.
297. Peiresc to Gassendi, 20 August 1633, *Lettres de Peiresc*, 4:349.
298. Peiresc to [Minuti], 11 October 1633, CBI, MS. 1874, f. 314v. "Je vous [Minuti] pris de faire effort pour avoir quelques . . . les memoires de la musique des Dreviz ou Turcz & Arabes et des Grecz Basili[ens]."
299. Peiresc to [Minuti], 11 October 1633, CBI, MS. 1874, f. 314v. "J'entendz que cez Grecz basiliens ont des livres rituelz de St. Jean damascene & d'un de leur colonie grand musicien qui les à mis en notes de musique. Il fauldroit en avoir quelque piece bien complette, quand ce ne seroit qu'une hymne ou bien un pseaulme avec leurs notes de musique & l'interpretation de la valleur desditz notes par quelqu'un qui entendoit un peu de nostre musique."
300. Peiresc to [Minuti], 11 October 1633, CBI, MS. 1874, f. 314v. "Vous aurez des portraitz de leurs instruments pour monstrer elles qui se chantent de caresme ou plustost un piece de chasque sorte."
301. Peiresc to Salvator, 11 October 1633, CBI, MS. 1874, f. 314v.
302. Peiresc to Tarquet, 11 October 1633, CBI, MS. 1874, f. 314v.
303. Peiresc to Magy, 12 October 1633, CBI, MS. 1874, f. 315r. "Ayant acquis grand credit en ce pais là, parmy ceux qui ont des livres aussy bien come avec les autres. Et qu'il est curieux jusques à ce point d'avoir, chez soy des *arbres di casse, de mirabolans, de choux pommez qui poussent une seconde foys leur pommes quand on l'a coupée* et choses semblables, dont la race seroit bonne a acquerir s'il se pouvoit commodement." It is people just like him who collected the materials cataloged in *Egypte & Provence: Civilisation, survivances et cabinetz de curiositez* (Avignon: Fondation du Musée Calvet, 1985).
304. Peiresc to Magy, 12 October 1633, CBI, MS. 1874, f. 315r. "Au reste j'oubliay de vous charger en voz instructions *dans un memoire concernant la musique de pardela;* que vous trouverez cy joinct sur lequel je vous prie de vous enquerir de quelques qui entende un peu de musique et qui peust mettre par escript ce que l'on desire scavoir de chantant des Grecz & des Cophtes que des Turcz & Arabes sil y a moyen d'en rien tirer."
305. Peiresc to Magy, 12 October 1633, CBI, MS. 1874, f. 315r.
306. Peiresc to Seghezzi, 12 October 1633, CBI, MS. 1874, f. 315r.
307. Peiresc to Seghezzi, 11 October 1633, CBI, MS. 1874, f. 315r.
308. Peiresc to Allemand, 12 October 1633, CBI, MS. 1874, f. 315v.

309. Peiresc to Jacques de Vendôme, 12 October 1633, CBI, MS. 1874, f. 315v.
310. Peiresc to Jacques de Vendôme, 12 October 1633, CBI, MS. 1874, f. 316r.
311. Peiresc to Jacques de Vendôme, 12 October 1633, CBI, MS. 1874, ff. 316r–v. "De faire marquer sur le papier et . . . notre musique le chant des Grecz, celles des Cophtes, celles des Maronites, celle des . . . [Nestorians/Georgians?] celles des Abyssins et de tous autres qui se peuvent pratiquer en entender en ce lieu la . . . avec la chant & les notes & characteres des . . . nations estranges dont une repetition en noz characteres et notes pour . . . a peu prez la prononciation, & le ton de leur parolles en leur langue . . . des portraitz d'Instrumentz faictz avec un grand soing. . . . [I]l ne fauldroit pas negliger de les faire portr[aire]."
312. Peiresc to Minuti, 12 October 1633, CBI, MS. 1874, f. 316v. "Avec des memoires de la musique de cez pais là pour en ayder le bon P. Mercene, et des espreuves en taille doulce de ses instrumentz, pour les faire voir aux curieux de la musique, et les induire à communiquer les portraicts et dimensions des leurs et s'il est possible quelque relation ou instruction des proportions de leurs tons, notes & characteres de musique et facon de chanter et sonner de leurs Instrumentz." Quoted in *Mersenne Correspondance*, 3:494–495.
313. They are found today in PBN, MS. 9531, ff. 238–288.
314. Peiresc to Minuti, 12 October 1633, CBI, MS. 1874, f. 316v. "Qui se meslage de chanter & de sonner des instruments que vous peusse donner quelques instructions sur cela." Imbert was the *premier commis* of Abel Servien (1593–1659), *secrétaire d'État* after 1631.
315. Peiresc to Minuti, 12 October 1633, CBI, MS. 1874, f. 317r. "S'il y avoit moyen de communiquer ce memoire de la musique a quelqu'un qui allast en Hierusalem dans le St. Sepulchre ou il y à de tant de differentes sortes de Chrestiens ce peult le vray lieu pour faire marquer la differences de chant des Grecz aux Cophtes, Armeniens, Maronites, Abyssins & autres, s'il s'y rencontrer quelqu'un un peu intelligent de Notre musique car il pourroit metter en nottes de notre musique l'air du chant different de tous ces peuples et en transcripre a part les notes de chacun selong leur escript pour les comparer aux n[ot]res."
316. Peiresc to Minuti, 12 October 1633, CBI, MS. 1874, f. 317r. "Je luy escriptz aussy pour le memoire de la musique, a fin qu'il y faire trouver en Hierusalem dans les St. Sepulchre si faire ce peu."
317. Peiresc to Mersenne, 13–15 October 1633, *Mersenne Correspondance*, 3:497.
318. Peiresc to Mersenne, 13–15 October 1633, *Mersenne Correspondance*, 3:498, 503. Peiresc must have learned about the dervishes from Minuti and identified the Moor as a gallerian in Marseille (Peiresc to Mersenne, 16 July 1634, *Mersenne Correspondance*, 4:241, 243). Elsewhere, Peiresc notes that this Persian ambassador was in reality a "simple merchant." That he was rewarded with a gift by Pope Clement VIII, despite being a Muslim, was used by Peiresc as an argument that the Protestant Samuel Petit should be rewarded by the church for his services as a student of oriental languages. Peiresc to Barberini, 2 July 1635, Rome, BAV, MS. Barb.-Lat. 6503, f. 141r.
319. Peiresc to Mersenne, 13–15 October 1633, *Mersenne Correspondance*, 3:499.

320. Peiresc to de Loches, 25 October 1633, CBI, MS. 1874, f. 317v. "Et de vous plus si vous aur[i]ez agreable de me mander un peu de r[elation?] . . . [Chose]s plus curieux que vous avez veu dans les Bibliotheques des Cophtes et . . ."

321. Peiresc to Minuti, 28 October 1633, CBI, MS. 1874, f. 317v. "Dans le paquet d'Alep, je fis joindre des images en taille doulce de divers instrumentz de musique pour voir si cez peuples en ont et semblement ou rapprochantz, et tascher d'avoir quelque relation exacte de ceux qu'ilz ont. Mais j'oubliay de vous prie comme je faictz presentement de vouloir faire cotté les noms quils donnent à noz instrumentz s'ilz en ont de semblant aux notres scavoir est pour notre luths, notre thiorbe, notre viole, notre violon, notre espinette, notre trompett, noz fluttes, noz cornetz, nos tunbales corneuses et autres, scavoir comment ilz les nomment, tant en Arabe et Turquesque qu'en Syriac, Armenien, Cophte & autres langues orientales. Et mesmes s'ilz en scavoir rendre les ethymologies en leur langue pour scavoir surquoy ont esté formez leurs noms a peu prez, il n'y auroit rien plus a descrire. Je vous prie de faire ceste enqueste, la plus curieusement & punctuellement car cest pour le servir non seulement de Vre bon P. Mercenne mais encore de l'Em.ce Cardinal Barberin."

322. Peiresc to Jacques de Vendôme, 28 October 1633, CBI, MS. 1874, f. 318r. "Je vous pris dernierement de nous donner quelque instructions des differentes sortes de chant & de musique des differentes sortes du Xretiens et autres religions qui se professent en cez païs là, vous nous ferez grande faveur de les nous envoye le plustost que vous pourrez. Et vous prie de faire cotter les divers noms que les y donnent [non] seulement aux instrumentz semblables aux notres comme luths, violons, espinettes, . . . [es] trompettes, cornetz, cornemeuses & autres, silz en ont, mais a ceux quilz . . . [p]ouvent avoir differantz aux n[ot]res de deçà."

323. Minuti to Peiresc, 21 October 1633, PBN, MS. F.fr. 9542, f. 15v.

324. Minuti to Peiresc, 21 October 1633, PBN, MS. F.fr. 9542, f. 16v. Peiresc to Aycard, 17 December 1633, CBI, MS. 1874, f. 40r. De l'Isle wrote directly to Peiresc about this case the following week: De l'Isle to Peiresc, 7 November 1633, CBI, MS. 1879, f. 223v.

325. Peiresc to Aycard, 17 December 1633, CBI, MS. 1874, f. 40r.

326. Peiresc to de Loches, 20 December 1633, CBI, MS. 1874, f. 319r.

327. Peiresc to Magy, 21 December 1633, CBI, MS. 1874, f. 319v. "Plaisir d'entendre ce que me mandez du mariage du Sr Vermeil avec la niepce du Roy d'A[byssinie] mais pour prendre asseurance en telles nouvelles il eust fallu marque la datte du temps [de la?] celebration & consommation d'icelluy, s'il estoit possible de l'apprendre, ou pour le moins de temps que la nouvelle en fut apporter au Cayre. Et si ne font pas des personnes qualifees ou de grande creance, comme il en vient aulcuneffois dans les caravanes auquel cas il est bon de cotter les noms de telles personnes sur la foy desquelz on appuye la certitude de telles choses quand elles sont tant soit peu estranges et hors des termes ordinaires et fauldroit aussy marquer la qualité de la caravane le lieu d'ou elle venoit qui en estoient les chefz et quel en estoit le fondz a peu prez et par consequent l'importance soit qu'elles vennent des Abyssins mesmes ou des Malgarbins, ou

des Daononro [interlinear: Dakydxri] ou bien du costé du Ayman, du Moukal & des Indes mesmes." That this suggested a broader epistemological agenda is immediately made explicit: "Quand vous en pourrez apprenent des curiositez notables, soit de l'histoire du temps ou des nouvelles de la nature. Ce que vous pourra servir d'advis a l'advenir."

328. Peiresc to Magy, 21 December 1633, CBI, MS. 1874, f. 319v. "Pauvres peuples un peu plus barbares & moins polys ou civilisez [que les] Francoys."

329. Peiresc to Magy, 21 December 1633, CBI, MS. 1874, f. 319v.

330. Peiresc to Magy, 21 December 1633, CBI, MS. 1874, f. 320r. "Je desire d'en voir l'invention. Et avec le temps et peu a peu, vous travaillerez aux autres choses ou articles de voz memoire."

331. Peiresc to Magy, 21 December 1633, CBI, MS. 1874, f. 320r.

332. Peiresc to Jean-Baptiste Magy, 22 December 1633, CBI, MS. 1874, f. 320r.

333. Peiresc to Seguetti, 22 December 1633, CBI, MS. 1874, f. 320v.

334. Peiresc to Gela, 22 December 1633, CBI, MS. 1874, f. 320v.

335. Peiresc to Minuti, 23–27 December 1633, CBI, MS. 1874, f. 320v.

336. Peiresc to Minuti, 23–27 December 1633, CBI, MS. 1874, f. 321r.

337. Peiresc to Minuti, 23–27 December 1633, CBI, MS. 1874, f. 321r. "Des grandes ruines et masures de belles villes quil y avoit autreffois dans ceste Asie mineure."

338. Peiresc to Minuti, 23–27 December 1633, CBI, MS. 1874, f. 321r. "De plus curieux en matiere de livres, antiquailles, et curiositez de nature."

339. Peiresc to Minuti, 23–27 December 1633, CBI, MS. 1874, f. 321v.

340. Peiresc to Minuti, 23–27 December 1633, CBI, MS. 1874, f. 321r. "De vive voix on peult beaucoup mieux s'arraisonne & donné a entendre, et qu'il seroit difficile de mettre par escript tout ce qui seroit bien a dire, sur tout pour les livres, & pour toutes sorte d'escripture ancienne. Il fauldroit, s'il estoit loysible moyenne que l'en eusse un peu de venir, car je me ferois partir à Marseille et bien plus loing pour en aller voir quelque chose, & y apprendre mille rares notices que j'ignoreray toute ma vie sans cela." Peiresc's priority on conversation is only worth noting because of his effort and fame as a letter-writer; conversation itself was generally praised. See Peter N. Miller, *Peiresc's Europe: Learning and Virtue in the Seventeenth Century* (New Haven, CT: Yale University Press, 2000), ch. 2.

341. Peiresc to Minuti, 23–27 December 1633, CBI, MS. 1874, f. 321v. "Mais je crois nullement, que vous en puissiez venir à bone estant ce que vous estes, il fauldroit quasi se pouvoir desguiser et transformer en Angloys au lieu de Francoys pour extorquer la recommandation cordiale et confidenter, ce que vous ne scaurez non plus faire que de puisse f[aire] minister au lieu de presbtre ou Religieux."

342. Peiresc to Minuti, 23–27 December 1633, CBI, MS. 1874, f. 321v.

343. Peiresc to Minuti, 23–27 December 1633, CBI, MS. 1874, f. 322r. "Un grand personage de mes amis qui escript sur cette matiere & preuve (tant en Italien qu'en Hebreu) si les pouviez trouver & et les plus complets que vous pourrez."

344. On their study of the Constantinople Polyglot Bible, see Miller, *Peiresc's Orient*, 216–217.

345. Peiresc to Minuti, 23–27 December 1633, CBI, MS. 1874, f. 322r.

346. Peiresc to Minuti, 23–27 December 1633, CBI, MS. 1874, f. 322r. "De peur qu'ilz ne vous . . . quelque mauvais tour soubs main pour se prevaloir de vos conquestes . . . une marche de jalousie sur moi ou plustost sur Mons.r . . . et sur toute la nation. C'est pourquoy il fault aller en cella bien discretement et avec de grandes reserves mentales et pretexter vos recherches restraintes tant seullement."

347. Peiresc to Minuti, 23–27 December 1633, CBI, MS. 1874, f. 322v. "Que si les Juifz y vouloient appliquer encores les leurs Bebieux [bibiaux?] vous me feriez encores plus de plaisir, ensemble ceux des autres nations qui resident en Constantinople, avec un peu de relation telle qui se peult faire avec les poidz & mesures de france s'il y en a la quelque usage entre ceux de n[ot]re nation."

348. Peiresc to Ehinger, 3 January 1634, PBN, MS. N.a.f. 5172, f. 204r. "Ma recherche est fort esloignée de tout ce que l'Arias Montanus et tous les autres modernes en ont escript."

349. Peiresc to Minuti, 23–27 December 1633, CBI, MS. 1874, f. 322v. "De prendre les noms Turquesques et Grecz vulgaires & autres que vous pourrez recueillir pour l'intelligence de l'usage de telles machines ou instrumentz."

350. Peiresc to Minuti, 23–27 December 1633, CBI, MS. 1874, f. 322v.

351. Peiresc to Minuti, 23–27 December 1633, CBI, MS. 1874, f. 322v.

352. Peiresc to l'Empereur, 24 December 1633, CBI, MS. 1874, f. 323r.

353. Peiresc to l'Empereur, 24 December 1633, CBI, MS. 1874, f. 323v.

354. Peiresc to Guez, 24 December 1633, CBI, MS. 1874, f. 323v.

355. Peiresc to Sabatier, 24 December 1633, CBI, MS. 1874, f. 323v.

356. Peiresc to Marcheville, 26 December 1633, CBI, MS. 1874, f. 605r. "Il me laissa entr'autres la version Italique de ce petit bordereau des diverses sectes Mahometaines de Memet Enim Ben Sadredin dont suis estre curieux de retenir coppie soubz votre adveu, et s'il eust de le texte Turquesque je n'eusse pas espargne la despense a le faire . . . il sera a propos de s'enquerir de verifier s'il estoit possible[,] la qualité & creance de l'autheur, en quel temps il vivoit, qui est celluy[,] à qui il addresse son oeuvre[,] a fin que cela servir de garentir de la verité de la piece, et que ce n'est point chose forger à plaisir a desseign de desroger a la religion Mahometain."

357. Peiresc to Marcheville, 26 December 1633, CBI, MS. 1874, f. 605v.

358. Peiresc to M. le Consul de Smyrne, 26 December 1633, CBI, MS. 1874, f. 324r.

359. Peiresc to Jean Magy, 1 January 1634, CBI, MS. 1874, f. 324r. In his accompanying letter to Jean Magy, Peiresc explained that he had written another letter when he realized that he had forgotten to raise the issue of papyrus. Peiresc to Jean-Baptiste Magy, 1 January 1634, CBI, MS. 1874, f. 324r.

360. Peiresc to Gela, 1 January 1634, CBI, MS. 1874, f. 324v.

361. Peiresc to Minuti, 9 January 1634, CBI, MS. 1874, f. 324v.

362. Peiresc to de Loches, 31 January 1634, CBI, MS. 1874, f. 325r. "Une relation fort exacte qu'il à eu du pais des Abyssins de la part tant d'un Pere Jesuite que du Sr Vermeil de qui il ne me dict pas une si grande fortune comme on avoit faict le bruit."

363. Peiresc to Minuti, 20 February 1634, CBI, MS. 1874, f. 327r.

364. Peiresc to Albert, 20 February 1634, CBI, MS. 1874, f. 328r. "J'ay bien de la peine de croire tout ce que l'on en a dict puis que vous en parlez si sobrement saichant comme je faicts qu'il est fort de voz amis et compare que ce soit de sa part que vous ayez eu la relation dont vous me faictes faveur puis que c'est a sa requisition que vous avez faict la recherche que vous faictes de livres et figures en taille doulce."

365. Peiresc to Albert, 20 February 1634, CBI, MS. 1874, f. 327v. "S'il ne tenoit qu'a cela pour obtenir la liberté du commerce avec Mr Vermeil, de faire avoir a cez Bassas qui commandent en Aegypte de cez libvres, quilz pourroient desire du nombre de ceux que j'envoys audit Sr. Vermeil je leur permetteois bien volontiers de leur en faire recouvre de pareilz." The story of this project is told in Miller, *Peiresc's Orient,* ch. 10.

366. Peiresc to Albert, 20 February 1634, CBI, MS. 1874, f. 328v. "Je tiens qu'il auroit bien du subiect, d'en tirer de la satisfaction par ce que la graveure en est fort proprement faict & capable de bien recreer l'oeuil et y a grande facilité d'y faire comprendre les regles de l'art aultant d'une seulle veüe quasi quand l'on ne sçauroit pas parler le langage du pais . . . et pense que s'ilz estoient bien visités & examinez il s'y trouveroit de bien curieuses pieces dont nous ne laisserions pas de retirer du fruict & du secours s'il nous en peult tomber en main comme j'y travailherai tousjours tant que je pourrai et me resoultz d'en escrire Mr Vermeil a fin qu'il y employe son credit ne doubtant point qu'il n'en puisse obtenir quasi aussi facilement comme nous pourrons lui faire avoir en eschange de tout ce qu'il pourra desirer de plus digne de cez quartiers de deca."

367. Peiresc to Albert, 20 February 1634, CBI, MS. 1874, f. 328v.

368. Peiresc to Magy, 27 February 1634, CBI, MS. 1874, f. 329r. "Ayant apprins que le Sr Vermeil qui est pussé au pais des Abyssines s'estoit addressé a luy pour le recouvrement de quelques *libvres* comme vous scavez j'en ay faict venir quelques uns, et luy en envoyer *une petite casette* de ceux que j'ay estimez plus proprie à l'usaige auquel il les pourra destiner, en attendant de luy en pouvoir envoyer plus grand nombre & un meilleur assortiment accompagner des autres curiositez qui pouroit estre mieux retenir en ce pais ou il est. Cependant je luy demander quelques *instruments* pour ma curiosité principalement *en matiere de libvres* m'imaginant qu'il s'y en doibt estre conserver bon nombre des plus curieux qui l'on scavoir rechercher, dont je luy demander des roolles & Inventaires et la communication de quelquesunes. Et seray bien ayse que vous puissiez voir mes memoires & instructions, avant qu'on les envoye s'il est possible."

369. Peiresc to Magy, 27 February 1634, CBI, MS. 1874, f. 329r.

370. Peiresc to Magy, 27 February 1634, CBI, MS. 1874, f. 329v. "Toutes cez mémoires & Instructions ne serent pas communiquez a d'autres s'il est possible de peur qu'ils me servent a me faire encherir la marchandise que je cherche et à donner les advis à des gentz qui praignent le party pour eulx comme il n'y est desia plusieurs foys advenus et qui m'en fassent demeurer frustrer. . . . Et de ne pas faire de dissimuler de courir sur votre marché & par consequent sur le mien, ce qui pourroit mesmes unire à voz autres affaires dont je serois bien marry."

371. Peiresc to Magy, 27 February 1634, CBI, MS. 1874, f.329v. "Qu'on ne scauroit jamais aller trop reservé en toute sorte de negociations ou il peult escheoir tant soit peu de jalousie et de concurrance a la recherche de toutes marchandises et a plus sorte raison de celles qui sont si curieuses, comme les livres."

372. I am advised by Prof. G. J. Toomer that "Ebenbitar" is Ibn al-Baytar (thirteenth century), who wrote on materia medica, most of which was connected with plants (derived mainly from Dioscorides); see Juan Vernet, in *Dictionary of Scientific Biography*, 16 vols. (New York: Charles Scribner's Sons, 1970–1980), 1:538–539. The "abridgement" alluded to by Peiresc could refer to a sixteenth-century Latin book edition of some of his writings published by Andrea Alpago, *De Limonibus, Tractatus Embitar Arabis, per Andream Bellunensem Latinitate Donatus* [Abdallah ibn Ahmad Ibn al-Baitar al-Malaqi Abu Muhammad Diya-al-din; Alpago, Andreas] (Paris: Petrus Chevalier, 1602). I am grateful to Prof. Toomer for sharing this information with me. "Maleyia" I cannot now identify.

373. Peiresc to Magy, 27 February 1634, CBI, MS. 1874, f. 329v.

374. Peiresc to Magy, 27 February 1634, CBI, MS. 1874, f. 330r. "Je pense qu'il debvra bien estre passé par l'estamine a travers de si estranges et loingtains pays . . . principalement s'il se trouve bien veritable que le *Sr Vermeil* y ayt acquis tant de credit comme l'on vous à dict. Mais j'en doubte un peu . . . un peu de libre accez a la personne du Roy ou de ses principaux ministeres."

375. Peiresc to Baulme, 27 February 1634, CBI, MS. 1874, ff. 330v–331r. "Sy vous en faictes faire article sur la pollixe de chargement de ce qu'envoyerez de dela possible que les que les [*sic*] douaniers ne feront pas difficulté de la croire a bonne foy; mais s'il estoit possible que le Capp.ne ou aultre des chefs du navire la peussent tenir en l'eau qui ne fust pas exposé aux visites de cez gents la il ne seroit que bon d'esviter qu'elle ne passe par leurs mains s'il est possible de crainte que tout cela ne se cesse [*sic*, for sache] et ne s'esgare. En l'ouvrant elle occupera si peu de place qu'elle se peult mettre comme un pacquet de lettres, mais s'ilz visitent aussy les lettres il ne fauldroit pas qu'elle fusse avec le communication des lettres ains la faire reserver pour estre rendue aprez tout a loisir & hors de la veüe de ceste gents si mal raisonables. Sy vous jugés qu'il se pratique en pareil cas que si vous estimez qu'elle peusse courir fortune en cette sorte il la vauldroit mieux faire inserer dans la polixe de chargement pour ce qu'elle est & faire advertir qu'on ne la laisse pas ouvrir sans y avoir l'oeuil par la faire conserver."

376. Peiresc to Seghezzi, 27 February 1634, CBI, MS. 1874, f. 330r.

377. Peiresc to Albert, 2 March 1634, CBI, MS. 1874, f. 331r.

378. Peiresc to Laurens, 2 March 1634, CBI, MS. 1874, ff. 331r–v.

379. Peiresc to Laure, 2 March 1634, CBI, MS. 1874, f. 331v.

380. Peiresc to Baulme, 2 March 1634, CBI, MS. 1874, f. 331v. "Donner l'aultre jour a mon homme ce mulletier qui voulloit partir luy fit oublier un memoire."

381. Peiresc to Minuti, [2 March 1634], CBI, MS. 1874, f. 332r.

382. Peiresc to Minuti, 7 March 1634, CBI, MS. 1874, ff. 332r–v. "Par ou vous pourrcz voir qu'il se court des fortunes icy prez, aussy bien qu'aux loingtains païs."

383. Peiresc to Magy, 12 March 1634, CBI, MS. 1874, f. 332v.

384. Peiresc to Guez, 19 March 1634, and Peiresc to Sabatier, 19 March 1634, CBI, MS. 1874, f. 333r.

385. Peiresc to Minuti, 9 April 1634, CBI, MS. 1874, f. 335r. "Ou toute les gens de negoce maritime estoi[e]nt perdue si la commerce est cessé si soudainement et sans pouvoir retirer leur facilitez engagé au Levant." Minuti's letter of 20 March seems not to have survived.

386. Peiresc to de Loches, 6 May 1634, 54 [= CBI, MS. 1874, f. 343v]. transcribed in *Mersenne Correspondance*, 5:155: "On me mande que c'estoit le sieur Georgio l'Armeno, que vous pouvez avoir cogneu, qui auroit entreprins pour l'amour de moy la recherche des livres cophtes et abyssins. Et qu'il avoit commencé un inventaire de tout ce qui se trouvoit de par de là ès lieux où il avoit de l'accez."

387. Peiresc to Magy, 15 May 1634, CBI, MS. 1874, f. 342v. "Tant est que cela me faict juger que ces Mores doibvent avoir de fort bons livres de musique. Et si celluy de qui vous avez ou celluy-là que vous nommez en vostre lettre Jann Lazaravam, si je l'ay sceu bien lisre, ou bien ce maistre de musique du Cayre nommé au dos des couvertures dudit libvre Sici Ottoman, sont curieux d'avoir des libvres de nostre musique de Crestienté, je leur en envoyeray de la plus melodieuse et de Paris et de Rome."

388. Mersenne to Peiresc, 14 May 1634, *Mersenne Correspondance*, 4:107.

389. Amnon Shiloah and Annie Berthier, "À propos d'un 'Petit livre arabe de musique,'" *Revue de musicologie* 71 (1985): 167n11. Peiresc's notes on the book are in PBN, MS. F.fr. 9531, ff. 223r–225r.

390. Peiresc to de Loches, 6 May 1634, 55 [= CBI, MS. 1874, f. 343v]. "Ce que je n'avois jamais veu en tous les livres imprimés et mss qui m'éstoient passez par mes mains. Ce qui nous a faict recognoistre que, parmy ces peuples barbares, il fault qu'il y ait eu des esprits bien desliés."

391. Peiresc to Arcos, 25 January 1634, CBI, MS. 1871, f. 360r [= *Lettres de Peiresc*, 7:118].

392. Peiresc to Magy, 15 May 1634, CBI, MS. 1874, f. 343r. "Qu'il s'estoit chargé de vous faire un inventaire des libvres de ce pais là pour y pouvoir choisir ce qui s'y trouveoit de mon goust."

393. Peiresc to Magy, 15 May 1634, CBI, MS. 1874, f. 343r.

394. Peiresc to Mersenne, 18 June 1634, *Mersenne Correspondance*, 4:178.

395. Peiresc to Magy, 15 May 1634, CBI, MS. 1874, f. 343r. Capigies were porters, or gatekeepers.

396. Peiresc to Minuti, 27 July 1634, CBI, MS. 1874, f. 349r.

397. Peiresc to Magy, 30 September 1634, CBI, MS. 1874, f. 356r.

398. Peiresc to Magy, 30 September 1634, CBI, MS. 1874, f. 356r. "Hors d'estat de retrouver si tost en voz Cartieres comme il auroit creu de sorte qu'il fault tascher de faire sans luy."

399. Allemand to Minuti [December 1634], CBI, MS. 1874, f. 274r.

400. Peiresc to Minuti, 1 October 1634, CBI, MS. 1874, f. 356r.

401. Fernoux to Peiresc, 28 October 1634, PBN, MS. Dupuy 661, f. 199v. "Les Turcs n'ont point l'usage de la musique et ne chantent que par nature, et font d'aussi beaux concerts, et aussi plaisans à l'oreille."

402. Peiresc to Fernoux, 3 November 1634, CBI, MS. 1874, f. 356v. "Tres doctes & fonciers & capables de faire honte aux plus grands musiciens en l'Europe."

403. He was born Pieter van Gool at The Hague in 1597 and became a Carmelite in 1626. In 1632 he was sent to Syria to learn Arabic. In 1643 he founded the mission of the Discalced Carmelites to Mount Lebanon, and became the superior at Mar Elicha, the convent he founded and whose location he chose. In 1649 he created a school to prepare students for the Maronite college in Rome. In 1644 he gave a funeral oration for Galaup-Chasteuil, whom he had brought to Mar Elicha in 1643. In 1652 he was called to Rome as a professor of oriental languages in the general seminar of the Carmelite missions. In 1663 he edited an Arabic edition of the *Imitation of Jesus Christ* and in 1671 was chosen by Sergius Risius, archbishop of Damascus, to translate the Vulgate into Arabic. He also then produced a *Doctrina Christiana* in Turkish (1673) and a history of the Carmelite mission in Lebanon from 1643 to 1659 which remains in manuscript, along with the letters he wrote back from Lebanon to his superiors. In 1675 he was sent as a visitor of the Carmelite missions to Malabar. He died on the way, in Surat.

404. Peiresc to Celestin de Sainte-Lidwine, 5 January 1635, in Raymond Lebegue, ed., *Peiresc: Lettres à divers; Supplément au tome VII* (Paris: CNRS, 1985), 127 [= CBI, MS. 1874, f. 361v]. "Si vous rencontriez là par hazard soit chez les moynes Grecs ou les drevitz quelque bon livre un peu ancien de la musique non seullement en grec, mais en arabe, ou autre langue orientale, principalement de ceux où se pourroient estre conservées quelques notes de l'ancienne musique, j'employerois volontiers mon argent. . . . M. vostre frere m'a faict offrir ce qu'il en a tant d'Avicenne que d'un autre en arabe, et j'en ay recouvré un troisiesme du Cayre en arabe aussy, que je luy ay envoyé pour le conferer sur les siens. . . . Et j'entendz qu'il s'en trouve là quelques bons volumes ez mans de quelque prebstre grec bien jaloux de les monstrer qu'à des amys bien confidentz. Je voudrois surtout un exemplaire bien fidelement transcript en portraict sur quelque bien ancien manuscrit des trois hymnes de Dionysius qui sont derriere l'Aristides avec les notes, parce qu'elles sont fort corrompues en tous les exemplaires que nous en avons peu avoir de par deçà. Vous feriez oeuvre bien meritoire envers le public si vous aviez donné moyen de restaurer ce beau secret de l'antiquité, y ayant des braves hommes qui travaillent maintenant en divers lieux de l'Europe sur la restauration de la plus excellent musique des anciens Grecs [et] Romains." This is fairly unprecedented; for later seventeenth-century European interest in Eastern music, see Bryan White, " 'Brothers of the String': Henry Purcell and the Letter-Books of Rowland Sherman," *Music and Letters* 92, no. 4 (2011): 519–581. I am grateful to Simon Mills for this reference.

405. Peiresc to Contour, 5 January 1635, and Peiresc to Allemand, 6 January 1635, CBI, MS. 1874, f. 362r. We learn Contour's name in MAD, 380 E-337.

406. Peiresc to Blanc, en Cypre, 6 January 1635, CBI, MS. 1874, f. 362v. "Vous pourriez bien descouvrire en quelque facon les habitudes qui pouroit avoir prinses ledit feu Sr. Espanet dans la Montagne."

407. Peiresc to Blanc, en Cypre, 6 January 1635, CBI, MS. 1874, f. 362v.

408. Celestin to Peiresc, 5 August 1635, PBN, MS. F.fr. 9539, f. 193r.

409. Peiresc to Golius, 24 April 1635, *Peiresc: Lettres à Saumaise*, 155–156.

410. Peiresc to Celestin, 29 April 1635, CBI, MS. 1873, f. 42r. "Principalement aux observations de la nature & de ses effects plus merveilleux ou la providence divine paroit tousiours plus admirable."

411. Peiresc to Celestin, 29 April 1635, CBI, MS. 1873, f. 42v. "Car l'aspect de cez païs là peult fournir de grandz arguments & moyens de penetrer dans la philosophie naturelle en peu plus avant que ne songent communement ceux qui s'y estudient pour le jourdhuy, tout aultrement que ne faisoient les anciens, mais non possible mieux qu'eulx, veu que le livre de la nature est le livre des livres, et n'y à rien de si concluant que les observations des choses mesmes dont le cours est si constant, quelques vicissitudes & revelations ou changementz qu'il y puisse avoir, ne ou la grandeur de Dieu paroisse davantage, et soit capable de nous faire eslever l'esprit humain quand tout est bien pesé & examiné comme il fault."

412. Peiresc to Celestin, 29 April 1635, CBI, MS. 1873, f. 42v. "S'il y avoit moyen de s'y aller promener, quelque jour de votre loysir, avec quelque janissaire ou autres personnes requises pour la seureté de votre compagnie, j'en ferois volontiers la despence."

413. Peiresc to Celestin, 29 April 1635, CBI, MS. 1873, f. 43r, f. 43bis. A methodized version of this "how-to" approach is the mémoire written for the Capuchin Cassien de Nantes, PBN, MS. Dupuy, 663, f. 157r.

414. Peiresc to Celestin, 29 April 1635, CBI, MS. 1873, ff. 43v–44r.

415. Peiresc to Celestin, 29 April 1635, CBI, MS. 1873, f. 44v.

416. Peiresc to Hazard, 10 July 1635, CBI, MS. 1874, f. 374r. Peiresc refers to Gaulmin as "votre maitre"—suggesting the connection to oriental studies. "Toutes les Instructions que vous pourrez de l'age, patrie, bonnes moeurs et doctrine de cet Evesque Isaac, en quel lieu vous l'avez cogneu, et speciallement de la cognoissance qu'il peut avoir de la langue Arabique & de la Latin ou autres, Et s'il à des inclinations plus curieuses que le commun, et d'ou est le tiltre de son Evesché, et en quel employ vous l'avez veu et quel à esté le subiect de son voyage à Rouen."

417. PBN, MS. Lat. 9340, f. 221v, dated 13 July 1635.

418. Peiresc to Mersenne, 17 July 1635, *Mersenne Correspondance*, 5:317.

419. Peiresc to Danmartin, 9 July 1635, CBI, MS. 1874, f. 374v; Peiresc to de Loches, 10 July 1635, CBI, MS. 1874, f. 375r.

420. Peiresc to de Loches, 17 July 1635, CBI, MS. 1874, f. 376r. "Ce petit que vous avez veu seullement un jour, duquel j'estime qu'il se tireroit bien plus de fruict que l'on ne croit, s'il y avait moyen de le bien interpreter, à cause des notes et des figures coloriées qui peuvent suppléer tout plein de secrets de l'ancienne musique des Grecs, dont la memoire et cognoissance sont ensevelies et perdues tout a faict."

421. Peiresc's notes on the content of the book with the three treatises are in PBN, MS. F.fr. 9531, ff. 227r–229r.

422. Peiresc to Celestin, 16 August 1635, Lebègue ed., 128 [= CBI, MS. 1874, f. 384]. "Saphadin, fort celebre musicien de cette nation et inventeur de leurs notes musicales. Mais il y a sur la fin du Persan ou il n'est pas aisé de mordre."

423. Peiresc to Celestin, 16 August 1635, Lebègue ed., 128 [= CBI, MS. 1874, f. 384]. "Sur tout s'il y avoit rien de traduit des autheurs grecs formellement et principalement concernant les notes des anciens vous me feriez un trez singulier playsir d'en faire prendre sur les lieux un peu d'interpretation tell quelle, s'il est possible a cause du Persan qui s'y rencontre souvent et des termes de l'art qui ne sont pas intelligible a des gens bien scavants dailleurs en ces langues orientales."

424. Celestin to Peiresc, 5 August 1635, PBN, MS. F.fr. 9539, f. 193r.

425. Peiresc to Celestin, 18 October 1635, and Peiresc to Pierre and Jean Constans, CBI, MS. 1874, f. 393bis v.

426. Peiresc to Venture, 18 October 1635, CBI, MS. 1874, f. 394r; Peiresc to Golius, 11 September 1635, *Lettres à Claude Saumaise*, 177.

427. In her copious notes, Agnès Bresson traces Peiresc's description of this project in parallel letters to Kircher and Naudé (*Lettres à Claude Saumaise*, 179–182).

428. Peiresc to Celestin, 14 November 1635, CBI, MS. 1874, ff. 396v–397r [partially printed in Lebègue et al., *Supplément au tome VII*, 129]. "Et puis que vous dict que il y a là des vieux Drevits et autres braves hommes doctes et bien curieux des bons livres en toutes sortes de sciences et specialement aux Mathematiques. . . . Il fault scavoir d'eux aussy par mesme moyen s'ils n'ont pas des livres de la bonne astronomie, où c'est que soyent induictes et enregistrées des observations des eclypses et autres phenomènes des siecles passez pour en pouvoir faire le calcul et la comparaison avec les notres comme je ne doubte pas qu'ils n'en ayant puisqu'ils ont des tables astronomiques comme celles du Roy Alphonse et autres auquel cas je vous supplie d'en prendre les noms des autheurs, le siecle qu'ils ont vescu et s'ils estoient a vendre ou a coppier je n'y espargnerois pas une piece d'argent si non a tout le moins voyez de vous faire cotter sur un papier quelqu'une des eclypses y enoncees et de prendre exactement toutes les circonstances de l'observation tant pour le vray poinct des epoques des moments de chaque phase qui avoir esté observee et reglee a la dimension de la hautteur de quelque estoile comme de la situation du lieu ou est faicte l'observation pour en scavoir la latitude ou haulteur du pole et la longitude a peu pres et de la qualité des instruments dont on s'est servy pour prendre lesdits dimensions."

429. Peiresc to Celestin, 14 November 1635, in Lebègue et al., *Supplément au tome VII*, 129 [= CBI, MS. 1874, f. 397r]. "Au reste, ne vous contenter pas d'estudier en Langue Arabique ains tascher de penetrer a la Persienne la plus avant que vous pourrez car cest en cette langue la que se trouvent escripts les livres de plus grands importance en ce Levant, principalement aux Mathematiques et en l'histoire et si mesmes pouver [*sic*] trouver quelque livre bien propre a faciliter la cognoissance de la langue Persienne ne le layser pas eschaper facilement et disposez librement de moy."

430. On the role of Persian texts in Arab cities in the seventeenth century, see Khaled El-Rouayheb, "Opening the Gate of Verification: The Forgotten Arabic-Islamic Florescence of the 17th Century," *International Journal of Middle Eastern Studies* 38 (2006): 263–281. I am grateful to Simon Mills for this reference.

431. Peiresc to Celestin, 14 November 1635, CBI, MS. 1874, f. 397v (omitted in Lebègue et al., *Supplément au tome VII*). "Je verois bien volontiers aussy celluy des libvres d'histoire qu'il à en son pouvoir, et qui sont au pouvoir des autres curieux d'Halep, et s'ils sont à vendre on y en pouroit cotter le prix."

432. Agathange to Peiresc, 25 July 1635, PBN, MS. F.fr. 9543, f. 257r [= *Correspondance de Peiresc*, 155].

433. Peiresc to Celestin, 17 November 1635, in Lebègue et al., *Supplément au tome VII*, 130 [=CBI, MS. 1874, f. 398v]. "Qui n'estoit pas si mauvaise comme plusieurs l'ont voulu faire a croire sur des faulx bruitz ou equivoques des noms de la volupté soubz lesquels il ne concepvoir rien moings que les sensualitez."

434. Peiresc to Celestin, 17 November 1635, CBI, MS. 1874, f. 398v (omitted in Lebègue et al., *Supplément au tome VII*).

435. See Zur Shalev, "Measurer of All Things: John Greaves (1602–1652), the Great Pyramid, and Modern Metrology," *Journal of the History of Ideas* 63 (2002): 555–575.

436. Celestin to Peiresc, 29 November 1635, PBN, MS. 688, ff. 19r–21v.

437. Peiresc to Celestin, 22 November 1635, CBI, MS. 1874, f. 399v. "Mais je regrette ce grand volume du recueil des Autheurs de la Musique qui vous est eschapper des mains si malheureusement pour estre emporter sy loing comme on vous à voulu faire accroire ce qui pourroit bien estre un artifice pour vous encherir. Il faudra vous en donner de garde & y veiller en son temps." The dates are confirmed in Peiresc to Golius, 19 November 1635, *Lettres à Claude Saumaise*, 217.

438. Peiresc to Celestin, 22 November 1635, CBI, MS. 1874, f. 400r. "Vous ne scauriez vous imaginer l'utilité de telles observations qui est tout aultre que celle des plantes & des autres choses naturelles, et quand on y à prins un peu de routtine il n'y à rien de si facile."

439. Peiresc to Celestin, 22 November 1635, CBI, MS. 1874, f. 400v. "Quand au voyage du Mont Casius puis que le premier dessein a si mal succedé, je ne suis d'advis que vous y soingiez plus[,] ayant a faire a la discretion de gentz si barbares & qui ne cherchent que des pretextes de ranconnements a tout & a trames. Et je ne suis pas assez grand seigneur pour fournir a la despence qu'il y faudroit." On Schikard see *Wilhelm Schickard, 1592–1635: Astronom, Geograph, Orientalist, Erfinder der Rechenmaschine*, ed. Friedrich Seck (Tübingen: Mohr, 1978); *Wissenschaftsgeschichte um Wilhelm Schickard: Vorträge bei dem Symposion der Universität Tübingen im 500. Jahr ihres Bestehens am 24. und 25. Juni 1977*, ed. Friedrich Seck (Tübingen: Mohr, 1981); *Zum 400. Geburtstag von Wilhelm Schickard: Zweites Tübinger Schickard-Symposion, 25. bis 27. Juni 1992*, ed. Friedrich Seck (Sigmaringen: J. Thorbecke, 1995).

440. Peiresc to Celestin, 22 November 1635, CBI, MS. 1874, f. 399v.

441. Peiresc to Celestin, 22 November 1635, CBI, MS. 1874, f. 400v. "A la bonne heure vous en fistes rappellez puis que m'estantz allez qu'à une journée d'Alep la despence à esté de plus de 80 escus (car pour rendre icy l'indempnité il nous fault rendu un escu pour piastre) a laquelle raison pour attendre le jour de l'ecclipse sur les lieux & revenir avec tout ce train. Il eust fallu despendre un millier d'escus qui eust esté trop cherement payer la coppie d'une inscription

antique qui s'y pourroit transcripre. Oultre que vous n'estierez jamais de la teste de cez espritz foibles et superstitueux, que vous n'y feussiez allé pour chercher les tresors qu'ils se sont figurez y estre, ou pour d'autres choses encores moins imaginables cappables de pretexter une avarice contre votre personne & contre tous les votres, voire possible contre toute la nation. C'est pourquoy je renonce a toutes les pretentions que j'y pourrois avoir, et vous supplie de n'y plus penser."

442. Peiresc to Celestin, 22 November 1635, CBI, MS. 1874, f. 404r. "Vous avez encore oublié de me dire la propre nom du votre venerable vieillard le drevis qui vous monstre en Arabe de qui vous vous louëz tant, lequel merite bien que son nom, sa patrie & ses recommandables qualitez ne soient pas desormais ignorées. . . . Et faudroit scavoir de luy s'il n'y a pas là des gentz de leur nation qui s'acheve et qu'importe l'observation bien precise d'une eclypse plus rares consequences qui s'en peuvent tirer en faisant la comparaison avec celles que les anciens ont observées durant les siecles passez. Et si l'on n'en pourroit pas scavoir les noms & la demeure et prendre des habitudes avec eulx."

443. Peiresc to Contour, 22 November 1635, CBI, MS. 1874, f. 401v. "Car en cez matieres là, les faultes mesmes et les equivoques servent davantage bien souvent que les bons coups ou du moins qui paraissent telz voir que les corrections bien qu'il soit tirez a propos de les voir aussy, quand on peu voir l'un & l'autre."

444. Peiresc to Contour, 22 November 1635, CBI, MS. 1874, f. 401v.

445. Peiresc to Contour, 22 November 1635, CBI, MS. 1874, f. 402r. "Bien souvent on à tellement proffité de la remarque des faultes qu'il a fallu choixsir la supposition & assertion de ce qui sembloit faulte, et laisser la correction en arriver quelque apparence & vraysemblance qu'elle peusse avoir."

446. Peiresc to Contour, 22 November 1635, CBI, MS. 1874, f. 402r.

447. Peiresc to Contour, 22 November 1635, CBI, MS. 1874, f. 402r. "Il suffice a d'observer a Alep, si l'on s'y trouver sans aller chercher aulcune montaigne esloigné pour ne donner de la jalousie, que si on se trouvoit en hierusalem ou en autre lieu celebre, la chose n'en servir que plus recommandable."

448. Peiresc to Contour, 22 November 1635, CBI, MS. 1874, f. 402r.

449. Peiresc to Constans, 22 November 1635, CBI, MS. 1874, f. 402v. "Je n'eusse eu garde de songer a un tel dessein si j'eusse peu prevoir des ombrages si mal fondez, mais estant a la gueale et a la discretion de gents si barbares & si desfiants et de si mauvais foy il ne fault rien tenir d'asseuré et se fault abstenir des actions des plus innocentes quand elles sont tant soit peu hors du grand chemin. C'est pourquoy je vous supplie et coniure trez instamment de ne pas souffre que le bon pere Celestin ne le Sr. Claret et encores moins qu'aulcunes de vous autres Mssrs ne autre de voz amys ou des miens s'engagent jamais au malheureux voyage de cette montagne dont il ne pourroit advenir que du mal et de desplaisir parmy une si grande superstition et de perfidie de ce monde la et dont j'aurois du regret estremement tout le temps de ma vie car cetz gents la ne scaurent pas faire des petites avaries ne de petits desplaisirs et l'importance est que la chose ne peult pas meriter de se hazarder a rien que ce soit ne pas mesmc de prendre tant de peine pour ne voir qu'une grotte et quelques figures ou inscriptions."

450. Peiresc to Constans, 22 November 1635, CBI, MS. 1874, f. 402v. "Oultre que je suis trop petit compagnon pour de telles depenses a plaisir puis que cette compagnie n'estant alle que jusques a la premiere journee d'Alep a neant moins despendu 86 piastres car a cette proportion la le voyage eust deub coustent mille ou douze cents piastres a quoy je me seroit trouvé bien court . . . le project de ce bon pere qui y alloit a si bonne foy et qui me m'escrivoit a un'aulne [*sic*] un peu trop grande pour moy ce qui me servira d'advis pour l'advenir de ne plus faire de telles dessein."

451. Peiresc to Constans, 22 November 1635, CBI, MS. 1874, f. 403r. "Et vous supplie de rompre la partye quand vous verrez un'autre foys qu'on s'y voudroit attacher, oultre le danger des avaries qui pourroient aller a la ruine de familles entieres. Car quelque parole qu'on eusse eüe du Mausolee mesmes ie pense qu'il eust este homme de faire tousiours l'avarie pour peu qu'il eust eu de pretxte."

452. Father Celestin describes him as "Dominus Claret pharmacopolam, virum in simplicium cognitione diversarumque rerum peritia excellentem." Celestin to Peiresc, 29 September 1635, PBN, MS. Dupuy 688, f. 19r. We possess a list of debts drawn up by Fabre in 1633. We also have documents colophoned by Balthasar Claret with a subscription saying that they were collated from the original materials in the Chancellery "by me, Balthasar Fabre." MACC, J 1736 [unfoliated]. When both the consul and vice-consul of Egypt were absent, Fabre filled the function. See Fabre [Claret] to Consuls of Marseille, 9 February 1633, MACC, J 548.

453. Peiresc to Constans, 22 November 1635, CBI, MS. 1874, f. 403r. "L'employ qui avez faict du Sr B. Claret que j'estime personne de merite fort singulier en sa profession."

454. Peiresc to Claret, 22 November 1635, CBI, MS. 1874, f. 400v. "Ayant affaire à des gents si ombrageux et si superstitieux et de si mauvaise foy qui servient bien ayses d'y avoir un preteste de vous mesfaire."

455. Peiresc to Venture, 22 November 1635, CBI, MS. 1874, f. 403v. There is an Andre Venture mentioned in an obligation acknowledged by the Patron Nicolas Crouset but I have not been able to determine the relationship between Jean and Andre (MACC, J 745, unfoliated).

456. Peiresc to Fabre, 21 May 1636, PBN, MS. N.a.f. 5172, ff. 72–73. This is the only letter Peiresc wrote to Balthazar Fabre.

457. Peiresc to Fabre, 21 May 1636, PBN, MS. N.a.f. 5172, f. 72r [autograph]; CBI, MS. 1874, f. 425r. "Je ne suis pas tel qu'on vous a voulu faire a croire, ny pour les moyens (car je n'ay pas de quoy despendre des 8,000 piastres à des affaires inutiles), ni pour la curiosité, laquelle ne consiste nullement à apprendre des nouvelles du monde. . . . Car je ne suis pas de qualité ni de condition pour y vacquer ni pour en faire capital, et bien moings pour me charger des despences qui y pourroient escheoir."

458. Peiresc to Fabre, 21 May 1636, PBN, MS. N.a.f. 5172, f. 72r [autograph]; CBI, MS. 1874, f. 425r. "Aussy seray je bien aise que vous en dezabuziez ceux qui vouldroient le revoquer en doubte, et croire les faux bruicts qui en ont esté

semez de par delà par gents qui ne me cognoissent pas et qui m'on prins pour un autre. C'est la verité que je suis un peu curieux, mais ce n'est principalement que des livres propres à ayder le public, et consequamment des anticailles, quand il s'en rencontre à prix si modéré que ma petite bourse y puisse aspirer sans incommodité, ou bien lorsqu'il y a moyen d'avoir des portraicts ou desseins fideles de celles qui ne sont pas en commerce, et specialement quand il y a de l'escripture grecque ou latine ancienne, telle que l'on trouve souvent sur les frontispieces des anciens temples et dans les marbres et vieilles mazures, je n'espargneray, quand il ne tient qu'a peu de chose, la despence d'un peintre pour les desseigner, si les frais n'en sont pas trop considerables."

459. Peiresc to Fabre, 21 May 1636, PBN, MS. N.a.f. 5172, f. 72v. "C'estoit pour cela, qu'ayant ouy dire qu'il se lisoit, tout plain d'escritture Grecque et Syriaque dans dans un petit Temple ou caverne de la plus haulte montaigne de cez quartiers là, un bon Religieux qui estant porté sur les lieux, m'ayant faict feste d'un petit voyage qu'il y vouloit aller faire pour Herboriser et cueillir des semences plus rares je le priais de prendre sa route du costé de ladit caverne, pour transcrire cette escriture s'il estoit possible, et de disferer son voyage au temps de l'eclipse, s'il ne luy estoit incommode pour tascher d'en proffitter l'observation, qui eust esté vraysemblablement plus belle et plus certaine, et moings subiecte a l'empeschement des brouillards, d'un lieu si relevé que celuy là, ou les anciens avoient creu que le soleil se levoit un quart d'heure plustost qu'ailleurs ce qui se recontroit lors plus à propos qu'en autre occasion d'aultant que l'ecclipse devoit durer encores au soleil levant. Ce qui pourroit rendre l'observation plus facile et plus indubitable au moings subiecte à erreur."

460. Peiresc to Fabre, 21 May 1636, PBN MS. Naf 5172, f.72v. "Mais les jalousie et la mauvaise foy de ceux qui gouvernent en ce païs là, ne sont pas compatibles à aulcun dessein qui vaille pour innocent qu'il soit. Et le bon religieux l'avoit voulu aggreger et mettre de la partie un peu trop de gents qui en avoient trop faicte de bruict parmy des peuples si desfiements et qui sont trop friands des occasions et des pretextes de faire des avanies et des ranconnements aux plus gents de bien."

461. Peiresc to Fabre, 21 May 1636, PBN MS. N.a.f. 5172, f. 72v: "Toutes les choses que le ne sont semblent des bagatelles ne lassoit pas tousjours pourtant."

462. Peiresc to Fabre, 21 May 1636, PBN, MS. N.a.f. 5172, f. 73r. Peiresc's number is wrong, but by the summer he is giving the right number, 300 leagues, or 100 miles. See Peiresc to Jacques Dupuy, 12 August 1636, *Lettres de Peiresc*, 3:542. A letter to the Capuchin Michelange de Nantes concerning the eclipse observation traveled in the same package. Peiresc to Michelange de Nantes, 22 November 1635, CBI, MS. 1874, ff. 40r–v. On this episode, see Peter N. Miller, "Mapping Peiresc's Mediterranean: Geography and Astronomy, 1610–1636," in *Communicating Observations in Early Modern Letters, 1500–1675: Epistolography and Epistemology in the Age of the Scientific Revolution*, ed. Dirk van Miert (Oxford: Warburg Institute Colloquia, 2013), 151–159.

463. Peiresc to Fabre, 21 May 1636, PBN, MS. N.a.f. 5172, f. 73r: "Mais il seroit pour tant à desirer que nous peussions avoir quelques autres observations des eclipses

faictes en ce païs là quand il y en aura. Afin de ne laisser aulcun regret à la correction desdits cartes & fauldroit qu'un Hasan y contribuast de son costé."

464. Peiresc to Celestin, 12 May 1636, CBI, MS. 1874, f. 416v.

465. See Bruce Masters, *The Origins of Western Economic Dominance in the Middle East: Mercantilism and the Islamic Economy in Aleppo, 1600–1750* (New York: New York University Press, 1988); Masters, "Aleppo: The Ottoman Empire's Caravan City," in Edhen Eldem, Daniel Goffman, and Bruce Masters, *The Ottoman City between East and West: Aleppo, Izmir, and Istanbul* (Cambridge: Cambridge University Press, 1999), pp. 17–78; Maurits H. van den Boogert, "European Patronage in the Ottoman Empire: Anglo-Dutch Conflicts of Interest in Aleppo (1703–1755)," in *Friends and Rivals in the East: Studies in Anglo-Dutch Relations in the Levant from the Seventeenth to the Early Nineteenth Century*, ed. Alastair Hamilton, Alexander H. de Groot, and Maurits H. van den Boogert (Leiden: E. J. Brill, 2000), 187–222. In all these the emphasis is on the later seventeenth century; Heghnar Zeitlian Watenpaugh, *The Image of an Ottoman City: Imperial Architecture and Urban Experience in Aleppo in the 16th and 17th Centuries* (Leiden: Brill, 2004), by contrast, does not focus so much on the human actors.

466. Celestin to Peiresc, 29 September 1635, PBN, MS. Dupuy 688, f. 21r.

467. Agathange to Peiresc, 25 July 1635, PBN, MS. F.fr. 9543, f. 257r [= *Correspondance de Peiresc*, 155].

468. Celestin to Golius, 22 February 1636, ABM, MS. 205 (1023), 262, 267; PBN, MS. Lat. 9340, f. 205v.

469. "Scripsum illum Mohamed Eltacwii, cujus mentionem alis fecit D.V., saepius converi, sed Bibliothecae suae catalogum, quem mihi promiserat, hactenus obtinere non potui: sane ut uno verbo dicam quod sentio, hominem illum versipellem esse et fraudulentum, non solum a Magistro meo Dervisio Ahemede, qui multis annis eodem usus est familiarissime, intellexi, sed etiam experientia cognovi." Celestin to Peiresc, 22 August 1637, ABM, MS. 205 (1023), 283.

470. This was published in P. M. Holt, *Studies in the History of the Near East* (London: Frank Cass, 1973), 44. I am very grateful to Gerald Toomer for sending me an emended transcription of the manuscript (Bodeleian MS. Pococke 432, f. 8) and for discussing with me the situation in Aleppo ca. 1636.

471. Celestin to Peiresc, 29 September 1635, PBN, MS. Dupuy 688, f. 21r. "*Cum senem quendam Dervisium, Magistrum scilicet meum*" and "Senem Dervisium Magistrum meum Arabicum in Geographicis versatissimum," f. 19r. The dervish himself had asked Pococke for a copy of "the printed geography" (G. J. Toomer, *Eastern Wisdome and Learning* [Oxford: Oxford University Press, 1996?], 123n30). I thank Simon Mills for pointing this out to me.

472. Celestin to Peiresc, 25 February 1636, ABM, MS. 205 (1023), 274.

473. G. J. Toomer, *Eastern Wisdome and Learning*, 122–123. This is how the copyist identifies himself in the colopohon to a copy of the *Conics*, which we independently know was transcribed for Golius in Aleppo (Leiden, MS. Or 14). See J. J. Witkam, *Inventory of the Oriental Manuscripts in the University of Leiden*, 25 vols. (Leiden: Ter Lugt Press, 2006–2008), 1:20. Martijn Theodor Houtsma, *Uit de Oostersche correspondentie van Th. Erpenius, Jac. Golius en*

Lev. Warner: Een bijdrage tot de geschiedenis van de beoefening der Oostersche letteren in Nederland (Amsterdam: Koninklijke Akademie van Wetenschappen te Amsterdam, 1887), distinguishes the letters of this Ahmad from that of another, studied in G. A. Wiegers, *A Learned Muslim Acquaintance of Erpenius and Golius: Ahmad b. Kasim al-Andalusi and Arabic Studies in the Netherlands* (Leiden: Faculteit der Godgeleerdheid Rijksuniversiteit, 1988).

474. Celestin to Peiresc, 25 February 1636, ABM, MS. 205 (1023), 277; Celestin to Peiresc, 22 August 1637 ABM, MS. 205 (1023), 284. I have learned a great deal from Simon Mills about the work of al-Akalshani and the context in Aleppo, in particular from an unpublished paper entitled "European Manuscript Collectors in the Ottoman Empire." I am grateful to him for allowing me to read it.

475. My inquiries of Suraiya Farouqi, Dana Sadji, and Charles L. Wilkens have not turned up anything on the Europeans in the Levant comparable to that of Nelly Hanna on merchant Cairo of that period (though we do not find the Europeans in her narrative either). Were they simply of no interest? Were they not discussed? Or has no one yet looked for these accounts in the right place?

476. Peiresc to Celestin, 12 May 1636, CBI, MS. 1874, f. 417r. "Je suis marry que vous ayez perdu le secours que vous receviez en voz petites consultations des langues orientales de votre Mister Pokak mais puisqu'il estoit si jaloux de ses livres et si mal sociable je ne suis pas marry qu'il vous ayt quitté la place et la parade, et pense bien que vous auriez maintenant de trez bonnes fortunes, et possible encore meilleures que celles des traictez fraternels ou je ne serois pas marry que vous eussiez employe les 60 piastres en mon nom parceque cella vous eut peu servir d'excuse et descharge a celluy qui le voulloit revendiquer quand vous eussiez dict de me l'avoir envoyé en France bien qu'il eussiez encore pour votre usaige, ces petites mensonges officieuses n'estant pas de si grand crimes qu'il s'en faille abstenir en la nécessité urgent pour le salut d'un bon livre qui est quelque foys comparable a celluy d'un homme puisque c'est la cresme et la travail de toute la vie de l'Autheur, et qu'il sagissoit lors de plusieurs grands hommes que avoient concouru et contribué a ce travail ce que vous dictes." This same image of Pococke is corroborated in the report of the English consul, John Wandesford (see Toomer, *Eastern Wisdome and Learning*, 69–70). I thank Simon Mills for this reference.

477. Peiresc to Celestin, 12 May 1636, CBI, MS. 1874, f. 417r. "Au temps a peu prez de l'exactesse des Massorets qui ont travaillé sur la bible Hebraïque ce qui n'est pas bien esloigné du nome que vous luy donnez encores mais je crains que ce soit chose plus recente de plus de 300 ans et composée en Hespagne plustost qu'en Levant si je ne me trompe, vous nous en pourrez esclaircir puis qu'il s'en trouve d'autres exemplaires."

478. "Index Librorum Arabicorum M.SS. quos Dominus Magister Pockack Anglus habuit Alepi à Mehmede. Ac eorum quos P. Celstinus misit ad Jac. Golium fratrem," PBN, MS. Lat. 9340, ff. 295r–301v.

479. PBN, MS. Lat. 9340, f. 293v. The document was dated 8 April.

480. Peiresc to Celestin, 12 May 1636, CBI, MS. 1874, f. 417r. To Golius, Peiresc had explained that he was having difficulty getting the volume translated

because of the "extravagance des termes de l'art, qui sont entremelez en cest ouvraige, et qui ne sont pas de la commune langue arabique, ains de la persiene, et possible de trop vieille origine pour estre facilement entendus par gentz, qui ne soint fort consumez en l'art mesme, quelque cognoissance qu'ilz ayent d'ailleurs, de l'une et l'autre langue." Peiresc to Golius, 8 May 1636, *Lettres à Claude Saumaise*, 262.

481. Peiresc to Celestin, 12 May 1636, CBI, MS. 1874, f. 417r. "Je veux dire non seulement celle de la Dinastie sarrasine mais la precedente des pays orientaulx selong les traditives du pays bien differentes de ce que les grecs en ont escrit."

482. See Miller, *Peiresc's "History of Provence,"* 84–85. Note that many years later, on his travels, Chateaubriand was praising the prospective edition of Arab historians of the Crusades translated by the Benedictine Dom Berthereau. It was never to appear. François de Chateaubriand, *Intinéraire de Paris à Jerusalem et de Jérusalem à Paris*, ed. Jean-Claude Berchet (Paris: Gallimard, 2005), 435.

483. Peiresc to Celestin, 12 May 1636, CBI, MS. 1874, ff. 417r–v. "Surtout je prends plaisir aux observations celestes qui ont esté marquées avec des bonnes epoques, comme des Eclypses de l'un et l'autre luminaire et autres Phoenomenes celestes, dont la comparaison avec les plus anciennes et avec les plus recentes peut servir a regler les mouvements des cieux qui sont la plus digne obiect de noz yeux."

484. Peiresc to Celestin, 12 May 1636, CBI, MS. 1874, f. 417v. "Et de faict j'entends que dans cet Orient il y a des sectes meslées du mahometisme, qui en ont retenu je ne sçay combien de maximes et des livres entiers . . . vous y trouveriez je m'asseure toute autre chose que ce dont on a accusé le pauvre Epicure quand on s'est arresté au bruit sans le voulloir cognoistre. . . . Attendu qu'on s'est imaginé que mettant son souverain bien en la volupté il n'y avoit que desbauche et toutefois il n'y avoit rien de si chaste que sa volupté d'esprit et non sensuelle ni de si temperant, car il ne viveoit la pluspart que de pain et d'eau comme les vieux Anacoretes."

485. Peiresc to Celestin, 12 May 1636, CBI, MS. 1874, f. 417v.

486. Peiresc to Venture, 8 May 1636, CBI, MS. 1874, f. 415v. "Cependant vous avez icy une lettre de change qui m'a esté envoyer d'Hollande de la part du Sr. Jac. Golius frere de ce bon P. Celestin pour la somme de 50 piastres payables par le Sr. Piscatoris de Marseille a qui je vous prie de la presenter, d'une part pour scavoir de luy le credit qu'il en à & la disposition au payement et ce qu'il voudra que je fasse pour la dessang en cela, car s'il veult que j'endosse la lettre originellement je le feray & s'il se contente de l'endossement que j'ay faict sur une coppie d'icelle cy jointe, vous li pourrez aussy contresigne selong mon ordre et retenier les deniers s'il vous plaist ou bien me renvoyer l'original de ladit lettre de change, aprez qu'il l'aura accepter a fin que je l'endosse si ce n'est qu'il ayant mieux que vous l'endosserez de ma part, comme vous le pourriez faire aussy." In a second letter written on this day, after reflecting, Peiresc decided it would be better for it to be countersigned and for Celestin to collect it in Aleppo from Mssrs. Constans (f. 415v).

487. Peiresc to Golius, 2 June 1636, *Lettres à Claude Saumaise*, 291.

488. "Mais la piece nous fut enviée par d'autres qui l'ont soubstraicte à la simplicité et bonté du P. Celestin, possible pour le porter en Angleterre." Peiresc to Golius, 2 June 1636, *Lettres à Claude Saumaise*, 291.

489. Simon Mills suggested to me that this might be MS. Pococke 26. http://www .fihrist.org.uk/profile/work/922db17a-d2b9-4f78-915f-f956e1b96917.

490. "Ainsi en la Musique il faut quelque sort d'accoutumance à ouir un air diverses fois et à divers jours pour y trouver enfin des douveures et delicatessees, au lieu des rudesses qui s'y rencontrent de prim'abbord; et c'est veritablement ce qui a souvent rebutté plusieurs de ceux de cette profession quand ils ont voulu mettre à éxécution des regles de l'ancienne theorie de la Musique, et qui a extorqué ces consentements genereux de quelques Nations toutes entieres a se delecter par accoutumance, et par predilection, les uns comme les Italiens à des chants plaintifs, les autres comme les Francois a des airs plus gaïs, et les autres a d'autres qualités bien differentes de celles là. Les habitudes se contractants insensiblement par imitation les unes des autres et par accoutumance, principalement quand il n'y a point d'affectation, et que les actes en sont frequemment reiterées." Peiresc to Chancellor d'Alegre, 22 July 1636, ABM, MS. 201 (1019), 453–454.

491. Peiresc to Celestin, 21 August 1636, CBI, MS. 1874, f. 426v.

492. Rewriting the letters, Celestin did not try the French maritime route again, but sent them directly to Venice for distribution. Peiresc to Golius, 29 November 1636, *Lettres à Claude Saumaise*, 341.

493. Constans to Peiresc, 6 January 1637, PBN, MS. F.fr. 9540, f. 139r.

494. Peiresc to Venture, 21 March 1637, CBI, MS. 1874, f. 443r.

7. Peiresc's Names, or, On Reading the Namescape

1. "Notre petit village de Peiresc s'appelle dans les vieux cadastres Latins Castrum de Petrisco." Leiden, Universiteitsbibliothek, MS. Vulcanius. 101. None of this material is found in the printed edition of these letters (*Lettres de Peiresc,* vol. 7) because Tamizey de Larroque worked from Peiresc's secretaries' copies of the letters, which often lack the subscriptions and postscripts of the originals.

2. CBI, MS. 1853, ff. 123r, 125r, 124r.

3. See William Stenhouse, *Reading Inscriptions and Writing Ancient History: Historical Scholarship in the Late Renaissance* (London: Institute of Classical Studies, School of Advanced Study, University of London, 2005), esp. 149–160.

4. On this see Roberto Bizzocchi, *Genealogie incredibili: Scritti di storia nell'Europa moderna* (Bologna: Il Mulino, 2009).

5. "Ma i nomi dei pittori, scevri dalla conoscenza diretta delle loro opere, sono nomi vuoti; e vuoti gli aneddoti, e vuote le descrizioni dei soggetti, e vuoti i guidizi di approvazione o di riprovazione, e vuoto l'ordinamento cronologico, perché pura aritmetica che non sta ad esprimere uno svolgimento reale, del quale non si realizza in noi il pensiero perché ce ne mancano gli elementi costitutivi." Benedetto Croce, "Storia, cronaca e false storie," in Benedetto

Croce–Renato Serra, *Polemica sulla storia,* ed. Alfonso Musci (Rome: Edizioni di Storia e Letteratura, 2012), 63–64.

6. "Prima il vivente, poi il cadavere; e far nascere la storia dalla cronaca tanto varebbe quanto far nascere il vivente dal cadavere." Croce, *Polemica sulla storia,* 68.

7. Aby Warburg, "Flemish Art and the Florentine Early Renaissance," in Warburg, *The Renewal of Pagan Antiquity: Contributions to the Cultural History of the European Renaissance,* trans. David Burtt (Los Angeles: Getty Publications, 1998), 286.

8. Ludwig Wittgenstein, *Tractatus Logico-Philosophicus,* trans. D. F. Pears and B. F. McGuinness, intro. Bertrand Russell (London: Routledge and Kegan Paul, 1961 [1921]), 3.22, 3.221, 13.

9. Wittgenstein, *Tractatus,* 4.0311, 22.

10. Hegel echoed Keats's poem to separate between dead and living and so demarcate the realms of antiquary and historian (Peter N. Miller, *Peiresc's Europe: Learning and Virtue in the Seventeenth Century* [New Haven, CT: Yale University Press, 2000], 153–154).

11. Ludwig Wittgenstein, *Philosophical Investigations,* trans. G. E. M. Anscombe (Oxford: Blackwell, 1958, 2nd ed.), I.55, 27e. For Henry James, it was only through art, and not through research, that the past could be grasped (James, *The Sense of the Past* [London: W. Collins Sons, 1917], 47–48).

12. "Dem Gedächtnis der Namenlosen ist die historische Konstruktion geweiht." Walter Benjamin, *Gesammelte Schriften,* ed. Rolf Tiedemann and Hermann Schweppenhäuser (Frankfurt: Surkhamp Verlag, 1991 [1974]), I.3, 1241. The sentence was part of a discarded draft toward his "Concept of History."

13. Carlo Ginzburg, *Threads and Traces: True, False, Fictive,* trans. Anne C. Tedeschi and John Tedeschi (Berkeley: University of California Press, 2012), 15.

14. Peiresc to Celestin, 22 November 1635, CBI, MS. 1874, f. 404r.

15. See Peter N. Miller, *Peiresc's "History of Provence": Antiquarianism and the Discovery of a Medieval Mediterranean,* Transactions of the American Philosophical Society 101, 3 (Philadelphia: American Philosophical Society, 2011), 20–22, 39, and esp. 31n51.

16. Christophe de Savigny, *Tableaux accomplis de tous les arts liberaux* (Paris, 1587, 2nd ed. 1619). See Annarita Angelini, *Metodo ed enciclopedia nel cinquecento francese: I* Tableaux *di Savigny,* 2 vols. (Florence: Leo S. Olschki, 2008), vol. 2; and Steffen Siegel, *Tabula: Figuren der Ordnung um 1600* (Berlin: Akademie Verlag, 2009). But while noting the Ramist switch from an arborial to a left-to-right mapping, neither addresses the question of "legibility" or compares these Ramist charts with genealogical forms (for instance, Siegel, *Tabula,* 78).

17. See Wolfgang Kaiser, "Extranéités urbaines, à l'époque moderne," in *Étrangers et sociétés: Représentations, coexistences, interactions dans la longue durée,* ed. Pilar González-Bernaldo, Manuela Martini, and Marie-Louise Pelus-Kaplan (Rennes: PUR, 2008), 77–86, sec. 2, "Le jeu des perspectives."

18. Hugo, *Ninety-Three* (New York: A. L. Burt, n.d., [1874]), part I, book III, ch.2, 66.

19. Michel de Certeau, *The Writing of History*, trans. Tom Conley (New York: Columbia University Press, 1988 [1975]), 74, 84–86. Stephen Bann's emphasis on Augustin Thierry's insistence that names brought one into direct contact with the past reflects exactly de Certeau's argument for the power of names, though it is unmentioned. Bann, *The Clothing of Clio: A Study of the Representation of History in Nineteenth-Century Britain and France* (Cambridge: Cambridge University Press, 1984), 29, 38.

20. Jacques Rancière, *The Names of History: On the Poetics of Knowledge*, trans. Hassan Melehy (Minneapolis: University of Minnesota Press, 1994 [French, 1992]), 1–3, 41.

21. Anthony Grafton, *What Was History? The Art of History in Early Modern Europe* (Cambridge: Cambridge University Press, 2007), 133–135.

22. I fully understand that introducing Proust as an "authority" might seem arch, but were I to feel the need for buttressing I could point to François Hartog's interpretation of Vidal-Naquet's recourse to "Proust historien" (Hartog, *Vidal-Naquet, historien en personne: L'Homme-mémoire et le moment-mémoire* [Paris: La Découverte, 2007]), 116 et passim.

23. Marcel Proust, *In Search of Lost Time*, vol. 6, *Finding Time Again*, trans. Ian Patterson (London: Penguin Books, 2003), 275.

24. J. Vendryes, "Marcel Proust et les noms propres," in *Mélanges de philologie et d'histoire littéraire offerts à Edmond Huguet* (Paris: Boivin, 1940), 120. See also Proust, *In Search of Lost Time*, vol. 1, *Swann's Way*, trans. Lydia Davis (London: Penguin, 2000), pt. 3, 403.

25. Proust, *Swann's Way*, 403. Biagio Salvemini suggests that in this category we see more of the breadth of names: "The *noms de pays* are not 'local names,' and they have little to do with personal names. They are names that emerge, disappear, flutter in the ocean of toponomastics, and that tend to capture the *esprit* of spaces not officialized as *départements* or *cantons* are" (pers. comm.). See also Salvemini, "Luoghi di antico regime: La classificazione dello spazio rurale nella storia e nella storiografia francese," in *Il territorio sghembo: Forme e dinamiche degli spazi umani in età moderna* (Bari: Edipuglia, 2006), 245–293.

26. "Les lettrés, les étymologistes de la langue, non des mots mais des noms." Marcel Proust, *The Guermantes Way*, trans. Mark Treharne (London: Penguin Books, 2002), 530. Proust may even have had some impact on the origins of onomastics as an academic field. Albert Dauzat, who presided over the first International Congress of Toponymy and Anthroponymy in 1938, published pivotal onomastic studies which directly followed Proust's terms: *Les noms de personnes* (1925), and *Les noms de lieux* (1926).

27. Proust, *Guermantes Way*, 539. "On peut dire que l'histoire, même simplement généalogique, rend la vie aux vielle pierres." The most recent brain research on the role of the angular gyrus seems to suggest that the role of names is part of our hardware: "Thus the name of an object, far from being just any other attribute of the object, seems to be a magic key that opens a whole treasury of meanings associated with the object." V. S. Ramachandran, *The Tell-Tale Brain: A Neuroscientist's Quest for What Makes Us Human* (New York: Norton, 2011), 181.

28. "Home is where one starts from. As we grow older / The world becomes stranger, the pattern more complicated / Of dead and living. Not the intense moment / Isolated, with no before and after / But a lifetime burning in every moment. / And not the lifetime of one man only / But of old stones that cannot be deciphered." "Little Gidding," *Four Quartets*. Arnaldo Momigliano, "Ancient History and the Antiquarian [1950]," in *Contributo alla storia degli studi classici* (Rome: Edizioni di Storia e Letteratura, 1955), 102.

29. Proust, *Guermantes Way*, 535. "Ainsi les espaces de ma mémoire se couvraient peu à peu de noms qui, en s'ordonnant, en se composant les uns relativement aux autres, en nouant entre eux des rapports de plus en plus nombreux, imitaient ces oeuvres d'art achevés ou il n'y a pas une seule touche qui soit isolée."

30. Proust himself seems to have thought in terms of the conventional "Tree of Jesse" model ("Names," in *Proust on Art and Literature 1896–1919*, trans. Sylvia Townsend Warner [New York: Carroll and Graf, 1984], 243–244).

31. Marcel Proust, *In Search of Lost Time*, vol. 5: *The Captive, The Fugitive* (London: Chatto and Windus, 1992), 156. "La curiosité amoureuse est comme celle qu'excitent en nous les noms de pays; toujours déçue, elle renaît et reste toujours insatiable" (*La Prisonnière*, 1:195).

32. Proust, *Swann's Way*, 284. George Bernard Shaw similarly described Joyce's *Ulysses* as "a document, the outcome of a passion for documentation that is as fundamental as the artistic passion." Quoted in Louis Menand, "Silence, Exile, Punning: James Joyce's Chance Encounters," *New Yorker*, July 2, 2012, 75.

8. The Problem of Detail

1. Marcel Proust, *Remembrance of Things Past,* trans. C. K. Scott Montcrieff and Terence Kilmartin (New York: Random House, 1982), 1:525. The new Penguin translation makes the mistake of translating "Académie des Inscriptions" as "Academy of Antiquities" with all the consequences of such an error. I thank Rachel Eisendrath for bringing this passage to my attention.

2. Framed slightly differently, the return to the "namescape" lies at the heart of Sabine Loriga's passionate *Le petit* x: *De la biographie à l'histoire* (Paris: Éditions du Seuil, 2010). I thank Danièle Tosato for bringing this book to my attention.

3. "Unde plus sapientiae ac utilitatis lectori, quam ex quavis alia narratione, accesserit. Ego, si omiserit, ne excusandum quidem existimaverim" (Daniel Morhof, *Polyhistor,* bk. I, ch. 19, sec. 4 [Lübeck, 1708 (1688)], 216).

4. "Ego certe eam ob causam magni facio vitam Peirescii a Gassendus scriptam, quod in omnes partes excurrat & se diffundat, quam noster ille forte in eo *micrologion* damnaverit" (Morhof, *Polyhistor,* bk. I, ch. 19, sec. 5, 216). For the current history of microhistory as a term, see the first pages of Carlo Ginzburg's "Microhistory: Two or Three Things I Know about It" (originally 1993) and republished in *Threads and Traces: True, False, Fictive,* trans. Anne C. Tedeschi and John Tedeschi (Berkeley: University of California Press, 2012), 193–196).

5. "Je ne méprise point qu'on épluche les antiquités jusqu'aux moindres bagatelles, car quelquefois la connaissance que les critiques en tirent, peut servir aux choses

plus importantes. Je consens par exemple, qu'on écrive même toute l'histoire des vestemens et de l'art des tailleurs depuis les habits des pontifes des Hébreux. . . . . et qu'on y joigne tout ce qu'on peut tirer des anciennes sculptures et des peintures encore faites depuis quelques siècles." Leibniz, *Schriften und Briefe zur Geschichte,* ed. Malte-Ludolf Babin and Gerd van den Heuvel (Hannover: Verlag Hansche Buchhandlung, 2004), 111.

6. Hayden White, *Metahistory: The Historical Imagination in Nineteenth-Century Europe* (Baltimore: Johns Hopkins University Press, 1973), 61. White is, so far as I know, the only one to have made the connection between the *Monadology* and the logic of historical research. This connection to microhistory, for example, is missed in the otherwise illuminating Matti Peltonen, "Clues, Margins, and Monads: The Micro-Macro Link in Historical Research," *History and Theory* 40 (2001): 347–359.

7. Leibniz, *The Monadology,* trans. Robert Latta, nos. 56 and 50, http://oregon state.edu/instruct/phl302/texts/leibniz/monadology.html.

8. In a letter to the Abbé Dubos in 1738 explaining his preference for writing a cultural history that focused only on the geniuses who advanced the arts and philosophy (quoted in Anthony Grafton, *The Footnote: A Curious History* [Cambridge, MA: Harvard University Press, 1999], 95).

9. See Johann Christoph Gatterer, "Von der Evidenz in der Geschichtskunde" (1767), in *Die Allgemeine Welthistorie die in England durch eine Gesellschaft von Gelehrten ausgefertiget worden: In einem vollständigen und pragmatischen Auszuge,* ed. Friedrich Eberhard Boysen, Alte Historie, vol. 1 (Halle: Gebauer, 1767), 1–38. On the eighteenth-century context, see Mark Philips, *Society and Sentiment: Genres of Historical Writing in Britain, 1740–1820* (Princeton, NJ: Princeton University Press, 2000).

10. Ludwig Wachler, *Geschichte der Künste und Wissenschaften seit der Wiederherstellung derselben bis an das Ende des achtzehnten Jahrhunderts: Fünfte Abtheilung. Geschichte der historischen Wissenschaften* (Gottingen: Vandenhoeck & Ruprecht, 1812), 1:viii.

11. "Der Vorliebe für Mikrologie und oft lästige Zusammenfügung zerstreuter Materialien zu," Wachler, *Geschichte der Künste und Wissenschaften,* 1:417.

12. "Dagegen theilen die Franzosen mit den Deutschen den Ruhm, vortreffliche Kritiker hervorgebracht zu haben, die, wenn sie auch oft sich bis zu Micrologien verirren, doch gründliche Aufschlüsse geben, wie *Ducange, Duchesne, Mabillon,* u.s.w." Friedrich Rühs, *Entwurf einer Propaedeutik des historischen Studiums* (Berlin: Realschulbuchhandlung, 1811), 272.

13. Johann Wolfgang Goethe, *Zur Farbenlehre,* ed. Peter Schmidt [= Münchner Ausgabe, vol. 10] (Munich: Hanser Verlag, 1989), 476, 577.

14. Goethe, *Zur Farbenlehre,* 476. Intriguingly, Voltaire had also singled out the example of Gassendi as biographer in a discussion of historiographical practice. "God preserve me from devoting 300 pages to the story of Gassendi!" was his prayer (quoted in Grafton, *The Footnote,* 95).

15. Johann Gustav Droysen, *Texte zur Geschichtstheorie: Mit ungedruckten Materialien zur "Historik,"* ed. Günter Birsch and Jörn Rüsen (Göttingen: Vandenhoeck and Ruprecht, 1972), 18.

16. Nietzsche, *On the Advantage and Disadvantage of History for Life*, trans. Peter Preuss (Indianapolis: Hackett Publishing, 1980), nos. 2 and 15.

17. Nietzsche, *On the Advantage and Disadvantage of History for Life*, 19.

18. Raymond Geuss, "Nietzsche and Genealogy," *European Journal of Philosophy* 2 (1994): 276, 282.

19. Alexander Nehemas, *Nietzsche: Life as Literature* (Cambridge, MA: Harvard University Press, 1985), 246n1, quoted in Geuss, "Nietzsche and Genealogy," 287; Ginzburg, *Threads and Traces*, 15.

20. On Petrarch: Aby Warburg, *Il primo Rinascimento italiano: Sette conferenze inedite*, ed. Giovanna Targia (Turin: Nino Aragno Editore, 2013), lxv, lxxxix. On the *Pathosformel*, 332: "Pathos als historisch antiquarischer echter Stil."

21. Walter Benjamin, *The Origin of German Tragic Drama*, trans. John Osborne (London: Verso, 1985), 29. I have corrected the translation that replaces "der mikrologischen Verarbeitung" with "minute precision," completely obscuring the force of Benjamin's intervention (see Benjamin, *Gesammelte Schriften*, ed. Rolf Tidemann and Hermann Schweppenhäuser, 13 vols. [Frankfurt: Surkhamp Verlag, 1991 (1974)], 1:1, 208).

22. Siegfried Kracauer to Gertrud Bing, 30 September 1958, quoted in *Siegfried Kracauer–Erwin Panofsky Briefwechsel 1941–1966*, ed. Volker Breidecker (Berlin: Akademie Verlag, 1996), 99; Siegfried Kracauer, *History: The Last Things before the Last*, completed after the author's death by Paul Oskar Kristeller (Princeton, NJ: Markus Wiener, 1995 [1969]), 118.

23. Carlo Ginzburg, "Microhistory: Two or Three Things That I Know about It," *Critical Inquiry* 20 (1993): 26–27; Ginzburg, *Threads and Traces*, 207–208.

24. For the general state of this question today, see the issue of *Le Débat:* "L'Histoire saisie par la fiction" (May–August 2011, 165).

25. Proust, *In Search of Lost Time*, vol. 6, *Finding Time Again* (London: Penguin, 2002), 350–351. Interestingly, Proust feels that it is not a microscope but a telescope that he uses, "but only because they [his subjects] were situated a long way away."

26. See, for example, the thirteen-page note on line 130 of John Shade's poem (Vladimir Nabokov, *Pale Fire* [New York: Berkley Books, 1985 (1962)], 76–89).

27. Braudel, "Note sull'economia del Mediterraneo nel XVII secolo," *Economia e Storia: Rivista Italiana di storia economica e sociale* 2 (1955): 140, 142.

28. "Thus the hypotheses, the doubts, the uncertainties became part of the narration. . . . Could the result still be defined as 'narrative history'? For a reader with the slightest familiarity with twentieth-century fiction, the reply is obviously yes." Ginzburg, "Microhistory," 24. Even Lukács, who disagreed with this, did so in terms that precisely echo our contrast between antiquaries who research and historians who write stories. See Lukács, "Narrate or Describe? A Preliminary Discussion of Naturalism and Formalism," in *Writer and Critic: And Other Essays*, ed. Arthur Kahn (Lincoln, NE: I-universe, 2005 [1970]), 110–146.

29. R. G. Collingwood, *The Idea of History* (Oxford: Oxford University Press, 1956 [1946]), Epilegomena, §2, 246.

30. Robert Alter, *Partial Magic: The Novel as a Self-Conscious Genre* (Berkeley: University of California Press, 1976).

31. Sabina Loriga makes this point very directly in the last paragraph of her excellent book: "Le dessein est, plus simplement, de cultiver une politique de confrontation avec la littérature, afin de conférer plus de profondeur et de variété au discours historique." Loriga, *Le petit* x, 272. This could be construed as a kind of reply to the question posed by Mark Salber Phillips (*On Historical Distance* [New Haven, CT: Yale University Press, 2013], 22).

9. The Postal Link

1. Marc Fumaroli, *Nicolas-Claude Fabri de Peiresc, prince de la République des Lettres* (Brussels: Pro-Peyresq, 1993).
2. Peiresc to Marc Antonio Lumaga, 7 December 1623, CBI, MS. 1874, f. 295r.
3. Gassendi, *Mirrour,* bk. 4, year 1627, 171. Typically, none of this finds its way into modern treatments such as Jacques Bottin, "Négoce et circulation de l'information au début de l'époque moderne," in *Histoire de la Poste: De l'administration à l'entreprise,* ed. Muriel Le Roux (Paris: Éditions Rue d'Ulm, 2002), 41–54.
4. CBI, MS. 1841, f. 342r, "*1627.* 16 September Deliberation de l'assemblee du Pais pour l'establishment d'un ordinaire a Lyon."
5. Eugène Vaillé, *Histoire générale des postes françaises: Tome II, De Louis XI à la création de la surintendance générale des postes (1477–1630)* (Paris: Presses Universitaires de France, 1949), 120–121.
6. Often asserted as typical, as in Peiresc to Andrault, 12 May 1628, CBI, MS. 1873, f. 130r (omitted in *Lettres de Peiresc,* vol. 7).
7. Peiresc to Minuti, 13 June 1634, CBI, MS. 1874, f. 345v.
8. Aycard to Peiresc, 12 October 1632, CBI, MS. 1871, f. 22r; Peiresc to Aycard, 17 October 1632, *Lettres de Peiresc,* 7:285 [= CBI, MS. 1871, f. 22r].
9. Evidence from his correspondence appears frequently in Eugène Vaillé's *Histoire générale des postes françaises,* 7 vols. (Paris: Presses Universitaires de France, 1947–1955).
10. Peiresc to Cayre, 28 [ ] 1619, CBI, MS. 1874, f. 631v. This letter is in a cahier of those addressed to the provost of the Cathedral of St. Sauveur at Aix.
11. Peiresc to Valbelle, 7 February 1628, CBI, MS. 1876, f. 366r.
12. Peiresc to Marcheville, [undated], CBI, MS. 1874, f. 604r.
13. A letter from Minuti written on 21 November arrived in Marseille by the first week in January. This merited no comment. Peiresc to Marcheville, 9 January 1634, CBI, MS. 1874, f. 606r.
14. Peiresc to Guez, 1 August 1628, CBI, MS. 1876, f. 368v.
15. Peiresc to Gaffarel, 22 August 1633, CBI, MS. 1873, f. 404v.
16. PBN, MS. N.a.f. 5169, f. 6r. By April 1624 there is another ordinaire, called "le Gascon" (f. 8r).
17. Peiresc to Aycard, 11 October 1635, CBI, MS. 1871, f. 54r.
18. Peiresc to Aycard, 11 October 1635, CBI, MS. 1871, f. 54v.
19. Peiresc to Suares, 17 December 1632, CBI, MS. 1876, f. 219v.
20. Peiresc to Aubery de Mesnil, 28 July 1630, CBI, MS. 1871, f. 425v. Peiresc writes "predecesseur," but this must be in error, as a letter of his to Gaffarel of

11 September 1633 refers to Lieu as "maitre des courriers du Roy a Lyon" (CBI, MS. 1873, f. 404v).

21. Peiresc to Guibberville, 9 April 1635, CBI, MS. 1877, f. 439v. "Attendu que les commoditez sont si rares d'icy à Carpentras (ou ceste ville na point de commerce) qu'il eust fallu trop long temps attendu le passage de gentz de congnoissance."

22. Peiresc to Petit, 6 May 1632, CBI, MS. 1875, f. 248r. "Sr de Gastines l'un des plus celebres marchands de Marseille qui m'est venu voir icy, m'a asseuré qu'il y à si grand commerce de Marseille a Nismes que tous le jours il se trouve des gentz de cognoissance qui vont & viennent d'un lieu à l'autre."

23. Peiresc to Petit, 23 July 1632, CBI, MS. 1875, f. 249r. In a subsequent letter, Peiresc identifies Artaut as a "marchand drapier" (Peiresc to Petit, 14 August 1632, CBI, MS. 1875, f. 249v).

24. Peiresc to Petit, 3 October 1633, CBI, MS. 1875, f. 262r.

25. Peiresc to Chavary, 3 October 1633, CBI, MS. 1875, ff. 262r–v; Peiresc to Messrs. les Comis de la Douane, 3 October 1633, CBI, MS. 1875, f. 262v.

26. Peiresc to Petit, 25 October 1633, CBI, MS. 1875, f. 262v.

27. Peiresc to Petit, 2 November 1633, CBI, MS. 1875, f. 263r.

10. The Last Mile (Mule Is King)

1. Peiresc to Aycard, 14 February 1632, CBI, MS. 1821, f. 265v.

2. Peiresc to Danmartin, 25 May 1628, CBI, MS. 1873, f. 124r; Viguier to Peiresc, 21 May 1628, CBI, MS. 1879, f. 684r, reporting the arrival of the letter announcing the arrival of the book. Viguier also brought Peiresc a copy of an inscription found in Ventavon, on the way to Pignerol (PBN, MS. Lat. 8958, f. 240).

3. Peiresc to Tarquet, 1 August 1629, CBI, MS. 1876, f. 357v.

4. Peiresc to Minuti, 13–18 October 1630, CBI, MS. 1876, f. 808v; Peiresc to Berengier "a Marseille au cartier de St Jehan prez la fontane," f. 808v.

5. Peiresc to Jean-Baptiste Magy, 3 August 1634, CBI, MS. 1874, f. 380r; Peiresc to Issaultier, 22 August 1635, CBI, MS. 1874, f. 385r.

6. Peiresc to Aycard, 29 March 1634, CBI, MS. 1871, f. 41v.

7. See the many references in Fernand Braudel, *The Mediterranean and the Mediterranean World in the Age of Phillip II*, vol. 2, trans. Siân Reynolds (New York: Harper and Row, 1972), 2:1368, and now Georges Livet, *Histoire des routes & des transports en Europe* (Strasbourg: Presses Universitaires de Strasbourg, 2003), 44.

8. Peiresc to Signier, 8 May 1621, CBI, MS. 1871, f. 107v.

9. A "billet" from de Gastines, for example, arrived by a "mulletier" (Peiresc to Aycard, 20 April 1634, CBI, MS. 1871, f. 42r).

10. Peiresc to Sestoy, 1 May 1635, CBI, MS. 1876, f. 842v.

11. Peiresc to Bartolle, 6 November 1629, CBI, MS. 1876, ff. 360r–v. "Il ne fault que prendre quelque mulletier qui sache le chemin d'Aubagne, Cuies & Signes par lequel il n'y à que neuf lieux de Marseille icy."

12. Peiresc to Bartolle, 8 November 1629, CBI, MS. 1876, f. 360v.

13. For example, Peiresc to Madame de Cuges, 13 November 1629, CBI, MS. 1876, f. 361v.
14. Peiresc to Madame de Cuges, 18 November 1629, CBI, MS. 1876, f. 790r.
15. Peiresc to Minuti, 23 April 1630, CBI, MS. 1876, f. 801r.
16. Peiresc to Astier, 11 November 1629, CBI, MS. 1876, f. 435r.
17. Peiresc to Honoré Tourtel, 16 June 1630, CBI, MS. 1876, f. 803v.
18. Peiresc to Baulme, 2 March 1634, CBI, MS. 1874, f. 331v.
19. Peiresc to Venture, 18 October 1635, CBI, MS. 1874, f. 394r.
20. Peiresc to Jean-Baptiste Magy, 27 February 1634, CBI, MS. 1874, f. 329r. "J'ay esté si pressé pour ne perdre la commodité du mulletrie du Rousseau que Je n'ay peu faire emballer du cassets et vous prier de la faire emballer a Marseille avec de la toille cerer pour la conserver."
21. Peiresc to Petit, 8 March 1633, CBI, MS. 1875, f. 253r.
22. Peiresc to Minuti, 13–18 October 1630, CBI, MS. 1876, f. 808v; Peiresc to Berengier "a Marseille au cartier de St Jehan prez la fontane," f. 808v.
23. Peiresc to Vallavez, 20 June 1630, CBI, MS. 1821, f. 465r.
24. PBN, MS. N.a.f. 5169, f. 13r.
25. Guillemin to Peiresc, 20 April 1629, PBN, MS. Lat. 8958, f. 238r.
26. Bovis to Peiresc, 8 March 1637, CBI, MS. 1878, f. 361r. In exchange Peiresc received a box and a "pot de sourbet," both likely from Jean Magy in Cairo. Bovis served similarly as an exchange point for M. Ruffi of Marseille (21 March 1637, CBI, MS. 1878, f. 362r). "Pisciolini" is probably a descendant of the Niccolò Pesciolini from San Gimignano who played an important role in the city's politics during the 1590s. I am grateful to Wolfgang Kaiser for pointing this out to me. See Kaiser, *Marseille im Bürgerkrieg: Sozialgefüge, Religionskonflikt und Faktionskämpfe von 1559–1596* (Göttingen: Vandenhoeck and Ruprecht, 1991).
27. De Gastines to Peiresc, 31 July 1629, PBN, MS. F.fr. 9537, f. 319r.
28. Peiresc to Magy, 14 July 1633, CBI, MS. 1874, f. 313r.
29. Peiresc to Vallavez, [between 4 and 11] March 1626, *Lettres de Peiresc*, 6:405.

11. Marseille's Merchants

1. Franz Bierlaire, *La Familia d'Érasme: Contribution à l'histoire de l'humanisme* (Paris: Vrin, 1968).
2. Most notably Steven Shapin, "The Invisible Technician," *American Scientist* 77 (1989): 554–63; Shapin, *A Social History of Truth: Civility and Science in Seventeenth-Century England* (Chicago: University of Chicago Press, 1994), ch. 8: "Invisible Technicians: Masters, Servants, and the Making of Experimental Knowledge."
3. See, for example, Anne Borgini, "Entre deux mondes: Les Marchands de Malte au XVIIe siècle," in *Hommes de l'entre-deux: Parcours individuels et portraits de groupes sur la frontière de la Méditerranée (XVIe–XXe siècle)*, ed. Bernard Heyberger and Chantal Verdeil (Paris: Les Indes Savantes, 2009), 23–42.
4. Wolfgang Kaiser, "Asymétries méditerranéennes: Présence et circulation de marchands entre Alger, Tunis et Marseille," in *Les Musulmans dans l'histoire de l'Europe: I: Une intégration invisible*, ed. Jocelyne Dakhlia and Bernard Vincent

(Paris: Albin Michel, 2011), 418–419; Kaiser, "Una missione impossibile? Riscatto e comunicazione nel mediterraneo occidentale (secs. 16–17)," in *Informazioni e scelte economiche*, ed. Kaiser and Biagio Salvemini [= *Quaderni storici*, 124 (2007), 20–21].

5. Even the many collective volumes on the subject have found no place for seventeenth-century Marseille. See, for example, Simonetta Cavaciocchi, ed., *I porti come impresa economica: Secoli XIII–XVIII* (Florence: Le Monier, 1988); A. Guimerà and D. Romero, eds., *Puertos y sistemas portuarios (siglo XVI–XX)* (Madrid: Ministerio de Fomento, 1996); A. Leroy and Ch. Villain-Gandossi, eds., *Stations navales et navigations organisées en Méditerranée* (Ollioules-Provence: Éditions de la Nerthe/Courtine, 2003); L. A. Ribot Garcia and L. De Rosa, eds., *Naves, puertos y itinerarios maritimos en la época moderna* (Madrid: Actas, 2003); *Il Mediterraneo delle città: Scambi, confronti, culture, rappresentazioni*, ed. Franco Salvatori (Rome: Viella, 2008). Nor has the last decade's turn in Mediterranean historiography toward the *sociétés littorale* brought any new attention to Marseille. See, for example, Gilbert Buti and Jacques Péret, "Gens de mer et sociétés littorales en France à l'époque moderne," in *La Recherche internationale en histoire maritime*, [= *Revue d'histoire maritime* 10–11 (2010)]: 135–158; it is not even mentioned in the otherwise fascinating Amélia Polónia, "European Seaports in the Early Modern Age: Concepts, Methodology and Models of Analysis," *Cahiers de la Méditerranée* 80 (2010): 17–39. This blind spot is bidirectional: even Ottomanist study of European merchants ignores Marseille, e.g., *Merchants in the Ottoman Empire*, ed. Surayia Faroqhi and Gilles Veinstein (Paris-Louvain: Peeters, 2008), which is only mentioned in the two post-1700 essays on Smyrna.

6. There is nothing for Marseille like André Lespagnol, *Messieurs de Saint-Malo, une élite négociante au temps de Louis XIV* (Rennes: PUR, 1997 [1990]), or, more recently, Amândio Jorge Morais Barros, "Oporto: The Building of a Maritime Space in the Early Modern Period," the summary of a thesis defended at Oporto University in the Faculty of Humanities, 20 October 2004, [http://www.brown.edu/Departments/Portuguese_Brazilian_Studies/ejph/html/issue5/html/barros_main.html], but even these do not engage with the sphere of merchants and knowledge.

7. Vallavez to Peiresc, 10 January 1631, CBI, MS. 1841, f. 484v.

8. Marriages in Marseille are listed as follows: those celebrated in the cathedral, which are the vast majority, are digested in MAD, 35 F 228 (males by name, 1574–1637) and 35 F 229 (males by chronology, 1574–1637); 35 F 230 (males by name, 1638–1669); and 35 F 231 (males by chronology, 1638–1669).

9. See Louis Bergasse, *Histoire du commerce de Marseille*, vol. 4: *1599–1660* (Paris: Plon, 1954), 195–196.

10. Are there other scholars who wrote to merchants in this way? The relatively recent literature of the history of science has done much to elevate the role of the artisanal, and of the hitherto anonymous laboratory assistants, but though they have gained an identity we still know very little about their intellectual lives. In Peiresc's case unlike, say, Boyle, he viewed the merchants as his partners, not his preparators.

11. Peiresc to Seghezzi, 15 September 1634, CBI, MS. 1874, f. 355r.

12. Wolfgang Kaiser, "Récits d'espace: Présence et parcours d'étrangers à Marseille au XVIe siècle," in *Les Étrangers dans la ville: Minorités et espace urbain du bas Moyen Age à l'époque moderne,* ed. Jacques Bottin and Donatella Calabi (Paris: Éditions de la Maison des Sciences de l'Homme, 1999), 299.

13. These were gathered up and reprinted in Geneva by Slatkine in 2 volumes in 1972.

14. Augustin Fabre, *Histoire des hôpitaux des institutions de bienfaisance de Marseille* (Marseille: Jules Barile, 1854), 210–216.

15. Peiresc to Malherbe, 6 October 1609, CBI, MS. 1874, f. 481r.

16. Cassagnes to Peiresc, 27 December 1620, in *Les Correspondants de Peiresc,* 2 vols. (Geneva: Slatkine, 1972), 2:732. Tamizey de Larroque published eight of his letters to Peiresc in *Les Correspondants de Peiresc,* 2:727–736, as an appendix to the letters of Antoine Novel. The manuscript is CBI, MS. 1774, ff. 386r–400v.

17. Borilly to Peiresc, 23 January 1637, MAD, 8 F bis 1, unpaginated [165].

18. For biographical and bibliographical information, see Tamizey de Larroque's introduction to his letters to Peiresc, *Les Correspondants de Peiresc,* 1:417–437; and Félix Vérany, *Balthazar de Vias: Sa vie et ses oeuvres* (Marseille: Imprimerie veuve Marius Olive, 1862). He was also the author of a neo-Latin poetic elegy of Peiresc's life, *In Clarissimum Virum Nicolaum Claudium Fabricium de Peiresc Senatorem Aquensem Epicedion* (Marseille, 1642).

19. MAD, 9 B 2, f. 41v.

20. Vias to Peiresc, 25 November 1626, in de Larroque, *Les Correspondants de Peiresc,* 1:448.

21. See Peter N. Miller, *Peiresc's Orient: Antiquarianism as Cultural History in the Seventeenth Century* (Farnham, UK: Ashgate, 2012), ch. 3.

22. On Ruffi's *History,* see Wolfgang Kaiser, "Le Passé refaçonné: Mémoire et oubli dans les histoires de Marseille, de Robert Ruffi à Louis-Antoine de Ruffi," *Provence historique* 193 (1998): 279–292.

23. Ruffi to Peiresc, 17 January 1637, 12 March 1637, 24 March 1637, ABM, MS. 211 (1029), 165–172.

24. Peiresc to Ruffi, 13 March 1634, ABM, MS. 211 (1029), 181.

25. Peiresc to Ruffi, 18 March 1634, ABM, MS. 211 (1029), 183.

26. CBI, MS. 1769, ff. 366r–v.

27. Antoine de Ruffi, *Histoire de la Ville de Marseille contenant tout ce qui s'y est passé de plus memorable de puis sa fondation* (Marseille, 1642).

28. Peiresc to Pierre Ruffi, 12 May 1630, CBI, MS. 1875, f. 754r.

29. For example: Prat of Marseille, CBI, MS. 1861, f. 166r; for Astier of Aix, CBI, MS. 1861, f. 124v; Arfeuille of Arles, CBI, MS. 1844, f. 21v.

30. Suffin is identified as a translator as early as 1621 (Cassagnes to Peiresc, 22 February 1621, in de Larroque, *Les Correspondants de Peiresc,* 2:733). He was a native of Famagusta on Cyprus (Wolfgang Kaiser, "Asymétries méditerranéennes: Présence et circulation de marchands entre Alger, Tunis et Marseille," in *L'Histoire des musulmans en Europe,* ed. Jocelyne Dakhlia and Bernard Vincent [Paris: Albin Michel, 2011], 417). He is working with Napollon in Algiers in 1628 (CBI, MS. 1777, ff. 111v, 113v, 115r) and Berengier in Tripoli in 1629 (MACC,

J 1910, piece 3, unpaginated). By 1633, however, a new position has been created at Marseille, "l'office de secrétaire-interprète des langues turque et arabe,"
and Pierre Borelly given it by Cardinal Richelieu on 29 July 1633. MAD, 9 B
2, f. 276.

31. "Rapport faict par Antoine Mazarat et Jean Fargues merchands sur la closture
du compte donne par le Sr Philibert de Bermond durant son exercise au consulate d'Egypte," 24 October 1634, MACC, J 550, piece 4 [unpaginated].

32. Laugeiret to Consuls of Marseille, MACC, J 731, unpaginated.

33. Biagio Salvemini, "Commerçants honorés, nobles marchands, parfaits négociants: Conflitti di designazione a Marsiglia fra la Fronda e la Rivoluzione," in
Il mediterraneo delle città, a cura di E. Iachello e P. Militello (Milan: Franco
Angeli, 2011), 93–209; Salvemini, "Storia e semantica di una 'professione': Appunti su negozio e negozianti a Bari fra Cinquecento e Ottocento," Meridiana 7
(1993): 43–111.

34. The document is quoted in full in Kaiser, "Récits d'espace," 300. For example,
Peiresc to Berengier, "A Marseille au cartier de St Jehan prez la fontane," f. 808v.

35. The Hague, Museo Meermano-Westreenianum, MS. C.10.30, 383, 405.

36. De Vento to Consuls of Marseille, 14 September 1607, MACC, J 544, piece 1
[unpaginated]. On the Vento family, see Sydney Aufrère, La Momie et la
tempête: Nicolas-Claude Fabri de Peiresc et la 'curiosité Égyptienne' en Provence
au début du XVIIe siècle (Avignon: Éditions A. Barthélemy, 1990), 98.

37. Peiresc to Vallavez, 24 May 1625, "Le premier consul de Marseille nommé
Vente est allé de par de là deputé de la ville de Marseille: Il est homme curieux
qui a de fort jolies singularitez et lequel m'obligea tout plain au dernier voyage
que je fis à Marseille, cette sepmaine saincte, m'ayant non seulement monstré
son cabinet, mais m'ayant laissé la disposition de certaines petites curiositez du
monde." Lettres de Peiresc 6:182–183.

38. Peiresc to Madame de Brèves, 12 May 1629, CBI, MS. 1874, f. 69v. "Un des plus
honnestes bourgeois de la ville & a qui on peut consigne cette affaire et toute
autre plus grande croyant qu'il vous y servira fidellement." Bergasse lists him
alongside a few other "seigneurs de moindre importance" in his discussion of
cabotage (Bergasse, Histoire du commerce de Marseille, 129).

39. Peiresc to Napollon, 6 November 1627, CBI, MS. 1873, f. 463r.

40. Peiresc to d'Espiot, 28 July 1633, CBI, MS. 1874, f. 570v.

41. Fort to Peiresc, 1 February 1630, PBN, MS. F.fr. 9540, f. 160r; 31 January 1630,
PBN, MS. F.fr. 9540, f. 162r.

42. Fort received two letters written on 28 January and two on 30 January. Fort to
Peiresc, 1 February 1630, PBN, MS. F.fr. 9540, f. 160r. On 31 January he re-
ceived three letters from Peiresc at the same time, 9:00 in the morning. Fort to
Peiresc, 31 January 1630, PBN, MS. F.fr. 9540, f. 162r.

43. MAD, 9 B 21. Gaëlle Lapeyrie notes that these two names, of all the merchants
of the period, do not appear in the archives of Pierre Gloton's that she has
studied (pers. comm.); see her "De la boutique au comptoir: La Trajectoire d'un
négociant toulousain en textile, entre traditions et nouveautés (vers 1600–
1620)," Rives méditerranéennes 29 (2008): 79–105.

44. Peiresc to Fort, 23 January 1631, CBI, MS. 1876, f. 810v.

45. Fort to Peiresc, 31 January 1630, PBN, MS. F.fr. 9540, f. 162r.

46. Letters from de Gastines to Peiresc are found in PBN, MS. F.fr. 9537 15 June 1629, f. 312; 28 June 1629, f. 313; 31 July 1629, f. 319; PBN, MS. F.fr. 9539 17 June 1632, f. 262; 6 March 1632, f. 263; [ ] June 1632, f. 269.

47. Father Michael to Minuti, 1 September 1635, PBN, MS. F.fr. 9543, f. 121r. Next to the address, in smaller letters, someone wrote "recomandee a la courtoizie de Mr de Gastines."

48. MAD, 201 E 72, f. 223v. His father's name was Guilleaume and the family seems to have come from Lanson, which would explain the absence of other members of this family in Marseille's parish records. For a century's marriages at the Cathedral de la Major, see 35 F 228–234. I have also checked the surviving records of the Churches of St. Laurent (35 F 101), St. Martin (35 F 252), and Notre Dame les Accoules (35 F 409) and found no de Gastines.

49. *Arrest du Conseil d'Estat du Roy portant cessation du droict de Cinq pour Cent qui se levoit sur les Marchandises venantes des Eschelles & pais d'Egypte* (n.p., n.d. [but after 1657]), 21 (preserved in MACC, J 1676). Parallel material can be found in PBN, MS. F.fr. 18593, 216ff. [1645].

50. "Factum du proces pendant au Conseil, Entre Jean Magy, Iean Louis Maurellet, Joseph & Mathieu Baumes freres & Iacques Sabain Machands de la ville de Marseille, Negotians en Allexandrie d'Egypte, defendeurs & demandeurs en Requete du 26 Febvrier dernier," PBN, MS. F.fr. 18593, f. 53r ("Julles de Gastines"), f. 297r ("M. Masse de Gastines").

51. De Gastines is not, for instance, listed by Bergasse among the "principal maisons de commerce de Marseille en relations avec le Levant." Bergasse, *Histoire du commerce de Marseille*, 4:94–95.

52. MAD, 9 B 12+[unpaginated], in "Rapport faict par Pierre Gallo patron de Tartane de ceste ville venu de Rome." This volume contains the declarations of cargo made by captains returning to Marseille between 1634 and 1637.

53. MAD, 9 B 12+[unpaginated], "Rapport faict par Jacques Calment patron de barque de Frontignan venu de Civitavecchia."

54. Peiresc to Danmartin, 24 December 1626, CBI, MS. 1873, f. 122r. He is also described this way in Peiresc to Vallavez, 18 November 1626, *Lettres de Peiresc*, 6:602.

55. Marc-Antoine Espagnet—Jean's father? Brother? Uncle?—is mentioned as a parlementaire in a letter of Peiresc to Malherbe of 1613. Peiresc to Malherbe, 28 August 1613, CBI, MS. 1874, f. 413v.

56. Pierre Viguier inherited the consulship of Tripoli, Cyprus, Beirut, Alexandretta, and the coast around Antalya from his father Jean in August 1624 (MAD, 9 B 2, f. 70v). Peiresc to Viguier, consul of Syria, 24 June 1627, CBI, MS. 1876, f. 615r.

57. Peiresc to Danmartin, 25 November 1627, CBI, MS. 1873, f. 122v.

58. Viguier to Peiresc, 21 May 1628, CBI, MS. 1879, f. 684r.

59. I tell this story in Peter N. Miller, *Peiresc's "History of Provence": Antiquarianism and the Discovery of a Medieval Mediterranean*, Transactions of the American Philosophical Society 101, 3 (Philadelphia: American Philosophical Society, 2011), 46–48.

60. I have only found his name given once, in "Extraict de lettre de Constantinople du 6 d Avril 1634 (escripte par le Sr Guillaume Guez au Sr Sabain a Livourne)," CBI, MS. 493, f. 231r. The *État Civil* lists marriages for a Laurent Guetz, son of Barthelemi on 13 May 1607, a Pierre Gues, son of Elzias on 27 May 1620, a Barthélemy Guez on 8 August 1621, and a Jean Guez on 22 May 1623 (MAD, 35 F 228).

61. He is Alvise in Peiresc to Gela, 27 February 1635, and Gela to Peiresc, 22 February 1635, CBI, MS. 1874, f. 365v. He is Alvigi in Peiresc to Seghezzi, 23 February 1637, CBI, MS. 1874, f. 441v. But note in Gela to de Thou, 14 April 1636, CBI, MS. 1810, f. 112, where the copy is signed as "G.L." (for Giovanni Luigi?).

62. Gela to Peiresc, 25 February 1637, CBI, MS. 1879, f. 15r.

63. "Du Pic de mesurage des habitans de l'Egypte," PBN, MS. Dupuy 661, f. 197r.

64. One letter from him to the consuls of Marseille survives (MACC, J 760, 24 April 1633).

65. Tarquet to [. . .], 10 March 1629, CBI, MS. 1876, f. 158r.

66. Peiresc to Venture, 22 November 1635, CBI, MS. 1874, f. 403v.

67. Peiresc to Piscatoris, 3 November 1629, CBI, MS. 1876, f. 359r. Letters of Forbin to Peiresc are preserved in CBI, MS. 1878, ff. 514–537.

68. Peiresc to Grange, 6 November 1629, CBI, MS. 1876, f. 359v.

69. Peiresc to Madame la Lieutenant de Valbelle, 6 November 1629, CBI, MS. 1876, f. 359v. Peiresc also wrote to his deputy, the Advocat Berardy (Peiresc to Berardy, 6 November 1629, CBI, MS. 1876, f. 359v).

70. Peiresc to Thibault, 13 February 1630, CBI, MS. 1876, f. 794r.

71. Peiresc to Mallon, 20 February 1630, CBI, MS. 1876, f. 795r.

72. Peiresc to Mallon, 20 February 1630, CBI, MS. 1876, f. 795v.

73. Minuti to Peiresc, 29 August 1630, PBN, MS. F.fr. 9542, f. 3r; Peiresc to Aymini, 26 February 1630, CBI, MS. 1876, f. 396v (postscript to letter begun on 20 February). Blanc, or his brother, first appears in 1626, while still in Marseille, and is paying out a *lettre de change* drawn on Peiresc's account (Blanc to Peiresc, 29 September 1626, CBI, MS. 1878, f. 346r).

74. Peiresc to Marquesi, 2 November 1630, CBI, MS. 1876, f. 809v

75. Peiresc to baron d'Alegre, 14 May 1630, CBI, MS. 1876, f. 801v.

76. Peiresc to Chastagnier, 17 May 1630, CBI, MS. 1876, f. 802r.

77. Peiresc to Celestin, 12 May 1636, CBI, MS. 1874, f. 416v. "Que le Sr de Gastines avoit oublié de vous faire tenir avant un voyage par luy faict a Paris."

78. Peiresc to Celestin, 12 May 1636, CBI, MS. 1874, f. 416v. "Voyant si miserablement interrompre [*sic*] le commerce que j'avois espere pouvoir entretenir entre vous et Mr votre frere plus seur et plus commode que partout autre voye. . . . Car le Sr Venture pensoit avoir choisy le plus asseuré de touts les navires qui partoient en flotte avec Lombardon, et quasi soubs la protection d'icelluy, et toutesfois."

79. *Monumenta Proximi-Orientis. III Palestine-Liban-Syrie-Mesopotamie (1583–1623)*, ed. Sami Kuri, S.J., Monumenta Historia Societatis Iesu, vol. 147 (Rome: Institutum Historicum Societatis Iesu, 1994), 317; Jean-Philippe Mochon, "Le Consul Général de France à Jérusalem: Aspects historiques, juridiques et politiques de ses fonctions," *Annuaire français de droit international* 42 (1996): 932. Minuti notes that he was no longer in Sidon and was told that he would

not be returning any longer "pro causa." Minuti to Peiresc, 20 July 1629, PBN, MS. F.fr. 9542, f. IV.

80. In the *État Civil* we learn that a Jean Lempereur, son of François, was married on 15 August 1632 (35 F 228).

81. Peiresc to l'Empereur, 19 September 1633, CBI, MS. 1876, f. 831r.

82. Peiresc to Minuti, 28 October 1633, CBI, MS. 1874, f. 317v. "Il m'apporter de cez amandes mais confittes, je les aymerois bien mieux sur l'arbre."

83. Peiresc to Issaultier, 8 December 1635, CBI, MS. 1874, f. 404v.

84. Peiresc to Paolo Seghezzi in Venetia, 23 February 1637, CBI, MS. 1874, f. 441v.

85. Peiresc to Pelissier, 25 April 1631, CBI, MS. 1876, f. 812v.

86. Peiresc to Pelissier, 24 June 1631, CBI, MS. 1876, f. 813v.

87. Pelissier to Peiresc, 23 July 1631, CBI, MS. 1879, f. 534r. "Je l'ay donné a Monsieur de Gastines a condition qu'il le vous donnera et en eschange de l'espée qu'il porte dernier de l'espaule gauche il m'en a donné une autre toutte dorée et pour son bonet et robbe longue il m'a donné ung pognard pistolet q'estoit a feu Monsieur le grand Prieur quy a esté a la Mecque."

88. Peiresc to Pelissier, 20 August 1631, CBI, MS. 1876, f. 816r. "C'est pourquoy je m'imagine pour vous excuser d'avoir prins de la terre pour des pierres precieuses ou rares, que vous estiez encores tout ravy de l'idolastrie ou vous avoir faict tomber (ce dictes vous) ce dervis ou santon des Chinois que vous avez trouvez si excellent & si capable d'esmouvoir de la pieté en vous, sur la contemplation de sa froide & devote mien. Mais je ne scay come elle peu estre compatible avec lesacré dont vous l'auriez."

89. Peiresc to de Gastines, 25 August 1631, CBI, MS. 1877, f. 239r.

90. Peiresc to Jean Berard, 2 November 1630, CBI, MS. 1876, f. 808v.

91. Ramatuelle Tourtel to Peiresc, 15 July 1633, CBI, MS. 1879, f. 584r.

92. CBI, MS. 1771, f. 182r. "Les armoiries du Sr Michel Tourtel Sr de Ramatuelle *1631.* se peuvent blasonner en cez termes"—and then they are depicted by Peiresc.

93. CBI, MS. 493, ff. 245r–v.

94. Peiresc to Bermond, 20 December 1630, CBI, MS. 1876, f. 810r. "Laquelles doibt faire grande honte aux Chrestiens qui ne scavent pas en cela se comporter aussy dignement que les infidelles."

95. Michelange de Nantes to Raphael de Nantes, PBN, MS. N.a.f. 10220, 119–120.

96. Durand to Peiresc, 7 September 1632, PBN, MS. F.fr. 9539, f. 223r. I have not been able to determine his first name.

97. He is referred to as "Consul Durand" in PBN, MS. N.a.f. 5169, f. 17r, "18 March 1626."

98. Sacco and Durand to Peiresc, CBI, MS. 1878, ff. 476–501v.

99. Peiresc to St. Jacob, 22 November 1635, CBI, MS. 1874, f. 404r.

100. Bovis to Peiresc, 15 January 1637, CBI, MS. 1878, 9537, f. 358r. A month later, Bovis wrote to say that Peiresc would soon see that sacristan, named Father Antoine, with his "autographe de la baleine avec quelque autre chose qu'il se promet" (Bovis to Peiresc, 7 February 1637, CBI, MS. 1878, f. 360r).

101. Bovis to Peiresc, 8 March 1637, CBI, MS. 1878, f. 361. "J'ay rendu votre lettre à Mr Magy que Mr Pisciolini ma envoyé chez nous et que l'avois prie de faire porter à l'homme qu'il vous envoya le coffinet et le pot de sourbet."

102. Bovis to Peiresc, 23 January 1637, MAD, 8 F 1 bis, unpaginated.

103. Bovis to Peiresc, 21 March 1637, CBI, MS. 1878, f. 362r.

104. "L'adresse du contenu cy dessus se sera à Monsieur Pesciolini a Marseille." PBN, MS. 8957, f. 253r.

105. Peiresc to Gilly, 18 September 1626, CBI, MS. 1873, f. 179r. "Que je n'estime gueres moins que les originaulx . . . sur ma feuille de papier."

106. PBN, MS. F.fr. 9532, f. 339v.

107. "Il s'est trouvé le sammedy 15. May 1632 à Beaugentier, ou estoit venu Maitre Claude Aman de Joinville Bossetier ou faiseur de trompetes, que j'avois envoyé querir à Toulon pour redresser ledit Phioles, qui avoient esté Bossellees à coups de pies par les ouvriers qui les avoient desterres. Aprez les avoir bien reparees, et remply les trous de maistyc ou de ciment." PBN, MS. F.fr. 9532, f. 339v.

108. Peiresc to Vallavez, [late May] 1626, *Lettres de Peiresc*, 6:543: "des gents du mestier qui sont fort de mes amys."

109. The Hague, Museum Meermano-Westreenianum, MS. c.10.30, 384–385.

110. Peiresc to Vallavez, all in *Lettres de Peiresc*, 6:21 May 1622, 27; 3 February 1625, 100; 17 February 1625, 107; 4 June 1625, 192.

111. Peiresc to Vallavez, 18 November 1626, *Lettres de Peiresc*, 6:601–602.

112. Peiresc to Vallavez, 20 November 1626, *Lettres de Peiresc*, 6:604.

113. MAD, 9 B 39+.

114. MAD, 9 B 12+. Similar records exist for 1611–1612 (9 B 10+) and 1613–1615 (9 B 11+).

115. There is no satisfactory treatment of this very important organization. Xavier Labat Saint Vincent, "La Chambre de Commerce de Marseille, trait d'union entre le corps d'ancien régime et l'institution consulaire moderne," in *Consolati di Mare and Chambers of Commerce*, ed. C. Vassallo (Msida: Malta University Press, 2000), 83–94, is focused entirely on the modern period.

116. *Arrest du Conseil d'Estat du Roy portant cessation du droict de Cinq pour Cent qui se levoit sur les Marchandises venantes des Eschelles & pais d'Egypte* (n.p., n.d. [but after 1657]), MACC, J 1676, 24. Parallel material can be found in PBN, MS. F.fr. 18593, 216ff. "Factum du proces pendant au Conseil, Entre Iean Magy, Iean Louis Maurellet, Joseph & Mathieu Baumes freres & Iacques Sabain Machands de la ville de Marseille, Negotians en Allexandrie d'Egypte, defendeurs & demandeurs en Requete du 26 Febvrier dernier" [1645].

117. *Arrest du Conseil*, 1.

118. *Arrest du Conseil*, 8.

119. *Arrest du Conseil*, 15. There was also a Guillaume Napolon "natif de ceste ville [Marseille] age du trente-deux ans ou environ" (PBN, MS. F.fr. 18593, f. 288v).

120. *Arrest du Conseil*, 27. The first recorded mention of Lambert in Egypt is in the letters patent authorizing the creation of a "Société ayant pour but le commerce des drogues, casse et séné" at Alexandria on 25 November 1614, MAD, 9 B 1+².

121. *Arrest du Conseil*, 16.

122. *Arrest du Conseil*, 18.

123. *Arrest du Conseil*, 18.

124. *Arrest du Conseil*, 18.

125. A glimpse of Fernoux in action can be gleaned from eight letters between 1611 and 1621 preserved in the MACC, J 545, and an additional nine between 1628 and 32 in J 547.

126. One thousand piastres were remitted on 9 December 1633. The entire sum was then retrocessed to the king's secretary, François Augist, on 18 May 1634. *Arrest du Conseil*, 19. "Lettre missive escrite par lesdits marchands residans au Caire audict sieur Comte de Brèves ledit jour 26. Aoust 1646."

127. *Arrest du Conseil*, 19.

128. *Arrest du Conseil*, 20.

129. *Arrest du Conseil*, 20.

130. MAD, 9 B 2, f. 707r.

12. Marseille's Merchant Families

1. Géraud Pourmarède, "Naissance d'une institution royale: Les Consuls de la nation française en Levant et en Barbarie aux XVIe et XVIIe siècles," in *Annuaire-Bulletin de la Société de l'histoire de France* 2002 (Paris: La Société de l'Histoire de France, 2003), 88–92, 96.

2. Peiresc to Aycard, 2 October 1633, CBI, MS. 1871, f. 36r; Peiresc to Salvator, [11] October 1633, CBI, MS. 1874, f. 314v, thanking him for taking care of Minuti during his Damascus sickness.

3. Peiresc to Grange [in Smyrna], 5 January 1635, CBI, MS. 1874, f. 363r.

4. Peiresc to l'Empereur en Constantinople, 22 Aug 1632, CBI, MS. 1873, f. 300r. A l'Empereur with a collection of medals in Marseille is described as "late" in Durand to Peiresc, 1 September 1632, PBN, MS. F.fr. 9539, f. 223r. Peiresc, who transmitted Durand's letter to his brother, added that Durand had already acquired all of the gold medals (Vallavez to Peiresc, 2 September 1632, PBN, MS. F.fr. 9539, f. 224v). This would seem to refer to the death of the other Jean l'Empereur.

5. Peiresc to l'Empereur [in Constantinople], 19 September 1633, CBI, MS. 1876, f. 831r.

6. *"Des manuscrits et forte belle choses."* Cassagnes to Peiresc, 14 July 1632, PBN, MS. F.fr. 9539, f. 222r [= *Les Correspondants de Peiresc*, 2 vols. (Geneva: Slatkine, 1972), 2:734].

7. Peiresc to Boerio, 3 August 1635, CBI, MS. 1872, f. 405v. Lambert is recorded as in business as early as 1614 in partnership for the "commerce des drogues" with Alexandria (Mar. Arch. Dept., Fonds de l'amirauté, 9 B 1+², f. 412r). It is perhaps for this reason that Bergasse identifies him as "Lambert de Gastine" (Louis Bergasse, *Histoire du commerce de Marseille*, vol. 4: *1599–1660* [Paris: Plon, 1954], 111).

8. Peiresc to de Thou, 28 February 1633, CBI, MS. 1876, f. 307v.

9. Pieresc to Gazille, 12 September 1627, CBI, MS. 1873, f. 462v. For evidence of an argument between them over an investment in a ship, see Peiresc to Napollon, 17 September 1627, CBI, MS. 1873, f. 462v.

10. Peiresc to Jean-Baptise Magy, 22 December 1633, CBI, MS. 1874, f. 320r. The same letter identifies Santo Seghezzi of Cairo and Sr. Gela of Marseille as brothers-in-law; also Peiresc to Gela, 22 December 1633, CBI, MS. 1874, f. 320v.

11. Oleg V. Volkoff, *À la recherche de manuscrits en Égypte*, Recherches d'archéologie, de philologie et d'histoire, 30 (Cairo: Institut Français d'Archéologie Orientale, 1974), 30.

12. Peiresc to de l'Isle, 16 July 1631, CBI, MS. 1876, f. 815r.

13. Minuti to Peiresc, 21 October 1633, PBN, MS. 9542, f. 16v.

14. Poumarède, "Naissance d'une institution royale," 111.

15. Peiresc to Esperit Laurens, 2 March 1634, CBI, MS. 1874, f. 331r. The letter identifies Jean Magy and Jacques Albert as Baulme's friends in Cairo. Laurens is named chancellor in the report of Antoine Mazarat and Jean Fargues, from Alexandria, 24 October 1634, MACC, J 550, piece 4 [unpaginated].

16. Peiresc to Galaup, 8 April 1631, CBI, MS. 1873, f. 440v.

17. Published as *Discours sur les arcs triomphaux, dressés en la ville d'Aix à l'heureuse arrivée de très chrestien, très grand et très juste monarque Louis XIII* (Aix: Jean Tholosan, 1624).

18. Estelle to Peiresc, 10 December 1629, CBI, MS. 1876, f. 793r.

19. Peiresc to Marquesi, 15 May 1630, CBI, MS. 1876, f. 802r; Peiresc to Marquesi, 20 November 1630, CBI, MS. 1876, f. 808v. Aymini to Peiresc, 5 March 1630, PBN, MS. F.fr. 9540, f. 120r.

20. I have only found his name given once, in "Extraict de lettre de Constantinople du 6 d Avril 1634 [escripte par le Sr Guillaume Guez au Sr Sabain a Livourne]," CBI, MS. 493, f. 231r.

21. Sydney Aufrère, "Peiresc et sa connaissance de l'Égypte," in *Peiresc, ou la passion de connaître*, ed. Anne Reinbold (Paris: Vrin, 1990), 145.

22. *Arrest du Conseil d'Estat du Roy portant cessation du droict de Cinq pour Cent qui se levoit sur les Marchandises venantes des Eschelles & païs d'Egypte* (n.p., n.d. [but after 1657]), MACC, J 1676, 25.

23. Peiresc to Paolo Seghezzi, 23 February 1637, CBI, MS. 1874, f. 441v; Peiresc to Boerio, 6 March 1637, CBI, MS. 1872, f. 410v.

13. Financing, Disbursing, Reimbursing

1. Peiresc to Pierre Dupuy, 29 December 1626, *Lettres de Peiresc*, 1:117.

2. Peiresc to Labbia, 25 October 1615, CBI, MS. 1874, f. 314v.

3. Peiresc to Labbia, 25 October 1615, CBI, MS. 1874, f. 314v.

4. Peiresc to Vic, 21 September 1612, CBI, MS. 1874, f. 574r.

5. Peiresc to Andrew Bruggiotti, 11 April 1617, CBI, MS. 1872, f. 529r.

6. Peiresc to Labbia, 9 March 1616, CBI, MS. 1874, f. 315v.

7. He is identified as "Marchant de la Ville de Marseille" in a quittance from 1582 copied out for Peiresc (CBI, MS. 1882, f. 261r). In 1624, Peiresc describes him as "Mr Signier, Escuyer a Marseille" (Peiresc to Bonnaire, 9 February 1624, CBI, MS. 1872, f. 149r—the same letter in which he asks the Roman *destinataire* to find him a copy of Galileo's *Saggiatore*). But note that he—or, perhaps, his father—is already serving as a respondent for Peiresc in a letter of 1608: "indriciare [*sic*] le lettere al S.or Segnier [*sic*] mercante in Marsilia" (Marco Rubin to Peiresc, 22 April 1608, PBN, MS. F.fr. 9540, f. 132).

8. Peiresc to Barclay, October 1620, CBI, MS. 1872, f. 101v.

9. Peiresc to Barclay, 19 July 1621, CBI, MS. 1872, f. 110v.

10. PBN, MS. N.a.f. 5169, f. 6v. November 13: "par M. Signier au Sr Lucas Torrius avec lettre de credit de 7 ou 8 l.t.; au Sr Raimon Marre à Vallance pour ledit credit a M. Signier."

11. Peiresc to Signier, 8 May 1621, CBI, MS. 1872, f. 107v.

12. Peiresc to Barclay, 4 November 1620, CBI, MS. 1872, f. 102r.

13. Peiresc to Eschinard, 2 June 1621, CBI, MS. 1873, f. 322r.

14. Peiresc to Eschinard, 18 January 1626, CBI, MS. 1873, f. 344r.

15. Peiresc to Marc Antonio Lumaga, 7 December 1623, CBI, MS. 1874, f. 295r. See also PBN, MS. N.a.f. 5169, f. 6v, for 17 November 1623.

16. Peiresc to Lumaga, 12 January 1624, CBI, MS. 1874, f. 295v.

17. Signier to Lumaga, 26 January 1624, CBI, MS. 1876, f. 305r.

18. As in, for example, Peiresc to Lumaga, 7 February 1625, CBI, MS. 1874, f. 299r.

19. Examples of this are Peiresc to Lumaga, December 1624 or January 1625, CBI, MS. 1874, f. 299r; Peiresc to Lumaga, 14 August 1625, CBI, MS. 1874, f. 300bis v.

20. Peiresc to Gasparo Molino and Francesco Rosa, 28 October 1625, CBI, MS. 1874, f. 759r; Signier to Molino and Rosa, 27 October 1625, CBI, MS. 1874, f. 759r.

21. Peiresc to Molino and Rosa, 5 January 1626, CBI, MS. 1874, f. 759v.

22. Signier to Molino and Rosa, 4 January 1626, CBI, MS. 1874, f. 759v.

23. Peiresc to Lumaga, 17 July 1626, CBI, MS. 1874, f. 300bis v. The letter also refers to another Venetian who could draw on the account, variously spelled "du Balas," "du Balens," and "du Bonlans."

24. Peiresc to Vallavez, 10 April 1626, *Lettres de Peiresc*, 6:446; [late] May 1626, *Lettres de Peiresc*, 6:543.

25. Peiresc to Lumaga, 29 October 1627, CBI, MS. 1874, f. 302r. Mary, Douaille, and Frayse or Freisse, Fraisse, or Freysse are mentioned in an earlier letter from Peiresc to Bonnaire (16 January 1626, CBI, MS. 1872, f. 180v). "Signori Mario, Douaille & Fraisse ò vero al Sr Ces. Lamberto et di Gastines." News of the change was also given in Peiresc to Pierre Dupuy, 23 January 1627, *Lettres de Peiresc*, 1:127.

26. Peiresc to Bonnaire, 24 April 1626, CBI, MS. 1872, f. 187r, where he describes them as "Mary, Douaille and Fraisse of Lyon and Marseille." I have only found their first names used in PBN, MS. N.a.f. 5169, f. 14r, "19 June 1625." At this point they are still being provided with letters of credit from Signier.

27. Guillaume d'Abbathia, a parlementaire in Toulouse, was advanced money by Peiresc through them in 1627 (Peiresc to Mary, Douaille, and Fraisse, 8 May 1627, CBI, MS. 1871, f. 7v); in 1628 he again was able to draw on credit "chez Sr Mary Douaille & Fraisse" (Peiresc to Sponde, 3 February 1628, CBI, MS. 1876, f. 215v). Fraisse was also asked to draw up a letter of credit to his "respondants" in Toulouse for Father du Val to draw upon, perhaps while at the seminary run by the Benedictines of St. Maur. CBI, MS. 1820, f. 412bis, ca. 1626.

28. Peiresc to Lumaga, 11 October 1628, CBI, MS. 1873, f. 303r.

29. Fraisse to Lumaga, 16 January 1627, CBI, MS. 1877, f. 28v.

30. Mary, Douaille, and Fraisse to Pettau, 3 September 1626, CBI, MS. 1874, f. 564r.

31. Peiresc to Plaignard, 20 June 1636, CBI, MS. 1876, f. 320v. Pichery also had a respondent in Lyon, Sr. René Gais.
32. Peiresc to Aubery de Mesnil, 11 June 1635, CBI, MS. 1871, f. 434r; Peiresc to Venture, 24 October 1635, CBI, MS. 1874, f. 393bis r.
33. Peiresc to Mary, Douaille, and Fraisse, 9 March 1629, CBI, MS. 1876, f. 158r.
34. Peiresc to Aubery, 17 March 1627, CBI, MS. 1871, f. 466r.
35. Lambert to d'Espiot, 30 March 1627, CBI, MS. 1871, f. 467r. Aubery to Peiresc, 21 April 1627, PBN, MS. F.fr. 9542, f. 233r. Aubery writes "Despiau"; the name is written "Guillaume des Piotz" in Peiresc to Holstenius, 2 June 1633, *Lettres de Peiresc*, 5:407. Louis d'Aubery is the brother of Aubery de Mesnil.
36. Peiresc to de Gastines, 20 July 1628, CBI, MS. 1877, f. 153v; copy of a letter of credit written by Lambert to Madame, the widow of the Prior de Lignage, 20 July 1628, CBI, MS. 1877, f. 153r.
37. Bovis to Peiresc, 23 January 1637, MAD, MS. 8 F bis 1, unpaginated [165].
38. Peiresc to Jacques Dupuy, 28 November 1634, *Lettres de Peiresc*, 3:230.
39. Peiresc to Pierre Bourdelot, 17 March 1634, *Lettres de Peiresc*, 7:703 [= CBI, MS. 1872, f. 443r. "personne grandement officieuse et qui sera bien ayse de vous pouvoir servir non seulement durant vostre sejour à Marseille, mais aussy durant celluy que vous pourrez faire à Rome, si vous l'employez, pour ce que vous vouldrez recepvoir du costé de Paris."
40. Peiresc to Bartolle, 8 November 1629, CBI, MS. 1876, f. 360v.
41. Bonnaire to Peiresc, 29 June 1629, PBN, MS. F.fr. 9539, f. 148r.
42. Peiresc to Marchand, 12 May 1630, CBI, MS. 1874, f. 565v.
43. Aubery to Peiresc, 20 May 1630, PBN, MS. F.fr. 9542, f. 265r.
44. Peiresc to Minuti, 3 June 1629, CBI, MS. 1876, f. 356r: "Il n'est pas de besoing d'en prendre de Mr Fraisse ny de Mr Salicoffres puis mesmes qu'il dict ne scavoir point de commodité de navire flamandz. Il vous fauldra faire la guerrir a l'oeuil."
45. Peiresc to Magy, 6 December 1634, CBI, MS. 1874, f. 359v.
46. Peiresc to Venture, 24 October 1635, CBI, MS. 1874, f. 393bis r.
47. "Credit de Gastines," 14 January 1631, CBI, MS. 1877, f. 239r.
48. Gastines to Peiresc, 31 July 1629, PBN, MS. F.fr. 9537, f. 319r.
49. Peiresc to de Thou, 28 February 1633, CBI, MS. 1877, f. 307v.
50. This corresponds to a big increase in Dutch shipping to the Levant in the early 1630s (Marie-Christine Engels, *Merchants, Interlopers, Seamen and Corsairs: The "Flemish" Community in Livorno and Genoa [1615–1635]* [Hilversum: Verloren, 1997], 213).
51. For example, Peiresc to Boerio, 10 April 1637, CBI, MS. 1872, f. 111v. Payments went from de Gastines to Ruts and Martin to Guillem Vandestraten in Genoa (Peiresc to Boerio, 9 June 1637, CBI, MS. 1872, f. 412r).
52. Peiresc to Gaffarel, 30 October 1634, CBI, MS. 1873, f. 415r.
53. *Monumenta Proximi-Orientis. V. Égypte (1591–1699)*, ed. Charles Libois, Monumenta Historica Societatis Iesu 152 (Rome: Institutum Historicum Societatis Iesu, 2002), 115.
54. Peiresc to Tarquet, 7 November 1629, CBI, MS. 1876, f. 360v.
55. Peiresc to Blanc, 16 November 1629, CBI, MS. 1876, f. 363r: "Telz que l'argent eust peu gaignee s'il eust esté employe en autre marchandise." The package was

none other than a Samaritan Pentateuch "qu'ilz [the two fathers] ont eue des mains de ce RP Michael Maronite par votre intercession" (Peiresc to Meynier, marchand francois a damas, undated [16 November 1629?], CBI, MS. 1876, f. 363r).

56. Peiresc to Estelle, 16 November 1629, CBI, MS. 1876, f. 363v.

57. Peiresc to Tarquet, 27 January 1630, CBI, MS. 1876, f. 792v.

58. Peiresc to Aurivelier, 27 January 1630, CBI, MS. 1876, f. 793r. A second letter, following up, and announcing receipt of a letter from Aymini sent to Sr. Galaup, was written on 2 February (Peiresc to Aurivelier, 2 February 1630, CBI, MS. 1876, f. 793v).

59. Peiresc to Estelle, 20 February 1630, CBI, MS. 1876, f. 797r. "A proportion du gain de l'autre argent employér en marchandise . . . d'ordonner la rembourcement a raison de 30 pour cent & m'a faict plaisir & je l'employeray tant plus librement une autrefois."

60. Peiresc to Tarquet, 20 February 1630, CBI, MS. 1876, f. 797r. "Mais à condition que vous accepterez *les charges nautiques come a faict Mr Cesar Lambert qui cognoist mon humeur & que je l'en employeray bien à l'advenir avec moins de regret & je ne vous en demeureray pas moins redevable . . . car sans doubte il y à fallu adjouster quelque supplement pour le redimer d'un Venitien qui avoit couru sur mon marché.*"

61. Peiresc to Gaffarel, 11 September 1633, CBI, MS. 1873, f. 405v.

62. Peiresc to Danmartin, 17 December 1627, CBI, MS. 1873, f. 123v. "On peu estre quitter a raison de vingt pour cent de l'argent que l'on prend en Cypre."

63. Peiresc to Jean-Baptiste Magy, 5 April 1636, CBI, MS. 1874, f. 413r. Masson gives 15 percent as the overall "change maritime" during the seventeenth century (*Histoire du commerce français*, 497).

64. Peiresc to d'Espiot, 12 May 1630, CBI, MS. 1874, f. 565v.

65. Peiresc to d'Espiot, 3 October 1631, CBI, MS. 1874, f. 567r.

66. Peiresc to Marchand, 3 June 1633, CBI, MS. 1874, f. 570v.

67. Peiresc to Estelle, 20 February 1630, CBI, MS. 1876, f. 797r.

68. Peiresc to Minuti, 3 March 1630, CBI, MS. 1876, f. 798r; the same figure is offered by Peiresc in his letter to Magy, 15 May 1634, CBI, MS. 1874, f. 342r.

69. Peiresc to Petit, 8 May 1635, CBI, MS. 1875, f. 274r.

70. Peiresc to Guez, 18 October 1632, CBI, MS. 1876, f. 825r. "Proportionnez a ce que la mesme somme pourroit avoir porte de profit au marchand qui la fornie si elle eust estre employer de marchandize sur la mesme navire."

71. For example, Peiresc to Aymini, 20 February 1630, CBI, MS. 1876, ff. 796r, 796v.

72. Jérôme de l'Isle, by contrast, was not so lucky. He purchased 2,000 piastres at the going rate of 42 sols per piastre from one Jehan Jaine at Marseille. Jaine, however, had purchased them at 30 sols per piastre, "a price more than 30 percent lower than what is charged by the good and ordinaries" of Flanders. The piastres, however, were fake. De l'Isle was caught in Sidon and punished by a 100 percent fine with interest. Minuti to Peiresc, 21 October 1633, PBN, MS. F.fr. 9542, f. 16v.

73. Ashtor calculates gross profits on copper at 25 percent, spices at 50 percent, and cotton from Egypt at 80 percent. But duties in the Levant, commissions to the

fattore, freight charges, and duties back in Venice—Peiresc's "frais, nolis et charges maritimes"—added up to 25 percent on spices and 34 percent on cotton, leaving net profits on spices of 25 percent and cotton of 45 to 50 percent. Eliyahu Ashtor, *Levant Trade in the Later Middle Ages* (Princeton, NJ: Princeton University Press, 1981), 417.

74. Peiresc to Jean-Baptiste Magy, 1 May 1634, CBI, MS. 1874, f. 339v.

75. Peiresc to Minuti, end of October or early November 1630, CBI, MS. 1876, f. 808v. We know his first name from Aix-en-Provence, Arch. Dept., B 3348, f. 545.

76. Peiresc to de l'Isle, 16 July 1631, CBI, MS. 1876, f. 815r. "Laissa perdre sur la mer fault d'avoir faict faire une semblable seureté, comme je l'en avois charger autreprendre Sr Charles Blanc son parent."

77. Peiresc to de Gastines, 25 August 1631, CBI, MS. 1877, f. 239r.

78. Peiresc to Tarquet, 18 November 1629, CBI, MS. 1876, f. 789v. "De rechercher quelques supplementz de ceux que j'ay receu."

79. Peiresc to Tarquet, 16 July 1631, CBI, MS. 1876, f. 815r. It is in this letter that Peiresc acknowledges never hearing back from the Capuchin in Sidon he had contacted at the suggestion of de Thou—the first mention of Gilles de Loches, who would later become such an important person for Peiresc.

80. Peiresc to Constans in Aleppo, 16 August 1635, CBI, MS. 1874, f. 383v. "En droicts de change et de remise conformes au proffit que le faict sur les marchandises portees sur le mesme navire." When Peiresc saw that the "droits de change" and "profits maritimes" were still not being charged to his account, he was embarrassed. Peiresc to Venture, 16 June 1636, CBI, MS. 1874, f. 419r.

81. For more on Pichery, see Agnès Bresson's note, *Lettres à Claude Saumaise,* 268n4.

82. Peiresc to Truillet, 11 July 1630, CBI, MS. 1876, f. 806v.

83. Peiresc to Venture, 8 May 1636, CBI, MS. 1874, f. 415v. "Cependant vous avez icy une lettre de change qui m'a esté envoyer d'hollande de la part du Sr. Jac. Golius frere de ce bon P. Celestin pour la somme de 50 piastres payables par le Sr. Piscatoris de Marseille a qui je vous prie de la presenter, d'une part pour scavoir de luy le credit qu'il en à & la disposition au payement et ce qu'il voudra que je fasse pour sa descharge en cela, car s'il veult que j'endosse la lettre originellement je le feray & s'il se contente de l'endossement que j'ay faict sur une coppie d'icelle cy jointe, vous li pourrez aussy contresigne selong mon ordre et retourner les deniers s'il vous plaist ou bien me renvoyer l'original de ladit lettre de change, aprez qu'il l'aura accepter a fin que je l'endosse si ce n'est qu'il ayant mieux que vous l'endosserez de ma part, comme vous le pourriez faire aussy." In a second letter written on this day, after reflecting, Peiresc decided it would be better for it to be countersigned and Celestin collect it in Aleppo from Messrs. Constans (f. 415v).

84. David de Willehem, for Jacob Golius to "la president du change." "M. Il vous plairra payer veu la presente, a Monsieur Peres Con.er du Roy au parlement d'Aix cinquante patacons ou pieces du huict selon le cours qu'ilz ont & vallent en Alep, & m'en donner advis, a la Haye ce 29 November 1635, David de Willehem, ainsy signe et au dessus est escript Monsieur Antoine Piscatoris Marseille." CBI, MS. 1874, f. 415v.

85. Peiresc to Magy, 27 July 1636, CBI, MS. 1874, f. 421v.

86. Peiresc to Celestin, 12 May 1636, CBI, MS. 1874, f. 416v. "Au reste comme lors que je fis payer a Marseille les premiers deniers que vous avez receus des S.rs Constans sur ma recommandation je n'avois poinct songé a m'en faire embourcer ains avois prins a singuliere faveur de vous rendre ce petit service, en attendante faire mieux si j'en rencontrois de meilleurs moyens. Je fus tout honteux de recevoir autre lettre de Mr Golius votre frere du dernier Novembre passé avec une lettre de change a Marseille pour tirer le rembourcement de 50 piastres que vous aviez eües, et ne me voullus pas mettre en debvoir de faire presenter ladicte lettre de change ne de faire exiger le payement de ladicte somme, mais ayant appris par votre despeche derniere du 25 dernier l'inquietude que vous vous donniez pour cella et que vous desirez l'avoir employee aux ordres que vous en aviez de Mr votre frere, craincte qu'il ne le print en mauvaise part et que les deniers ne courassent fortune de se perdre avec l'interruption du commerce aprez y avoir mieux pense j'ay creu qu'il valloit mieux la mettre en surette et envoyay la lettre de change audict Sr Venture pour en retirer le payement comme il a faict en intention que vous vous en puissiez prevalloir encores en levant quand vous voudrez a quoy Mrs Constans ne feront pas de difficulté je m'asseure." This is the plan as presented to Jacob Golius in a letter of 8 May (*Lettres à Claude Saumaise*, 263–264).

87. Among the insurers of a voyage to Egypt of Michel Tourtel, Sr. de Ramatuelle, on 1 February 1634 was "Nicolas Rutz." MAD, Fonds de l'amirauté, 9 B 21, f. 685r. Niklaes Ruts, later Dutch consul in Marseille, was originally from Amsterdam and married into the Swiss merchant family of Zollikofer (Salicoffres), who were from St. Gall and active in Marseille for almost a century. His business partners were the Martens family, also from Holland. Lynn Hunt, Margaret C. Jacob, and Wijanard Mijnhardt, *The Book That Changed Europe: Picart and Bernard's "Religious Ceremonies of the World"* (Cambridge, MA: Belknap Press of Harvard University Press, 2010), 90, 334n4. For Ruts as consul, see O. Schutte, *Repertorium der Nederlandse vertegenwoordigers residerende in het buitenland 1584–1810* (The Hague: M. Nijhoff, 1976), 71.

    A ship returning from Alexandria in 1637 carried goods traded on the account of "Ruts & David Martin." MAD, Fonds de l'amirauté, 9 B 12+, unpaginated. David Martin, "natif de Amsterdam" but living in Marseille for more than seventeen years, PBN, MS. F.fr. 18593, f. 282. "Nicolas Ruts et Durand Martin" are identified as "deux marchands hollandais," Aix-en-Provence, Arch. Dept., B 3350, f. 713v, dated 18 July 1636.

88. Peiresc to Venture, 2 June 1636, CBI, MS. 1874, f. 418v.

89. But we know nothing about this company. Marie-Christine Engles mentions a Ruts who traded at Palermo and another at Messina but nothing at Marseille in Engles, *Merchants, Interlopers, Seamen and Corsairs: The "Flemish" Community in Livorno and Genoa (1615–1635)* (Hilversum: Verloren, 1997).

90. PBN, MS. N.a.f. 5169, f. 7v, 1 March 1624: "par mon frere à M. Signier avec la lettre de Bordeaux."

91. Peiresc to du Val, 1 February 1625: "Je vous ay promis affermer Guistres à 2,000 livres comme il estoit." Quoted in Ant. de Lantenay [Antoine-Louis Bertrand], *Peiresc: Abbé de Guitres* (Bordeaux: Feret et Fils, 1888), 50.

92. De Lantenay, *Peiresc: Abbé de Guitres,* 50, 55, 63, 111.
93. Guillemin to Peiresc, 5 March 1628, CBI, MS. 1879, f. 77r.
94. PBN, MS. N.a.f. 5169, f. 17v, 18 April 1626.
95. PBN, MS. N.a.f. 5169, f. 22v, 6 January 1627.
96. PBN, MS. N.a.f. 5169, f. 32r, 5 April 1628.
97. Peiresc to Guez, 4 April 1629, CBI, MS. 1876, f. 376v.
98. Peiresc to Meynard, 4 April 1629, CBI, MS. 1876, ff. 376v–377r.
99. Taillevant to Guez, 4 April 1629, CBI, MS. 1876, f. 377r. This complex transaction is summarized in a paragraph of Peiresc's letter to Vallavez, 5 April 1629, *Lettres de Peiresc,* 6:633.
100. Peiresc to d'Espiot, 21 October 1632, CBI, MS. 1874, f. 568v.
101. Peiresc to Guez, 8 October 1633, CBI, MS. 1876, f. 833r. "Selon les occurences qui s'en pourroit presenter de temps a autre . . . a qui je donne quelquefois des commission a mes amis autant de plus . . . nous à assignez à prendre de vous tant de compte de mon frere de Valavez que du mien."
102. Peiresc to Guez [at Constantinople], 10 July 1631, CBI, MS. 1876, f. 809v. "En tirant lettre de change sur moy ou sur Mr de Gastines de Marseille."
103. Peiresc to Jean-Baptiste Magy, 5 April 1636, CBI, MS. 1874, f. 413r: "Et n'y à que cez Angloys qui traffiquent de Bordeaux a Marseille."
104. Peiresc to Jean-Baptiste Magy, 2 June 1636, CBI, MS. 1874, f. 418v. Peiresc had written on 25 May (f. 418v) that Mssrs. Ruts and Martin had written that they had already made a payment of 50 piastres. In June, Peiresc was asking them to pay another 40 to close a bill of 135 piastres, indicating that another 40 piastres must have been paid in between.
105. Peiresc to Aubery de Mesnil, 23 February 1635, CBI, MS. 1874, f. 698v. "N'y ayant pas de lieu revoquer en doubte les pretentions de son eminence pour peu qu'il aye de fondement sans encourri un grand crime." Aubery de Mesnil was the brother of Louis d'Aubery. For Peiresc and Guîtres, see Lantenay, *Peiresc: Abbé de Guîtres,* and Peter N. Miller, "Further Thoughts on the 'Ethics of the Historian': Peiresc and the Benedictines of Saint-Maur," in *Europäische Geschichtskulturen um 1700 zwischen Gelehrsamkeit, Politik und Konfession,* ed. Thomas Wallnig, Ines Peper, Thomas Stockinger, and Patrick Fiska (Berlin: De Gruyter, 2012).
106. Peiresc to Aurivilier, 27 January 1630, CBI, MS. 1876, f. 793r. "Je m'imagine que ce sera le surplus que vous aurez possible fraye quoyque c'en soit M. Fort vous baillera votre indempnité." Aurivilier seems to have made a show of being unwilling to accept the reimbursement. He also, perhaps less chivalrously, claimed that he could not release the medals Aymini purchased for Peiresc because they had supposedly not been included in Peiresc's quittance (Peiresc to Tarquet, 2 February 1630, CBI, MS. 1876, f. 794r).
107. Peiresc to Minuti, end of October or early November 1630, CBI, MS. 1876, f. 808v.
108. Peiresc to Thibault, 13 February 1630, CBI, MS. 1876, f. 794r.
109. Peiresc to Thibault, 4 January 1632, CBI, MS. 1876, f. 817v.
110. Peiresc to Fort, 23 January 1631, CBI, MS. 1876, f. 810v.
111. Fort to Peiresc, 1 February 1630, PBN, MS. F.fr. 9540, f. 160r.
112. Fort to Peiresc, 31 January 1630, PBN, MS. F.fr. 9540, f. 162r.

113. For example, there is no indication of these letters in PBN, MS. N.a.f. 5169, f. 43r.

114. Fort's letter to Rocafort went out on 2 April 1629. PBN, MS. N.a.f. 5169, f. 39v, 2 April 1629; Fort to Peiresc, 27 May 1629 [24 May in N.a.f. 5169], CBI, 1816, f. 240r. Peiresc succinctly described this on the flyleaf as "augmentation du credit donné au P. Jean François Provincial des Minimes" (f. 240v). In his initial letter of 8 May, Jean François had acknowledged making contact with Roquefort (CBI, 1816, f. 243r).

115. On this project more generally, see Peter N. Miller, *Peiresc's "History of Provence": Antiquarianism and the Discovery of a Medieval Mediterranean*, Transactions of the American Philosophical Society 101, 3 (Philadelphia: American Philosophical Society, 2011).

116. Marengo to Peiresc, 26 August 1629, CBI, MS. 1879, f. 311r.

117. Peiresc to Aubéry du Mesnil, 30 March 1628, CBI, MS. 1871, f. 483v.

118. Peiresc to Carrayre, 5 June 1633, CBI, MS. 1876, f. 827r.

119. Peiresc to Gela, 28 January 1636, CBI, MS. 1874, f. 410r: "Ma bisogna che hoggidi in Egitto si facino savoir questi monumenti dell'antiquita del solito prezio. trovandovisi 400 piastres di questa reliquie come ella dice."

120. Peiresc to Jacques de Vendôme, 31 January 1636, CBI, MS. 1874, f. 411r. "Ou bien 150# pour l'ayder aux plus urgentes necessitez quand bien il voudroit bouger de là. & sans une aultre somme de 200# que Madame sa Mere avoit vouleu luy faire tenir a mesmes fins."

121. Peiresc to Vallavez, 18 July 1626, *Lettres de Peiresc*, 6:579.

14. Sanson Napollon

1. King Henri IV identifies him as a "corsous naturalizés et habitans en nostre dicte ville de Marseille," quoted in Wolfgang Kaiser, "Négocier la liberté: Missions françaises pour l'échange et le rachat de captifs au Maghreb (XVIIe siècle)," in *La Mobilité des personnes en Méditerranée de l'Antiquité à l'époque modern*, ed. Claudia Moatti and Wolfgang Kaiser (Rome: École Française de Rome, 2004), 506. On the Corsican Marseillais, see Michel Vergé-Franceschi, "Les Corses de Marseille du XVIe au XVIIIe siècle: Des intermédiaires entre chrétiens et musulmans," in *Hommes de l'entre-deux: Parcours individuels et portraits de groupes sur la frontière de la Méditerranée (XVIe–XXe siècle)*, ed. Bernard Heyberger and Chantal Verdeil (Paris: Les Indes Savantes, 2009), 43–60.

2. Napollon to Consuls of Marseille, MACC, J 866, 28 November 1615, 6 February 1616, 6 November 1616, and 14 December 1617.

3. On the consulates, see Julien Pillaut, *Les Consulats du Levant: I, Smyrne (1610–1900), Satalie de Caramanie (1607–1814)* (Nancy: Imprimerie Berger-Levrault, 1902); *Les Consulats du Levant: II, Larnaca (1673–1900)* (Nancy: Imprimerie Berger-Levrault, 1902); *Les Consulats du Levant: III, Alep-Seïde-Tripoli de Syrie (1548–1900)* (Nancy: Imprimerie Berger-Levrault, 1902); François-Charles Pouqueville, "Mémoire historique et diplomatique sur le commerce et les établissements français au Levant," in *Mémoires de l'académie des inscriptions*, vol. 10 (Paris: Imprimerie Nationale, 1833).

4. Aix-en-Provence, Arch. Dept., B 3346, f. 665: "lettres de noblesse pour Sanson Napollon, ecuyer de Marseille, en raison de ses services comme consul a Alep, Saint-Germain-en-Laye, Octobre 1623."

5. Olivier Olivmapier [interpreter at Pera] to Loménie, 11 May 1624, PBN, V Cents Colbert, MS. 483 (formerly Dupuy MS. 475), f. 90: "sigr. Sanson Napolon conssolo a Smirna."

6. Napollon to Consuls of Marseille, 24 January 1624, MACC, J 1565, unpaginated.

7. Napollon to Consuls of Marseille, 27 April 1624, MACC, J 1565, unpaginated. "Je suis en Constinoble despuis le moys de Mars," in *Journal et correspondance de Gédoyn "Le Turc,"* ed. A. Boppe (Paris: Typographie Plon-Nourrit, 1909) is an invaluable source for the details of French oriental policy in the Ottoman lands, and in particular the relations between the ambassador in Constantinople and the consulate of Aleppo between 1610 and 1624.

8. Napollon to Consuls of Marseille, 10 May 1624, MACC, J 1565, unpaginated; 26 July 1624.

9. Napollon to Consuls of Marseille, 10 June 1624, MACC, J 1565, unpaginated.

10. CBI, MS. 1777, ff. 84r–v. It is hard to square this set of dates with those provided by de Grammont, which have him leaving Smyrna on 4 July 1624 and arriving in Tunis on 12 August. H.-D. de Grammont, *Relations entre la France & la Régence d'Alger au XVIIe siècle: Deuxième partie; La Mission de Sanson Napollon (1628–1633)* (Algiers: Adolphe Jourdan, 1880), 9.

11. I have been unable to find documentation of this incident in the Peiresc archive, the Archive of the Chambre de Commerce de Marseille, the Archives Departementales des Bouches-du-Rhône, or any number of manuscripts in the Bibliothèque Nationale de France. But it must, tantalizingly, be out there somewhere.

12. Mémoire drawn up by Sr. Picardière for Napollon "pour son voyage d'Alep." PBN, V Cents Colbert, MS. 483, f. 185v.

13. Gédoyn to Consuls of Marseille, [ ] April 1624, MACC, J 889, unpaginated. "Je me suis trouvé grandement scandalisé de l'entreprise dudit Sr Napollon qui scavoit que j'avois commission expresse du Roy pour cet affaire."

14. At the bottom of a letter to M. de Guise of 19 April 1625 on negotiations with Barbary, Cesy writes, "Jai donné charge au Sr Samson Napollon" (71v). A letter of the same day, 19 June 1625, to the consuls of Marseille confirms the sending of Napollon (72r). A letter of Cesy to Napollon telling him of the plan to send him to Barbary has the date "1625" next to "Au Sr Napollon" (73r). PBN, MS. F.fr. 16164.

15. PBN, MS. F.fr. 16164, ff. 76–110.

16. PBN, MS. Lat. 8957, f. 110r.

17. For instance, Peiresc to Gazille, 7 April 1627, CBI, MS. 1873, f. 461r, specified "en la maison de Mons.r Napollon a Marseille."

18. Peiresc to Napollon, 12 August 1627, CBI, MS. 1873, f. 461v.

19. Cited in Kaiser, "Le rachat de captifs au Maghreb," 521.

20. Peiresc to Napollon, 6 November 1627, CBI, MS. 1873, f. 463r.

21. Peiresc to Gazille, 16 May 1629, CBI, MS. 1873, f. 468r.

22. Peiresc to Napollon, 6 November 1627, CBI, MS. 1873, f. 463r.

23. Treaty of Algiers and France, 18 September 1628 (ff. 91–93), Napollon's "Verbal de la négociation du traitté d'Alger," 17 September–1 October 1628 (ff. 95–99v). A copy of the latter is PBN, MS. Dupuy 429, ff. 139–148.

24. Mustafa to Napollon, 29 May 1628, CBI, MS. 1777, f. 107; Amoda to Napollon, 1 February 1629, CBI, MS. 1777, ff. 111, 113. The colophon to these last adds that the translations by Honoré Suffin in Marseille were done on 4 April.

25. Bechar Bassa to Napollon, 5 May 1629, PBN, MS. Dupuy 429, f. 149.

26. CBI, MS. 1777, f. 103r. The captains plying the route to Genoa and Livorno were Patron Fabiano, Patron du Mas, and Patron Matau of Toulon.

27. *Bastion de France* I (1929), 7–11; *Bastion de France* 7 (1932), 311–318. Both originals are in PBN, MS. F.fr. 16164.

28. The conflict between them broke into print in 1632. See "Responce des Consuls de Marseille, A une lettre qui leur a esté escripte par le Corse Sanson" (15. vi.1632), PBN, MS. F.fr. 16164, ff. 165–172.

29. Vergé-Franceschi, "Les Corses de Marseille du XVIe au XVIIIe siècle," 53.

15. Naturalizing Merchants

1. Peiresc to Piscatoris, 3 November 1629, CBI, MS. 1876, f. 359r. "Si M. le Lieutenant de l'Admirauté eust este a Marseille je luy eusse recommander votre affaire et si vous me faicte scavoir la . . . je tascheray de vous y rendre toute la recommandation qui pourra dependre de moy." Peiresc to Madame la Lieutenant de Valbelle, 6 November 1629, CBI, MS. 1876, f. 359v. Peiresc also wrote to the Advocat Berardy, who was the deputy of Valbelle, also on 6 November 1629, CBI, MS. 1876, f. 359v.

2. De l'Isle to Peiresc, 7 November 1633, CBI, MS. 1879, f. 225r.

3. Gazille to Peiresc, 30 January 1627, CBI, MS. 1879, f. 13r.

4. See Peter N. Miller, *Peiresc's Orient: Antiquarianism as Cultural History in the Seventeenth Century* (Farnham, UK: Ashgate, 2012), ch. 6.

5. Peiresc to Eschinard, 6? March 1623, CBI, MS. 1873, f. 327r. A letter from an official, perhaps in Secretary of State Loménie's office, confirmed to Eschinard that his children would have the rights of Frenchmen even though they were domiciled in Rome—rewarded for his service in the Mediterranean by denizenship across the Alps. Lucas to Eschinard, 13 April 1624, CBI, MS. 1873, f. 335v. In Peiresc's log of outgoing mail we find for 14 August a letter sent to M. Sceu, "Secretaire du roy" with "*la signature de* la pension d'*Eschinard.*" PBN, MS. N.a.f. 5169, f. 5v.

6. Peiresc to Guittard, 20 December 1626, CBI, MS. 1873, f. 648r; to Guittard, 8 April 1627, CBI, MS. 1873, f. 652v.

7. Peiresc to le Tenneur, 3 December 1628, CBI, MS. 1876, f. 327v. For Menestrier, see Aix-en-Provence, Arch. Departmentales, B 3347, f. 1270.

8. Peiresc to Issaultier, 1 December 1635, CBI, MS. 1874, f. 404v.

9. Peiresc to Marchand, 5 December 1636, CBI, MS. 1874, f. 577v; mémoire at f. 578r.

10. Peiresc to Gela, 18 August 1634, CBI, MS. 1874, f. 352v.

11. Peiresc to Magy, 6 December 1634, CBI, MS. 1874, f. 359v. "Et fault tire ce que vous pourrez par le moyen dudit Sr. Santo puis qu'il l'est declaré françois tout à faict, et qu'il me tesmoinge tant de bonne volonté."

12. Peiresc to Jean-Baptiste Magy, 21 January 1634, CBI, MS. 1874, f. 324v. "M. J'escriptz a M. le Lieutenant pour l'affaire que vous desiriez & ay escript à mon fre[re pour] recommander encore de vive voix."

13. Peiresc to Magy, 14 July 1633, CBI, MS. 1874, f. 313r.
14. Magy to Peiresc, 15 July 1633, CBI, MS. 1777, f. 374r.
15. In a letter to Aycard of 4 July 1633, Peiresc writes that Magy had lived in Cairo for ten years (CBI, MS. 1871, f. 34v).
16. Peiresc to Villeauxclercs, 8 July 1635, CBI, MS. 1876, f. 628v. "Il s'est employé en cez pais là a me faire recouvrer quelques vieux libvres escripts à la main que j'ay payez assez cherement mais dont neantmoins j'ay esté bien satisfaict & content."
17. Peiresc to Magy, 12 September 1635, CBI, MS. 1874, f. 360v; Peiresc to Jean-Baptiste Magy, 26 September 1635, CBI, MS. 1874, f. 388r.
18. Peiresc to Jean-Baptiste Magy, 29 September 1635, CBI, MS. 1874, f. 388v.
19. Peiresc to Jean-Baptiste Magy, 7 October 1635, CBI, MS. 1874, f. 393r.
20. Peiresc to Jean-Baptiste Magy, 12 October 1635, CBI, MS. 1874, f. 393bis r. The news was sent to Magy in Cairo in a letter of late October, indicating that the arrest was published on the 26th of the month, and the registration made in due formalities and the Cour des Finances signed off, waiting only for obtaining a "grace particuliere" (Peiresc to Magy, [26 October 1635], CBI, MS. 1874, f. 395r). Some preliminary papers must have reached Magy earlier, because he thanked Peiresc for the successful effort on his behalf in a letter of 29 October 1635 (Magy to Peiresc, 29 October 1635, PBN, MS. F.fr. 9542, f. 111r).
21. Gabriel Audisio, *Étranger au XVIe siècle: France, Provence, Apt* (Geneva: Droz, 2012), 193, 183, and more generally on Marseille 149–154.

16. North Africans in Marseille

1. Wolfgang Kaiser, "Les *Hommes de crédit* dans les rachats de captifs provençaux (XVIe–XVIIe siècles)," in *Le Commerce des captifs: Les Intermédiaires dans l'échange et le rachat des prisonniers en Méditerranée, XVe–XVIIIe siècle*, ed. Wolfgang Kaiser (Rome: École Française de Rome, 2008), 291n2.
2. De Brèves to Consuls of Marseille, 21 January 1617, MACC, J 1862, unpaginated.
3. Peiresc to Barclay, 3 July 1619, CBI, MS. 1872, f. 93v [= *Lettres de Peiresc*, 7:395]. Peiresc presented this public demonstration as the concluding act to the treaty negotiated by Guise with Algiers the previous year.
4. Vallavez to Peiresc, 29 December 1620, CBI, MS. 1878, f. 110r. For this, see Gillian Weiss, *Captives and Corsairs: France and Slavery in the Early Modern Mediterranean* (Stanford, CA: Stanford University Press, 2011), 16–17; Wolfgang Kaiser, "Asymétries méditerranéennes. Présence et circulation de marchands entre Alger, Tunis et Marseille," in *Les Musulmans dans l'histoire de l'Europe*, ed. Jocelyne Dakhlia and Bernard Vincent (Paris: Albin Michel, 2011), 429–435.
5. Vias to Peiresc, 15 February 1628, in *Les Correspondants de Peiresc*, 2 vols. (Geneva: Slatkine, 1972), 1:21–22.
6. Peiresc to Pelletier, 25 September 1627, CBI, MS. 1875, f. 221r.
7. Peiresc to de Thou, 12 February 1628, CBI, MS. 1876, f. 367v.
8. Vallavez to Peiresc, 11 April 1627, CBI, MS. 1878, f. 146v.
9. Peter N. Miller, *Peiresc's Orient: Antiquarianism as Cultural History in the Seventeenth Century* (Farnham, UK: Ashgate, 2012), 154.
10. CBI, MS. 1769, f. 349.

11. See Miller, *Peiresc's Orient,* ch. 3.

12. Peiresc to Berengier, 20 December 1630, CBI, MS. 1876, f. 810r. Peiresc speculated that it might have been the house of one "Centurion." We learn Berengier's first name from Lange Martin to Consuls of Marseille, 15 September 1629, MACC, J 1408, unpaginated.

13. Peiresc to Loménie, 8 August 1633, CBI, MS. 1874, f. 184v.

14. Peiresc to Mersenne, 16 July 1634, *Mersenne Correspondance,* 4:243.

17. Northerners in the Mediterranean

1. On the "Northern Invasion," see Fernand Braudel, *The Mediterranean and the Mediterranean World in the Age of Phillip II,* trans. Siân Reynolds (New York: Harper and Row, 1972), pt. 2, sec. III, ch. 3, "Trade and Transport: The Sailing Ships of the Atlantic"; Molly Greene, "Beyond the Northern Invasion: The Mediterranean in the Seventeenth Century," *Past and Present* 174 (2002): 42–71; Maria Fusaro, "After Braudel: A Reassessment of Mediterranean History between the Northern Invasion and the Caravane Maritime," in *Trade and Cultural Exchange in the Early Modern Mediterranean,* ed. Maria Fusaro, Colin Heywood, and Mohamed-Salah Omri (London: I. B. Tauris, 2010), 1–22.

2. I will not dwell on this here, as it is a theme that has been touched on in several of my essays on Peiresc's oriental studies. But it suffices as a place holder to note that when Peiresc was assembling books to send to Gédoyn, they included Greek books from England and Arabic ones from Holland (Peiresc to Aubery, 24 August 1629, CBI, MS. 1871, f. 54v).

3. "C'est pour venir au bout d'un desseing qu'ilz ont faict depuis 5 ou 6 ans qui est de ruyiner le negoce de notre nation pour relever d'aultant plus celluy de la leur n'ayant point de plus puissant obstacle que les françois." Montolieu to de Gastines, 14 February 1634, CBI, MS. 1777, f. 152r.

4. Vallavez to Peiresc, 19 November 1619, CBI, MS. 1878, f. 101r. "Et m'en a faict tesmoigner des ressentiment par des Anglois habitez à Marseille." On the English "colony" in Marseille, see Louis Bergasse, *Histoire du commerce de Marseille,* vol. 4: *1599–1660* (Paris: Plon, 1954), 124–125.

5. CBI, MS. 1777, f. 61r. The document lists 447 Dutch ships, 193 French [Atlantic and Mediterranean ports], 56 German, 278 Baltic, 60 English, 120 Spanish, 60 Provence-Languedoc. The document, tellingly, is dated 1621. Michel Fontenay, "Le Commerce des Occidentaux dans les échelles du Levant au XVIIe siècle," in *Relazioni economiche tra Europe e mondo Islamico secc. XIII–XVIII/Europe's Economic Relations with the Islamic World 13th–18th Centuries,* ed. Simonetta Cavaciocchi (Florence: Le Monnier, 2007), 525. Another estimate from Algiers gives 963 as the number of ships seized between 1613 and 1622, of which 447 were Dutch and 253 French (Godfrey Fisher, *Barbary Legend: War, Trade and Piracy in North Africa, 1415–1830* [Oxford: Clarendon Press, 1957], 190). I thank Wolfgang Kaiser for this reference. Gérard van Krieken says nothing about Marseille, or about anything North African other than Algiers, and nothing on the period 1628–1655. But for 1618 to 1620 he cites the seizure of more than a hundred Dutch ships; in 1620 they constituted

76 of 125 prizes (van Krieken, *Corsaires & marchands: Les Relations entre Alger et les Pays-Bas 1604–1830* [Paris: Bouchene, 2002 (1999)], 26).

6. Bergasse, *Histoire du commerce de Marseille*, 4:121. Two of these carried letters from Father Celestin to Peiresc (Celestin to Peiresc, 8 April 1636, PBN, MS. Lat. 9340, f. 205r).

7. CBI, MS. 1775, f. 40v. "Il nous auroit esté dit Que toutes les annees il aborde audit Tolon quinze ou vingt, et par fois trente vaisseaux flamandz chargez ordinairement d'harangz, merluches, guitran, graisses, plomb et autres choses semblable."

8. Peiresc to Valois, 1 January 1634, PBN, MS. N.a.f. 5172, f. 201v. "Mais vous verrez qu'il ne se contente pas de cela, ains traictant à la turquesque et à la mode du Bassa d'Aegypte qui a faict payer au François la banqueroutte d'un Suisse nommé Croy, pour ce qu'il parloit un peu françois aussy bien qu'Allemand."

9. The full title is "Advertissement qu'on donne touchant la navigation, trafic, pescheries, commerce qu'autres choses apartenantes à la mer du Nort et de la mer Oceane, & des Indes ou trafiquent & habitent les Rebelles de sa Majesté," CBI, MS. 1775, f. 110r.

10. Jonathan Israel, "The Phases of the Dutch *Staatsvaart* 1590–1713: A Chapter in the Economic History of the Mediterranean," *Tijdschrieft voor Geschiedenis* 99 (1986): 1–30.

11. Vallavez to Peiresc, 10 August 1621, CBI, MS. 1878, f. 119r; Peiresc to Vallavez, 25 May 1625, *Lettres de Peiresc*, 6:185.

12. Peiresc to Dupuy, 17 July 1627, *Lettres de Peiresc*, 1:296. When he eventually laid hands on his transcriptions from the thirteenth-century statutes of Marseille, he found nothing on shipwrecks. Peiresc to Dupuy, 2 August 1627, *Lettres de Peiresc*, 1:317. His probably referring to "Memoire de la forme & maniere que les officiers de l'Admirauté de la ville de Marseille ont accoustumé proceder au faict des naufrages, survenuz tant aux mers dudit marseille que autres lieu de la coste de Provence et Languedoc." CBI, MS. 1775, f. 140r. labeled *"ADMIRAULTÉ."*

13. Peiresc to Pierre Dupuy, 12 October 1626, *Lettres de Peiresc*, 1:76.

14. De Thou to Pierre Dupuy, 28 May 1628, PBN, MS. Dupuy 703, f. 125r.

15. Peiresc to Minuti, 9 April 1634, CBI, MS. 1874, f. 335r; Peiresc to de Loches, 9 April 1634, *Correspondance de Peiresc*, 37 [= CBI, MS. 1874, f. 335v].

16. Aycard to Peiresc, 8 March 1634, CBI, MS. 1821, f. 311r.

17. We know of "David Martin natif d'Amsterdam marchant habitué en ceste ville despuis dix sept ans ou environ age de trente huict ans ou environ" (PBN, MS. F.fr. 18593, f. 282r).

18. Peiresc to Boerio, 7 November 1635, CBI, MS. 1872, f. 407r. Ruts and Martin seem to have been involved in the Genoese trade (Peiresc to Boerio, 6 February 1636, CBI, MS. 1873, f. 408r). William was no doubt related to Thomas Vandestraten from Frankfurt, but living in Marseille for over forty years. PBN, MS. F.fr. 18593, f. 131r.

19. Peiresc to Boerio, 9 June 1637, CBI, MS. 1782, f. 412r.

20. For the Dutch trade in Marseille and Toulon, see Hermann Wätjen, *Die Niederländer im Mittelmeergebiet zur Zeit ihrer höchsten Machtstellung*. Abhandlungen zur Verkehrs- und Seegeschichte im Auftrage des hansischen Geschichtsvereins. Bd II (Berlin: Karl Curtis, 1909), 125–128.

21. Rubens to Pierre Dupuy, 20 April 1628, in *Correspondance de Rubens et documents épistolaires concernant sa vie et ses oeuvres,* ed. Charles Louis Ruelens and Max Rooses, 6 vols. (Antwerp: Veuve de Backer, 1887–1909), 4:435; Peiresc to Rubens, 1 June 1628, PBN, MS. N.a.f. 5172, f. 149v.

22. Peiresc to Rubens, 3 June 1625, PBN, MS N.a.f. 5172, f. 135r: "S'aspettano con grand'impatienza gli vassal[i] di Hollandi i Normandia."

23. Peiresc to Rubens, 10 August 1623, *Correspondance de Rubens,* 3:234. "Et per conto della vettura io credo che sara facilissima per via del mare soppra le navi che vanno di Holland a Marsiglia dove si puo faire il ricapita al Sr Gasparo Seguiran [*sic,* Signier] che havera cura di paragre il porto et farmi condurre a salvamento la casetta in Aix."

24. Rubens to Vallavez, 19 September 1625, *Correspondance de Rubens,* 3:387. "Non mancando in Anversa corrispondenza sicurissima con Marsiglia per farglila capitare al mio rischio."

25. Peiresc to Rubens, 11–12 February 1624, *Correspondance de Rubens,* 3:277. "Ma se V.S. vuol mandare alcuna cosa per mare come potrebbe essere la cassetta dello stromento del suo compare potra valersi del Sr Guil. van Steenwinckel d'Amsterdam, corrispondente delli Sg.i Baltasare Boyer et Abrah[am] Stayar di Marsiglia facendo la soprascritta a me, et a detti Sg.i Boyer et Stayar liquali mela manderano qui."

26. Baltasar Boyer and Abraham Stayar, Marseille, to Guillaume van Steenwinckel, Amsterdam, 4 February 1624, *Correspondance de Rubens,* 3:278. "Personnage de grand mérite et à qui [nous?] désirons extremement pouvoir rendre quelque digne service . . . de faire tenir en aggrégation quelques caissettes ou autre chose qu'il a cheminées par voye d'Amsterdam."

27. Peiresc to Steenwinckel, 4 February 1624, *Correspondance de Rubens,* 3:278.

28. Peiresc to Rubens, 31 March 1628, PBN, MS. N.a.f. 5172, ff. 143r–144r. Jan Nancelot was Dutch consul in Toulon around 1632. Wätjen, *Die Niederländer im Mittelmeergebiet zur Zeit ihrer höchsten Machtstellung,* 113. Peiresc to Rubens, 12 November 1627, PBN, MS. N.a.f. 5172, f. 143r. "S'hanno di ricapitare a V.S. in Anverza con la presente certi rami et legnami di lentisco, accennati per altra via, che saranno consegnati al capitan d'una nave flamente che sta hora di partenza nel porto di Tollone per andare a cotesta volta. Et farà la polizza di carica in Tollone il Sig.r Chaberto, con mentione del nome del cappitano suddetto et della quantità o peso di detti legnami, si come del tempo che sarà di partenza."

29. Peiresc to Rubens, 23 May 1625, *Correspondance de Rubens,* 3:359.

30. Peiresc to Mesnil Aubray, 18 September 1635, CBI, MS. 1874, f. 716v. "De ce costé la leurs lettres vont plus librement que de nostre et possible sans passer par tant de formalitez."

31. Peiresc to Loménie, 18 April 1634, CBI, MS. 1874, f. 190r.

32. Peiresc to Petit, 3 June 1635, CBI, MS. 1875, f. 275r.

33. See H.-D. de Grammont, *Relations entre la France & la Régence d'Alger au XVIIe siècle. Première partie: Les deux canons de Simon Dansa (1606–1628)* (Algiers: Adolphe Jourdan, 1879); Alexander H. de Groot, "Ottoman North Africa and the Dutch Republic in the Seventeenth and Eighteenth Centuries," *Revue de l'Occident musulman et de la Méditerranée* 39 (1985): 131–147.

34. Peiresc to Malherbe, 26 December 1609, CBI, MS. 1874, f. 499v; 4 November 1609, CBI, MS. 1874, f. 485r.

35. This was true on land as well. In a letter to Aycard, Peiresc compared the self-help of Provençaux negatively with that of the Protestants, who when allowed to build their own fortresses did, and were quite formidable. Peiresc to Aycard, 24 November 1622, CBI, MS. 1871, f. 54v.

36. De Thou to Dupuy, 5 August 1628, PBN, MS. Dupuy 703, f. 141r. As he himself exclaimed to Dupuy, though the waters off Alexandria were teeming with corsairs, "nos vaisseaux farançois sont si legers & si bons de la voile que j'espere que nous n'aurons point de disgrace de ce costé la." De Thou to Dupuy, PBM, MS. Dupuy 703, f. 158r.

37. Peiresc to Constans, 10 May 1636, CBI, MS. 1874, f. 418r: "J'aymeray mieux que vous me les envoyez par des Navires Flamans ou Anglois quand vous en aurez la commodité asseuree avec d'autres choses chargees pour Marseille que par des Provençaulx qui ne se scavent pas battre en mer, aussy peu allants a vuide comme faisoit Lombardon comme revenants chargez et ne scavent pas aller en flotte et de conserve comme les autres, mais quand vous non aurez pas d'autres que de Provencaulx, je ne suis d'advis que vous perdiez les occasions de me faire tenir ce que vous pourrez par eux a tout hazard s'ils pourrent arriver à bon port ou non."

38. Magy to Peiresc, 29 October or November 1635, PBN F.fr. 9542, ff. 110r–112v.

39. Peiresc to Magy, [probably 5 January 1635], CBI, MS. 1874, f. 363r.

40. Peiresc to Jean-Baptiste Magy, 13 May 1635, CBI, MS. 1874, f. 368r: "Patron Durbec pilot de Navire Anglois de M. de Gastines que debvoit partire le 17 Avril priant Dieu qu'il puisse." The letter to Jean Magy of 17 May follows (368r–v). By 28 May, Peiresc could write that Durbec's ship had made Livorno on the 20th, where it was being held for quarantine. Peiresc to Agathange de Vendôme, 28 May 1635, CBI, MS. 1874, f. 372v (from the postscript omitted in the printed edition).

41. Peiresc to Magy, 10 August 1635, CBI, MS. 1874, f. 382v. "Car encor que je n'eusse pas leur cognoissance particuliere et que leur humeur semble si rude & si brusque, elle voulu bien mieux que les notres par ce qu'ils sçauvent mieux combatte & disputir leur honneur leur facultez & leur vie . . . noz Provencaux ne sont pas si soigneaux & si jaloux."

42. Peiresc to Magy, 10 August 1635, CBI, MS. 1874, f. 382bis v. "Car cez gents là sont plus hardiz et plus aguerris que les notres et ne laisront pas dieu aydant de s'en acquitter aussy fidelement pour le moins si dieu voulu benie noz bons & Innocens souhaitz pour ce regard."

43. De Thou to Dupuy, 28 May 1628, PBN, MS. Dupuy 703, f. 124v.

44. Peiresc to Magy, 27 July 1636 CBI, MS. 1874, f. 421v.

45. Peiresc to Magy, 6 December 1634, CBI, MS. 1874, f. 359v; Peiresc to Jean-Baptiste Magy, 7 December 1634, CBI, MS. 1874, f. 357r.

46. Peiresc to Jean-Baptiste Magy, 24 December 1635, CBI, MS. 1874, f. 407bis r: "[le] vaisseau Angloys de Sr Gela."

47. MACC, J 1664, pp. 1–8. Among the merchants prominently named as using northern shipping was Jean Magy.

48. Martin to Consuls of Marseille, [1?] February 1628, MACC, J 1408, unpaginated. "Car les flamandz & anglois charter sur noz vaisseaux soit en allexandrette que allexandrie."

49. Martin to Consuls of Marseille, 11 April 1629, MACC, J 1408, unpaginated.

50. Peiresc to Minuti, 27 December 1633, CBI, MS. 1874, f. 321v. "Il faudroit quasi si pouvoir desguiser et trasformer en Angloys au lieu de francoys pour extorquer la recommandation cordiale et confidente, ce que vous ne scauriez non plus faire que de puisse . . . minister au lieu de prebtre et relligieux."

51. Peiresc to Aycard, 28 April 1634, CBI, MS. 1871, f. 42r.

52. Peiresc to Hazard, 26 August 1635, CBI, MS. 1874, f. 386r. "Sur une flotte Hollandoise qui est allée en ce pais la, capable de ruiner l'armée Turquesque et l'espagnol quand elles seroient jointes."

53. Peiresc to Constans, 16 August 1635, CBI, MS. 1874, f. 383v. The ship used by Ruts and Martin was the Dutch galleon *Bleu*, captained by P. Dol (Peiresc to Venture, 24 October 1635, CBI, MS. 1874, f. 393bis r).

54. Peiresc to Jean-Baptiste Magy, 5 November 1636, CBI, MS. 1874, f. 434r.

55. Peiresc to Magy, 7 December 1634, CBI, MS. 1874, f. 357r; Father Celestin, 16 August 1635, CBI, MS. 1874, f. 384r.

56. Peiresc to Pierre and Jean Constans, 5 January 1635, CBI, MS. 1874, f. 360v.

57. Peiresc to "Le nom fu laissé en blanc," in Sidon, 20 August 1635, CBI, MS. 1874, f. 385r: "Voir si pour s'en revenir il avoit besoing d'argent nous vous remboursserions trez voluntiers tout ce que vous trouveriez bon de luy fournir jusques a 100 et 200 piastres si besoing estoit en mon particulier, lesquelles je remboursseray punctuellement a Messrs Ruts et Martin avec les changes et proffits maritimes telles que l'argent pourroit porter au present voyage de cez navires flamands sur lesquelles j'aymerois bien mieux qu'il se peult embarquer à son retour que sur touts autres parce qu'ils sont plusieurs qui viennont de conserve et qui ne s'abandonnent jamais et scavent bien mieux combattre que noz Marseilleois." In a letter of 24 October 1635 to M. Venture, who was the Marseille-based contact for Constans in Aleppo, Peiresc asked after letters that were destined for Aleppo and were to be carried via Ruts and Martin, while another had told him that other letters for Aleppo had been sent via Sidon *by de Gastines*—suggesting that Gastines had some "commodité" for Sidon but not for Aleppo (CBI, MS. 1874, f. 389r). And there is at least one piece of evidence for the firm of Ruts and Martin, not Gastines or Lambert and Gastines, supplying Jean Magy in Egypt with cash (Peiresc to Magy, 25 May 1636, CBI, MS. 1874, f. 418v; Peiresc to Jean-Baptiste Magy, 2 June 1636, CBI, MS. 1874, f. 418v).

58. Peiresc to Galaup, 20 August 1633, CBI, MS. 1873, ff. 446r–v.

59. Procureur-Général Chasteuil to Ruts and Martin, 20 August 1633, CBI, MS. 1873, f. 446v.

60. Peiresc to Jean-Baptiste Magy, 5 April 1636, CBI, MS. 1874, f. 413r. "Mais depuis Noel que l'argent est en mains de mon ageant de Bordeaux il n'a peu trouver moyen de le faire remettre à Marseille par lettre de change, & j'avoys prié Messrs Ruts, & Martin de l'employer par le moyen de quelque marchand anglois de ses amys, de le faire venir de ce pays-la[,] vous priant de les en solliciter

pour faire souvenir s'il vous plaist pour voir si nous pourrions anticiper la venir de cez derniers qeu j'avois destinez à l'acquittement de votre part & autres du Levant. Et n y à que cez Angloys qui traffiquent de Bordeaux à Marseille."

61. Peiresc to Guillemin, 24 March 1636, *Lettres de Peiresc,* 5:187.

62. Peiresc to Guillemin, 20 May 1636, *Lettres de Peiresc,* 5:189. "C'est [*sic*] advis m'ayant esté donné par un marchand flamand qu'il falloit chercher à Marseille cette commodité de le faire remettre au pair par les Angloys, lesquels seuls y pouvoient trouver leur compte et que les aultres marchands ne le pouvoient faire sans droict de remise." They were still seeking a way as late as 29 July 1636 (*Lettres de Peiresc,* 5:194).

63. Peiresc to Guillemin, 12 August 1636, *Lettres de Peiresc,* 5:198.

64. Peiresc to Menestrier, 4 May 1634, *Lettres de Peiresc,* 5:703.

65. Peiresc to de Thou, 28 May 1635, CBI, MS. 1877, f. 449v. "C'est la verité qu'il n'appartient quasi plus qu'a eulx & aux Angloys de naviger puis que les autres se scavent si peu deffendre et m'imaginer que deshormais il faudra noliquer des Anglois & Flamandz pour negocier en Levant."

66. Peiresc to de Thou, 28 May 1635, CBI, MS. 1877, f. 449v. "Aussy que l'avoit faict cez moys passez Mr de Gastines qui nolisa si heureusement un Navire Angloys qui nonobstant la peste d'Alexandrie il est dieu mercy arrivée à bon port à Ligourne."

67. MACC, J 1664, pp. 1–10.

68. When the Dutch were sending their first ambassador to Algiers in 1622, he also went to Marseille, where he took ship for the crossing. Gérard van Krieden, *Corsaires et marchands: Les Relations entre Alger et les Pays-Bas 1604–1830* (n.p.: Éditions Bouchine, 2002 [1999]), 30.

69. Peiresc to Celestin, 16 August 1635, CBI, MS. 384r: "Que par noz navires francoys qui ne se battent pas si bien en Mer et ne scavent pas aller de conserve comme les flamands et principa[lement] durant la guerre d'Espagne." There was also the direct route from Aix to Paris, and then to Holland (Peiresc to Celestin, 29 April 1635, *Lettres de Peiresc* 7:855 [=CBI, MS. 1873, f. 42r]; the date is incorrectly given as 1633 in the printed edition). Sometimes Celestin employed Dutch ships to carry his mail to Marseille, and from there intended that it be sent overland by Peiresc (for instance, Peiresc to Celestin, 12 May 1636, CBI, MS. 1874, f. 410v).

70. Peiresc to Celestin, 12 May 1636, CBI, MS. 1874, f. 416v. "Que le Sr de Gastines avoit oublié de vous faire tenir avant un voyage par luy faict à Paris."

71. Peiresc to Celestin, 12 May 1636, CBI, MS. 1874, f. 416v. "Voyant si miserasblement interrompre le commerce que j'avois espere pouvoir entretenir entre vous et Mr votre frere plus seur et plus commode que partout autre voye . . . accidents que ne sont quasi pas esvitables. Car le Sr Venture pensoit avoir choisy le plus asseuré de touts les navires qui partoient en flotte avec Lombardon, et quasi soubs la protection d'icelluy, et toutesfois . . ."

72. Peiresc to Aubery de Mesnil, 18 September 1635, CBI, MS. 1874, f. 716v. "De ce costé la leurs lettres vont plus librement que de nostre et possible sans passer par tant de formalitez." His Chemsedin was sent overland from Marseille. Peiresc to Golius, 2 June 1636, *Lettres à Claude Saumaise,* 290.

73. Peiresc to Golius, 29 November 1636, *Lettres à Claude Saumaise,* 341. "Car durant quasi toute l'année, les Marseillois n'avoient expedié aulcun navire de ce costé là, ce qui l'avoit tenu en grande peine."

74. Celestin to Peiresc, 30 September 1636, ABM 205 (1023), 279. During this time he did, however, receive two letters from his brother—by way of Venice.

75. Magy to Peiresc, 29 October 1635, PBN, MS. F.fr. 9542, ff. 110r–v. "Et de plus que le pere Agatange m'en a donné le courage de le faire pour une consideration que dans le port n'y avoit aucun autre vaisseau, et à cause de la peste qu'estoit en ce temps sur ce pays peu d'esperance d'en venir d'autres et vostre ordre est que cy tost que ly aura quelque chosse preste de le vous envoier ce qu'avons faict . . . et vous qui avés tout pouvoir de me commander, vous direi que d'aussitost ay ressu lesdits livres le vous ay envoyés pour ne manquer a voz commandementz" (f. 111r).

76. Peiresc to Magy, 27 July 1636 CBI, MS. 1874, f. 422r. "& sur la plaincte que je vous avois faict de ce que le Grand Volume du Psaultier avoit esté hazardé sur Patron Baille sont veritablement je n'avois pas de raison de me plaindre si ceste commodité là s'estoit presenter la premiere, mais vous ne vous souvenez pas bien que par le Navire Anglois vous m'escripvistes que l'on avoit appresté pour m'envoyer tant ledit Psautier que les 4. Evangiles que vous me pouvez vous re-souldre de me faire tenir par des gentz si rebarbatifz comme estoient cez Anglois. Et puis par Apostille ou en un billet adjoustastes qu'en fin à la persuasion du R. P. Agathange et contre votre propre sentiment vous hazardez par ceste voye là le volume des 4. Evangiles et touteffois je vous avois prié par les mesmes Angloys de m'envoyer par eux ce que pourriez desirer de sorte que cet ordre là estoit preferable à tout autre consideration, & si l'eussiez suivy vous n'eussiez pas aprez eu occasion de vous servir de la commodité du patron Baille qui s'estoit desia monstrée bien malheureuse puis qu'il avoit laissé perdre ma balle de livres sur le Nil en allant d'icy là et cela seul le debvoit exclure de tout autre employ pour mon compte et tout de mesme pour celle du Sr Hugon Bermond sy vous avez quelque chose en main a son despart puis que je desirerois que vous l'en feissiez porteur son retour par l'Italie ne vous en debvoit pas empescher at-tendu que c'estoit mon ordre et que j'avois choisy sa personne et sa fidelité outre qu'à ceste heure ses navires. . . . Italie en revenant d'Aegypte. Et que de la il ne leur manque pas de bonnes commoditez de me faire tenir icy ce qu'en veuillent de sorte."

77. Peiresc to Magy, 8 August 1636, CBI, MS. 1874, f. 424v. "Navire flamand ou il ne pourroit pas courir de fortune comme sur les barques Marseilleises de ge-lines mouilliérs qui abbandonnent tout au premier coup de canon."

78. Peiresc to Magy, 24 December 1635, CBI, MS. 1874, f. 406r. "Mais j'ay eu de la peyne à tirer de luy ceste lettre tant les gents sont peu serviable, & peu officieux ayant bient trouvé *plus d'honnesteté en les Anglois qu'y vous avoit semblé sy rebar-batifs* quy prindrent le soing de me faire tenir de ligourne vos lettres & de *m'apporter fort fidellement le vollume des quatres evangiles* qui ma bien donné de la satisfaction & pourra m'en donner davantage à l'advenir."

79. Peiresc to Salicoffres (à Marseille), 9 March 1629, CBI, MS. 1876, f. 158r; Peiresc to Seghezzi, 6 December 1634, CBI, MS. 1874, f. 358r.

80. Peiresc to de Thou, 25 April 1629, CBI, MS. 1876, f. 354v. "Il y a long temps que ses superstitions de noz marinieres m'empeschent d'en faire apporter une bien entier & bien conservé comme j'avois des soignée . . . car ils faire mocquer de tous ces scrupules."

81. Peiresc to Salicoffres, 9 March 1629, CBI, MS. 1876, f. 158r. "Par le moyen de voz navires flamandaz dont les pilotes & cappitaines ne sont pas si scrupuleux que nos provenceaux."

82. Peiresc to Magy, 7 December 1634, CBI, SM. 1874, f. 357v. "Cez Angloys ne feroient pas tant de scrupule que les provencaulx de la charger sur les navires." This point was echoed in an exactly contemporary letter to Seghezzi (Peiresc to Seghezzi, 6 December 1634, CBI, MS. 1874, f. 358r).

83. Peiresc to Fernoux, 13 May 1629, CBI, MS. 1876, f. 158v.

84. Peiresc to Issaultier, 13 April 1630, CBI, MS. 1876, f. 799v.

18. Ship's Captains and *Patrons*

1. See most recently Ian Mclean, *Scholarship, Commerce, Religion: The Learned Book in the Age of Confessions, 1560–1630* (Cambridge, MA: Harvard University Press, 2012).

2. The exception is the sovereign treatment by Biagio Salvemini, "Storia e semantica di una 'professione': Appunti su *negozio* e *negozianti* a Bari fra Cinquecento e Ottocento," *Meridiana* 7 (1993): 43–111.

3. Bergasse notes that "captain" was used for vaisseaux, polacres, *galions, galères,* and *frégates,* while *"patron"* was employed on barques, tartanes, *felouques, pinques,* and bateaux. Louis Bergasse, *Histoire du commerce de Marseille,* vol. 4: *1599–1660* (Paris: Plon, 1954), 181.

4. Only the list of Marseille-based ships provides their names and those of their captains; from the other home ports only the type of ship is given (barque, polacre, etc.). CBI, MS. 1775, ff. 22r–24r. According to Morineau, the number of ships actively visiting the Levantine ports in the second half of the seventeenth century is more or less the same as early in the century. The number he gives is seventy-one. Michel Morineau, "Flots de commerce et trafics français en méditerranée au XVIIe siècle (jusqu'en 1669)," *XVIIe siècle* 86–87 (1970): 43.

19. Tasks Entrusted to Captains

1. Peiresc to de Thou, [6 September 1628], CBI, MS. 1876, f. 371r.

2. Peiresc to Lieutenant de Valbelle, 27 May 1629, CBI, MS. 1876, f. 356r.

3. Peiresc to Valbelle, 26 July 1629, CBI, MS. 1876, f. 357r.

4. Peiresc to Captain Roubaud, 26 July 1629, CBI, MS. 1876, f. 356v.

5. Peiresc to Roubaud, 1 August 1629, CBI, MS. 1876, f. 357r.

6. Minuti to Peiresc, 29 August 1629, PBN, MS. F.fr. 9542, f. 2v.

7. Peiresc to Bartolle, 6 November 1629, CBI, MS. 1876, f. 360r.

8. Peiresc to Bartolle, 6 November 1629, CBI, MS. 1876, f. 360v.

9. Peiresc to Gela, 29 May 1634, CBI, MS. 1874, f. 345r.

10. L'Empereur to de Thou, 31 May 1634, CBI, MS. 1777, f. 149r.

11. Peiresc to Petit, 21 March 1634 and 7 April 1634, CBI, MS. 1875, f. 268v.

12. Peiresc to Magy, 15 September 1634, CBI, MS. 1874, f. 355r.

13. Peiresc to Giovanni Alvise Gela, 22 February 1635, CBI, MS. 1874, f. 365v.

14. Peiresc to Aycard, 18 March 1634, CBI, MS. 1871, f. 41v. For this, see Peter N. Miller, *Peiresc's Orient: Antiquarianism as Cultural History in the Seventeenth Century* (Farnham, UK: Ashgate, 2012), ch. 10. But then it turned out that the navire *Ste. Anne* had arrived in a timely way at Siracusa, but with so much charged for Messina it had to go there. As it had to pass the quarantine, and as Messina was not capable of supporting this operation, the ship was forced to sail on to Livorno to do the quarantine, and then to return to Messina to unload, before finally setting course for Marseille. Peiresc to Petit, 6 March 1635 and 10 March 1635, CBI, MS. 1875, f. 273r.

15. For instance, Patron Paschal told Peiresc about a giant waterspout he saw in the Isles of Lerins. Peiresc to Granier, undated [after 26 February 1636], CBI, MS. 1873, f. 581v. Peiresc's information about currents and tides in the Mediterranean came largely from captains.

16. PBN, MS. F.fr. 9532, f. 266r.

17. CBI, MS. 1774, f. 386r.

20. Port Practices

1. "Il fauldrà proprement empacquetter le tout, et l'enfermer dans quelque boitte bien cachetté fagot ou casette addressée au sieur de Peiresc avec une enveloppe pardessus, addressée à Mr de Valbelle Con.er du Roy et lieutenant general de l'admiraulté, à Marseille, pour la faire tenir auditz Sr de Peyresc. & recommander la boitte, ou cassette, ou fagot, au Sr Estelle Consul à Seyde, ou bien aux autres consuls de la Nation qui se trouveront sur les lieux d'ou l'on vouldrà envoyer lesditz fagots, ensemble, aux Capitaines des Navires qui se chargeront de les apporter." CBI, MS. 1821, f. 486v ("Memoires pour les medailles & pierreries precieuses gravees, qui peuvent rechercher et recouvrer en Levant").

2. PBN, MS. Lat. 8957, f. 257r. A full tun contained 252 gallons.

3. The *Arret* of the Parlement of Provence of 10 January 1622 required all *patrons* and mariners returning from the Levant or North Africa to stop and establish their "patentes de santé" before being allowed to disembark. Quoted in Daniel Panzac, *Quarantaines et lazarets: L'Europe et la peste d'Orient (XVIIe–XXe siècles)* (Aix: Edisud, 1986), 33n7.

4. The standard work on the subject, Françoise Hildesheimer, *Le Bureau de la santé de Marseille sous l'ancien regime* (Marseille: Fédération Historique de Provence, 1980), notes that the archives of the Santé contain only two pieces earlier than 1647, and a third, from 1640, that is a list of the intendants (17). Working from departmental and communal archives, she offers a brief, deeper reconstruction of its history for the sixteenth and seventeenth centuries (18–20).

5. Peiresc to Minuti, 14 April 1630, CBI, MS. 1876, f. 800r. "Et afin de n'estre pas obligé a des purifications desditz livres & de voz mommies [*sic*], si la mer ne les a moullez, il seroit bon de les laisser dans leur premier emballage et de prendre

certifficat des intendentz des commerce & des consuls & intendants de la santé de Cassis comme on ne les à point desballez afin que en bruslant les enveloppes nous soyons quittes de toutes ces formalitez." We know, for example, that purification by vinegar destroyed two letters sent by Father Celestin in Aleppo to his brother Jacob Golius at Leiden, and their uncle, Jean Hemelaers, cathedral canon at Antwerp. Peiresc to Leonard Danmartin, 9 July 1635, CBI, MS. 1874, f. 374r.

6. Minuti to Peiresc, 14 April 1632, ABM, MS. 207 (1025), 251. "Deux boites, envelopées dans un sac de cuir scellées de mon sceau."

7. Peiresc to Jean-Baptiste Magy, 27 April 1634, CBI, MS. 1874, f. 339r. I am grateful to Jérôme Delatour for pointing out to me the definition contained in Magnien, *Dictionnaire des productions de la nature et de l'art, qui font l'objet du commerce de la France* (Paris: Antoine Bailleul, 1809), 2:772.

8. Peiresc to Dupuy, *Lettres de Peiresc,* 2:225–226. For a discussion of how items were labeled by medieval merchants, see Jessica Goldberg, *Trade and Institutions in the Medieval Mediterranean: The Geniza Merchants and Their Business World* (Cambridge: Cambridge University Press, 2012), 181.

9. Peiresc to de Thou, 29 April 1630, CBI, MS. 1876, f. 801v. The objects included one of the Samaritan Pentateuchs that Minuti acquired for Peiresc in the Levant. Peiresc to Minuti, 23 April 1630, CBI, MS. 1876, ff. 800r–v.

10. Peiresc to Minuti, 23 April 1630, CBI, MS. 1876, f. 800v.

11. Peiresc to Aycard, 24 October 1632, CBI, MS. 1871, f. 22v, referring to materials from Sidon carried by Sr. Issaultier.

12. Peiresc to [Dupuy], 30 June 1629?, CBI, MS. 1877, f. 225r.

13. Peiresc to Aycard, 14 August 1632, CBI, MS. 1871, f. 16r.

14. Peiresc to Aycard, undated and unfinished, but likely mid-August 1632, CBI, MS. 1871, f. 17r. "Tant pour sa personne que pour tout ce qui estoit chargé sur son navire & s'excuser sur la liberté du commerce de Constantinople."

15. Peiresc to Jean-Baptiste Magy, 28 May 1635, CBI, MS. 1874, f. 373r.

16. Peiresc to Constans, 22 November 1635, CBI, MS. 1874, f. 402v.

17. Peiresc to St. Jacob, 22 November 1635, CBI, MS. 1874, f. 404r.

18. Peiresc to Viguier, 22 November 1635, CBI, MS. 1874, f. 404r.

19. Peiresc to Issaultier, 15 May 1630, and Peiresc to Marquesi, 15 May 1630, CBI, MS. 1876, f. 802r.

20. Peiresc to de Thou, 5 June 1630, CBI, MS. 1876, f. 802v.

21. Peiresc to de Thou, 17 June 1630, CBI, MS. 1876, f. 804r. Giving the history of the outbreak in Cassis, Peiresc explained that the disease was confined to the Chateau for about forty days; after the first outbreak which he had told de Thou about, the alarm was really felt. And then all of a sudden there was an outbreak of five or six fatalities. At this point, everyone scattered who could, and all the ships as well, Jacques de Vendôme's included.

22. Peiresc to Vallavez at Lyon, 20 June 1630, CBI, MS. 1821, f. 466r. "Au Cartue de Ste Marthe de Mr Jean Roux dict le bonnestir ou il se retiré." This letter is not published in *Lettres de Peiresc.*

23. Peiresc to de Thou, 29 April 1630, CBI, MS. 1876, f. 801v. "De tres bonnes habitudes par tout l'Italie et Constantinople & quasi par toute la coste de la mer mediterranée."

24. Peiresc to Truillet, 11 June 1630, CBI, MS. 1876, f. 803r; 16 June 1630, CBI, MS. 1876, f. 803v.
25. Peiresc to Alfant [*sic*], 16 June 1630, CBI, MS. 1876, f. 804r.
26. Peiresc to Vicard [viguier and abbot of St. Victor at Sixfours], 16 June 1630, CBI, MS. 1876, f. 804r.
27. Peiresc to Castagnie, 24 June 1630, CBI, MS. 1876, f. 806r. Peiresc later learned that the plants were delivered to a Mazerac in Port Miou, the *calanque* adjacent to Cassis, and wrote with care instructions for the plants (Peiresc to Mazerac, 26 June 1630, CBI, MS. 1876, f. 806r).
28. Peiresc to de Thou, 17 June 1630, CBI, MS. 1876, f. 805v.
29. Peiresc to de Thou, 17 June 1630, CBI, MS. 1874, f. 804r. Letters to Truillet explaining what he wanted handed on to Jacques de Vendôme and where he wanted letters to be sent for de Gastines, Tarquet, and Bermond the Younger can be found at ff. 803v (16 June 1630) and 803r (11 June 1630).
30. Peiresc to M. le commandeur de Venterol a Malthe, 20 June 1630, CBI, MS. 1876, f. 806r.
31. Peiresc to Castagnier, 24 June 1630, CBI, MS. 1876, f. 806r.
32. Peiresc to Mazerac, "au Cartier de pourmieu prez de Cassis ou il est en quarantaine," 26 June 1630, CBI, MS. 1876, f. 806r.
33. Peiresc to Mazerac, 29 June 1630, and Peiresc to Truillet, 5 July 1630, CBI, MS. 1876, f. 806v.
34. Peiresc to de Thou, 30 June 1630, CBI, MS. 1876, f. 804v.
35. Peiresc to Estelle, 20 February 1630, CBI, MS. 1876, f. 797r. "Et a tous autres juges & officiers de la coste de ce pais ou lesditz navires pourroient abborder & descharger." Chabert is mentioned as early as 1627 (Peiresc to Lumaga, 22 September 1627, CBI, MS. 1874, f. 302r), and eleven letters from him to Peiresc are preserved from April 1627–December 1628 (CBI, MS. 1878, ff. 417–431).
36. Peiresc to Mazerac, 26 June 1630, CBI, MS. 1876, f. 806r.
37. Peiresc to Pelissier, 20 August 1631, CBI, MS. 1876, f. 815r.
38. Peiresc to Aycard, 20 February 1633, CBI, MS. 1871, f. 27r.
39. Peiresc to de Thou, 26 July 1630, CBI, MS. 1876, f. 807v. "Ce chetif lieu cy est maintenant devenu le grand chemin des postes, ou des routtes pour les Ambassadeurs de Rome, de Constantinople, (et si je l'osois dire) des Indes."

21. Setting Sail

1. Peiresc to de Thou, 16 December 1628, CBI, MS. 1876, f. 374v.
2. Peiresc to Emanuel da Costa Casseretz, 11 August 1630, CBI, MS. 1874, f. 11v.
3. Peiresc to Minuti, [23 August 1632], CBI, MS. 1876, f. 821r. In fact, there was a day's delay, which gave Peiresc time to write the long letter that followed.

22. Merchant Routes

1. Michael McCormick, *The Origins of the European Economy: Communication and Commerce 300–900* (Cambridge: Cambridge University Press, 2000), 502. Shockingly, there is no discussion of maritime routes in Georges Livet, *Histoire des routes & des transports en Europe* (Strasbourg: Presses Universitaires de Strasbourg, 2003).

2. Nicolas Bergier, *Histoire des Grands chemins de l'Empire Romain* (Paris, 1622). The dedication to Peiresc is at sig. ***4v.

3. Peiresc to Malherbe, 16 August 1609, CBI, MS. 1874, f. 478r.

4. Peiresc to Guez [in Marseille], 6 September 1628, CBI, MS. 1876, f. 372r.

5. CBI, MS. 1769, f. 242v.

6. A. Danmartin to Jerosme de Dorne, 29 March 1635, CBI, MS. 1777, f. 367r.

7. We can see this from the surviving volume of shipping insurance contracts from this period, MAD, 9 B 21.

8. CBI, MS. 1821, ff. 490–491v, "Memoires des plus jolies curiositez qui se peuvent recouvrer des Isles Canaries, et particulierement de celluy de Teneriffe, Madere, & du Fer."

9. Peiresc to M. de la Tuillerie, undated, CBI, MS. 1873, f. 425r: "Il y a de l'apparence qu'il seroit canal pour aller aborder en Sardaigne & se joindre a ceux d'Italie avant que revenir en nos coste."

10. Peiresc to Rubens, 2 June 1629, PBN, MS. F.fr. 5712, f. 152r.

11. Gastines to Peiresc, 18 June 1629, PBN, MS. F.fr. 9537, f. 312.

12. MAD, 9 B 21, f. 327v. "Faire canal sans toucher a Mourges ni a Villefranche." Panzac, by contrast, for the eighteenth century, describes "naviguer en droiture" as "très rare" (Daniel Panzac, *Commerce et navigation dans l'empire Ottoman à XVIIIe siècle* [Istanbul: Les Éditions Isis, 1996], 81).

13. François Galaup to Jean Galaup, 29 October 1631, in *Les Correspondants de Peiresc*, 2 vols. (Geneva: Slatkine, 1972), 2:329.

14. François Galaup to Jean Galaup, 29 October 1631, in *Les Correspondants de Peiresc*, 2:330; François Galaup to Jean Galaup, 11 September 1632, in *Les Correspondants de Peiresc*, 2:333. But Marcheville had made a side trip to Delos, as well, to see the ancient sculptures there.

15. Peiresc to Aycard, 5 October 1632, CBI, MS. 1871, f. 21r.

16. François Galaup to Jean Galaup, 11 September 1632, in *Les Correspondants de Peiresc*, 2:333–334.

17. Thus, Ambassador Marcheville's party reached Malta, and then some went via Rome and others headed directly for Marseille (Peiresc to Loménie, 25 July 1634, CBI, MS. 1874, f. 193r).

18. Peiresc to Malherbe, 4 November 1609, CBI, MS. 1874, f. 485v. Peiresc knew full well about caravans in Asia and Africa; for the latter, see the discussion of the "caravan d'Acroui" (Peiresc to Magy, 27 July 1636, CBI, MS. 1874, f. 421v). The "maritime caravan" of which much is now being written by maritime historians was something else, a feature of the late seventeenth and eighteenth centuries. Gilbert Buti defines the practice as a collective coastal tramping, or long-distance cabotage. He distinguishes this from a specifically Venetian or Maltese "caravan." See Buti, "Aller en caravane: Le Cabotage lointain en Méditerranée, XVIIe et XVIIIe siècles," *Revue d'histoire moderne et contemporaine* 52 (2005): 7–38; Buti, "La Caravane maritime provençale aux XVIIe et XVIIIe siècles: Un *voyage à l'aventure* organisé?," in *Stations navales et navigations organisées en Méditerranée*, ed. André Leroy and Christiane Villain-Gandossi (Ollioules: Nerthe, 2004), 135–150. Daniel Panzac, *La Caravane maritime: Marins et marchands ottomans en Méditerranée 1580–1830* (Paris: Éditions

du C.N.R.S., 2004), despite its title, is almost entirely focused on the later seventeenth and eighteenth centuries.

19. Peiresc to Tarquet, 7 November 1629, CBI, MS. 1876, f. 361r.

20. Peiresc to Gela, 27 February 1635, CBI, MS. 1874, f. 365v. The *Ste. Anne* eventually did arrive (Peiresc to Magy, 26 May 1635, CBI, MS. 1874, f. 372r).

21. Peiresc to de Thou, 31 July 1635, CBI, MS. 1877, f. 463r. The context for this is the Spanish seizure of the Isles de Lerins. De Thou himself used the phrase to describe the value of the English heavy ships (De Thou to Dupuy, 5 August 1628, PBN, MS. Dupuy 703, f. 140v).

22. Peiresc to Jacques Dupuy, 26 May 1636, *Lettres de Peiresc*, 3:682.

23. Peiresc to de Thou, 19 March 1635, CBI, MS. 1877, f. 413r. On the bottom of f. 413r begins "Instruction de l'Abbaye de St Honoré de Lerins," which continues on f. 435r and concludes on the bottom of that page. De Thou had asked for this information in his letter to Peiresc of 23 February 1635 (PBN, MS. F.fr. 9537, f. 354v).

24. CBI, MS. 1860, f. 337r.

23. Mapping the Mediterranean

1. While I am not entirely comfortable with David Abulafia's vision of global "Mediterraneans" (in *Rethinking the Mediterranean*, ed. William V. Harris [Oxford: Oxford University Press, 2005], 64–93), it is a very useful prompt for thinking. A version of this section was published as Peter N. Miller, "Mapping Peiresc's Mediterranean: Geography and Astronomy, 1610–1636," in *Observation in Early Modern Letters, 1500–1675: Epistolography and Epistemology in the Age of the Scientific Revolution*, ed. Dirk van Miert (Oxford: Warburg Institute Colloquia, 2013), 135–160.

2. For an account of the chronology of the production of the *Siderius Nuncius*, see Horst Bredekamp, *Galilei der Künstler: Die Sonne, Der Mond, Der Hand* (Berlin: Akademie Verlag, 2007).

3. Vallavez to Hondius, 17 March 1610, CBI, MS. 1874, f. 21r.

4. "Escrivant au lecteur que par singuliere affection à la Geographie Messrs. m'ont communiqué la chart susdicte, ou autrement j'useray quelque aultre moyen pour n'estre ingrat du faveur que Messieurs m'auront faits." Hondius to Vallavez, 26 August 1611, PBN, MS. F.fr. 9540, f. 166r. This was the heyday of Hondius as a globe manufacturer and as the continuator of Mercator's *Atlas*.

5. "Afin que joignant leur esloignement du poinct ou nous sommes en ce pais je peusse affirmer sans crainte a combien de degré de longitude nous sommes scitués et tirer de suite en suite par la difference du lieu ou nous sommes avec tout aultre lieu de la terre le vrai degré de longitude qu'il luy apartient; et par ce qu'il n'y a nation au monde laquelle fasse de si belles & illustres navigations que la vostre, je desirerois bien de sçavoyr s'il se prepare quelque voyage ou soyt d'employer personnes aulcunement entandues en geografie & cappables de nous rapporter deux ou troys vrayes observations de la hautteur du polle aux Azores et d'une aultre choze quy n'est pas plus difficille apprandre que la hautteur polayre ensemble quelque estimation semblable faicte au cap de Bonne

Esperance & en quelques aultres endroiz de la terre de plus cignallés d'aultant que je leur fayrois tenir des memoyres & instructions pour cest effect qui leur en renderoyent la recherche fort aisee & au retour vous pouroient vous assurer que de tous les lieux d'ou ilz me rapporteroyent des observations que je demande, j'en determineroys le vray degré de longitude." Peiresc to Hondius, 24 October 1611, CBI, MS. 1874, f. 22v. This compares very closely with the content of the well-known letter of Lancelot Voisin de la Popelinière to Joseph Scaliger of 4 January 1604, printed in Scaliger, *Epistres françoises,* ed. Jacob de Reves (Harderwijk, 1624) bk. 2, no. 70, 303–307. Scaliger seems to have been a focal point also for Guillaume le Nautonier, Geographer Royal to Henri IV, when seeking eclipse observation data for cartographic purposes, as in his letter to Scaliger of later February 1606, printed in Scaliger, *Epistres,* bk. 2, no. 68, 466–476. I thank Dirk van Miert for bringing these to my attention. There is now a new edition of these letters, *The Correspondence of Joseph Justus Scaliger,* ed. Paul Botley and Dirk Van Miert with Henk Jan de Jonge (Geneva: Droz, 2012,), 8 vols.

6. G. Bigourdan, *Histoire de l'astronomie d'observation et des observatoires: Première partie; De l'origine à la fondation de l'observatoire de Paris* (Paris: Gauthier-Villars et Cie., 1918), 44, describes the theory behind this.

7. Peiresc had him do some practice observing in Marseille in order—presumably— to check on his methods. This practice material, preserved by Peiresc, is entirely in Lombard's hand, and called by him "Observationes de Lombard," Peiresc adding "faictes a MARSEILLE." These were day-by-day observations, with drawings, of the relative positions of the Jovian system on the consecutive days of Friday, 25 November through Friday, 2 December 1611 (CBI, MS. 1803, ff. 262r, 265r). It is possible, of course, that Lombard arrived in Marseille a month before actually sailing in order to find passage and await propitious winds. Even so, the short distance between Marseille and Aix meant that oversight by the master would have still been possible.

8. CBI, MS. 1803, f. 251v.

9. CBI, MS. 1803, f. 254r: "Je vous ay faict 3 observations lesquelles je vous envoye." The letter is at f. 253v.

10. Lombard to Peiresc, 8 January 1612, CBI, MS. 1803, f. 254r: "Une ville bien forte a tout outrance et y a de beaux ports, et ramply de geans que ne s'adonnent que à la lubricité de ce monde."

11. CBI, MS. 1803, f. 255r.

12. CBI, MS. 1803, ff. 255v–257r.

13. CBI, MS. 1803, f. 261r.

14. "Et je vous assure que cella m'á fort degouste de aller naviger et sy dieu me faict la grace de retourner a nostre maison jamais la maire [*sic*] ne me tiendra plus a son sujet" (CBI, MS. 1803, f. 254r).

15. In pointing to precisely this conjunction of astronomy and geography in the seventeenth and eighteenth centuries, Peter Dear states the principle that the Lombard expedition so perfectly illustrates: "Place did not merely describe, as previously, *where* things were; place could now, perhaps, help to explain *why* things were." P. Dear, "Space, Revolution, and Science," in *Geography and Revolution,* ed. D. N. Livingstone and C. W. J. Withers (Chicago: University of Chicago Press, 2005), 27–42, at 40.

16. In all this we might take Peiresc as a paradigm of what has recently attracted notice: local geographies of the new science. See, for example, *Instruments, Travel and Science: Itineraries of Precision from the Seventeenth to the Twentieth Centuries*, ed. M.-N. Bourguet, C. Licoppe, and H. Otto Sibum (London: Routledge, 2002); D. N. Livingstone, *Putting Science in Its Place: Geographies of Scientific Knowledge* (Chicago: University of Chicago Press, 2003); *Spektakuläre Experimente: Praktiken der Evidenzproduktion im 17. Jahrhundert*, ed. H. Schramm, L. Schwarte, and J. Lazardzig (Berlin: Walter de Gruyter, 2006).

17. It has been a recent "discovery" of historians of science that the Mediterranean was "scientifically discovered" in the nineteenth century. *L'Invention scientifique de la Méditerranée: Égypte, Morée, Algérie*, ed. Marie-Noëlle Bouguet, Bernard Leptit, Daniel Nordman, and Maroula Sinarellis (Paris: Éditions de l'École des Hautes Études en Sciences Sociales, 1998).

18. "Parce que cela serviroit grandement pour regler la chronologie, et verifier si le calcul respond bien exactement à celuy que Ptolomée et les autres ont faict sur des pareilles observations au mesme lieu que vous estes, ou bien proche." Peiresc to Agathange de Vendôme, 17 May 1635, *Correspondance de Peiresc avec plusieurs Missionaires et Religieux de l'ordre des Capucins 1631–1637*, ed. P. Apollinaire de Valence [Paris: Picard, 1891], 137–138.

19. Labeled by Peiresc for filing purposes "636. 8 Juin. Instructions de M. Gassend au R. P. Ephrem de Nevers capucin et a Frère Alexandre d'Angoulesme pur les observations célestes," it was published by P. Humbert, "Un manuscrit inédit de Gassendi," *Revue des questions scientifiques* 53 (1934): 5–11.

20. We also possess letters written by Peiresc to individual correspondents reporting to them on the night's events, for instance, Peiresc to Luillier, 28 August 1635, CBI, MS. 1873, f. 269v; Peiresc to Naudé, 29 August 1635, CBI, MS. 1775, f. 12r. In a letter to Luillier of 12 January 1636, Peiresc reported on Gassendi's receipt of the local eclipse reports but not yet of the existence of a Gassendian recension of them (CBI, MS. 1873, f. 273v).

21. P. Gassendi, *Opera Omnia*, 6 vols. (Lyon, 1658), 6:85–90 (Gassendi to Diodati), 90 (Gassendi to Peiresc), and 4:274–280 (the astronomical diary).

22. CBI, MS. 1832, ff. 33r–35r at f. 33r.

23. Peiresc's letter to Athanasius Kircher of 8 October 1635 complaining about his shoddy technique has been published in *Lettres à Claude Saumaise*, 180–182n15. Similarly, Peiresc complained to one of the French merchants based in Aleppo about the poor results obtained by the Capuchin Father Michelange de Nantes there. Peiresc to Contour, CBI, MS. 1873, ff. 401v–402r.

24. Those observations made at Aix were by Peiresc, with assistance from Théophile Minuti, Antoine Agarrat, Simon Corberan, and Honoré Bouche, at Digne by Gassendi, at Paris by Ismail Boulliau, at Rome by Athanasius Kircher, Melchior Inchofer, and Gasparo Berti, at Naples by Camillo Glorioso and Juan Ladron de Guevarra, at Cairo by the Capuchin Agathange de Vendôme and his Venetian dragoman Giovanni Molino, and at Aleppo by the Discalced Carmelite Celestin de Sainte Lidwine, the Capuchin Michelange de Nantes, and the chancellor of the French merchant community, Baltasar Fabre. La Mothe le Vayer's secondhand account informed him of the Jesuit observation in Quebec. Gassendi to Diodati, 7 April 1636, CBI, MS.

1832, ff. 24–29. Gassendi's language in his *Commentarii* is identical (Gassendi, *Opera Omnia*, 4:275–280).

25. Gassendi to Peiresc, undated, CBI, MS 1832, f. 34v: "Alterum est, inde constare, quam nimis multum tabulae, chartaeque Geographicac omnes illa AE-gypti, ac Syriae loca a nobis removeant." This exact wording is found in Gassendi to Diodati, CBI, MS. 1832, f. 28v.

26. J. L. Heilbron, *The Sun in the Church: Cathedrals as Solar Observatories* (Cambridge, MA: Harvard University Press, 2001), pp. 74–75.

27. See Gassendi, *Solstitialis altitudo Massiliae seu proportio gnomonis ad solstitialem umbram observata Massiliae anno 1636, pro Wendelini voto*, in Gassendi, *Opera Omnia*, 4:523–536.

28. CBI, MS. 1832, f. 21r: "*1636*. Julii. P. GASSENDUS ad GOD.VENDELINUM DE SOLSTICIO MASSILIENSI et ECLIPSI LUNAE 28. Aug. *1635* ex qua convincitur Error in Tabulis Geographicis Leucarum 300 plus minus inter Massilam et Alexandrinum." Interestingly, Peiresc had excerpted *only* the part dealing with the implications for Mediterranean cartography, *not* the actual experiment performed in Marseille, indicating what was most important to him.

29. Peiresc to Jacques Dupuy, 12 August 1636, *Lettres de Peiresc*, 3:542.

30. CBI, MS. 1777, f. 366r. "Que *des Isles St. PIERRE a Marseille, les courant* de la mer les jettoient en ponant, et que les marinieres marseilloys, incistoient à donner une quarte a la droicte, pour s'en deffendre selon leur routtine."

31. Peiresc to Gassendi, 20 December 1633, *Lettres de Peiresc*, 4:394.

32. Peiresc similarly invokes the experience of mariners when trying to explain the phenomenon of hot winds at sea (Peiresc to La Hoguette, 6 September 1633, *Philippe Fortin de La Hoguette, Lettres aux frères Dupuy et à leur entouage [1623–1662]*, ed. Giuliano Ferretti, 2 vols. [Florence: Leo S. Olschki Editore,1997], 1:323–328; CBI, MS. 1809, ff. 182–183) and currents in the Mediterranean, "confirmé par noz matelots" (Peiresc to Pierre Dupuy, 9 January 1634, *Lettres de Peiresc*, 3:10).

33. Peiresc to Jacques Dupuy, 12 August 1636, *Lettres de Peiresc*, 3:542: "Au reste, les observations que Mr Gassend alla faire à Marseille dernierement et les instructions qu'il y print des mariniers plus experimentez, au faict de la navigation dans la Mediterranée, joinct aux observations que je fis faire de l'eclipse du moys d'aoust de l'année passée, tant en Alep et au Cayre qu'a Thunis, Naples, Rome, et ailleurs, luy a donné de quoy faire apparoir par bonnes et valables demonstrations d'une erreur en toutes noz cartes marines de plus de 2 ou 300 lieues d'entre Naples et la Palestine qu'il y a de trop dans les cartes, à quoy la routtine des mariniers avoit trouvé un remede dont ils n'avoient jamais sceu comprendre la cause et la raison." That Peiresc might have viewed this project as Gassendi's *in execution* is also registered in the fact that in the economy of his wider correspondence he left it to Gassendi to spread the news. See Peiresc to Cassiano dal Pozzo, 31 July 1636, postscript, *Peiresc: Lettres à Cassiano dal Pozzo*, ed. J.-F. Lhote and D. Joyal (Clermont-Ferrand: Adosa, 1989), 249.

34. Peiresc to d'Arcos, 20 July 1636, *Lettres de Peiresc*, 7:182; CBI, MS. 1871, ff. 380v–381r; autograph draft, PBN, MS. N.a.f. 5172, ff. 78r–79r: "Les plus experts mariniers de Marseille qui se trouverent à cette observation, et ceux mesmes qui

font les cartes marines estoient ravis, et quasi hors d'eux de voir resouldre si
facilement la difficulté qu'ils n'avoient jamais sceu entendre ne comprendre,
pourquoy il leur falloit donner un quart de vent à la gauche en leur course de
ponant en levant jusques en Candie, et deux quarts de la Candie en Cypre et par
de là, et qu'au retour il en falloit faire aultant et du mesme costé, dont vous
verrez la demonstration bien clair et bien facile en l'extraict que j'ay faict
transcrire pour l'amour de vous, d'une lettre de Mr Gassend to Wendelin."

35. Gassendi, *Opera Omnia*, 4:534–535.

36. This story of pilots' relying on experience to correct cartographic theory is an
exact parallel to the one told by Arndt Brendecke in *Imperio e información:
Funciones del saber en el dominio colonial español* (Frankfurt am Main:
Iberoamericana/Vervuert, 2012) [trans. of *Imperium und Empirie: Funktionen
des Wissens in der Spanischen Kolonialherrschaft*], 202–217: "La verdad de las
pilotos." I thank Biagio Salvemini for bringing this book to my attention.

37. There seem to have been both a Balthasar Claret and Balthasar Fabre in Aleppo
at the time. We possess a list of debts drawn up by Fabre in 1633. We also have
documents colophoned by Balthasar Claret with a subscription saying that they
were collated from the original materials in the Chancellery "by me, Balthasar
Fabre." MACC, J. 1736 [unfoliated]. When both the consul and vice-consul of
Egypt were absent, Fabre filled its function. See Fabre to Consuls of Marseille,
9 February 1633, MACC, J 548. Determining who Peiresc was actually referring
to is not straightforward.

38. Peiresc to d'Arcos, 20 July 1636, *Lettres de Peiresc*, 7:182 and CBI, MS. 1871, ff.
380v–381r.

39. Peiresc to Fabre, 21 May 1636, PBN, MS. N.a.f. 5172, f. 73r. "En pensant faillir
neantmoings ce leur sembloit quand ils donnoient une quarte à la gauche par
leur course de Malthe en Candie, et deux quartes du mesmes costé de la Candie
en Cypre. Et prattiquant à leur retour, le mesme proportion de la declination à
la gauche sans qu'il en peussent rendre, ne comprendre aulcune raison . . .
depuis que l'obligation de cette eclipse (telle qu'elle a peut estre faicte) à ouvert
le chemin a la cognoissance de cette verité auparavant incogneue durant tant de
siecles a faulte d'un homme qui eust eu la curiosité et le courage de faire observer
une eclipse en ce païs là, en mesme temps qu'en celuy cy. Au moyen de quoy
deshormais les cartes se pourront reparer et rendre si correctes que sans donner
cez quartes ou doubles quartes de vent a gauche, l'on pourra suivre les mesmes
routtes que la carte donnerà." See also Peiresc to Dupuy, 12 August 1636, *Lettres
de Peiresc*, 3:542–543.

40. Gassendi, *Mirrour*, year 1636, pp. 251–252. This is an abridged but in parts still
word-for-word version of the letter to Wendelin of 15 July 1636 whose concluding pages turn from the experiment of Pytheas to Mediterranean cartography: Gassendi, *Opera Omnia*, 4:532–534. Peiresc had himself written to Wendelin in May 1636, informing him of the important implications of the
observation for cartography (Peiresc to Wendelin, 18 May 1636, CBI, MS. 1876, f.
509r): "Ou vous verrez l'erreur de toutes les cartes geographiques, & globes ter-
restres en la scituation des lieux & proportions des distances beaucoup moindres
en effect qu'on ne les supposoit, puis qu'il s'en fait un grand tiers du chemin

entre cy & les pais du Levant. Je feray à l'advenir tous mes effortz pour en faire continuer les observations aux occurrences qui se pourroit presenter."

41. Peiresc to Holstenius, 2 July 1636, *Lettres de Peiresc*, 5:445.

42. In the August 1636 letter to Jacques Dupuy he asked him and his brother to look in Paris for two navigation manuals, the first by an unnamed Spaniard which he had been unable to locate, and the second the additional parts or volumes of Willem Janszoon Blaeu's extremely rare *Le Flambeau de la navigation, monstrant la description & delineation de toutes les costes & havres de la mer occidentale, septentrionale & orientale* (Amsterdam, 1620). Peiresc to Jacques Dupuy, 12 August 1636, *Lettres de Peiresc*, 3:543.

43. "Mind that in the nautical charts this island is located badly: it should be almost 100 miles farther south, because it is barely at 35 degrees latitude, which I have often proved myself using the astrolabe. Damiata, which lies exactly on a line south-north, is at 31 degrees, which is a difference of only 4 degrees—that equals 280 miles—and charts give Cyprus as 390 miles from Damiata. And this is why many ships have put to land between Rossetto and Damiata thinking, thanks to the charts, to be 100 miles away from where they actually are" (quoted in C. Astengo, "The Renaissance Chart Tradition in the Mediterranean," in *The History of Cartography*, vol. 3: *Cartography in The European Renaissance* [Chicago: University of Chicago Press, 2007], 196n129).

44. Astengo, "The Renaissance Chart Tradition," 196–197. The subsection "The Axis of the Mediterranean," 194–199, condenses "L'asse del Mediterraneo nella cartografia nautica dei secoli XVI e XVII," *Studi e ricerche di geografia* 18 (1995): 213–237. Bartolomeo Crescenzio discusses the problem in *Nautica Mediterranea* (Rome, 1602), 175–178.

45. Astengo, "The Renaissance Chart Tradition," subsection "Marseilles," 232–235.

46. J.-M. Homet, "Cartes marines," in *Rivages & terres de Provence: Cartographie d'une province,* ed. Mireille Pastoureau, Jean-Marie Homet, and Georges Pichard (Avignon: A. Barthélemy, 1991), 27–45, at 32: "Disparait la dernière génération des cartographes artistes et marins, cumulant un peu de science et beaucoup d'art. La genération suivante des 'géographes' sera celle des savants: astronomes voyageurs pour les grandes cartes du monde, des pilotes hydrographes pour les cartes régionales."

47. See Christopher Drew Armstrong, "Travel and Experience in the Mediterranean of Louis XV," in *Rethinking the Mediterranean*, ed. W. V. Harris (Oxford: Oxford University Press, 2005), 243–244, 246.

48. "Et j'estime que la pluspart des montagnes qui bordent toutes cez grandes mers suivent les mesmes allignementz à peu prez, et particulierement celle de vostre carte d'Affrique." Peiresc to d'Arcos, 30 May 1636, *Lettres de Peiresc*, 7:175.

49. There is no indication of authorship and it is currently impossible to establish this. D'Arcos is the obvious and likely source of these materials, though they are not mentioned in the surviving correspondence.

50. There are distinct views: a rough pencil sketch of the center city with Peiresc's inked-in identification of sites from classical ("Castra Scipionis") as well as modern history ("Byrsa," "Tunis") (CBI, MS. 1831, ff. 423v–424r); a finished, indexed drawing of the wider site of Tunis-Carthage (ff. 428r, 429r); a rough

sketch by Peiresc with his annotations identifying locations from the Roman siege of Carthage (f. 430v); and detailed maps of Tunis (ff. 431r, 432r).

51. CBI, MS. 1831, ff. 423v–424r; 430v. On the latter he notes the location of a causeway built by Scipio across the harbor.

52. Writing on the back of a very finished drawing of the site of Carthage, he wrote, "Ce dessein, ne s'est pas faict si iustement, que la faulte du papier, de l'ait fait reussir plus court tant soit peu qu'il ne devoit. Mais le II est fort iuste." CBI, MS. 1831, ff. 432v.

53. PBN, MS. Dupuy 663, f. 154r. "Il y a quelques difficultez pour accorder le dire des anciens autheurs avec le plan de Carthage qui a esté faict selon l'estat de present."

54. CBI, MS. 1831, f. 428.

55. PBN, MS. Dupuy 663, f. 154r. The memorandum is in fact keyed to the maps, referring to the scale indicated on the map and identifying a specific place, "ou elle est marquée dans le Plan" (154v). The author seems to claim authority of the map as well: "Car nous en eussions tiré le Plan de la forme desdicts Ports" (155v). The precise location of Tunis-Carthage so as to correct the bookish cartography is a main theme of the memorandum.

56. "De monter pour cet effect sur diverses montagnes ou collines plus eslevées d'alentour pour mieux recognoistre non seulement la conformation et figure des lieux, mais à peu prez la proportion des distances, *et symmetrie* qu'il y peult avoir, possible beaucoup *plus semblable que le griffonement cy joint, à un vase tel qu'Aristide avoit choisy pour le comparer.*" Aristides devoted six orations to Smyrna; the passage Peiresc refers to is in Oration XVII, the so-called first Smyrnaean Oration (Aelius Aristides, *The Complete Works*, 2 vols., ed. Charles A. Behr [Leiden: Brill, 1981], 2, 6) where the comparison is to "spouted bowls."

57. "Quadrent fort bien à ce que les orphevres & autres artisantz appellent goderons, à la circonference d'un plat ou d'un petit bassin . . . supposé que l'un & l'autre mot Grec & Latin soient prins en la propre signification des sources des ruisseaux & des rivieres, la plus part desquelles previennent de diverses veynes & surgeons, l'assemblage desquelz est capable de former une riviere & ruisseau environné en sa teste de plus ou moins grand nombre de moindre reuisseaux dont les particulieres souces breschent la terre qui borde la terreste de la riviere qui plus m . . . et rompantz la rondeur de ce bord par leur enfoncement dans le terrain, . . . forment la representation de divers petitz portz ou demy ronds pleins d'eau et la mesme figure des bassins goderonnez" (CBI, MS. 1809, ff. 169r–v). This is excerpted from Peiresc to Valois, 6 November 1633, PBN, MS. N.a.f. 5172, ff. 201v–202r [= CBI, MS. 1876, ff. 465r–v].

58. Elsewhere, Peiresc supplied Greek sources and etymologies, citing Isidore of Seville's *Etymologies* or *Origines* (bk. 2, ch. 6), PBN, MS. F.fr. 9532, f. 427r.

59. "Et d'aultant que nous appellons communement en langue françoise *un godet,* Ce que les anciens appelloient *poculum,* je ne scay si le mot de *Goderon* ne seroit point venu de quelque allusion ou diminutif de godet, comme si plusieurs petitz godetz, ou goderons assemblez, formoient un plus grand godet goderonné, ou bien environné de goderons ou de petitz godetz." CBI, MS. 1809, f. 169v.

60. "Ou vous prendrez plaisir de voir la grande conformité qu'ilz on avec un grand port environné de plusieurs petitz portz, quand elles sont remplies d'eau." Peiresc to Valois, 6 November 1633, PBN, MS. N.a.f. 5172, ff. 201v–202r [= CBI, MS. 1876, ff. 465r–v]. This part of a much longer letter is excerpted in MS. 1809, ff. 169–171, with the drawing of the port at f. 170r.

61. Peiresc to Villeauxclercs, 24 April 1637, CBI, MS. 1876, f. 631r. "En faire le desseing en taille doulce affin de confirmer la memoire plus vive & plus fideles de toutes les belles actions qui ont donné tant de reputation aux armies du Roy & aux ordres que sa Ma.té y avoit donnez."

62. David Jaffé, "Mellan and Peiresc," *Print Quarterly* 7 (1990): 168–175.

63. "Une belle grande Carthe du plain des Isles de Lerins avec tous les travaux tant des ennemys que des notres, & toute la disposition des armées navalles tant de sa Ma.té que des Ennemys." Peiresc to Villeauxclercs, 24 April 1637, CBI, MS. 1876, f. 631r.

64. Jules Lieure, *Jacques Callot: Catalogue raisonné de l'oeuvre gravé*, 2 vols. (San Francisco: Alan Wofsy Fine Arts, 1989 [1924–1927]), 26. The copy in the Cabinet des Estampes (Res.) of the Bibliothèque Nationale in Paris was believed unique.

65. Peter N. Miller, *Peiresc's "History of Provence": Antiquarianism and the Discovery of a Medieval Mediterranean,* Transactions of the American Philosophical Society 101, 3 (Philadelphia: American Philosophical Society, 2011), 49–53 and 56–61.

24. Sicily

1. Goethe, *Italian Journey, The Collected Works,* vol. 6, ed. Thomas P. Saine and Jeffrey L. Sammons (Princeton, NJ: Princeton University Press, 1989), 181.

2. Peiresc to Cassiano, 2 August 1635, in Peiresc, *Lettres à Cassiano dal Pozzo,* ed. Jean-François Lhote and Danielle Joyal (Clermont-Ferrand: Adosa, 1989), 197.

3. Menestrier to Peiresc, 19 December 1634, *Lettres de Peiresc,* 5:739–740, copy in CBI, MS. 1821, f. 70.

4. Peiresc to Menestrier, 1 February 1635, *Lettres de Peiresc,* 5:757–759.

5. Peiresc to Cassiano, 2 August 1635, *Lettres à Cassiano dal Pozzo,* 198–201.

6. Peiresc to Pierre Bourdelot, 21 March 1635, CBI, MS. 1821, ff. 221r–v.

7. The standard work on this project is David Freedberg (with Andrew Scott), *Fossil Woods and Other Geological Specimens: The Paper Museum of Cassiano dal Pozzo, Natural History Series, III* (London: Harvey Miller Publishers, 2000).

8. Peiresc to La Ferrière, 30 May 1635, CBI, MS. 1871, ff. 462v–463r. "Principalement s'il est veritable comme je le tiens qu'il s'y trouve bien prez des coquillages, et aultres petrifications maritimes pour en voir la situation, & posture dans le voysignage de ce boys si c'est a costé, & comme en mesme couche de Rocher ou de terrain comme niveau ou autrement ou bien plus hault ou plus bas que la veine ou sont les troncs de boys."

9. Peiresc to La Hoguette, 6 September 1633, Philippe Fortin de La Hoguette, *Lettres aux frères Dupuy et à leur entourage (1623–1662),* ed. Giuliano Ferretti, 2 vols. (Florence: Leo S. Olschki Editore, 1997), 1:323–324 (the original is CBI,

MS. 1809, ff 182–184v). "Mais ce que j'y trouve le plus estrange est de voir que le feu puisse venir de si profond, comme il fault qu'il vienne, puis qu'il a faict eslever des isles au milieu de la mer, et faict ouvrir des gueulles de feu au mitan d'icelles, comme on raconte d'aulcunes de celles de la mer de Naples aussy bien que de celle de la Grece. . . . Et sembleroient induire je ne sçay quelle necessité de correspondance de l'un à l'autre, par dessoubz le lict de la mer, puis que dans icelle se trouvent les isles bruslantes du Wulcan et de Stromboly." The Semien range does contain once-active volcanoes.

10. Peiresc to La Hoguette, 6 September 1633, La Hoguette, *Lettres,* 324. "Estant bien certain que leur chaleur provient du feu qui est par dessoubz, ainsy qu'il s'est veriffié aux bains de Pozzuolo à l'endroict desquelz s'ouvrit une gueulle de feu soubzsterrain au temps du pape Paul III, dont les baveures formerent une montagne bien haulte dans 24 heures, laquelle j'ay veue jusques au sommet où il est demeuré une forme de grand theatre ou de chauderon, dont la gueulle s'est refermée par le croulement des terres de ça et de là que les pluyes y ont trainées."

11. Peiresc's "Memoire des plus jolies curiositez qui se peuvent recouvrer des Isles Canaries, et particulierement de celles de Teneriffe, Madere, & du Fer" (CBI, MS. 1821, ff. 490–491) makes no mention of this history of volcanism, though it does show that Peiresc had thought seriously about the natural history of the Canaries.

12. Peiresc to La Hoguette, 6 September 1633, La Hoguette, *Lettres* 1:325. "Si tant est que la matiere où s'entretiennent cez feux sousterrains soit assez profonde dans la terre pour prendre quelque correspondance d'un lieu à l'autre, par dessoubz la mer Rouge, comm'il semble qu'il y en ayt du mont Aethna au Vesuve et aux autres lieux d'autour de Pozzuolo, aussy bien qu'avec le Vulcan et le Stromboli."

13. "Le feu a esté capable de pousser des montaignes et des isles nouvelles, où il s'ouvroit des souspiraulx de feu sousterrain embrasé par dessoubz la mer. Il se soit poussé de semblables montaignes ou enleveures par dedans le fondz de la mer d'entre la Sicile et la Syrie qui ne soient pas arrivées assez hault pour paroistre sur le niveau des ondes marines, et pour s'entr'ouvrir comme les autres" (Peiresc to La Hoguette, 6 September 1633, La Hoguette, *Lettres* 1:325). It was at Pozzuolo that Pomponio Leto found giant bones—showing how the argument had evolved in the century between them. Grafton, *What Was History? The Art of History in Early Modern Europe* (Cambridge: Cambridge University Press, 2007), 104.

14. "Lesquelles, estant heritées par le gros de la mer, agitées du siroc soient cappables d'imprimer quelque mouvement de compression dans les plus profondes entraillez de cez fournaises bruslantes, en sorte qu'elles en irritent le bruict et en augmentent la fumée et les flammes à leur gueulle, toutes et quantes fois que le vent syroc se met sus, et les fassent paroistre si long temps à l'advance comme l'on dict" (Peiresc to La Hoguette, 6 September 1633, La Hoguette, *Lettres* 1:325).

15. "Car le mariniers n'en ont point de signes plus certains que ceux là, ce disent ilz, et c'estoit vraysemblablement sur quelques pareilles experiences qu'estoit fondée l'ancienne fable du regne d'Aeole sur les ventz, s'il pouvoit en predire certainement quelques uns par telz signes de ces montagnes bruslantes, la cessation des quelz pouvoit induire la succession des ventz contraires selong la

commune vicissitude des choses de ce monde" (Peiresc to La Hoguette, 6 September 1633, La Hoguette, *Lettres* 1:325).

16. "Que s'il pouvoit estre loysible de supposer une communication soubsterraine aussy bien du mont Aetna, en ceux de la Grece et de la Palestine, qui ont bruslé ou produit des eaux chaudes, et avec ces autres d'autour de la mer Rouge, supposant aussy que telz feux, en fondant cez matieres grasses et bytumineuses se forment une crouste ou une espece de bource ou de fourreau capable de soustenir l'eau marine et de l'empescher d'entrer dans cez cavernes enflammées, comme la charge et froideur de l'eau pourroit empescher ce feu de percer telle crouste, si ce n'est par quelque accident extraordinaire" (Peiresc to La Hoguette, 6 September 1633, La Hoguette, *Lettres* 1:326).

17. "Il seroit bien plus facile de comprendre et de conceptvoir que la mer Mediterranée, se trouvant agitée du costé de la Syrie et portée vers la Sicile, fît une si grande charge sur cez antres ou cavernes enflammées couvertes de la mer, qu'elle y fist assez de compression pour en exprimer la fumée et les flammes et le bruict extraordinaire qui precede le vent syroc de certain temps plus ou moins long, selon que le vent est plus ou moins fort et impetueux. Car ce heurt de la mer, trouvant des matieres obeissantes en quelque façon pour la molesse ou graisse d'icelles et compriment le vuide sousterrain, en faict sortir comme par une syringue la fumée et les flammes et le bruict par les gueulles du mont Aethna, et de ceux du Vulcan et de Stromboli et autres, dont la fumée couvre incontinant la mer et est portée par le syroc subsequent jusques à nostre coste de Provence vers Frejus et les isles d'Yeres, jusqu'où elle conserve sa puanteur et noirceur" (Peiresc to La Hoguette, 6 September 1633, La Hoguette, *Lettres* 1:326).

18. "Et qui sçayt sy les eaux pareillement bruslantes ou bouillantes que la montagine vomit par diverses ouvertures laterales, qui formerent des torrents lesquelz firent des grands ravages et creusements des terres et noyerent des grandes campagnes, ne vindrent pas de ces eaux engloutties de ceste maniere comme des rivieres destournées, à ce qu'on presuppose." Peiresc to La Hoguette, 6 September 1633, La Hoguette, *Lettres* 1:327.

19. CBI, MS. 1821, f. 198.

20. "Je m'en approchay avec horreur et admiration et puis asseurer que ce que les oreilles oyent de ce terrestre Phlegeton, n'arrive pas a exprimer ce que les yeux voyent. La matiere qui coulle est comme le metail liquifié qui coulle de la fournaise pur faire une piece de fonte, fort rouge et fort ardante laquelle peu a peu s'endurcit a mesure qu'elle s'esloigne de son origine. C'est un meslange de fer de plomb, de terre, de sel, et de soufle. Je fus curieux de m'approcher a quattre doigts du fer, de jeter des pierres contre, et d'y plonger quelque piece de bois que s'allumé en peu de temps, et neantmoins c'estois esloigné de la source du feu deux lieues environ estant un peu dessus le grand Chesne ou la belle quercia (que V.R. pourra voir au plan que je luy envoyé et qu'elle portera s'il luy plaist de ma part au R.P. provincial quand elle ira a la congregation aprez qu'elle l'aura veu et faict voir au votres et a noz amys.) Le feu en cet endroict ou ie le consideriois avoit au moins 1000 pas de largeuer." Antoine Leal to P. Hugues Guile [rector of the Jesuit college at Aix], 18 March 1636, CBI, MS. 1810, f. 104v; another letter, of the same date, describes his tour of Sicily at greater length,

ff. 102–103; partial copy in CBI, MS. 1821, f. 270; additional full copy in PBN, MS. Dupuy 488, ff. 172–173.

21. Gassendi, *Mirrour*, year 1633, pp. 90–91.

22. Compare Montaigne, "On the Cannibals," in *Essays*, ed. M. A. Screech (Harmondsworth, UK: Penguin, 1990), 229–230; and Peiresc to Cassiano dal Pozzo, 2 August 1635, *Lettres à Cassiano dal Pozzo*, 199. In addition to Plato, *Timaeus*, see Ovid, *Metamorphoses*, XV, 315–345.

23. Yushi Ito, "Earth Science in the Scientific Revolution" (PhD diss., University of Melbourne, 1985); Ito, "Hooke's Cyclic Theory of the Earth in the Context of Seventeenth Century England," *British Journal for the History of Science* 21 (1988): 295–314; R. Rappaport, "Hooke on Earthquakes: Lectures, Strategy and Audience," *British Journal for the History of Science* 19 (1986): 129–146.

24. Richard Waller, ed., *Posthumous Works of Robert Hooke* (1705; facs. New York: Johnson Reprint Corp., 1969), p. 321. "There is no Coin can so well inform an Antiquary that there has been such or such a place subject to such a Prince, as these will certify a Natural Antiquary, that such and such places have been under the Water, that there have been such kinds of Animals, that there have been such and such preceding Alterations and Changes of the superficial Parts of the Earth: And methinks Providence does seem to have design'd these permanent shapes, as Monuments and Records to instruct succeeding Ages of what past in preceding. And these written in a more legible Character than the Hieroglyphicks of the ancient *Egyptians*, and on more lasting Monuments than those of their vast Pyramids and Obelisks. And I find that those that have well consider'd and study'd all the remarkable Circumstances to be met with at *Teneriffe* and *Fayale*, do no more doubt that those vast Pikes [*sic*] have been raised up by the Eruption of Fire out of their tops, than others that have survey'd the Pyramids of *Egypt*, or the Stones on *Salisbury* Plain do doubt that they have been the effects of Man's Labours."

25. People in Motion

1. Claudia Moatti and Wolfgang Kaiser, eds., *Gens de passage en Méditerranée de l'Antiquité à l'époque moderne: Procédures de contrôle et d'identification* (Paris: Maisonneuve & Larose, 2007); Moatti, ed., *La Mobilité de personnes en Méditerranée de l'Antiquité à l'époque moderne: Procédures de contrôle et documents d'identification* (Rome: École Française de Rome, 2004); E. Natalie Rothman, *Brokering Empire: Trans-Imperial Subjects between Venice and Istanbul* (Ithaca, NY: Cornell University Press, 2011); Bernard Heyberger and Chantal Verdeil, eds., *Hommes de l'entre-deux: Parcours individuels et portaits de groupes sur la frontière de la Méditerranée (XVIe–XXe siècles)* (Paris: Les Indes savantes, 2009).

2. The lists of possible goods to acquire were "Empreintes de diverses petites figurettes, placques . . . ou il s'en trouve a vendre communement au Grand Cayre" (CBI, MS. 1821, ff. 480–481); "Empreintes de mcdailles grecques & samaritaines antiques pour servir d'instruction au pere Minuti" (CBI, MS. 1821, f. 482); "Memoire sur les mommyes et les aultres curiositez Eegyptiennes qui se

peuvent rechercher au grand Cayre et ez environs" (CBI, MS. 1821, ff. 483–484); and "Memoires pour les medailles & pierreries precieuses gravees, que peuvent rechercher et rencontrer en Levant" (CBI, MS. 1821, ff. 486–487). These last two are in Peiresc's hand and parts are printed in Sidney Aufrère, *La Momie et la tempête: Nicolas-Claude Fabri de Peiresc et la "curiosité Égyptienne" en Provence au début du XVIIe siècle* (Avignon: Éditions A. Barthélemy, 1990), 172–177.

3. "Instructions baillées au R. P. Théophile Minuti s'en allant en Pellerinage à Hierusalem avec dessein de voir le Levant et l'Aegypte et les livres et autres curiositez qu'il désire faire avoir au Sieur de Peiresc son serviteur qui le supplie" (CBI, MS. 1821, ff. 488 489).

4. There is the fragment of a letter addressed to a [Mait]re [Dominiqu]e l'hoste," Lambert's *commis* in Cairo dated 14 July 1633, thanking him for the assistance he provided with acquiring a mummy and other antiquities in Egypt, as Peiresc had heard from Lambert, recently returned from there, and Minuti (CBI, MS. 1874, f. 311r).

5. Sr. le Gris died in 1634, providing a terminus ad quem to this memo (Peiresc to Magy, 15 September 1634, CBI, MS. 1874, f. 354v).

6. PBN, MS. N.a.f. 5174, ff. 25r–v.

7. CBI, MS. 1864, f. 256r. The original is printed in Aufrère, *La Momie et la Tempête*, 106–107.

8. CBI, MS. 1864, f. 257r. "Venitien qui ayme fort les francois, et est naturalisé, il demeure *au Caire*, il est *beau frere du Sr Gella* qui demeure a Marseille pres St Jaume de l'Espagne. Ce Santo Seguetti a tant d'habitudes dans l'Egypte qu'il y est plus puissant que le Basha et peut facilement faire recouvrere et a meilleur prix que nul aultre tout ce qu'il y a de curieux et particulierement *des livres* . . . il se fault adresser *a Mr Payen de Marseille* qui a son frere audit Marseille Patron de Polacre, qui a son trafic a Damas et fort curieuse. Et au cas que Mr Payen n'y fuit pas il y a *Mr Truc* qui supplera a son deffault. Il est maintenant a Marseille."

9. PBN, MS. Lat. 8957, f. 256v.

10. "*1636*. 22. Octobre/du RP LEONARD DE LA TOUR/et du RP MACLOU DE/Cappucins revenants du Levant/le P. Leonard ayant sesjourné xii ans/et a Scio viii ans." CBI, MS. 1777, f. 365r.

11. CBI, MS. 1777, f. 365r. "Le Sr STEPHANO GIUSTINIANO de Scio, qui est si fort accreditté sur les lieux, et qui à esté esclave du G.S. *avec des Angloys* qui avoient faict *le voyage de Moscovie par le lieu de la pesche des morües* que dans des barques couvertes de draps et de peaux oultre le boys et les Vitres pour se deffendre de l'extremité du froit . . . *que le nez gelé* en le moustrant a la grille et que *au vent froid,* succede un *vent si chaud qu'on estouffe.*" In addition to the memo's index, we know that Stefano Giustiniani of Chios was in Aix with the Capuchins for a legal case. The memo likely dates from that moment. Peiresc to Aycard, 31 October 1636, CBI, MS. 1871, f. 67v.

12. PBN, MS. Lat. 8957, f. 253r.

13. CBI, MS. 1821, f. 140r. "*Prince de Botera* qui a sa maison a *CASTELVETRAMO* a 25 milles de Palerme, a le plus riche cabinet d'antiquitez de toute la Sicile. Et estoit deputé en Espagne pour affaires reliques. Castel Vetramo est une grande villasse . . . le Sr Chartres y fut au temps des raisins au commancement du moys

d'Aoust avant la feste de Trapani de la my Aoust . . . Don *Joseph de Balsamo* Messinoys, deputé en Espagne pour la division del Regno, pour obtenir deux viceroys ou deux parlements. Fort curieux de Peintures, Desseins & medailles . . . Sr *Jacques Zagry* marchand a *Palerme* a Cassaro, marchand de vers Bordeaux marié sur les lieux qui fait Grand negoce, et est fort courtoys et officieux, traffique de Diamants de toutes choses, il est homme propre a faire vendre de cez oz de geant, il conservoit les deniers du Sr Chartres. . . . *Giacomo Maringo libraire de Palerme* al Cassaro, celuy qui a imprimé *le Paruta* et peult rendre raison de ce que sont devenus de ses memoires. Il a afforce medailles et autres curiositez." I am grateful to Biagio Salvemini for identification of the prince of Butera.

14. Peiresc to Gaffarel, 19 July 1633 and [13] October 1633, CBI, MS. 1873, f. 404r.

15. Peiresc to Schikard, 29 August 1634, [letter 5a, otherwise unpaginated], Württembergische Landesbibliothek, Stuttgart, MS. 563, f. [3]v.

16. On Iona, see the introduction in J. Carmignac, ed., *Évangiles de Matthieu et de Marc traduits en hébreu en 1668 par Giovanni Battista Iona retouchés en 1805 par Thomas Yeates* (Turnhout: Brepols, 1982).

17. *Monumentum Romanum,* ed. Jean-Jacques Bouchard (Rome, 1639), 89.

18. Aycard to Peiresc, 22 November 1633, CBI, MS. 1821, f. 85r. "Ce Granatin (qui est venu querir son pere)."

19. Aycard to Peiresc, 2 November 1633, CBI, MS. 1821, f. 89: "Je ay [*sic*] aprins toutes ces particularites de celuy que les a conduitz en ceste ville pour le Sr d'Arcos. Il ne m'en donne autres instructions que celles que ie vous ay envoyé par ma precedente." A major monograph-like essay on d'Arcos has just been published by Jocelyne Dakhlia, "Une archéologie du même et de l'autre: Thomas-Osman d'Arcos dans la Méditerranée du XVIIe siècle," in *Les Musulmans dans l'histoire de l'Europe,* ed. Jocelyne Dakhlia and Wolfgang Kaiser (Paris: Albin Michel, 2013), 2:61–163.

20. For a discussion, see Peter N. Miller, "Thinking with Thomas Browne: Sebald and the *Nachleben* of the Antiquarian," in *The World Proposed: Sir Thomas Browne,* ed. Reid Barbour and Claire Preston (Oxford: Oxford University Press, 2008), 311–312.

21. In a note to himself, Peiresc recorded that he received from Aycard of Toulon two chameleons in a crate on 18 October 1633 accompanied by a letter from d'Arcos written on 25 September and a copy of his "Histoire du commancement du monde." Peiresc added that he had earlier received another book "de sa facon," containing a "Relation des pais d'Affrique fort ample." Peiresc went on to note that the male died on 31 October and the female on 10 November. CBI, MS. 1821, f. 91r. See Paul Sebag, *Tunis au XVIIe siècle: Une cité barbaresque au temps de la course* (Paris: L'Harmattan, 1989), 50–52; Sadok Boubaker, *La Régence de Tunis au XVIIe siècle: Ses relations commerciales avec les ports de l'Europe méditerranéenne, Marseille et Livourne* (Zaghouan: Ceroma, 1987), 172–174.

22. CBI, MS. 1821, f. 89r. "*Mustapha de Cardennas* qui se dict *Roy des Andaluz,* ou Grenadins sortis d'Espagne, qui se tient à la *Bourombaille* maison de plaisance qu'il a bastie a six lieues de Tunis, et les Grenadins y ont faict village pour estre prez de luy en bon nombre. Son pere avoit esté tresorier des derniers Royaulx en

Espagne et prevoyant l'expulsion des Grenadins avoit envoyés es facultez de hors avec son fils à l'advance, du costé de Toulouse *Jacques Vallent du Martigues* a esté 4. ans esclave a la Bourombaille, *et disoit avoir trouvé en terre de cez Cameleons, en labourant la terre pour server du blé.*" Peiresc repeated all this in a letter to d'Arcos (Peiresc to d'Arcos, 25 January 1634, *Lettres de Peiresc,* 7:118 [= CBI, MS. 1871, f. 360r]).

23. Peiresc to Mersenne, 18 June 1634, *Mersenne Correspondance,* 4:180.

24. Mersenne to Peiresc, 2 July 1634, *Mersenne Correspondance,* 4:227.

25. CBI, MS. 1821, f. 127; PBN, Dupuy MS. 669, f. 81. Other sources were the captain, Patron Paschal, and the vice-consul in Algiers, Pion.

26. "At Constantinople, M. the Count Marcheville and the Captain Gilles of Marseille who piloted the ship *Dauphin* on which he returned, and who stayed in the port there for six full months on his last voyage, have attested to us as a well-known, indubitable, thing, and which one saw daily." PBN, MS. Dupuy 669, f. 83; Novel to Peiresc, 10 December 1633, in *Les Correspondants de Peiresc,* 2 vols. (Geneva: Slatkine, 1972), 2:699–700.

27. CBI, MS. 1777, f. 366r.

28. "Record a patron Paschal soubz l'adveu de Mr de Gastines de Marseilles." CBI, MS. 1821, f. 34r.

29. Peiresc to Bouchard, [early 1631], *Lettres de Peiresc,* 4:62. Peiresc got Galileo's *Discorso del flusso e reflusso,* written in 1616, in 1627. The theme comes up again in Galileo's *Dialogue on the Two Chief World Systems* (1634).

30. Peiresc to Galileo, 17 April 1635, CBI, MS. 1873, f. 450r [= *Galileo Opera,* ed. Antonio Favaro (Florence: Barbèra, 1890–1909; repr. 1929–1939 and 1964–1966), 16:261].

31. Peiresc to Seguiran, undated, CBI, MS. 1876, f. 163r. But since the Spanish fortified the islands in 1635, the letter must date from the end of 1634 or beginning of 1635.

32. There is a letter to "D. Severo di Napoli" dated 27 March 1632 that is sixteen folio pages long and might have been a printed text in the form of a letter, CBI, MS. 1821, ff. 178–193. It is preceded by a later note giving the titles of those three volumes with which it was bound: Giovan Bernardino Giuliano, *Trattato del monte di Vesuvio & de suoi incendii* (Naples, 1632); Pietro Castelli, *Incendio del monte Vesuvio* (Rome, 1632); F. Giulio Caesare Braccini, *Incendio fattoci nel Vesuvio a XVI. di decembrio 1631 e delle sue cause et d'effetti* (Napoli, 1632). Also, CBI, MS. 1821, f. 195: "De Incendiis Montium Aetnae ac Vesuvii." For a recent study of this eruption, see Sean Cocco, *Watching Vesuvius: A History of Science and Culture in Early Modern Italy* (Chicago: University of Chicago Press, 2014), ch. 2.

33. Aycard to Peiresc, 10 February 1632, CBI, MS. 1821, f. 266r, and 14 February 1632, f. 265r.

34. CBI, MS. 1864, f. 263r; CBI, MS. 1864, ff. 256r and 263v. Written to Philippe Fortin de la Hoguette, all of these were lumped together as "cez Marseilloys." Peiresc to La Hoguette, 6 September 1633, in *Philippe Fortin de La Hoguette, Lettres aux frères Dupuy et à leur entouage (1623–1662),* ed. Giuliano Ferretti, 2 vols. (Florence: Leo S. Olschki Editore, 1997), 1:323–328; CBI, MS. 1809, ff. 182–183.

35. On this, see Olivier Raveux, "Les Marchands orientaux et les langues occiden-
    tales au XVIIe siècle: L'exemple des Choffelins de Marseille," in *Langues et
    langages du commerce en Méditerranée et en Europe à l'époque moderne,* ed. Gil-
    bert Buti, Michèle Janin-Thivos, and Olivier Raveux (Aix: Presses Universitaires
    de Provence, 2013), 99–114.
36. These references were communicated to me privately by Dr. Raveux. I am
    grateful for his kindly assistance.
37. Peiresc, *Histoire abrégée de Provence & autres textes,* ed. Jacques Ferrier and
    Michel Feuillas (Avignon: Aubanel, 1982), 306–307.
38. PBN, MS. F.fr. 9530, f. 262r.
39. Peiresc to Aycard, 11 January 1633, CBI, MS. 1871, f. 26r. In a following letter,
    Peiresc asked Aycard to take two curious visiting Germans who wanted to see
    oranges to the gardens of some of his friends. Peiresc to Aycard, 27 January
    1633, CBI, MS. 1871, f. 26r.
40. Peiresc to Vallavez, 25 May 1625, *Lettres de Peiresc,* 6:186; Peiresc to Vallavez,
    14 June 1625, *Lettres de Peiresc,* 6:196–197; also Domenico Maiolo to Peiresc,
    16 May 1625 and 1 August 1625, CBI, MS. 1879, f. 327r.
41. Peiresc to Vallavez, 25 May 1625, *Lettres de Peiresc,* 6:187. Upon their departure
    they also carried letters from Peiresc to the lieutenants of Brignoles and Antibes
    on their behalf. PBN, MS. N.a.f. 5169, f. 13r, "15 May," spelled "Mayolo."
42. PBN, MS. N.a.f. 5169, f. 23r, 10 February 1627.
43. Fabritio Sbardoni to Peiresc, 3 December 1629, ABM, MS. 212 (1029), 98. His
    archive also preserves a questionnaire sent from Cassiano dal Pozzo on behalf
    of Giovanni Battista Ferrari seeking information about the oranges and lemons
    of Provence (PBN, MS. F.fr. 9542, f. 46r).
44. "Memoire delli Agrumi ou Orangeries, qui se peuvent recouvrer de Candie et
    possible de Reggio et de Naples," PBN, MS. Lat. 8957, ff. 257r–v. Dating is es-
    tablished by the next item in the archive, a letter to Michel Tourtel of 16 De-
    cember 1630 which mentions the preparation of the mémoire for immediate use
    (PBN, MS. Lat. 8957, f. 257v).
45. PBN, MS. N.a.f. 5169, f. 43r, 6 February 1630; on 7 May they carried a letter to
    Toulon.
46. PBN, MS. N.a.f. 5169, f. 46r, 9 February 1631.
47. Peiresc to Aycard, 12 February 1633, CBI, MS. 1871, f. 27r. This episode begins
    in a letter of Peiresc to Guillemin, 16 January 1633, *Lettres de Peiresc,* 5:106.
    Peiresc was a little skeptical as to whether the jasmine was really yellow jasmine
    or Indian jasmine, noting that it was he who had in fact introduced it to Italy
    ("Au reste vostre Marchand d'orengiers a beau vous asseurer des Jassemein
    jaulnes pour le moins de celluy des Indes qui est odorant car il n'y en a en tout
    de l'Italie que ceux J'en ey envoyé"); Peiresc to Aycard, 1 February 1633, CBI,
    MS. 1871, f. 26v. In his letter of 20 February, Peiresc noted that while he had
    received his orange trees, Domenico Drague "n'a point voulu bailler de son
    pretandu Jassemin Jaulne en sorte que nous ne scaurions juger s'il à dit vray ou
    non" (Peiresc to Aycard, 20 February 1633, CBI, MS. 1871, f. 27v).
48. Alvares to Peiresc, 18 November 1633, ABM, MS. 201 (1019), 357.
49. Peiresc to Guillemin, 16 January 1633, *Lettres de Peiresc,* 5:106.

50. Peiresc to Villeauxclercs, 5 December 1634, CBI, MS. 1876, f. 625r. "Le simple transito est fort favorable en matiere de commerce par toute la Chrestienté, et je seroys bien asseuré que ce bon homme n'en abusera nullement." The safe transit was duly received. Aix-en-Provence, Archives Départementales, B 3349, f. 940: "Permission à Domenico Majolo, natif de Maurizio (rivière de Genes) à expédier en Hollande et aux Pays-Bas quinze ou seize ballots d'orangers et autres arbustes et lui accordant libre transit, sauf l'obligation de faire vérifier au bureau de Lyon. St Germain-en-Laye, 15 Decembre 1634."

51. Peiresc to Boerio, 30 December 1634, CBI, MS. 1872, f. 401v. I am grateful to Biagio Salvemini for his discussion of these issues.

52. Peiresc to Villeauxclercs, 2 January 1635, CBI, MS. 1876, f. 625v; Peiresc to Villeauxclercs, 3 February 1635, CBI, MS. 1876, f. 627v.

53. He had earlier taken an interest in their fate when they had gotten caught up in the dragnet of the admiral of the Levant against Genoese shipping in 1625. Peiresc to Vallavez, 25 May 1625, *Lettres de Peiresc*, 6:187–188.

54. Peiresc to Galaup, 20 August 1633, CBI, MS. 1873, ff. 445v–446r. According to Peiresc he was the son of a brother of the mother of Gabriel Sionite and was the son of the Georgio son of Gamerio who was the uncle of the Amira who was the brother of his father [!]. Peiresc to Hazard, 26 August 1635, CBI, MS. 1874, f. 386r.

55. De Loches to Peiresc, 14 September 1635, PBN, MS. F.fr. 9541, f. 286v [= *Correspondance de Peiresc*, 175].

56. Peiresc to Sionite, 26 August 1635, CBI, MS. 1874, ff. 385r–v.

57. Peiresc to Hazard, 26 August 1635, CBI, MS. 1874, f. 386r. Eventually, Sionite warmed and Gamerio went to visit him in Paris (Peiresc to Sionite, 2 October 1635, CBI, MS. 1874, f. 392v).

58. Peiresc to Piscatoris, 12 October 1635, CBI, MS. 1874, f. 393bis r.

59. Sergio Gamerio to Peiresc, 23 February 1636, ABM, MS. 205 (1022), 62.

60. Peiresc to Luillier, 16 July 1635, CBI, MS. 1874, f. 267v.

61. Peiresc to La Ferrière, 14 August 1635, CBI, MS. 1872, f. 465r.

62. Peiresc to M. de la Tuillerie, 30 October 1634, CBI, MS. 1873, f. 414v. This is the first mention I have found of a Marseillais consul in Venice.

63. Peiresc to Gaffarel, 30 October 1634, CBI, MS. 1873, f. 415r.

64. Peiresc to Jacques Dupuy, 7 November 1634, CBI, MS. 1877, f. 402r. For the description—but not a first name—see CBI, MS. 1875, f. 754r.

65. Peiresc to Gaffarel, 29 December 1634, CBI, MS. 1873, f. 416r.

66. Peiresc to Gaffarel 28 [January] 1635, CBI, MS. 1873, ff. 416v–417r. "Aprez toutes cez petits finesses chettives dont il a usé." Part of the legal case was assisted by the fact that one of Peiresc's servants had mislaid it.

67. Peiresc to Piscatoris, 12 October 1635, CBI, MS. 1874, f. 393bis r.

68. Peiresc to Jerome de Dorne, 9 July 1635, CBI, MS. 1874, ff. 374r–v. "Au deffault de quoy ayant sceu que dans le desordre de la purification des marchandises du Levant arrivées sur les navires dernieres venez à Marseille (a cause du soupcon de la maladie contagieuse qui est en cez païs la) l'on avoir rencontré certaines petrifications et croustes de pierre asséz extravagantes qu'on disoit vous appartenir, j'euz la curiosité d'en demander la vëue, qui m'en fut fort courtoisement accordé de bonne foy."

69. Peiresc to Jerome de Dorne, 9 July 1635, CBI, MS. 1874, f. 374v. "Jugeant bien que cela à esté la plus part recueilly au rivage de quelque mer, soit la rouge ou autre plus esloigné ou de quelque rivière qui coul au long de montaignes metalliques ou cappables de la formation de pierres de la dureté, pesanteur et couleur des presentes."

70. Peiresc to Leonard Danmartin, 9 July 1635, CBI, MS. 1874, f. 374v. The rest of the letter reflects on the loss of Father Celestin's letters to his brother in Leiden and uncle in Antwerp during the purification process. Peiresc asked Danmartin "d'aultant que vous estes des intendants de la santé" to seek in detail after them since he might owe the sender money.

71. Peiresc to Danmartin, 21 July 1635, CBI, MS. 1873, f. 125r.

72. Peiresc to Danmartin[?], [late July 1635], CBI, MS. 1874, f. 379r. The item is marked as an insertion but the body of the letter seems missing, and perhaps was on the missing ff. 378–379.

73. Peiresc to Danmartin[?], [late July 1635], CBI, MS. 1874, f. 379r. The item is marked as an insertion but the body of the letter seems missing, and perhaps was on the missing ff. 378–379. The identification of the Turk as the Aleppan named Mattouk Chiasaan is in PBN, MS. F.fr. 9530, f. 119r.

74. MACC, J 745, preserves an "IOU" from Nicolas Crouset to Andre Venture dated 29 January 1632.

75. PBN, MS. F.fr. 9532, f. 43r.

76. Peiresc refers to him "being gone" to Marseille, from which he would return in three days (Peiresc to Petit, 3 June 1635, CBI, MS. 1875, f. 274v).

77. Peiresc to Petit, 3 June 1635, CBI, MS. 1875, f. 274v.

78. Peiresc to Mersenne, 5 May 1635, *Mersenne Correspondance*, 5:168. "Nous avons icy un Turc naturel, for intelligent, qui nous y eust peu donner quelque addresse aussy tost que tout aultre, lequel a esté en Perse et avec qui j'eusse employé un Provençal pour l'ayder et servir de truchement de ce qui ne seroit pas tant intelligible pour nous au discours de ce Turc."

79. Peiresc to Mersenne, 17 July 1635, *Mersenne Correspondance*, 5:316.

80. Peter N. Miller, *Peiresc's Orient: Antiquarianism as Cultural History in the Seventeenth Century* (Farnham, UK: Ashgate, 2012), ch. 3.

81. Peiresc to Jacques de Vendôme, 31 January 1636, CBI, MS. 1874, f. 410v. "Ce vaillant Capp.ne Maronite qui s'est rendu si celebre au service du pauvre Esmir Facardin."

82. D'Arcos to Peiresc, 30 June 1633, PBN, MS. F.fr. 9540, f. 83v [= *Les Correspondants de Peiresc*, 2:211].

83. The main lines of the plot can be recovered from Peiresc's letters to Cardinal Barberini of 18 May 1633 (Rome, BAV, MS. Barb.-Lat. 6503, f. 48r), 3 November 1633 (f. 70r), 4 October 1635 (ff. 153v–154r).

84. Gilles de Loches to Vallavez, 18 April 1638, ABM, MS. 206 (1024), 310.

85. Peiresc to Seghezzi, 14 May 1634, CBI, MS. 1874, f. 341r. A later letter to Gela suggests that Giorgio l'Armeno had made a long stay at Damiette (Peiresc to Gela, 14 May 1634, CBI, MS. 1874, f. 341v).

86. Cassien de Nantes to Peiresc, 7 September 1635, PBN, MS. F.fr. 9542, f. 197 [= *Correspondance de Peiresc avec plusieurs Missionaires et Religieux de l'ordre*

des Capucins 1631–1637, ed. Apollinaire de Valence (Paris: Alphonse Picard, 1891), 170].

87. Peiresc to Molino, 1 November 1636, CBI, MS. 1874, f. 432v. The eclipse observations arrived in Molino's letter of 27 June, long after the eclipse itself, which occurred on 28 August 1635. Taking the height of the sun at noon, especially on the solstice, made it possible to calculate the latitude most precisely, which was important if one's goal was to check information in ancient geographers like Ptolemy, who took Alexandria as his point of orientation.

88. Peiresc to Magy, 17 May 1635, CBI, MS. 1874, f. 368v.

89. CBI, MS. 1864, f. 256r.

90. Peiresc to Aquin Mustapha, 14 July 1633, CBI, MS. 1876, f. 829v.

91. "Sarebbe cosa degna di grand reflessioni se vi si incontrassero l'istessi accidenti in tempo medesimo, o non troppo lontanto l'un dall'altro, in tanta distanza de luoghi, et quantità d'aqua del mare che ne fanno la separatione" (CBI, MS. 1876, f. 830r).

92. "Con l'aiuto di quali si puonno sciogliere molte difficoltà et contradittioni fra gli authori antiqui che n'hanno trattato" (CBI, MS. 1876, f. 830r).

93. Peiresc to Mustapha, 14 July 1633, CBI, MS. 1876, f. 830r. "Havendo io per le mani un trattato de ponderibus & mensuris de gli antiqui, dove ho examinato con piu esatezza che non s'era fatto piu ancora tutte l'authorità prencipali delli scrittori antiqui Greci & Latini in questa natura et vi ho aggionto parecchi sperienze notabili & di molto rilievo." In a letter to Ehinger in Vienna, Peiresc even more precisely defined his work, explaining that "my research is very far from all that Arias Montano and the other moderns have written" because he worked from unpublished materials. Peiresc to Ehinger, 3 January 1634, quoted in Bresson, "Peiresc et le cercle humaniste d'Augsbourg," 254.

94. Peiresc to Barberini, 5 December 1634, Rome, BAV, MS. Barb.-Lat. 6503, f. 108v.

26. Ottoman Empire News

1. Peiresc to Malherbe, 25 May 1610, CBI, MS. 1874, f. 491v. "On a fait une information à Marseille sur le dire de tous les mariniers qui sont venus d'Espaigne."

2. CBI, MS. 1816, f. 487r; PBN, MS. Dupuy 429, f. 124r. On news, see John-Paul A. Ghobrial, *The Whispers of Cities: Information Flows in Istanbul, London, and Paris in the Age of William Trumbull* (Oxford: Oxford University Press, 2013); and Johann Petitjean, *L'Intelligence des choses: Une histoire de l'information entre Italie et Méditerranée, XVIe–XVIIe siècles* (Rome: École Française de Rome, 2013). For Venice, in particular, see Filippo di Vivo, *Information and Communication in Venice: Rethinking Early Modern Politics* (Oxford: Oxford University Press, 2007).

3. Césy to d'Herbault, 23.viii.1627, CBI, MS. Dupuy 772, ff. 145v, 126r.

4. CBI, MS. 1816, ff. 486r–v, 488; PBN, MS. Dupuy 429, f. 123r, "De Constantinople le 18. Mars 1628."

5. CBI, MS. ff. 44–59; PBN, Dupuy MS. 429, "Divers Memoires servans a l'histoire de Turquie," signed P. Dupuy 1636, ff. 103–115. The volume contains many items that would have come directly from Peiresc.

6. CBI, MS. 1777, ff. 66r–70v.

7. For example, CBI, MS. 1777, ff. 83r–v.

8. PBN, MS. Dupuy 429, f. 129. "Un vaisseau arrivé a Marseille parti de Smirne le 4e Mars rapporte qu'au mois de febvrier dernier a Constantinople, les Janissaires s'estantz mutinez. . . . Vous voyez comme c'est Empire vu à l'Empire par la desobeissance & rebellion. Et il semble que cez gents là sont sur le point d'exercer leur fer contre leurs propres entrailles, vous aurez sceu l'arrivé a Marseille de la Pelicorne chargé de bled."

9. Minuti to Peiresc, 7 September 1632, PBN, MS. F.fr. 9542, ff. 5r–7r.

10. CBI, MS. 1777, f. 117r. This is a copy of the section of Minuti's letter to Peiresc of 5 November 1632 that begins "Pour des nouvelles" (PBN, MS. F.fr. 9542, f. 9v).

11. PBN, MS. F.fr. 16163, "Memoires/Lettres, Instructions, Comptes ordonnances, ordres du Roy, Jugemens, Arrests &c/Touchant les debtes contractées par Mr de Cesy Amb.r a Constantinople pour l'affaire d'Alep. Contestations pour raison de ce entre ledit sieur et les Deputez de Marseille./Mesme pour le payement de ce qui luy estoit promis tous les ans par ceux de Marseille./Mémoires, lettres &c. touchant l'arrivee du Sr de Marcheville a Constantinople, son procedé durant son sejour, et son partement." See also MACC, J 1776, J 1840.

12. Peiresc to Gaffarel, 25 July 1634, CBI, MS. 1873, f. 412bis r. "Comme les deputez de Marseilles pour le payement des debtes de Mr de Cesy."

13. MACC, J 1810.

14. L'Empereur to de Thou, 5 May 1634, CBI, MS. 1777, f. 125r. The mustering of the Ottoman army was a constant topic of discussion in letters from Constantinople; see CBI, MS. 493, f. 173r.

15. L'Empereur to de Thou, 31 May 1634, CBI, MS. 1777, f. 149r.

16. For a scholarly overview, see P. Paolo Carali, *Fakhr ad-Din II Prencipe del Libano e la Corte di Toscana 1605–1635,* 2 vols. (Rome: Reale Accademia d'Italia 1936-XIV, vol. 1: *Introduzione storica, documenti europei e documenti orientali tradotti;* Michel Chebli, *Fakhreddine II Maan, Prince du Liban (1572–1635)* (Beirut: Publications de l'Université Libanaise, 1984 [1946]).

17. Minuti to Peiresc, 10 April 1633, PBN, MS. F.fr. 9542, f. 14r.

18. Minuti to Peiresc, 1 September 1633, PBN, MS. F.fr. 9542, f. 20r.

19. Minuti to Peiresc, 21 October 1633, PBN, MS. F.fr. 9542, f. 17v; Peiresc to Aycard, 17 December 1633, CBI, MS. 1871, f. 40r.

20. De l'Isle to Peiresc, 7 November 1633, CBI, MS. 1879, f. 223v.

21. Allemand to Minuti, [December 1634], CBI, MS. 1874, f. 274v. Excerpts from letters written from Sidon in December 1634 and January 1635 were grouped by Peiresc under the title "Esmir Facardin." CBI, MS. 1777, f. 120r.

22. CBI, MS. 493, ff. 260r, 272r.

23. Peiresc to Aycard, 1 October 1635, CBI, MS. 1871, f. 54r. We learn his first name in Jacques de Vendôme to Peiresc, 7 March 1636, PBN, MS. F.fr. 9542, f. 157v.

24. Peiresc to de Thou, 16 July 1635, CBI, MS. 1877, f. 461r. "Qui nous est confermé du costé de Cypre & de Seyde & de Smyrne."

25. For example, Peiresc to Loménie, 19 December 1633, CBI, MS. 1874, f. 187bis r; 10 January 1634, f. 187bis v; 28 March 1634, f. 189v; 28 October 1636, f. 225r.

Sometimes Peiresc would retail the same information to two correspondents on the same day, e.g., to de Thou and Loménie on 31 July 1635 about the taking of that valuable prize by Tuscan pirates (Peiresc to Loménie, 31 July 1635, CBI, MS. 1874, f. 209r).

26. Payment for the debts accumulated by Césy and de Marcheville was being enforced and disputed in the 1650s and for Marcheville in the 1640s (MACC, J 1775–1777). On the embassy, see Alastair Hamilton, "'To Divest the East of all Its Manuscripts and all Its Rarities': The Unfortunate Embassy of Henri Gournay de Marcheville," in *The Republic of Letters in the Levant* [= Intersections: Leiden Yearbook for Early Modern Studies], ed. Alastair Hamilton, Maurits H. van den Boogert, and Bart Westerweel (Leiden: Brill, 2005), 123–150.

27. PBN, MS. Dupuy 429, ff. 130r–131v. This volume contains many pieces that can be sourced to Peiresc, though there is no parallel copy in the Peiresc archive. Other reports from Constantinople are dated to 26 May 1632 (f. 132r), 14 March 1632 (f. 133r), and 11 January 1634 (f. 135r).

28. Peiresc to Aycard, 4 December 1633, CBI, MS. 1871, f. 38r. All Peiresc reported, though, was news of a particularly bad fire in Constantinople.

29. Peiresc to Minuti, 9 April 1634, CBI, MS. 1874, f. 334v.

30. D'Angusse had spoken to him in generalities of a plan for a tax to be raised at Marseille for *16 years* to eliminate Césy's debt (Peiresc to de Thou, 15 October 1635, CBI, MS. 1876, f. 380v).

31. Montolieu to Guez, 22 January/14 February 1634, CBI, MS. 1777, ff. 153r–155r; Montolieu to Gastines, 14 February 1634, CBI, MS. 1777, f. 152r; Montolieu to [Consuls of Marseille], 14 April and 4 May 1634, CBI, MS. 1777, ff. 144r–146v.

32. Peiresc to Minuti, 9 April 1634, CBI, MS. 1874, f. 334v.

33. Guez to Peiresc, 17 May 1634, CBI, MS. 1777, f. 156r; materials at 153–155.

34. L'Empereur to de Thou, 5 May 1634, CBI, MS. 1777, ff. 125r–126.

35. Montolieu to [Consuls of Marseille], 14 April 1634, CBI, MS. 1777, ff. 140–144; Montolieu to [Consuls of Marseille], 4 May 1634, CBI, MS. 1777, ff. 144r–146v; Montolieu to Guez, 22 January/14 February 1634, CBI, MS. 1777, ff. 153r–155.

36. Montolieu to de Gastines, 14 February 1634, CBI, MS. 1777, f. 152r.

37. Peiresc to Aycard, 29 March 1634, CBI, MS. 1871, f. 41v. A letter from Minuti of 9 April that arrived much later would have replaced one rumor of Marcheville's demise with another: "Mons.r de Marcheville avoit esté veritablement condamné à mort mais que sa vie avoit esté mise à ranson de cent mille piastres fournies par tout les ambassadeur Chrestiens et recouvrables sur toutes les nations de la Chrestienté qui ont commerce en ce pays la dont il y à de grande consolation a Marseille ou toute les gens de negoce maritime estoient perdus si la commerce est cessé si soudainement" (Peiresc to Minuti, 9 April 1634, CBI, MS. 1874, f. 335r).

38. Peiresc to de Thou, 28 August 1635, CBI, MS. 1876, f. 379r. "Toute les facilitez des françois ont esté saissy derechef en Constantinople pour les debtes du Mons.r de Cesi . . . la totale ruine du commerce de France non seulement en Constantinople mais par tout le Levant."

39. Peiresc to de Thou, 31 July 1635, CBI, 1877, f. 463r.

40. Minuti to Peiresc, 26 August 1633, PBN, MS. F.fr. 9542, f. 19v.

41. Peiresc to de Thou, 5 December 1634, CBI, MS. 1877, f. 408v.

42. Peiresc to de Thou, 25 September 1635, CBI, MS. 1876, f. 380r: "Les Angloys ont bien ruiné le negoce qui s'establissoit en la mer rouge."

43. Peiresc to Barberini, 5 December 1634, Rome, BAV, MS. Barb.-Lat. 6503, ff. 108r–v.

27. Time and Timings

1. Fernand Braudel, *The Mediterranean and the Mediterranean World in the Age of Phillip II,* trans. Siân Reynolds, 2 vols. (New York: Harper and Row, 1972), 1:366–367; Mario Scaduto, "La corrispondenza dei primi gesuiti e le poste italiane," *Archivum Historicum Societatis Iesu* 19 (1950): 237–253; Johann Petitjean, *L'Intelligence des choses: Une histoire de l'information entre Italie et Méditerranée (XVIe–XVIIe siècles)* (Rome: École Française de Rome, 2013), [ch. 6].

2. Peiresc to Holstenius, 9 April 1637, PBN, MS. 5172, f. 79r [= CBI, MS. 1873, f. 175r], omitted in *Lettres de Peiresc,* 5:473.

3. Minuti to Peiresc, 14 April 1632, ABM, MS. 207 (1025), 251. "Je ne l'estime pas si bon a la voile."

4. Federigo Melis, "Intensità, e regolarità nella diffusione dell'informazione economica generale nel Medieterraneo e in Occidente alla fine del Medioevo," in *Histoire économique du monde méditerranéen, 1450–1650: Mélanges Fernand Braudel* (Toulouse: Privat Éditeur, 1973), 405ff: Alexandria to Venice in thirty-eight days; Beirut to Venice in thirty-nine days; Alexandria to Genoa in forty-six days; Beirut to Barcelona in fifty-two days. In spring and fall the travel time from Alexandria to Venice dropped to thirty days.

5. Peiresc to de Thou, 29 March 1634, CBI, MS. 1877, f. 371v.

6. Estelle in Sidon wrote on 10 December that the book was going aboard ship (Estelle to Peiresc, 10 December 1629, CBI, MS. 1876, f. 793r), and Peiresc wrote that the book arrived in Marseille on 27 January 1630 (Peiresc to Tarquet, 27 January 1630, CBI, MS. 1876, f. 792v).

7. Peiresc to Aycard, 20 November 1632, CBI, MS. 1871, f. 17v.

8. Peiresc to Beaumont, 5 April 1633, CBI, MS. 1876, f. 825v.

9. Peiresc to Petit, 15 May 1635, CBI, MS. 1875, f. 274r.

10. Peiresc to Celestin, 22 November 1635, CBI, MS. 1874, f. 399r.

11. Peiresc to Marcheville, 24 April 1633, CBI, MS. 1876, f. 604v.

12. Peiresc to D'Avaulx, 16 June 1629, CBI, MS. 1871, f. 399r; de Thou to Peiresc, 30 May 1629, CBI, MS. 1777, f. 552r. In a letter to Louis Aubery of 1 June 1629, Peiresc explained further that de Thou had to wait twenty days in Malta for his onward passage (Peiresc to Aubery, CBI, MS. 1871, f. 507v).

13. Peiresc to de Thou, 8 January 1635, CBI, MS. 1877, f. 418v.

14. De Thou to Dupuy, 30 October 1628, PBN, MS. Dupuy 703, f. 145r. "Si le vent est favorable, la presente vous sera rendue dans peu de temps, car je l'envoie par l'occasion d'une barque qui part dans un jour ou deux, & quoi que ce lieu soit esloigné de Marseille de pres de mil lieües, si est ce que ce chemin la se fait quelquefois en moins de quinze jours."

15. Pierre Golius to Jacob Golius, 22 February 1636, ABM, MS. 205 (1023), 261.

16. Minuti to Peiresc, 20 July 1629, PBN, MS. F.fr. 9542, f. 1r. He notes that he arrived at Sidon on 28 June; we know that Peiresc was still writing to him on 3 June in Marseille.

17. François Galaup to Jean Galaup, 29 October 1631, in *Les Correspondants de Peiresc*, 2 vols. (Geneva: Slatkine, 1972), 2:329.

18. P. Adrian de la Brosse to P. Raphael de Nantes, 25 November 1629 (from Beirut), PBN, MS. N.a.f. 10220, f. 95.

19. P. Gilles de Loches to P. Raphael de Nantes, 15 December 1630 (from Cairo), PBN, MS. N.a.f. 10220, f. 103r.

20. Gilbert Buti, "Contrôles sanitaire et militaire dans les ports provençaux au XVIIIe siècle," in *Gens de passage en Méditerranée de l'Antiquité à l'époque moderne: Procédures de contrôle et d'identification,* ed. Claudia Moatti and Wolfgang Kaiser (Paris: Maisonneuve & Larose, 2007), 163.

21. See the figures in Yvelise Bernard, *L'Orient du XVIe siècle a travers les récits des voyageurs français: Regards portés sur la société Musulmane* (Paris: Éditions de l'Harmattan, 1988), 80–82. But note that while these were not the shortest travel times, most were longer, and not only those with combined land-sea itineraries.

22. François de Chateaubriand, *Itinéraire de Paris à Jérusalem et de Jérusalem à Paris,* ed. Jean-Claude Berchet (Paris: Gallimard, 2005), 483.

23. P. Michelange de Nantes to P. Raphael de Nantes, 24 January 1633 (from Aleppo), PBN, MS. N.a.f. 10220, f. 123r. Trivellato also gives forty days as the usual benchmark for a letter to go from Livorno to Aleppo (Francesca Trivellato, *The Familiarity of Strangers: The Sephardic Diaspora, Livorno, and Cross-Cultural Trade in the Early Modern Period* [New Haven, CT: Yale University Press, 2009], 258).

24. Peiresc to Aycard, 18 October 1636, CBI, MS. 1871, f. 66v.

25. De Thou to Peiresc, 7 July 1629, CBI, MS. 1777, f. 551r.

26. Pierre Hartzwick to Peiresc, 18 April 1631, CBI, MS. 1879, f. 154r.

27. Peiresc to Dupuy, 1 May 1634, *Lettres de Peiresc,* 3:95.

28. Peiresc to Holstenius, 29 August 1631, *Lettres de Peiresc,* 5:380.

29. Peiresc to Aycard, 7 September 1636, CBI, MS. 1876, f. 64r.

30. De Thou to Dupuy, 3 May 1629, PBN, MS. Dupuy 703, f. 161v; Peiresc to de Thou, 15 October 1635, CBI, MS. 1876, f. 380r.

31. Peiresc to Magy, 6 January 1635, CBI, MS. 1874, f. 363r. "Avec plus d'impatience que ne font les Juifs leur Messie."

32. Peiresc to de Loches, 20 March 1634, *Correspondance de Peiresc,* 33 [= CBI, MS. 1874, f. 334v]. "Ce qui facit apprehender quelque nouvelle avanie de ces Barbares."

33. Peiresc to Seghezzi, 14 May 1634, CBI, MS. 1874, f. 340v.

34. Peiresc to de Loches, 24 July 1634, *Correspondance de Peiresc,* 75 [= CBI, MS. 1874, f. 348v].

35. Peiresc to Minuti, 9 January 1634, CBI, MS. 1874, f. 324v: "Je ne scay si la nouvelle est croyable, car difficilement en pouvoir en avoir l'advis a la cour dans la fin de decembre si la chose estoit advenue depuis le 21 Novembre, si l'on n'avoit envoyé quelque courrier exprez."

36. For example, Peiresc to Boerio, 17 December 1634, CBI, MS. 1872, f. 391v.

37. Douglas Carruthers, "The Great Desert Caravan Route, Aleppo to Basra," *Geographical Journal* 52 (1918): 157–184, is charming, if dated.

38. Peiresc to Aycard, 5 February 1633, CBI, MS. 1871, f. 27r.

39. Peiresc to Aycard, 5 June 1633, CBI, MS. 1871, f. 31v; Minuti to Peiresc, 18 April 1633, PBN, MS. F.fr. 9542, f. 15r.

40. Peiresc to Aycard, 17 December 1633, CBI, MS. 1871, f. 40r.

41. Peiresc to Aycard, 18 March 1634, CBI, MS. 1871, f. 41v.

42. Tavernier thought it extraordinary that it took sixty-four days from Aleppo to Basora; Pietro della Valle needed sixty-nine days. Paul Masson, *Histoire du commerce français dans le Levant au XVIIe siècle* (Paris: Hachette, 1896), 376. Pedro Texeira took forty days of travel (not including forced stops), *The Travels of Pedro Texeira*, trans. William F. Sinclair (London: Hakluyt Society, 1902), xxii–xxiii.

43. CBI, MS. 1777, f. 390r. "*D'Alep* en Bassora par le desert en 33 jours/De *Bassorà* par mer à Muscat, en sept jours/De *Muscat a Ormes* par mer en une jour à peu prez./De *Muscat à Goa* on passe en 15 jours, a peu prez./De Goa on va à *Surate*, qui est un port du Mogor, ou à *Gaya*, qui est moings mercantile./De Gaya à *Lahor* y a 8 ou 10 jours de chemin. De Surate il y a moings." From the Poggio Bracciolini–Nicolo Conti account of travel to India, we can extract the following times: from Babylon, twenty days down the Euphrates, then eight days across country to Basra; four days from Basra to the Gulf; five days' sail to Calchon and then Hormuz; Hormuz to India, one hundred miles; thirty days' sail to "Cambay" in the second gulf beyond the mouth of the Indus; Scotora to Aden, fifteen days; Aden to Ethiopia (Berbera port), seven days; thirty days Berbera to Jidda. *Travelers in Disguise: Narratives of Eastern Travel by Poggio Bracciolini and Ludovico de Varthema*, trans. John Winter Jones, intro. Lincoln Davis Hammond (Cambridge, MA: Harvard University Press, 1963).

44. PBN, MS. F.fr. 9532, f. 42. "Du Cayre à la Meque en coute 35 journees à cheminer nuit & jour dans les deserts. de la Meque au Senan capitale du Hiemen quarante journees, & quarante journees pardelà à Moucal port de mer de l'Hiemen quinze journees [*sic*]."

45. Alvares to Peiresc, 12 June 1633, PBN, MS. F.fr. 9539, ff. 256r–v.

46. Alvares to Peiresc, 22 August 1633, PBN, MS. F.fr. 9539, f. 254v: "*Fernand Nunes est en le plus grand autorité dans le dealcan . . .* me disent de goa que *entierement gouverna ce Pais la.*" Note Peiresc's elaborate seventeen-point summary of the letter on the flyleaf (f. 255v).

47. Peiresc to Alvares, 9 October 1633, CBI, MS. 1871, f. 335r [omitted in *Lettres de Peiresc*]: "Comme j'ay la patience d'attendre des années entieres les advis des Indes, Je n'en doibz pas moins avoir pour attendre les advis de mes amys, lorsque leurs affaires leur peuvent permettre de se souvenir de moy. . . . Ce que je suis contrainct de pratticquer moy mesmes bien souvent a cause de mes infirmitez et indispositions, et des occupations que me donner ma charge, qui me ferois bien souvent de differe des sepmaines & des mois entieres ce que j'aymerois bien mieux avoir faict des le lendemain."

48. Peiresc to Minuti, 7 June 1633, CBI, MS. 1876, f. 827v. "Tant plus on s'esloignoit des pais de cognoissance et ou s'estend le commerce des provençaux."

49. Minuti to Peiresc, 20 July 1629, PBN, MS. F.fr. 9542, f. IV.
50. Peiresc to de Loches, 10 July 1634, *Correspondance de Peiresc*, 63 [= CBI, MS. 1874, f. 346v]. "Leur commerce y estant beaucoup plus frequent que ne peult estre le nostre. Ce qui ne peult pas estre du costé d'Affrique, où il ne tiendra qu'à nous de prendre pied si nous voulons, et d'y maintenir un commerce fort frequent et fort commode."

28. Corsairs

1. On the *course*, see the works of Salvatore Bono, Peter Earle, Michel Fontenay, Alberto Tenenti, Daniel Panzac, and most recently Molly Greene, *Catholic Pirates and Greek Merchants: A Maritime History of the Early Modern Mediterranean* (Princeton, NJ: Princeton University Press, 2011), and Gilbert Buti, ed., *Dictionnaire des corsairs* (Paris: Éditions CNRS, 2012).
2. Peiresc to Captain Roubaud, 26 July 1629, CBI, MS. 1876, f. 356v.
3. Molini to Peiresc, 22 July 1623, CBI, MS. 1879, ff. 352r–v.
4. For the French expeditions, see, for example, Peiresc's letters to Malherbe from the summer of 1609 (18 July 1609, CBI, MS. 1874, f. 473v; 25 July 1609, f. 476r; 16 August 1609, f. 478r).
5. "Divers Memoires Servans a l'Histoire de Turquie. ALGER," dated 1635. PBN, MS. Dupuy 429.
6. Peiresc to Loménie, 27 April 1628, CBI, MS. 1874, f. 154r.
7. Aubery to Peiresc, 12 May 1629, PBN, MS. F.fr. 9542, f. 25r. He lamented that one of them carried some of his cases.
8. Peiresc to Loménie, 6 December 1633, CBI, MS. 1874, f. 186v. It is worth noting the wider consequence mentioned by Peiresc: adducing a loss of of 25,000 écus on the ship, one of the investing merchants, "Saurier" declared bankruptcy. This cost his Marseillais colleagues 70,000 écus, but the total "ruin" was 120,000 écus including his "correspondances" in Lyon and beyond. Even bankruptcies are valuable maps of trade. A subsequent letter stated the total loss in the seizure of the *St. Lazare* at 50,000 écus (Peiresc to Loménie, undated [December 1633], CBI, MS. 1874, f. 187v).
9. Peiresc to Loménie, 9 June 1637, CBI, MS. 1874, f. 235r.
10. Peiresc to Gilles de Loches, 20 December 1633, CBI, MS. 1874, f. 318v. "Seigneur. que nonobstant dez que le Capt.ne francoys et patron Crivellier de la Ciottat se furent mis à la veille un de ses Corsaires se mit en . . . [même] temps a le suyvre ce qui occasionna ledit Mustafa Bey de saisir le General de ses Cor[saires] . . . mettre a la chaisne et de faire tirer les cannons du chateau sur lesdit corsaires en sorte . . . navires francoys eurent des moyens d'eschapper. depuis son arrivée le Consul Berm[ond] . . . /[Mssrs.] Agu et La Baye se sont recociliez dont on espere bien de soulagement de peu de [. . .]." This part of the letter is omitted from the part printed in *Correspondance de Peiresc*, and the date is there given incorrectly as 1631 instead of 1633.
11. Peiresc to Saumaise, 4 April 1634, quoted in Sidney Aufrère, *La Momie et la tempête: Nicolas-Claude Fabri de Peiresc et la "curiosité Égyptienne" en Provence au début du XVIIe siècle* (Avignon: Éditions A. Barthélemy, 1990), 67, citing

PBN, MS. F.fr. 22536, f. 68. The passage is not found in the letter published in *Lettres à Claude Saumaise,* which is based on the secretary's copy in CBI, MS. 1876.

12. Peiresc to Magy, 17 May 1635, CBI, MS. 1874, f. 368v. "Si cez desordres ne sont reparez il faudra abbandonner tout le negoce de Levant."

13. François Galaup to Jean Galaup, 11 September 1632, in *Les Correspondants de Peiresc,* 2 vols. (Geneva: Slatkine, 1972), 2:334.

14. Cassagnes to Peiresc, 27 December 1620, *Les Correspondants de Peiresc,* 2:732.

15. Minuti to Peiresc, 15 March 1633, PBN, MS. F.fr. 9542, ff. 11r–v. "Je promits au dit Martegan qu'il le payeroit mais il se mocqua de moy."

16. Minuti to Peiresc, 10 April 1633, PBN, MS. F.fr. 9542, f. 14r.

17. Peiresc to Minuti, 7 June 1633, CBI, MS. 1876, f. 828r.

18. Peiresc to Allemand, 7 June 1633, CBI, MS. 1876, f. 829r. "Quant au vol des voz bonnetz et des hardes du RP Théophile. J'employeray tout mon credit pour vous en faire tirer la raison soit du costé de Malthe ou de ce pais icy, au cas que voz corsaires y reviennent vous asseurant qu'ilz y seront receuz comme ils meritent. . . . Si nous scavons asseurement leurs noms qualitez et origine ou demeurant."

19. Peiresc to Aycard, 7 June 1633, CBI, MS. 1871, f. 31v [= *Lettres de Peiresc,* 7:300–301]. "Fut volé par une barque du Martigues armé en guerre soubz la banniere de Malthe, où il n'y avoit que 27 personnes, un venitien, un malthois, et le reste de Provençaux, dont le capitaine est, ce dict-on, de la Ciotat ou du Martigues mesmes, sans qu'il en aye peu apprendre le nom. Il estoit dans une barque toute chargée de mariniers chrestiens, grecs et maronites, et furent tous despouillez et laissez tous nudz en chemise sans rien pouvoir obtenir de ces volleurs, que son seul breviaire et mes memoires."

20. Peiresc to Aycard, 19 June 1633, CBI, MS. 1871, f. 33v.

21. Peiresc to Gaffarel, 28 November 1633, CBI, MS. 1873, ff. 408r–v. "J'ay creu vous devoir advertir que ce sont comme je pense de mauvais garnementz & bien indignes de ceste grace aussy bien que leur Capp.ne pour avoir exercé des inhumanitez & impietez non seulement envers des pauvres Chrestiens Grecz et Maronites qui estoient dans une saique [caïque] partir de Seyde l'année derniere pour aller en Cypre, laquelle ilz prendrent le 23 Novembre 1632 au Cap de St Andrea de Cypre vis a vis de la Caramanie et la pillierent et saccagerent a leur volonte et sans discretion quelconque. Mais ilz ne vouloient pas espargne un bon P. Minim Provencal nommé le P. Théophile Minuti que possible vous cognoissez comme il est bien cogneu par tout ce Levant, a qui ilz enlevent toutes ses hardes et le miennes chemises, a peine luy ayant laissé ses breviaire, un petit cahier de memoires qu'il avoit du moy, quelques protestations qu'il sceut faire de sa patrie, et bien qu'il fist apparence qu'une caisse de marchandises de bonnetz rouges qu'on luy avoient recommandé appartenent au Sr Iean Louys Allemand de Marseille et qu'elle debvoir estre consigné a un marchand venitien, aux salines de Cyprus, pour le comte dudit Allemand Provencal. Mais cez Canailles qui n'estoient que 27 en combien dont il n'y avoit qu'un Malthois & un Venitien tous les autres 25 estoient provençaux furent si desnaturez & impitoyable que les Turcz ne feurent pas si barbares qu'eux. Car ilz laissoient ce pauvre bon Pere

avec cez autres pauvres Grecs et Maronites exposez en son lieu desert sans vivres & mesmes sans eau que se peust boivre[,] leur ayant emporté jusques aux barrils. Tous lesquelz furent trois sepmaines a ne vivre que de champignons et autres choses que la terre leur pouvoit fournir honteusement ay cu grande peine de trouver seulement de l'eau, jusques à tenir que des Turcz qui passoient prez de là, envent pitié d'eulx et les en tirerent les ayant menez au lieu ou il y avoit de l'eau et leur ayant charitablement desparty de leurs vivres et donné moyen de prendre le chemin des lieux habité ou ilz trouverent du secours. Et le bon pere estoit passé pour la seconde fo[is?] en Levant, au service de Mr le Comte de Marcheville jusques en Constantinople. Et aprez quelques mois de sesiour en ceste grande ville estoit retourné du coste de Seyde & de la terre Ste pour y continuer des recherches de bons livres pour l'amour de moy, comme il en auroit desia tiré de bien rares et bien dignes d'estre conservez de son premiere voyage. . . . Croyant bien qu'il ne vous seroit pas difficile d'apprendre là le nom de ce marchand Venitien residant aux salines de Cypre et de son correspondant a Venise qui vous pourroit fournir plus de certitude des particularitez de l'affaire et de la qualité, nombre & valleur a peu prez de ceste marchandises dont je voudrois bien avoir faict faire la raison aux marchands pour en descharger de regret ce bon pere a qui le public est si redevable aussy bien que moy en mon particuliere."

22. Peiresc to Minuti, 20 February 1634, CBI, MS. 1874, f. 327r.

23. From the 1687 "Mémoire d'Ortières," quoted in Michel Fontenay, *La Méditerranée entre la Croix et le Croissant: Navigation, commerce, course et piraterie (XVIe–XIXe siècle)* (Paris: Classiques Garnier, 2012), 190; chart on 201.

29. Ransoming

1. For ransoming, see Wolfgang Kaiser, ed., *La Rançon* (Paris: Hypotheses, 2006), 343–358. For slavery and captives, see W. Kaiser, ed., *Le Commerce des captifs: Les Intermédiaires dans l'échange et le rachat des prisonniers en Méditerranée, XVe–XVIIIe siècle* (Rome: École Française de Rome, 2008); Giovanna Fiume, *Schiavitù mediterranee: Corsari, rinnegati e santi di età moderna* (Milan: Bruno Mondadori, 2009); Molly Greene, *Catholic Pirates and Greek Merchants: A Maritime History of the Early Modern Mediterranean* (Princeton, NJ: Princeton University Press, 2010); Gillian Weiss, *Captives and Corsairs: France and Slavery in the Early Modern Mediterranean* (Stanford, CA: Stanford University Press, 2011), and the references there.

2. CBI, MS. 1777, ff. 101–102, for the list of slaves redeemed by Napollon and f. 102bis with the amounts contributed by different Provençal towns toward a fund for randoming. Sadok Boubaker, "Réseaux et techniques de rachat des captifs de la course à Tunis au XVIIe siècle," in Kaiser, *Le Commerce des captifs*, 26–32.

3. Peiresc to Aycard, 29 April 1635, CBI, MS. 1871, f. 51v.

4. Peiresc to d'Arcos, 30 December 1632, CBI, MS. 1871, f. 358r. In the immediately following letter to the prior of the abbey of St. Victor at Marseille, Peiresc expressed surprise, and even disbelief, at the news that d'Arcos had converted to Islam and taken the name "Osman" (Peiresc to Martin, Prieur claustral de l'abbaye de Saint-Victor, 28 December 1632, CBI, MS. 1871, f. 358v).

5. Peiresc to Gazille, 24 October 1628, CBI, MS. 1873, f. 365r, on the fate of Louis Apvril of Aix.

6. Peiresc to Napollon, 26 November 1628, CBI, MS. 1873, f. 365r.

7. Peiresc to d'Arcos, 14 January 1635, CBI, MS. 1871, f. 367v. "Petit filz d'une personne qui ay le nourice dans notre maison a Boisgency & dont toute la famille a tousjours affecté quelques dependance de nous & des notres."

8. Peiresc to d'Arcos, 23 March 1637, CBI, MS. 1871, ff. 381v–382r.

9. Peiresc to Berengier, 22 March 1637, CBI, MS. 1871, f. 382v. For Berengier's earlier mission to Tripoli, see MACC, J 1910, piece 1, unpaginated.

10. Peiresc to Philippe Andruges, ministre du convent de la St Trinité de Montmorency ou a Messrs ses Collegues, 24 April 1637, CBI, MS. 1871, f. 383r.

11. Fiume, *Schiavitù mediterranee,* 75–76. For Napollon, CBI, MS. 1777, f. 99v.

12. CBI, MS. 1777, ff. 101–102.

13. CBI, MS. 1777, f. 102v.

14. CBI, MS. 1777, f. 99r.

15. Peiresc to Aycard, 29 April 1635, CBI, MS. 1871, f. 51v; Peiresc to Jean-Baptiste Magy, 11 October 1635, CBI, MS. 1874, f. 393bis r.

16. Peiresc to Lombard, 9 November 1635, CBI, MS. 1871, f. 56v.

17. Peiresc to Jean-Baptiste Magy, 26 May 1635, CBI, MS. 1874, f. 372r; Peiresc to Gela, 4 September 1635, CBI, MS. 1874, f. 386v.

18. Peiresc to Aycard, 26 November 1635, CBI, MS. 1871, f. 57r.

19. Eugène Tisserant, *Patrologia Orientalis,* vol. 10, ed. R. Graffin and F. Nau (Paris: Firmin-Didot et Cie, 1915), app. 2, pp. 217–222.

20. "Car outre que c'est pour l'eglise et pour le service de Dieu, qui sçait bien recompenser ce qui se donne pour luy, j'espere que nous tirerons encore de ce convent-là quantité de bons livres anciens." Agathange de Vendôme to Peiresc, 18 March 1634, *Correspondance de Peiresc,* 25. The practice of swapping old manuscripts for newly made ritual artifacts or books began with the beginning of antiquities collections. See Francesco Scalamonti, *Vita Viri Clarissimi et Famosissimi Kyriaci Anconitani,* ed. and trans. Charles Mitchell and Edward W. Bodnar (Philadelphia: American Philosophical Society, 1996), para. 71.

21. Agathange de Vendôme to Peiresc, 18 March 1634, ABM, 201 (1019), 50: "Il faut que le calice soit mediocre, la coupe dorée par dedans, comme aussy le plat qui sert de patene, qui ne doibt avoir par dedans graveure ni ciseleure aucune, mais estre bien poli et doré, le fond tout plat et egal jusques aux bords, qui doibvent estre eslevés d'un pouce."

22. Peiresc to de Thou, 28 May 1635, CBI, MS. 1877, f. 449v: "L'on me faict esperer un volume des octaples, qui jetteroit bien de la poudre aux yeux des plus subelins [*sic*] en matiere de livres, j'y feray jouer tous les ressortz dont je me pourray adviser, dieu aydant."

23. Peiresc to Jean-Baptiste Magy, 12 May 1635, CBI, MS. 1873, f. 46v.

24. Agathange de Vendôme to Peiresc, 25 July 1635, *Correspondance de Peiresc,* 154.

25. Peiresc to Jean-Baptiste Magy, 7 August 1635, CBI, MS. 1874, f. 380r.

26. Peiresc to Jean-Baptiste Magy, 10 August 1635, CBI, MS. 1874, f. 382bis v.

27. Peiresc to Gela, 4 September 1635, CBI, MS. 1874, f. 386v: "Del resto io ho fatto far un calyx d'argento per mandare à quei padri d'Aegitto che mi hanno favorito

di certi libri, et ho preggatto il R. P. Theophilo d'incaminarsi à Marsiglia per veder con l'accuso di V.S. et del Sr G. B. Magy, si doverà imbarcare su questa polacra, che stava in procinto di mettersi alla vella per Alessandria ò se si dovera aspettar che parta il Capp.ne Crouset preggandola di raccommandarlo in Alessandria & al Cayro a suoi corrispondenti."

28. Peiresc to Jean-Baptiste Magy, 5 September 1635, CBI, MS. 1874, f. 386v.

29. Peiresc to Agathange, 10 August 1635, CBI, MS. 1874, f. 389r. "Car les Anglois ne se laisser pas faire peur, comme noz provencaulx. Et je ne pense pas que j'eusse jamais rien receu de ce pais là, si la bonne moeurs des Cappitaines des navires n'eust aultant faict apprehender les corsaires par eulx rencontrez comme eulx pouvent apprehender lesdits Corsaires."

30. Peiresc to Jean-Baptiste Magy, 12 September 1635, CBI, MS. 1874, f. 386v. "Qui m'ont voulu gratiffié de ce volume en diverses langues dont vous m'avez faict feste de si long main." Confirmed in Peiresc to Jean-Baptiste Magy, 24 December 1635, CBI, MS. 1874, f. 413r: "J'ay envoye le callice des bon P. P. Cophtes par le Capitaine Pierre Caillon qui a touché a Malte."

31. Peiresc to Jean-Baptiste Magy, 26 September 1635, CBI, MS. 1874, f. 388r.

32. Peiresc to Jean-Baptiste Magy, 29 September 1635, CBI, MS. 1874, f. 389r. "Car nous scavons desia que ce Cap.ne Baile avoit eu si peu de courage qu'au lieu de se preparer à combattre a la rencontre des corsaires il leur avoit abandonné sa barque prez de Malte." The sad fact is that Magy himself acknowledged this principle, writing a few months earlier that "le Pere Agathange trouve à propos que ie vous envoye les quatre Evangelistes en Arabe et en Siriaque par le Capitaine Anglois." Jean-Baptiste Magy to Peiresc, 15 March 1635, ABM, MS. 207 (1025), 21.

33. Peiresc to Jean-Baptiste Magy, 29 September 1635, CBI, MS. 1874, ff. 389r–v: "Et si vous eussiez suivy l'article de mes instructions que je vous ay faict recommandé vous n'eussiez envoyé ce volume du Saultier [sic] aussy tost que le traicté en fut conclu moyenant le Calyce ce que vous pourriez faire par le vaisseau Anglois. . . . Nous avions sceu par mesme moyen qu'il avoit esté si malheureux en allant et si mal prevoyant qu'il avoit embarqué ce qu'il portoit en Egypte sur une germe [sic] que avoit faict naufrage dans le Nil."

34. Peiresc to Jean-Baptiste Magy, 26 September 1635, CBI, MS. 1874, f. 388r.

35. Peiresc to Gela, 26 September 1635, CBI, MS. 1874, f. 398v: "Cioè il nome del corsaro, il nome del Vascello di Livorno, et di chi ci commanda e da donde sia, il luogo et il tempo dove, et quando il corsaro presse Baille & dove il corsaro e stato ripreso acciò ch'io possa scrivere & tentare ogni mezzo possibile di ricuperar quel mio libro." In this letter Peiresc confirms that the chalice was intended in trade for the Psalter.

36. Peiresc to Pion, 29 September 1635, CBI, MS. 1871, f. 390v.

37. Peiresc to d'Arcos, 30 September 1635, CBI, MS. 1871, f. 372v.

38. Peiresc to Luguet, 30 September 1635, CBI, MS. 1871, f. 373r.

39. Peiresc to Bayon, 30 September 1635, Lettres de Peiresc, 7:514–516 [= CBI, MS. 1871, f. 372v.]: "Comme font souvent les corsaires, qui n'ont que faire des livres." "Je vous donne cez indices là pour ayder à les suivre à la piste."

40. Peiresc to Luguet, 8 October 1635, CBI, MS. 1871, f. 373r.

41. Peiresc to Bayon, 14 October 1635, *Lettres de Peiresc*, 7:517 [= CBI, MS. 1871, f. 373r]. "Qui n'estoit pas assez forte pour attaquer ceste polacre . . . qu'elle avoit esté vendue en bloc à un marchand corse habitüé à Livourne, mais que le Basha de Tripoly avoit retenu le ceste de l'Escrivain qui estoit le Sr Faysan, lequel asseure que mon livre estoit dans sa ceste, qu'il estoit relié en cuir rouge pasle de la longuer d'un pan et demi, de la largeur d'un pan et quart et de la hauteur de quatre doits ou environ." Peiresc had a copy made for himself of a letter from the basha of Tripoli to the premier president of the Parlement of Provence, complete with a very detailed copy of the basha's seal and monogram (CBI, MS. 1777, f. 118). The basha was originally general of the galleys of Algiers and bore the name Ibrahim-Arabadji, which was metamorphosed by the Marseillais into "Rapagoy." *Lettres de Peiresc*, 1:393n2.
42. Peiresc to Gela, 10 October 1635, CBI, MS. 1874, f. 393v.
43. Peiresc to Jean-Baptiste Magy, 11 October 1635, CBI, MS. 1874, f. 393bis r.
44. Consuls of Marseille to Jacques Beau, 13 October 1633, MACC, J 1910, unpaginated. He was still there six months later (Beau to Consuls of Marseille, 8 May 1634, MACC, J 1910.
45. Peiresc to Bayon, 14 October 1635, *Lettres de Peiresc*, 7:517.
46. Mamet Basha to Consuls of Marseille, 8 May 1634, MACC, J 1910, unpaginated.
47. Peiresc to Bayon, 17 October 1635, *Lettres de Peiresc*, 7:520. "À quoy je le servirois de bon coeur pour l'inclination que j'ay à servir le public et promouvoir la liberté et seureté du commerce qui s'en va en ruine, s'il n'y est bientost remedié; et lors ceux qui vivent de leurs courses n'y trouveroient pas leurs comptes et se trouveroint bien mieux sans hazard quelconque au payement des grands droits qu'ils en retireroient avec le commerce libre chez eux."
48. Mamet Basha to Consuls of Marseille, 8 May 1634, MACC, J 1910, unpaginated.
49. Peiresc to Bayon, 17 October 1635, *Lettres de Peiresc*, 7:518–521 [= CBI, MS. 1871, ff. 373v–374v].
50. Peiresc to Fay[s]an, 18 October 1635, CBI, MS. 1871, f. 374v.
51. Peiresc to Luguet, 18 October 1635, CBI, MS. 1871, f. 374v.
52. Peiresc to Le Beau, 18 October 1635, CBI, MS. 1871, f. 375r.
53. Peiresc to Le Beau, 24 October 1635, CBI, MS. 1871, f. 376v.
54. Peiresc to Jean-Baptiste Magy, 24 October 1635, CBI, MS. 1874, f. 394v.
55. Peiresc to Magy, 26 October 1635, CBI, MS. 1874, f. 395r.
56. Peiresc to Piscatoris, 24 October 1635, CBI, MS. 1874, f. 394v.
57. Peiresc to Lombard, 9 November 1635, CBI, MS. 1871, f. 56v. "En quel temps il partit de Rhodes et quelles retraites et correspondances il pouvoit avoir soit du coste du Tripoly ou de l'Alexandrie ou bien de celluy d'Argers ou de Thunis, de quel age il est, de quel païs et quelle profession il auroit faicte puis qu'on dict qu'il entendoit quelque chose en mes livres lesquels toutesfois restoient qu'a l'usage des chrestiens la plus part mais n'ay pas des Chrestiens Catholiques." For Peiresc's identification of him, see Peiresc to Aycard, 26 November 1635, CBI, MS. 1871, f. 57r.
58. Peiresc to Jean-Baptiste Magy, 24 December 1634, CBI, MS. 1874, f. 405v.

59. Peiresc to Jacques de Vendôme, 31 January 1636, CBI, MS. 1874, f. 410v: "Et de ne s'estoit pas advisé (en recouvrant d'eulx son navire & les personnes) de rede-mandre un petit fagot de vieux livres qu'il avoit à moy qui me les eussent compté que le demandre comme plusieurs autres passagers qui demandent leurs livres & papiers les obtiendrent sans rien payer, et quand il en eust fallu payer quelque rancom il la pouroit faire payer par celluy qui faict la charge de consul des fran-cois a Rhodes & les y laisser plustost en gaige ou se les eusse bien tost envoyé r'achepter ou desgaiger."

60. Bayon to Bayon, 26 August 1636, CBI, MS. 1874, f. 435v.

61. Bayon to Peiresc, 29 September 1636, PBN, MS. F.fr. 9539, ff. 179–180v.

62. Bayon to Peiresc, 29 September 1636, PBN, MS. F.fr. 9539, ff. 179–180v.

63. Peiresc to Bayon, 12 December 1636, CBI, MS. 1874, f. 435r. Writing to Luguet, Peiresc explicitly asked if Bayon in his letters mentioned anything about the recovery of his book (Peiresc to Luguet, 11 December 1636, CBI, MS. 1874, f. 435r).

64. Peiresc to Luguet, 21 December 1636, CBI, MS. 1874, f. 437r. Peiresc even asked Luguet to transcribe the part of any letter he wrote to Bayon that might concern his book.

65. Peiresc to Petit, 17 December 1636, PBN, MS. N.a.f. 5172, f. 98v [= CBI, MS. 1875, f. 279v].

66. Peiresc to Bayon, 26 April 1637, *Lettres de Peiresc*, 7:522–523 [= CBI, MS. 1871, f. 383r]. "Sans nerveures sur le dos c'est a la maniere de Levantins, qui y em-ployent de bien plus gros cuir, que nous & sans aulcuns cartons . . . qu'elle doibt avoir couru trop de fortune & possible passé par trop de mains pour la pouvoir suyvre a la piste."

67. Peiresc to Bayon [in Marseille], 26 April 1637, CBI, MS. 1871, f. 384r.

68. Peiresc to Bayon, 26 April 1637, *Lettres de Peiresc*, 7:524 [= CBI, MS. 1871, f. 383v]. Even in defeat Peiresc never forgot the rules of the game: he asked Bayon how much he had spent on the Dutch book in order to properly reimburse him.

69. Peiresc to Diodati, 11 May 1637, quoted in Ernesta Caldarini, "Notizia sul carteggio tra N. C. de Peiresc ed Elia Diodati," *Studi Urbinati* 39 (1965): 448: " 'Il a un genie bien different et s'y amusera à bien d'aultres recherches que Mr Holstenius. . . . Je m'imagine que Mr Holstenius en tirera plus que du Vatican et avec plus de liberté." For Peiresc's relationship with Kircher, see Peter N. Miller, *Peiresc's Orient: Antiquarianism as Cultural History in the Seventeenth Century* (Farnham, UK: Ashgate, 2012), ch. 7.

70. Peiresc to Dormalius, 6 March 1637, CBI, MS. 1873, f. 172r.

71. Oleg V. Volkoff, *À la recherche de manuscrits en Égypte*, Recherches d'archéologie, de philologie et d'histoire, 30 (Cairo: Institut Français d'Archéologie Orientale, 1974), 42.

72. The original, with decipherment, dated 29 October, (BAV, MS. 6681), in Tisserant, *Patrologia Orientalis*, 10:221: "Le Grand Maitre envoie par son maitre de pages a Votre Eminence le livre de tant de langues dont le sieur Hol-stein doit l'avoir entretenue."

73. BAV, MS. Barb.-Lat. 6488, f. 46v, quoted in Tisserant, *Patrologia Orientalis*, 10:221: "Il salterio di cinque lingue già è stato inviato dal Granmastro per un

fra servente, mastro de' paggi, con ordine di presentarlo a V. Emin. come m'avisa Monsig. Inquisitore da Malta."

74. Goezald's letter to Jean Morin of 1 August 1637 mentions that Holstenius was then in Malta (*Antiquitates Ecclesiae Orientalis* [London, 1682], 267).

30. End Points

1. "Afin d'en envoyer des empreintes par differantes voyes à Marseille de peur que si les unes se perdent, on n'en demeure pas despourveu, ains qu'on en puisse avoir aultant par une autre voye." CBI, MS. 1821, f. 486v ("Memoires pour les medailles & pierreries precieuses gravees, qui peuvent rechercher et recouvrer en Levant").

2. Peiresc to Minuti, 23 August 1632, CBI, MS. 1876, f. 824v. "Y adjousta a costé un peu de recommandation a Marseille a Monsr de Valbelle et Mr de Gastines et pour Toullon a M. [A]ycard et le Capitaine Tourtel."

3. Peiresc to l'Empereur at Constantinople, 7 March 1634, CBI, MS. 1873, f. 300v.

4. CBI, MS. 1821, f. 456v. "Pour faire tenir les lettres on peult escrire./A Mr de Peiresc./Recommander les lettres, à Marseille, Tollon, & tous autres lieux de la Coste maritime de Provence, aux Srs lieutenants, de Seneschal, de l'admiraulté et autres juges, et officiers du roy, pour les faire tenir audit Sr de Peiresc./Recommander les premieres enveloppes, aux consuls de la nation Françoise establis, tant en Alep, Seyde, Smyrne, et au Cayre, que ailleurs. Pour faire tenir en Provence audit Sr. de Peiresc./Mesmes si l'occasion s'en presente aux consuls de la nation Françoise establis à Lisbone, Seville, Valance, Barcellone, & tous autres ports de la coste d'Espagne, pour faire tenir à Marseille."

5. "Quand mesmes de Seyde on trouveroit commodité asseuree pour envoyer de pardeça les curiositez qu'on y auroit recouvrees, il seroit bien meilleur que de les charrier d'envoyer les propres originaulx en Aegypte, pour ne les exposer à d'autres dangers qui ne sont que trop frequents partouts cez païs orientaulx." CBI, MS. 1821, f. 486v ("Memoires pour les medailles & pierreries precieuses gravees, qui peuvent rechercher et recouvrer en Levant").

6. "Votre employe en Levant pouvait tirer quelque advantage des correspondances que nous trouverés bon d'essayer et entretenir non seulement aux plus grandes eschelles mais aux lieux les plus escortés, et les moings frequentés." Peiresc to de Thou, 7 February 1635, CBI, MS. 1877, f. 425r.

7. Peiresc to Valbelle, 7 February 1628, CBI, MS. 1876, f. 367r.

8. Peiresc to de Thou, 12 February 1628, CBI, MS. 1876, f. 367v. Peiresc notes that Guez in Marseille had already agreed to put 1,000 écus of credit at de Thou's disposal. Napollon, in turn, is described as knowing the "Intendant des Jardines & plusieurs Bassaux" at Constantinople.

9. Peiresc to de Thou, [6 September 1628], CBI, MS. 1876, f. 371r.

10. Peiresc to Sabatier, 12 January 1633, CBI, MS. 1876, ff. 825r–v. A parallel letter was written to Guillaume Guez in Constantinople the same day, asking the same questions (Peiresc to Guez, 12 January 1633, CBI, MS. 1876, f. 825v).

11. Peiresc to Sabatier, 20 September 1633, CBI, MS. 1876, f. 832v. If he was unable to get one, Peiresc was happy to have a picture, "avec leurs couleurs & a peu

prez de la grandeur des animaulx sy vous avez la de peintre [*sic*] qui la voulut & le s'eust faire."

12. Nelly Hanna, *Making Big Money in 1600: The Life and Times of Isma'il Abu Taqiyya, Egyptian Merchant* (Syracuse, NY: Syracuse University Press, 1998); Hanna, *In Praise of Books: A Cultural History of Cairo's Middle Class, Sixteenth to the Eighteenth Century* (Syracuse, NY: Syracuse University Press, 2003); Daniel Goffman, *Izmir and the Levantine World, 1550–1650* (Seattle: University of Washington Press, 1990).

13. Peiresc to Hainhofer, 17 October 1633, PBN, MS. N.a.f. 5172, 199r, quoted in Agnès Bresson, "Peiresc et le cercle d'Augsbourg," *Sciences et techniques en perspective*, 2nd ser. 9 (2005): 242.

14. Aubery to Peiresc, 12 September 1629, PBN, MS., F.fr. 9542, f. 259r: "J'ay remarqué à Rome la quantité d'amis que vous entretenies à tous les ordinaires et comme vous estiez ponctuel. Je veulx croire que par la France & particulairement à Paris, c'est tout autre chose. Je scais que par ce moyen on entretient et confirme les amities. Mais vous n'avez nullement besoing de cela, ayant des qualités si attrayantes que par le seul recit que chacun faict d'icelles tous les galants hommes sont portes d'affection à vous servir." In 1629, Peiresc had eighteen correspondents in Rome (one of whom was just passing through). For comparison, he had thirty-three in Paris.

15. Eschinard is first mentioned by Peiresc in a letter to Paolo Gualdo of 13 October 1614 (*Lettere di uomini illustri* [Venice, 1744], 241–242).

16. A biographical study of Eschinard is now being undertaken by Cees de Bondt in the context of his work on "Caravaggio's Tennis Match," and I am extremely grateful to him for sharing much information with me.

17. Peiresc to Eschinard, 29 June 1616, CBI, MS. 1873, f. 311r.

18. Peiresc to Eschinard, 16 April 1616, CBI, MS. 1873, f. 311v.

19. Peiresc to Eschinard, 2 August 1617, CBI, MS. 1873, f. 316v. Brugiotti published *Specimen des caractères de l'imprimerie du Vatican* (1628), a subject that would have interested Peiresc greatly.

20. Aubery to Peiresc, 28 November 1626, PBN, MS. F.fr. 9542, f. 220r.

21. Peiresc to Marchand, 2 July 1635, CBI, MS. 1874, f. 574v.

22. Aubery to Peiresc, 6 March 1627, PBN, MS. F.fr. 9542, f. 226r; 21 April 1627, f. 233r. D'Espiot also reimbursed on the account of the archbishop of Aix, suggesting that Peiresc offered his purchasing network as a gift to the cleric: "*Ledit Sr Lambert escrive icy a son amy que il m'a donne aux occasions ce que je luy demanderay pour votre conte.*"

23. Aubery to Peiresc, 28 May 1627, PBN, MS. F.fr. 9542, f. 236r: "Parce qu'il n'escript que de mois en mois & par la voye d'Avignon."

24. Peiresc to Galaup, 11 May 1633, CBI, MS. 1873, f. 444v. "Et que par le moyen du Sr. Guill. d'Espiot respondant à Rome du Sr. de Gastines a Marseille, il y aura bon moyen de luy faire tenir en Levant tout ce que nous pourrons obtenir pour luy de notre S.P. le Pape & de Messeurs. les Em.ces Card.aux de la Congregation de Propaganda Fide ausquelz j'en feray faire instance la plus ardante que je pourray."

25. Peiresc to Jacques de Vendôme, 12 May 1633, CBI, MS. 1876, f. 826r. "Je le feray consigner dans Rome en mains du Sr. Guill. d'Espiots [*sic*] marchand pour le

faire tenir en Levant par le correspondance et entremise qu'il a avec Mr de Gastines de pareille parent de Mr de l'Isle de Seyde, à qui il l'envoyera, ou bien à Mr
Tarquet le consul ou tel autre que Mr Amirà voudra choisir de pardela pour luy
faire annuellement remettre sa pension."

26. Peiresc to Holstenius, 9 April 1637, PBN, MS. 5172, f. 79r [= formerly CBI, MS.
1873, f. 175r], omitted in *Lettres de Peiresc* 5:473.

27. CBI, MS. 1821, f. 33r, dated 26 August 1634. The memo spells out, step-by-step,
the passage to Rome and the relevant personae, then the stages and tasks for
the return, then what needed to be done before departing for Civitavecchia,
and what to be done at sea ("Patron Paschal est prié d'observer tant qu'il
pourra tous les jours en un petit memorial les lieux ou il se trouvera le veu
qui aura regné le jour & la nuict, Et la courante de mer qui aura peu estre
cognoissable. Et de quel costé elle venoit & chargeoit le plus. Sur tout si elle
n'est pas plus ordinairement du Levant au Ponant que au contraire. Specialement sur le Cap de Nolis & dans les Destroictz de Corseque & de l'Elba"
(33v–34r).

28. Peiresc to Rossi, 5 May 1634, CBI, MS. 1875, f. 571v. Alternatively, if Rossi had a
Roman address, Peiresc could communicate with him via letters sent to any of
his many Roman correspondents, such as Menestrier or Bonnaire (f. 572r).
When letters of Rossi from 5 and 8 August arrived in Marseille only in early
October, Peiresc blamed the climate, noting that "mentre durano i caldi sonno
rarissime le commodità di passaggio adrittura" (Peiresc to Rossi, 6 October
1634, CBI, MS. 1874, f. 573r).

29. Peiresc to Rossi, 3 July 1634, CBI, MS. 1875, f. 572r.

30. Peiresc to Malatesta, 25 August 1634, CBI, MS. 1875, f. 573r. Peiresc understood
that to make it worth the captain's while, it would be useful also to obtain per-
mission for him to pick up goods—in this case, alum—in Rome for export to
Marseille. Peiresc asked for this, too. Peiresc explained all this in the letter to
Rossi that accompanied one to Malatesta (Peiresc to Rossi, 25 August 1634,
CBI, MS. 1875, f. 573r). On Rome and the alum trade, see Jean Delumeau,
L'Alun de Rome, XVe–XIXe siècle (Paris: SEVPEN, 1962).

31. Rossi to Peiresc, 22 September 1634, PBN, MS. F.fr. 9539, f. 271v.

32. Peiresc to Barberini, 28 October 1634, Rome, BAV, MS. Barb.-Lat. 6503, f. 104r.

33. Typically, Peiresc to Boerio, November 1634, CBI, MS. 1872, f. 390v, was
brought to Boerio by Mattieu Fredeau, the painter, who was passing through
Genoa en route to Bologna, Rome, and Naples.

34. Peiresc to Eschinard, 20 September 1627, CBI, MS. 1873, f. 348r.

35. Peiresc to Bonnaire, 24 April 1626, CBI, MS. 1872, f. 187r.

36. Peiresc to Marc Antonio Lumaga, 7 December 1623, CBI, MS. 1874, f. 295r.

37. Peiresc to Bartolomeo Lumaga, 4 July 1633, CBI, MS. 1876, f. 459r; Peiresc to
Aubery, 18 July 1633, CBI, MS. 1871, f. 550r.

38. Hainhofer to Lumaga, 5 June 1633, CBI, MS. 1876, f. 459v. On Peiresc's Augsburg connections, see Bresson, "Peiresc et le cercle humaniste d'Augsbourg,"
173–258; for Hainhofer in particular, see 193–194.

39. Peiresc to Lumaga, 15 August 1634, CBI, MS. 1874, f. 474r.

40. Peiresc to Bonnaire, 24 April 1626, CBI, MS. 1872, f. 187r.

41. Of Avignon, he wrote, "Il s'y pert souvent des semaines toutes entiers pour attendre que les despeches puissent revenir de la" (Peiresc to Eschinard, 27 July 1628, CBI, MS. 1873, f. 325v).

42. Peiresc to Menestrier, 30 June 1633, *Lettres de Peiresc*, 5:642. "Il a tous les jours des commoditez fort opportunes de Genes à Marseille où il escript d'ordinaire à Mr de Gastines." De Gastines, for his part, described Tridi as "un des honnestes et courtois hommes que j'aye jamais cognu," and asked Peiresc to intervene on his side in a legal dispute. Gastines to Peiresc, 6 March 1632, PBN, MS. F.fr. 9539, f. 263r.

43. Peiresc to Bouchard [early 1631], *Lettres de Peiresc*, 4:63.

44. CBI, MS. 1872, ff. 390–413.

45. François-Auguste de Thou to Peiresc, 7 July 1629, CBI, MS. 1777, f. 551r.

46. E.g., Peiresc to Sabran, 30 December 1633, CBI, MS. 1876, f. 6v, on mail to Cardinal Barberini that had gone missing.

47. Peiresc marks these differences in a letter to Boerio of 17 December 1634, CBI, MS. 1872, f. 391v.

48. Peiresc to Suares, 8 September 1633, CBI, MS. 1876, f. 227v. "Moyennant une certain gratiffication que je baille d'ordinaire aux courriers, tant en l'allent qu'en revenant, soit que mes pacquet [*sic*] soient gros ou petits. . . . Et voz Messieurs d'Avignon ne laissent pas de faire payer le port ric a ric comme s'y c'estoient."

49. "Estimant qu'il seroit plus commode a mez amis pour le moins de la famiglie de son Em.ce de porter leurs lettres en sa Secretaire que en d'autres vieux [*sic*]." Peiresc to Suares, 8 September 1633, CBI, MS. 1876, f. 228r.

50. Peiresc to Boerio, 26 December 1634, CBI, MS. 1872, f. 401r.

51. Peiresc to Boerio, 6 February 1636, CBI, MS. 1872, f. 408r: "Et si in Cracovia si havesse corrispondenza con qualche amico assai curioso per tal commissioni gliela darei molto volentieri con offerta di servirlo in scambio dovunque fosse possibile." For other examples of Genoese in Kraków, see Fernand Braudel, *The Wheels of Commerce: Civilization and Capitalism* (New York: Harper and Row, 1986 [1979]), 2:165.

52. Peiresc to R. P. Maximilian, 3 January 1636, CBI, MS. 1876, f. 13r.

53. See Peter N. Miller, *Peiresc's "History of Provence": Antiquarianism and the Discovery of a Medieval Mediterranean*, Transactions of the American Philosophical Society 101, 3 (Philadelphia: American Philosophical Society, 2011).

54. Peiresc to Boerio, 7 September 1634, CBI, MS. 1872, f. 389r. Boerio had connected Peiresc with Father Agostino Schiaffino, whose long letter of 4 January 1634 contains long lists of Genoese historical sources (PBN, MS. F.fr. 9540, ff. 106–108r).

55. Peiresc to Boerio, 10 October 1634, CBI, MS. 1872, f. 390v.

56. Peiresc to Boerio, 25 February 1637, CBI, MS. 1872, f. 410v, referring to the trip of Giovanni [Jean] Issaultier of Marseille.

57. Peiresc to Welser, 22 November 1601, PBN, MS. N.a.f. 5172, f. 207r.

58. Peiresc to Ciotti, 10 July 1604, CBI, MS. 1873, f. 83r; 24 August 1604, CBI, MS. 1873, f. 83r.

59. Peiresc to Ciotti, 28 October 1613, CBI, MS. 1873, f. 83v. Two lists of titles can be found in CBI, MS. 1875, one dated to 28 October 1615 (f. 302r) and connected to a letter listing books sent to him by Pignoria which contained various printing imperfections (f. 300r). The other is undated (ff. 301r–v).

60. Peiresc to Pignoria, 4 January 1616, CBI, MS. 1875, f. 308r.

61. Peiresc to Pignoria, 28 October 1615, PBN, MS. N.a.f. 5172, f. 104 [= CBI, MS. 1875, f. 299] and 104v [f. 299v]. He tells Pignoria in a later letter, "Et pigliar il dannaro necessario dal Sr Abbioso" in order to purchase telescopes. Peiresc to Pignoria, 23 December 1618, CBI, MS. 1875, f. 356v.

62. Peiresc to Gaffarel, 28 November 1633, CBI, MS. 1873, f. 408r.

63. Peiresc to Gaffarel, 3 May 1633, CBI, MS. 1873, f. 403r.

64. Peiresc to M. de la Tuillerie, 15 January 1636, CBI, MS. 1873, f. 422v.

65. Peiresc also noted that if the items were too heavy they would not be able to go overland. He did not specify the alternative maritime routing. Peiresc to Gaffarel, 21 August 1634, CBI, MS. 1873, f. 413v.

66. Peiresc to Gela, 9 November 1635, CBI, MS. 1874, f. 396v.

67. Peiresc to Bourdelot, 2 March 1636, CBI, MS. 1872, f. 474r.

68. Peiresc to Gela, 24 February 1637, CBI, MS. 1874, f. 442r. "Pelissieri che fu amazzato in Venetia l'anno passato. . . . Di volerle mandare per la via del mare, quando se ne presentera commodita opportuna per Marsiglia adrittura o per la via delli ricapiti di Livorno a Genoa."

69. Peiresc to Seghezzi "in Venetia," 23 February 1637, CBI, MS. 1874, f. 441v.

70. Peiresc to M. de la Tuillerie, 14 April 1637, CBI, MS. 1873, f. 427r. Apparently, Pelissier had collected a series of marble fragments ("tables") with Greek inscriptions that had recently arrived in Venice from Greece. (Peiresc noted that he had seen things like this when he had been in Venice decades earlier, but had not paid sufficient attention.) Pelissier had apparently also collected for him some Greek and Arabic coins, as well as some ancient engraved gems.

71. Peiresc to M. de la Tuillerie, 14 April 1637, CBI, MS. 1873, f. 427r. "Je ne cognoissois plus de curieux en ce pais la, depuis que j'y ay perdu mes vieilles cognoissances du procurator Federigo Contarini, & du Sr Giovanni Mocenigo il Zoppo, lesquelz avoient les plus riches cabinets de mon temps plus de 30 ans y à, et prenoient plaisir de m'envoie monstrer jusques icy bien souvent de leur plus precieuses raretez."

72. Peiresc to M. de la Tuillerie, 24 July 1635, CBI, MS. 1873, f. 420r. This probably refers to one "Mattou Sassan" or "Mattouk Chiassan," described in PBN, MS. F.fr. 9530 f. 119r, dated 10 May 1635, as a native of Aleppo. He is also described in exactly this way in a letter from Peiresc to the French ambassador to Venice in July 1635 (Peiresc to M. de la Tuillerie, 24 July 1635, CBI, MS. 1873, f. 420r). We know from a memorandum in Peiresc's collection that Peiresc met Chiassan on 19 October 1632 (PBN, MS. F.fr. 9532, f. 43r). Mention of Aleppo is omitted in Peiresc's reference to a "Turc naturel que nous avons icy" (Peiresc to Petit, 29 May 1635, CBI, MS. 1875, f. 274v).

73. In his splendid study, Petitjean describes Malta and its Inquisitorial archive as a "maritime observatory," but for support cites the arrival of a Marseillais vessel

with news—not among the four indexed references to Marseille in his book (*L'Intelligence des choses*, 404).

74. Peiresc to M. General Commandeur de Venterol, 20 June 1630, CBI, MS. 1876, f. 806r. Peiresc wrote the next month to assure him that the packet had been delivered. Peiresc's zealousness was purposive—there would always be Provençal shipping passing through Malta and a happy contact there would always be helpful—but also an affirmation of history—he invoked the "wishes of the late M. Callas my father and uncle who had performed their service to the late M. de Paris and all your illustrious house" (Peiresc to Venterol, 19 July 1630, CBI, MS. 1876, f. 807r).

75. Aubery to Peiresc, 28 May 1627, PBN, MS. F.fr. 9542, 28 May 1627, f. 238v.

76. Jacques de Vendôme to Peiresc, 22 November 1635, PBN, MS. F.fr. 9542, f. 164r. "Comme de bouche vous aura refert le Sr *Capitaine Beaussier* qui en fut porteur."

77. Jacques de Vendôme to Peiresc, 7 March 1636, PBN, MS. F.fr. 9542, f. 157v.

78. Agathange to Peiresc, 10 October 1636, PBN, MS. F.fr. 9543, f. 253r. "Je passe beaucoup de temps aveq un chevallier apellé Mons.r Labbia qui est en reputation d'entendre beaucoup aux mathematique & astronomie." The astronomical observations he undertook there are included in this letter.

79. See Michel Fontenay, *La Méditerranée entre la Croix et le Croissant: Navigation, commerce, course et piraterie (XVIe–XIXe siècle)* (Paris: Classiques Garnier, 2012), 162.

80. Peiresc noted that he was writing to the ambassador by the next ordinaire, which left on Friday in the evening for Lyon, and from Lyon to Venice the following Wednesday (Peiresc to Guez, 1 August 1628, CBI, MS. 1876, f. 368v). Similarly, he received a letter from the French ambassador, d'Avaux, via M. Jacquet of Lyon (Peiresc to de Thou, 4 August 1628, CBI, MS. 1876, f. 369r).

81. Peiresc to Marcheville, 15 June 1631, CBI, MS. 1874, f. 602r. "Votre sesiour en Constantinople y attira les plus grands hommes de l'Europe & vous donnera moyen de restaure les bonnes lettres. Je me suis marry que de ne pouvoir assez promettre de santé pour un si long voyage car rien ne me pourroit retenir en une telle opportunité que je me fusse de la partir quand ce ne seroit que pour servir une personne & les gens de lettres."

82. " 'To Divest the East of all Its Manuscripts and All Its Rarities': The Unfortunate Embassy of Henri Gournay de Marcheville," in *The Republic of Letters in the Levant* [= *Intersections*, vol. 5], ed. Alastair Hamilton, Maurits H. van den Boogert, and Bart Westerweel (Leiden: Brill, 2005), 123–150.

83. Peiresc to l'Empereur [in Constantinople], 10 July 1631, CBI, MS. 1876, f. 809v.

84. Peiresc to Guez, 19 March 1634, CBI, MS. 1874, f. 333r; Peiresc to Sabatier, 19 March 1634, CBI, MS. 1874, f. 333r.

85. Peiresc to Minuti, 11 July 1631, CBI, MS. 1876, f. 814v. "Il y dresse une maison et y envoyera souvent des navires, et sans cela tousiours la voye de Marseille fournira afforce commoditez pour vous donner de voz nouvelles. Et quand vous aurez esté sur les lieux que vous aurez faict voz resolutions fournisées de ce que vous voudriez entreprendre ou devenir, lors que vous serez en volonté de passer en la

Palestine nous y raffreschirons les ordres convenables le mieux que nous pourrions pour votre contentement. Et vous, envoyerons ce que trouverez bon."

86. Peiresc to Minuti, 23 August 1632, CBI, MS. 1876, f. 821v.

87. Peiresc to Procureur-General Chasteuil, 30 November 1632, CBI, MS. 1873, f. 443r.

88. Marcheville to Peiresc, 16 September 1632, PBN, MS. F.fr. 9542, f. 165r. "Je vous jure, que quoyque j'aye estudié et recherché à vous en faire voir quelques preuves, depuis notre separation, que je n'ay rien encor trouvé, dont j'y puisse satisfaire."

89. Peiresc to Grange, 13 May 1637, CBI, MS. 1874, f. 445bis v: "Des derniers temps de l'Empire de Constantinople, elles ne sont pas si curieuses comme sont les plus anciennes, qui sont des meilleurs ouvriers, & plustost de metail jaulne, que du rouge comme sont celles."

90. Peiresc for Jean Grange, 5 January 1635, CBI, MS. 1874, f. 363r: "Memoire au sieur Jehan Grange allant à Smyrne, et au sieur François Grange son cousin. Neveux du sieur Baltasar Grange."

91. CBI, MS. 1809, f. 170r.

92. PBN, N.a.f. 5169, f. 28v.

93. See Miller, Peiresc's "History of Provence."

94. PBN, N.a.f. 5169, f. 29r.

95. PBN, N.a.f. 5169, f. 29v.

96. Minuti to Peiresc, 15 March 1633, PBN, MS. F.fr. 9542, ff. 11v–12r.

97. See now Stefan Weber, "La Fabrique d'une ville portuaire ottomane: Les acteurs du développment urbain de Sidon entre le XVIe et le XVIIIe siècle," in *La Loge et le fondouk: Les Dimensions spatiales des pratiques marchandes en Méditerranée*, ed. Wolfgang Kaiser (Paris: Éditions Karthala, 2014), 21–70.

98. Paul Masson, *Histoire du commerce français dans le Levant au XVIIe siècle* (Paris: Hachette, 1896), 383.

99. Four letters from Estelle to the Consuls of Marseille dating 1635–1637 are found in MACC, J 761. On Tarquet's visits to Sidon, see Géraud Poumarède, "Naissance d'une institution royale: Les consuls de la nation française en Levant et en Barbarie aux XVIe et XVIIe siècles," *Annuaire-Bulletin de la Société de l'histoire de France: Année 2001* (Paris: Honoré Champion, 2003), 104–105.

100. Pères Leonard and Joseph to Ingoli, 12 March 1626, in M. de Vaumas, *Lettres et documents du Père Joseph de Paris concernant les missions étrangères (1619–1648)* (Lyon: Imprimerie Express, 1942), 51.

101. Peiresc to Galaup, 11 May 1633, CBI, MS. 1873, f. 444v.

102. Jacques de Vendôme to Peiresc, 15 June 1633, PBN, MS. F.fr. 9542, f. 162r.

103. Peiresc to Aymini, 26 February 1630, CBI, MS. 1876, f. 396v (postscript to letter begun on 20 February).

104. Peiresc to de l'Isle, 16 July 1631, CBI, MS. 1876, f. 815r.

105. Minuti to Peiresc, 7 September 1632, PBN, MS. F.fr. 9542, f. 7r. "*J'ay trouvé plus de cortoisie en la personne de Monsr. le consul Tarquet que non pas en celle de Monsr. l'ambassadeur. Il est vray que le bon homme ne peche pas par malice, je l'ay laissé si pauvre qu'il n'avoit pas un double pour faire boullir sa marmitte.*"

106. Minuti to Peiresc, 29 August 1629, PBN, MS. F.fr. 9542, f. 2r.
107. Peiresc to Meynier, [16 November 1629], CBI, MS. 1876, ff. 363r–v: "leur histoire, leur Calendrier et leurs reglements et facons de vivre en leur sectes."
108. Minuti to Peiresc, 5 November 1632, PBN, MS. F.fr. 9542, f. 9r.
109. Minuti to Peiresc, 10 April 1633, PBN, MS. F.fr. 9542, f. 13v: "Il est assés [*sic*] pauvre et a beaucoup de peine de vivre."
110. Peiresc to Aycard, 1 November 1632, CBI, MS. 1871, f. 22v.
111. Minuti to Peiresc, 5 November 1632, PBN, MS. F.fr. 9542, f. 8v.
112. Minuti to Peiresc, 15 March 1633, PBN, MS. F.fr. 9542, f. 12v; Minuti to Peiresc, 10 April 1633, PBN, MS. F.fr. 9542, f. 13v.
113. Minuti to Peiresc, 26 August 1633, PBN, MS. F.fr. 9542, f. 19r. "*Durant deux bons moys j'y ay esté malade ou Monsieur Salvator* neveu de Monsieur d'Aycard *m'a* autant *assisté* et plus que si j'eusse esté son propre frere, dont je luy en demeure grandement obligé."
114. Minuti to Peiresc, 18 April 1633, PBN, MS. F.fr. 9542, f. 15r.
115. Allemand to Minuti, [undated], CBI, MS. 1878, f. 274r. "Comme feu Salvator voullant faire ung autre mestier que le sien est allé voir l'auttre monde par ung sault bien perilheux."
116. A list of those attending a meeting at the consulate on 30 April 1631 is found in an extract from a register of the chancellery of the consulate: Robert Contour, Anthoine Allemand, Luc Mouchin, Jean Jullien, Gabriel Venture, Laurent Bermond, Michel Frejure, Anthoine Bayon, Pierre Dupont, Clement Mazurat, Pantellin Gratian, Ludovic Hou, Jean Saxe, Loys Paul, and Loys Raymond. MACC, J 892, unpaginated. A meeting one month later included Andre Guigonet, Jean Berelle, Claude Danin, Jacqnon Mazanod, Anthoine Lombardon, Juan Romick, and Estienne Boisson. MACC, J 892, unpaginated. Masson gives a figure of forty for 1630, declining to fifteen in 1653 (*Histoire du commerce français,* 378). For more on the French community, see Stefan Knost, "Les *Francs* à Alep (Syrie), leur statut juridique et leur interaction avec les institutions locales (XVIIe–XIXe siècle)," in *Gens de passage en Méditerranée de l'Antiquité à l'époque moderne: Procédures de contrôle et d'identification. L'Atelier Méditerranéen,* ed. Claudia Moatti and Wolfgang Kaiser (Paris: Maisonneuve & Larose, 2007), 243–262.
117. Peiresc to de Thou, 22 February 1630, CBI, MS. 1876, f. 794v.
118. Peiresc to Mallon, 20 February 1630, CBI, MS. 1876, f. 795r. "Mais principalement je desirerois de ceux de leur chronologies & histoires & de leur religion, et kalendriers mesmes quand ils seront escripts en parchemin, & qu'ils seront anciens bien que je ne suis pas d'advis que vous negligiez pour tant ceux qui ne sont escripts en papier . . . vous pourrez assez recognoistre a peu prez la maniere de celles sur quoy peu eschoir ma curiosité." Peiresc echoed this same sense of priorities in the contemporary letter to Daniel Aymini (MS. 1876, f. 796r). In that letter to Mallon, Peiresc also provided a fascinating description of the kind of coins and medals he desired. He had prepared a sheet of engravings for Minuti, but for those of copper he suggested taking everything that had Samaritan, Greek, or Syriac characters, even in large format (weighing up to 9 or 10 écus).

119. Peiresc refers to l'Archier as Fort's "parent"; Peiresc to Mallon, 20 February 1631, CBI, MS. 1876, f. 810v.

120. Mallon to l'Archier, 25 April 1631, CBI, MS. 1876, f. 816v.

121. Peiresc to Thibault, 4 January 1632, CBI, MS. 1876, ff. 817r–v.

122. Peiresc to Mallon, 12 August 1632, CBI, MS. 1876, f. 818r.

123. Mallon to Peiresc, 8 April 1632, PBN, MS. F.fr. 9542, f. 102r.

124. These assemblies were standard practice; Estelle tells the consuls of Marseille, "J'ay faict assemblée la Nation dans la maison consulaire comme il est de coustume."

125. Others included Ulric Cron de St. Gal, Antoine Mazerat, Loys Bayard, Geremie Bollins, Jacques Cappon, Laurens Escalonze, Jean Magy, Cap. Thomas Rougier, Cap. Barthélemy Bansel, Bertrand Bree, Jacomo d'Alloisio, and Pietro Ceconnulli. MACC, J 547.

126. MACC, J 731, unpaginated, dated 5 February 1634. The list is also divided by social category. Thus, "nobles" Jacques D'Altoviti and Anthoine de Caudolle; "sieurs" Esperit Laurens, Denis de la Garde, Lazarin Langy, and Gorgi Calamara; "merchantz cappitaine" Anthoine Courtes (Marseille), Jaulmet Martin, Anthoine Carbonel, Anthoine Fabre (La Ciotat), Jehan Audibert (Sixfours), Francois Rous, Ambroise Guache, Pierre Denans, Jehan Aubert, Pierre Quiesset, Phelip Giremonde, Nicollas Guigou, Honnoré Porquier, Gabriel Audibert, and François Mailhet.

127. Some biographical information can be found in Sidney Aufrère, *La Momie et la tempête: Nicolas-Claude Fabri de Peiresc et la "curiosité Égyptienne" en Provence au début du XVIIe siècle* (Avignon: Éditions A. Barthélemy, 1990), 105–108.

128. Peiresc to Magy, 6 December 1634, CBI, MS. 1874, f. 359r. The top-secret memos intended for Minuti were never seen by him. PBN, MS. Lat. 9340, ff. 110–113.

129. "Le Sr Jean Magy de Marseille qui à esté longtemps en Aegypte et jusques à une vintaine d'annees." PBN, MS. F.fr. 9530, f. 279r.

130. Ramatuelle to Peiresc, 15 July 1633, CBI, MS. 1879, f. 584r.

131. Peiresc to Jean-Baptiste Magy, 12 May 1635, CBI, MS. 1873, f. 46v.

132. Peiresc to Magy, 15 September 1634, CBI, MS. 1874, f. 354v.

133. Peiresc to Jean-Baptiste Magy, 27 April 1634, CBI, MS. 1874, f. 339r. "Un caffas remply de plusieurs curiositez, une caisse dans laquelle y à deux arbres, et outre ce un libvre en moresque, une figure de porcelaine et un genre de sorbet et que dans les caffes il y à divers pacquetz sachetz, ou gobelletz, pleins de semences diverses pieces de poidz et mesures à peser & mesurer un coquemar de cuivre, ou eschauffoire, un fanal, 7 massons [. . . ?], 12. langues de buffle que je ne scay que ce cest, une couffre con quasi 35. medailles 32. idoles et autres chosettes." I am especially grateful to Jérôme Delatour for his discussion of these exotic objects.

134. Peiresc to Magy, 6 December 1634, CBI, MS. 1874, f. 360r.

135. Magy to Peiresc, 9 July 1633, CBI, MS. 1777, f. 372r; Magy to Peiresc, 7 July 1633, CBI, MS. 1777, f. 376v. I thank Barbara Karl for discussing this with me.

136. Peiresc to Jean-Baptiste Magy, 24 April 1636, CBI, MS. 1874, f. 414r.

137. CBI, MS. 1864, f. 223r; Magy to Peiresc, ABM, MS. 207 (1025), 19.

138. CBI, MS. 1864, f. 225r.

139. PBN, MS. F.fr. 9530, f. 279r. "Le Sr Jean MAGY de Marseille qui à esté longtemps en Aegypte et jusques à une vintaine d'annees dict y avoir veu divers
vases et utensils en commun usage, de forme fort semblable ou approchante
aux anciens, entr'autres."

140. PBN, MS. F.fr. 9530, f. 101r. "Le Sr Magy de Marseille revenu d'AEgypte, estant a Aix le 30 Juin 1633 recognent les fragments antiques de divers utensils,
vases & machines semblables à ceux dont les Turcs se servent encors."

141. PBN, MS. F.fr. 9532, f. 187r.

142. See Peter N. Miller, *Peiresc's Orient: Antiquarianism as Cultural History in the
Seventeenth Century* (Farnham, UK: Ashgate, 2012), ch. 6.

143. PBN, MS. F.fr. 9532, f. 42r. "Ex Moresque du Cayre/au rapport du Sr. Jean
Magy filz d'Agostin de Marseille/le 29 Juillet *1633* à Aix." Likely *June* 29.

144. CBI, MS. 1864, f. 263. The terms are translated in Aufrère, *La Momie et la
tempête,* 290–291.

145. CBI, MS. 1864, f. 261.

146. Peiresc to Magy, 10 August 1635, CBI, MS. 1874, f. 382r. See Anne Boud'hors,
"François Daniel: Un 'marchand d'Égypte' provençal au service des premiers
orientalistes français," in *Hommages à Jean Leclant,* ed. Catherine Berger,
Gisèle Clerc, and Nicolas Grimal (Cairo: Institut Français d'Archéologie Orientale, 1994) [= *Bibliothèque d'étude* 106 (1994)], 19–27.

147. Minuti to Peiresc, 18 April 1633, PBN, MS. F.fr. 9542, f. 15v.

148. Peiresc to Thomas de Saint-Calan, 10 April 1634, CBI, MS. 1876, f. 338r.

149. MACC, J 1664, unpaginated. Alexandria: Michel Mercurin, Mary Laugeret,
Jean de Lagarde, Hugon Bermond, Jean Antoine Picquet, Jean German, Lazarin
Langy, Antoine German, and Barthélemy Chabert. Cairo: Jean Faugues, Louis
Bayard, Peirre Andre Baron, Jean Magy, Dominique l'Hoste, Laurence de Croii,
Langy Aufant, Pierre de Mercurin, Barthélemy Hugue, Louis Vignon, Antoine
Mazarat, and Annibal Gibiet.

150. MACC, J 1676. Interestingly, while his signature is found in a letter of
1 February 1656, it is absent in a letter of 5 February 1657 on the same subject
with the same other group of signatories. Does this mark out the year of his
death?

151. The best comprehensive treatment remains Paul Masson, *Histoire des établissements et du commerce français dans l'Afrique barbaresque (1560–1793)* (Paris: Hachette, 1903).

152. Peiresc to Aycard, 7 September 1636, CBI, MS. 1871, f. 64r. All these names are
intertwined in the same sentence concerning a shipment that did not reach its
destination. Berengier was plying the Marseille-Tunis route, connecting
d'Arcos with de Gastines at least as early as 1633 (Peiresc to Aycard, 6 April
1633, CBI, MS. 1871, f. 29v).

153. E.g., Peiresc to Gazille, 31 October 1628, CBI, MS. 1873, f. 465v, reporting on
the shipment of some letters for Napollon.

154. For instance, the materials in CBI, MS. 1777.

155. Boubaker, *La Régence de Tunis,* 147.

156. Berengier to Peiresc, 15 May 1627, CBI, MS. 1878, f. 328r. For background, see Paul Sebag, *Tunis au XVIIe siècle: Une cité barbaresque au temps de la course* (Paris: L'Harmattan, 1989).

157. Olivier to Peiresc, 20 April 1620, PBN, MS. Lat. 8957, f. 169r. The inscriptions followed (ff. 170–171), with drawings and identifications. The place was close to Tunis and called by the Moors "Billedgirit."

158. Pierre Grandchamp, *La France en Tunisie au XVIIe siècle* (Tunis: Imprimerie Aloccio, 1921–1933), 4:166. D'Arcos is a source, but only a small one, in Yvan Debbasch, *La Nation française en Tunisie (1577–1835)* (Paris: Éditions Sirey, 1957), which is mostly devoted to the eighteenth century; he illustrates the category of "renegade" in Sebag, *Tunis*, 48. See now the treatment of d'Arcos, fully realized in the monograph-like essay of Jocelyn Dakhlia, "Une archéologie du même et de l'autre: Thomas-Osman d'Arcos dans la Méditerranée du XVIIe siècle," in *Les Musulmans dans l'histoire de l'Europe*, ed. Jocelyne Dakhlia and Wolfgang Kaiser (Paris: Albin Michel, 2013), 2:61–163.

159. See Miller, *Peiresc's Orient*, ch. 8.

160. The book was *Historia Josephi Patriarchae, ex Alcorano, Arabice. cum triplici versione Latina* (1617). Peiresc to d'Arcos, 22 March 1633, CBI, MS. 1871, f. 358v [= *Lettres de Peiresc*, 7:107–108]. Peiresc reported that Erpenius had planned to do a new edition of the Koran but was interrupted by death. Peiresc had begun looking for a Koran in November (Peiresc to Aycard, 21 November 1632 and 30 November 1632, CBI, MS. 1871, f. 23v) and found one by the end of January (Peiresc to Aycard, 1 February 1633, CBI, MS. 1871, f. 26r). It was a rare and dear copy: "Vous ne scauriez croire la peyne que i'ay eüe de recouvrer ce livre, dont l'edition est perdue longtemps y a en sorte que les libraires n'ont pas de honte de le tenir à 30 & 40 escus" (f. 26v).

161. CBI, MS. 493, f. 238r.

162. On Tripoli in the eighteenth century, see Daniel Panzac, *Commerce et navigation dans l'empire Ottoman à XVIIIe siècle* (Istanbul: Les Éditions Isis, 1996), 129–156.

163. Durand to Peiresc, 5 November 1626, CBI, MS. 1878, f. 497r.

164. Peiresc prepared for them a mémoire identifying Torrius as a student of Lipsius to whom the late Schilderus bequeathed his papers. They were to find him, get his address, and send him Peiresc's best wishes. ABM, MS. 212 (1030), 443.

165. Peiresc to Torrius, 26 February 1626, ABM, MS. 212 (1030), 439.

166. Peiresc to Torrius, 28 September 1626, ABM, MS. 212 (1030), 441 (copy says from CBI, MS. 1810, f. 114).

167. Novel to Peiresc, 10 December 1633, in *Les Correspondants de Peiresc*, 2 vols. (Geneva: Slatkine, 1972), 2:699–700.

168. The figures are from Louis Bergasse, *Histoire du commerce de Marseille*, vol. 4: *1599–1660* (Paris: Plon, 1954), 89.

169. Peiresc to Alvares, 4 July 1633, CBI, MS. 1871, f. 34r. "Car je ne cognois personne en ce pais la, et les Marseillais y ont fort peu de correspondance reglé." But there was not *no* contact: an insurance contract of 26 January 1633, for instance, covers traffic to Spain and then on to Lisbon and Madeira (MAD, 9 B 21, f. 307r).

170. Peiresc to Menestrier, 16 June 1633, *Lettres de Peiresc,* 5:639.
171. Peiresc to Tourtel, 16 December 1630, PBN, MS. Lat. 8957, f. 257v.
172. PBN, MS. Lat. 8957, f. 255r.
173. Alvares to Peiresc, 22 August 1633, PBN, MS. F.fr. 9539, f. 254v.
174. Alvares to Peiresc, 18 November 1633, ABM, MS. 201 (1019), 557. The name is given here as Domenico de Olivares.
175. Peiresc to Alvares, 9 October 1633, CBI, MS. 1871, f. 335r [omitted in *Lettres de Peiresc*].
176. Peiresc to Alvares, 28 November 1633, *Lettres de Peiresc,* 7:32–34 [= ABM, MS. 201 (1019), 560].

31. Merchants as Intellectual Partners

1. The most recent insight into this world is Anthony Grafton, *The Culture of Correction in Renaissance Europe* (London: British Library, 2011).
2. Vittore Branca, *Mercanti scrittori: Ricordi nella Firenze tra Medioevo e Rinascimento* (Milan: Rusconi, 1986); Christian Bec, *Les Marchands écrivains: Affaires et humanisme à Florence 1375–1434* (Paris: Mouton, 1967). Bec's compelling presentation of the convergence between Florentine humanists and merchants circa 1400 devotes only a single paragraph and two examples to the subject of "collaboration intellectuelle." The first is carrying letters and the second, acquiring manuscripts, both on behalf of the same scholar, then chancellor of Florence, Coluccio Salutati (368–369).
3. C. Secrétan, *Le "marchand philosophe" de Caspar Barlaeus: Un éloge du commerce dans la Hollande du Siècle d'Or; Étude, texte et traduction du Mercator sapiens* (Paris: Honoré Champion, 2002).
4. As, for example, the fine collection of essays, *Merchants and Marvels: Commerce, Science, and Art in Early Modern Europe,* ed. Pamela H. Smith and Paula Findlen (London: Routledge, 2002).
5. For the collections, see Peiresc's repeated requests of Minuti to obtain copies from l'Empereur's collection, as well as the inventories of coins and inscriptions held by the Vento and de Vias families (The Hague, Museo Meermano-Westreenianum, MS. 10.c.30, 383). This orientation toward Marseille is omitted in the otherwise splendid discussion of Provençal collections of Egyptian materials in *Égypte & Provence: Civilisation, survivances et "cabinetz de curiositez,"* ed. Marie-Pierre Foissy-Aufrère (Avignon: Musée Calvet, 1985), 182–188.
6. Even in the brilliant essays of Pierre Jeannin, this dimension of the merchant is nonexistent. See his *Marchands d'Europe: Pratiques et savoirs à l'époque moderne,* ed. Jacques Bottin and Marie-Louise Pelus-Kaplan (Paris: Éditions Rue d'Ulm, 2002), especially "La Profession de négociant entre le XVIe et le XVIIIe siècle," 281–308.
7. Peiresc to Gela, 13 January 1636, CBI, MS. 1874, f. 409v.
8. Peiresc to Seghezzi, 6 December 1634, CBI, MS. 1874, f. 358v. "Et si le riesche questo tentativo bisognarebbe haver gran curiosita di far raccogliere tutte quelle altri cose della supelettili antiqua che troveranno apprezzo delli mummie, soprà tuttò di libri che s'inchiadevano tal volta in scatolini e basi di figure di legno."

9. Seghezzi to Peiresc, 30 September 1635, CBI, MS. 1874, f. 409v. "Tutte cose di poco *rilievo ma di qualche curiosità* per essere tanto antiche."

10. Peiresc to Alvares, 1 August 1633, CBI, MS. 1871, f. 334v. "Mais comme la commerce des gents de negoce est plus libre que des autres, il vous sera plus aysé d'en venir a bout maintenant qu'à moy." This letter is omitted from those to Alvares printed by Tamizey de Larroque in vol. 7 of *Lettres de Peiresc*.

11. CBI, MS. 1777, ff. 127r–v.

12. Peiresc to Gaffarel, 4 July 1633, CBI, MS. 1873, f. 403r: "Il n'y a aucun mal que la deffense de la prattica, qui n'est pas un petit Impedimentum rerum bene agendarum, car les bonnes lettres ont de besoing d'une correspondance et communication plus libre et sans entremise de tant de truchementz et tierces personnes." Peiresc's negative view of the "pratique du palais" reflects his distinct perspective. See Wolfgang Kaiser, "Une aristocratie urbaine entre la plume et l'épée: Les 'nobles marchands' de Marseille, XVIe–XVIIe siècles," in *Le Second Ordre: L'Idéal nobiliaire: Hommage à Ellery Schalk*, ed. Chantal Grell and Arnaud Ramiere de Fortanier (Paris: Presses de l'Université de Paris-Sorbonne, 1999), 166.

13. Peiresc to Pierre Dupuy, 17 January 1630, *Lettres de Peiresc*, 2:230.

14. Peiresc to Pierre Dupuy, 7 September 1628, *Lettres de Peiresc*, 1:712.

15. Peiresc to Pierre Dupuy, 25 April 1634, *Lettres de Peiresc*, 3:89.

16. Peiresc to Golius, 8 May 1636, *Lettres à Claude Saumaise*, 261.

17. Peiresc to Petit, 7 April 1634, CBI, MS. 1875, f. 268v: "Nous avons eu de grande apprehensions d'une rupture entiere du commerce avec le Turc ou vous scavez que je pretends des interests plus sensibles que les marchands sur les bruictz venuz du costé de Constantinople."

18. "... non solum negotia mercatorum Interrupta sed etiam commercia literarum." Father Celestin to Jacob Golius, 8 April 1636, PBN, MS. Lat. 9340, f. 205r.

19. Peiresc to Gaffarel, 22 August 1633, CBI, MS. 1873, f. 405r.

20. Peiresc to Boerio, 6 February 1636, CBI, MS. 1873, f. 408r.

21. Peiresc to Marchand, [early March 1633], CBI, MS. 1874, f. 570r.

22. Peiresc to Contour, 22 November 1635, CBI, MS. 1874, f. 401v. "Mais pour des scrupules que j'ay souvent rencontrez en cas pareil, prevenantz de la difficulté qui se rencontrer en ces operations, quand il fault executer des choses en pratique qui semblent si aysées en Theorie."

23. Peiresc to Constans, 22 November 1635, CBI, MS. 1874, f. 403r. "Et vous supplie de rompre la partye quand vous verrez un'autre foys qu'on s'y voudroit attacher, oultre le danger des avaries qui pourroient aller à la ruine de familles entieres."

24. Peiresc to Gela, 6 March 1635, CBI, MS. 1874, f. 367r: "Io ho veduto altre volte in Venetia gran quantità di Caviaro, che fanno comm' intendo cert' ovi di pesci di color negro si per sorte vivanda del gusto di V.S. et ch'ella ne havesse in casa sua, o qualche suo amico ben confidente, che fosse ben recente & ben saporito ella mi carebbe un favore singolarissimo dispartiremene una libra ò duoi ... ma intendo che si non habbiamo un poco di caviaro, non gustata quasi in maniera alcuna il restante sendo il solo gusto di S.Em.za ma bisogna che sia ben recente & non rancido."

25. Peiresc to Gela, 15 March 1635, CBI, MS. 1874, f. 367v.

26. Peiresc to Gela, 6 December 1636, CBI, MS. 1874, f. 435r; Peiresc to Gela, 12 December 1636, CBI, MS. 1874, f. 435v. On 4 January 1637, Peiresc asked Gela for another one (CBI, MS. 1874, f. 440v).

27. PBN, MS. F.fr. 9532, f. 67v. "Le Sr. Henrique Alvares à qui j'escripts, ensemble *Les Orfevres et Joyelliers* de Paris ou les Corraliens qui font trouver argent dans Paris sur des engagements de pierreries auront ou scauront les lieux ou se pour-ront trouver des *vases de pierres precieuses,* et *de ceux mesmes d'argent antiques* que l'on faict souvent fondre pour les convertir en vaisselle d'argent à la mode courant."

28. PBN, MS. F.fr. 9532, f. 67v. "Chez les celebres droguistes et Apoticaires ils en tiennent souvent pour ennobler leurs monstres de boutique, lors qu'ils pre-parent la theriaque, la confection d'alchelmes et autres plus recommandables compositions."

29. An otherwise unknown Dr. Barbec from Cologne "qui a esté un an avec moy," made mathematical instruments for Peiresc's nephew (Peiresc to Bonnaire, 18 September 1626, CBI, MS. 1872, f. 191v). A bronze equestrian figure given to him by M. Agut was said to have been brought from Sidon, and Peiresc thought it functioned as a kind of wine pitcher because of a cover and hole on the neck of the horse. "M. Suchet," whom we know from a series of studies he did with Peiresc on casting and molding (CBI, MS. 1821), thought there had once been a candle-holder on the head of the rider but that it had been removed. PBN, MS. F.fr. 9532, f. 230v. On the occasion of there being an opening for the posi-tion of Maitre fondeur de l'Arsenal à Lyon, Peiresc wrote a letter of recommen-dation to his friend the archbishop identifying Suchet as "l'un des maitres fon-deurs du Roy, notre bon voysin et des meilleurs amys de notre maison." Peiresc to Richelieu, 13 February 1634, CBI, MS. 1875, f. 499r. Suchet was also particularly skilled with artillery (Peiresc to Aubery, 7 May 1630, CBI, MS. 1871, f. 520r).

30. PBN, MS. F.fr. 9530, f. 119r. The merchant was Laurens Bermond. Peiresc's lan-guage is quite precise: "la version Françoise recueillir de son discours." Peiresc's commentary was done on 10 May 1635. The description is on f. 119r, the tran-scription of the four verses on the outside of the cup is on f. 119v, and interlinear translations of the six verses on the inside are on f. 120r and f. 121r.

31. Peiresc to Petit, 2 November 1633, CBI, MS. 1875, f. 263r: "qui escript bien ce charactere."

32. Peiresc to Gilly, 18 September 1626, CBI, MS. 1873, f. 179r: "Que je n'estime gueres moins que les originaulx . . . sur ma feuille de papier."

33. This is documented in the lovely and important exhibition *Égypte & Provence,* ed. Aufrère and Loury.

34. PBN, MS. F.fr. 9532, f. 111r. "À esté apporté d'Aegypte à Marseille par un des ancestres duditz Sr Vento qui avoit esté Consul d'Alexandrie."

35. Peiresc to l'Empereur, 14 February 1629, CBI, MS. 1876, f. 375v. This likely re-fers to Peiresc's ongoing study of ancient weights and measures.

36. Peiresc to l'Empereur, 29 March 1634, CBI, MS. 1873, ff. 301r–v.

37. Pelissier to Peiresc, 2 August 1635, CBI, MS. 1821, f. 304r; PBN, MS. Lat. 8957, f. 143r.

38. For example, PBN, MS. F.fr. 9532, ff. 63–64. See the long letters on the experiment written by Guillemin to Peiresc, 10 June 1633, PBN, MS. F.fr. 9532, ff. 357r–363r, and 6 January 1633, ff. 369–371v and the associated "Memoire de ce que j'ay remarqué au Tresor de St Denys, pendant mon sejour du premiere et seconde de Janvier 1633" (364–368). Also Guillemin to Peiresc, 7 May 1633, PBN, MS. F.fr. 9538, f. 19r.

39. The letters of Guillemin to Peiresc in PBN, MS. F.fr. 9538, constitute the parallel to the overseas researches undertaken by merchants.

40. PBN, MS. F.fr. 9532, f. 68. "En allant dans les *vielles eglises,* de riche et ancienne fondation, il fault tousjours voir la sacristie, et les reliques, avec quoy il se trouve souvent des *vases fort precieux* de pierres fines, et quelque *foys d'argent* qui meriteroient d'en prendre la mesurage, & le dessein, s'ils paroissent bien antiques. Mesmes des calyces quand ils ont des ances des deux costez, comme ceux de St. Denys."

41. Peiresc to Pallavicino, 7 September 1634, CBI, MS. 1872, f. 389r.

42. Peiresc to Boerio, 25 February 1637, CBI, MS. 1872, f. 410v. "Discorso sulla piu celebri vasi antiqui in Italia."

43. Peiresc to Boerio, 6 March 1637, CBI, MS. 1872, f. 410v.

44. Peiresc to Gaffarel [early October] 1633, CBI, MS. 1873, ff. 406v–407r: "Il avoit la disposition des clefs de communication sy particuliers que il [*sic*] voulut car il fit ouvrier la chaste d'argent ou estoit l'Evangile de St Marc par une orfevre & fit d'autres experiances que n'estoit pas moins difficiles que celles que je demande maintenant." Peiresc thought water better than millet because water was not subject to compression. See also Peiresc to Gaffarel, 21 August 1634, CBI, MS. 1873, f. 413r.

45. "Que si vous pouvez trouver le moyen de voir entre les joyaulx de Grand Seigneur les vases qu'il doibt avoir d'Agathe & autres pierres precieuses, cela meriteroit bien d'en prendre un peu de relation et de portraict s'il estoit possible que s'il estoit loisible d'en faire mesurer la contenans du ceux du vase, il y auroit bien plus a discourir. Il ne faudroit que les faire remplir d'eau ou autre liqueur quelconque ou bien du millet ou autre menu grain, et puis faire mestre la mesme liqueur ou grayn dans un autre vase quel que ce puisse estre et le faire compare & adiustre a peu prez, a la juste contenance de l'eau qui aura remply le vase antique de pierre precieuse, et puis m'envoyer ce modele, soit de fer blanc ou d'estaing ou autre matiere, sur lequel je puisse faire examiner la cappacité ou mesure de l'antique, et vous verrez un jour que ce ne sera inutilement, dieu aydant. Il s'en trouve par foys de fort antiques, qui sont d'argent fort enrichis de figures et d'escripture, dont la maniere est si differente de la vaisselle d'argent moderne, qu'il n'est pas malaysé de les recognoistre quand ce ne seroit qu'a la seul polisseure qui estoit plus grande anciennement de beaucoup qu'a present. Vous y pourrez faire adviser & s'il s'en rencontre il faudroit user de la mesme diligence, et s'il estoit possible & loisible en faire mouller des empreintes pour mieux gouster la maniere des figures et autres ouvraiges & enrichissementz et ne fault pas negliger les platz et escuellons que si peuvent rencontrer antiques non seulement d'argent, mais aussy de cuivre & de pierre bien precieuses, dont les modelles au desfault des originaulx ne laisront

pas de nous ayder en noz recherches." Peiresc to Marcheville, 24 April 1633, CBI, MS. 1874, f. 604v.

46. Alvares to Peiresc, 18 November 1633, ABM, MS. 201 (1019), 357. "Le modelle de l'Agathe que je vous ay envoyé la masure. . . . Le vase d'Agathe on l'attend icy tous les jours, et venant je tireray le modelle parfaitement come me mandés en fer blanc, de mesme ayant receu celuy de Venise."

47. Peiresc to Minuti, 22 August 1632, CBI, MS. 1876, f. 818v.

48. PBN, MS. F.fr. 9532, f. 38r.

49. PBN, MS. F.fr. 9532, f. 46r. "Examen GEMMEDRUM POCILLORUM aut SCYPHUNCULORUM qui ex India Memphim aduchunt qui comparavunt Caesar Lambertus et Belgenciacum attulit *1632* 18 Augusti."

50. PBN, MS. F.fr. 9532, f. 43r. "Sur la relation d'un Turc nommé MATTOUK CHIASSAN d'Alep, que le Sr. Crouset gendre du Sr. Audifredy m'amene icy le 19 Octobre *1632*."

51. D'Arcos to Peiresc, 30 June 1633, PBN, MS. F.fr. 9540, f. 83v [= *Les Correspondants de Peiresc*, 2 vols. (Geneva: Slatkine, 1972), 2:211].

52. PBN, MS. F.fr. 9532, f. 42r. "Leditz Sr. MAGY me dict que cez vases viennent la plus part des Indes, ou du païs d'Adan ou Heden de l'Arabie Heureuse ou c'est que les peuple s'en servent pour boire de l'eau de canelle dont il se boit une extreme quantité en ce païs là."

53. See Hélène Desmet-Grégoire, "Origine et evolution des objets du café a Marseille aux XVIIe et XVIIIe siecles," *Provence Historique* 38 (1988): 70, and Sadok Boubaker, *La Régence de Tunis au XVIIe siècle: Ses relations commerciales avec les ports de l'Europe méditerranéenne, Marseille et Livorne* (Zaghouan: Ceroma, 1987), 107, arguing for 1660 and 1657, respectively.

54. PBN, MS. F.fr. 9532, f. 42r. This resembles the record of a conversation between Peiresc and the rabbi of Carpentras, Salomon Azuby. See Peter N. Miller, *Peiresc's Orient: Antiquarianism as Cultural History in the Seventeenth Century* (Farnham, UK: Ashgate, 2012), ch. 6.

55. PBN, MS. F.fr. 9530, f. 279r. "Le Jean Magy de Marseille qui à esté longtemps en Aegypte et jusques à une vintaine d'annees dict y avoir veu divers vases et utensils en commun usage, de forme fort semblable ou approchante aux anciens, entr'autres." "Les femmes se servent fort de cette machine." For the dating, see also Peiresc to Gassendi, 3 July 1633, *Lettres de Peiresc*, 4:322.

56. PBN, MS. F.fr. 9532, f. 187r, entitled "Mesures de Bronse Arabesques."

57. PBN, MS. F.fr. 9532, f. 254. There is no mention here of Magy, and we know that on this day Peiresc hosted Gilles de Loches on his way back from Egypt, so it is possible that the information derived from their conversation.

58. Lambert to Peiresc, 20 November 1634, PBN, MS. F.fr. 9532, f. 122r. "Le *Grand Picq est le picq general & ordinaire de villes du Grand Seigneur* pour les marchands qui passe directement en Constantinoble, le Caire, Allep, Damas, Saide & autres de son obeissance; et pour ce que vande les francs qui sont les francesi, i espagnolz, Italiens, anglois, flamans, Allemands & autres qui negotie de pardela." Peiresc carefully indexed the flyleaf: "*1634*. 20. Novembre./DIFFERANCE DES POIDS/dont on fait le quintal de chasque marchandise dans le Caire et ailleurs quasi partout le Levant./sur la relation de Mr Cesar Lambert."

59. Lambert to Peiresc, 20 November 1634, PBN, MS. F.fr. 9532, f. 123r.
60. Peiresc to Cassien de Nantes, 17 May 1635, *Correspondance de Peiresc*, 134–135.
61. PBN, MS. F.fr. 9532, f. 124v. "Il fault examiner si toutes cez differances ne peuvant pas proceder de quelque usage de mesurer les especes dans des vases ou mesures qui produisent cette diversité de poids, comme la differance du vin à l'huille, au miel, au froment, et autres denrees tant liquides que seiches, susceptibles de mesurage."
62. Peiresc to Seghezzi, 6 December 1634, CBI, MS. 1874, f. 357v. In this he goes beyond what he asked of Fernoulx on 3 November 1634 (CBI, MS. 1874, f. 356v).
63. Peiresc to Seghezzi, 6 December 1634, CBI, MS. 1874, f. 358r.
64. Peiresc to Seghezzi, 6 December 1634, CBI, MS. 1874, f. 358r. "Ma per ciò che sonno tutte guaste la maggior parte le mummie che si veggono in quelle grotte già aperti & scoperti, bisognarebbe far cercare et aprire qualche grotta vergine & non aperta di molti anni, dove si trovarebbono senz'altro, cose isquistissime non solamente per le mummie ma per le lor vesti, & ornamenti per gli idoli, vasi[,] libri et altri cosi. . . . Et si le riesche questo tentativo bisognarebbe haver gran curiosita di far raccogliere tutte quelle altri cose della supelettili antiqua [*sic*] che troveranno apprezzo delli mummie, soprà tuttò di libri che s'inchiadevano tal volta in scatolini et basi di figure di legno."
65. Peiresc to Seghezzi, 25 April 1636, CBI, MS. 1874, f. 423r: "Et s'ella usera diligenza apprezzo cotesti mori di campagna, se ne scuoprirà senz' altro qualche d'una piu facilmente ch'ella non crede mirando solamente alla proportione delle distanza delle bocche o buggi, dell'altre grotte già scoperte & alla drittura dell'ordine di detti buggi, sapendo io sicuramente che solevano gli antiqui osservar scrupulosamente coteste misure ugguali nelle distanze di coteste grotte destinate à sepolture quasi in questa forma à poco appresso ò altra non troppo differente. Anzi si VS Ill.ma ci attende vi si potria trovar qualche cosa preciosa et degna d'essio presentata a Prencipi grandi, et a cotesti Governatori in cui casi ne basterebbe haveva un schizzo o dissegno in carta."
66. Peiresc to Seghezzi, 25 April 1636, CBI, MS. 1874, f. 423r. "Ma vorrei ben ch'ella si rendesse un poco piu curiosa di far cercar grotta vergine di coteste mummie, nelle quali si trovarebbono sicuramente et vasi et scatoli et scrigni pieni di libretti ò volumetti et mummie preciose, & resti proprie di quei secoli, & ogni altra suppellectile, che potrebbe essere di sommo giovamento al pubblico, non potendosi conservar cotesti monumenti di materia tanto fragile et di poca duratione in qualsi vogli altro paese che in cotesto, dove non piove, et dove l'humidità del Nilo non arriva all'altezza di coteste grotte intagliate nel sasso vive dove si sono conservata la mummie piu di due migliaria d'anni con tutti li suoi pannicoli, carni et pitture senza corruptione alcuna."
67. Karl H. Dannenfeldt, "Egyptian Mumia: The Sixteenth Century Experience and Debate," *Sixteenth Century Journal* 16 (1985): 163–180; Dannenfeldt, "Egypt and Egyptian Antiquities in the Renaissance," *Studies in the Renaissance* 6 (1959): 7–27; Philip Schwyzer, "Mummy Is Become Merchandise: Literature and the Anglo-Egyptian Mummy Trade in the Seventeenth Century," in *Re-Orienting the Renaissance*, ed. Gerald Maclean (London: Palgrave Macmillan, 2005), 66–87. I am grateful to Katja Reetz for these references.

68. Peiresc for Jean Grange, 5 January 1635, CBI, MS. 1874, f. 363r:

> Memoire au sieur Jehan Grange allant à Smyrne, et au sieur François Grange son cousin. Neveux du sieur Baltasar Grange.
>
> De m'envoyer au Printemps s'il est possible quelque nombre de cameleons vivants, tant gros, petits, masles, et femelles, et tant des gris que des verdastres, par quelque navire ou barque qui vienne a droicture, et qui les fasse languir en mer le moings, que faire ce pourra, et de moyener que les puisse avoir s'il est possible avant l'esté.
>
> Et de s'informer de quels endroits on les apporte a peu près, si c'est des montagnes, ou des vallees, ou des plaines voisines, de quoy ils vivent qu'on aye peu recognoistre. Si on en passe jamais l'hyver dans les maisons combien on les vend, a peu pres; parmi quels arbrisseaux on les trouve. S'ils ne sont jamais au long des ruisseaux, si on les tient pas dans ces caves l'hyver, si l'on ne'n trouve pas dans la terre en labourant, & combien profond dans terre ils crusent leurs tanieres, si personne e[u]st jamais plainet d'avoir esté picqué, d'aulcun de tels animaux, ou blessé d'aulcun venin ou mauvaise qualité qu'il ayt.
>
> J'entends qu'il s'en trouve quantité envers les champs aux environs de Smyrne, et de Cic, et ailleurs et qu'ils ne se vendent pas grand chose.

69. Peiresc to Gela, 26 April 1636, CBI, MS. 1874, f. 414r. "Per dipingere la testa sola separatamente della giusta grandezza con la giusta lungezza della corna, & la proportione della fronte, & della radice & distanza di dette corna fra di loro. Ma bisognava far coteste diligenze quando sara giunto l'animale in Pariggi, dio giovante. Intanto la preggo di mandarmi una giusta misura della lunghezza di dette corna per farme la comparazione sulla pittura, insieme della lunghezza della testa, dubitando che il pittore, l'habbia tenuta forzi un poco piu piccola del naturale, a proportione della lunghezza & altezza del corpo di tutto l'animal, che è nobilissimo veramente."

70. It is illustrated in *The Paper Museum of Cassiano dal Pozzo,* Quaderni Puteani 4 (n.p.: Olivetti, 1993), 158.

71. Peiresc to Pion, 29 September 1635, CBI, MS. 1874, f. 391.

72. Peiresc to Constans, 13 May 1635, CBI, MS. 1873, f. 46v. "Pour apprendre la vraye situation de ce pays la sur la globe terrestre."

73. Peiresc to Contour, 22 November 1635, CBI, MS. 1874, f. 401v. "De ce qu'il à observé avec toutes ses circonstances et plustost la plumitif, ou minute primative que ce qui pourroit estre plus au net."

74. Peiresc to Contour, 22 November 1635, CBI, MS. 1874, f. 402r. "Qu'il m'en fault faire la comparaison, avec les observations qu'en avoit faictes en mesme temps le RP Agathange en Aegypte, Mr de Chasteuil au Liban, un autre de mes amys à Thunis, et plusieurs autres a Rome, Padoue, Naples, Florence, a Paris, en Hollande en Allemagne & ailleurs, que nous donnerons moyens de regler sur la carte les vrayes distances d'un lieu à autre de sorte que, parlant d'Alep, si son observation me manque il me fauldra contenter de ce peu que m'en à peu mander sur le credit de sa memoire le R. P. Celestin & le Sr. B. Claret ce qui ne

se pourra pas faire sans parler de luy, et dire qu'il eusse bien peu fournir quelque chose de meilleure s'il eust voulu. Dont il auroit du reproche de la posterité car dieu sçait quand on rencontera d'autres occasions de faire accorder tant de gents ensemble a faire en un instance de pareilles observations en des lieux du monde si esloignez les unes des autres."

75. Peiresc to Claret, 21 May 1636, PBN, MS. N.a.f. 5172, f. 72r [autograph]; CBI, MS. 1874, f. 425r. Father Celestin describes him as "Dominus Claret pharmacopolam, virum in simplicium cognitione diversarumque rerum peritia excellentem." Celestin to Peiresc, 29 September 1635, PBN, MS. Dupuy 688, f. 19r.

76. On this, see more fully Peter N. Miller, "Mapping Peiresc's Mediterranean: Geography and Astronomy, 1610–1636," in *Communicating Observations in Early Modern Letters, 1500–1675: Epistolography and Epistemology in the Age of the Scientific Revolution,* ed. Dirk van Miert (London: Warburg Institute Colloquia, 2013), 135–160.

77. Peiresc to Wendelin, 18 May 1636, CBI, MS. 1876, f. 509r. "Il se trouve si peu de gents capables de faire des observations assez exactes pour y fonder des importantes consequences."

78. Pierre Humbert, "Un manuscrit inédit de Gassendi," *Revue des questions scientifiques* 53 (1934): 5–11 [= CBI, MS. 1832, ff. 30–32]; "Instructions pour observer au deffault des esclipses, le passage de la lune sur quelque estoile fixe et la haulteur du soleil, aux solstice et consequemment celle de l'elevation du pole" (CBI, MS. 1832, ff. 147r–v).

79. Peiresc to Giovanni l'Armeno, 1 November 1636, CBI, MS. 1874, f. 432v. "Et quando passera in Alessandria in qual si voglia staggione che sia, la preggo di prendere l'altezza del sole meridiana quanti giorni potrà, & mandarmene la relation punctuale, di quanto ella haverà osservato, et di già mi mandi su il suo Astrolabio ò di cartone, ò di metallo, per giudicare se è tale che vi si possa prendere confidenza."

80. Peiresc to Mallon, 20 February 1631, CBI, MS. 1876, f. 810v. Although it was possible that the person who supplied him with his collection of silver and copper coins had in fact made a long study of those coins and medals, Peiresc tended to think that they were "triailles portées de Venise ou d'ailleurs." These were brought to the Levant in order satisfy market demand in exchange for which they took in good silver and gold. This provides a fascinating insight into the state of the market for antiquities, already in the 1630s, in the Levantine cities.

81. See my discussion of Peiresc's attentiveness to historical headgear in Miller, *Peiresc's Orient,* "Introduction: Peiresc and History," 24–29.

82. Peiresc to Mallon, 20 February 1631, CBI, MS. 1876, f. 811r: "Et qui ont des testes couronées d'un simple ruban sont coustumement meilleures a garder, et celles de cest grosseur qui sont d'argent bien fin & ont des testes d'empereures couronnes de laurier ou de Rayons, soit qu'elles ayent les lettres grecques & Latines. Mais entre celles d'or celles qui sont fort grosses et espoisses sont les meilleures quand elles sont des poids d'environ dix escus et qu'elles sont bien elaborrées & de bon relief et bon dessein. Des autres plus petites celles qui ont pareillement des testes ceintes ou couronnees d'un simple ruban ou bandelotte

et qui ont des lettres grecques bien apparentes voir les plus petites d'or sont tres bonnes quand elles sont bien espoisses pour la largeur & bien nettes & bien travaillees s'il s'en trouve d'or ou il y a avec une couronne d'espines entrelasser avec la croix, je serois bien ayse d'en avoir."

83. "C'est une marchandise si sujete a fraude que je ne serois vous en donne commission puis que vous n'en avez pas peu acquerir une si grande praticque & connoissance qu'il faudroit pour oser attacquer des plantes." Peiresc to Minuti, 23 August 1632, CBI, MS. 1876, f. 824r.

84. Quoted in Aby Warburg, "Francesco Sassetti's Last Injunctions to His Sons," in *The Renewal of Pagan Antiquity: Contributions to the Cultural History of the European Renaissance,* trans. David Britt, intro. Kurt W. Forster (Los Angeles: Getty Publications, 1999), 237.

85. John Donne, "A Lecture upon the Shadow," in *Donne: Poetical Works,* ed. Herbert J. C. Grierson (Oxford: Oxford University Press, 1979 [1929]), 64.

86. "Pries dieu quy donne du repos a mon esprit inquietté par les gouttes quy me *tiennent depuis le jour de l'an quy dans [moins] d'ung mois sera revolleu,* mais plus pour voir que ma fortune est plus estropiée que moy, je la voudrois bien tenir pour indifferante, mais je suis que rarement dans ceste posteure ma philosophie ne m'ayant pas encores bien affermy. Pardonnes a ceste sailhie et faictes moy voir pour vos commendements. Que vous me rendes dignes de Votre souvenir ce quy pretend sur toutes les chozes du monde." Allemand to Minuti, [December 1634], CBI, MS. 1878, f. 274v. This sentiment takes us straight back to the diaries of Florentine merchants studied by Gene Brucker (*Two Memoirs of Renaissance Florence: The Diaries of Buonaccorso Pitti and Gregorio Dati* [Long Grove, IL: Waveland Press, 1991 (1967)]).

32. Before *Statistik*

1. I discuss this in Peter N. Miller, *Peiresc's Orient: Antiquarianism as Cultural History in the Seventeenth Century* (Farnham, UK: Ashgate, 2012), 312–316.

2. Classic is Howard F. Cline, "The *Relaciones Geográficas* of the Spanish Indies, 1577–1586," *Hispanic American Historical Review* 44 (1964): 341–374.

3. See, for instance, José de Acosta, *Natural and Moral History of the Indies,* ed. Jane E. Mangan (Durham, NC: Duke University Press, 2002), esp. bks. 4 and 6. I am grateful to Anthony Grafton for bringing this point to my attention.

4. CBI, MS. 1777, ff. 60–61r. The document lists 447 Dutch ships, 193 French ["ponant et levant"], 56 German, Baltic 278, English 60, Spanish 120, Provence-Languedoc 60. The document, tellingly, is dated 1621, the last year of the Twelve Years' Truce between Spain and the United Provinces.

5. Diego de Haedo, *Topographia e historia general de Argel* (1612); *Africa overo Barbaria. Relazione al doge di Venezia sulle reggenze di Algeri e di Tunisi del dragomano Gio. Battista Salvago* (1625).

6. They were published, with the assistance of the Dupuy brothers, as *Trois relations d'Egypte et autre mémoires curieux des singularitez dudit pays* (Paris, 1651).

7. The figure of 100,000 was given by Baltasar Vias in a letter to Peiresc of 21 March 1626 (London, British Library, Add. Mss. 19272, ff. 70r–71r).

8. CBI, MS. 1864, ff. 225r–v.

9. "Un memoire qu'il a dressé de l'Estat des provinces de l'Egypte, dont il n'avoit faict grand feste autrefois, disant l'avoir apprins avec grand peine de ceux qui hantent aux lieux publiques ou sont les actes & registres des droictz du Gr. Seign. lesquelz caressent & festinent pour en apprendre ce qu'ilz peuvent a bastons rompus" (Peiresc to de Thou, 5 June 1635, CBI, MS. 1877, f. 450v).

10. "Si vous aviez reservé coppie des memoires que vous avez dressés journellement de Charnassé je serois bien ayse d'en avoir un extraict. Mais de vous donner la peyne de les dresser vous mesmes de rechef comme vous dictes vouloir faire c'est ce que je vous supplie tres humblement de ne voulois [*sic*] pas faire pour moy seul attandeu qu'oultre que je n'en vaulx pas la peine j'en ay quasi sur le mesme subjet dressees par le Sr Cesar Lambert & par plusieurs aultres qui peuvent aulcunement suffire a ma curiosité sans vous donner de la peine et vous desrober pour cela du temps qui vous est sy cher." Peiresc to Albert, 20 February 1634, CBI, MS. 1874, f. 328v.

11. Peiresc to de Thou, 15 October 1635, CBI, MS. 1876, f. 380v. "Une relation assez particuliere des pais d'Egypte. Je n'ay recouvré fraischement une plus succincte mais bien exacte et bien certaine ce dict on."

12. For background on the merchants, see Oleg V. Volkoff, *À la recherche des manuscrits en Égypte,* Recherches d'archéologie, de philologie et d'histoire, 30 (Cairo: Institut Francais d'Archéologie Orientale, 1974); Sidney Aufrère, *La Momie et la tempête: Nicolas-Claude Fabri de Peiresc et la "curiosité Égyptienne" en Provence au début du XVIIe siècle* (Avignon: Éditions A. Barthélemy, 1990), 97, 99, 104, 120.

13. PBN, MS. Dupuy 669, ff. 215–236. "Relation de Cesar Lambert de Marseille de ce qu'il a veu de plus remarquable és annees 1627.28.29.30 & 31 *au Cayre en Alexandrie & autres villes d'Egypte.*"

14. "C'est ce qui rend le negoce du Cayre si miserable, & par consequent la ville moins fleurissante" (PBN, MS. Dupuy 669, f. 216v).

15. Albert's mémoire is found in V Cents Colbert MS. 483 [= PBN, MS. Dupuy 475], ff. 554–556; PBN, MS. Dupuy 669, ff. 239–251v.

16. PBN, V Cents Colbert MS. 483, f. 559v.

17. "Rentree des marchandises de Turquie, comme des grains, huiles, savon, amandes & autres marchandises qui viennent de Gaza, de Seide & de Damas, qui payent toutes dix pour cent." PBN, V Cents Colbert MS. 483 [= PBN, MS. Dupuy 475], f. 559v.

18. PBN, V Cents Colbert, MS. 483, f. 559v.

19. Copies are found in CBI, MS. 1777, ff. 157–161; PBN, V Cents Colbert MS. 483 [= PBN, MS. Dupuy 475], ff. 554–564; PBN, MS. Dupuy 669, ff. 253–258.

20. CBI, MS. 1777, f. 157r. "Lieu trez grand, ou autres fois alloit le Bascha de Constantinople. A present il est gouverné par un Sangiat de Cayre qu'y envoye le Bascha lequel se gouverne par le mesme conseil dudit Cayre. Il tient soubs luy 14. gouverneurs pour 14. petites provinces et lorsque la riviere du Nil croist elle rend toutes sortes de bled sans fin."

21. "Sont absoluts et n'y a point d'appellation ny pour la vie ny pour le bien des gents."

22. CBI, MS. 1777, f. 158r.
23. "Une Reddebe qui est la mesure du bled d'Egypte revient en France un charge de 300 livres de poids environ." CBI, MS. 1777, f. 158v.
24. CBI, MS. 1777, f. 158v.
25. CBI, MS. 1777, ff. 160r–161r.
26. August Ludwig Schlözer, *Theorie der Statistik: Nebst Ideen ueber das Studium der Politik ueberhaupt* (Göttingen: Vandenhoeck and Ruprecht, 1804), 86.
27. On this, see Justin Stagl, *A History of Curiosity: The Theory of Travel 1550–1800* (Chur, Switzerland: Harwood, 1995), 127; Michael C. Carhart, *The Science of Culture in Enlightenment Germany* (Cambridge, MA: Harvard University Press, 2008).

33. Peiresc's Mixing in Cairo's Consular Politics

1. The relations of Gédoin and Deshayes were printed; the observations of La Picardière remain in manuscript (such as PBN, V Cents Colbert MS. 485, ff. 125, 137, 184, 205, 229; also MACC, J 891, piece 5 [unpaginated], Pierre d'Olivier to Consuls of Marseille, 28 February 1631. For a history of the consulates, see G. M. Saint-Yves, *Les Consulats du Levant et leurs origines* (Paris: Imprimerie Nationale, 1901) [extrait du *Bulletin de géographie historique et descriptive,* nos. 1–2 (1900)].
2. De Brèves's choice of Du Ryer to replace Gabriel Fernoux, whom he had appointed, was rebuffed by the consuls, provoking a series of angry letters from de Brèves (MACC, J 129). See Alastair Hamilton and François Richard, *André Du Ryer and Oriental Studies in Seventeenth-Century France* (London: Arcadian Library, 2004).
3. Géraud Poumarède, "Naissance d'une institution royale: Les Consuls de la nation française en Levant et en Barbarie aux XVIe et XVIIe siècles," *Annuaire-Bulletin de la Société de l'histoire de France: Année 2001* (Paris: Champion, 2003), 117n349.
4. Peiresc to Bermond, 7 June 1633, CBI, MS. 1876, f. 829r.
5. Peiresc to de Thou, 5 December 1634, CBI, MS. 1877, f. 408v. "Je ne le cognoys que par reputation, mais je n'ay veu personne de tous ceux qui ont negotié de ce costé la, qu'il en dict tout le bien qui se peut imaginer accepté les parans du consul qui a esté tiré de charge lequel n'aura pas esté trop bon mesnager s'il est vray ce qu'on dict."
6. Peiresc to Gela, 12 February 1635, CBI, MS. 1874, f. 364v.
7. Much correspondence can be found in PBN, MS. F.fr. 16161, "Lettres de du Ryer consul d'Egypte/de Bermond Consul, et d'un sien frere/et de Santo Segezi consul du Caire/escrittes d'Alexandrie, et du Caire a Mr de Cesy Ambassadeur a Constantinople tant sur les affaires du Consulat, et de la nation que sur les affaires particulieres dudit sr de Cesy; mesmes touchant quelques nouvelles et occurences du pais depuis 1623 jusques a 1644," ff. 176ff.
8. Peiresc to de Thou, 13 February 1635, CBI, MS. 1877, f. 426r.
9. Peiresc to de Thou, 13 February 1635, CBI, MS. 1877, f. 426v. "En somme je pense que c'est un tres dangereux conseil et ne trouve aulcune raison qui n'y repugne, supposant les choses en l'estat qu'elles sont comme il ne se peult pas

dissimuler sans trahir les intheretz de la France quy sont plus attachez aux cor-respondances des marchants françois, qu'a la formalité de l'origine & n'ayant d'aultre homme quy s'est mis a l'abry du nom françois, & qui ne luy a poinct faict de dezhonneur jusques icy."

10. Peiresc to de Thou, 1 May 1635, CBI, MS. 1877, ff. 442v–443r.

11. Magy to Peiresc, 29 October 1635, PBN, MS. F.fr. 9542, ff. 111v–112r. "Je ne le puis croire, car d'ici personne que soit marchand n'a faict de plaintes contre de luy cy quelque canaille pour ne luy avoir voulleu averer cais mechansetez estant ceux qu'on a ruiné nostre nation d'honneur et de bien on faict quelques fauces informations pour nous priver du bien recevons du gouvernement de nostre dict frere consul pour nous remestre dans un labarinte que sera la ruine totale de nostre ditte nation en ce pays cy. . . . Sy Mons.r nostre consul y a dict d'aller moderement s'a esté pour leur bien ou le puis dire que sans son respect eussent eu de travail, car Tur[c]s, Mores, Greq. Juifs Coffestis murmuroyent contre eux don en luy donnant les avis pour les garder de mal."

12. Laugeiret to Consuls of Marseille, 18 December 1634, MACC, J 731, piece 1, unfoliated. Jean Jacques Laugeiret was the chancellor of the French consulate in Alexandria.

13. Seghezzi to Consuls of Marseille, 13 September 1634, MACC, J 550, piece 1, unpaginated. The original letter was written in Italian. In the original, Seghezzi writes that Bermond profited from the rental of those taverns ("Si affitava ta-verne, et il Sr. Bermond ne haveva questo Beneficio non riguardando che se in esse taverne si fosse amazatto qualche Turcho, come facilmente tra huomini imbriachi").

14. "Puisque ce n'est pas mon naturel, & au contraire c'est de faire bien a ceulx qui m'ont fait du mal." Seghezzi to Consuls of Marseille, 11 October 1634, MACC, J 550, unpaginated.

15. Seghezzi to Consuls of Marseille, 11 October 1634, MACC, J 550, unpaginated.

16. Report of Antoine Mazarat and Jean Fargues, 24 October 1634, MACC, J 550, unpaginated.

17. Seghezzi to Consuls of Marseille, 16 December 1634, MACC, J 550, unpaginated.

18. Seghezzi to Consuls of Marseille, 24 April 1635, MACC, J 550, unpaginated.

19. Bermond to Consuls of Marseille, 13 August 1633, MACC, J 549, unpaginated. "La malice & meschancette de ceulx qui m'ont vouleu callonier."

20. Peiresc to de Thou, 14 May 1635, CBI, MS. 1877, f. 447r. "Un peu de memorial ou instruction de l'estat present des affaires du negoce de Levant."

21. Peiresc to de Thou, 29 June 1635, CBI, MS. 1877, f. 454v.

22. Seghezzi to de Thou, 30 September 1635, PBN, MS. F.fr. 9542, f. 146r.

23. Seghezzi to de Thou, 30 September 1635, PBN, MS. F.fr. 9542, f. 146v. *De me faire tenir quelque formalité de lettres patentes du Roy ou Conseil portants tels ordres suffisants a faire contenir noz negotiants en leur debvoir.*" The animal would subsequently occupy a lively place in Peiresc's correspondence.

24. We can identify him from a document in MACC, J 731.

25. Peiresc to de Thou, 18 April 1636, CBI, MS. 1876, f. 385v: "Et si Mr de Brèves ne si laisse a ce coup dessiller les yeux pour se trouver de ce coste la, tout a bon

essiant il y perdra plus que tous les autres & quand il aura senty le coup, il ne sera plus temps d'y chercher des remedes."

26. Seghezzi to Peiresc, 30 September 1635, ABM, MS. 212 (1030), p. 123.

27. Gela to Peiresc, 31 December 1635, PBN, MS. F.fr. 9542, f. 147v.

28. Seghezzi to Peiresc, 12 February 1636, PBN, MS. F.fr. 9542, f. 148r.

29. Christophe de Bermond to Consuls of Marseille, 4 November 1635, MACC, J 551, unpaginated.

30. Aix-en-Provence, Archives Départementales, B 3351, f. 18, dated 4 October 1636.

31. Oleg V. Volkoff, *À la recherche de manuscrits en Égypte*. Recherches d'archéologie, de philologie et d'histoire, 30 (Cairo: Institut Français d'Archéologie Orientale) (Cairo, 1974), 82.

32. Marc Bloch, "Pour une histoire comparée des sociétés médiévales," in *VIe Congrès International des Sciences Historiques: Résumés des communications présentées au congrès* (Oslo: Comité du Congrès, 1928), 119–121.

33. Marc Bloch, *The Historian's Craft* (New York: Random House, 1953), 42.

34. For a brilliant analysis of Bloch's *Ex Libris,* see Ulrich Raulff, *Marc Bloch: Un historien au XXe siècle* (Paris: Éditions de la Maison des Sciences de l'Homme, 2005 [German ed. 1995]), 271–288.

34. Peiresc and Travel

1. Including a manuscript account by Christophorius Furerius; Claude Thormont, *Voyage du Levant* (1610); *Relation de voyage au Levant faict par le Baron de Beauvau* (1608); *Viaggio da Venetia al santo Sepolcro e al monte Sinai* (1600); Jean Mocquee, *Voyages en Afrique, Asie, Indes Orientales* (1617); Henri Castela, *Les Voyages du seigneur de Villamont* (1598, 1603). George Sandys he got in 1626 from Cardon in Lyon (*Lettres de Peiresc*, 6:466). This subject is discussed in Sidney Aufrère, *La Momie et la tempête: Nicolas-Claude Fabri de Peiresc et la "curiosité Égyptienne" en Provence au début du XVIIe siècle* (Avignon: Éditions A. Barthélemy, 1990), 139–140.

2. Peiresc to Blanc, 30 July 1619, CBI, MS. 1872, f. 326r; *Les Voyages Fameux du Sieur Vincent Le Blanc Marseillois* (Paris, 1648).

3. Bergeron to Peiresc, 15 January 1627, PBN, MS. F.fr. 9539, f. 214v.

4. For details of this project, see Peter N. Miller, *Peiresc's Orient: Antiquarianism as Cultural History in the Seventeenth Century* (Farnham, UK: Ashgate, 2012), "Introduction: Peiresc and History," 17–18. A transcript of a table of contents survives in Peiresc's archive, CBI, MS. 1777, ff. 166r–177.

5. These are all found in CBI, MS. 1777: Maurand's manuscript includes many pen-and-ink sketches, as well as watercolor illustrations of places along the itinerary (ff. 179–220v); "Discours du voyage faict en Levant par le sieur de Beaulieu de Pairsac, par le commandement du feu roy Henry le Grand" (ff. 277–307v); Feine de Montferran's voyage (ff. 222–239v); and the "*1598:* Voyage de Perse" (ff. 242–276). The ethnographic details in Feine de Montferran's journey fascinate Peiresc; he underlines a discussion of how Indians train cormorants to fish in the river, and put a ring around their necks so they cannot swallow the food, but must bring it to their masters (f. 237).

6. CBI, MS. 1777, ff. 332–341. This seems to be one of two known manuscript copies (the other is PBN, MS. F.fr. 9670, ff. 67–74) of what is now printed in *Mémoires d'un voyage aux Indes Orientales 1619–1622: Augustin de Beaulieu, un marchand normand à Sumatra*, ed. and intro. Denys Lombard (Paris: Maisonneuve & Larose, 1996).

7. CBI, MS. 1777, f. 255r: "Le lieu est appelle Brisseton, nous seiourassmes le reste du jour."

8. Peiresc to Pierre Dupuy, 26 May 1628, *Lettres de Peiresc*, 1:621.

9. "TERRE SAINCTE/*1608* [*sic.*, 1618?]/VOYAGE DU Sr. RAIMONDIN/EN HIERUSALEM," CBI, MS. 1777, f. 309 r.–v.

10. Wickham depicts these villages on the cover of his *Framing the Early Middle Ages: Europe and the Mediterranean, 400–800* (Oxford: Oxford University Press, 2005).

11. These references occur at ff. 310r, 314r, and 329r.

12. Minuti to Peiresc, 15 March 1633, PBN, MS. F.fr. 9542, f. 11r. This compares to the inventory list of clothing items sent back by Peiresc from Paris to Aix in October 1623: "Un rac de cuir plain de chimses d'un valet. Un manteau bleau d'un laqauy. Un habit noir, une chemisette rouge, 2 chemises, 4 calisons, 2 coiffes de nuict et un bonnet de nuict." CBI, MS. 1869, f. 93r.

13. Minuti to Peiresc, 21 October 1633, PBN, MS. F.fr. 9542, f. 16v. *"Mes provisions que je porte quand a moy en mon voyage, que consistent en biscuit, vin, huille, d'eau de vie, vinegre, sel, lentilles, fayols, ris, poutarques, couvertes de lict, capot* et beaucoup d'autres choses a ce fait grandement necessaires car au pays du Turc on ne trouve point d'hostellerie ny le plus souvent du pain."

14. De l'Isle to Peiresc, 7 November 1633, CBI, MS. 1879, f. 223r. "Toutte ces provisions quy consistent en un peu de biscuit des Ognions et un pilu de legume avec une petite pignatte pour fert son pottaige. Je ne scay comme ce bon homme peu subsister de voyage en ce pays sans manger de la viande ou pour le moins du beurre et des oeufs. Avec toutte cest chettive vie qu'il faict, il est, Dieu Messias, en tres bonne sante et a bonne Mine avec sa grand barbe qu'il y vien quazy jusques a la ceinture. Il est accorder pour sa monture d'icy en Constantinople pour vingt sept piastres." A copy of this letter is at CBI, MS. 493, f. 220r.

15. Joan-Pau Rubiés, "Instructions for Travellers: Teaching the Eye to See," *History and Anthropology* 9 (1996): 165, 167–176, now collected in *Travellers and Cosmographers: Studies in the History of Early Modern Travel and Ethnography* (Aldershot, UK: Ashgate, 2007). For the English reception of Peiresc, see Peter N. Miller, *Peiresc's Europe: Learning and Virtue in the Seventeenth Century* (New Haven, CT: Yale University Press, 2000), 45–48.

35. Where Mediterranean Meets Orient

1. De Brèves to Puysieux, 12 May 1619, MACC, J 1862, unpaginated. "Les subiectz du Roy trafficans par les mers de Levant ou pour mieux dire sur la mer mediterranée."

2. Egypt in Provence was the subject of the exhibition and catalog *Égypte & Provence* in 1985. For new interest in the wider Mediterranean, see Sabine du

Crest, "Les Réseaux méditerranéens de l'exotique indien autour de Peiresc: Érudition antiquaire et hybridation artistique," in *La Méditerranée sur la route des Indes: Savoirs, mémoire, imaginaire, réseau* (Aix: Presses Universitaires de Provence, forthcoming).

3. Nuno Vassallo e Silva, "Precious Stones, Jewels and Cameos: Jacques de Coutre's Journey to Goa and Agra," in *Goa and the Great Mughal*, ed. Jorge Flores and Nuno Vassallo e Silva (Lisbon: Calouste Gulbenkian Foundation, 2004), 116–133; Susan Stronge, "The Land of 'Mogor,'" in Flores and Vassallo e Silva, *Goa and the Great Mughal*, 144; João Teles e Cunha, "Hunting Riches: Goa's Gem Trade in the Early Modern Age," in *Portuguese, Indian Ocean and European Bridgeheads 1500–1800: Festschrift in Honour of Prof. K. S. Mathew*, ed. Pius Malekandathil and Jamal Mohammed (Tellicherry, India: Institute for Research in Social Sciences and Humanities of MESHAR, 2001), 267–304; Francesca Trivellato, "The Exchange of Mediterranean Coral and Indian Diamonds," in Trivellato, *The Familiarity of Strangers: The Sephardic Diaspora, Livorno, and Cross-Cultural Trade in the Early Modern Period* (New Haven, CT: Yale University Press, 2009), ch. 9, 224–250.

4. *"Treasury of the World": Jeweled Arts of India in the Age of the Mughals*, ed. Manuel Keene and Salam Kaoukii (London: Thames and Hudson, 2001).

5. Charles de la Roncière, "Un artiste français à la cour du Grand Mogol," *Revue hebdomodaire* (1905): 182.

6. Peiresc to Bishop of Mans, 6 April 1637, *Lettres de Peiresc*, 7:558 [= CBI, MS. 1872, f. 411r]. "Pour se randre plus expert & plus recommandable, en son art d'orfevrerie & de diamanterie, ou s'il est randu si excellent, qu'il a emporté la preferance par tout ou il a faict du sesiour sur touts les autres ouvrieres de sa vocation."

7. Peiresc to Bergeron, 29 December 1626, *Lettres de Peiresc*, 7:592 [= CBI, MS. 1872, f. 325r]. "La cognoissance de cez pais là semble bien estre aussy agreable que aulcune aultre de tout l'Orient."

8. Peiresc to Bergeron, 18 November 1629, CBI, MS. 1872, f. 327v. "C'est un homme trez bien advisé et trez veridique, ce qui me facit avoir une bonne esperance de son labeur."

9. "4.Avril.1626, achepte pour 6.Suizadas/de Nicolas Jaloux de la Verdiere lapidaire/qui a faict un voyage aux Indes, Babylone, Ormus, Goa & aux Royaulmes de Dealcan et Golganda, duquel il a emport le Rubies qu'il m'a vendre, les roys y sont Mahometans mais le peuples la plus part Idolastres des serpents, veaux, & autres Animaux comme les AEgyptiens." The Hague, Museo Meermano-Westreenianum, MS. C.10.30, 391. For the discussion of Hinduism in the circle of Peiresc, see Joan-Pau Rubiés, *Travel and Ethnology in the Renaissance: South India through European Eyes, 1250–1625* (Cambridge: Cambridge University Press, 2000), chs. 9, 10.

10. "*Pseudocarbunculus Indicus,* . . . è Regno Golgondensi Morgoris tributario, anno *1622*, allata." "Il m'en a depuis faict avoir deux autres plus jolis mentionnez cy devant" (C.10.30, 391).

11. The Hague, Museo Meermano-Westreenianum, MS. C.10.30, 392. A first, undated letter from Peiresc to "Nicolas Jaloux de Laverdière, marchant lapidaire a

Marseille," refers to a projected trip to Constantinople, while a second, dated 22 January 1627, both refers to a letter from Jaloux dated 20 January and invites him to come look at Peiresc's collection (CBI, MS. 1874, f. 36r).

12. "Il debvoit repartir pour un autre voyage en Perse le 20. Aoust *1627* sur la barque de Patron Viguier parent du Consul d'Alep." The Hague, Museo Meermano-Westreenianum, MS. C.10.30, 392.

13. PBN, MS. N.a.f. 5169, f. 28v.

14. Peiresc to Pierre Dupuy, 12 February 1628, *Lettres de Peiresc,* 1:533.

15. Gallous [*sic*] to Peiresc, 10 November 1627, CBI, MS. 1777, f. 86r. "Je fais estat avec que dieu aydant *de partir dans deux moys pour la Perse & puis passé oulture.*"

16. Peiresc to Jaloux, 18 July 1630, CBI, MS. 1874, f. 11r.

17. Peiresc to [Minuti], 11 October 1633, CBI, MS. 1874, f. 314r.

18. "Gentilhomme François au service du Roy le Grand Mogor & en son absence au Sr. Loys Herryard son filz. A Lahore . . . M. H. Alvares a Paris, rue Michel le Comte," printed in Sneyders de Vogel, *Philologus* 39 (1955): 6–8. See also on Herryard, Sir E. D. Maclagan, "Four Letters by Austin of Bordeaux," *Journal of the Punjab University Historical Society* 4, no. 1 (1916): 3–17; Herryard's travels with von Poser are highlighted by William Irvine, "Augustin of Bordeaux," *Journal of the Royal Asiatic Society* (1910): 1343–1345; H. Beveridge, "Von Poser's Diary in Persia and India," *Imperial and Asiatic Quarterly Review,* 3rd ser. 29, no. 57 (1910): 96–100.

19. "D'aller voyager par les Royaumes Orientaux, & ne trouvant en Agypte, Arabie, Mesopotamie, Babylone, Perse chose digne d'un Roy, j'ay passé outre vers ce Roy des Indes dict communement Grand Mogor ou Mougoul." Herryard to du Tour, 26 April 1625, CBI, MS. 1777, f. 354r.

20. CBI, MS. 1777, ff. 361r–v. "Je luis fis un *trono* real ou il y a autre plusieurs *milions d'or* e d'argent et plusieurs autro invansions, comme de talier un *diamant de 100 guilats.*" "Augustin Houaremand, qui est un nom que le Roy m'a donné. En persian veu dire inventeur des ars."

21. Herryard to du Tour, 26 April 1625, CBI, MS. 1777, ff. 354r–v.

22. Herryard to du Tour, 26 April 1625, CBI, MS. 1777, f. 355r.

23. It was probably based on this information that Peiresc crafted the genealogical table of Jahangir's family (CBI, MS. 1777, f. 353v).

24. Herryard to Bermon, 9 March 1632, CBI, MS. 1777, ff. 352–353. Note that Peiresc translated Herryard's narrative of the family relations between Jahangir's children into tabular form (353v).

25. Jean-Baptiste Tavernier, *Travels in India,* ed. William Crooke, [trans. Vallenine Ball,] 2 vols. (Oxford: Oxford University Press, 1925 [2nd ed.]), bk. 1, ch. 7, 88.

26. CBI, MS. 1777, f. 390r: "A *Gaspar da Costa Casseretz*/ausente a Fran.co Tinoco de Carvallo/E em ausensia d'ambos a Ruy. Lopes da Silva que de Sr g.de [?]/ Em Goa." Peiresc adds beneath, "India Oriental," and continues from there in his hand: "*Fernand Nunes ou Guill. Corner* de Hamfort en Hollande qu'a un frere a Paris nommé *Mr Alvarez Flamand* qui sc *tient rüe Michel le Comte./ Manuel de la Costa* Casseretz, qui a une soeur marie audit Alvarez et qui est frere dudit Gaspar de Costa."

27. PBN, MS. N.a.f. 5169, f. 60r.
28. James Boyajian has traced the shape of the Alvares de Luna family in Goa, Paris, Amsterdam, and Hamburg from the records of the Inquisition in Lisbon (Boyajian, *Portuguese Trade in Asia under the Habsburgs, 1580–1640* [Baltimore: Johns Hopkins University Press, 1993], 138–139). It is possible that the correspondence with Peiresc represents the only other archival source. I thank Sanjay Subrahmanyam for this reference. Wim Klooster has identified for me a "Manoel da Costa" who had his daughter Anna baptized in the Reformed Church in Recife on 27 August 1653 (C. J. Wasch, ed., "Een doopregister der Hollanders in Brazilië," *Algemeen Nederlandich Familieblad* 5 [1888]: 141–144, 169–172, 197–200, 225–228, 253–256, 281–284; 6 [1889]: 1–4, 25–28, 49–52, 73–77). The absence of the "Casseretz" might indicate that this is a different person. Portuguese Sephardim were also known for their role in the contemporary international diamond trade. See Luís Crespo Fabião, "Subsídios para a história dos chamados 'Judeus-Portugueses' na indústria dos diamantes em Amsterdão nos séculos XVII e XVIII," *Revista da Faculdade de letras* [Universidade de Lisboa], 3rd ser. 15 (1973): 455–517; Herbert I. Bloom, *The Economic Activities of the Jews of Amsterdam in the Seventeenth and Eighteenth Centuries* (Port Washington, NY: Kennikat Press, 1969 [1937]), 40–44; and more generally Francesca Trivellato, "Jews of Leghorn, Italians of Lisbon, and Hindus of Goa: Merchant Networks and Cross-Cultural Trade in the Early Modern Period," in *Commercial Networks in the Early Modern World,* ed. Diogo Ramada Curto and Anthony Molho, European University Institute Working Paper HEC No. 2002/2, 76.
29. Peiresc to Gaspar da Costa, [18 July 1630], CBI, MS. 1874, ff. 10v–11r.
30. Peiresc to Jaloux, 18 July 1630, CBI, MS. 1874, f. 11r.
31. Peiresc to Fernand Nunes and Manuel da Costa Cassaretz, 19 July 1630, CBI, MS. 1874, f. 11r. "Si nobles et si excellent pour le reglement de la chronologie & de l'histoire."
32. Peiresc to Emanuel da Costa Casseretz, 11 August 1630, CBI, MS. 1874, f. 11v; Peiresc to Bermond le Cadet, 11 August 1630, CBI, MS. 1874, f. 11v.
33. CBI, MS. 1821, ff. 453r–456v.
34. CBI, MS. 1821, f. 454r.
35. CBI, MS. 1821, f. 454v. "Il fauldroit en prendre quelque griffonement des plus belles fabriques, et des figures et bas reliefs qui s'y voyent encores, et sur tout des inscriptions, qui y peuvent estre soit Grecques ou barbares, autres que Arabiques." To Vermeil, Peiresc had explained the way to make "squeezes" of inscriptions: "Que s'il s'en pouvoit avoir des portraicts bien fidèlement représentéz et que pour les caracteres d'escripture l'on trouvast moyen de les contretirer en y plaquant dessus des feuilles de papier mouillé doubles ou simples, selon que le papier est plus ou moins mince ou assez fort pour résister à la mouilleure et souffrir qu'avec un mouchoir pressé dessus quand le papier est encore mouillé; il puisse s'imprimer dans le creux des lettres et en retenir la figure en le laissant quasi seicher sur la pierre." CBI, MS. 1821, f. 472v.
36. "S'il s'y trouve des petites coquilles cannellees comme celles qui sont les plus communes en noz mers de deca. S'il y en a de cornües, comme celles qui se

trouvent icy petrifiées. S'il y a des limassons fort delliez et fort larges. Contre ceux qui se trouvent icy petrifiez, dont la coquille doibt estre tenue comme du papier, ou comme la coque d'un oeuf tout au plus. S'il y a des animaulx de mer faicts come la poincte d'un doigt, ou le fer d'un espier, ou d'un dard, qui s'attache aux Rochers. Recueillir de touts cez sortes de coquillages, et sur tout de ceux qui sont comme des limasses à diverse étages percées d'un petit trou par ou passe un petit nerf, sur quoy les Chinois s'exercent volontiers à faire diverses graveures de feuillages, et oyseaux, ou en vouldroit qui ne fussent pas tra-vaillez." CBI, MS. 1821, f. 455r.

37. Peiresc to Bermond, 26 December 1630, CBI, MS. 1876, f. 810r: "La conserva-tion de commerce parmy les armes qui est une marque de bonne foy laquelles doibt faire grande honte aux Chrestiens qui ne scavent pas en ce la se comporter aussy dignement que les infidelles."

38. Peiresc to de Thou, 26 July 1630, CBI, MS. 1876, f. 807v.

39. Peiresc to Alvares, 15 May 1633, *Lettres de Peiresc*, 7:29 [= CBI, MS. 1871, f. 333r].

40. Alvares to Peiresc, 12 June 1633, PBN, MS. F.fr. 9539, ff. 256r–v.

41. Peiresc to Alvares, 4 July 1633, CBI, MS. 1871, f. 333v [omitted in *Lettres de Peiresc*]. Peiresc asks for "quelque morceau de Roche ou soient demeurez atta-chez quelques rubis pour petits qu'ils soient, pourveu qu'ilz soient de belle cou-leur et de bonne dureté, afinque je puisse juger de la nature de la mere roche des montagnes où ils naissent, comme j'en ay de celle des diamans, esmeraudes et autres, et encore des saphirs. Mais ce n'est pas des orientaulx. . . . Et les es-timerois bien davantage si les grains de Rubis & de Saphirs y paroissent en leur naturelle figure enchassez dans la roche sans aucun artifice de roue ou de main d'homme ainsy que je leur en fis voir des monstres lorsqu'ilz me vindrent voir à Boisgency."

42. Peiresc to Alvares, 4 July 1633, CBI, MS. 1871, ff. 333v–334r. "S'il estoit loisible d'apprendre voz correspondances dans Lisbonne ou semble s'il y en à aussi je les scaurois volontiers pour y prendre mes addresses quand il y va par foys des barques de Marseille pour les prins de me faire recouvrer pour mon argent des plantes & fruictz des Indes quand il en arrive de fraiz en sorte qu'on en puisse esprouvé le goust et en conserver la race de ceux qui se peuvent domestiquer dans des vases ou potz de terre. . . . Car je ne cognois personne en ce pais la, et les Marseillois y ont fort peu de correspondance reglé encores que par foys il y ailt des barques dont les marinieres ne peuvent pas s'acquitter des commissions si commodement comme ceux du pais ne avoir les addresses et credit qu'il y fault aulcuneffois pour cela."

43. Alvares to Peiresc, 22 August 1633, PBN, MS. F.fr. 9539, f. 254v: "*Fernand Nunes est en le plus grand autorité dans le dealcan . . . me disent de Goa que entierement gouverner ce Pais la.*" Note Peiresc's elaborate seventeen-point summary of the letter on the flyleaf (255v).

44. Peiresc to Alvares, 9 October 1633, CBI, MS. 1871, f. 335r [omitted in *Lettres de Peiresc*].

45. Peiresc to Alvares, 28 November 1633, *Lettres de Peiresc*, 7:33 [= ABM, MS. 201 (1019), 560].

46. Peiresc to Aycard, 11 October 1633, CBI, MS. 1871, f. 36v.

47. Peiresc to Aycard, 20 April 1634, CBI, MS. 1871, f. 42r.

48. Peiresc to Vermeil, 25 February 1634, CBI, MS. 1821, f. 470. This letter was published in Caix de Saint-Aymour, *Histoire des relations de la France avec l'Abyssinie chrétienne sous les règnes de Louis XIII et de Louis XIV* (Paris: A. Faivre et H. Teillard, 1886), 273–288, but from an inferior copy of the letter (CBI, MS. 1876, ff. 550–554, with silent omissions and errors; Peiresc's autograph draft is CBI, MS. 1821, ff. 468–743). The letter and associated boxes of gifts were sent to Jacques Albert in Cairo, who was to handle the transshipment to Vermeil. See Peiresc to Albert, CBI, MS. 1874, ff. 327v–328v. Raymond Lebègue, who never missed an opportunity to score Philippe Tamizey de Larroque for his sloppy editorial practices, excised this portion of the letter from his *Supplement au tome VII de l'édition Tamizey de Larroque* (Paris: Éditions du CNRS, 1985), 15.

49. Roxani Heleni Margariti, *Aden and the Indian Ocean Trade: 150 Years in the Life of a Medieval Arabian Port* (Chapel Hill: University of North Carolina Press, 2007).

50. Peiresc to Vallavez, 19 March 1626, *Lettres de Peiresc,* 6:427; PBN, MS. N.a.f. 5169, f. 17r, 18 March 1626; Louis Deshayes, *Voyage du Levant fait en l'année 1621* (Paris, 1624).

51. Signier to Peiresc, 20 March 1626, CBI, MS. 1879, ff. 636r–v. "Q'une compagnie de trois cens mille escus seroint peu de cas & on ne la scauroit faire de dix mil car il fault que vous sachiez que noz vaisseaux qui alloit en Levant & qui sont porter quatre cens mille escus aujourdhuy se contentent d'ilz porter quinze ou vingt mille pour le plus oultre qu'il estime notre nation la pire du toutes impatiente & incapable de pouvoir de[meuré?] a un payes & y a davantaige que les angloys nous font la bar . . . & vont charger les soyes a Ormuz & puis peu de jours on est ve[nu] en vaisseau a Londres avec six cens balles & en l'estat que nous sommes n'y a nul de noz vaisseaux que en peult aporter trente & sy autres fois un seul en à apporter quinze cens je croys que feu Mr de Viaz & Durand vous en diroit le mesme veritable."

52. In terms of scale, the smaller French boats carried a slight inventory; when Captain Baille's polacre was lost near Malta, its cargo was valued at only 3,000 écus. Magy to Peiresc, 29 October 1635, PBN, MS. F.fr. 9542, f. 110v. Looking at some of the surviving maritime insurance contracts, one of the largest values was for a ship going to Egypt in 1631, the *patron* was Barthélemy Issaultier, frequently mentioned by Peiresc, and its content was only being insured for 9,000 écus (MAD, 9 B 21, f. 84r).

53. Edhem Eldem, Daniel Goffman, and Bruce Masters, *The Ottoman City between East and West: Aleppo, Izmir, and Istanbul* (Cambridge: Cambridge University Press, 1999), 32.

54. Vias to Peiresc, 21 March 1626, London British Library, Add. MSS. 19272, ff. 70r–71r.

55. Fernoux to d'Oppède, 20 November 1627, PBN, MS. Dupuy 429, f. 125r. "Pays du Yemen, Royaulme de L'Arabie heureuse, scituée à l'entrée de la mer Roue, vis à vis de l'Ethiopie, ou abordent tous les vaisseaux qui viennent des Indes, chargez d'espisseries & autres marchandises de grand prix, de quoy les ministres du

Grand Seigneur tiroient un grand revenue pour les doüanes qu'ilz avoient faict establir audit Yemen en un lieu qui s'appelle Moca, qui est sur la mer."

56. Fernoux to d'Oppède, 20 November 1627, PBN, MS. Dupuy 429, f. 125v.

57. Peiresc to de Thou, 25 April 1629, CBI, MS. 1876, f. 354v: "Ceste affaire de l'Hyemen est de de trez grande importance si on l'eust mesnager mais on l'aura sans doubte laissé ruiner comme celle d'Erzeron." The context here suggests what we learn later of the province's rebellion against its Ottoman suzerains.

58. The initial argument was made for the eighteenth century in André Raymond, *Artisans et commerçants au Caire au XVIIIe siècle*, 2 vols. (Damascus: Institut Français de Damas, 1973), and then for the seventeenth century in Nelly Hanna, *Making Big Money in 1600: The Life and Times of Isma'il Abu Taqiyya, Egyptian Merchant* (Syracuse, NY: Syracuse University Press, 1998), 19, 75, 81.

59. Peiresc to de Thou, 12 December 1629, CBI, MS. 1876, f. 827r. "Dont plusieurs sont si estranges & si dignes de remarques qu'il s'y recognoist des plantes qui ne se trouvent qu'au fonds de la mer rouge, & des grandes coquilles ou limaçons pareilz à ceux de nacre qui se peschent avec les perles orientales dont les Chinois font de si beaux godets, et qui plus est des fruicts marins aussy curieux et aussy bigearres qu'on en scavoit concepvoir."

60. The best exploitation of this set of facts is in S. D. Goitein and Mordechai A. Friedman, *India Traders of the Middle Ages: Documents from the Cairo Geniza; "India Book" Part One* (Leiden: Brill, 2007); and Margariti, *Aden and the Indian Ocean Trade*.

61. "Cez vases"—Peiresc's old interest—"de *Bezoar mineral* se font *au Hiemen* audelà de la mer rouge ou il y a *une montagne* toute entiere de cette pierre qu'ils appellent IASA ou GEZA. Les ouvriers travaillent en des cabanes aux champs, la maison mesme du Sultan est couverte de Chaulme. . . . Chiassan d'Alep, de bonne famille avoit esté sur les lieux au païs du Hiemen, et avoit veu travailler de cez vases, scier les pierres, et les travailler au Tour." PBN, MS. F.fr. 9532, f. 43r.

62. PBN, MS. F.fr. 9532, f. 43r.

63. Peiresc to Gaffarel, 1 October 1633, CBI, MS. 1873, f. 406r: "L'on les apporte du Montka [*sic*] et les marchands disent que les mines n'en sont pas esloignées."

64. CBI, MS. 1777, f. 374r: "1633. 7 Juill. IEAN MAGY avec le memoire des livres & graines/pour le ROY D'AETHIOPIE" [= ABM, MS. 207 (1025), 3]. "Vous sçaurés qu'au Moucal on a tué Camson Basha, et que le Grand Seigneur a perdu tout le pais de l'Ayaman."

65. PBN, MS. F.fr. 9532, f. 42r. "Ex Moresque du Cayre au rapport du Sr. Jean Magy filz d'Agostin de Marseille."

66. This section was subtitled "Leditz Sr. MAGY me dict que cez vases viennent la plus part des Indes, ou du païs d'Adan ou Heden de l'Arabie Heureuse ou c'est que les peuples s'en servent pour boire de l'eau de canelle dont il se boit une extreme quantité en ce païs là." PBN, MS. F.fr. 9532, f. 42r.

67. "Le chef du païs de l'Hiemen nomme, Basnisius Hiemani de la race des anciens princes de ce païs là, s'estant rebellé contre la Sultan entretient sa milice en les norissant seulement et leur distribuant des places au paradis, dont il pretend avoir la disposition en qualité de cherif, descendeu de la race de Mahomet et s'est emparé de la ville de Senam qui estoit la capitale & demeure du Bassa. . . . De la

vient l'encens, myrrhe, aloes, coroe, Zedoign, coque de Levant, nux vomique, tulleries de cotton, Indiannes. Baulme noir. Indigo. Le Cavvy que les Mores appellent Ben." PBN, MS. F.fr. 9532, f. 42r.

68. Peiresc to Magy, 17 May 1635, CBI, MS. 1874, f. 368v. "Concernant l'estat present du païs de l'Hiemen et des pieces venez de l'Abais au Suaquez [sic], sur quoy il à bien à discourrir." Peiresc added that Magy was not to tell the Venetian consul anything. Peiresc to Magy, 10 August 1635, CBI, MS. 1874, f. 382bis v, thanking him for news of Suaquin and Moucal.

69. Peiresc to Magy, 27 July 1636, CBI, MS. 1874, f. 422r. "Celle de la caravane de Dacroy de laquelle je vouldrois bien avoir de une relation bien particuliere."

70. We see this also in the contemporary letters of the French Capuchin Cesair de Roscoff, for example, to Raphael de Nantes, 26 November 1630, PBN, MS. N.a.f. 10220, f. 106r; 24 January 1632, f. 109.

71. Peiresc to Albert, 20 February 1634, CBI, MS. 1874, f. 329r. "Les aultre pais plus loingtains et plus estranges par tout . . . les caravannes qui abordent au Cayre soit du coste de l'Afrique ou des Abyssins, ou de coste du Moucal de l'Arabie ou des Indes."

72. Peiresc to Pelissier, 25 April 1631, CBI, MS. 1876, f. 812v.

73. Peiresc to Pelissier, 5 June 1631, CBI, MS. 1876, f. 813v. "Tous ceux qui se mesle de negoce ont droit et debvoir de l'aller salluer."

74. Peiresc to Pelissier, 24 June 1631, CBI, MS. 1876, f. 813v.

75. Pelissier to Peiresc, 23 July 1631, CBI, MS. 1879, f. 534r. "Pour *ce dervis et saint chinois* il est perfectement bien fait et a quelque chose de Pie et religieus [sic] a soy qu'il ne scait dire et qu'aussy je ne puis facilement comprendre je l'ay posé droit couché a travers et en diverses fassons, mesmes dans la bouete [boite], m'imaginant l'avoir sepulturé m'avoit telement attiré mes sens a sa contemplation, que j'en ay esté plus d'une heure idolatre."

76. Peiresc to Pelissier, 20 August 1631, CBI, MS. 1876, f. 816r: "Que vous estiez encores tout ravy de l'idolastrie ou vous avoir faict tomber (ce dictes vous) ce dervis ou santon des Chinois que vous avez trouvé si excellent & si capable d'esmouvoir de la pieté en vous, sur la contemplation de sa froide & devote mine. Mais je ne scay comme elle peut estre compatible avec le sacré dont vous l'armez. Lorsque je pourray aller a Marseille je seray bien ayse de le voir. . . . Car je serois bien marry que Mr de Gastines s'en prinast comme vous dictes pour l'amour de moy puis que la piece luy tient lieu de tant d'autres belles choses qu'il vous a donnes en troque." Another part of the letter urged him not to go to Italy in the summer because of the persistent risk of plague.

77. CBI, MS. 1777, ff. 128r–v:

> Que si l'on vouloit establir quelque correspondance et commerce en la ville du Moucal hors de la bouche de la mer rouge, pour peu qu'on luy donnast de secours pour y subsister, il s'y offriroit volontiers, et donneroit moyen d'en tirer avec le temps toutes les plus precieuses marchandises qui peuvent venir non seulement de l'Arabie heureuse qui y est joignante, mais des Indes dont le Traffic et traject y est grand et ordinaire. Et de l'Etiopie mesmes qui a un port à l'autre costé du bord de ladit Mer Rouge.

C'estoit de ce lieu du Moucal que souloient venir au Cayre autres foys toutes ces Grandes richesses des Indes qui y abordoient et qui se vouloient espandre par toute la Chrestienté, et dont le commerce et la correspondance pourroient se restablir plus facilement qu'il ne semble par l'entremise et le credit du Sr Santo Seghezzi à present consul de la nation Françoise dans le Cayre, qui y a plus de creance que n'eut de long temps aulcun autre consul. Et par la bonne volonté et disposition dudit Pellissier qui ne s'y esparnerà pas, et qui pourroit y prendre le soing de ce qui y seroit adressé tant à Goa que autres ports des Indes, ou qui en viendroit audit lieu du Moucal pour passer au Cayre et en Chrestienté.

Le traject estant fort ordinaire de Goa au Moucal, et de Moucal au Suez ou à la Mecque, comme les caravanes ordinaires aussy du Cayre au Suez et à la Mecque. Et se tireroit par ce moyen de Grandes commoditez encore de l'Aethiopie par le moyen des ports qu'abouttissent tant à la Mer Rouge que dehors icelle, et par les correspondances qu'on y pourroit prendre avec le Sr Vermeil, qui s'est estably en cette cour là, et qui seroit bien aise de maintenir le commerce en Chrestienté par la voye du Moucal et du Cayre plustost que par celle du Portugal et de l'Espagne.

78. Peiresc to de Seguiran, 9 December 1634, CBI, MS. 1876, f. 163v. "Au Monquas [Moucal] qui est quasi a l'embouscheure de la mer Rouge ou toutes les Indes orientales abordent a cette heure les Turcs cy sont desrechef assurés de cette ville là comme des pais d'allentour, je vous en feray un jour la relation et projets."

79. Peiresc to Villeauxclercs, 7 February 1635, CBI, MS. 1876, f. 628v.

80. Aix-en-Provence, Archives Départementales, B 3350, f. 119v, letter patent giving the office "de joaillier et antiquaire du Roi" to Benoit Pelissier of Aix, dated Chantilly, 14 March 1635.

81. Peiresc to de Thou, 7 February 1635, PBN, MS. N.a.f. 5172, f. 47r [= CBI, MS. 1877, f. 425r]: "& si ces Messrs. les intendants du commerce soubs l'authorité de Monseigneur le Em. Card.al Duc [Richelieu] leur surintendant General trouvoint du jour a son establissement en la ville du Moucal pour la correspondance aux Indes et en l'Ethiopie, auquel cas il ne pourroit peult estre pas se passer de quelque secours jusques a ce qu'il eust pourveu aux moyens de si entretenir de son Gain possible ne seroit il pas inutile pour le public d'ouvrir ce chemin là pour n'estre pas obligé de passer par les mains des Espanols & Portugais et pense que la correspondance du Sr Santo Seghezzi au Caire pourroit faire valloir cette sorte de negociation dans la creance qu'il c'est acquis de pardelà, comme vous scavés." The letter concluded with a thoughtful description of Pelissier as a person.

82. Peiresc to de Thou, 13 February 1635, PBN, MS. N.a.f. 5172, ff. 48v–49r [= CBI, MS. 1877, ff. 426v–427r.] [Margin:] "J'avois oublié de vous dire que je vous escrivis cez jours passés par le Sr Benoit Pellissier sur une proposition qu'il faict d'aller rendre au Montqual en Arabie Heureuse ou a esté transferé le commerce qui soulloit estre a Aden et ou abordent aforces barques & marchandz des Indes tant de Goa que de Callicut & de plus loing & mesme de l'Aethiopie qui est de l'aultre costé de l'embboucheure de la mer Rouge. C'estoit par la que souloient

venir au grand Cayre les plus grandes . . . de l'Orient. Sy cella se restablissoit comme il ne semble pas sy difficille le commerce en seroit fort abregé & fort reglé avec les marchandz françois de Goa & du Mogor & du consulat du Caire en vauldroit mieux. Cet homme est assez industrieux & a d'honnestes garantz de ceste ville. Difficillement trouvera on des personnes de meilleure condition qui voulussent s'aller exposer de la sorte. C'est pourquoy je pense qu'il ne le fault pas negliger, & quand mesmes il en cousteroit quelque chose pour le commence-ment soit au roy ou a Mr de Brèves possible la despense n'en seroit pas toute perdüe, ne comparables a celles de cez Mssrs qui ont l'advantage non seulement d'estre sur les lieux, mais d'estre dans les interestz mesmes dudit negoce."

83. Peiresc to Alvares, 8 February 1635, CBI, MS. 1871, f. 336r [omitted in *Lettres de Peiresc*]. "Saichant les habitudes & correspondances que vous avez aux Indes Orientales et ayant apprins le dessein qu'avez le Sr. Benoit Pelissier de ceste ville d'Aix, d'aller faire quelque residence en la ville du Moucal qui est du costé de l'Arabie heureuse assez proche d'Aden au delà de la bouche de la mer rouge ou le commerce & le traject [est] si frequent avec ceux d'Ormus & de Goa. J'ay creu que vous ne seriez pas marry de le cognoistre et que possible trouveriez vous bon d'entretenir quelque sorte de correspondance avec luy quand ce ne seroit que pour avoir des nouvelles de voz amys de cez pays des Indes par ceste voye là, qui est la plus brefve, attendu que du Moucal a la Mecque au Suez, et au Cayre, le commerce est fort frequent et que du Cayre à Marseille il l'est encore davantage. Il a fort voyagé en ce Levant et faict profession et negoce particuliere de tout plein de pierreries et autres choses qui peuvent aulcunement tombé soubz votre goust. C'est pourquoy j'ay creu que vous n'auriez pas desagreable qu'il vous fasse offre de son service, et qu'il trouveroit chez vous ce bon accueil."

84. Pelissier to Peiresc, 2 August 1635, CBI, MS. 1821, ff. 304r–v. "Mon camerade Monsieur Jacob Vermeils frere de celuy qui se treuve en l'Ethiopie."

85. Peiresc to Magy, 10 August 1635, CBI, MS. 1874, f. 382bis v.

86. Peiresc to Magy, 7 October 1635, CBI, MS. 1874, f. 393r.

87. Peiresc to M. de la Tuillerie, 9 November 1635, CBI, MS. 1873, f. 422r.

88. Peiresc to Gela, 9 November 1635, CBI, MS. 1874, f. 396v.

89. Peiresc to M. de la Tuillerie, 17 June 1636, CBI, MS. 1873, f. 423r. To Gela, in 1637, Peiresc wrote that Pelissier "fu amazzato in Venetia l'anno passato" (24 February 1637, CBI, MS. 1874, f. 442r).

90. Peiresc to Seghezzi in Venetia, 23 February 1637, CBI, MS. 1874, f. 441v.

91. None of this material is known even to the most recent study of Yemen in the seventeenth century, C. G. Brouwer, *Al-Mukha: Profile of a Yemeni Seaport as Sketched by Servants of the Dutch East India Company (VOC) 1614–1640* (Amsterdam: D'Fluyte Rarob, 1997).

36. At the Still Point

1. "Instructions des différentes sortes ou qualitez du coral qui se pesche en nos mers, données de la part du sieur Jean Caulne, de la Ciottat, qui en fait traffic particulier," PBN, MS. Dupuy 661, f. 223. I am grateful to my friend Jérôme Delatour for helping identify the place.

2. Gassendi seems to put the location on the other side of Sixfours, off Cape Sicié. This is a contradiction we cannot resolve. Gassendi, *Vita Peireskii,* in *Opera Omnia,* 6 vols. (Lyon, 1658), 5:295; Gassendi, *Mirrour,* 162. Coral fishing was an old maritime occupation of Marseille. See P. Giraud, "Les Lenche à Marseille et en Barbarie," *Mémoires de l'Institut historique de Provence* 13 (1936): 10–57; 14 (1937): 107–139; 15 (1938): 53–86; and more recently P. Gourdin, "Le Corail maghrébin à l'époque moderne," in *Corallo di ieri, corallo di oggi,* ed. J.-P. Morel, Cecilia Rondi-Costanzo, and D. Ugolini (Bari: Edipuglia, 2000), 55–68; H. B. Hassine, "Les Concessions françaises du corail en Afrique barbaresque," *Mésogéios* 7 (2000): 238–259. Cyriac of Ancona reported encountering coral fishers from Marseille off the coast of Epirus in September 1448. See Cyriac, *Later Travels,* ed. Edward W. Bodnar (Cambridge, MA: Harvard University Press, 2003), 345, fragment 46.

3. PBN, MS. N.a.f. 5169, f. 10r, 6 September 1624: "À Sr Menestrier avec la coral en une boitte."

4. "J'ay autrefois eu ce plaisir la moy mesmes en personne d'aller voir cette pesche, ou j'observay mille petites singularitez de la nature, que je me repent bien de n'avoir redigé par escrit de frasiche memoire comme cela le meritoit, les autheurs n'ayant pas traictté cette matiere si exactement comme je l'eusse pû faire." Peiresc to Suares, 25 September 1628, PBN, MS. Dupuy 661, ff. 224r–v. Peiresc remained attracted to coral. In October 1628 he sent to his brother a piece of "coral arbor" (PBN, MS. N.a.f. 5169, f. 36v).

5. For more on this story, see Peter N. Miller, "Major Trends in European Antiquarianism, Petrarch to Peiresc," in *The Oxford History of Historical Writing,* ed. José Rabasa, Masayuki Sato, Edoardo Tortarolo, and Daniel Woolf (Oxford: Oxford University Press, 2012), 3:252.

6. The epistemic possibilities of fiction for historians are assessed in *Le Débat* 165 (2011); *Critique* 767 (2011); *Vingtième siècle* 112 (2011); Johann Petitjean, "Raconte-moi une histoire: Enjeux et perspectives (critiques) du narrativisme," *Tracés: Revue de sciences humaines* 13 (2007): 185–200; Christophe Granger, "L'Imagination narrative, ou l'art de raconter des histoires," in *À quoi pensent les historiens: Faire de l'histoire au XXIe siècle,* ed. Christophe Granger (Paris: Éditions Autrement, 2013), 149–164; François Hartog, *Croire en l'histoire* (Paris: Flammarion, 2013), 163–224.

Appendix A. Peiresc in History, 1637–1932

1. Jacques Morgues, *Les Statuts et Coustumes du Pays de Provence* (Aix, 1642), sig. ã2v; Pierre-Joseph de Haitze, *Histoire de la ville d'Aix,* 6 vols. (Aix, 1889 [1660]), 4:43–44, 283–284; Jean-François de Gaufridi, *Histoire de Provence* (Aix: Charles David, 1694), 67, 399–400; Jean Scholastique Pitton, *Histoire de la Ville d'Aix Capitale de la Provence* (Aix, 1666), 9, 54, 613–14, 680; Honoré Bouche, *La Chorographie ou description de Provence et l'histoire Chronologique du Meme Pays,* 2 vols. (Paris, 1736 [1669]), 1:sig. biii r, 35, 63, 76, 91, 95–96, 123, 158, 200, 217; 2:910–911. Bouché was a protégé of Peiresc (Peiresc to Bourdelot, 26 December 1634, CBI, MS. 1872, f. 448r) and contributed a memorial poem

in Occitan to the *Panglossia* section of the *Monumentum Romanum,* ed. Bouchard (Rome, 1638), 107–108.

2. Gabriel Naudé, for example, proclaimed in a letter to Jacques Dupuy, "For myself, I think that it [publication of Peiresc's letters] would be the most learned and curious work that we would have had for the last 500 years, and that is also the opinion of Cavalier [Cassiano] dal Pozzo" (Naudé to Dupuy, 3 May 1638, quoted in *Lettres de Gabriel Naudé à Jacques Dupuy [1632–1652],* ed. and intro. Phillip Wolfe [Edmonton: Alta, 1982], p. 53). Nevertheless, neither Dupuy, nor Naudé when he was librarian to Cardinal Mazarin, made any effort to gather, let alone publish, Peiresc's letters. (Peiresc's heir, Claude Fabri, even offered Pierre Dupuy the whole lot [10 April 1646, PBN, MS. Dupuy 830, f. 264). Naude's formal eulogy, in the form of a letter to Gassendi, was published in Pierre Gassendi's foundational *Vita Nicolai Fabricii de Peiresc, Senatoris Aquisextiensis Vita* (Paris, 1641), as were eulogies embedded in the works of other contemporaries: Claude Saumaise, Pierre Borilly, Athanasius Kircher, and Marin Mersenne. Jean-Jacques Bouchard's *Laudatio Funebris Claudii Fabri Peirescii* was first published separately in Venice (1638), then in the *Monumentum Romanum,* which he edited (1638), and then again the following year, apart, in Aix (1639). The superiority of Gassendi's biography was recognized immediately. Gui Patin wrote on 4 September 1641 that "Peiresc étoit un grand personnage: l'auteur l'est pareillement": *Lettres de Gui Patin,* ed. J.-H. Revillé-Parise, 3 vols. (Paris, 1846), 2:82–83; Daniel Morhof proclaimed it the best life of a scholar ever written: *Polyhistor* (Lübeck, 1708 [1688]), 50; and it was the explicit model for other scholars' lives, such as Robert Boyle: *Robert Boyle by Himself and His Friends: With a Fragment of William Wotton's Lost Life of Boyle,* ed. and intro. Michael Hunter (London: William Pickering, 1994), xxxiv–xxxvii, xlix, li, lx, 62.

3. Richard Yeo, *Notebooks, English Virtuosi, and Early Modern Science* (Chicago: University of Chicago Press, 2014), 106.

4. Benjamin Rand, "The Epistle Dedicatory," in Gassendi, *Mirrour,* [A3v].

5. Pepys to Evelyn, 9 January 1692, in *Private Correspondence and Miscellaneous Papers of Samuel Pepys,* ed. J. R. Tanner, 2 vols. (London: G. Bell and Sons), 1:51.

6. Bayle to Mazaugues, 3 April 1699, CBI, MS. 439, f. iv.

7. Francis W. Gravit, *The Peiresc Papers* [= University of Michigan Contributions in Modern Philology 14] (Ann Arbor: University of Michigan Press, 1950), 11.

8. Gravit, *The Peiresc Papers,* 16. Bégon, who was intendant of La Rochelle, knew enough of Peiresc to write to Louis Thomassin de Mazaugues of his "si grand vénération pour la mémoire de l'incomparable M. de Peyresc" (CBI, MS. 440, f. 3r).

9. Peiresc's name is of central importance for Spon. See Spon, *Recherches curieuses d'antiquité contenues en plusieurs dissertations* (Lyon, 1683), but esp. at 177–178; in *Miscellanea Eruditae Antiquitatis* there are thirty references to objects in the Peiresc collection, and Spon prints Peiresc's essay on the tripod found in Fréjus in 1629 (118–120); in *Réponse à la critique publiée par M. Guillet* (Lyon, 1679) Peiresc serves as *the* example of the study of material culture: Spon's *Angeiografia* (70–80). Montfaucon reproduced many Peiresc images in his *Antiquité expliquée* and cataloged his manuscripts: Montfaucon, *Bibliotheca Bibliothecarum Manuscriptorum Nova,* 2 vols. (Paris: Briasson, 1739), 2:1181–1189. Mabillon cites Peiresc

out of Gassendi in *De Re Diplomatica* (Paris, 1681), 135, 143, and mentions him twice in the *Iter Italicum* (1687), entries for 4 July and 28 December 1685. I thank Ingo Herklotz for bringing this last reference to my attention.

10. Charles Patin, *Relations historiques et curieuses des voyages* (Paris, 1695 [2nd ed.]), 114.

11. Antoine Schnapper, *Le Géant, la licorne, la tulipe: Collections françaises au XVIIe siècle* (Paris: Flammarion, 1988), 139. For Peiresc's Egyptian collection in particular, see Sidney Aufrère, *La Momie et la tempête: Nicolas-Claude Fabri de Peiresc et la "curiosité Égyptienne" en Provence au début du XVIIe siècle* (Avignon: Éditions A. Barthélemy, 1990), 212–217.

12. Gravit, *The Peiresc Papers*, 52–53.

13. He cites Gassendi "in Peirescii vita" for the judgment that Welser and not Peiresc was the author of the famous anti-Venetian *Squitinio* of 1606 (*Gottfried Wilhelm Leibniz: Schriften und Briefe zur Geschichte*, ed. Malte-Ludolf Babin and Gerd van den Heuvel [Hannover: Verlag Hahnsche Buchhandlung, 2004], 626).

14. See Leibniz's letters to the Abbé Nicaise of 23 December 1698 and 16 June 1699, in *Lettres de divers savants à l'Abbé Claude Nicaise*, ed. E. Caillemer (Lyon: Association Typographique, 1885), 73, 77.

15. Leibniz, *Schriften und Briefe zur Geschichte*, 24. "Die wichtigste Stütze für das Selbstbewußtsein, mit entsprechender Methodik der historischen Evidenz nahekommen zu können, liefert die antiquarische Arbeit, die Sammlung und philologisch exakte Bearbeitung des Quellenmaterials."

16. G. W. Leibniz, *Protogaea: De l'aspect primitif de la terre et des traces d'une histoire très ancienne que renferment les monuments mêmes de la nature/Sive de prima facie telluris et antiquissimae historiae vestigiis in ipsis naturae monumentis dissertatio, ex schedis manuscriptis viri illustris in lucem edita*, trans. Bertrand de Saint-Germain, ed., intro., and notes Jean-Marie Barrande (Toulouse: Presses Universitaires du Mirail, 1993), ch. 39, 139. The context is alluviation produced by a combination of silt-carrying rivers flowing north to south, and maritime currents running east to west.

17. J. G. Graveius to Nicaise, 31 March 1698, in *Lettres de divers savants à l'Abbé Claude Nicaise*, 177; C. F. Neickel, *Museographia, oder Anleitung zum rechten Begriff und nützlicher Anlegung der Museorum, oder Raritaten-Kammern* (Leipzig, 1727), 224–227.

18. The best account is in Louis Thomassin de Mazagues to Nicaise, 13 August 1696, *Lettres de divers savants à l'Abbé Claude Nicaise*, 177–182.

19. Huet to Nicaise, 16 February 1696, in *Lettres de divers savants à l'Abbé Claude Nicaise*, 250n1.

20. *A Collection of Curious Discourses Written by Eminent Antiquaries upon Several Heads in Our English Antiquities. Together with Mr. Thomas Hearne's Preface and Appendix to the Former Edition*, 2 vols. (London, 1771), I:iii, v.

21. On Caylus, see Marc Fumaroli, "Arnaldo Momigliano et la réhabilitation des 'antiquaires': Le comte de Caylus et le 'retour à l'antique' au XVIIIe siècle," in *Momigliano and Antiquarianism: Foundations of the Modern Cultural Sciences*, ed. Peter N. Miller (Toronto: University of Toronto Press, 2007), 178–179; on Winkelmann, see Élisabeth Décultot, *Johann Joachim Winckelmann: Enquête sur la genèse de l'histoire de l'art* (Paris: Presses Universitaires de France, 2000), 219, 225.

22. For Sterne, see Peter N. Miller, *Peiresc's Europe: Learning and Virtue in the Seventeenth Century* (New Haven, CT: Yale University Press, 2000), 221n108. For Johnson, see *The Idler*, ed. W. J. Bate, John M. Builitt, and L. F. Powell, in *The Yale Edition of the Works of Samuel Johnson*, 16 vols. (New Haven, CT: Yale University Press, 1963), vol. 2, no. 64, 14 July 1759, 202.

23. M. Paris, *Éloge de Nicolas-Claude Fabry de Peiresc, Conseiller au Parlement de Provence* (n.p., n.d. [1783]).

24. See G. M. Adkins, "The Renaissance of Peiresc: Aubin-Louis Millin and the Postrevolutionary Republic of Letters," *Isis* 99 (2008): 675–700; Jacques Ferrier, "Monuments consacrés à la mémoire de Peiresc," in *L'Été Peiresc*, ed. Jacques Ferrier (Avignon: Aubanel, 1988), 31–36. On Provençal antiquarianism before and after the French Revolution see L. W. B. Brockliss, *Calvet's Web: Enlightenment and the Republic of Letters in 18th Century France* (Oxford: Oxford University Press, 2002); *Les Antiquaires du Midi: Savoirs et mémoires XVIe–XIXe siècle*, ed. Véronique Krings and Catherine Valenti (Paris: Éditions Errance, 2010).

25. *Opere varie italiane e francesi di Ennio Quirino Visconti*, ed. Giovanni Labus, 4 vols. (Milan: Co'torchi della Società Tipogr. de'Classici Italiani, 1827–1831), 2:146–147; *Amalthea oder Museum der Kunstmythologie und bildlichen Alterthumskunde*, ed. C. A. Böttiger, vol. 1 (Leipzig: G. J. Göschen, 1820), xxviii–xxix. Gottsched, in 1750, cited Peiresc, but in a discussion of natural history, and out of Gassendi. See sec. 7 of the "Prolusio Academica," which precedes the *Singularia Vindobonensia* (Leipzig, 1749/50). I thank Annamaria Lesigang for this reference.

26. He praises André Duchesne for making genealogy into family history, Guillaume Catel's (of Toulouse) history of Languedoc based on old documents and on local history, Honoré Bouche's "brave antiquarian investigations" (without noticing the repeated exaltation of Peiresc in Bouche's mouth); describes Antoine de Ruffi's history of Marseille as possessing an "almost astounding completeness and a clarity" hardly equaled by "any other specialist historian of that time"; and calls Pierre d'Hozier (1592–1660) of Marseille the pioneer of heraldry, and the Sainte Marthe brothers masters of genealogy. Ludwig Wachler, *Geschichte der Künste und Wissenschaften seit der Wiederherstellung derselben bis an das Ende des achtzehnten Jahrhunderts. Fünfte Abtheilung. Geschichte der historischen Wissenschaften*, 2 vols. (Göttingen: Johann Friedrich Rower, 1812), 2:577, 588–589, 593, 599.

27. I. C. D'Israeli, *Curiosities of Literature and the Literary Character Illustrated* (New York: D. Appleton, 1846), 440; Daniel Morhof, *Polyhistor* (Lübeck, 1714 [1688]), 930, sec. 1; Ludwig Wachler, *Geschichte der Künste und Wissenschaften*, 1:viii.

28. Taxile Delord, *Histoire du Second Empire (1848–1869)* (Paris: G. Ballière, 1869), 245. M. Fourtoul, named "professeur de littérature étrangère" at Aix, was just putting the final touches to this when the Revolution broke out. What happened to the project we do not know.

29. Tamizey de Larroque's projected publication of Peiresc's letters was announced in a seance of the Academie des Inscriptions et Belles-Lettres of 10 January 1879 (Philippe Tamizey de Larroque, *Les Correspondants de Peiresc. I. Dubernard:*

Une lettre inédite écrite d'Agen a Peiresc en 1628 [Agen: P. Noubel–Fernand Lamy, 1879], 5).

30. Arnaldo Momigliano, "Ancient History and the Antiquarian" [1950], in *Contributo alla storia degli studi classici* (Rome: Edizioni di Storia e Letteratura, 1955), 69.

31. Peiresc was "einer der universalsten Menschen der modernen Zeit, der erste archäologische Kritiker, mehr durch seine Briefe und persönlichen Verkehr als durch Schriften wirksam. In ihm vereinte sich die damals zuerst in Europa zum Durchbruch kommende Naturforschung mit Sprachgelehrsamkeit und mit Kunstsinn. Ein Unstern hat über seinen gewaltigen literarischen Nachlass gewaltet, der selbst noch heute nicht ausgenutzt ist." Karl Bernhard Stark, *Systematik und Geschichte der Archäologie der Kunst* (Leipzig: Teubner, 1880), 110.

32. Henri Leclerq, "Peiresc," in *Dictionaire d'archéologie chrétien et de liturgie*, ed. F. Cabrol, 15 vols. (Paris: Letouzey et Ané, 1939), 14:1–39.

33. "Die grosse und bleibende Bedeutung des Mannes für die Archäologie liegt zunächst in seiner universalen wissenschaftlichen Stellung, die ihn ebensosehr die Universalgeschichte im Zusammenhang der Ethnographie und Geographie als Zielpunkt für die monumentalen Studien, wie eine vorurtheilsfreie, empirische und experimentirende Naturforschung, eine scharfe, vergleichende, prüfende Beobachtung der Objekte als nothwendige Voraussetzung eben dieser Studien betrachten liess. Dazu kam ein entschieden künstlerischer Sinn, der in fortwährendem Verkehr mit Künstlern geübt ist und nichts weniger als einseitig blos das Alte um des Alters willen bewundert." Karl Bernhard Stark, *Handbuch der Archäologie der Kunst* (Leipzig: W. Engelmann, 1880), 132.

34. "Der Vergleich zunächst derselben Objektgattungen wie der Münzen in möglichster Fülle, dann aller verschiedenen Gattungen ward von ihm fort und fort geübt," Stark, *Handbuch*, 133.

35. Publication of seven of the planned ten volumes began in 1888 and ended in 1898. In the first half of the twentieth century the publication of letters took a back seat to more synthetic treatments in the work of Raymond Lebègue and Pierre Humbert, but in its second half Agnès Bresson, Daniel Lhote, and Francesco Solinas have been responsible for editions of Peiresc's letters to Claude Saumaise, Cassiano dal Pozzo, Girolamo Aleandro, Lelio Pasqualini, and Cardinal Francesco Barberini. Tamizey also published as separate fascicules the letters of some of the individual correspondents to Peiresc, usually with a substantial introduction. These were gathered up and published by Slatkine in two volumes in 1972.

36. Henri Berr, *Du Scepticisme de Gassendi* [*An jure inter scepticos Gassendus numeratus fuerit* 1898], trans. Bernard Rochot (Paris: Albin Michel, 1960), discusses Peiresc repeatedly, e.g., 18n, 80, 86, 115–116.

37. Henri Berr, Comment, in *Pierre Gassendi 1592–1655: Sa vie et son oeuvre*, Centre International de Synthèse (Paris: Albin Michel, 1955), 142.

38. Marc Bloch, *L'Ile-de France* (Paris: Revue de Synthèse Historique, 1913); Lucien Febvre, *La Terre et l'évolution humaine* (Paris: Renaissance du Livre, 1922).

39. Henri Berr, *L'Histoire traditionnelle et la synthèse historique*, 2nd ed. (Paris: Librairie Félix Alcan, 1935), ch. 1, "Analyse et synthèse: Un érudit; Philippe

Tamizey de Larroque." The contrast is with ch. 2, "La Conception de la synthèse en histoire: Discussion avec un historien 'historisant.' "

40. Henri Berr and Lucien Febvre, "History," in *Encyclopaedia of the Social Sciences*, editor-in-chief Edwin R. A. Seligman, associate editor Alvin Johnson (New York: Macmillan, 1937), 363.

41. Durkheim, "Preface," *Année Sociologique* I (1897): ii; Bloch, "Pour une histoire comparée des sociétés européennes" [1928], in *Mélanges historiques*, 2 vols. (Paris: Service d'Édition et de Vente des Publications de l'Éducation Nationale, 1963), 1:16–40. See Laurent Mucchielli, "Psychologie des peuples, races, régions et milieu social: Problèmes scientifiques et enjeux disciplinaires d'une théorie de l'histoire autour d'Henri Berr et de la *Revue de Synthèse Historique* (1890–1925)," in *Henri Berr et la culture du XXe siècle*, ed. Agnès Biard, Dominique Bourel, and Eric Brian (Paris: Albin Michel, 1997), 81–110.

42. For Braudel's account of the importance of Berr for him, see Fernand Braudel, "Personal Testimony," *Journal of Modern History* 44 (1972): 454–461.

43. William H. McNeill, "Fernand Braudel, Historian," *Journal of Modern History* 73 (2001): 141. Bailyn argued earlier that it was not a single, coherent book (Bernard Bailyn, "Braudel's Geo-History—A Reconsideration," *Journal of Economic History* 11 [1951]: 277–282); J. H. Hexter scored Braudel's casualness with the statistics that festoon the volume (Hexter, "Fernand Braudel and the Monde Braudellien," *Journal of Modern History* 44 [1972]: 516); Trevor-Roper insisted on its proximity, rather than distance, from Ranke's nineteenth-century model (H. R. Trevor-Roper, "Fernand Braudel, the Annales, and the Mediterranean," *Journal of Modern History* 44 [1972]: 475); Hans Kellner assumed that its disorganization was so systemic as to be intentional and therefore declared it "the principal example of the anatomy, or Menippean Satire, in this century" (Kellner, "Disorderly Conduct: Braudel's Mediterranean Satire," *History and Theory* 18 [1979]: 222).

44. Georges Huppert, "La Liberté du cerveau: Notes on the Psychology of Historical Erudition," in *Mélanges en l'honneur de Fernand Braudel*, 2 vols. (Toulouse: Privat, 1976), 1:267, 270. This argument, in this place, resembles Jacob Bernays writing about seventeenth-century antiquarian practices of comparison in a Festschrift honoring Theodor Mommsen's invention of comparison! (Bernays, "Die Gottesfürchtigen bei Juvenal," in *Commentationes Philologae in Honorem Theodori Mommseni Scripserunt Amici* [Berlin: Weidmann, 1877], 563–569).

45. Paul Ricoeur, *Time and Narrative*, trans. Kathleen McLaughlin and David Pelhauer, 2 vols. (Chicago: University of Chicago Press, 1984), 1:99–111 and 208–217; Jacques Rancière, *The Names of History*, trans. Hassan Melehy (Minneapolis: University of Minnesota Press, 1994 [1992]), 41, 99.

46. Fernand Braudel, "Personal Testimony," *Journal of Modern History* 44 (1972): 452. For empire-builders like Febvre in the 1930s and Braudel in the 1950s, insisting on this dichotomy was a form of divide-and-conquer (Hexter, "Fernand Braudel," 508).

Acknowledgments

"**S**ome name, read long ago in a book, contains among its syllables the strong wind and bright sunlight of the day when we were reading it." I remember a Saturday night in late autumn or winter—I think it was 2003, but it could have been 2004—with Marc Fumaroli on the rue de l'Université, when we had a long talk about Peiresc and he encouraged me to think about the Mediterranean. It wasn't quite Lucien Febvre's famous suggestion about the relationship between Philip and the Sea, but it had the same effect on me.

But was that the beginning? Maybe it was really ten years earlier, when I first saw the pages I would later come to read so carefully. That was on a trip that connected me, or reconnected me, with people whose names still breathe with mine. From Carpentras and Aix-en-Provence I went to Florence and Joan-Pau Rubiés, then to Bern and Béla Kapossy, and finally to Berlin and Tony Grafton. In the two decades that have followed I have shared with them the pleasures of friendship, thinking, and family. I have learned so much from them that some parts of what this has become must surely be theirs as well.

Proust also reminds us that "a book is a great cemetery where the names have been effaced from most of the tombs and are no longer legible." I first encountered Istvan Hont when he listed for me everything I had gotten wrong in the first seminar paper I ever delivered, at Cambridge. Who, in our age of false politeness, would not love, finally, to meet someone who always told the truth? It was love ever since. Somewhere in this book is his stone—or maybe it is the book itself—silently marking the gift he gave me.

Many are the names I can remember, but over these two decades, alas, there have been many more who have generously given of their time and knowledge whom I cannot. I met Ann Blair, Paula Findlen, and Martin Muslow the first time I ever spoke about Peiresc in public. Later, I talked about Peiresc and his world with Timothy J. Reiss, Jacob Soll, Andrew Abbott, and David Freedberg. Donald R. Kelley encouraged my first steps in this direction. From even further back in time, around the dining room

617

table in 7 North Terrace, Bill Sherman showed me some of the things you could do with manuscripts. Alain Schnapp, Horst Bredekamp, and Carlo Ginzburg shaped my work as writers, even before they did so as conversationalists and friends. Bernard Bailyn, in the years of writing this book, has been an important inspiration. Aleš Debeljak told me to read Predrag Matvejević, and Stuart Schwartz put *Far Tortuga* before my eyes.

A draft of this book was written during a long, extremely cold month in Marseille as a guest of Jean Boutier at the École des Hautes Études en Sciences Sociales. Walking up and down the narrow lanes of Le Panier day after day and circulating around the port between bouts of writing helped blur the distance between Peiresc's time and mine. I am grateful to Jean and to Arundhati Virmani for the exceptional hospitality they showed me during my stay there. Wolfgang Kaiser invited me several times to Paris as I worked on finishing this book and shared with me his unparalleled knowledge of Marseille and the Mediterranean. During the two decades in which my work has taken me to Paris, Jean-Robert Armogathe has been always the most generous of hosts.

Readers of this book in manuscript deserve special thanks. Anthony Grafton, Marc Fumaroli, Wolfgang Kaiser, David Nirenberg, Jean Boutier, Francesca Trivellato, Biagio Salvemini, Ulrich Raulff, Ann Blair, Suraya Farouqui, Hannah Baader, and Gerhard Wolf read through the entire text, and the first four of them read it twice. Twice! For these Herculean feats, let alone for their wise and helpful comments, I am in debt to them all. Joan-Pau Rubiés, Noel Malcolm, and Simon Mills read sizable chunks and offered valuable criticism. I hope I have learned the lesson in Andrew Abbott's observations about an earlier version of the Introduction. Hannah Baader and Gerhard Wolf organized a study day around the finished book manuscript at the Kunsthistorisches Institut in Florence, surely one of the greatest gifts a scholar can be given. For many years now, Jérôme Delatour, who knows the erudite scene in early seventeenth-century Paris as well as anyone, has freely shared that knowledge with me, and also his exceptional skills at deciphering lost hands. We have sat together many times over these manuscripts these past fifteen years, and he has always made time for my pleas for help. Andrew Wylie read this book in manuscript and offered comments as a thoughtful reader long before he earned my further admiration for wanting to help a book of this sort into print. My dear Sabine MacCormack, *z"l*, once told me, as I stood before an abyss, to go off and write the kind of book I could not have before facing it. I have again tried to live up to her high teaching.

I wish to thank all my colleagues at the Bard Graduate Center for their indulgence with my Peiresc for so long, but also for their perceptive observations about the project. The library, led by Heather Topcik with Karyn Hinkle, has always kept me happily up to my ears in books and articles. A group of students have over the years assisted in preparing images and organizing data: Christine Wilmot, Yenna Chan, Martina D'Amato, Antonia Behan, and Maude Bass-Krueger. I am especially grateful to Antonia and Maude for work they have done in the final stages of the preparation of the manuscript. Elena Pinto Simon has been my colleague and collaborator in academic administration for almost a decade; I can truly say that without her generous and graceful shouldering of a heavy burden this book would not now be finished.

Nearing the end I realized that the Peiresc story is a kind of reverse Odyssey: this hero stayed home while his words wandered the sea-ways. Perhaps this, too, attracted me to him. For home, for me, has always been a place of great happiness. I thank my wife, conversation partner, and colleague, Deborah Krohn, for all the many things she has taught me; for all the different paths of life that flow into this book. My mother-in-law, Barbara Krohn, in turn made her home mine and opened new pleasures to me. My mother, Professor Naomi Churgin Miller, has, like a promontory visible from afar, been the landmark I have navigated by for my entire life. My father, Samuel Miller, is long gone, but every time I go to Aix in search of Peiresc I always slow when I pass the phone box at the bottom of the Cours Mirabeau in which I once stood, very early one June morning, a young man lingering for a moment more of childhood, while my father narrated from afar the last minutes of the final game of a basketball championship lost by our shared love.

Although my children were born into their world, not mine, it feels now that I owe them everything in mine. If I began by dedicating this book to them by way of Peiresc's reach for the heavens, let me end it now with Dante's: *l'amor che muove il sole e l'altre stelle.*

Index